The Family Handyman

Home Improvement 2004

The Family Handyman

Home Improvement

2004

by The Editors of *The Family Handyman* magazine

THE FAMILY HANDYMAN HOME IMPROVEMENT 2004
Executive Editor: Spike Carlsen
Managing Editor: Mary Flanagan
Archives: Shannon Hooge
Contributing Designers: Teresa Marrone, Bruce Bohnenstingl
Contributing Copy Editor: Amy Orchard
Marketing Director: Michael J. Kuzma

Editor in Chief: Ken Collier
Vice President, General Manager, U.S. Publishing Group: Bonnie Bachar

Warning: All do-it-yourself activities involve a degree of risk. Skills, materials, tools, and site conditions vary widely. Although the editors have made every effort to ensure accuracy, the reader remains responsible for the selection and use of tools, materials, and methods. Always obey local codes and laws, follow manufacturer's operating instructions, and observe safety precautions.

ISBN 0–7621–0598–4

Address any comments about *The Family Handyman Home Improvement 2004* to:
Editor, Home Improvement 2004
2915 Commers Drive, Suite 700
Eagan, MN 55121

To order additional copies of *The Family Handyman Home Improvement 2004,* call 1-800-344-2560.

For more Reader's Digest products and information, visit our Web site at www.rd.com.

Printed in the United States of America.
1 3 5 7 9 10 8 6 4 2

ABOUT THIS BOOK

and *The Family Handyman* magazine

If you've ever wondered if the do-it-yourself way of life is gaining or losing ground in America, consider these statistics:

- Two-thirds of all major home improvement projects (building decks, room additions, major remodeling) are done by do-it-yourselfers.
- Home improvement product sales reached over 200 billion dollars in 2003. DIY purchases accounted for 70% of those dollars.
- Of households planning on tackling home improvement projects in 2003, the annual amount budgeted was $3,796, up 31% from 2000.
- A recent survey discovered more women would rather spend their leisure time on a home improvement project than at a mall. (Shocking, perhaps, but true!)
- And last, but not least, each issue of *The Family Handyman*—the most read, most instructive, most

down-to-earth magazine in the do-it-yourself world—was read by 4.5 million people per month in 2003.

It's clear to us that doing-it-yourself is not only alive and well, but thriving.

The Family Handyman Home Improvement 2004 organizes the best articles and departments found in the pages of *The Family Handyman* magazine from November, 2002 through November, 2003 into a single, convenient volume. You'll find hundreds of hints, tips and repairs and dozens of projects designed for the do-it-yourselfer. But as you tackle these home improvement projects, you'll find other things as well: a feeling of accomplishment, the knowledge that the job was done right, a "homier" home and a few extra dollars in your billfold.

Good luck in all your projects!

Spike Carlsen and *The Family Handyman* magazine

Contents

Safety 8

1 WALL, CEILING & FLOOR PROJECTS

Handy Hints 10
Built-Up Chair Rails 12
You Can Fix It 16
Painting Woodwork 18
Simple Stenciling 22
Ask Handyman 24
Craftsman Trim 27
Snap-Together Wood Flooring . .32

2 KITCHEN, BATHROOM & LAUNDRY ROOM PROJECTS

Cabinet Facelift 38
Handy Hints 43
Clutter-Free Laundry Room 44
Great Goofs 51, 59, 66
Gallery of Ideas 52
Built-In Pantry Cabinets 54
Ask Handyman 58
Tile Tub Surround 60
Undercabinet Lighting 66
Wordless Workshop 72

3 WIRING & ELECTRICAL

Hang a New Ceiling Fixture 74
Great Goofs 78
Ask Handyman 79
You Can Fix It 82
Using Tools: Stripping Wire . . .84
Get Wired 88

4 PLUMBING

Ask Handyman 96
Replace a Dishwasher 100
You Can Fix It 104
Handy Hints 109
How to Clear Clogged Drains . .110
Great Goofs 114

5 INTERIOR REPAIRS & APPLIANCES

Ask Handyman 116
Washing Machine Leaks 120
You Can Fix It 125
Handy Hints 128
Using Tools: Insulate 130

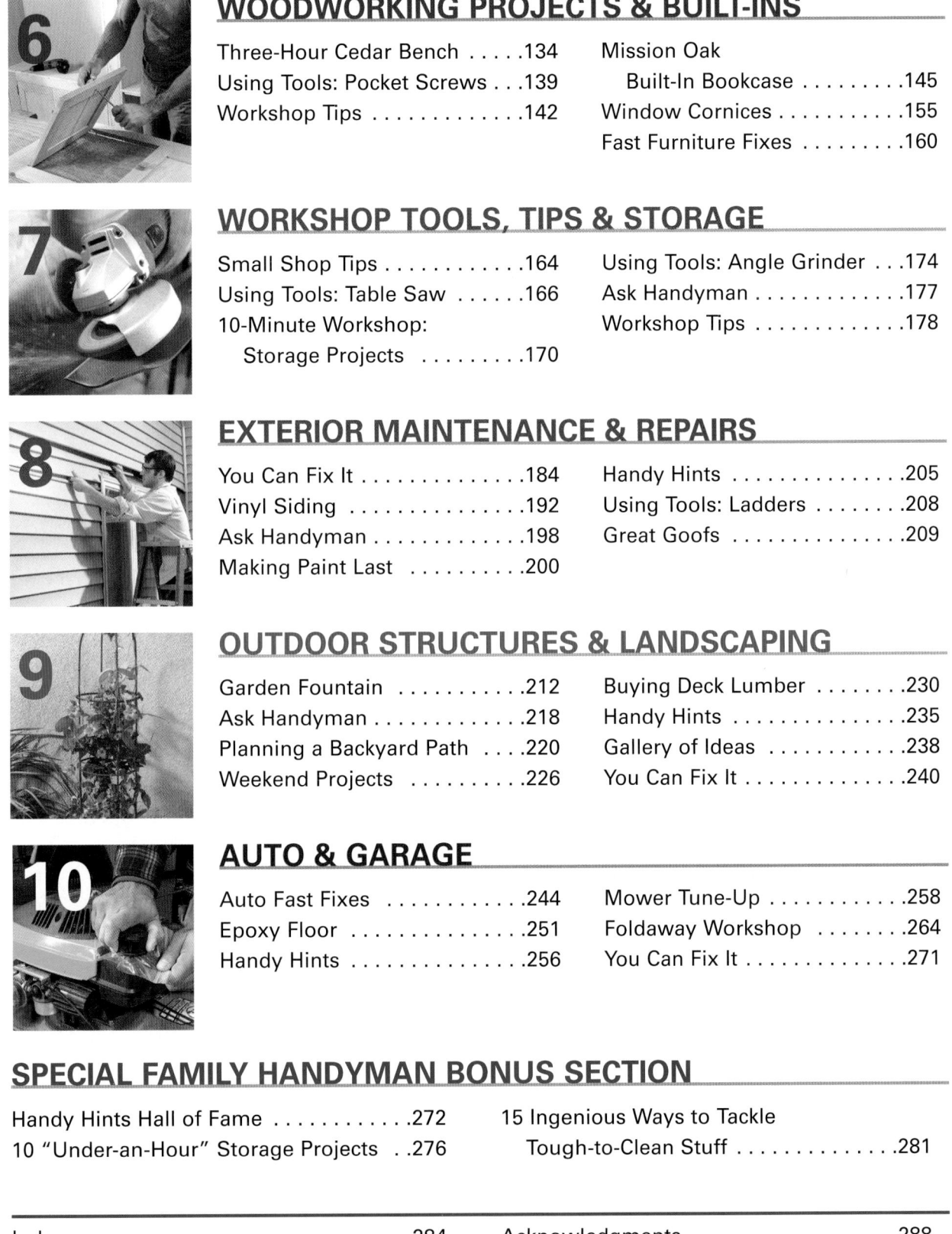

WOODWORKING PROJECTS & BUILT-INS

Three-Hour Cedar Bench 134
Using Tools: Pocket Screws . . .139
Workshop Tips 142

Mission Oak
    Built-In Bookcase 145
Window Cornices 155
Fast Furniture Fixes 160

WORKSHOP TOOLS, TIPS & STORAGE

Small Shop Tips 164
Using Tools: Table Saw 166
10-Minute Workshop:
    Storage Projects 170

Using Tools: Angle Grinder . . .174
Ask Handyman 177
Workshop Tips 178

EXTERIOR MAINTENANCE & REPAIRS

You Can Fix It 184
Vinyl Siding 192
Ask Handyman 198
Making Paint Last 200

Handy Hints 205
Using Tools: Ladders 208
Great Goofs 209

OUTDOOR STRUCTURES & LANDSCAPING

Garden Fountain 212
Ask Handyman 218
Planning a Backyard Path 220
Weekend Projects 226

Buying Deck Lumber 230
Handy Hints 235
Gallery of Ideas 238
You Can Fix It 240

AUTO & GARAGE

Auto Fast Fixes 244
Epoxy Floor 251
Handy Hints 256

Mower Tune-Up 258
Foldaway Workshop 264
You Can Fix It 271

SPECIAL FAMILY HANDYMAN BONUS SECTION

Handy Hints Hall of Fame 272
10 "Under-an-Hour" Storage Projects . .276

15 Ingenious Ways to Tackle
    Tough-to-Clean Stuff 281

Index 284

Acknowledgments 288

SAFETY

Tackling home improvement projects and repairs can be endlessly rewarding. But, as most of us know, with the rewards come risks. DIYers use power tools, climb ladders and tear into walls that can contain big and hazardous surprises.

The good news is, armed with the right knowledge, tools and procedures, homeowners can minimize risk. As you go about your home improvement projects and repairs, stay alert for these hazards:

Aluminum wiring

Aluminum wiring, installed in about 7 million homes between 1965 and 1973, requires special techniques and materials to make safe connections. This wiring is dull gray, not the dull orange characteristic of copper. Hire a licensed electrician certified to work with it. For more information visit www.inspect-ny.com/aluminum.htm.

Asbestos

Texture sprayed on ceilings before 1978, adhesives and tiles for vinyl and asphalt floors before 1980 and vermiculite insulation (with gray granules) all may contain asbestos. Other building materials, made between 1940 and 1980, could also contain asbestos. If you suspect that materials you're removing or working around contain asbestos, contact your health department or visit www.epa.gov/asbestos for information.

Backdrafting

As you make your home more energy-efficient and airtight, existing ducts and chimneys can't always successfully vent combustion gases, including potentially deadly carbon monoxide (CO). Install a UL-listed CO detector.

Buried utilities

Call your utility companies to have them mark underground gas, electrical, water and telephone lines before digging. In many areas it takes just one call.

Five-gallon buckets

Since 1984 over 200 children have drowned in 5-gallon buckets. Store empty buckets upside down and store those containing liquids with the cover securely snapped.

Lead paint

If your home was built before 1979 it may contain lead paint; a serious health hazard, especially for children six and under. Take precautions when you scrape or remove it. Contact your public health department for detailed safety information or call (800) 424-LEAD to receive an information pamphlet.

Spontaneous combustion

Rags saturated with oil finishes like Danish oil and linseed oil, and oil-based paints and stains can spontaneously combust if left bunched up. Always dry them outdoors, spread out loosely. When the oil has thoroughly dried, you can safely throw them in the trash.

1 Wall, Ceiling & Floor Projects

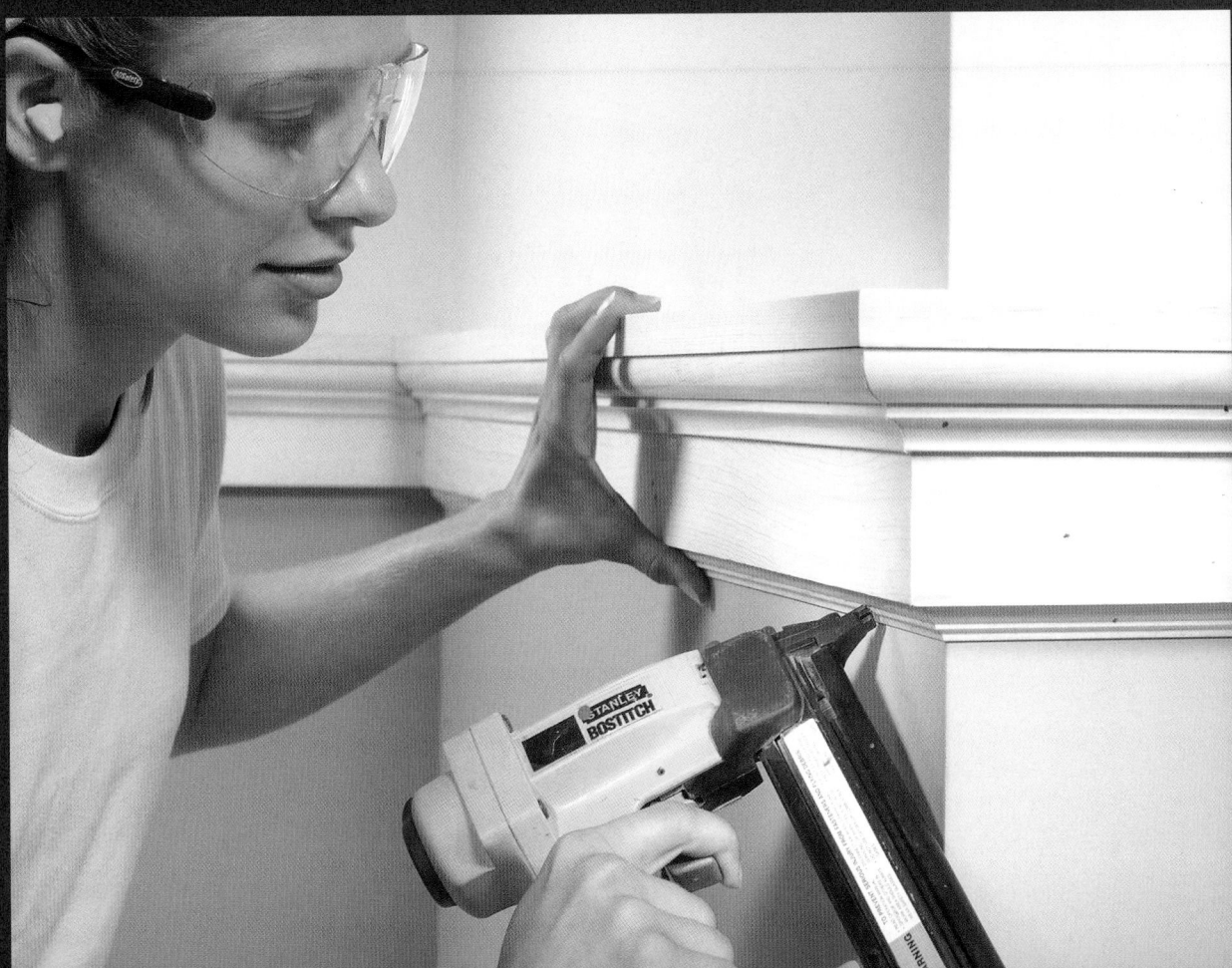

IN THIS CHAPTER

Handy Hints 10
   Pie-tin paint catcher, coat-hanger stirrer, sawdust wood filler

Built-up Chair Rails 12

You Can Fix It 16
   Repair a drywall crack and damaged metal corner bead

Painting Woodwork 18

Simple Stenciling 22

Ask Handyman .24
   Oil-based polyurethane over water-based?, building a drywall arch, flaking paint, repair cracks in drywall and more...

Craftsman Trim 27

Snap-Together Wood Flooring 32

Handy Hints® from our readers

NUTTY STAIN MIXER

When you open a fresh can of oil-based wood stain, drop in two medium-size steel nuts. Before staining, shake the can to thoroughly stir the contents. You'll hear the nuts banging around on the bottom when the pigments are well mixed.

HOT MELT GLUE

PIE-TIN PAINT CATCHER

Catch the paint that always seems to run down the side of the can. Hot-glue a disposable aluminum pie tin to the bottom of the paint can. When you're done painting, you can throw the pie tin away or save it and use it again.

PAINT CAN REMINDER

Before you put that paint can away, draw a line on the side of the can to indicate how much paint is left. Then write the name of the room you painted and the date on the lid.

KITCHEN MIXER BEATER BORROWED FROM NEIGHBOR

MUD MIXER

Powdered drywall setting compound sets up quickly, so there's no time to fool around while mixing. Chuck an old beater from a kitchen mixer into a cordless drill. It'll cut your mixing time in half and fluff up the compound like whipped cream.

COAT HANGER STIRRER

A plastic coat hanger makes a dandy power mixing attachment. Cut the bottom so that you have a long "J," insert it in a drill and start mixing.

PAINT BRUSH DRIP STOPPER

When you wipe your paint brush against the inside of the can, paint fills the rim and eventually runs down the side and onto the floor. Solve the problem by wiping the paint against a heavy rubber band wrapped around the center of the can. Excess paint will drip back into the can without making a mess or gumming up the lid.

PAINT BRUSH SOAKER

One good way to clean oil-based paint from a brush is to let the brush hang in paint thinner. Make a brush holder from a metal coat hanger. Cut the coat hanger and bend it around the threads of a jar. Then bend the hanger as shown. The brush will hang without getting into the paint sediment at the bottom of the jar.

SAWDUST WOOD FILLER

Make your own wood filler by mixing sawdust and wood glue. Apply the filler to holes and small imperfections, and sand it smooth when it's dry.

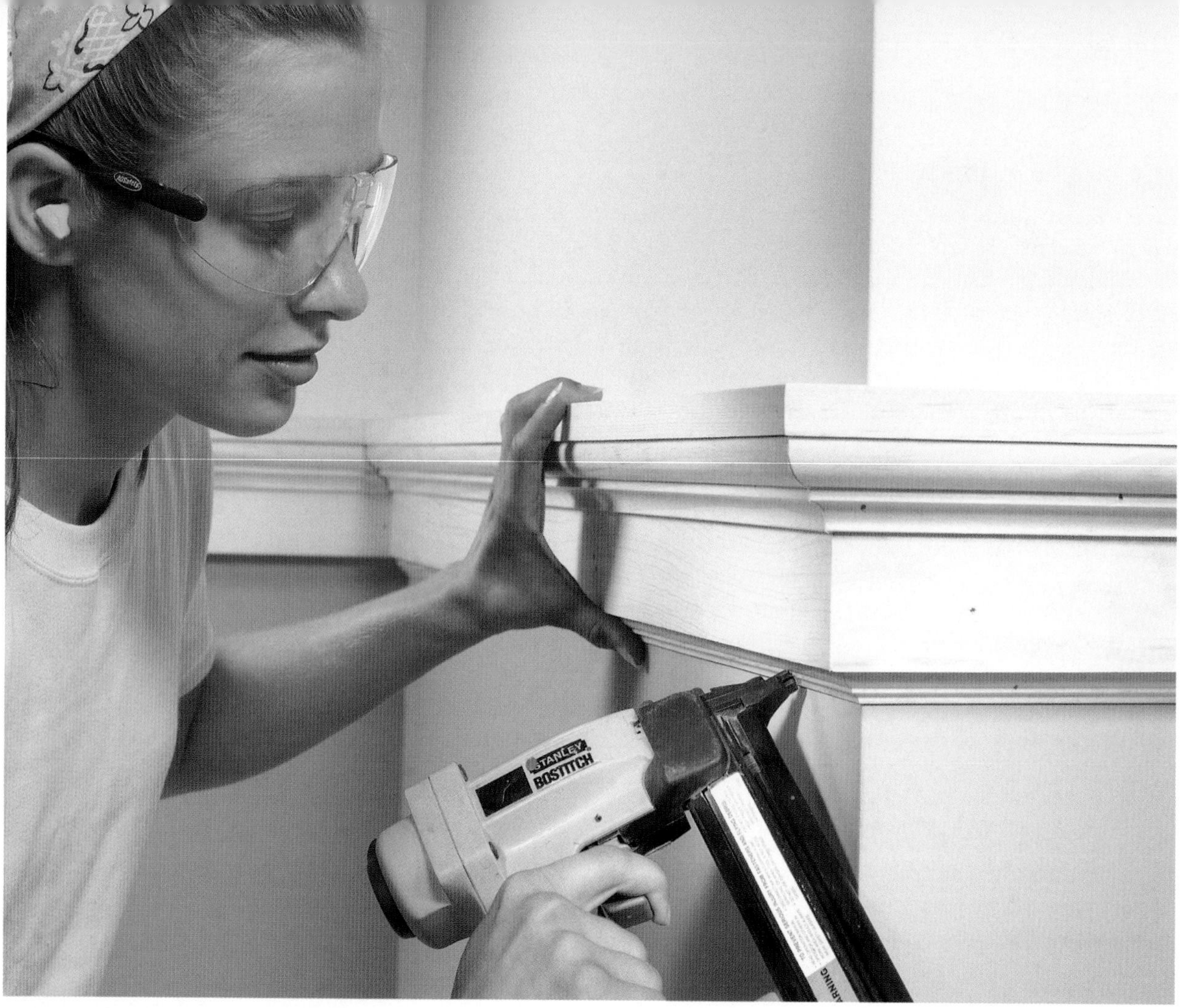

BUILT-UP
CHAIR RAILS

Make this elegant chair rail from two stock moldings and two simple boards

by **Spike Carlsen**

A chair rail can do a lot more than protect your walls from jostled chairs. A well-designed chair rail is an attractive accent and provides a clean dividing line so you can paint the upper part of a wall and wallpaper the lower. But this project's most attractive feature may be its simplicity.

We'll show you how to install a chair rail made from two simple boards and two moldings. See p. 15 to find ways of dealing with different types of molding.

Soft pine for simple cutting

Since we planned to paint our chair rail, we used pine moldings and clear boards. They're also available in oak.

We used a safe, simple, $35 hand-powered miter box, since soft pine boards and moldings cut easily. If you're working with oak or a large room, rent or buy a power

miter saw for more accuracy.

You can hand-nail all the boards and moldings, but we chose to hand-nail only the 1x4 horizontal rails. We used a small air-powered brad nailer to secure everything else. With brad nailing, there's less chance of splitting wood or leaving ugly hammer marks.

Decorative chair rails look best about one-third of the way up a wall. If in doubt, place a few strips at varying heights to get a feel for the right proportion.

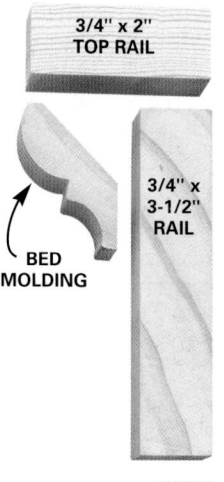

3/4" x 2" TOP RAIL

BED MOLDING

3/4" x 3-1/2" RAIL

GLASS BEAD MOLDING

The rails form the structure

Make marks equal distances above the floor in all the corners of a room (**Photo 1**) as well as next to all door and window casings. Connect these marks using white chalk in a chalk box, then locate and mark the studs. First install the horizontal 1x4s (the actual dimensions are 3/4 in. x 3-1/2 in.). Cut the rails to length, hold them in place, and then predrill small holes based on the stud marks on the wall. Align the top edge with the chalk line, then nail the rails using 8d finish nails. You can use simple square cuts where they meet at inside corners (**Photo 4**).

Tip If you live in an old house with slanted floors, use a 4-ft. level to draw lines around the room, making sure that by the time you come full circle, the starting and ending heights are the same.

Your outside corners will look neatest if you miter them. Align one board with the chalk line and trace along the wall to mark the back where it intersects the corner. Use your miter saw to cut the angle, leaving the board about 1/8 in. too long, then temporarily tack it in place (**Photo 3**). Use a small test piece with a 45-degree angle to see if the other mitered 1x4 will meet it right. If it won't, use your miter saw, sanding block or belt sander to adjust both miters until they fit.

Next, cut the 3/4-in. x 2-in. top rails and nail them to the 1x4 rails. Test-fit the ends of the boards on the inside corners (**Photo 4**), then cut to fit. If several layers of drywall compound hold the boards out from the wall, sand or plane the board edges until they fit tight. At the outside corners, again use miters and "test pieces" to get a tight fit.

The moldings add pizzazz

Cutting and installing the bed molding is the most challenging part of the project, since it perches at an angle to the rails. As you work, keep picturing how it will sit against the rails after it's installed. There are three details you need to contend with:

Outside corners. Outside corners meet with simple 45-degree miters. Position an overly long piece of bed molding in place, then make a little "tick" mark on the back lower edge where the 1x4s meet at the corner. This is the short side of your miter. Position the molding in your miter saw upside down (**Photo 6**) and use clamps or cam pins to hold the molding square to the fence. Set the saw at 45 degrees, line up the tick mark with the blade and carefully make the cut. It's easy to screw up here—remember that your tick mark will be the *shortest* part of the miter. After one piece is cut and tacked in place, use a test piece to make certain the second piece will meet it at the correct angle.

Inside corners. Since inside corners are rarely square, mitered moldings usually leave a gap. It's best to run one piece square into the corner (that's the easy one!) and then "cope" a second piece to butt into it. The best way is to cut a 45-degree angle on a molding, then use that profile as a guide for cutting out the shape. For a detailed explanation of this procedure, see "Using Tools," Sept. '02, p. 31. To order a copy, see page 288.

1 MAKE marks and snap chalk lines 32 to 36 in. off the floor. Locate studs with a stud finder or by probing with a finish nail, then mark other studs at 16- or 24-in. increments.

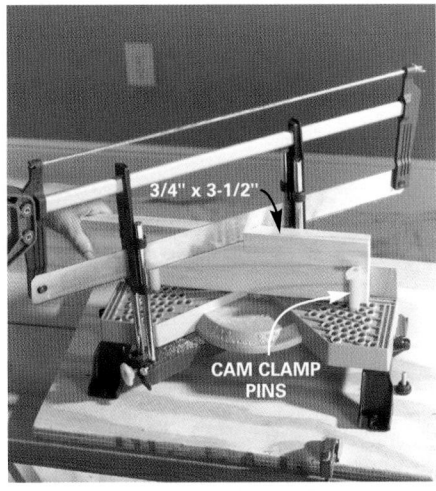

2 CUT the 1x4 horizontal rails to length. Make square cuts where the rail butts a wall or window or door casing. Make 45-degree miters (shown) at outside corners.

3 TEST-FIT corner pieces to ensure a tight fit. Cut one piece about 1/8 in. too long, then tack it in place. Use a mitered "test piece" to see how the corners will fit, then use a belt sander, miter saw or sanding block to fine-tune the angles.

Returns. You need to "cap" the ends where the chair rail overlaps window and door casings. Cut the long piece of molding at a 45-degree angle so the long point is 1/8 in. shy of the outside corner (**Photo 8**) of the top rail. Then miter a small piece to turn the corner and "return" the molding to the horizontal rail. It's like an outside corner, but the second piece is really small. Glue and tape the piece in place. You'll bust it if you try to nail it.

The smaller glass

bead molding, which covers any gaps between the wall and bottom of the 1x4 rail, is a breeze compared with the bed molding. Cut and test-fit the outside corners the same as you've done with other outside corners. Since the molding is so small, you can miter (rather than cope) the inside corners.

Puttying, priming and painting

Fill the nail holes and gaps with sandable wood putty, then smooth all surfaces with fine-grit sandpaper. Lightly run the sandpaper along the edges of the boards to ease them.

If you have gaps larger than 1/8 in. where the 1x2 rail meets the wall, run a small bead of paintable caulk in the gap. Prime, then paint the wood. You're done. ⌂

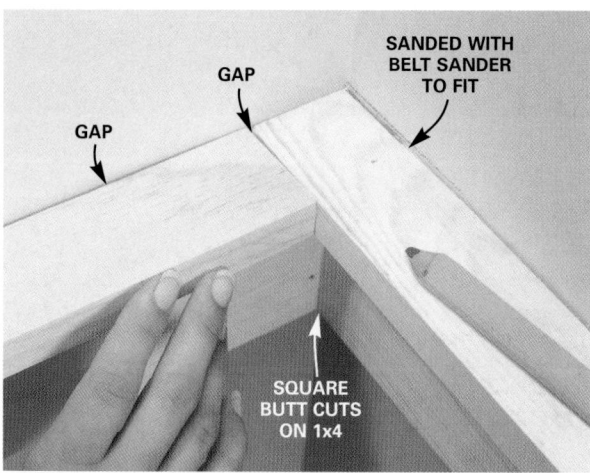

4 INSTALL the 3/4-in. x 2-in. top rails. Test-fit pieces and cut ends so they fit tightly against walls and one another. Scribe and sand edges so top rails fit snugly against walls.

5 NOTCH the ends of the top rails so they extend 5/8 in. onto door and window casings. Use 3d nails or 1-3/8 in. brads to secure the top rail to the rail below.

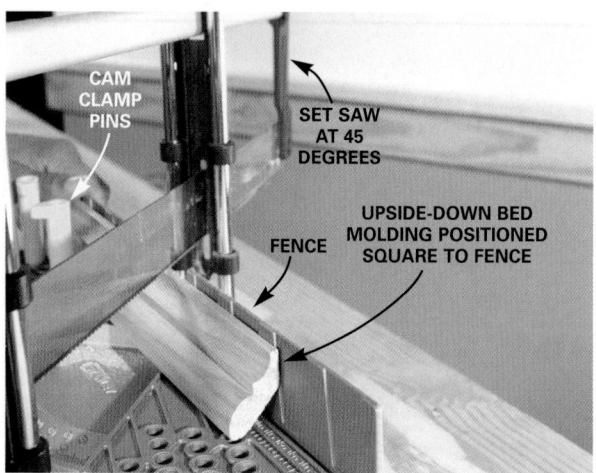

6 CUT and install the bed molding. Place the molding upside down and hold it tightly against the fence of the miter box with clamps or cam pins. Secure the moldings in place with 3d finish nails or brads.

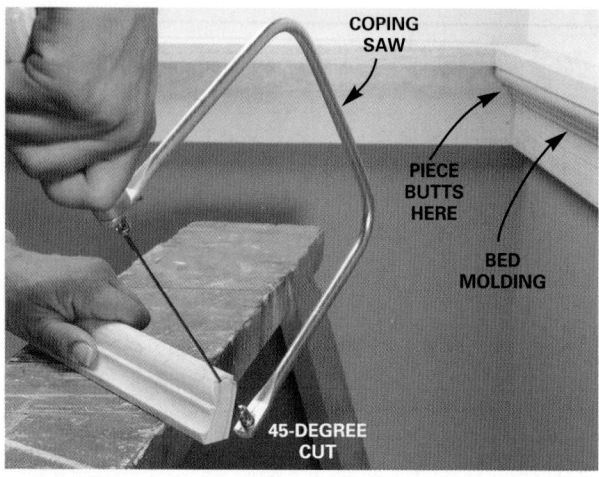

7 COPE one of the pieces where moldings meet at inside corners. Cut a 45-degree angle, then use that profile as a guide for cutting. Angle your saw to remove more wood from the back of the molding than from the front.

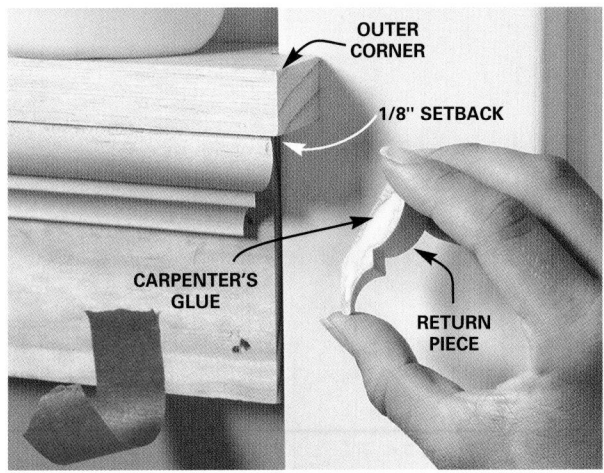

8 GLUE returns in place where the bed molding overlaps window or door casings. Tape them in place. Don't nail them; they'll break.

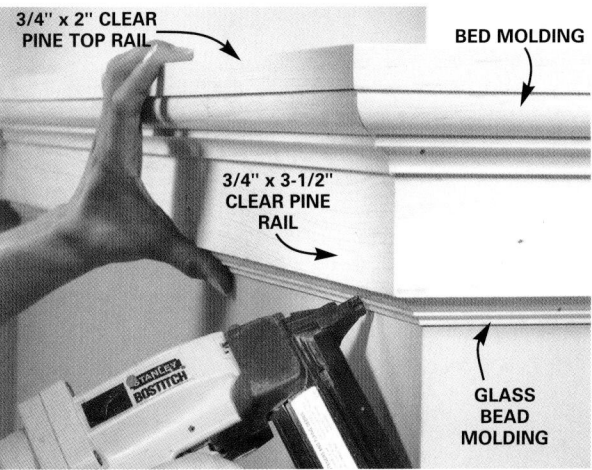

9 SECURE the glass bead molding in place with 1-in. brads. Press this flexible molding tightly against the wall so it covers any gaps between the wall and rail.

10 PUTTY all nail holes and gaps, then sand the rails and moldings smooth. Ease the exposed rail edges with sandpaper to create a more durable "paint edge." Caulk any gaps between the wall and top rail. Prime and paint.

Tip If you have moldings with a cope or angle on one end and a square cut on the other, always cut the cope or angle first. After you test-fit and fine-tune the piece, you can make the final (simpler) square cut to create the right length.

More simple chair rail ideas

A chair rail like the one we show is thicker than most contemporary moldings it butts to. Here are a couple of ideas for dealing with common situations:

■ If your existing door and window moldings are thin, you can cut out a small section of casing at chair rail height, install a thicker rosette, then butt the chair rail into that. Rosette blocks are made by House of Fara (a brand carried by many home centers). Visit the company's Web site at www.houseoffara.com or call (800) 334-1732 to find a dealer.

■ Use single, flat chair rail moldings that don't protrude past the casings. There are many embossed or fluted moldings that will work.

■ You can run a thicker band of wood, say a 1/2-in. x 1-1/2 in. strip, entirely around existing casings to provide a thicker edge to butt the chair rail to.

You can use different moldings and boards in any of hundreds of combinations to create your own chair rail. Always try to match the look, feel and scale of the other moldings in the room.

You Can Fix It™

1 TAP the corner bead straight with a smooth hammer (don't worry if you bury it in the wall a little). Use a level to check straightness and to make sure the bead doesn't protrude past the finished wall.

2 FILE OFF any sharp edges left on the corner bead with a mill file.

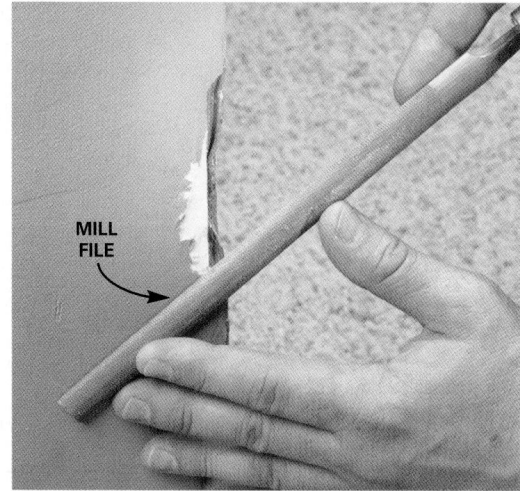

MILL FILE

With rambunctious kids or clumsy adults banging stuff around, something eventually smashes into the wall and damages the corner bead. Damaged metal corner bead can be fixed quickly with quick-setting patching compound (a 4-lb. box costs $3) and the common tools we show here. When the powdered quick-setting compound is mixed with water, a chemical reaction causes it to harden faster and stronger than premixed drywall compounds. This speeds up repair time and offers extra protection from future mishaps.

Photos 1 and 2 show how to bend the corner bead back in place and remove any sharp burrs. You can't get a smooth finish if any part of the metal bead sticks out. When the wall was originally finished, a strip of tape may have been run over the corner bead flange and adjoining gypsum board. If this tape is loose from the accident, cut it and any other loose plaster away and patch the damaged area. Use a fan to increase air circulation and speed up drying time. You may be able to match the paint (most home centers need a chip the size of a quarter to match the color), but chances are you're going to have to repaint the entire wall to hide the repair.

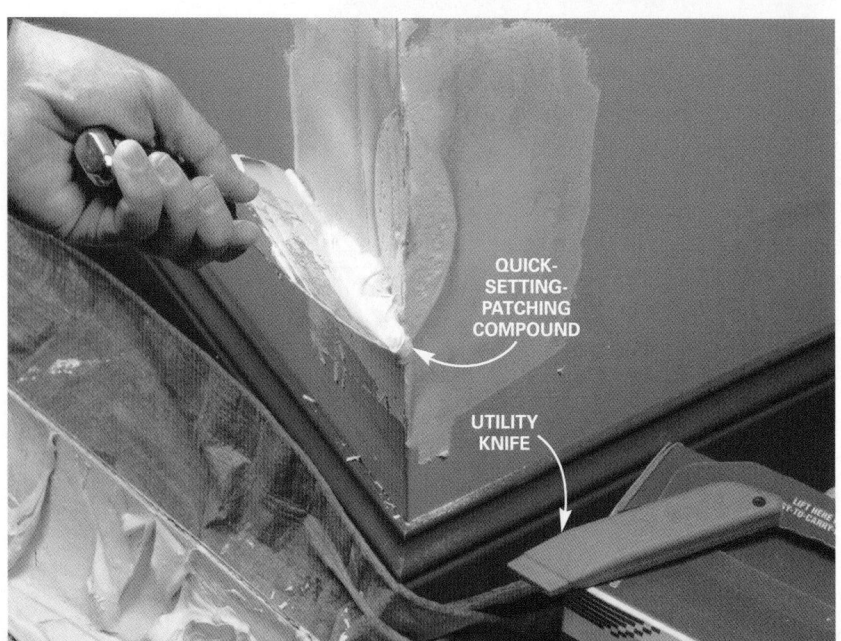

QUICK-SETTING-PATCHING COMPOUND

UTILITY KNIFE

3 PUT a tarp down and cut away any loose paint or paper around the damaged area with a utility knife. Mix some quick-setting patching compound until it's as smooth as warm butter, then fill in the damaged area. Let the compound harden, then recoat. Sand the area smooth after it's dry.

REPAIR A DRYWALL CRACK

CRACK

As homes settle, cracks may radiate from the corners of doors and windows. Whether your walls are made of plaster or drywall, you can repair the cracks in two steps over a day or two—and get the area ready to sand and paint. Use paper tape; it's stronger than fiberglass tape for wall repairs. For cracks more than 1/4 in. deep, clean out the loose material and use a quick-setting crack filler like Durabond to build up the area level with the wall. Then use the steps shown in Photos 2 and 3 to fix it.

For more information about tape-setting compounds and taping techniques, see "Drywall Taping," April '01, p. 35. To order a copy, see p. 288.

1 CUT a V-notch through the full length of the crack, 1/8 to 1/4 in. deep, removing all loose wall material. Protect woodwork with masking tape.

2 EMBED paper tape in joint compound using a 6-in. taping blade. To avoid trapping air bubbles under the tape, moisten the paper tape with water, lay it over the crack and squeeze excess compound and air from underneath with the blade. Apply an additional thin layer of compound and feather it off 2 in. on both sides of the tape. Let dry.

MOIST DRYWALL TAPE

3 APPLY a second (and third, if necessary) coat of compound, smoothing it out 6 to 7 in. on both sides of the joint. Smooth the compound to a thin, even coat using long, continuous strokes with a 12-in. taping blade. Allow the repair to dry thoroughly, sand it smooth (avoid exposing the tape) and paint it.

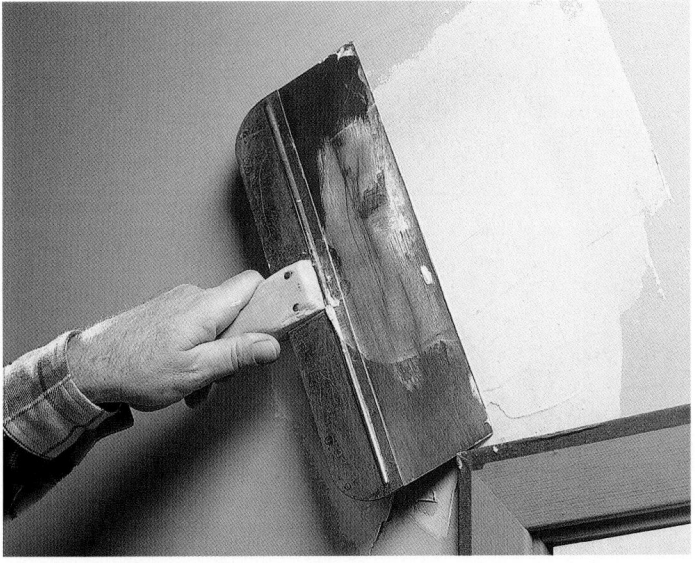

PAINTING
WOODWORK

Brushing on a silky smooth finish takes patience and attention to detail. Here's how.

by **Carl Hines**

Having trouble getting your paint to look smooth? Welcome to the club. Painting woodwork so it has a flawless, glossy sheen is challenging. In this article, we'll show you some techniques and tricks that'll produce top-notch results.

For great painted woodwork, good surface preparation and good brushing technique are essential. We'll show you how to accomplish both plus what to add to the paint to help it lie smoother.

Many pros still rely solely on oil-based paints because they dry slowly and allow brush marks to flatten out. But you can achieve similar results with high-quality latex paint. Today's formulations cover and brush out well. You won't have the strong odor of oil that'll drive you out of the house for days. And latex also offers the advantage of fast drying and easy soap and water cleanup.

Latex paint is available in a range of sheens from flat to high gloss. Because you want your wood trim to wear well, we recommend eggshell or semigloss. The downside to these shiny finishes is that every bump and scratch shows through. Good prep is critical.

Tip — Stiff putty knives work better for scraping; flexible putty knives work better for filling.

Preparation, preparation

A coat of paint won't fill or hide cracks, chips and other surface defects, and it won't smooth an existing rough surface. You have to fill and smooth the woodwork first.

Wash the woodwork with a TSP solution (or TSP substitute) to remove grease and grime. Mix according to the directions on the package and scrub with a sponge or rag. Be sure to rinse well with clear water to remove residues.

Next examine the surface for loose and cracked paint that'll need scraping. Many scraper types are available, but a 2-in. stiff putty knife works well for small areas (**Photo 1**). When you're done scraping, you'll be left with a rougher surface and a few more scratches and gouges than when you started. Don't worry—you'll fix these areas next.

For dents and chips deeper than about 1/8 in., we like to use a two-part polyester resin. One example is Minwax wood filler ($6 at hardware stores and home centers). It sticks well, doesn't shrink and sands easily. It's also the best material for rebuilding chipped corners. Auto body fillers also work well.

Scoop out a golf ball–size amount onto a scrap piece of wood or cardboard. Add the correct amount of hardener (follow the directions) and mix thoroughly but quickly (**Photo 2**). The resin only has a 5- to 10-minute working time.

For finer scratches and chips, use spackling compound. (Ready Patch by Zinsser is one brand used by many pros.) Don't use a lightweight compound; it doesn't stick to painted wood as well.

"Spot-prime" the filler and any bare wood with a latex primer. This step is worth the effort because it helps you see imperfections. Check your work by holding a bright light (trouble light or flashlight) close to the woodwork (**Photo 5**). Every small bump and scratch will jump out. Circle the defects with a pencil, then go back to the filler and sanding steps. Spot-prime and finish-sand these reworked areas.

Prep work requires patience, especially

1 REMOVE all loose or cracked paint with a stiff putty knife. Work in various directions to get underneath the loose paint.

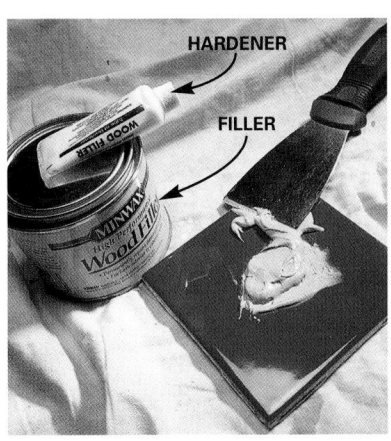

2 FILL nicks and gouges with a two-part wood filler. Mix it thoroughly (following label directions) with a 2- or 3-in. flexible metal or plastic putty knife.

3 PICK UP a dab of putty with the knife and apply it to the gouges. Press and smooth the filler into the scraped area. Leave the filler slightly higher than the surrounding surface.

4 SAND the filler flush to the painted surface with 100- or 120-grit sandpaper or a medium sanding sponge. Make sure to eliminate all ridges. Then finish-sand with 180-grit sandpaper or a fine sanding sponge. Spot-prime the filler and any bare wood.

5 HOLD a utility light close to the surface, and circle any imperfections with a pencil. Fill, sand and spot-prime these areas. Finally, lightly sand the entire surface with the 180-grit paper to ensure that the new paint will stick.

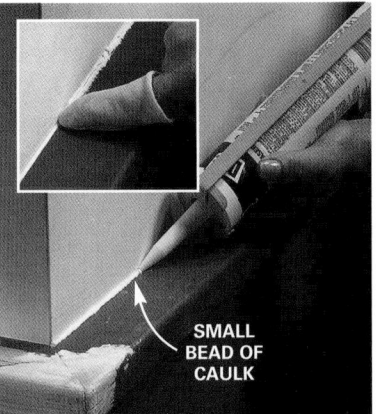

6 APPLY a small bead of paintable caulk to the crack between the wood and the wall. Smooth the caulk with a damp rag wrapped around your finger. Wipe the edges to remove any ridges of caulk.

when you have to go back to an earlier step. What you decide is acceptable here is what you'll get in the finish coat. But keep in mind that the most critical eye will probably be yours.

Finish up the prep work by lightly sanding all areas that haven't been scraped and spot-primed. Use 180-grit paper or the fine sanding sponge. This will smooth out previous brush marks and scuff the surface to help the new coat of paint stick. Then wipe down the whole surface with a damp cloth to remove all the dust.

> **CAUTION:** Paint dust and chips from lead paint are hazardous. If your home was built before 1977, the year lead paint was banned, call your local public health department and ask about paint testing details and safe scraping, sanding and cleaning techniques.

Caulk

Now that the filling, sanding and priming are done, caulk any long cracks and gaps (**Photo 6**). Use an acrylic latex caulk; it adheres well, remains flexible and cleans up with water. Cut the caulk tube at the very tip to leave a very small hole. You'll have better control of the caulk. Apply a bead of caulk that protrudes slightly, then wipe it with a damp cloth wrapped around your finger. Wipe excess caulk off the cloth so you don't smear it on either side of the joint. You may have to wipe several times to produce a smooth, clean caulk line.

The paint and the brush

Don't undermine all the time and effort you've put into the prep work by using cheap brushes and paint. Buy the best. With proper cleaning, a high-quality brush will last for

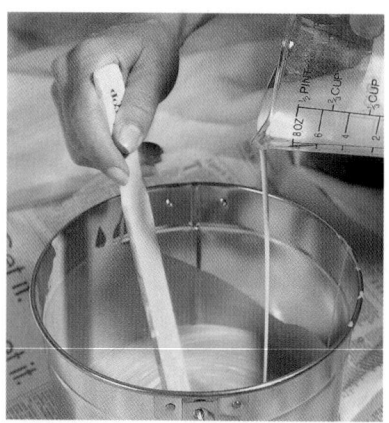

7 POUR a quart of paint into the pail and add a latex additive (such as Floetrol) for smoother results. Follow the label's instructions for the correct amount. Mix thoroughly.

8 DIP the brush bristles 1 to 2 in. into the paint to load the brush. Lightly tap the tip of the brush against the sides of the pail to shake off excess paint.

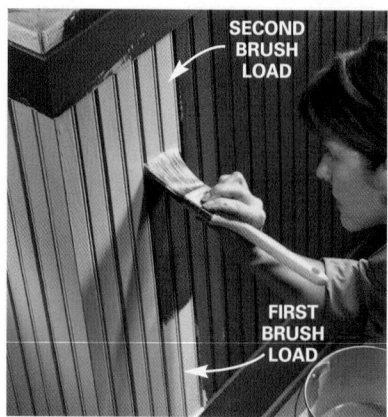

9 START at the top of the board with the loaded brush and stroke down toward the middle. When the brush begins to drag, stop and reload.

years. In most cases, you'll find the highest quality paint and tools (and good advice) at specialty paint stores.

While we recommend latex, it does have one weakness: It dries quickly. The longer the paint remains wet, the better it flows and flattens, leaving a smooth surface. We recommend that you use an additive that slows down the drying process and helps the paint lie smooth. (Floetrol is one common choice; $6 per quart at most paint stores.) Read the directions for the amount to add.

For best results from brushing, don't dip directly from the can. Pour a quart of the paint into a 4- or 5-qt. pail. This is your working paint that will move around with you. Add the measured amount of additive and mix well (**Photo 7**). From this pail you can dip and tap your brush without splattering. Good-quality paints are ready to use out of the can and don't need thinning with water. Be sure to have the paint store shake the can so it's well mixed, then stir the paint occasionally as you use it.

Brushing technique

The sequence in brushing is to quickly coat an area with several brush loads of paint, and then blend and smooth it out by lightly running the unloaded brush tip over it (called "tipping"). See **Photos 9 – 11**. Try to coat a whole board or section, but don't let the paint sit more than a minute before tipping.

The more paint the brush carries, the faster you'll coat the woodwork. But you want to avoid dripping. So after dipping, tap the tip of the brush against the pail, like the clapper of a bell (**Photo 8**). For a drier brush, try dragging one side over the edge of the pail.

Hold the brush at about a 45-degree angle, set the tip down where you want to start and pull it gently over the surface with a little downward pressure (**Photo 9**). Here's where the good brush pays off. The paint will flow smoothly

onto the surface with little effort on your part. A common mistake is to force paint out of the brush after it becomes too dry. The goal is a uniform thickness but not so thick as to run or sag. With practice, you'll quickly find the ideal thickness. If the new color doesn't hide the old, it's better to apply a second coat than to apply the paint too thick. Continue the next brush load from where the last stroke left off, or work backward, say from an inside corner back into the wet paint.

When "tipping," avoid dabbing small areas as this leaves marks in the paint. Make long strokes. The brush will leave a slight track of parallel ridges, but they'll lie down before the paint begins to skin over (**Photo 11**).

> **Tip** Brush marks in the old paint are particularly annoying and have to be sanded out, not filled.

Masking off and cutting in

Often the boards you're painting butt against a different

Choosing a brush

As with paint, buy quality when you shop for brushes. You'll spend $10 to $15 per brush. My favorites for trim are a 2-1/2 in. straight brush and a 1-1/2 in. angle brush for detail work and cutting in. Whether to use a straight or an angled brush is an individual choice. For latex, buy a synthetic bristle brush with "exploded" tips. A good brush draws a decent "load" of paint into the bristles and applies it smoothly onto the work surface.

STRAIGHT TIP

ANGLE TIP

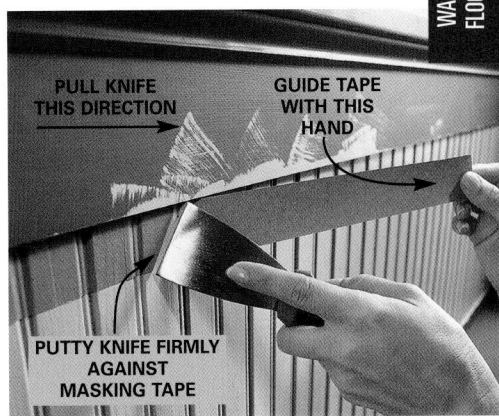

10 "TIP" the wet paint by lightly setting the tip of the brush against the wet paint at the top of the board and lightly stroking down the whole length of the board. Hold the brush almost perpendicular to the surface for this stroke.

11 THE FINE brush strokes left after tipping will flow together until the paint begins to skin over.

12 APPLY painter's masking tape to protect finished surfaces before brushing on the second color. Carefully position the tape and push it tight against the surface with a stiff putty knife. Be sure the paint underneath has thoroughly dried.

paint color or a wall. There are a couple of ways to leave a sharp, crisp line.

Masking off with tape is one method. Lay painter's tape tight to the line where your new coat of paint will end (**Photo 12**). Push the tape tight against the surface with a stiff putty knife to prevent the wet paint from bleeding (running) underneath the tape. Brush the woodwork, letting the paint go partially onto the tape, then tip. Remove the tape when the paint is dry.

The pros usually skip the masking tape and just cut in with a brush; it's faster. With some practice and a steady hand, even an amateur can get very sharp lines. Learn with a smaller brush (1-1/2 in.) and go to a wider brush as you gain control. Dip the brush and scrape one side on the pail. Hold the dry side of the brush toward the line and slowly draw the brush along (**Photo 13**). Support your arm to steady it, and keep the stroke moving. Use gentle downward pressure; you want the bristles to splay out slightly as you stroke. You'll find you can control the paint line by varying the pressure you apply to the brush.

When the brush is dry, reload and start where the previous stroke ended. Sometimes you'll have to go back over a section where the paint is shy of the line. Complete cutting in and then coat the rest of the piece.

Finishing up

Whether one coat will suffice depends on the paint used and the color. If the first coat of paint looks streaky or transparent, a second coat is necessary. Let the previous coat of paint dry overnight, then lightly sand with 180- or 220-grit paper or a fine sanding sponge. Wash the dust off the surface with a damp cloth, let dry and brush on another coat.

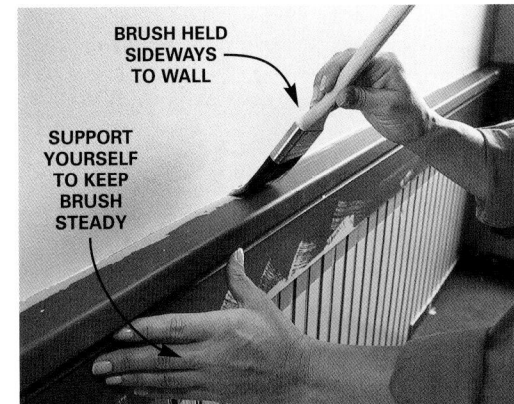

13 LOAD the 1-1/2 in. brush with paint and drag one side over the edge of the pail. Holding the dry side of the brush toward the wall, carefully set the tip of the brush close to the wall line. Apply a little pressure and pull the brush along the line. Guide the paint up to the line by manipulating the pressure and position of the brush's tip as you pull it along.

Tip Use special painter's masking tape. It's more expensive, but it's less likely to damage the surface when removed. Don't leave it on for more than a couple of days or it'll harden and be tougher to remove.

Buyer's Guide
- Minwax wood putty. (800) 523-9299. Available at home centers.
- Ready Patch by William Zinsser & Co. (732) 469-8100. www.zinsser.com. Available at most paint stores.

SIMPLE
STENCILING

Beautiful walls from an ancient art

by **Eric Smith**

Stenciling is a traditional decorative technique that perfectly complements a Craftsman-style room. And it's perfectly easy to learn, too. If you can handle a paint brush and a tape measure, you can quickly master the techniques for applying an attractive, simple border. And with a little practice, you can tackle complex patterns using multiple stencils and colors—and even create your own designs.

The key tools are a special stenciling brush ($10; **Photo 2**) and the stencil and paint. A wide variety of each are available at craft and art supply stores. You can also find stencil patterns at bookstores or on the Internet, or even buy stencil blanks and cut your own with an X-Acto knife. We bought our stencil, a pattern called Ginkgo Frieze, from www.fairoak.com for $42. Match the brush size to the area being filled within the stencil. We used a 1/2-in., medium-size brush, which is a good, all-purpose size. You can use almost any paint— artist acrylics, wall paints or the special stenciling paints sold at craft and art supply stores. We used artist acrylic paint for our stencil.

Plan the layout

Position your stencil on the wall at the desired height and mark the alignment holes or top edge. Then snap a light, horizontal chalk line around the room at that height. We used blue chalk for photo clarity, but make sure that whatever color you use wipes off easily. Or use faint pencil marks, which can be easily removed or covered later.

The key to a good layout is to avoid awkward pattern breaks at doors, windows and corners. To work out the best spacing, measure the stencil pattern and mark the actual repetitions on the wall. Vary the spacing slightly as needed to make the pattern fall in a pleasing way. Or if your stencil has multiple figures, you can alter the spacing between them like we did. Start your layout at the most prominent part of the room and make compromises in less visible areas. Draw vertical lines at the pattern center points to make positioning easier.

Dab on the paint

Tape the stencil pattern up on the alignment marks (**Photo 1**) and put a small quantity of paint on a paper plate. Push the stenciling brush into the paint just enough to coat the tips of the bristles, then pat off the excess on a dry cloth or newspaper, making sure the paint spreads to all the bristles as you do so (**Photo 2**). The brush should be almost dry— remember, it's easier to add paint than it is to take it away.

Lightly dab on the paint (**Photo 3**). Hold the stencil pattern with your free hand to keep it still and flat. Don't worry about getting paint on the stencil, but avoid wiping or stabbing too hard around the edges. You can cover the cutout completely or work for shading effects. Cover nearby cutouts with masking tape so you don't accidentally get paint in them (**Photo 5**).

Mistakes are easy to correct. You can lift the stencil (**Photo 4**) and wipe off any paint that's smeared under the edge with a damp paper towel, or touch it up later with wall paint. If you wipe some of the stenciled area away, just lay the stencil down again and touch up.

Our stencil design called for two colors, so we masked off the cutout where the second color would go, stenciled on the first color all the way around the room, then went back and added the second color, following our original alignment marks (**Photo 5**). Additional colors and even additional stencil patterns can be added in this manner. ⌂

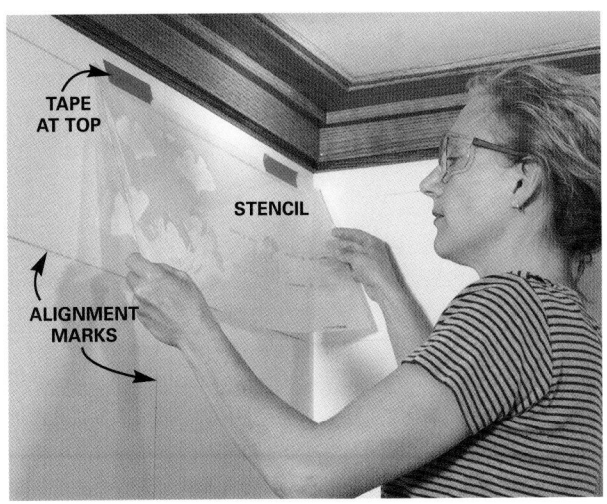

1 SNAP lines on the wall to align with the alignment marks on your stencil. Tape the stencil in place along the top edge with removable masking tape.

2 DAB the special stenciling brush into the paint, then pat off the bristles on a dry cloth. Leave the brush almost dry.

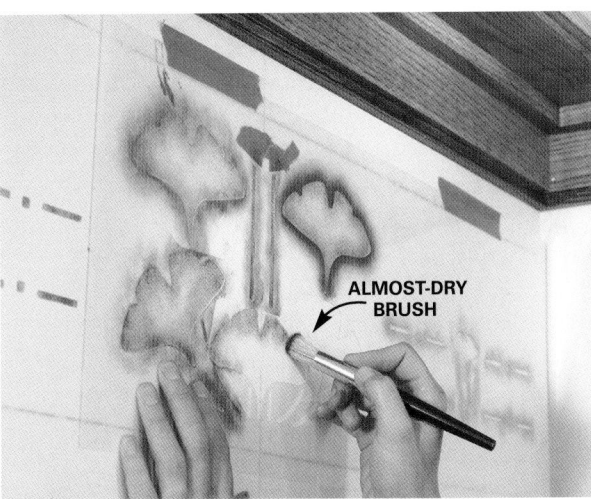

3 APPLY the paint to the stencil with light dabbing and swirling motions until the stencil area is covered. Work in from the edges, brushing toward the center.

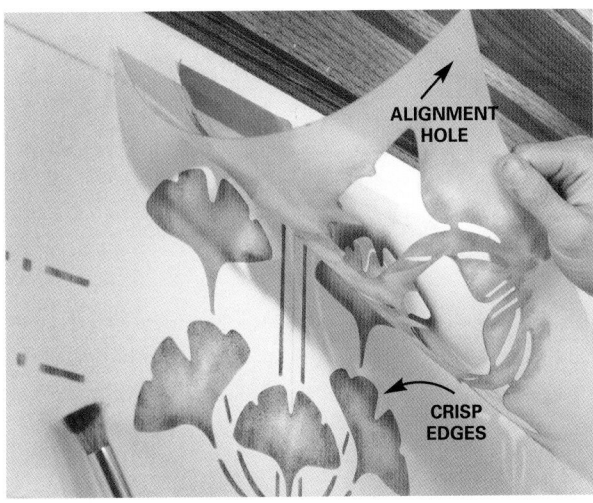

4 LIFT the stencil up on the tape hinges and check for paint drips and for clear, sharp edges. Lay the stencil back down and touch up if necessary.

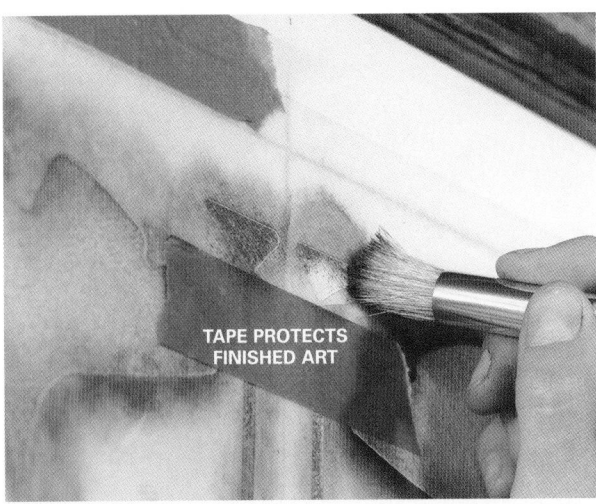

5 ALLOW the first color to dry, then tape the stencil up on the same marks and apply the second color. Cover nearby areas of the stencil to avoid getting paint in them.

Ask Handyman™

BUILDING A DRYWALL ARCH

I'm considering converting a plain arch into a curved arch. What's the best way to do this?

This is a relatively straightforward project that requires some carpentry and drywall taping skills. You'll need to frame a curved arch, bend and fasten a strip of drywall to the curved framing, and then install a flexible corner bead. None of these steps is difficult, but it's fussy work.

First cut away the drywall inside the opening to expose the framing. Don't worry if you break it back a few inches on the walls. Next determine the style and size of the arch (half circle, partial circle or ellipse) and make a pattern out of cardboard. Tape this up in the opening to make sure it looks OK and leaves enough headroom.

Use this template to mark out and cut two 1/2-in. thick plywood arches. Next cut a 6-ft. 2x4 down to 2-1/2 in. wide (or 2 in. narrower than the total wall thickness). Cut one top block and two side blocks and nail them to the door framing. Center them so that the 1/2-in. plywood arches will sit flush with the existing framing. Now nail the arched plywood into place on both sides.

Cut short arch blocks and screw them between the plywood arches about every 6 in. Cut strips of 1/8-in. hardboard (such as Masonite) and nail them to the arch blocks following the curve of the plywood. Use short drywall or underlayment nails. The hardboard provides a smooth, solid backer for the drywall and eliminates creases. Run it all the way down the sides to the floor.

Next fasten the drywall over the face of the arch. Let it overhang into the archway and then cut out the curve of the arch with a drywall or keyhole saw.

Then cut a strip of dry-

wall the same width as the total thickness of the wall. If you're using regular 1/2-in. drywall, wet the backside of the strip to help it bend. Lay it between sawhorses so it can sag as the water soaks in. You may need to wet it several times and let it slowly bend for an hour or two.

Another option is to buy 1/4-in. drywall that's designed to bend. Look for it at drywall suppliers (see "Drywall Supplies" in your Yellow Pages).

Start 6 in. below the curve of the arch, pushing the drywall firmly against the hardboard. Drive a pair of nails every 6 in. into your blocking around the curve. Then use straight strips to finish the sides.

Apply flexible plastic corner bead (also available at drywall suppliers) to both edges. Run it all the way to the floor. Start at one end and fasten the bead with a staple gun, driving 9/16-in. long staples every 3 inches. Keep the bead centered on the corner and tight to the drywall. This step gives the arch its final shape, so take your time.

Finally, mix up some setting-type joint compound and cover the corner bead. Apply second and third coats of joint compound, letting it dry between coats. Sand, paint and then go relax. You've earned it!

To reduce time spent soaking a drywall strip into a curve, buy 1/4-in. drywall that's designed to bend.

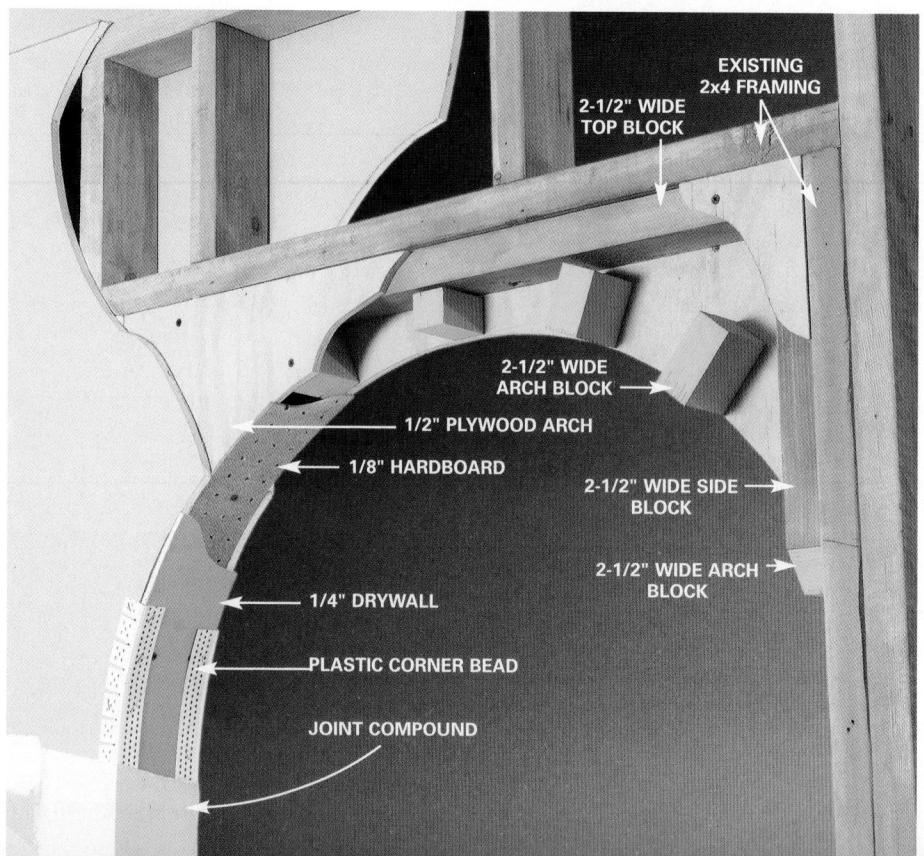

1/4" DRYWALL

EXISTING 2x4 FRAMING

2-1/2" WIDE TOP BLOCK

2-1/2" WIDE ARCH BLOCK

1/2" PLYWOOD ARCH

1/8" HARDBOARD

2-1/2" WIDE SIDE BLOCK

2-1/2" WIDE ARCH BLOCK

1/4" DRYWALL

PLASTIC CORNER BEAD

JOINT COMPOUND

CAN OIL-BASED POLYURETHANE BE USED OVER WATER-BASED?

Would it be OK to apply a coat of oil-based polyurethane over the original water-based poly on my hardwood floor?

I called several flooring wholesalers and veteran floor finishers and they assured me that you can do it if the original coating has completely cured. Since the curing period for water-based poly is 30 to 60 days, your floors are OK to recoat. You'll have to lightly buff the old finish with a power buffer to prepare it for the new polyurethane.

Rent a power buffer ($40) and buy a fine (150-grit) screen (shown at right). Use a light touch to avoid cutting through the finish and into the stained wood. Before applying the polyurethane, vacuum the floor thoroughly and then wipe up the remaining dust with a cloth dampened with mineral spirits.

Ventilate the area well and wear a respirator rated for organic fumes (follow the label warnings on the polyurethane can) when applying the finish. Stay off it overnight and give it a few days to cure before bringing in furniture or laying rugs down (or they may stick permanently!).

150-GRIT SANDING SCREEN

HOW DO I REPAIR CRACKS IN DRYWALL?

There are fine cracks in the walls over the corners of several windows and doors in my family room addition. The cracks run from the window trim up to the ceiling. Before I repaint the room, is there a permanent fix?

If you just spackle over the cracks and go your merry painting way, the cracks will certainly reappear. Like the tip of an iceberg, the surface crack is only the visible part of the problem. The drywall is cracked all the way through because of movement of the structural framing. This is common in new construction as the wood dries out and the addition settles. Often this movement stops after a few years, but sometimes it doesn't.

While I can't guarantee a permanent fix, this approach will give you the best shot at it.

1. Cut open the crack with a utility knife. Be bold and aggressive. You want to widen the crack to about 1/8 in. almost all the way through the drywall.

You may find that the surface crack is right on top of a joint between two pieces of drywall. Be sure to cut open the joint and clean it out.

2. Use a setting-type joint compound to fill the huge canyon you've carved into your wall. Let it dry and sand it flush with the wall.

3. Apply drywall tape and three coats of joint compound. See "Drywall Taping," April '01, p. 35, for detailed instructions. To order a copy, see p. 288.

FASTENING WOOD PANELING

How do I fasten 4x8 sheets of wood paneling to a plaster wall?

You can glue the panels with construction adhesive applied with a caulking gun. But for the glue to hold, the surface of the wall must be sound. Remove peeling and loose paint with a scraper or wire brush. The paneling can span minor holes (the size of a dollar bill), but you'll need to patch larger damaged areas.

Next, cut and fit the panel. Then apply the adhesive to the back. Lay a bead around the perimeter of the panel 1 or 2 in. from the edge, then fill in with a series of parallel glue lines spaced 8 in. apart. Push the panel firmly against the wall to spread the glue, then pull the panel away from the wall for about one minute to let the adhesive become tacky. Finally, push the panel back against the wall so the glue grabs and holds them tight. Position it carefully; the panel won't move much at this point. Drive colored paneling nails only where needed to hold the panel tight to the wall.

Ask Handyman™

PEELING PAINT

The paint on the siding outside my bathroom keeps peeling. I've scraped, primed and repainted, but within a year it's peeling again. What can I do?

If the peeling is limited to the area outside your bathroom, chances are that moisture is working its way through the wall and lifting the paint. Baths and showers generate a lot of humidity, and some of that water vapor is probably working its way through the drywall, insulation, sheathing and even the building paper. From there it continues into the wood siding, and it's just a matter of time until the paint peels.

Correct this problem right away, not only so the paint will stick but because the moisture may cause mold to grow inside your walls, especially in colder climates.

The first step is to reduce the humidity in the bathroom. Weather permitting, open a window while you're showering or bathing. If you've got a bath fan, be sure to use it and make sure it's actually working. Let it run for at least 10 to 15 minutes after you're done showering.

The second step is to stop the water vapor from moving into the wall. In moderate and cold climates, you normally install a sheet of plastic as a vapor barrier behind the drywall. In your case, it's probably missing. Instead of tearing out the drywall to install one, simply repaint your wall with a primer that's designed to act as a vapor barrier (BIN primer sealer is one good choice available at most paint stores). Then apply a standard finish coat. In humid areas (see map), skip the vapor barrier and rely on the bath fan.

And third, let the wall and siding dry out for a couple of months during warm weather before prepping and repainting the siding.

It's a cold-weather problem

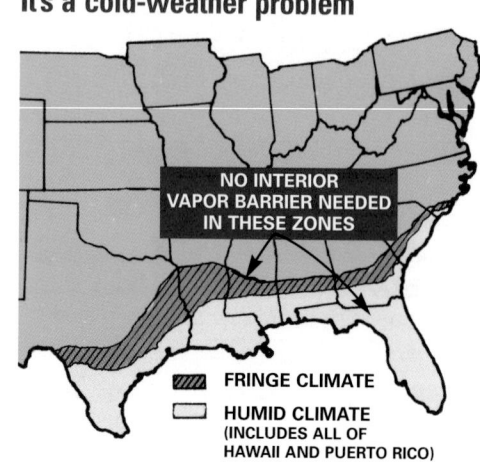

NO INTERIOR VAPOR BARRIER NEEDED IN THESE ZONES

▨ FRINGE CLIMATE
☐ HUMID CLIMATE (INCLUDES ALL OF HAWAII AND PUERTO RICO)

The Problem: Peeling paint

The Cause: High bathroom humidity

MOISTURE MOVING THROUGH WALL

The Solutions:

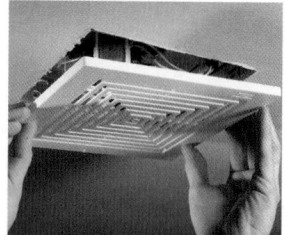

Vent the moisture

Add a vapor barrier

CRAFTSMAN
TRIM

Simple shapes make for easy but stylish moldings

by **Jeff Gorton**

Simplicity is the hallmark of Craftsman-style trim. And that's what makes it the perfect trim project for every DIYer, even if you have limited carpentry experience. There are no fancy shapes or store-bought moldings—just square-edged pieces of trim that are easy to make and assemble. Although each molding is simple, the combined effect gives the room a distinctive, hand-crafted look. In this article, we'll show you how to cut out and assemble the square-edged moldings to make the window and door trim, baseboard, cove and plate rail you see in the photo below.

The trim may look complex, but because it's built up from multiple pieces, it's actually quite easy to install. The 1/2-in. square moldings that run against the floor and along the edges of the cove bend easily to conform to irregular surfaces and hide gaps. In addition, most of the inside corner pieces simply butt together and don't require miters or bevels. You'll still have to work carefully to get nice-fitting joints, but the small size of the individual pieces makes them easier to cut and fit.

In addition to basic hand tools, you'll need a table saw to rip the thin strips from larger boards and a miter saw to make crisp, clean cuts in the hardwood. We used a bench-top planer to remove saw marks and to reduce the thickness of the 3/4-in. stock to 1/2-in. for some of the trim pieces (**Photo 2**). If you don't own a planer, hire the lumberyard or a local woodworker to plane these pieces for you. We recommend an air-powered trim nailer (**Photo 5**), which not only speeds up the work but also makes it much easier to get tight-fitting joints. You can rent a nailer and compressor for about $50 per day or buy a kit containing both for about $300.

We're using "plain sawn" red oak for this project rather than the more expensive "quarter sawn" that was common for Craftsman trim. It's readily available at home centers and most lumberyards. To simplify your planning, all the pieces are either 1x4s (3/4-in. x 3-1/2 in. actual size) or can be cut from 1x4s. The key to using plain sawn oak is to select the boards for similar appearance and attractive grain patterns. Straight-grained pieces usually look best and should be reserved for prominent locations. Use the less attractive wood for baseboards in areas that will be hidden by furniture. If you have a better selection of wider boards, 1x6s for example, buy these instead and rip them on the table saw to make your moldings. Expect to spend about $35 for an average window, $35 per door, about $3.50 per linear foot of base and about $4.50 per linear foot of cove or shelf.

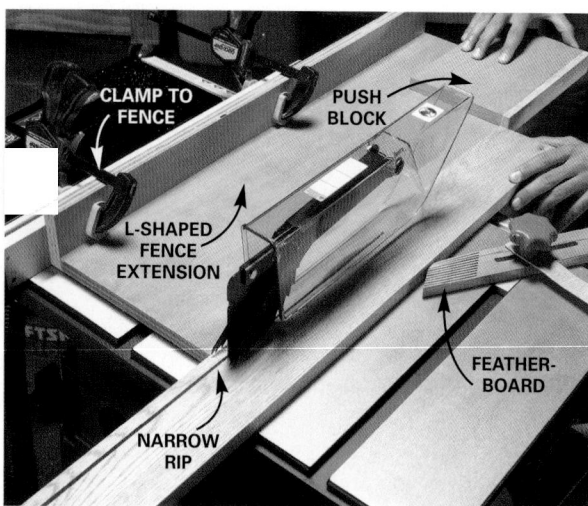

1 RIP narrow strips for the cove, base and casing using the setup shown. Leave blade guard in place and use the push block to complete the cut.

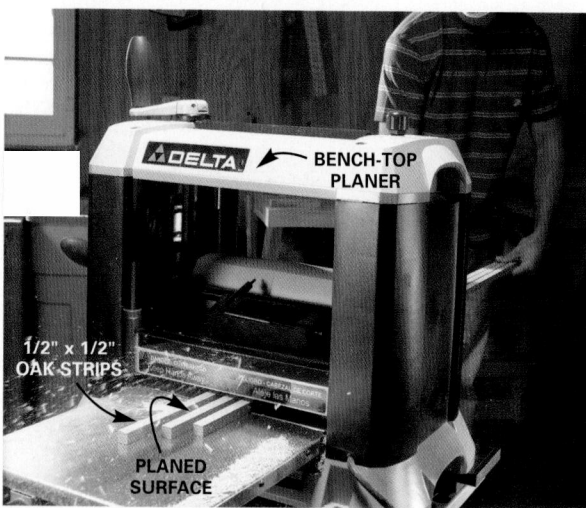

2 PLANE the cut edges to remove saw marks. Then plane some of the strips to 1/2 in. thick as needed.

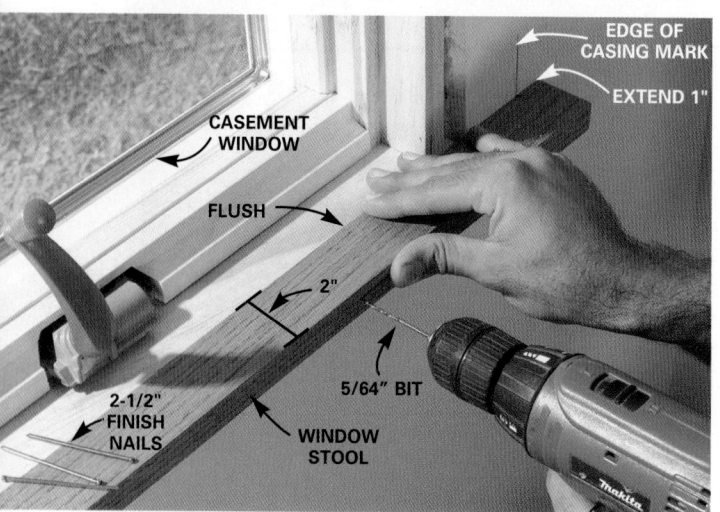

3 POSITION and predrill the window stool. Then add glue and nail it to the window frame. Snug the 1x4 apron up under to the stool and nail it in place.

Start the project by measuring the doors, windows and walls of your room and calculate the quantities of each piece of trim you'll need. Then rip all the pieces to width on your table saw (**Fig. A** and **Photo 1**). Add 1/8 in. extra to the width to allow for planing. To rip thin strips safely without removing the blade guard, clamp an extension to your table saw fence and use a custom-made push block like the one shown in **Photo 1**. When all the pieces are ripped, run them through the planer to remove saw blade marks from the edges. Then separate the pieces that need to be reduced to 1/2 in. thick and plane them down (**Photo 2**). Run them through the planer about four or five times, removing no more than 1/16 in. with each pass until they measure 1/2 in. thick.

Door and window trim

Trim the doors and windows first. Start by making a series of light marks every 12 in. along the jambs, 3/16 in. in from the inside edge with a sharp pencil, to indicate the edge of the trim (inset, **Photo 4**). On windows, install the stool first. We added a stool to a casement (crank-out) window by simply gluing and nailing it to the jamb (**Photo 3**). The stool on double-hung windows (windows where the sashes slide up and down) usually rest on top of the sill. You have to notch the ends to fit against the wall.

Measure between the jambs and add 9-3/8 in. to determine the length of the stool (1 in. beyond the side casings). Then center it on the window and glue and nail it to the jamb (**Photo 3**). It's difficult to get the stool and frame perfectly flush. Predrill the stool with a 5/64-in. bit and continue the hole 1/4 in. into the frame. Keep the frame and stool aligned while you drill. Cut the 1x4 apron 2 in. shorter than the stool. Center it on the window and snug it up to the bottom of the stool before nailing it to the framing under the window. For a durable, tight-fitting trim job, especially when working with 3/4-in. trim, it's essential to nail into the wall framing. Use a stud finder to locate the edges of studs and other framing around windows, doors and ceiling edges. When nailing through drywall into the framing, use 2-1/2 in. finish nails. If you're hand nailing, predrill the oak with a 5/64-in. bit.

Mark and cut side casings (**Photo 4**). Be sure to trim the end that rests on the stool for a tight fit before marking the top. Drive 1-1/2 in. nails every 16 in. into the jambs along the inside edge and 2-1/2 in. nails through the outside edge into the wall framing. Complete the window by assembling the head jamb and nailing it in place (**Photo 6**). Don't use a power nailer to attach the fillet to the jamb. Instead drill 5/64-in. pilot holes through the fillet and drive 2-in. long finish nails by hand (the same technique you used to attach the stool in **Photo 3**). With the exception of the stool, trim out doors just like windows.

Fig. A: Trim Details

COVE

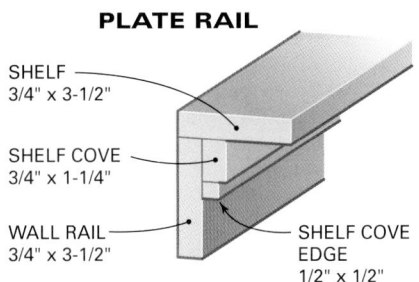

CEILING PIECE
3/4" x 3-1/2"

WALL PIECE
3/4" x 3-1/2"

INSIDE CORNER
3/4" x 3/4"

COVE EDGE
1/2" x 1/2"

COVE EDGE
1/2" x 1/2"

PLATE RAIL

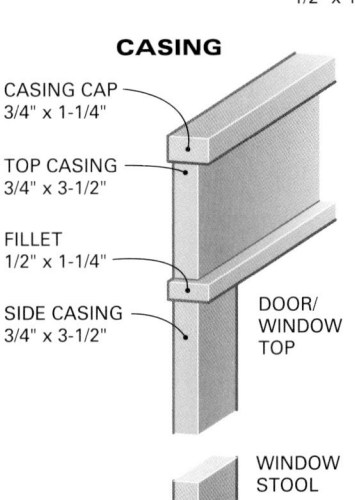

SHELF
3/4" x 3-1/2"

SHELF COVE
3/4" x 1-1/4"

WALL RAIL
3/4" x 3-1/2"

SHELF COVE
EDGE
1/2" x 1/2"

CASING

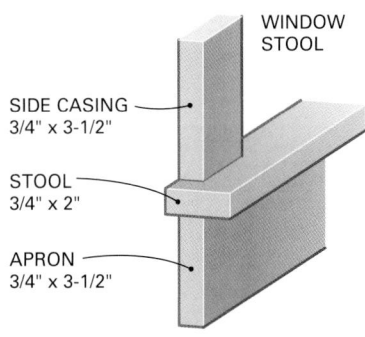

CASING CAP
3/4" x 1-1/4"

TOP CASING
3/4" x 3-1/2"

FILLET
1/2" x 1-1/4"

SIDE CASING
3/4" x 3-1/2"

DOOR/
WINDOW
TOP

WINDOW
STOOL

SIDE CASING
3/4" x 3-1/2"

STOOL
3/4" x 2"

APRON
3/4" x 3-1/2"

BASEBOARD

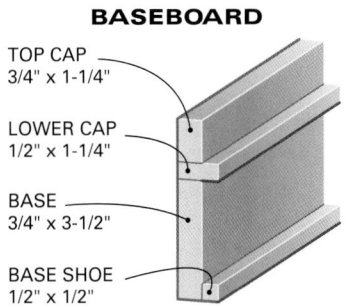

TOP CAP
3/4" x 1-1/4"

LOWER CAP
1/2" x 1-1/4"

BASE
3/4" x 3-1/2"

BASE SHOE
1/2" x 1/2"

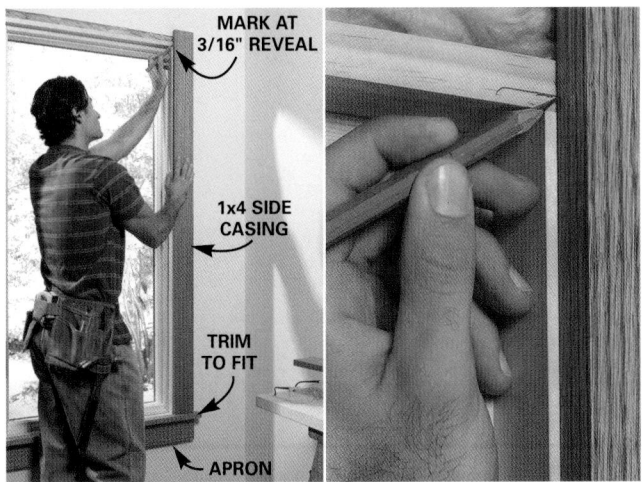

MARK AT
3/16" REVEAL

1x4 SIDE
CASING

TRIM
TO FIT

APRON

4 MARK the jambs to allow a 3/16-in. reveal. Cut side casings about 1/2 in. too long and fit them to the sill. Then mark and cut the top of the casings and tack them in place.

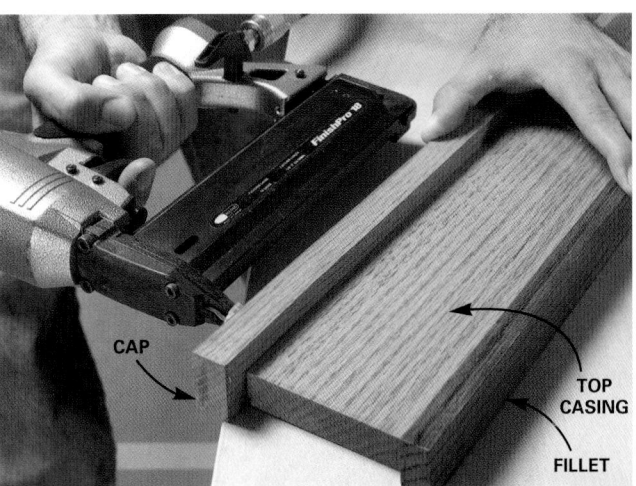

CAP

TOP
CASING

FILLET

5 MEASURE to the outside edges of the side casings and cut the top casing to this length. Add 1 in. for the cap and fillet and nail these pieces to the top and bottom of the casing.

EDGE
OF
CASING

WINDOW
TOP CASING

6 CENTER the completed assembly in place over the side casings. Predrill 5/64-in. holes through the fillet and nail it to the window frame with 2-in. finish nails. Nail along the top of the 1x4 into the wall framing with 2-1/2 in. finish nails.

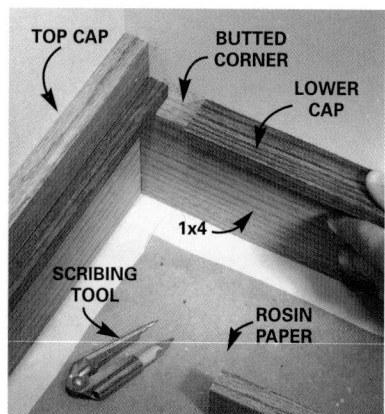

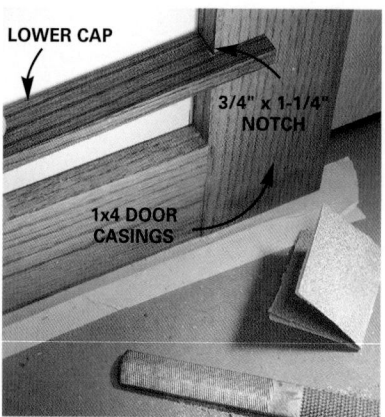

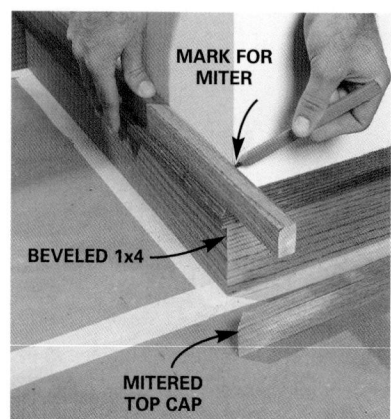

7 BUTT the baseboard at inside corners. Adjust for a tight fit by scribing a line and cutting to it. Nail the 1x4 to the wall studs, the lower cap to the 1x4 and the cap to the wall.

8 NOTCH the lower cap to overlap the casing by 1-1/4 in. Cut the notches a little undersized with a handsaw and file and sand to the lines.

9 HOLD outside corner pieces in place, mark and miter them. Complete the baseboard by cutting the base shoe and nailing it to the baseboard.

Baseboard

The baseboard consists of a 1x4 with a two-piece cap and a square molding (base shoe) that covers gaps at the floor (**Fig. A**). Before you start installing the base, locate the center of the wall studs with a stud finder or other method and mark their locations on the floor (mark on the paper used to protect the floor, or use strips of masking tape). Run the first piece of base wall to wall. Then cut square ends on the adjoining pieces and butt them into the first piece. If there's a gap at the butted joint, use a scribing tool (**Photo 7**) to mark the base and then recut it along the scribed line. Miter the base to fit around outside corners. Cut boards a few inches too long and mark in place whenever possible. Then make your cut about 1/16 in. beyond the mark to allow for fine adjustments. Mark, cut and fit both sides of outside corners before nailing either piece to the wall.

Nail the 1/2-in. x 1-1/4 in. lower cap down to the 1x4

base. Use a sharp handsaw to notch the lower cap to overlap door casings (**Photo 8**). This is a highly visible joint, so work for a tight fit. Once again, butt inside corners and miter outside corners. Cut and fit the top cap using the same technique as the 1x4 base. On floors without carpet, finish the baseboard by installing the square base shoe molding along the floor. Press the molding tight to the floor to cover gaps and nail it to the baseboard with 1-1/4 in. finish nails.

Cove

The cove molding consists of five pieces. Start by locating and marking the wall studs and ceiling framing members. If you put the marks about 4 in. from the wall and ceiling corner, they'll be hidden by the trim. You probably won't find any ceiling framing along two of the walls that run parallel to the ceiling joists. **Photo 12** shows how to attach the trim to the ceiling along these walls.

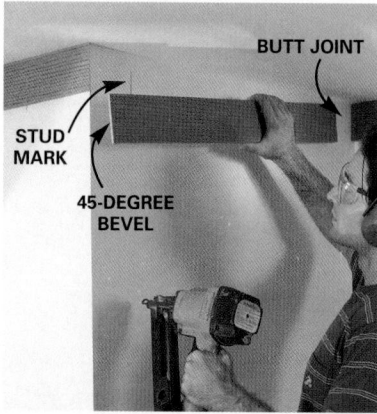

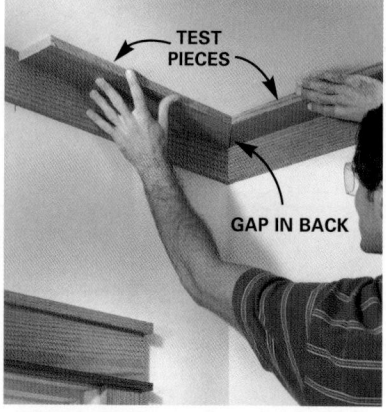

10 MARK the studs, then butt the 1x4s to the ceiling and nail them. Butt and scribe inside corners (see Photo 7) and miter outside corners.

11 USE a pair of 2-ft. long test boards to establish an accurate miter saw setting. Then cut and fit the ceiling boards and nail them to the ceiling framing.

12 ALONG walls without ceiling framing, use construction adhesive and temporary braces to attach the boards.

13 COVER gaps by fitting and nailing the 3/4 x 3/4-in. piece and the 1/2 x 1/2-in. edge pieces. Butt the inside corners and miter outside corners.

14 DRAW horizontal marks around the room and add the plate rail following the details in Fig. A. Notch the ends to overlap the casing as shown.

Start the installation by installing the 1x4 against the wall. This is exactly like installing the baseboard, except you'll need a ladder. Next install the 1x4 flat to the ceiling. Miter the inside and outside corners. Walls are rarely perfectly square to each other, so for a perfect fit you'll probably have to adjust the angles a fraction of a degree. Use a pair of test boards cut at 45 degrees to test the fit (**Photo 11**). If there's a gap, adjust the miter box angle slightly until they fit. Complete the cove by nailing the three remaining square profile moldings to the 1x4s (**Photo 13**).

Plate rail

We installed the plate rail 14 in. down from the top of the door head casing. Begin by marking this distance on the wall. Then measure down from the bottom of the cove molding and use this measurement to mark the height of the molding around the remainder of the room. A pencil mark every 4 ft. and at the corners is sufficient. This method is usually better than leveling because the rail will be parallel to the ceiling. Once again locate and mark the

stud locations. Installation is similar to the base and cove. Nail up the rail first. Then notch the shelf to overlap door and window casings by 1-1/2 in. and nail it down into the 1x4. Use 1-1/2 in. brads or finish nails. Next cut the shelf cove and nail it to the rail. Overlap this piece 3/4 in. onto door and window casings. Complete the plate rail by nailing the shelf cove edge to the rail (**Photo 14**).

Finishing tips

Sand the boards and trim pieces with 120-grit sandpaper followed by 180-grit and stain them before installation. We used Zar brand Provincial oil stain for most of the trim. For the darker-stained pieces, we used Zar Dark Mahogany. When all the moldings are installed, brush on a coat of sanding sealer. Then putty the nail holes with soft Color Putty. Mix two colors of putty to get a match if necessary. Lightly sand the surface with 220-grit sandpaper after the sealer dries. Vacuum off the dust and recoat with the polyurethane or varnish of your choice. Use the same brand of finish for the seal coat and the final coat. ⌂

SNAP-TOGETHER
WOOD FLOORING

This clever fastening system simplifies floor laying. No glue, no nails. You can do it in a weekend.

by **Jeff Gorton**

Here's a wood floor that's so easy to install you can complete an average-size room in a weekend. The joints just snap together. Simple carpentry skills and a few basic tools are all you need to cut the floorboards and notch them around corners.

In this article, we'll show you how to prepare your room and lay the snap-together flooring. The flooring we're using is similar to snap-together laminate floors except that it has a surface layer of real wood. The 5/16-in. thick flooring has specially shaped tongues and grooves that interlock to form a strong tight joint without glue or nails. Once assembled, the entire floor "floats" in one large sheet. You leave a small expansion space all around the edges so the floor can expand and contract with humidity changes.

Wood veneer floors cost $5 to $15 per sq. ft., depending on the species and thickness of the top wood layer. Most home centers sell a few types of snap-together floors, but you'll find a better selection and expert advice at your local flooring retailer. You can also buy flooring on-line.

Before you go shopping, draw a sketch of your room with dimensions. Make note of transitions to other types of flooring and other features like stair landings and exterior doors. Ask your salesperson for help choosing the right transition moldings for these areas.

You'll need a few special tools in addition to basic hand tools like a tape measure, square and utility knife. We purchased an installation kit from the manufacturer ($40) that included plastic shims, a tapping block and a last-board puller, but if you're handy you could fabricate these tools. A pull saw works great to undercut door-jambs and casing (**Photo 3**). It's difficult to get close enough to the floor with a standard handsaw. You'll also need a circular saw and a jigsaw to cut the flooring, and a miter box to cut the shoe molding. A table saw and power miter saw would make your job easier but aren't necessary.

Make sure your floor is dry

Don't lay this type of floor over damp concrete or damp crawlspaces. Check all concrete for excess moisture. As a starting point, use the plastic mat test shown in **Photo 1**. Even though some manufacturers allow it, professional installers we spoke to advised against installing floating floors in kitchens, full or three-quarter baths, or entryways, all areas where they might be subjected to standing water.

1 TEST for excess moisture in concrete floors by sealing the edges of a 3-ft. square of plastic sheeting to the floor with duct tape. Wait 24 hours before you peel back the plastic to check for moisture. Water droplets on the plastic or darkened concrete indicate a possible problem with excess moisture. Ask your flooring supplier for advice before installing a wood floor.

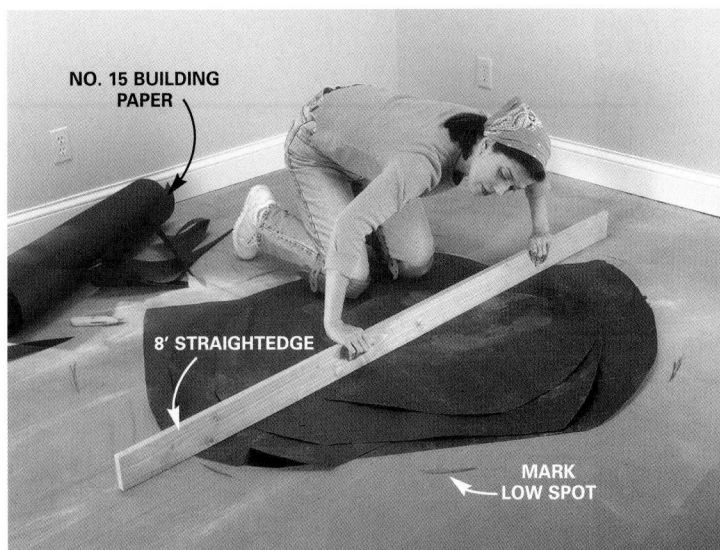

2 CHECK for low spots in the floor with an 8-ft. straightedge and mark their perimeter with a pencil. Fill depressions less than 1/4 in. deep with layers of building paper. Fill deeper depressions with a hardening-type floor filler available from flooring stores.

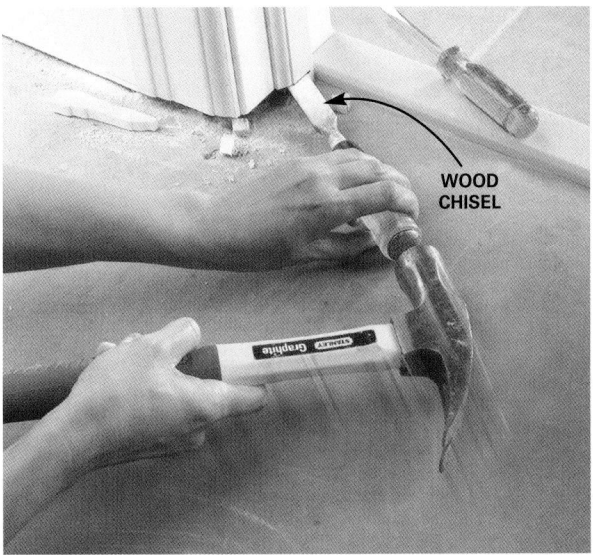

3 UNDERCUT doorjambs and casings (door moldings) to make space for the flooring to slip underneath. Guide the saw with a scrap of flooring stacked on a piece of underlayment.

4 BREAK and pry out the cutoff chunks of jamb and casing with a screwdriver. Use a sharp chisel or utility knife to complete the cut in areas the saw couldn't reach.

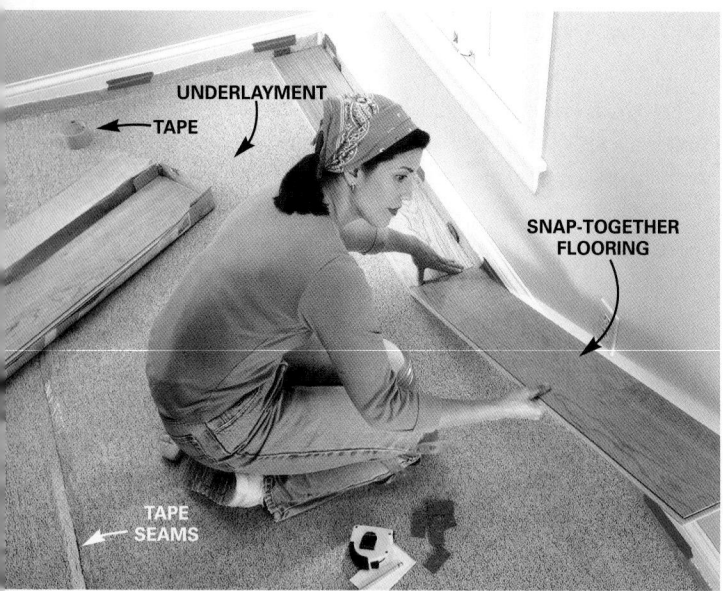

Labels: UNDERLAYMENT, TAPE, SNAP-TOGETHER FLOORING, TAPE SEAMS

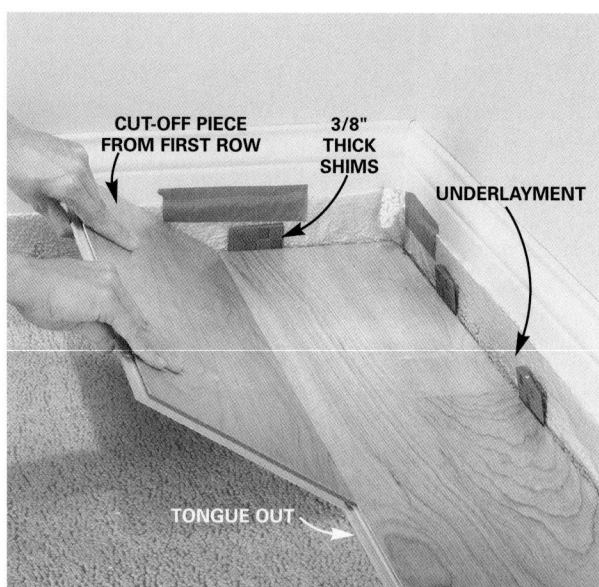

Labels: CUT-OFF PIECE FROM FIRST ROW, 3/8" THICK SHIMS, UNDERLAYMENT, TONGUE OUT

5 UNROLL the underlayment and lap it up the baseboards or walls 2 in. Temporarily secure the edges with masking tape. Butt the sheets together and seal the seams with the tape recommended by the manufacturer. Cut the first row of boards narrower if necessary to ensure that the last row of flooring will be at least 2 in. wide. Then start the installation by locking the ends of the first row of flooring together. Measure and cut the last piece to fit, allowing the 3/8-in. expansion space.

6 START the second row with the leftover cutoff piece from the first row, making sure the end joints are offset at least 12 in. from the end joints in the first row. With the board held at about a 45-degree angle, engage the tongue in the groove. Push in while you rotate the starter piece down toward the floor. The click indicates the pieces have locked together. The joint between boards should draw tight.

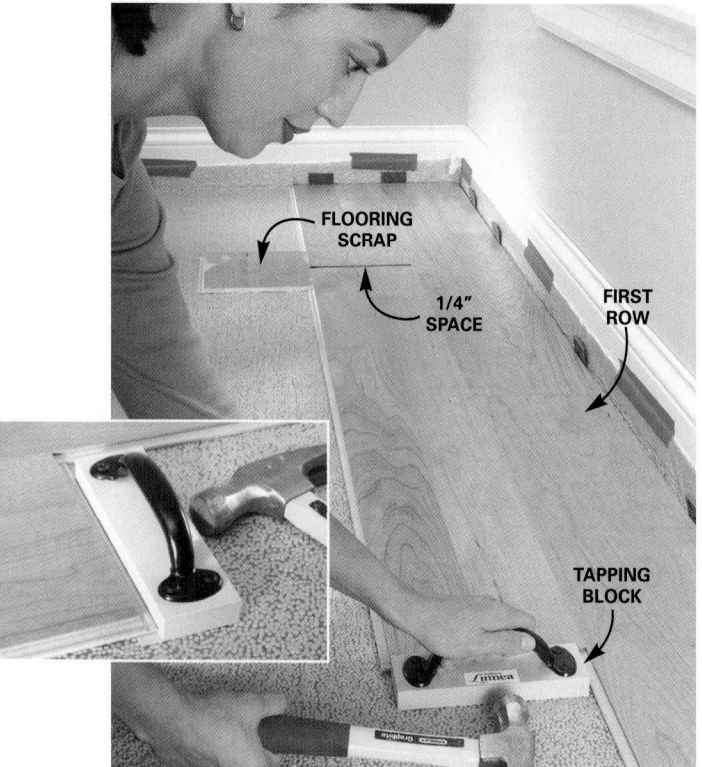

Labels: FLOORING SCRAP, 1/4" SPACE, FIRST ROW, TAPPING BLOCK

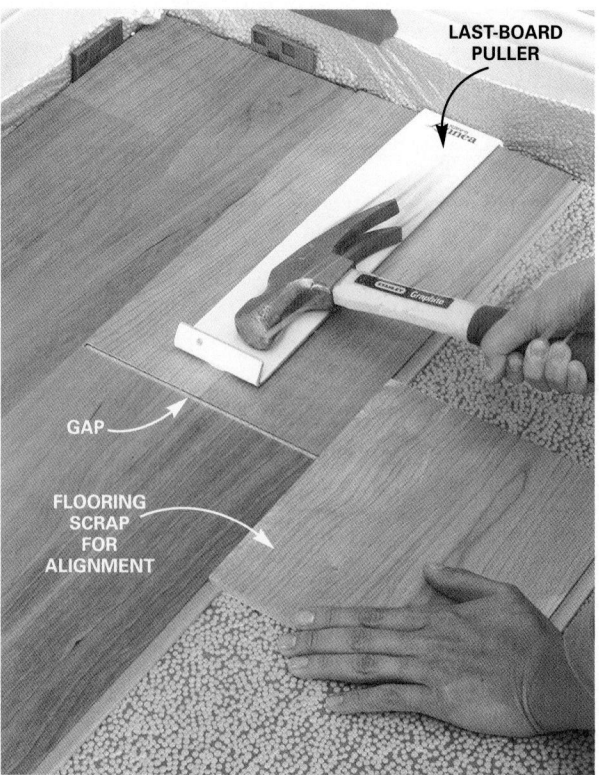

Labels: LAST-BOARD PULLER, GAP, FLOORING SCRAP FOR ALIGNMENT

7 LEAVE a 1/4-in. space between the next full piece of flooring and the previous piece. Snap this piece into the first row. Snap a scrap of flooring across the ends being joined to hold them in alignment while you tap them together. Place the tapping block against the end of the floor piece and tap it with a hammer to close the gap.

8 CLOSE a gap at the end of the row by hooking the last-board puller tool over the end of the plank and tapping it with a hammer to pull the end joints together.

Prepare your room for new flooring

You have to make sure the existing floor is smooth and flat before installing a floating floor overtop. Clear the old floor, then smooth it by scraping off lumps and sweeping it. If you have wood floors, now's the time to fix squeaks and tighten loose boards by screwing them to the joists with deck screws. Check the floor with an 8-ft. straightedge and mark high spots and depressions. Sand or grind down ridges and fill low spots (**Photo 2**). Most manufacturers recommend no more than 1/8-in. variation in flatness over an 8-ft. length.

Allowing the floor to expand and contract freely is critical. Leave at least a 3/8-in. expansion space along the edges. You can hide the gap under the baseboards or leave the baseboards in place and cover the gap with shoe molding or quarter round as we did. Cover the expansion

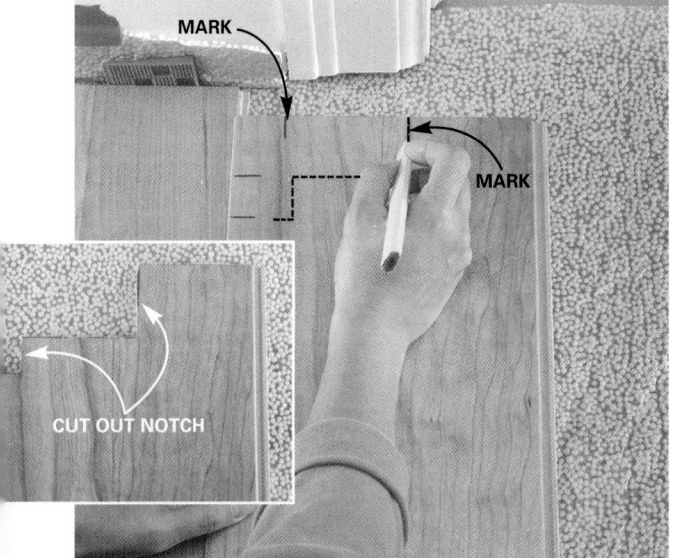

9 **PLAN** ahead when you get near a doorjamb. Usually you have to slide the next piece of flooring under the jamb rather than tilt and snap it into place. To accomplish this, you must slice off the locking section of the tongue from the preceding row with a sharp utility knife before installing it.

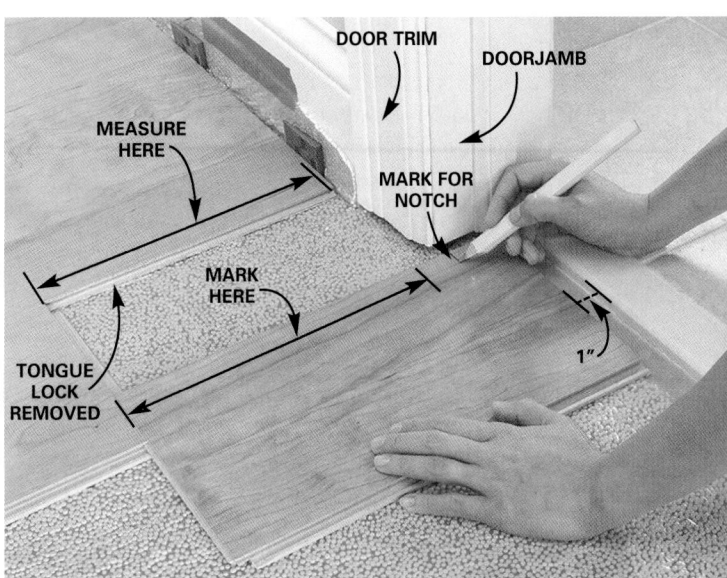

10 **CUT** the plank to be notched to length, allowing a 1-in. space for the future transition piece. Align the end with the end of the last plank laid and mark 3/8 in. inside the jamb to make sure the flooring extends under the door trim.

11 **ALIGN** the flooring lengthwise and mark for the notches in the other direction, allowing for the floor to slide under the doorjamb about 3/8 in. Connect the marks with a square and cut out the notch with a jigsaw.

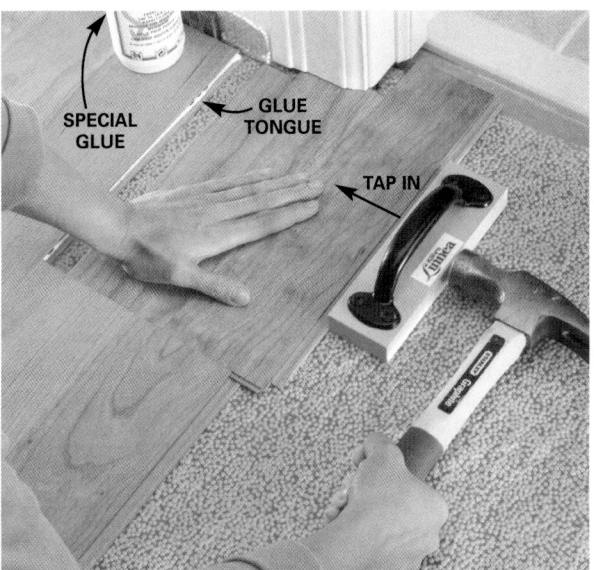

12 **APPLY** a thin bead of the manufacturer's recommended glue along the edge where the portion of the tongue was removed. Slide the notched piece of flooring into place and tighten the glued edge by pounding on the special tapping block.

space at openings or transitions to other types of flooring with special transition moldings (**Photo 13**). Buy these from the dealer.

Finally, saw off the bottoms of doorjambs and trim to allow for the flooring to slide underneath (**Photo 3**). Leaving an expansion gap at exterior doors presents a unique challenge. In older houses, you could carefully remove the threshold and notch it to allow the flooring to slide underneath. For most newer exterior doors, you can butt a square-nosed transition piece against the threshold.

Floating floors must be installed over a thin cushioning pad called underlayment (**Photo 5**). Underlayment is usually sold in rolls and costs 25¢ to 50¢ per sq. ft. Ask your flooring dealer to suggest the best one for your situation. Some types combine a vapor barrier and padding. Install this type over concrete or other floors where moisture might be a problem. Others reduce sound transmission.

Take extra care when installing underlayment that includes a vapor barrier. Lap the edges up the wall and carefully seal all the seams as recommended by the manufacturer. Keep a roll of tape handy to patch accidental rips and tears as you install the floor.

After the first few rows, installing the floor is a snap

You may have to cut your first row of flooring narrower to make sure the last row is at least 2 in. wide. To figure this, measure across the room and divide by the width of the

exposed face on the flooring. The number remaining is the width of the last row. If the remainder is less than 2, cut the first row narrower to make this last row wider. Then continue the installation as shown in **Photos 6 – 8**.

You can't use the same tilt-and-snap installation technique where the flooring fits under doorjambs. You have to slide the flooring together instead. **Photos 9 – 12** show how. If the opening requires a transition molding, cut the flooring short to leave space for it (**Photo 13**).

Complete the floor by cutting the last row to the correct width to fit against the wall. Make sure to leave the required expansion space. Finally, reinstall the baseboards if you removed them, or install new quarter-round or shoe molding to cover the expansion space (**Photo 14**). ⌂

CONSTRUCTION ADHESIVE

SQUARE NOSE TRANSITION

TEMPORARY WEIGHTS

BAND OF ADHESIVE

NAIL SET

4D FINISH NAILS

13 CUT a transition molding, in this case a square nose transition, to fit between the doorstops or jambs. Spread a bead of construction adhesive only on the area of the concrete floor that will be in contact with the transition piece. Set the transition in place and weight it down overnight.

14 COMPLETE the flooring project by trimming off the protruding underlayment with a utility knife and installing shoe molding. Predrill 1/16-in. holes through the shoe. Then nail the shoe molding to the baseboard with 4d finish nails. Set and fill the nails. Do not nail down into the flooring.

2 Kitchen, Bathroom & Laundry Room Projects

IN THIS CHAPTER

Cabinet Facelift 38

Handy Hints 43
   Drip eliminator, super shelf liner,
   thyme saver and more...

Clutter-Free Laundry Room 44

Great Goofs .51

Gallery of Ideas 52
   Whirlpool tub, new vanity & sink,
   tile countertop

Built-In Pantry Cabinets 54

Ask Handyman 58
   Can I renew a scratched
   countertop?, painting ceramic tile
   and more...

Great Goofs .59

Tile Tub Surround 60

Great Goofs .65

Undercabinet Lighting 66

Wordless Workshop 72
   Ironing board cabinet

CABINET FACELIFT

Simple, attractive kitchen upgrades you can do yourself—without replacing your cabinets

by **Spike Carlsen**

Take a look, a really close look. At first glance it may be hard to recognize, but the kitchen in the small photo is the same as the one below it. The cabinet "boxes," the countertop, the layout, the flooring, the sink and the window haven't changed a whit. Better yet, once the materials were in hand, this transformation took place in just a few days—without putting the kitchen out of commission. The frosting on the cake? The total cost for upgrading the cabinets was $2,100 (not including the wall tile).

With the average full-scale kitchen remodeling project costing more than $30,000 (and about one-third of that amount spent on cabinetry), you can see we got a big impact for a small cost.

Whether you tackle one or all of these cabinet upgrades, you'll increase the visual appeal of your kitchen quickly, inexpensively and with minimum hassle.

BEFORE

AFTER

If you're pleased with the basic layout and function of your kitchen but want to update the look—and add a few new features—read on. We'll show you how paint, new cabinet doors and drawer fronts, moldings and a few accessories can transform your kitchen.

Most of the projects require only a drill, basic hand tools and intermediate DIY savvy, although a power miter saw and pneumatic finish nailer allow you to cut and install the crown molding faster.

Bear in mind, these upgrades won't fix cabinets that are falling apart, create more storage space or make your kitchen easier to navigate. But if you want to give your kitchen an inexpensive yet dramatic facelift, here's how.

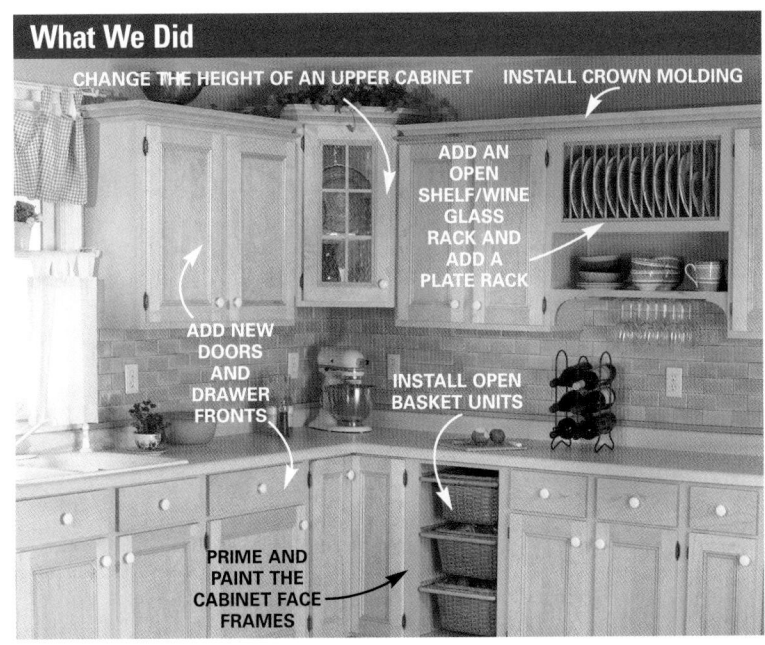

What We Did

CHANGE THE HEIGHT OF AN UPPER CABINET

INSTALL CROWN MOLDING

ADD AN OPEN SHELF/WINE GLASS RACK AND ADD A PLATE RACK

ADD NEW DOORS AND DRAWER FRONTS

INSTALL OPEN BASKET UNITS

PRIME AND PAINT THE CABINET FACE FRAMES

KITCHEN, BATHROOM & LAUNDRY ROOM PROJECTS

Add an open shelf, wine glass rack and plate rack

If you have a short cabinet flanked by two taller cabinets, you can add this combination shelf/wine rack.

We cut the shelf to length, then added mounting strips on each end. We cut four 9-in. sections of wine glass molding from a 3-ft. length (see Buyer's Guide, p. 42), then glued and nailed them to the bottom of the pine shelf. We also cut curved brackets from each end of a 1x6 maple board and cut the center 1 in. wide to serve as shelf edging. Finally, we installed the unit by driving screws through the mounting strips and into the cabinets on each side.

To display your plates and keep them accessible and chip-free, build and install this plate rack. The total cost of materials? Under $10.

To create the two plate rack "ladders," measure the cabinet, then build each ladder so the finished height equals the height of the inside of the cabinet. The finished width should be equal to the width of the face frame opening. Drill 3/8-in. holes, 3/8 in. deep in 3/4-in. x 3/4-in. square dowels and space them every 1-1/2 in. Cut the dowels to length, add a drop of glue in each hole, insert the dowels, then use elastic cords or clamps to hold things together until the glue dries.

A drill press comes in handy, but you can get excellent results using the same tools we did: a cordless drill, a steady hand and a 3/8-in. drill bit with masking tape wrapped around it as a depth guide for the holes in the rails.

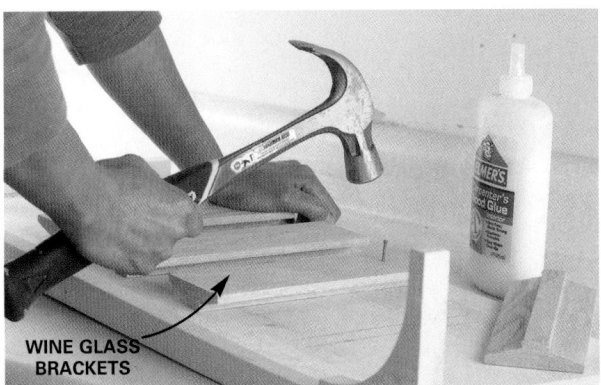

WINE GLASS BRACKETS

Build a shelf to fit snugly between the cabinets on each side. We used a jigsaw to create curved brackets, nailed wine glass brackets to the bottom of the shelf, then installed the entire unit as one piece.

3/4" x 3/4" RAILS   1-1/2" SPACE   DOWELS INSET INTO 3/8" DEEP HOLES

3/8" DOWELS

Cut, assemble and install the two plate rack "ladders." Use short screws to secure the ladders in the cabinet opening. We set the rear ladder 4 in. away from the back of the cabinet and the front ladder snug against the back of the face frame.

Paint your cabinet face frames

Proper preparation and sanding between coats are the keys to a smooth, durable paint job on your cabinet face frames.

Oil paints arguably create the smoothest surface, since they dry slowly and "self-level" as brush stroke marks fill in. However, this slow drying time means they're more vulnerable to dust. Cleanup is also more of a hassle. Latex paints dry quickly and may show brush strokes more, but additives like Floetrol (The Flood Co., 800-321-3444) improve "brushability."

After priming, paint the cabinets with a gloss or semigloss paint. Apply a thin first coat, let it dry, then lightly sand with 120- or 180-grit sandpaper. Wipe the surface, then apply a second coat. Two or three thin coats are better than one or two thick ones.

If you have a gas stove, turn off the gas for safety while using mineral spirits, shellac or oil paints, and provide plenty of ventilation.

PIGMENTED SHELLAC PRIMER

SANDING BLOCK WITH 120-GRIT PAPER

Clean the cabinet face frames with mineral spirits, then scrub them with household ammonia and rinse. Fill holes with spackling compound, then sand with 120-grit sandpaper. Vacuum the cabinets, then prime them with a pigmented shellac. Lightly sand the dried primer.

Add new doors and drawer fronts

We had a local cabinet shop make our new doors and drawer fronts the exact same dimensions as the old ones. We used the same hinges and mounting holes in the face frames to ensure the right fit.

You can have your components made locally or by one of the companies listed in the Buyer's Guide, p. 42.

Existing drawer fronts can be attached in a number of different ways. We were able to simply pry off the old and screw on the new. If yours can't be removed, you'll need to use a circular saw to cut all four edges of the drawer front even with the edges of the drawer box, then apply the new drawer front directly over the old. This will make your drawers 3/4 in. longer; make certain your drawer hardware and cabinets can accommodate the extra length. If not, you may need to install new drawer hardware or new drawer "boxes."

Mount the hinges to the doors, then mount the doors to the face frames using the existing screw holes. Most hinges allow for some up-and-down movement and tilt so the doors can be adjusted evenly.

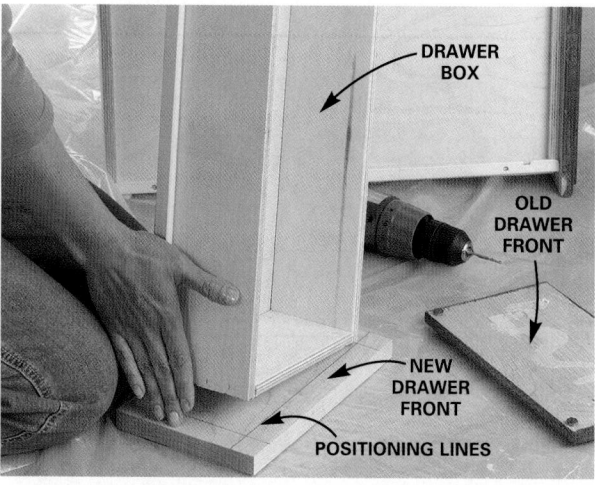

DRAWER BOX

OLD DRAWER FRONT

NEW DRAWER FRONT

POSITIONING LINES

Replace the old drawer fronts. We pried off the old front using a chisel and a flat bar, marked the position of the drawer box on the back of the new drawer front, then joined the two using carpenter's glue and screws.

Raise an upper cabinet

To break up the monotony of a row of cabinets, change the height of one or more upper cabinets. This provides more "headroom" for working and more space for lighting and appliances, as well as creates a more interesting and varied look.

In order to raise a cabinet, your cabinets must be the modular kind such that each cabinet is an independent "box" screwed to adjacent ones. Earlier "builder cabinets," with the entire row of cabinets built and installed as one unit, aren't easily separated. We elevated our corner cabinet 3 in., temporarily propped it up with scrap lumber, drilled pilot holes for new screws, then reattached it. A cabinet

To raise a cabinet, remove the shelves and doors and then the screws securing it to the wall and cabinets on either side. Raise the cabinet, temporarily prop it in place, drill new pilot holes, then reinstall the screws.

that's been in place a long time may need a sharp rap with a hammer to free it from paint and grime that have "glued" it in place.

Install open basket units

The "Base 18" baskets we installed (see Buyer's Guide, p. 42) came with two side tracks that could be cut narrower to accommodate cabinets ranging in width from 15-7/8 in. to 17-7/8 in. "Base 15" baskets fit cabinets with an inside width of 12-7/8 in. to 15-7/8 in. Measure carefully, cut the basket tracks to width, then install them as shown.

Remove cabinet hardware, then the rails where you want to create an open cabinet. A fine-tooth pull saw works well for removing the dividers, since it lies flat against the cabinet frame as it cuts. Sand the area to create a smooth surface.

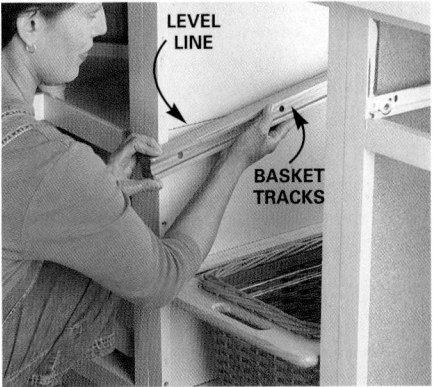

Cut the tracks to the proper width, then level them in both directions and screw them to the sides of the cabinet.

Install crown molding

Crown molding comes in many profiles and sizes; we installed rope molding (see Buyer's Guide, below). If your face frames aren't wide enough on top to nail the molding to, nail strips of wood to the top edge to provide a nailing surface.

Raising the corner cabinet created a challenge where the moldings on each side butted into it. We held the upper part of the crown molding back a few inches, but extended the thin rope molding portion so it butted into the corner cabinet.

For more detailed information on cutting and installing crown molding, see "Window Cornices," July/Aug. '01, p. 48. To order a copy, see p. 288. 🏠

see "Window Cornices," July/Aug. '01, p. 48. To order a copy, see p. 288.

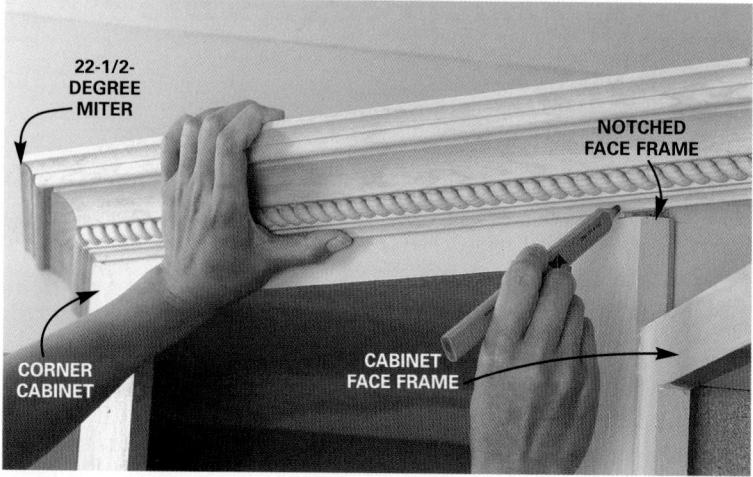

Position and mark each piece of crown molding as you work your way around the kitchen. Make small notches in the top corners of the face frames so the moldings lie flat against the sides of the cabinets when installed.

Cut the crown molding by placing it upside down and securing it at the correct angle with a clamp and wood scrap.

Buyer's Guide

All the products used in this project are readily available through catalogs, the Internet and specialty woodworking stores. Here are a few sources:

Cabinet doors and drawer fronts

A local cabinetmaker made our 13 maple doors and six drawer fronts for $1,500. Expect to pay about $20 per square foot for custom doors, slightly less for the drawer fronts. You could also have a company specializing in cabinet refacing measure and order the doors for you.

There are a variety of mail order sources you can explore:

- Custom Kitchen Cabinet and Refacing Co.: (888) 407-3322, www.reface.com
- Jackson Custom Woodworks: (866) 261-7643. www.jacksoncustom.com
- Kitchen Door Depot: (877) 399-5677, www.kitchendoordepot.com
- Kitchen Doors Online: (877) 887-0400, www.kitchendoors-online.net
- Rockler Custom Door and Drawer Front Program: (800) 279-4441, www.rockler.com

Crown molding, bun feet, baskets, wine glass molding

- We ordered our maple rope crown molding (No. 53639, $77.99 per 8-ft. length), wicker baskets (No. 47527, $70.00 each), wine glass molding (No. 22210, $10.99 per 36-in. piece) and bun feet (No. 70410, $10.59 each) from Rockler (800-279-4441, www.rockler.com).
- Outwater (888-688-9283, www.outwater.com) and Woodworker's Supply (800-645-9292, www.woodworker.com) sell similar items.

Miscellaneous

- The porcelain pulls, dowels for the plate rack, primer and paint were bought at a home center.
- We ordered the wall tile (Newport, Sage Green by Walker Zanger Ceramics, 877-611-0199, www.walkerzanger.com) from a local tile shop.

Handy Hints® from our readers

THYME SAVER

Does your stew boil over every time you're distracted for five minutes looking for the right spice? My spices were jammed into a drawer with only the tops visible until I took an hour to make this nifty rack that slips neatly into the drawer. I made it with leftover scraps of 1/4-in. and 1/2-in. plywood from my shop. Now I spend less time cleaning the burners and more time stirring the pot!

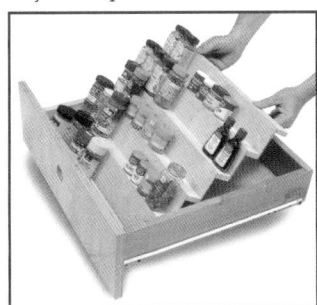

SUPER SHELF LINER

Looking for the ultimate shelf liner for your kitchen cabinets? Use the translucent plastic sheets made for fluorescent light panels in suspended ceilings. They're sold at most home centers in 2 x 4-ft. sheets and can be cut to fit the shelves. They're easy to wipe clean, and pots and pans slide easily on them.

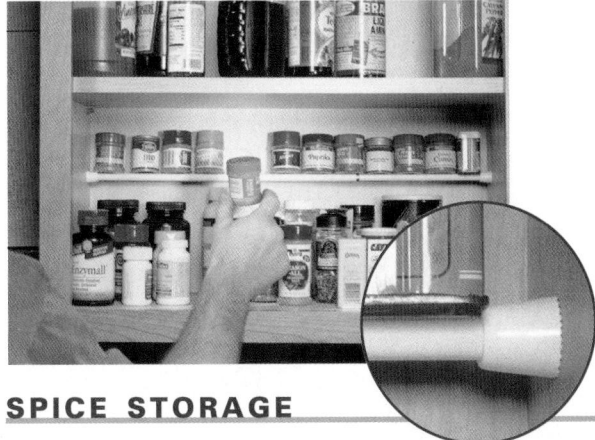

SPICE STORAGE

Small spice containers use shelf space inefficiently and are difficult to find when surrounded by taller bottles and items. Use a small spring-tension curtain rod ($3) as a simple shelf. It's easy to install and strong enough to support the spices.

SHE'S AT THE END OF HER ROPE

DRIP ELIMINATOR

The drip, drip, drip of a leaky faucet or shower head can drive a person to the brink of insanity. Here's a temporary fix that'll help you get a peaceful night's sleep. Hang a rope from the leaky fixture so the water drips onto the rope and runs silently down to the drain.

GROUT SQUEEZE BOTTLE

I installed an ornate tile border in my bathroom but couldn't float the grout between the tiles because of the raised details. My wife gave me a clean, empty mustard bottle to try. It worked like a champ! I filled it up and squeezed the grout between the tiles. You can cut the tip to get a better angle or increase the volume. P.S. It also works great for porous stone because it doesn't fill the pores with grout.

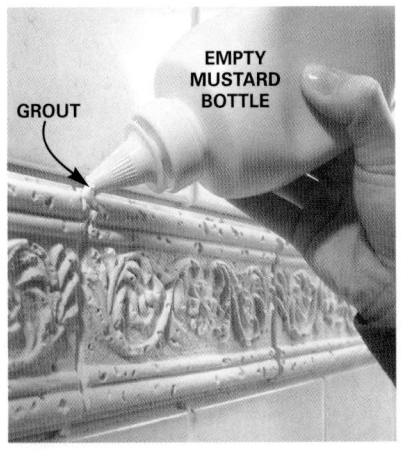

GROUT

EMPTY MUSTARD BOTTLE

CLUTTER-FREE
LAUNDRY ROOM

These fast and easy projects create a pleasant, efficient work area

by **David Radtke**

Why do you think the idle rich have always had their maids do their laundry while they go for a drive in the country? My hunch is if they had a laundry room outfitted like this one, they'd send the maids out for a drive and they'd be whistling at home sorting their own socks.

Closet rod and shelf/Fold-away folding table

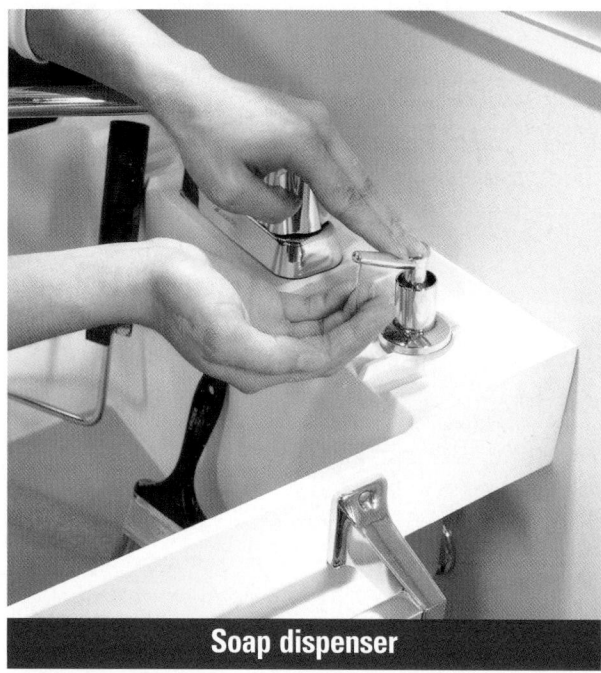

Soap dispenser

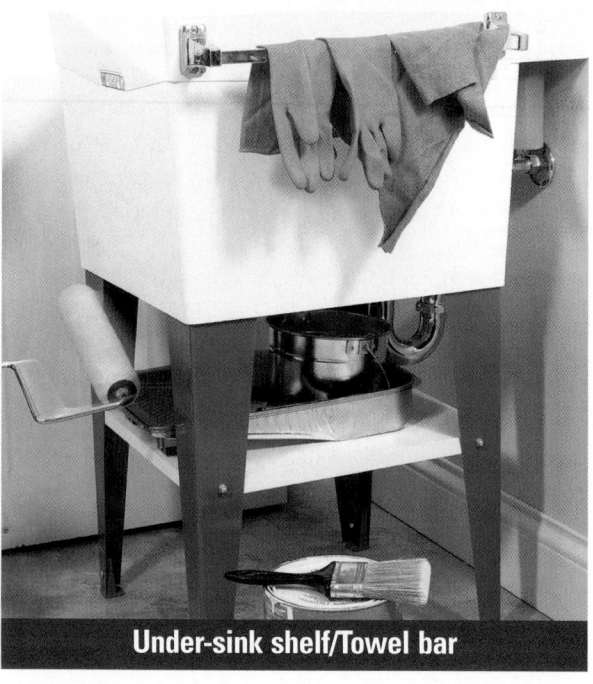

Under-sink shelf/Towel bar

All-purpose wall cabinet

Closet rod and shelf

You can get these great-looking Lido Rail chrome brackets and rod at home centers or buy them on-line. One source is www.aubuchonhardware.com.

This project will save you hours of ironing and organizing. Now you can hang up your shirts and jackets as soon as they're out of the dryer—no more wrinkled shirts at the bottom of the basket. You'll also gain an out-of-the-way upper shelf to store all sorts of odds and ends.

Just go to your home center and get standard closet rod brackets, a closet rod and a precut 12-in. deep Melamine shelf (all for about $25). Also pick up some drywall anchors, or if you have concrete, some plastic anchors and a corresponding masonry bit. Follow the instructions in **Photos 1 and 2**.

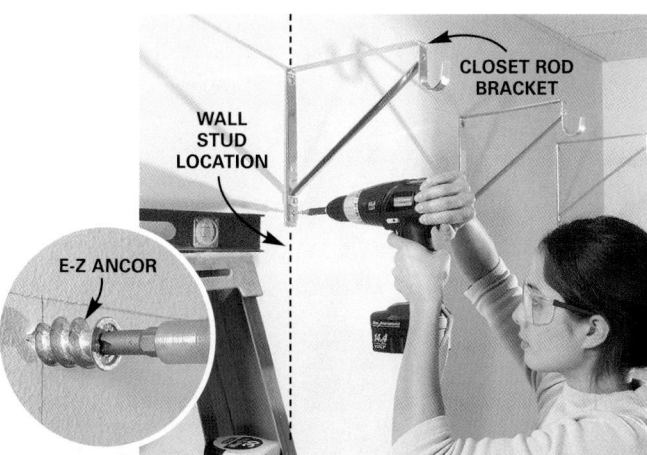

1 DRAW a level line about 78 in. above the floor and locate the studs behind the drywall. Fasten at least two of your closet rod brackets into wall studs (4 ft. apart) and then center the middle bracket with two 2-in. long screws into wall anchors (inset).

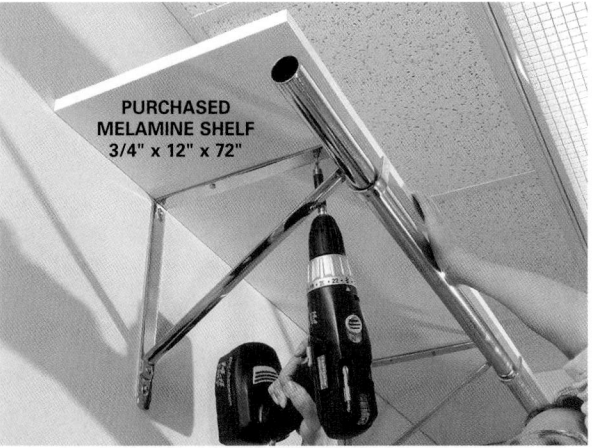

2 FASTEN your 12-in. deep Melamine shelf onto the tops of the brackets with 1/2-in. screws. Next, insert your closet rod, drill 1/8-in. holes into the rod, and secure it to the brackets with No. 6 x 1/2-in. sheet metal screws.

Soap dispenser

You can buy a soap dispenser in the kitchen section at home centers. Expect to pay about $12 to $25.

Get rid of that gross bar of soap that sits on the backsplash of your sink. Buy a soap dispenser at a home center and mount it to your acrylic tub. You'll need a drill, a 1-1/4 in. hole saw and liquid hand soap. Keep in mind you can put any liquid soap in the dispenser. A spot remover would be handy for prewash scrubbing.

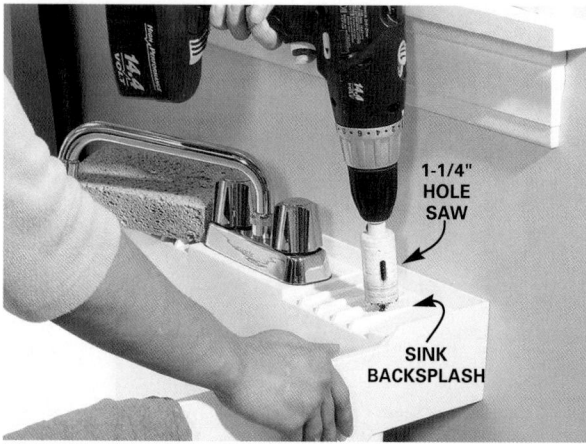

1-1/4" HOLE SAW

SINK BACKSPLASH

1 DRILL through the backsplash of your acrylic laundry tub with a hole saw. Measure precisely so you'll have clearance for the soap bottle below. Choose a hole saw just a bit larger than the threaded base of the pump.

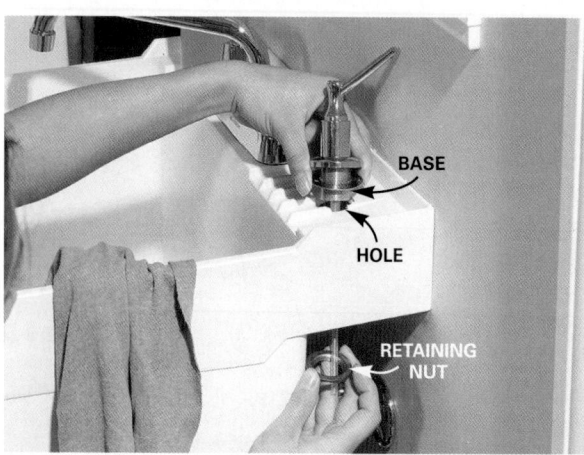

BASE

HOLE

RETAINING NUT

2 INSERT the threaded pump base into the hole and tighten the retaining nut to the underside of the backsplash. Fill the soap bottle with the liquid soap of your choice and thread it onto the base of the pump.

Towel bar

If you're looking for a basic towel bar like ours, your best bet is to go to a hardware store. Expect to pay about $8.

Get those messy rags out of the sink and onto a towel bar so they can actually dry. Shop for an easy mounting towel bar that you can shorten if you like. We picked one up at the hardware store that had easy mounting holes right on the face of the mounting plate and a removable bar. We cut the bar with a hacksaw so it would fit nicely on the side of the sink. While you're at the hardware store, buy stainless steel mounting bolts, washers and acorn nuts to mount the bar. We used 7/8-in. No. 8-24 bolts.

ACORN NUTS

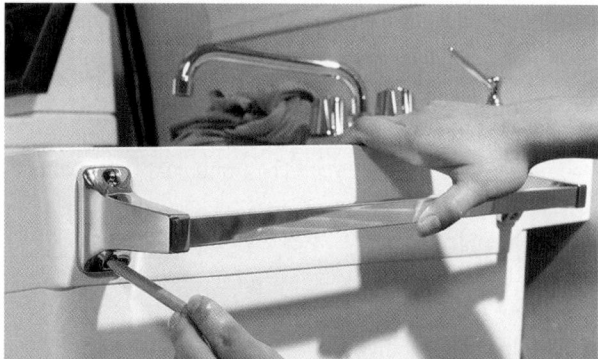

1 MARK the location of your towel bar on the thick rim near the top of the sink. You may need to shorten the bar first by pulling the bar from the ends and trimming it to about 16 in.

ACRYLIC LAUNDRY TUB

2 DRILL clearance holes at your marks and fasten the towel bar ends to the sink with bolts, washers and acorn nuts.

Under-sink shelf

You may have the materials for this project laying around your workshop or garage!

Tired of moving all that stuff under the sink every time you mop the floor? Just buy a Melamine closet shelf ($5) from a home center and a length of suspended-ceiling wall angle (sorry, it only comes in 10-ft. lengths, but it's cheap and you can have it cut for transport). Also pick up four 1/2-in. No. 8-24 bolts, washers and nuts. Follow Photos 1 – 3.

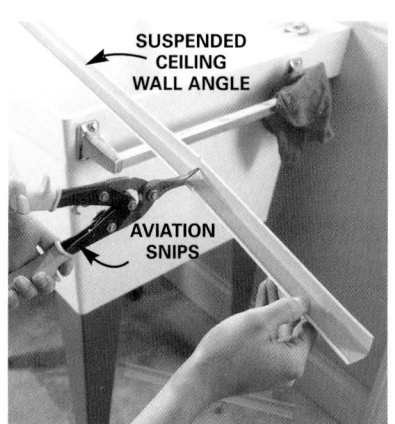

1 USING an aviation snips, cut two lengths of suspended ceiling channel to support the undersink shelf.

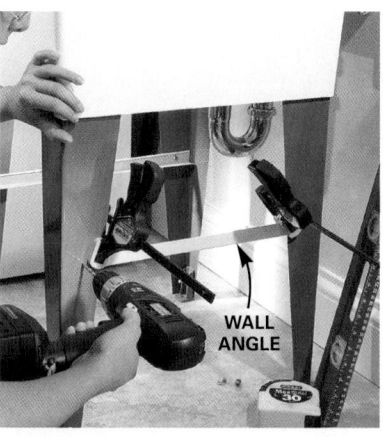

2 CLAMP pieces of ceiling wall angle to your sink legs (about 11 in. from the floor) and drill through with a 3/16-in. bit. Insert 1/2-in. long No. 8-24 bolts and thread on acorn nuts to cover sharp bolt edges.

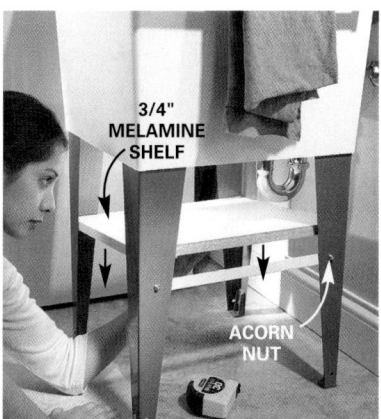

3 CUT a shelf from 3/4-in. Melamine board and drop it onto the angle braces. You may need to notch your shelf if the sink trap is in your way. Paint the raw edges of the board to protect them from moisture.

Fold-away folding table

You'll need to order the clever fold-away brackets for this project. Get them at Rockler Hardware (800-279-4441), part No. 29819 ($19.99).

This 2 x 5-ft. table is a handy option for any laundry room. Located right across from the washer and dryer, it's the perfect place for sorting colors before washing and folding the clothes as soon as they're dry. We chose heavy-duty brackets that'll hold more than 100 lbs. and neatly fold the top down (preventing future clutter).

You can get the countertop (and end cap) at a home center or maybe you can salvage one from a friend who's getting new countertops. Also buy three 8-ft. pine boards—a 1x2, a 1x3 and a 1x4—as well as some wood screws. You'll need 1-1/4 in. and 2-1/2 in. wood screws for mounting the wall cleats and the countertop stiffeners. Follow Photos 1 – 6 for clear step-by-step instructions.

UNDERSIDE OF COUNTERTOP BLANK

1 BUY a 6-ft. plastic laminate countertop blank from a home center. Measure in 1-1/2 in. from the backside, and draw a straight line. Cut this section away with a circular saw equipped with a sharp blade. Trim the countertop to length, cutting from the backside. We cut ours 5 ft. long so we could support it with only two laundry table brackets. Longer tables will sag without an additional bracket. Space the brackets no farther than 32 in. apart.

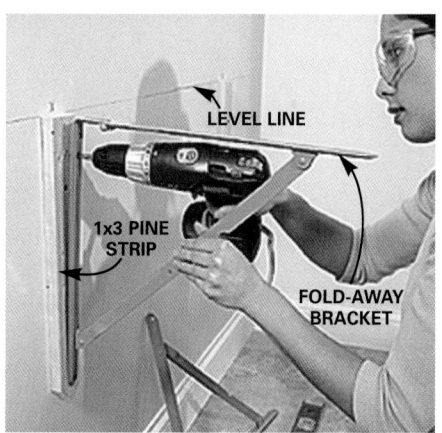

3 DRAW a level line 1-1/2 in. below the finished height of your laundry table. We made ours 33 in. high including the thickness of the top. Screw 1x3 pine strips to the wall into the studs behind. If you have a concrete wall, predrill holes for anchors and then screw the steel laundry table brackets to the strips and wall with 2-1/2 in. screws.

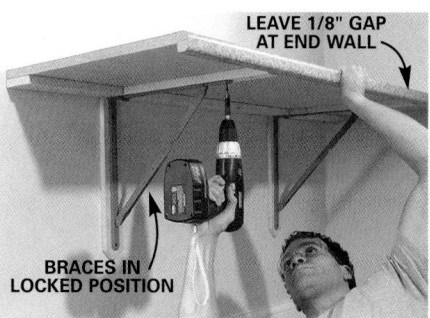

2 GLUE and screw 3/4-in. thick pine supports to the underside of the countertop. Use a 1x4 along the back and 1x2s at your bracket locations. The supports will stiffen the countertop and provide better backing for the bracket screws.

4 SET the top onto the brackets and screw them into the pine cleats (use 1-1/4 in. screws) under the table. Remember to keep about 1/8-in. clearance between the wall and the end for wiggle room as you lift and close the table. This will keep your wall from scarring each time you lift and close the tabletop.

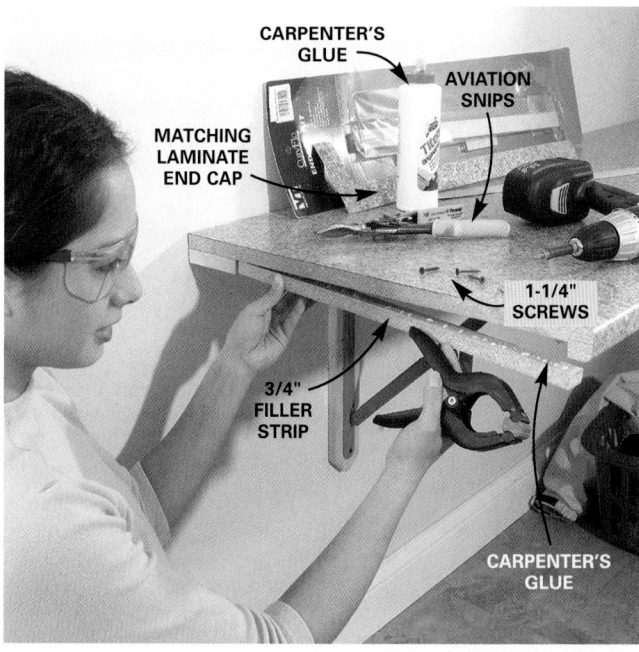

5 GLUE and screw the 3/4-in. thick filler strips to the exposed bottom edge of the counter. Align the filler strip so it's flush with the edge of the top.

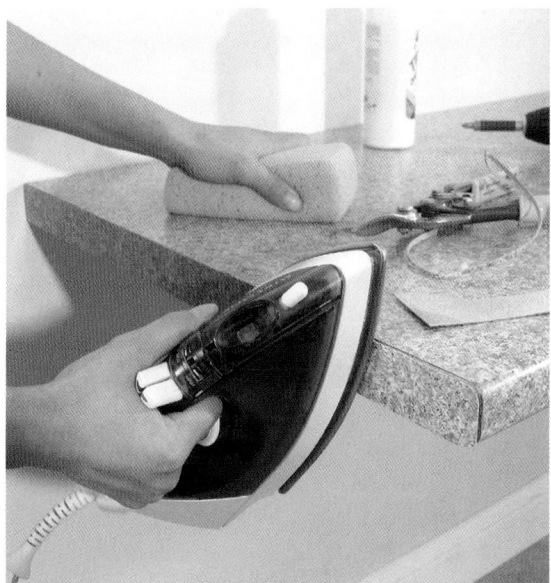

6 TRIM the laminate end cap with aviation snips to fit the size of the end panel. Set your iron on medium heat and slide it across the whole end panel until the glue bonds. Ease any sharp edges with a smooth-cutting metal file.

All-purpose wall cabinet

We chose an easy-to-clean Melamine wall cabinet from a local home center—no painting required. Expect to pay about $100.

You can make that wall space above the washer and dryer into a valuable dust-free storage space by adding a utility wall cabinet. We chose a 54-in. wide, 24-in. high and 12-in. deep cabinet available at home centers. It's prefinished inside and out, so it'll be easy to clean.

Chances are, you'll have a dryer vent or some other obstruction right where you want your cabinet. To solve this problem, we simply cut away the back and inserted a 4-in. galvanized duct as a liner to give the cabinet a 1-in. clearance from the dryer vent, preventing heat from building up inside the cabinet. With the liner in place, the vent is isolated behind the cabinet, keeping everything inside cool and clean. Follow the step-by-step how-to in **Photos 1 – 5**.

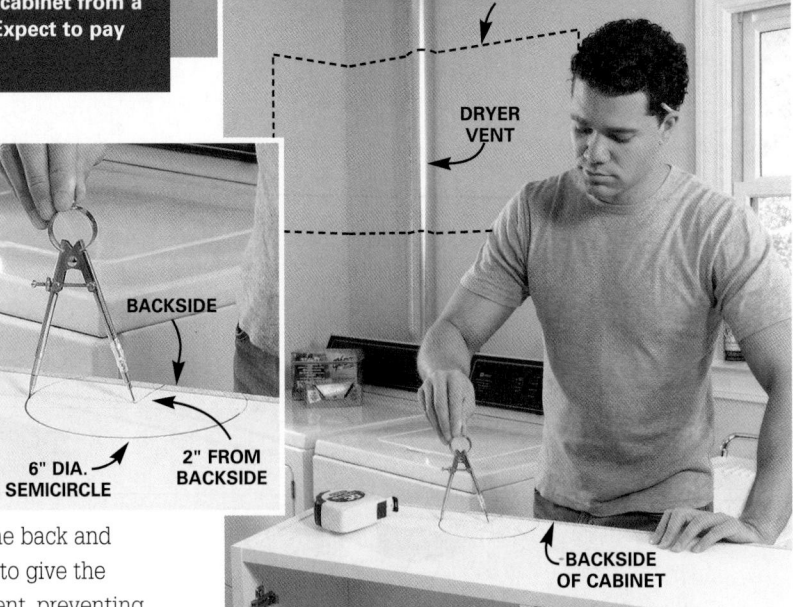

1 DRAW a 6-in. diameter circle 2 in. in from the back edge of your cabinet to correspond with the location of your dryer vent. Flip the cabinet upside down and draw the same circle to correspond with the top.

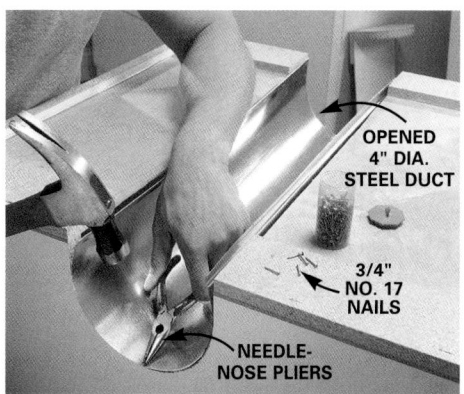

2 CUT slots 6 in. apart on the back of the cabinet that align with the edges of the semicircles. Set your circular saw for a 2-in. depth of cut. Then use a jigsaw to cut along the circles at the top and bottom of the cabinet.

3 NAIL a 4-in. steel vent pipe to the cabinet to act as a liner for the dryer vent. Use No. 17 wire nails 3/4 in. long. This liner will prevent heat buildup inside the cabinet and allow the contents of the cabinet to stay cool.

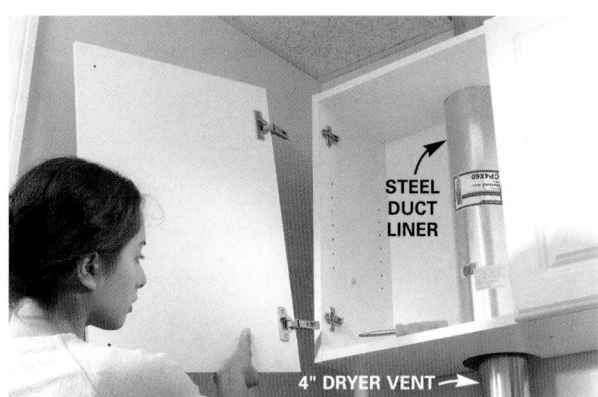

4 LEVEL AND SCREW a temporary 1x4 cleat to the wall studs with 2-1/2 in. drywall screws. The cabinet will rest on the cleat and your partner will be able to slide the cabinet left or right to align it. Once you have it where you like it, screw it to the studs with the cabinet screws provided.

5 REATTACH the cabinet doors and drill holes for your door pulls. You'll need to cut your shelves for the cabinet with a jigsaw to fit around your new vent shield.

Great Goofs™

Not-so-careful work crew

Our family likes to work on projects together, so when our bathroom needed remodeling, I thought it would be great to have our boys (ages 2, 4, 5, 7 and 9) help out with the demolition. I was a bit worried that the boys might damage something, but my husband reassured me that there was nothing they could ruin. We armed them with safety glasses, hammers and pry bars, and with a little instruction, set them to work. They were having a blast.

I checked on them every five minutes to make sure everything was going well and to tell them what a great job they were doing. After an hour, I went into the laundry room adjacent to the remodeling project. I couldn't believe my eyes. There were several huge holes in the laundry room wall. We now have an even bigger remodeling project on our hands. Seems the boys could swing those hammers harder than we thought.

Gallery of Ideas

WHIRLPOOL TUB

Your fantasy may be a soothing soak at the end of the day in a gleaming, polished spa. Your reality is a chipped, scratched-up tub and walls that are a mold-flecked embarrassment. But fantasies can come true by transforming that decaying bathtub area into a relaxing spa.

What makes this project both possible and easy to tackle are whirlpools you can now buy that fit into a standard tub space and install with little more hassle than a regular tub.

Project Facts:
Cost: $1,000 for tub, faucet and other plumbing materials
Skill level: Intermediate plumbing, electrical and carpentry skills
Time: 2-3 days for installing tub; 2-3 days for installing tile and finishing details
Special tools: Tubing cutter, soldering torch

NEW VANITY & SINK

Sinks and vanities get more use—and abuse—than any other fixture in your house. It's no wonder they can look tired and run-down after five or ten years. Fortunately, changing a vanity is relatively easy, and if you paint the walls at the same time, you can achieve a stunning transformation.

BEFORE

There is a wide range of tops, faucets and vanities available. But regardless of whether you spend $300 or $5,000 for your components, the installation details remain basically the same

AFTER

Project Facts:
Cost: About $2,500
Skill level: Intermediate plumbing and carpentry skills
Time: One weekend
Special tools: Basic plumbing and carpentry tools

TILE COUNTERTOP

Want to give your kitchen a timeless natural beauty? Consider putting in your own tumbled stone or ceramic countertops and backsplash. The project is within reach of an average do-it-yourselfer and you get the beauty of stone for a modest price.

Specialty tile shops offer a mouth-watering array of tiles to choose from, as well as expert design help in many cases. All the other materials are readily available at your local home center.

Project Facts:

Cost: $10-$25 per square foot for materials
Skill level: Intermediate carpentry and tile-laying skills
Time: 3-4 days
Special tools: Wet-cut tile saw

To order photocopies of complete plans for the projects shown here, call 715-246-4344 or write to:
Copies, The Family Handyman, P.O. Box 83695, Stillwater, MN 55083-0695.
Many public libraries also carry back issues of *The Family Handyman* magazine.

BUILT-IN PANTRY CABINETS

Triple your storage space and add a touch of class

by **Travis Larson**

I n most small bathrooms, all of the plumbing is on one wall and the door swings against a blank wall. Often, there's a closet on the other side of the blank wall to steal space from. If you don't have a closet, you'll have to decide if you can give up 1 or 2 ft. of floor space in the other room and go to the trouble of framing, drywalling, taping, painting and trimming a false wall to conceal the unsightly cabinet backs.

You can either add one or two cabinets to a wall using the method we show. If you want to add more, it's better to reframe the entire wall. You'll need a full 14-1/2 in. wide stud space for each cabinet in the blank wall (that space will be expanded to 15-1/2 in. wide). It's easiest to go into the bathroom and find the studs with a stud finder to see how many 14-1/2 in. stud spaces are available.

When a bathroom backs against a closet, there are rarely electrical cables inside the wall. We show cutting an inspection hole to check for cables or other obstructions (**Photo 1**). You can usually reroute an electrical cable if there is one.

If you have carpeting, unhook it from the tack strips and pull it and the padding back a couple of feet. You'll have to cut them both around the cabinets (or false wall), then staple down the padding and push the carpet onto new tack strips when you're through with the project.

> **Tip**
>
> Sometimes a stud will bow in the center. If it bows toward the opening, push it into position and hold it there by running drywall screws through the drywall into the stud.

3"
BATHROOM DRYWALL
① CUT INSPECTION HOLE
③ SAW ALONG STUDS
② CUT 3" FROM TOP AND BOTTOM

1 REMOVE the closet rod and shelf from the closet behind the bathroom wall. Cut a rough inspection hole, then check for electrical cables by peering down into the stud spaces with a flashlight. Cut horizontally between the studs 2 to 3 in. from the ceiling and the baseboard. Then cut out drywall using the studs as a guide.

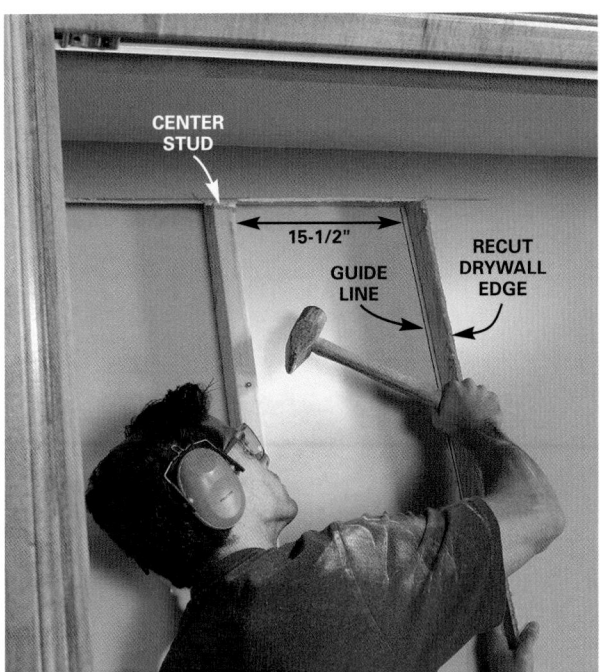

2 DRAW a line along the studs on the backside of the drywall, and then use a 2-lb. maul to pound the side studs over until each opening is 15-1/2 in. wide. Use the line as a guide to tell when the stud has moved about 1 in. Pound mostly at the very top and bottom of the stud to slide it along the plates. Smaller taps between the top and bottom will loosen the grip of drywall screws or nails. Toe-screw the studs to the plates with 3-in. screws and cut off the overhanging drywall edge.

3 SUBTRACT 5 in. from the depth of the cabinets and draw lines on the floor to mark the cabinet backs. Use the lines to position the bottom row of 2x4 cribbing. Center the middle 2x4 over the center stud so it supports both cabinets. Position the outside 2x4s even with the side studs. Overlap the rows at the corners and nail them together with 10d nails.

4 DRAW level lines on the backside of the bathroom drywall to mark the top and bottom of the cabinet face. (Base your layout on the cabinet face frame. The recessed toe-kick does not protrude into the bathroom.) Poke a drywall saw through the drywall to mark the corners of each cabinet.

5 USE the corner cuts from inside the bathroom to redraw the top and bottom cuts, adding 1/4 in. to the top and bottom for wiggle room. Cut out the bathroom drywall from the bathroom side. Remove the thin strip of drywall that covers the center stud (Photo 6).

Chop off the tack strip in front of the wall openings with a chisel and reuse it at the back of the cabinets.

Crib up the cabinets with overlapping 2x4s to establish the cabinet height (**Photos 3 and 4**). At a minimum, keep the bottom of the face frame 2-1/2 in. above the bathroom base trim. That way you won't have any trim or tilework to hassle with inside the bathroom. If you use shorter cabinets, adjust the height for convenience and the best appearance.

Finishing around the cabinet backs is optional if they're in a closet. You can build a separate wall (**Photo 13**) or put drywall directly against the cabinet backs. If you lay drywall against the cabinets, don't use screws or nails because they'll penetrate the cabinet backs. Instead, glue the drywall to the cabinet backs with construction adhesive and use paper-flanged corner beads that you tape on instead of nail. To minimize taping, stand the drywall sheets upright so you won't have seams to tape. Cut the drywall to fit tightly into existing drywall at walls and the ceiling and caulk those seams with paintable caulk. That way you'll only have to tape and sand the corner beads for painting. ⌂

6 TACK four 1/2-in. thick spacer blocks about 6 in. in from the top and bottom edges of the opening, then screw 1x2 stop blocks across both bays with 3-in. screws.

7 REMOVE the doors, drawers and shelving from the cabinets and slip them into the stud spaces to make sure they'll fit.

8 SCREW the bathroom-side drywall into the shifted studs. Push back the cabinets a few inches and screw 2x4 blocking to the drywall at the top and bottom for trim backing.

9 RIP the 3/4-in. filler strip to 1-3/4 in. wide and cut it the exact length of the cabinet face frames. Slip the filler into the opening, then place it between the cabinets. Pull the cabinets against the stop blocks.

Tip

Check the existing doorstop to make sure the knob doesn't hit the new cabinets. If a standard stop isn't adequate, use hinge- or floor-mounted stops.

10 CLAMP the filler strip flush with the face of the cabinet frames and with the top and bottom. You may have to shim under the cabinet bases to get the tops and bottoms aligned. Then drill pilot, clearance and screwhead countersink holes and screw both cabinets to the filler strip with 2-1/2 in. screws spaced about every 12 in.

11 HOLD the face frames tight against the stop blocks with clamps and screw the cabinets to the studs with 2-1/2 in. screws spaced about every 12 in. Be careful not to overtighten the screws and pull them through the cabinet sides.

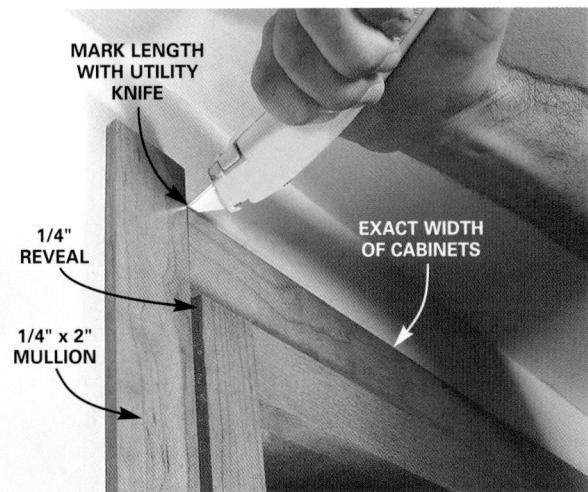

12 CUT the 1/4-in. thick x 2-in. wide mullion strips the exact width of the top and bottom of the cabinets and nail them on with 1-1/2 in. brad nails. Then mark the side trim for length and cut and nail it to the side studs.

Buyer's Guide

■ Medicine and utility cabinets: Dura Supreme Designer Series. Door style: Homestead door. Wood: Cherry. Finish: Harvest Cherry. (888) 711-3872. www.durasupreme.com

■ EZ-Toggle drywall anchors: Find them at any home center or hardware store. Smith Fastener Co., (800) 764-8488. www.smithfast.com

13 FRAME 2x4 stud walls directly behind the cabinets. Nail the bottom plates into the subflooring and the top plates into the ceiling framing with 10d nails. Use construction adhesive to glue any plates and studs that join surfaces that don't have underlying framing. Hang and tape the drywall and corner bead, then paint.

Ask Handyman™

HOW CAN I RENEW A SCRATCHED COUNTERTOP?

I've got a cultured marble countertop in my bathroom that's quite scratched up and shabby looking. Can I do anything to make it look like new?

How about close to new? I was disappointed by how quickly mine lost its shine, so one day I took out my auto polisher and went at it. What a difference.

Cultured tops are made of polyester resin with a clear topcoat (called the gel coat). This is the same material that's used with fiberglass and it buffs out beautifully. Removing the faucet makes it easier to buff the top.

First wet-sand with 1,000-grit paper (available at auto parts stores) to remove small, shallow scratches and surface stains. Don't try to remove deep scratches or deep stains. You'll risk sanding right through the gel coat. Rinse and dry the top.

Next, buff with Meguiar's Medium-Cut Cleaner (also available at auto parts stores). The buffing can be done by hand, but a small power buffer is much easier. Finally, protect the restored finish with a coat of Hope's Cultured Marble Polish (available at Home Depot and bath specialty stores). Follow the label directions.

MOUNTING A TOWEL BAR ON CERAMIC TILE

I want to install a ceramic towel bar in my tiled shower. How do I cut out the existing tile to make a space for it?

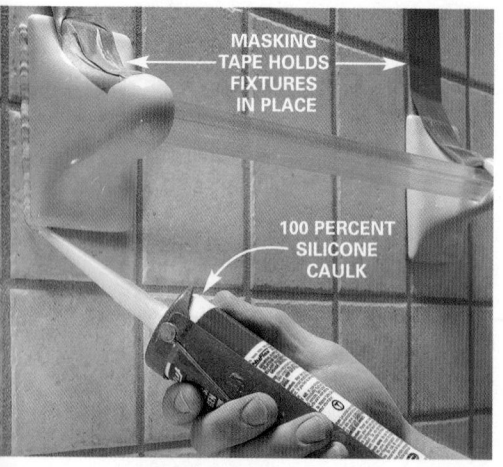

You don't have to. In the past, ceramic fixtures such as towel bar holders and soap dishes were cemented right to the wall and the tile was fitted around them. Now most are designed to be glued to the face of the tile with 100 percent silicone caulk. The only tricky part is holding them in place until the silicone sets up.

First thoroughly clean the tile with denatured alcohol. Lay a bead of caulk on the back of the fixture, push it into place and secure it with masking tape. Let the caulk stiffen for an hour or so and then add caulk around the perimeter. Use a wet finger or rag to smooth the caulk joint. Let it sit overnight before you pull the tape. Remember to put the rod in before setting the second fixture.

PAINTING CERAMIC TILE?

The tile around my bathtub and shower looks old and dated. Can I paint it rather than tear it out?

Yes, ceramic tile can be painted, but I wouldn't paint bathroom tile, especially if the room has a shower. Paint usually fails first at edges where moisture creeps behind it, and a tiled wall is nothing but edges. The paint will most likely crack at the grout joints and allow moisture to work its way in. Soon you could have a wall of flaking paint.

If you're dead set on doing this, clean the tile well with TSP or a TSP substitute, then apply a primer rated for ceramic tile. There are many in the marketplace, so call a full-service paint store, explain your situation and consider their recommended product.

First test the primer on a small area of cleaned tile. Let the primer dry for a few days and then try to scrape it off with your fingernail. If it comes off rather easily, try another primer.

Once the tile is primed, topcoat it with a semigloss 100 percent acrylic paint.

ETCHING BATHROOM WINDOW GLASS

My bathroom window faces the neighbor's house. Any suggestions on how to let in light but not prying eyes? I don't like the look of curtains or shades.

TAPE OFF SASH

ONE PASS: LIGHT ETCH

TWO PASSES: HEAVY ETCH

The easiest way is to apply a translucent window film. (See March '00, p. 15. To order a copy, see p. 288.) A more complex but also more attractive method is to etch (frost) the glass. It'll obscure the view yet still let light through.

You can etch glass with a rented sand blaster ($60), or contact a glass and mirror supplier that offers this service. Look in the Yellow Pages under "Glass."

The sand blaster makes a lot of dust, so work outside in a well-ventilated area. Ask the rental shop for operating instructions, and be sure to wear a face shield, a dust mask, gloves and long sleeves.

Practice on scrap glass. You control the etch by varying the air pressure, the distance you hold the blaster nozzle from the glass and the speed at which you move the nozzle. Make several passes to increase the depth of the etch.

Etch the inside face of the window glass. Protect the sash with several layers of masking tape.

Use masking tape on the clear glass if you're etching a pattern. The design possibilities are unlimited. Keep in mind that you'll void the glass warranty if you do this on double-pane windows. And don't etch tempered glass, that is, the glass in doors and in certain low windows.

Great Goofs™

Look out below!

I volunteered to help paint a friend's bathroom. The room was small, so I carried the door down to the basement and set it up on sawhorses. I moved a few boxes and a clothesbasket to get more elbow room. I carefully brushed on some glossy enamel paint and stepped back to admire the sheen. Just then, a shower of clothes came from the ceiling right onto the door. Then I realized why the clothesbasket was there in the first place. I'd set up the door right under the clothes chute!

A NON-SLIP SHOWER BASE

I have a fiberglass shower with a slick floor. How can I roughen the surface to make it safer?

Apply safety tape to the shower floor. You can buy strips of this self-sticking, non-slip material at most hardware stores. Clean the shower floor and let it completely dry to ensure that the tape adheres. Run parallel strips spaced about 4 in. apart across the shower floor.

NATURAL STONE TILE

Tile a tub surround with beautiful marble tile in a weekend— it won't cost a fortune

by Eric Smith

You can add the elegance of natural stone to your bathroom without the steep cost of custom design and highly skilled professional installation. Now natural stone is as affordable as it is beautiful. Home centers and tile shops carry a huge selection of marble, limestone and granite for the same price as regular ceramic tile. And the installation techniques are virtually the same as for ceramic. The only special tool you need is a wet saw with a diamond blade, which you can rent for $40 per day at any tile dealer or tool rental store. In fact, you can buy an inexpensive but adequate diamond blade wet saw for as little as $100.

In this article, we'll walk you through the basic tiling process, start to finish, including layout techniques, cutting and drilling and tips for setting it accurately. You don't need advanced skills for this project. Tile work is mostly a matter of careful planning and attention to detail. If you've worked with ceramic tile, you can work with stone tile.

The tile for our tub project cost $900 and additional materials ran about $150. Depending on the stone you choose, the cost of this project could range from $250 to $2,500. Expect to spend at least two days doing the installation work. For details of the tearout and tub replacement, see "Whirlpool Tub in a Small Bathroom," Oct. '03, p. 58. To order a copy, see p. 288.

Design options

For our tub surround, we chose polished 12-in. square marble tile and unpolished 1-in. square limestone accent tiles. We cut the 4-in. square accent tiles and 3 x 12-in. border tiles from the 12-in. marble. You can mix and match stone or buy ready-made patterns at tile stores. Tile dealers usually have sample displays where you can find ideas, or they'll steer you to designers who can guide you through the vast maze of materials. Just keep a few basics in mind: Lay out each wall on graph paper, tile for tile; start the pattern from a center line (**Photo 5**); and use tiles that are all the same thickness and that use the same

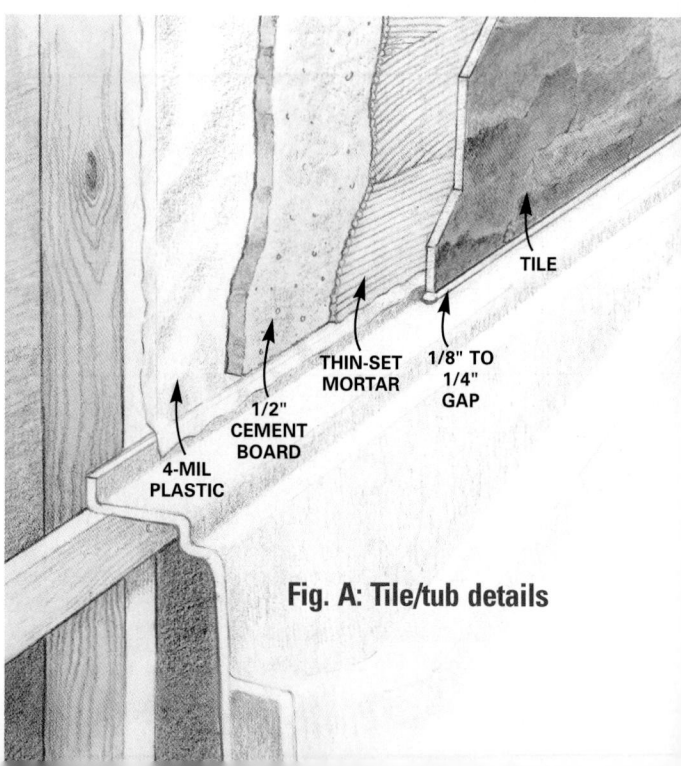

Fig. A: Tile/tub details

TILE

THIN-SET MORTAR

1/8" TO 1/4" GAP

1/2" CEMENT BOARD

4-MIL PLASTIC

VAPOR BARRIER

PLYWOOD OVER TUB

1 MARK the tub wall lengths on the cement board and score one side with a utility knife. Snap at the line and cut the fiberglass mesh backing, just as you would with drywall. Smooth ragged edges with the knife or drywall rasp.

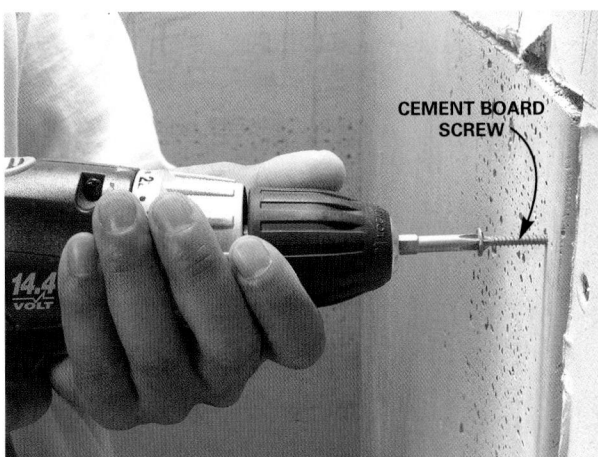

CEMENT BOARD SCREW

2 FASTEN the cement board to the studs with special 1-1/4 in. screws (or 1-1/2 in. roofing nails). Keep fasteners 1/2 in. from the edges, and install nailers in the corners if necessary to ensure adequate backing.

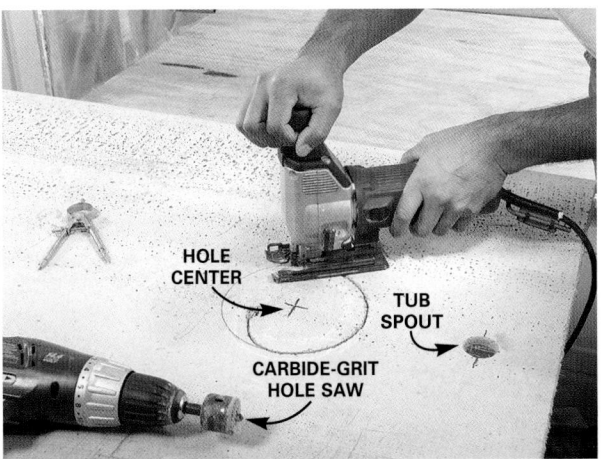

HOLE CENTER

TUB SPOUT

CARBIDE-GRIT HOLE SAW

3 MEASURE and mark the hole centers, then use a compass to trace them. Cut the spout and shower head holes with a 1-1/4 in. carbide-grit hole saw, and larger holes and curves with a carbide-grit jigsaw blade.

Tip Protect the tub! Tubs are easily chipped and scratched, and expensive to repair. Cover the tub with tape around the edges, and lay a 58-in. long piece of 1/2-in. plywood over rigid insulation or heavy cardboard on the tub rim. Replace it with a dropcloth during tiling, and check frequently in the bottom of the tub for debris that might scratch the finish.

grout. Plan to use unsanded grout for grout lines up to 1/8 in. wide and sanded grout for wider lines. The grout lines in our pattern ranged from 1/16 in. to 1/8 in.

Prices for natural stone range from $2 per sq. ft. to $200 per sq. ft. But keep in mind that expensive stone isn't necessarily better. It's just less common. Granite is much harder and more durable than marble and limestone, but curves and holes are tougher to cut and require somewhat different techniques. You have to use diamond-blade tools only, not the carbide-grit hole saws and jigsaw blades we show here for marble.

Install the tile backer

The first step is installing tile backer on the wall. We like to use cement board for areas that have to withstand frequent wetting such as a shower, but other types of tile backers will work as well. Check with your local building inspector for the approved types in your region. Add blocking if necessary to make sure your cement board ends catch at least 1/2 in. of framing. And add extra blocking to catch screws from grab bars if you intend to put some up. Small quantities of moisture can wick through tiled walls, and grout and caulk may develop cracks over time from building movement, so staple either a No. 15 felt or 4-mil polyethylene vapor barrier behind the cement board.

Measure each section of wall, subtract 1/4 in. to compensate for rough edges, and cut the cement board (**Photo 1**). Cement board consists of two layers of fiberglass mesh sandwiched around a cement and sand core. You score one side to cut the fiberglass mesh, then snap it like drywall. You'll dull your knife blades, so have a few extra handy or buy a special carbide scoring tool ($8) that'll last a lot longer. Set the cement board

CARBIDE-GRIT JIGSAW BLADE ($10)

on the tub flange, then screw it to the studs about every 8 in. with special cement board screws (available at tile stores and home centers).

It's easiest to make clean hole cutouts or curves with a carbide-grit jigsaw blade ($10) and a 1-1/4 in. carbide-grit hole saw (about $10). But in a pinch, you can use the crude, messy method of scoring the front and back of the hole and breaking it out with a hammer.

Use a special alkali-resistant mesh tape ($5 at tile dealers) and thin-set mortar to cover the joints (**Photo 4**), including the joint at the drywall. Use regular joint compound in areas that won't be fully covered by tile. Prime regular joint compound before tiling.

Mark the tile layout

Draw a plumb line at the center of the back wall, then measure over to the side to see how many tiles will fit. You want to end up with at least half a tile at each corner, so depending on the size of your tile, either place the edge of your first tile at the center line, or center a tile over it as we did (**Photo 5**).

If your tub is perfectly level, draw a level horizontal line at the height of one tile plus 1/8 in. (for caulk) above the rim. If the tub isn't level, find the low point, and start your horizontal guideline from that point. You'll then have to shave most tiles in the bottom row as you go to maintain the 1/8-in. gap. This is where the diamond saw comes in handy!

Draw additional lines for feature tiles or pattern changes. Remember to double-check horizontal and vertical lines to make sure they form true squares. Any sloppiness with the level at this point will cause headaches later during tiling.

Lay out the end walls so that cut tiles

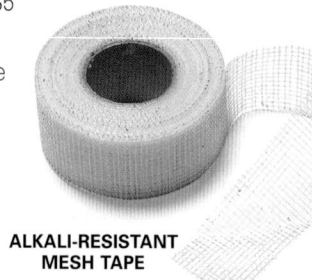

ALKALI-RESISTANT MESH TAPE

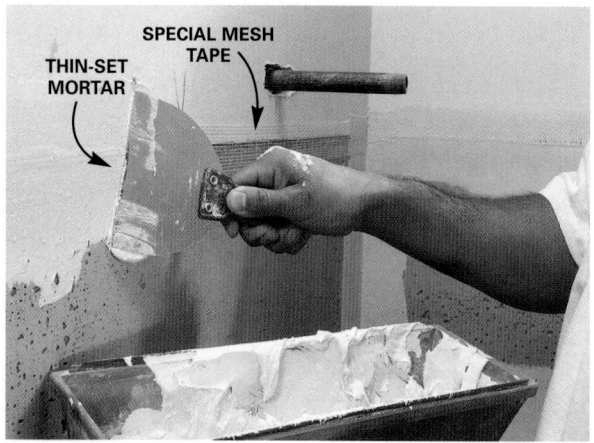

4 TAPE cement board joints with special mesh tape. Mix a batch of thin-set mortar and cover the tape with one thin coat.

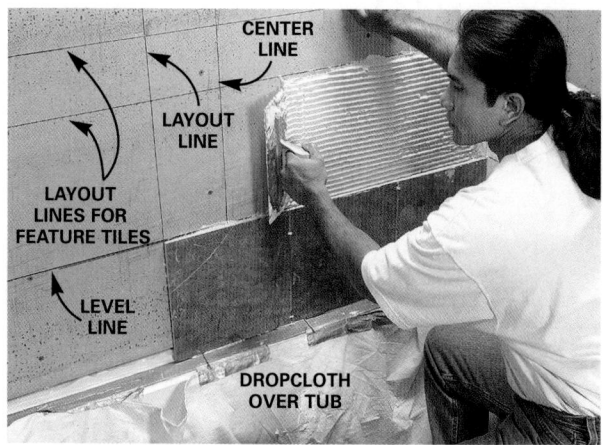

5 MARK level and plumb layout lines. Evenly spread several square feet of thin-set mortar with a 1/4-in. x 3/8-in. notched trowel held at about a 45-degree angle. Shim the first row about 1/8 in. above the tub to allow space for caulk.

6 ALIGN the tile with your layout lines and push each in firmly. Pull one off occasionally to make sure you're getting complete coverage.

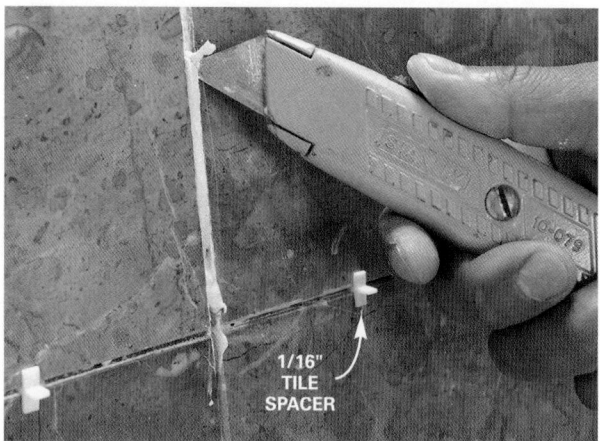

7 SCRAPE excess mortar out of the joints before it hardens. If mortar oozes out above the tile surface, spread it a little thinner by flattening the angle of the trowel.

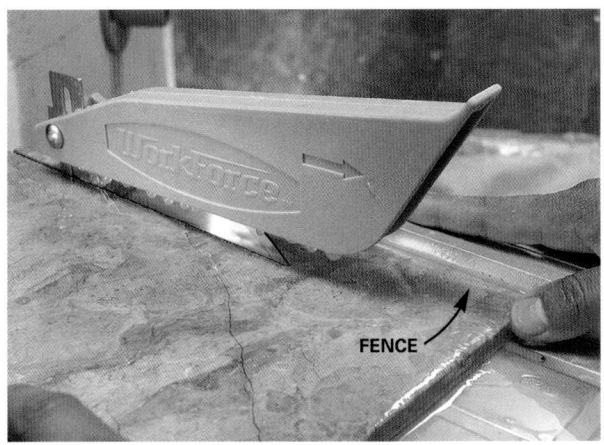

8 SET the fence to width and make straight cuts with a diamond blade wet saw. Cut slowly. Smooth the cut edges of marble with 200-grit wet/dry sandpaper.

SPOUT CUTOUT

FAUCET CUTOUT

9 CUT the hole for the tub and shower spouts with the 1-1/4 in. carbide-grit hole saw. Use light pressure to avoid cracking the tile.

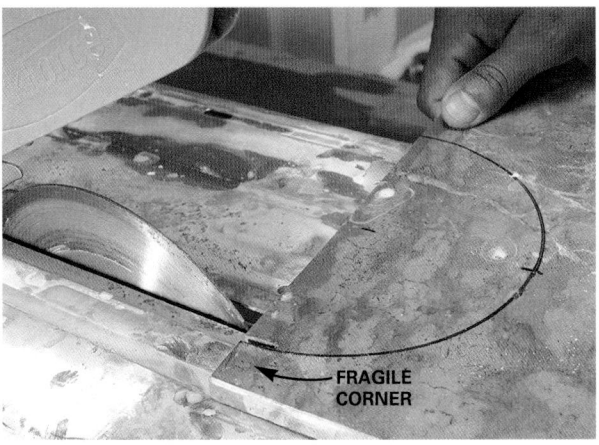

FRAGILE CORNER

10 START cuts near narrow edges with the wet saw to avoid breaking the tile. Grind rough edges smooth if necessary with the saw blade.

1/2" PLYWOOD

11 CLAMP the marble to 1/2-in. plywood to provide full support. Then cut through both with a carbide-grit blade. Cover the saw base with painter's tape to avoid scratching the tile.

fall in the corner, where they're less obvious. Our installation called for a 3-in. border tile, which we ran down the side of the tub, so we drew a plumb line 3-1/8 in. from the tub (remember to leave a caulk gap next to the tub), then worked back to the corner with full tiles, ending up with a 7-in. cut tile. The two basic rules for layouts are to hide cut edges whenever possible, and to make a layout that looks symmetrical and pleasing to the eye.

Hold to these lines as you work up the walls, and make slight adjustments in the corner tile cuts and grout lines as you go. Stand back every once in a while to look over the wall, and straighten any tiles that seem off.

Install the tile

Mix the mortar according to instructions on the bag. Marble and natural stone are installed with thin-set mortar mixed with latex additives for better bonding. Use white mortar for light-colored stone; darker mortars can darken the stone.

Use a 1/4 x 3/8-in. square notch trowel for 12-in. square marble tile. Hold the trowel at a 45-degree angle to create deep ridges (**Photo 5**). Spread no more than you can tile in 15 minutes or so. If the mud skins over and doesn't adhere, scrape it off and put a fresh batch on.

Use 1/8-in. spacers to hold the first row of tiles up off the tub (we used nails), then place tile spacers ($5) between the tiles to create even grout lines. Thin-set mortar doesn't grab right away; the tiles will slip down if unsupported. We used 1/16-in. spacers for tight grout lines between the 12-in. squares and 1/8-in. spacers in the decorative band (**Photo 12**). The 1-in. tiles were mounted on mesh. We used 4d finish nails to anchor them until the mortar set (**Photo 12**).

Cutting techniques

Cuts are simple and straightforward with a diamond blade wet saw (**Photo 8**). But push the tile through slowly. Part of the visual charm of marble is its flaws and fracture lines,

1 " SQUARE
LIMESTONES

1/8"
GROUT
LINES

1/16"
GROUT LINES

12 LAY in the special feature tiles following layout lines. Use bigger spacers if the grout lines are wider, or tap in nails to keep small tiles from slipping.

Tip

Don't mix the whole container of grout at once. Start with a quarter or third of a container, and mix more as you need it.

HAZE

13 FORCE grout into the joints with a rubber float, scraping diagonally across the tiles. Wipe off excess with a damp sponge. Polish off the light haze with a dry rag after the grout stiffens.

but these are also weak points where the stone can easily break, especially at the end of a cut. You may have to cut in from each end about an inch before completing cuts (**Photo 10**). Saw cuts leave slightly rough edges. Smooth these with 200-grit wet/dry sandpaper. (For granite, use a special rub stone.)

Cutting the holes for the tub spout, faucet and shower head can be tricky (**Photos 9 – 11**). Some marble tiles are fragile, so fully support the tile with plywood when cutting or drilling it. And work carefully near brittle edges and corners. Keep in mind that you can have a tile store do these cuts for you if you don't want to attempt them.

TILE SPACERS

Grouting pulls it all together

After the tiles have set for at least a day, the wall is ready to grout. Pull out all the spacers and clean off any mortar on the tile faces or projecting from the grout lines. Then coat the marble with a grout remover or tile sealer ($15) to prevent staining and to make grout removal easier.

Mix the grout (with water only for marble) to a smooth peanut butter consistency, and let it sit for the time listed in the directions. Remix, then work it into the grout joints with a special grout float ($10; **Photo 13**). This is fairly hard work—use two hands and pack the joints full. Then scrape the edge of the float diagonally across the tile to remove excess.

Stop after about 15 minutes and clean the grout off the surface with a damp (not wet) tiling sponge ($3), rubbing it in a circular motion. Be careful not to wipe out the grout from the joints. Keep a little grout on hand to fill in air bubbles and voids. Rinse the sponge often, but don't worry about getting the tile perfectly clean yet.

Wipe grout into the joint between the trim and drywall to create a finished-looking edge. Then clean all grout from the corners and the joint along the tub. You'll caulk these joints later (**Photo 14**).

After an hour, polish the haze off the tile with a dry towel. Some of the grout lines may look a little sloppy—rub the edges with the towel to sharpen the lines. Then wet down the tile and grout lines once a day for the next few days to help the grout cure. Finally, apply a tile sealer ($15) according to manufacturer's directions.

14 PRESS tape along each side at all the corners. Squeeze caulk into the joints, smooth them, then immediately remove the tape.

LIMESTONE TRIM →

15 ATTACH stone or tile trim to the front edge of the tub with silicone to cover an uneven floor/tub joint.

Caulk and finish

After the grout has dried for at least a day, fill all corners with a caulk designed for tubs and tile. (Check tile stores for a color that matches your grout.) Taping the edges of the caulk lines gives you cleaner, more precise caulk lines (**Photo 14**). Just remember to remove the tape as soon as you finish smoothing. Caulk starts skinning over within a few minutes, and if you wait too long, the tape will smear caulk on the wall.

Caulk the joint between the tub base and floor as well. The floor under our tub had a 1/4-in. sag in the center that was too large for a good-looking caulk joint. So we covered the edge with a limestone trim piece—a standard floor threshold with one edge cut square (**Photo 15**).

Finish details

If you wish, buy soap dishes or towel bars and mount them with silicone at comfortable heights. Tape them in place overnight until the silicone sets, then caulk around the edges.

Finally, install the faucet trim and tub and shower spouts, plug in the tub, and enjoy the fruits of your labor— if you can get in before someone else does! 🏠

Great Goofs™

Indoor bobsledding

I purchased a Jacuzzi tub to replace the old cast iron tub in our upstairs bath. We got the 300-lb. tub out of the bathroom and then decided to gently lower it down our wood staircase to get it outside. We wrapped a blanket around the legs at the upper end of the tub so my wife could guide that end with a firm hold on the blanket. I was to be at the lower end of the tub. Well, all was going fine until one of the stair nosings broke, causing the tub to jerk and get away from us. It started careening down the stairs, and to avoid being bowled over, I hopped into the tub and rode it all the way down. It broke all the nosings before smashing into the wall at the bottom of the stairs. Luckily my wife and I both made it through without a scratch, but unfortunately our remodeling project grew by leaps and bounds. When I told my father the story, he said we should have left the tub in place, broken it up with a sledgehammer and then carried down the pieces.

UNDERCABINET
LIGHTING

Add dramatic countertop lighting in a weekend without tearing up your walls to get your wiring in

by **Jeff Gorton**

Adding undercabinet lighting is a nearly perfect kitchen improvement project. In less than a weekend, you can add fixtures that provide bright, even light to every dim recess of your countertop. No more strained eyeballs when chopping and cooking. And you'll love the dramatic ambience provided by halogen or xenon fixtures. Teamed up with a dimmer, these fixtures can set the mood for a romantic dinner or give off a soft glow for that midnight raid on the refrigerator.

In this article, we'll show you a unique method of wiring undercabinet lights that eliminates disruptive wall tear-out and minimizes the difficult job of fishing cables from your attic or basement. Even though we've simplified the job by showing you how to easily route the cables, this is still an intermediate to advanced wiring project. Don't try it unless you understand basic wiring techniques.

Of course, the best time to install wiring for undercabinet lights is during a kitchen remodel, before the walls are covered with drywall. But if you want undercabinet lighting and aren't planning any major renovations, don't despair. The wiring plan we show in this article is designed to work in almost any kitchen, and can be installed without visible damage to the walls. And since we're using the inside of the base cabinets to run wires,

you don't even need access to a basement or attic.

The National Electrical Code requires that plastic-sheathed cable (commonly called Romex) be protected in areas where it's subject to abuse. Since we're running the cable in the back of cabinets where pots and pans could bump it, we've chosen to be safe and run the cable inside a flexible steel conduit (called "flex"). We'll show you how to cut and install flex and then how to pull the cable through it. If you can run the plastic-sheathed cable high in the cabinets or behind drawers, you may not need conduit. Ask your local electrical inspector which method is acceptable.

FLEX CONNECTOR

Even though the wiring is simple, you'll still have to tie in to a source of power to provide 120 volts for the lights. We'll tell you how to locate a suitable circuit. But if you're uncomfortable with this part of the job, consider hiring an electrician to bring power to the junction box (**Fig. A**), and then complete the remainder of the wiring yourself, following **Figs. A and B** and the photos. In either case, check with your local building department to see what type of electrical permit and what inspections are required.

Fig. A: Undercabinet Wiring

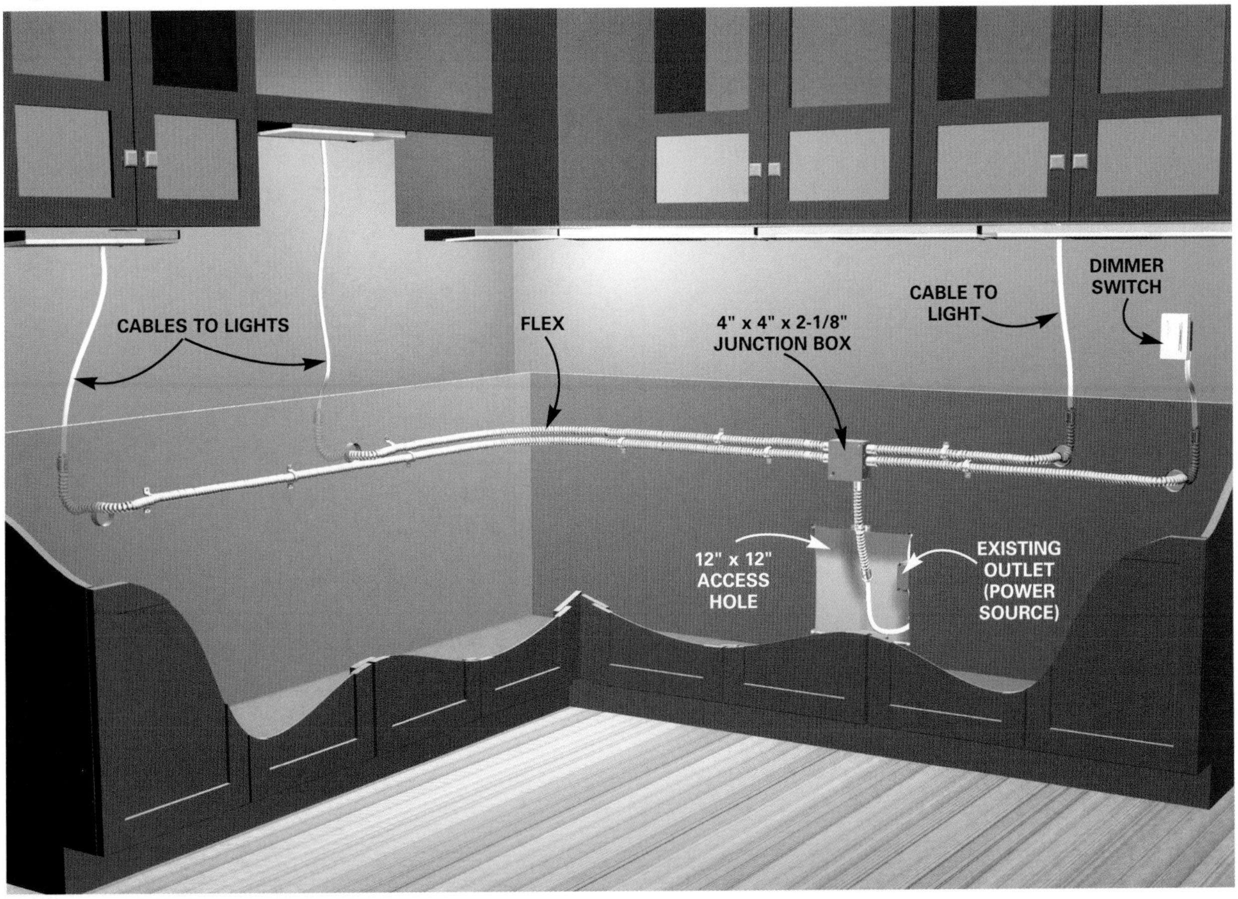
CABLES TO LIGHTS
FLEX
4" x 4" x 2-1/8"
JUNCTION BOX
CABLE TO
LIGHT
DIMMER
SWITCH
12" x 12"
ACCESS
HOLE
EXISTING
OUTLET
(POWER
SOURCE)

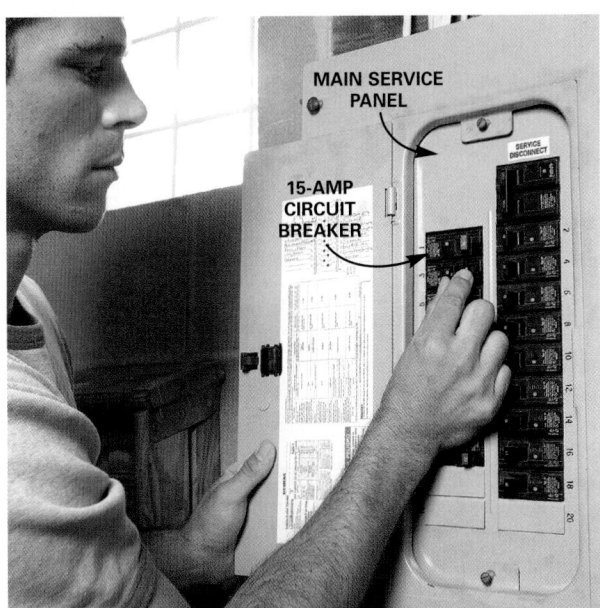

MAIN SERVICE
PANEL
15-AMP
CIRCUIT
BREAKER
SERVICE
DISCONNECT

1 FIND a nearby outlet in the wall opposite the backside of the cabinets and plug in a radio. Find the circuit by turning off circuit breakers until the radio goes off.

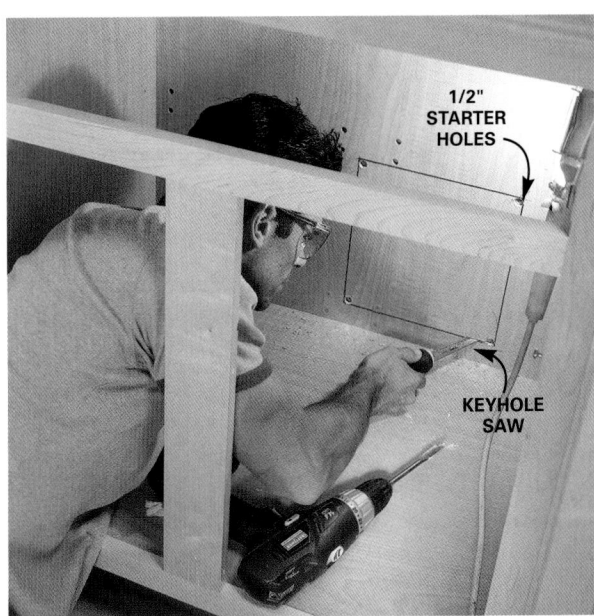

1/2"
STARTER
HOLES
KEYHOLE
SAW

2 DRILL starter holes and cut a 12-in. hole in the back of the cabinet to gain easy access to the outlet (power source). Keep the cut shallow to avoid nicking wires.

CAUTION: If you have aluminum wiring, call in a licensed pro who is certified to work with it. This wiring is dull gray, not the dull orange that's characteristic of copper.

Expect to spend a day running the flex, pulling in the plastic-sheathed cables and installing the lights. In addition to standard hand tools, you'll need a voltage tester ($3), a wire stripper ($5), a hacksaw and a drill with both 1/2-in. and 1-1/8 in. spade bits. If you plan to mount the switch in a tile backsplash like ours, buy a glass bit ($7 to $10) for cutting the switch hole. Otherwise, a sharp keyhole saw ($8; Photo 2) will work for cutting the hole for the new switch as well as the access hole in the back of the cabinet. All these tools are available at a hardware store or home center.

Finding power

There are many potential power sources, but unfortunately the electrical code prohibits any connections to "dedicated" circuits. This rules out the 20-amp small-appliance circuits in your kitchen (you can't use the countertop outlets for power) or dining areas, 20-amp laundry room circuits and 20-amp bathroom circuits. If a light switch box has a hot, neutral and ground, you can

SHARED WALL WITH KITCHEN

take power from it. Other possibilities include a junction box in the basement or an outlet on the other side of the wall from the cabinets (we used a hallway outlet). Make sure there's a protected route to get an electrical cable from your chosen power source into the base cabinets.

Even though the new undercabinet lights don't need much power, make sure they won't overload an existing circuit. This process is tedious and may take you several hours, but it's a necessary step for a safe job. Here's how you do it. To determine whether the circuit you want to use can handle the additional lights without overloading, first shut off the circuit in the main panel. Then go through the house turning on lights and other electrical

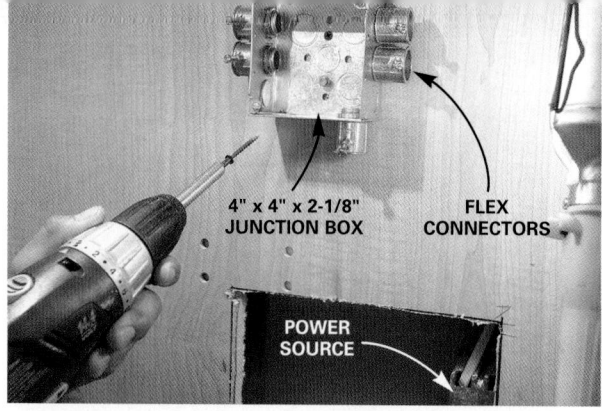

4" x 4" x 2-1/8" JUNCTION BOX · FLEX CONNECTORS · POWER SOURCE

3 ATTACH flex connectors to a junction box according to your plan (Fig. A) and screw it to the back of the cabinet. Align the connectors so the screws point out.

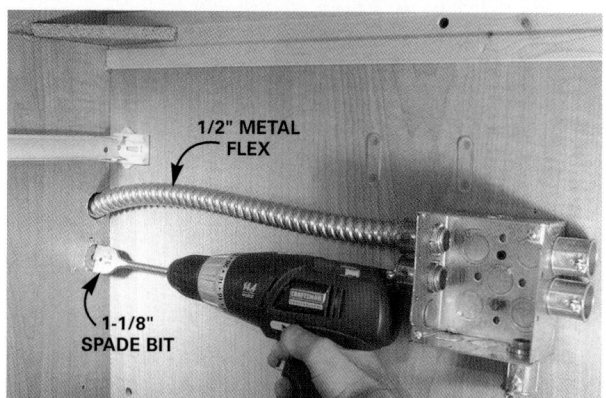

1/2" METAL FLEX · 1-1/8" SPADE BIT

4 DRILL 1-1/8 in. holes in the cabinet sides and feed flex from the metal junction box to each switch and light location.

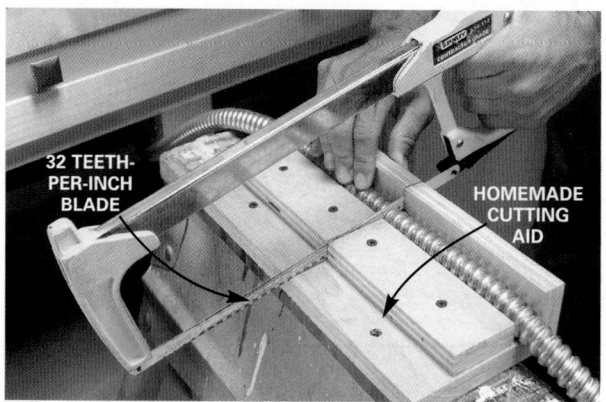

32 TEETH-PER-INCH BLADE · HOMEMADE CUTTING AID

5 MARK the flex and cut it off with a hacksaw to the desired length. Build a cutting guide as shown.

Buying undercabinet lights

The top-of-the-line fixtures we're installing use low-voltage xenon bulbs. The fixtures cost about $35 per linear foot, about 20 percent more than similar halogen fixtures. But the xenon bulbs last many times longer, burn cooler and don't require special handling like halogen bulbs. Each of our fixtures has a built-in electronic transformer to power the low-voltage xenon bulbs but is powered by standard 120-volt current. Xenon bulbs are dimmable but require a special electronic dimmer ($40). Basic fluorescent fixtures are much cheaper, about $10 per ft., but usually can't be dimmed. The wiring method we show works for any 120-volt undercabinet light.

Plan to install a continuous row of lights for the most evenly distributed light. Some types of undercabinet lights are provided with plug-in connectors to join fixtures end to end. Others, like the ones we're using, can be joined by running wires from one fixture to the next. Wire them together according to the manufacturer's instructions.

items. Add up the wattage of everything that doesn't go on, that is, everything that's on that circuit. Then add the wattage of the lights you'll be adding. We recommend a maximum connected load of 1,440 watts for a 15-amp circuit and 1,920 watts for a 20-amp circuit. (The circuit amperage is stamped on the breaker or fuse.) If the total amperage exceeds these amounts, find a different circuit. If you're confused, call in a licensed electrician to help with this part.

Finally, check to make sure the electrical box is large enough to accommodate the wires you'll be adding (see "Calculating Box Sizes," at right). If the box is too small, replace it with a larger one.

After you've chosen the electrical box to tie in to, turn off the circuit breaker or unscrew the fuse that controls the circuit. Some electrical boxes contain more than one circuit. Before doing any work in the box, test all the wires with a non-contact voltage tester to make sure they're "dead."

Plan the wiring route

The first step is to determine which base cabinet you'll run the power into. To locate the position of the outlet in the base cabinet, chuck an 8-in. length of coat hanger into your drill and drill a hole alongside the outlet and through

the back of the cabinet. Then mark a 12-in. square and cut an access hole (**Photo 2**) directly behind the electrical box. A sharp keyhole saw works well. Make sure to keep the cut shallow to avoid hitting electrical or plumbing lines. Next screw the junction box to the back of the cabinet just below the level of the drawer (**Photo 3**). The 4 x 4 x 2-1/8 in. deep metal box we're using is large enough to accommodate the wires shown. If your installation requires more cables, calculate the box size needed and buy a larger junction box if necessary.

Drill 1-1/8 in. holes through the cabinet sides and run 1/2-in. flex for each light or group of lights, for the switch and for the power (**Photo 4 and Fig. A**). Allow an extra 6 in. of flex where it enters the walls. Ream the cut end of

Calculating box sizes

To figure the minimum box size required by the National Electrical Code, add: 1 for each hot and neutral wire entering the box, 1 for all the ground wires combined, 1 for all the clamps combined, and 2 for each device (switch or receptacle, but usually not light fixtures) installed in the box. Multiply this figure by 2 for 14-gauge wire and 2.25 for 12-gauge wire to get the minimum box volume in cubic inches. Plastic boxes have the volume stamped inside.

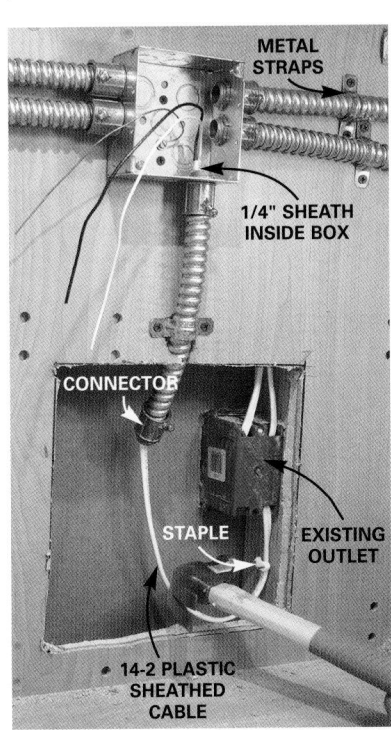

6 RUN a cable from the outlet (power source) to the junction box, stripping 12 in. of sheathing off each end. Staple it within 8 in. of the box.

7 PULL cables through the flex. Use a fish tape for long runs. Leave plenty of cable for running up the walls to the light fixtures.

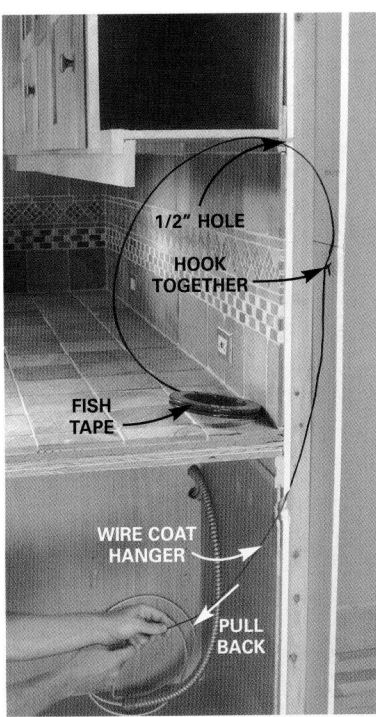

8 DRILL a 1/2-in. hole under the wall cabinet and push in the fish tape. Drill a 1-1/8 in. hole through the base cabinet and wall and push in a wire coat hanger to catch the fish tape. Pull the fish tape down, attach the cable and pull it up.

the flex to remove burrs and install flex connectors on both ends.

You may have to pull your stove away from the wall or slide your dishwasher out so you can run the flex behind them. Make sure to route it where it won't interfere when you slide the appliances back into place. If you have an inaccessible corner, you may have to cut an access hole in the side of the cabinet in order to run the flex. Route the cable through the attic or basement if necessary to get across areas that aren't connected by base cabinets.

Push or use a fish tape to pull the plastic-sheathed cable through the flex (**Photos 7 and 8**). Allow an extra 12 in. of cable at the junction box and several feet beyond where the cables should end. It's better to waste a few feet of cable than to end up short.

After the cable is pulled into the flex, drill holes in the back of the base cabinet (**Photo 8**) and the bottom of the wall cabinet (**Photos 8 and 10**) and cut the hole for the switch (**Photo 11**). Fish the cable up to these locations (**Photo 8**). The fishing method we show in **Photo 8** also works for insulated walls. You'll just have to work a little harder to hook the fish tape with the hanger. Using your saw, ream the hole through the back of the cabinet at an angle to better fit the flex. Push the end of the flex into the wall and secure the flex with straps placed every 4-1/2 ft. and within 12 in. of every hole in the cabinet and within 12 in. of the junction box (**Photo 6**).

Mount the fixtures and make final connections

The final step is to mount and connect the light fixtures and connect the wires in the switch box, outlet box and

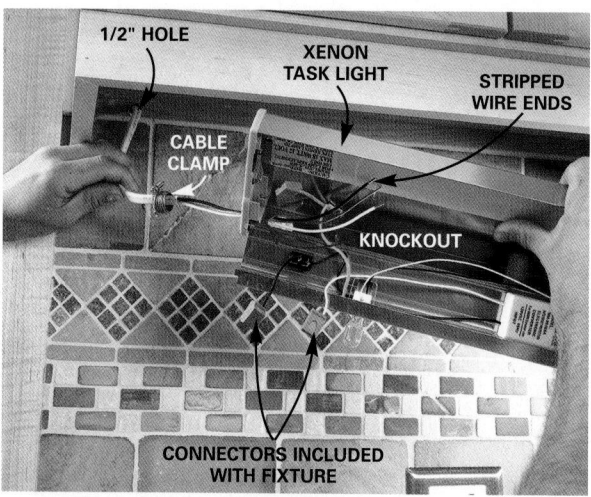

9 SECURE the cable to the fixture with a cable clamp. Connect the wires according to the manufacturer's instructions.

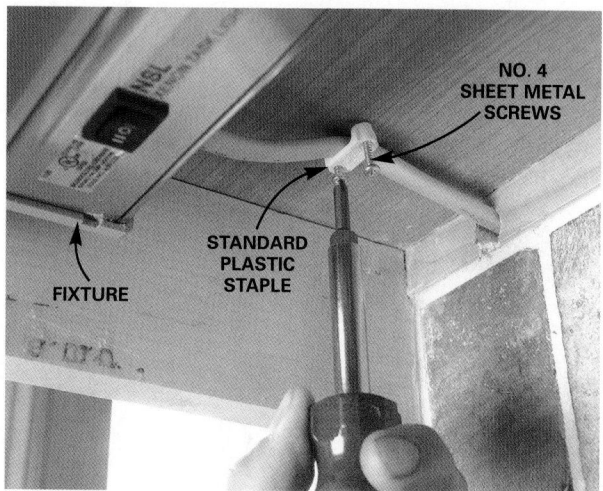

10 SCREW the fixture to the cabinet bottom and fasten the cable to the cabinet with a standard staple and No. 4 sheet metal screws.

11 MARK the switch box profile on the backsplash. Drill a series of holes with a glass bit and chip out the tile and wallboard.

12 PUSH the cable into a remodeling box and mount it in the wall.

junction box. **Photos 13 and 14** and **Fig. B** show how. Double-check the wires in the outlet box with a non-contact voltage tester to make sure the power is off before making the final connections in this box.

If possible, install a dimmer in place of a regular switch. Check with the manufacturer to find out whether a regular dimmer, a magnetic dimmer or an electronic dimmer is required. Then follow the package instructions for connecting the dimmer.

When you're through connecting the wires in the junction box according to **Fig. B**, screw a metal cover plate to the junction box. Then close up the hole in the back of the cabinet by screwing an oversized square of 1/4-in. plywood over the opening. 🏠

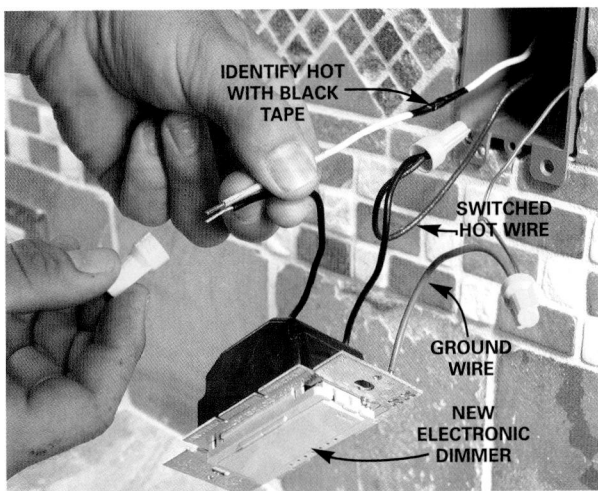

13 CONNECT the dimmer or switch according to the manufacturer's instructions. Fold the wires into the box and fasten the dimmer and cover plate.

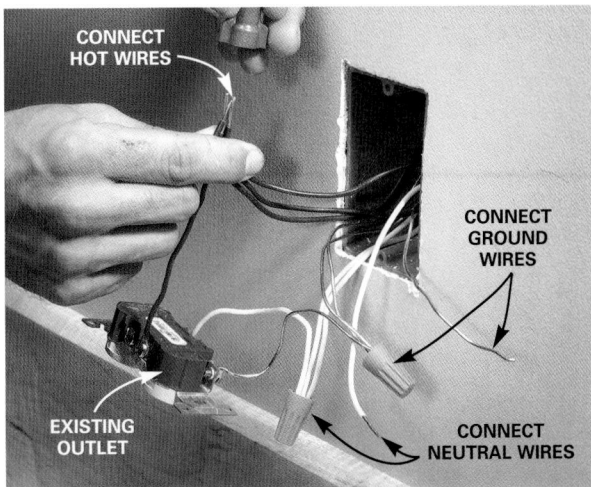

14 CONNECT the new wires to the existing wires in the outlet box, black to black (hot), white to white (neutral) and the bare ground wires. Reinstall the outlet.

Fig. B: Connections at Junction Box

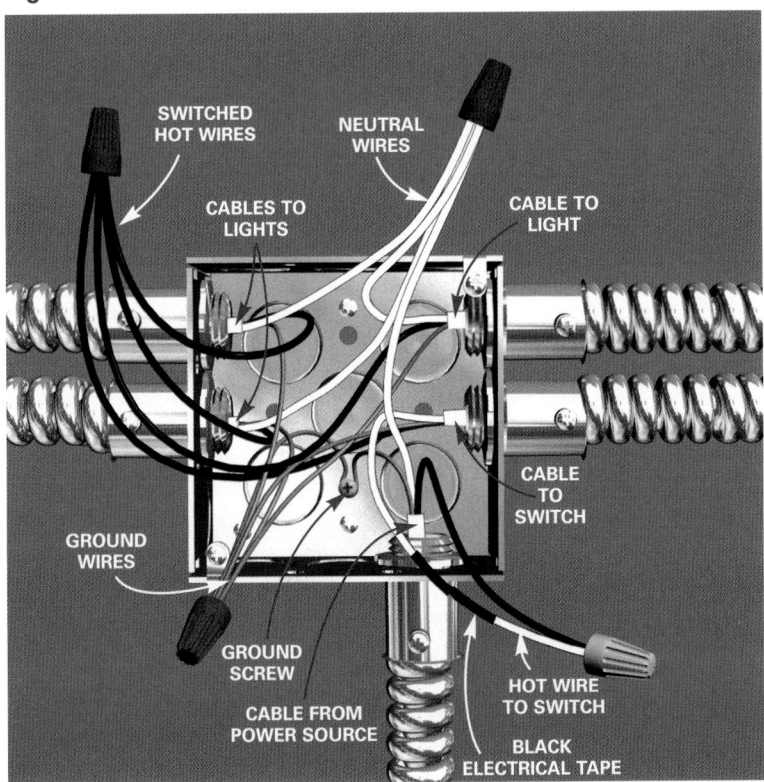

Connect the power source to the switch and from the switch to the hot wires (black) to the lights.

Buyer's Guide

The following companies manufacture undercabinet light fixtures. You'll find the ones in this article and others at local lighting retailers and on-line.

- ■ NATIONAL SPECIALTY LIGHTING (NSL): (800) 527-2923. www.nsl-ltg.com. We used NSL Xenon Task Lights in this article.
- ■ ALKCO: www.alkco.com
- ■ KICHLER LIGHTING: (888) 659-8809. www.kichler.com

Wordless Workshop™

by **Roy Doty**

IRONING BOARD CABINET

3 Wiring & Electrical

IN THIS CHAPTER

Hang a New Ceiling Fixture 74

Great Goofs 78

Ask Handyman .79
Replacing two-slot outlets,
power from a switch box,
better garage lighting and more...

You Can Fix It 82
Tighten a loose outlet,
update a doorbell

Using Tools: Stripping Wire 84

Get Wired! 88
Installing phone and coaxial cable

HANG A NEW
CEILING FIXTURE

Nothing spoils a dinner party like a chandelier in the pasta or a sudden blackout. Here's how to hang it safely and securely.

by **Jeff Gorton**

Installing a new light fixture is a great way to instantly change a drab room into a dazzling one. Lighting showrooms and catalogs have a wide variety of fixtures to tempt you. And even though the bag of parts included with some fixtures may look daunting, the electrical connections are simple enough for even a beginner.

But poor installation techniques can result in a poten-

tially lethal shock or fire. In this article, we'll help you choose a fixture that will mount safely on your electrical box and then show you the best techniques for testing a ground and connecting the wires. We've even included photos of the two most common mounting systems to help you make sense of all those little parts.

The temperature rating of your existing wires will affect which type of fixture you can install. Before you go shopping, read the following section.

Learn the temperature rating of your existing wires

It's hard to believe, but many of the light fixtures now sold at home centers and lighting showrooms can't be safely installed in most houses wired before 1985. These fixtures are clearly labeled with a warning that reads "For supply connections, use wire rated for at least 90 degrees C." The reason is simple: Fixtures with this label generate enough heat to damage the insulation on older wires and cause a fire hazard. Wires manufactured after 1985 are required to have coverings that can withstand the higher temperature.

If you know your wiring was installed before 1985, don't use fixtures requiring 90-degree-rated supply wires. To confirm that you have 90-degree-rated supply wire, look at the cable jacket or wire insulation. If you have plastic-sheathed cable (often referred to as Romex), look for the letters NM-B or UF-B printed on the plastic sheath. If your wiring is fed through conduit, look on the wire insulation for the letters THHN or THWN-2. If you're still unsure, either call an electrician or choose a fixture that isn't labeled with a supply wire temperature requirement.

Heavy fixtures require strong boxes

If you choose a heavy light fixture (the one we bought weighed in at a hefty 25 lbs.), check your electrical box to make sure it will support the weight. The National Electrical Code (NEC) allows you to hang up to 50 lbs. from any electrical box that is threaded to accept No. 8-32 machine screws for attaching the crossbar (**Fig. A**). This includes almost every type of ceiling box. For practical purposes, make sure your electrical box is securely fastened to solid framing before you hang a new light fixture

UNSCREW
CROSSBAR

OLD LIGHT
FIXTURE

1 TURN off the power to the light fixture at the main circuit panel. Remove the nut or screws securing the dome-shaped canopy and lower it.Then remove the screws securing the crossbar to the electrical box and lower the fixture.

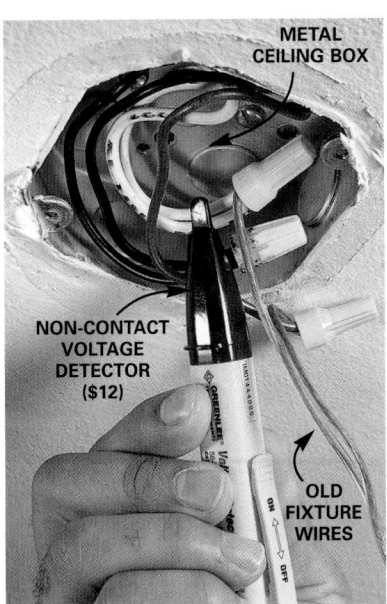

METAL
CEILING BOX

NON-CONTACT
VOLTAGE
DETECTOR
($12)

OLD
FIXTURE
WIRES

2 TEST the wires. Move the tip of a non-contact voltage detector near each wire to make sure the power to all wires in the box is turned off (make sure the light switch is turned on). If the tester lights, switch off circuit breakers or loosen fuses one at a time until the tester light goes off. Disconnect the wires from the light fixture. Leave other wires connected and tucked into the electrical box.

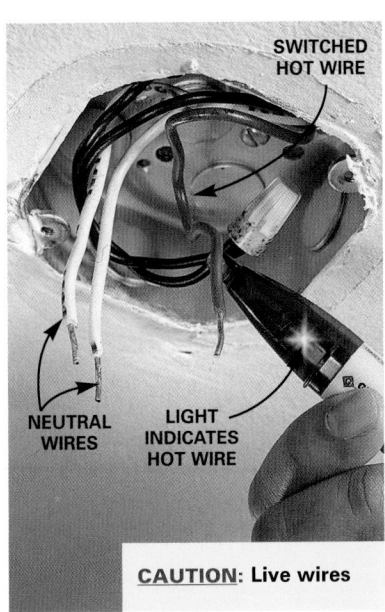

SWITCHED
HOT WIRE

NEUTRAL
WIRES

LIGHT
INDICATES
HOT WIRE

CAUTION: Live wires

3 TEST FOR GROUND: STEP 1. Turn the power to the light back on at the main circuit panel (the light switch is still on). Use the non-contact tester again to make sure there is power to the colored (hot) wire.

from it. If your light fixture weighs more than 50 lbs., it has to be supported independent of the electrical box. An easy solution is to install a fan brace box (about $15 at home centers and hardware stores) that's

Calculating box sizes

To figure the minimum box size required by the National Electrical Code, add: 1 for each hot and neutral wire entering the box, 1 for all the ground wires combined, 1 for all the clamps combined, and 2 for each device (switch or receptacle, but usually not light fixtures) installed in the box. Multiply this figure by 2 for 14-gauge wire and 2.25 for 12-gauge wire to get the minimum box volume in cubic inches. Plastic boxes have the volume stamped inside.

designed to be installed without cutting any additional holes in your ceiling. Check the label to make sure the box is designed to support more than 35 lbs. See "Ceiling Fan," May '01, p. 52, for complete instructions on installing a fan brace. To order a copy, see p. 288.

Most ceiling boxes are large enough

The NEC dictates how many wires and clamps you can safely put in an electrical box. Typical 1-1/2 to 2-in. deep octagonal or round ceiling boxes are quite large and overcrowding is rarely a problem. Even so, you should run through the calculations to be sure. See "Calculating Box Sizes," left. But if you encounter a round box that's only 1/2 in. deep, replace it. Once again, the easiest way to install a new electrical box in an existing ceiling is to use a special fan brace and box made for retrofitting.

Ground the light fixture to avoid dangerous electrical shocks

Because most light fixtures are metal or have exposed metal parts, they need to have an equipment ground to be safe. First you have to make sure a grounding means is available (**Photos 3 and 4**). If your house is wired with plastic-sheathed cable with a bare copper ground wire, you're probably covered, but test it to be sure, using the same procedure we're using to test the metal box. Once you've determined that a ground exists, it's simply a matter of making sure that all the metal parts— electrical box, fixture-mounting strap and light fixture—are securely connected to the ground (**Photos 5 and 8**). If your crossbar doesn't have a threaded hole for a ground screw, connect a ground wire to it with a special grounding clip.

Make sure you get the polarity right

The two lamp cord wires on many hanging light fixtures are hard to tell apart. However, it's critical to correctly identify the neutral wire and connect it to the neutral wire(s) in the box. Connecting it to the hot will energize the threaded bulb socket and create a potential shock hazard. See **Photo 8** for clues to identifying the neutral fixture wire.

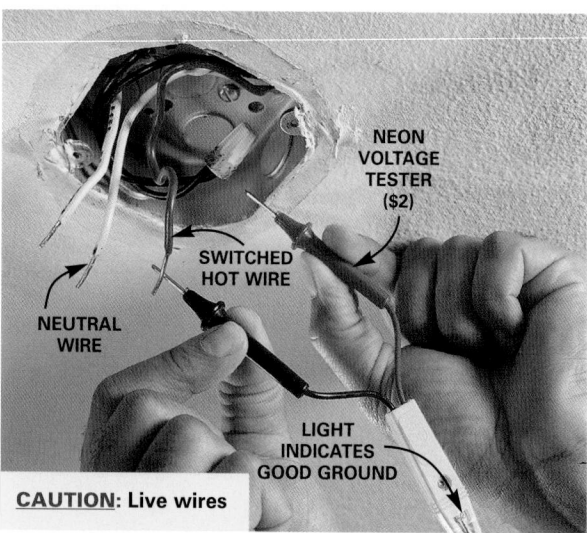

NEON VOLTAGE TESTER ($2)

SWITCHED HOT WIRE

NEUTRAL WIRE

LIGHT INDICATES GOOD GROUND

CAUTION: Live wires

4 **TEST FOR GROUND: STEP 2.** Touch the leads of a neon voltage tester between the hot wire and the metal box (or between the hot wire and bare copper ground wire if you have one). If the tester lights, the metal box or bare copper wire is grounded and you can proceed. If the tester doesn't light, indicating there is no ground, call in a licensed electrician to supply one. (It's often difficult.) **TURN OFF THE POWER AT THE MAIN CIRCUIT PANEL BEFORE CONTINUING.**

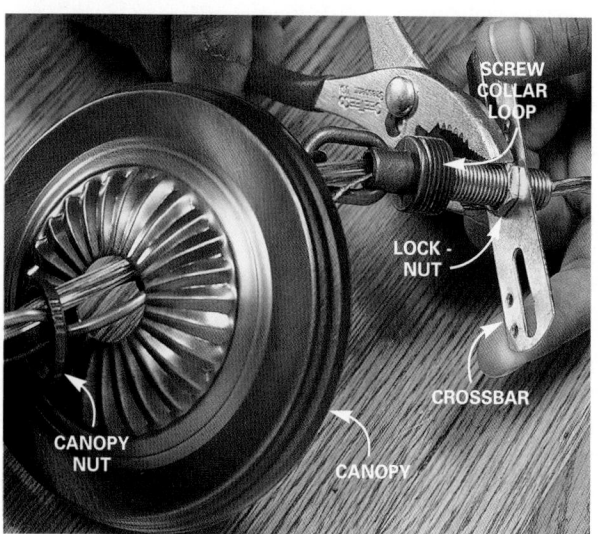

SCREW COLLAR LOOP

LOCK - NUT

CROSSBAR

CANOPY NUT

CANOPY

6 **PREASSEMBLE** the mounting strap assembly. Align the back of the canopy (the side that fits against the ceiling) with the crossbar and adjust the length of the pipe until about 3/8 in. of the threads on the screw collar loop extend through the canopy. Lock the threaded pipe in this position by tightening the locknut against the crossbar.

Reduce overhead work by preassembling parts on the ground

You'll save time and aching arms by assembling and adjusting the mounting hardware before you climb the ladder. The photos on p. 77 show the two most common mounting systems. In either case, the trick is to thread the machine screws or threaded rod into the crossbar first. Then slide the canopy over the screws or rod. Align the

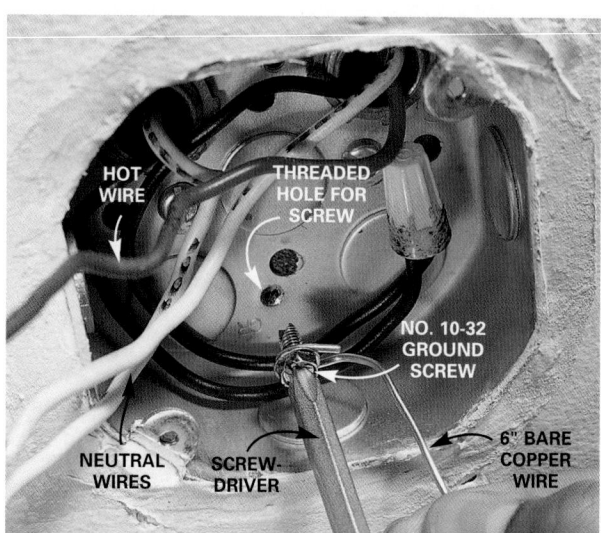

HOT WIRE

THREADED HOLE FOR SCREW

NO. 10-32 GROUND SCREW

NEUTRAL WIRES

SCREW-DRIVER

6" BARE COPPER WIRE

5 **ATTACH** a ground wire to the metal box if it's not already present. Wrap the end of a 6-in. length of bare copper wire around a No. 10-32 ground screw and drive it into the threaded hole in the bottom of the box. Wrap the wire at least three-quarters of the way around the screw in a clockwise direction. Tighten the screw to secure the ground wire.

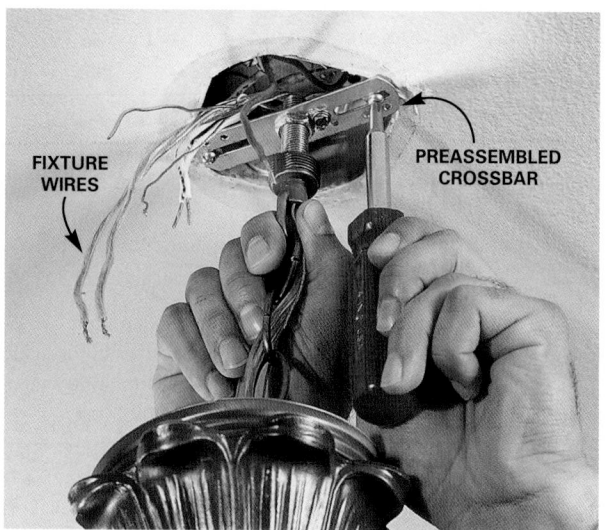

FIXTURE WIRES

PREASSEMBLED CROSSBAR

7 **POSITION** all the wires to one side of the crossbar. Then screw the crossbar to the electrical box with the screws. You'll need a helper to support the fixture while you do this.

crossbar with the back of the canopy and adjust the length of the screws or rod to protrude about 1/4 to 3/8 in. through the canopy. Tighten the locknut(s) to hold the screws or rod in this position. For hanging fixtures, adjust the length of the chain by removing lengths, but don't cut the wires shorter until you've hung the fixture and confirmed that it's the right height.

Reconnect the same wires

After testing to make sure none of the wires in the box are hot (**Photo 2**), disconnect the hot, neutral and ground (if your old fixture has one) from your old fixture and leave other wires bundled in the box. Reconnect the new fixture to these same wires (**Photo 8**). If the old wires have twisted or damaged ends, cut them off and remove 1/2 in. of the insulated covering with a wire-stripping tool. Connect

Fig. A: Two mounting systems

Whether your light fixture is held to the box with screws or a threaded pipe, the two mounting systems shown here, the key to an easy installation is assembling and adjusting the parts before you crawl up on the ladder. To do this, first thread the screws or pipe through the crossbar. Then, while the fixture is still on the ground, line up the crossbar with the top of the canopy and adjust the screws or pipe in or out until about 1/4 to 1/2 in. is protruding through the canopy. Mount the crossbar to the electrical box, then connect the wires and finally the fixture.

Mounting with a threaded pipe

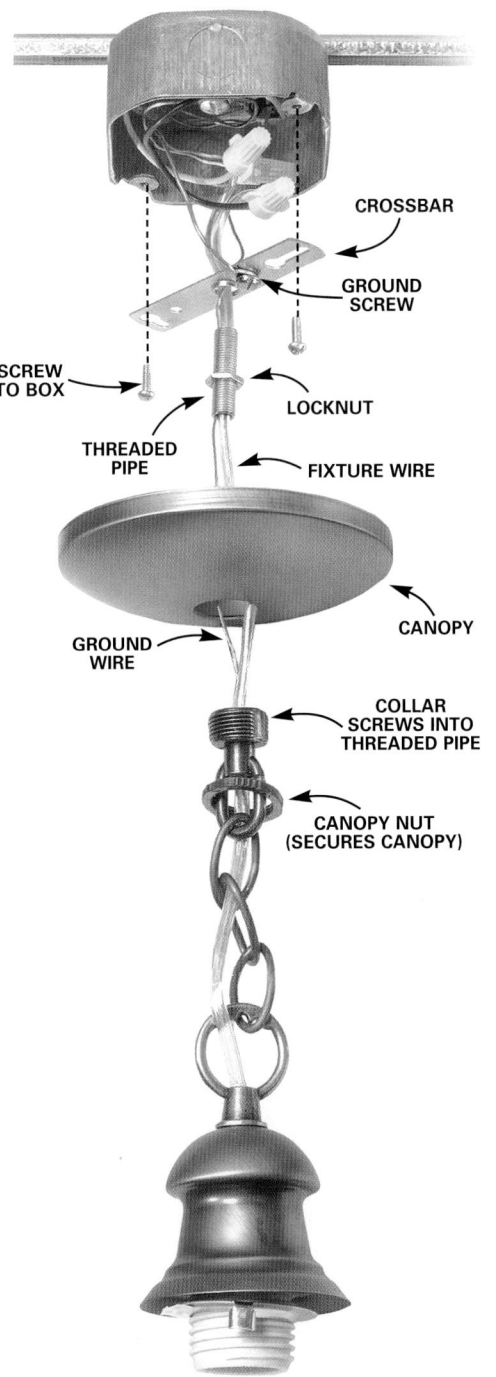

CROSSBAR

GROUND SCREW

SCREW TO BOX

THREADED PIPE

LOCKNUT

FIXTURE WIRE

GROUND WIRE

CANOPY

COLLAR SCREWS INTO THREADED PIPE

CANOPY NUT (SECURES CANOPY)

Mounting with screws and cap nuts

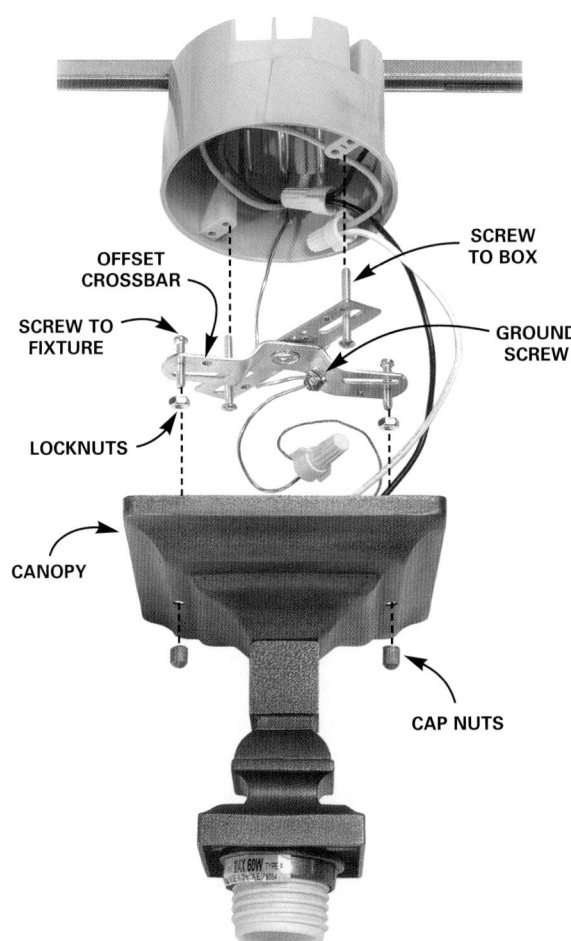

OFFSET CROSSBAR

SCREW TO BOX

SCREW TO FIXTURE

GROUND SCREW

LOCKNUTS

CANOPY

CAP NUTS

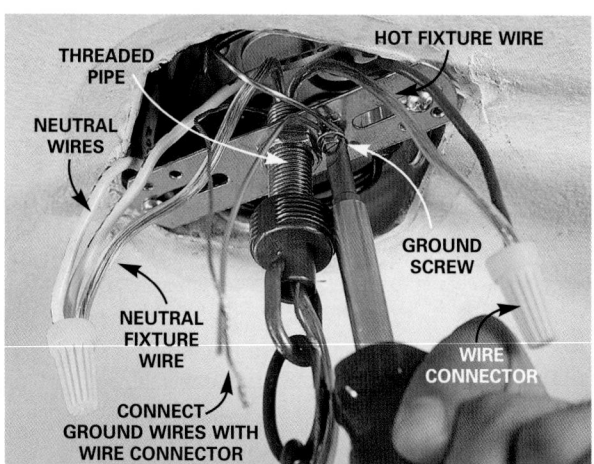

THREADED PIPE
NEUTRAL WIRES
HOT FIXTURE WIRE
GROUND SCREW
NEUTRAL FIXTURE WIRE
WIRE CONNECTOR
CONNECT GROUND WIRES WITH WIRE CONNECTOR

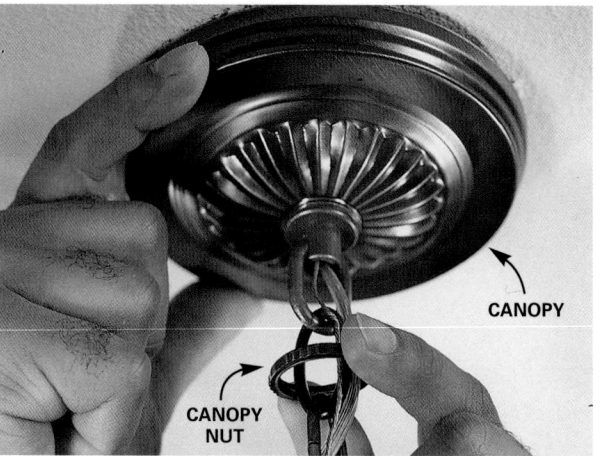

CANOPY
CANOPY NUT

8 CONNECT the neutral wire from the light fixture to the neutral white wire(s) in the box. If your fixture is wired with lamp-style cord rather than white (neutral) and black (hot) wires, identify the neutral wire by looking for silver conductors, writing, squared corners, or ribs or indentations on the insulation. The unmarked wire is the hot wire. Connect it to the colored (usually black or red) hot wire in the box. Complete the hook-up by looping the ground wire clockwise around the ground screw on the crossbar, tightening the screw, and connecting the end of the wire to the ground wire from the light fixture.

9 FOLD the conductors into the ceiling box and slide the canopy over the protruding threaded support. Secure it with the decorative nut to complete the installation.

> **CAUTION:** If you have aluminum wiring, don't mess with it! Call in a licensed pro who's certified to work with it. This wiring is dull gray, not the dull orange that's characteristic of copper.

the wires from the new fixture with appropriately sized wire connectors. Read the packaging to determine the correct size. When you connect stranded fixture wire to solid wire, extend the stranded end about 1/8 in. beyond the solid wire before you twist on the wire connector. Stranded wire occasionally clogs the threads in a connector, preventing a tight grip. Discard the connector and use a new one if it spins freely without tightening.

Complete the installation by installing the canopy (**Photo 9**). If it doesn't fit tight to the ceiling, readjust the screws or threaded rod. Add light bulbs, switch on the power, and turn on the switch to check out your work. ⌂

Great Goofs™

Fan-tabulous job!

When my son turned 7, I decided to build a special bed/shelving/desk project to fit into his small bedroom. Having read previous goofs in your magazine, I was careful to use knockdown hardware so I could get this sizable project in and out of the room. When the big day arrived to install this 6-ft. high beauty, my son climbed up the ladder to the bunk. My wife turned on the light to admire the project and the ceiling fan nearly took his head off. I'd completely forgotten about the fan in the middle of the room. We moved the project into every conceivable configuration and still the fan spun over the bed. The fan just wasn't in the plan!

Ask Handyman™

BETTER GARAGE LIGHTING

I plan to start woodworking in my garage, but the two bare bulbs in the ceiling are too dim. What's the best solution?

To efficiently light up a two-car garage, remove the bare-bulb porcelain fixtures (remember to turn off the power first) and replace each with an 8-ft. fluorescent fixture. (We recommend one 8-ft. fixture per vehicle space.) We like the type that use 4-ft. bulbs; the 8-ft. bulbs are difficult to handle. One choice, the Philips Alto, costs about $3. You can position the new lights to mount right over the existing ceiling boxes.

Keep in mind that not all fluorescent lights work in cold weather. Select your fluorescent fixture based on the lowest temperature in your garage. Refer to starting temperatures printed on the ballast (**see photo at top right**). Regular magnetic ballasts in standard T12 fluorescent fixtures (which have 1-1/2 in. diameter lamps) are not recommended for temperatures below 50 degrees F.

If the temperature in your garage drops below 50 degrees, buy fixtures with electronic ballasts (not electromagnetic) because they start in temperatures down to 0 degrees F and lower. We recommend you buy fixtures that take size T8 lamps (1 in. wide), which are more energy efficient. They cost more initially but will save you money over time. Avoid energy-saver T12 lamps; they need a minimum of 60 degrees to operate properly.

When buying bulbs, especially for a woodworking shop where you need to see the true color of paints and stains, ask for lamps with a CRI (color rendering index) of 85 or above. This number usually isn't printed on the bulb or packaging, but it's listed in the bulb company's product catalog (and on some Web sites).

Once you know the exact ceiling fixture location, drill a 7/8-in. hole in the base of the fluorescent light's metal housing, directly over the existing ceiling box. Buy a 1/2-in. electrical bushing (at home centers and hardware stores) and snap it into the newly drilled hole so sharp

Look for the cold starting temperature, which is only printed on the ballast label.

8' T8 FLUORESCENT FIXTURE (4' LAMPS)

WOW, I CAN SEE!

metal edges won't cut into wires. Then attach the fixtures to the drywall ceiling by screwing them directly into ceiling joists.

Note: Make sure a ground wire is present and fasten it to the metal body of the fluorescent fixture.

Ask Handyman™

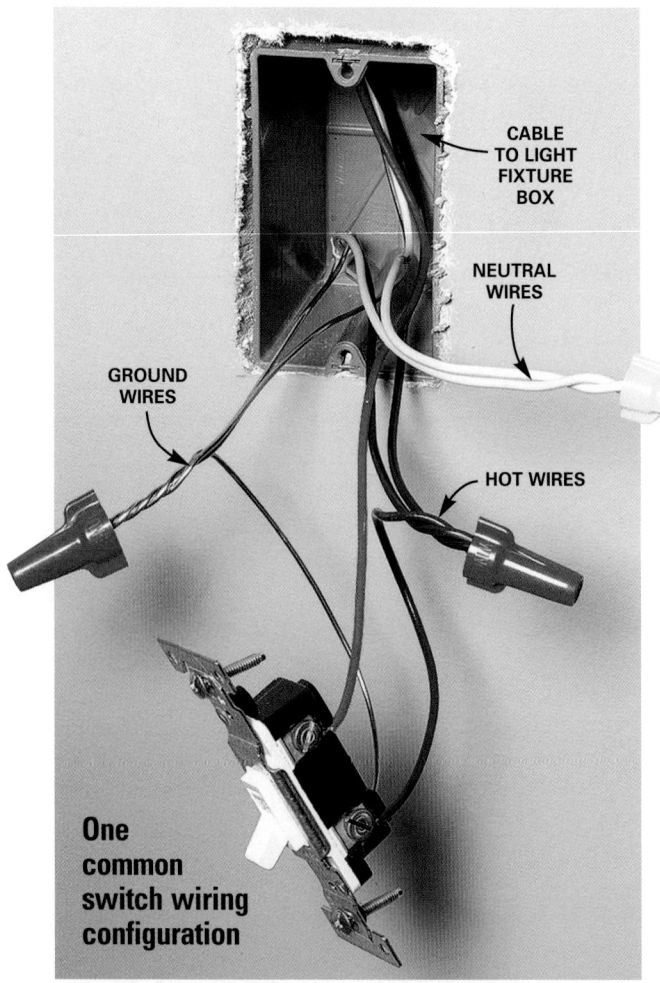

CABLE TO LIGHT FIXTURE BOX

NEUTRAL WIRES

GROUND WIRES

HOT WIRES

One common switch wiring configuration

POWER FROM A SWITCH BOX

I'm adding a new receptacle in my family room. Can I tie in to nearby switch box wires?

Sometimes. First, check to see if the box contains a circuit you can tie into. Turn off the power to the switch box, remove the switch plate and unscrew the switch so you can examine the wires. If there's a pair of neutral (white) wires that aren't connected to the switch, you're in luck (see photo). You can then add the new black wire to the black, the white to the white, and the ground to the ground wires. However, keep in mind that the switch box might contain other wires or have improper connections. If you're not sure, look elsewhere or call a licensed electrician to advise you.

Second, do a wire count to make sure the box is big enough for the three new wires (see chart). The box size (in cubic inches) is often stamped on the inside of the back. If it's not, measure the width, height and depth of the box and multiply to calculate its volume. If the box isn't large enough, replace it with a larger one or look for another place to tie in.

How to calculate box size

1 COUNT the wires coming into the box shown in the photo.

1 red wire	1
2 black wires	2
2 white wires	2
All ground wires (count as 1)	1
1 switch (counts as 2)	2
Total	**8**

2 ADD cable for the new receptacle:

1 new black wire	1
1 new white wire	1
1 new ground wire (combined with other ground wires)	0
Total	**2**

8 + 2 = 10 Total wire count with new cable

3 FOR 14-gauge wires, multiply by 2 cu. in. (For 12-gauge, multiply by 2.25)

Minimum box size needed:
10 x 2 = 20 cu. in.

DO I NEED TO MOVE MY ELECTRICAL BOXES?

I'm installing wood wainscot paneling in my dining room. Do I need to move the electrical outlets to make them flush with the paneling?

You sure do. You could move the boxes out, but you'd have to cut the wall open. It's easier to use a plastic or steel extension ring. They're available up to 1-1/4 in. deep.

To install an extension ring, first turn off the power to the receptacle at the main panel, then remove the cover plate and unscrew the receptacle from the box. Pull the receptacle away from the box (don't disconnect the wires). If you're using a steel ring, press a grounding clip onto it and connect a 6-in. grounding wire. Connect the other end to the ground pigtail. Fasten the receptacle back to the box using the longer screws that come with the extension ring.

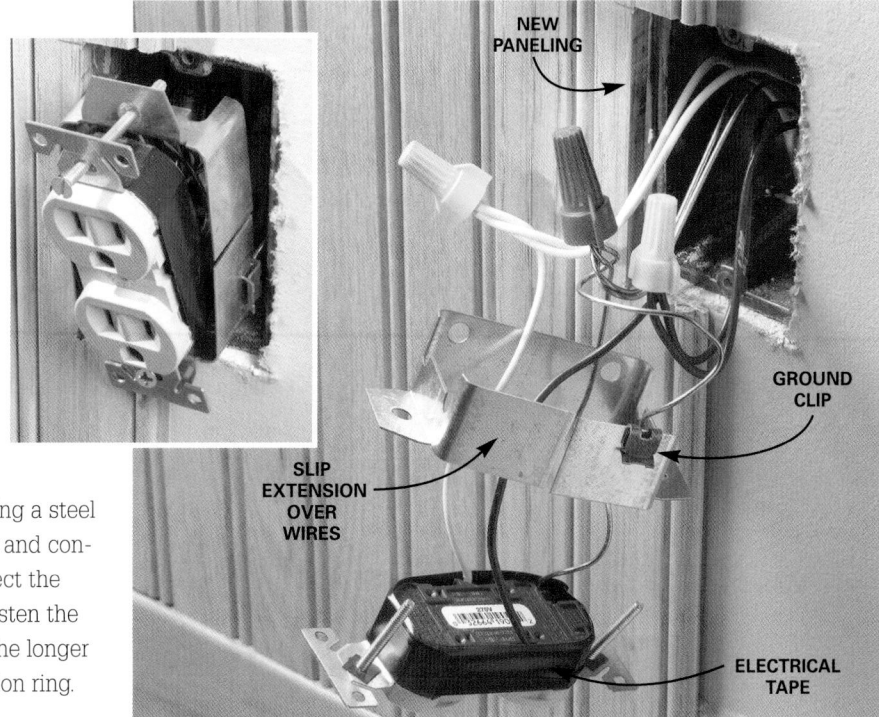

NEW PANELING

GROUND CLIP

SLIP EXTENSION OVER WIRES

ELECTRICAL TAPE

REPLACING TWO-SLOT ELECTRICAL OUTLETS WITH THREE-SLOT

Is there a way to change my two-slot outlets to three-slot so I don't have to use adapters on my three-prong plug ends?

Yes, there is, but the best way isn't easy. The two slots in your outlet represent the hot and neutral wires. Since the mid-1960s, the electrical code has required a third slot for an equipment ground, which adds shock and fire protection. The best way to get this protection is to run that third wire, which is usually bare copper or wire with green insulation, from the outlet box back to the grounding bar in your main electrical panel. However, you usually have to open walls or floors to get the wire in—a big job. Sometimes grounding can be done in other ways, but they're often tricky and require the expertise of a licensed electrician.

A second way is to install a GFCI outlet. This device will give you better safety protection than the equipment ground, without running the third wire. However, this method has drawbacks. Many types of modern electrical equipment, such as air conditioners and computers, won't operate properly without an equipment ground, which is why you're required to label any GFCI that doesn't have one. (The labels are included with the GFCI device; see the label above.)

It's unsafe to use adapters that convert three-prong plugs to two-prong ones, because as normally used, the adapters bypass the safety features of the equipment ground.

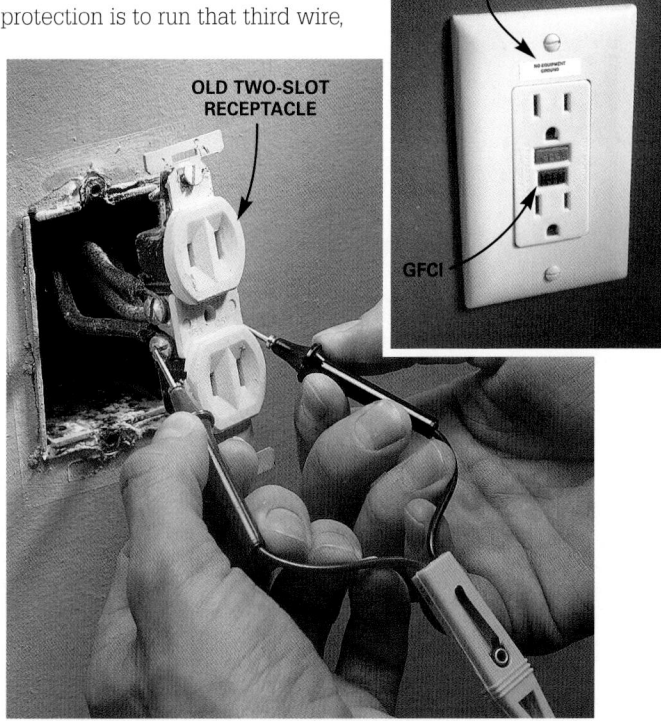

"NO EQUIPMENT GROUND" LABEL

OLD TWO-SLOT RECEPTACLE

GFCI

You Can Fix It™

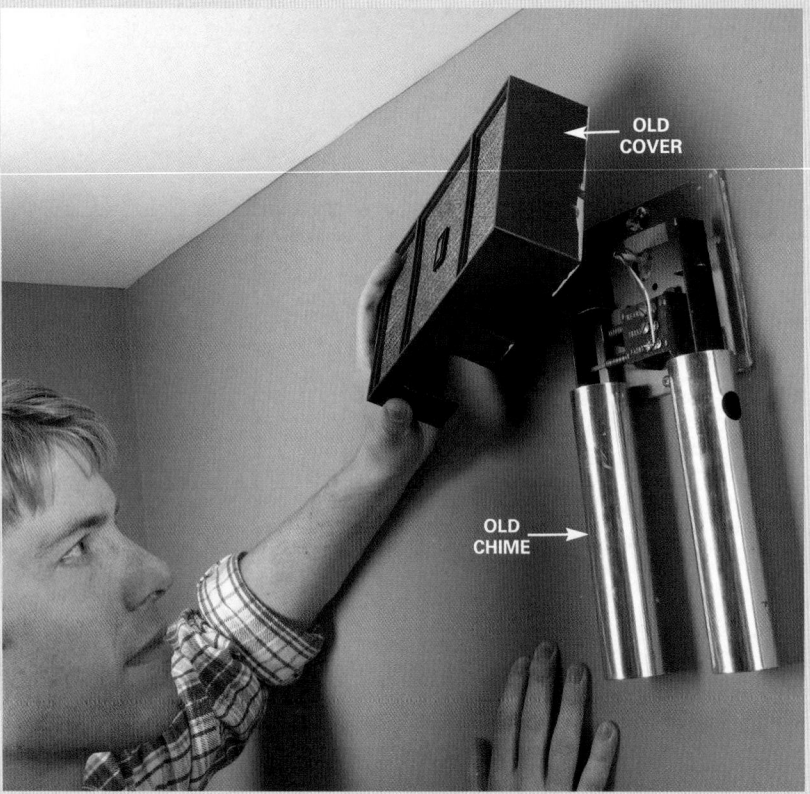

1 TURN OFF the power and lift off or unscrew the old chime cover.

UPDATE AN OLD DOORBELL CHIME

Tired of that old, worn doorbell button or the sound of the chime? Replacing the doorbell components is simple. New doorbell buttons ($2 to $10) and wired or wireless doorbell chimes ($10 to $80) are available at hardware stores and home centers.

The doorbell is powered by a small transformer mounted somewhere in your house, usually close to the main panel. It's connected to a standard electrical circuit. Shut off power to the old doorbell by turning off the main power or flipping the individual circuit breakers and testing the doorbell until it stops working.

You can replace the chime in about 10 minutes (Photos 1 – 4). The three wires—one from the transformer and one from each button—

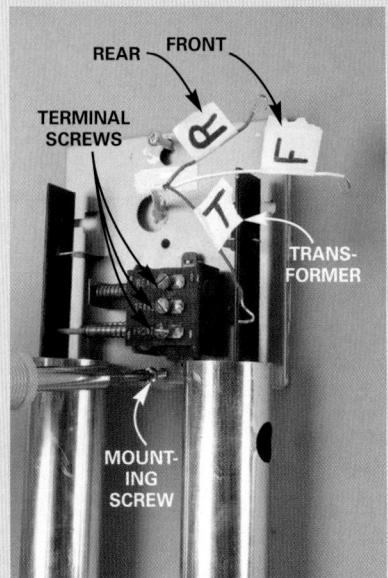

2 LABEL the individual wires with masking tape and the letter on the screw terminal. Unhook all the wires, remove the mounting screws and discard the old chime.

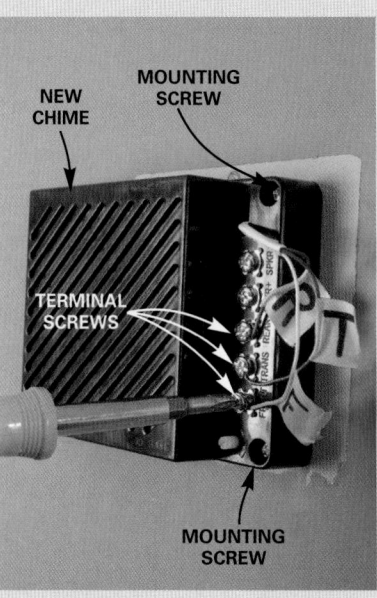

3 MOUNT the new chime to the wall with the enclosed hardware. Hook the wires to the corresponding terminal screws on the new chime.

4 REST the new chime cover over the new chime, turn on the power and test the doorbell.

are connected to the corresponding terminal screws. Label them so you can hook them up correctly to the new chime.

Mounting the new button(s) (Photo 5) probably will involve drilling new mounting holes, and their size will be specified in the instructions.

The trickiest part of the job is working with the old doorbell wires. The wire sheathing can flake off, or the wires can break and become very short. And it's usually impossible to pull in new bell wires. If the wires are too short for the new button, widen the hole with a chisel or utility knife and then extend the wire length with additional 18-2 doorbell wire and a couple of small wire connectors. Or try a different style button that requires less wire length. If all else fails, pick up a wireless doorbell that comes with a battery-powered button.

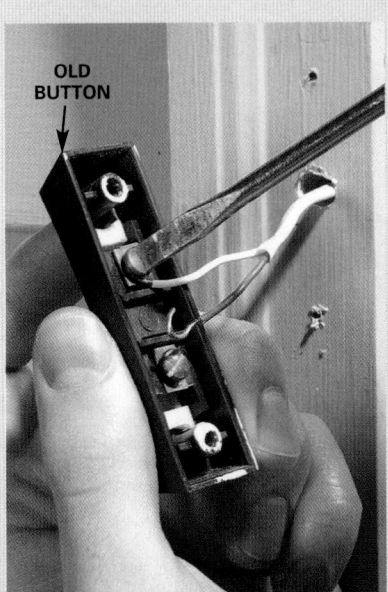

5 REMOVE the mounting screws, then unscrew the terminal screw wires and discard the old button. Wrap the wires clockwise around the new button terminal screws, tighten them and mount the new button.

TIGHTEN A LOOSE OUTLET

A loose outlet pushes in every time you insert a plug. Often it happens because the cutout around the outlet box is too big. When the drywall is taped, gaps around the electrical boxes are filled with mud, which supports the outlet ears. In a heavily used outlet, this mud breaks loose, leaving the outlet ears unsupported. Eventually the cover plate cracks. A scrap of 12- or 14-gauge electrical wire and a few common tools are all you'll need to lock that outlet down tighter than a pit bull's jaws.

Start by shutting off the power to the outlet (**Photo 1**). Photos 2 and 3 show how to convert scrap electrical wire into a coiled spacer, which will bridge the gap between the outlet and the electrical box. Once the spacer is completed, install it between the outlet and electrical box as shown in **Photo 4**. **Note:** If the face of the box isn't flush with a wood or combustible-material wall, or the box is more than 1/4 in. behind a drywall wall, you must add a box extender (50¢).

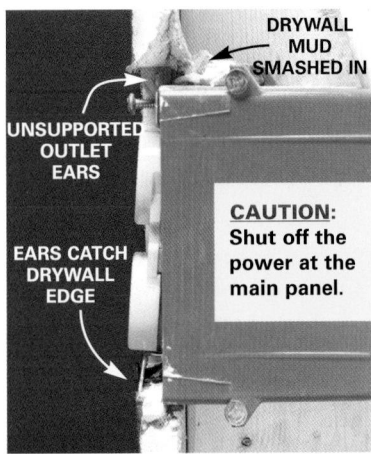

1 TURN off the power at the main panel and remove the broken cover plate. The drywall is often broken behind the outlet ears, leaving them unsupported.

2 STRIP the exterior sheathing off a 12-in. scrap of 12- or 14-gauge electrical cable and remove one of the individual wires. Twist the wire into a tight coil with a needle-nose pliers.

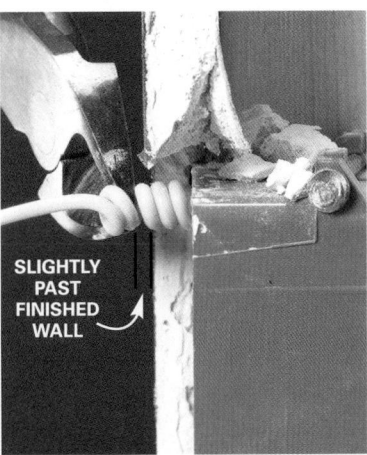

3 PRESS the coiled end tight to the outlet-mounting screw hole. Snip the coil so it extends just past the wall; the insulation will compress slightly when tightened.

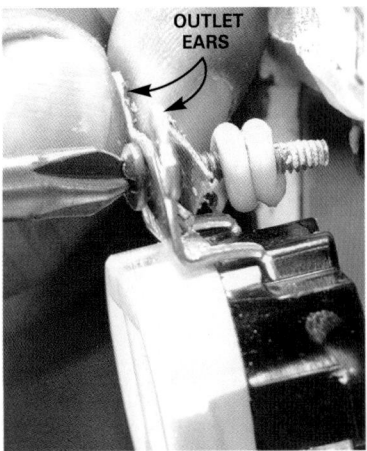

4 SLIDE the coil spacer over the outlet-mounting screw. Screw the outlet down until the outlet ears are flush to the wall.

Using Tools: Stripping Wire

TOOLS & TRICKS FOR WIRE & CABLE

Safe, durable electrical connections begin with clean, accurate wire stripping. You have to remove the outer layer of plastic without nicking or slicing the insulation or wires underneath; otherwise, your connection might break or an electrical short might occur.

In a pinch, you can strip almost any wire or cable with nothing more than a sharp pocket knife or utility knife. We'll show you how to do this safely and carefully. But for fast, accurate stripping, we recommend the specialized stripping tools we demonstrate in this article. They're afford-able and easy to use, and they produce high-quality results.

All the tools we show are available at home centers and electrical supply stores. Buy each as you need it, and you'll soon have exactly what you need for any home wiring task.

Cords

Cable

Communication

Underground

Electrical cords

A knife works best for stripping sheathing from cords. It takes a sharp blade, a steady hand and concentration to control the depth of the cut precisely. But once you master the technique, you'll be surprised how quickly and accurately you can remove cord sheathing.

We're showing the technique on a cord, but it also works on plastic-sheathed cable. Practice with the blade extended (**Photo 1**) or barely visible to see which technique works best for you.

When it comes to stripping individual wires, a wire stripping tool ($9; **Photo 3**) is faster and more accurate, but in a pinch you can use a knife. With all of these tech-niques, the key is to control the depth of the cut to avoid cutting or gouging the metal conductor.

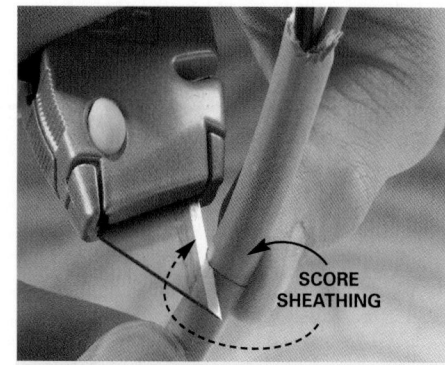

SCORE
SHEATHING

__CAUTION:__ Use the sharp knife blade very, very carefully

1 SCORE a circle around the cable jacket, but don't cut all the way through the plastic. This technique may look danger-ous, but it's safe as long as you apply very light pressure with the knife and keep your thumb on the opposite side of the cord. Carefully guide the knife around the cable until you reach your starting point.

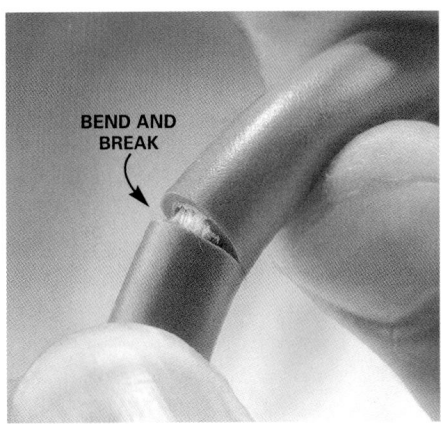

BEND AND BREAK

2 BEND the cable at the scored line to break the plastic covering. Bend it the opposite way to tear the other side and slide it off. Inspect the insulation on the wires underneath to make sure the blade didn't nick them. If you see slices, cut off the cable and try again.

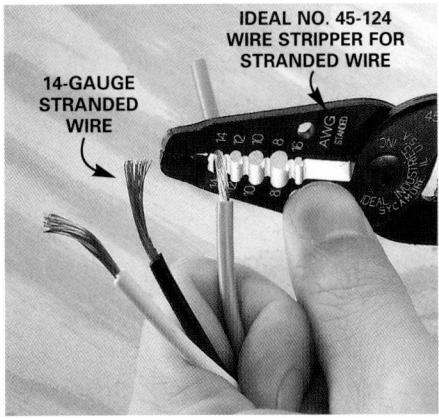

IDEAL NO. 45-124
WIRE STRIPPER FOR
STRANDED WIRE

14-GAUGE
STRANDED
WIRE

3 ALIGN the wire with the notch that matches the wire gauge and squeeze to cut the insulation. Then hold the wire with one hand while you push the stripper with your thumb to remove the insulation.

Plastic-sheathed cable

Stripping plastic-sheathed (NM, for nonmetallic) type cable is a two-step process. First you remove the outer plastic sheathing. Then you strip the individual conductors. There are many methods to remove the plastic sheath. The stripping tool we're using is unique because it combines both sheathing removal and wiring stripping in one tool (**Photo 1**) and works perfectly for both tasks. It's well worth the $20 price if you do any amount of home wiring. Otherwise, buy a simpler $9 stripper similar to the one in **Photo 3** (left, center photo) but designed for solid wires, and use a knife or other method to remove the outer sheathing.

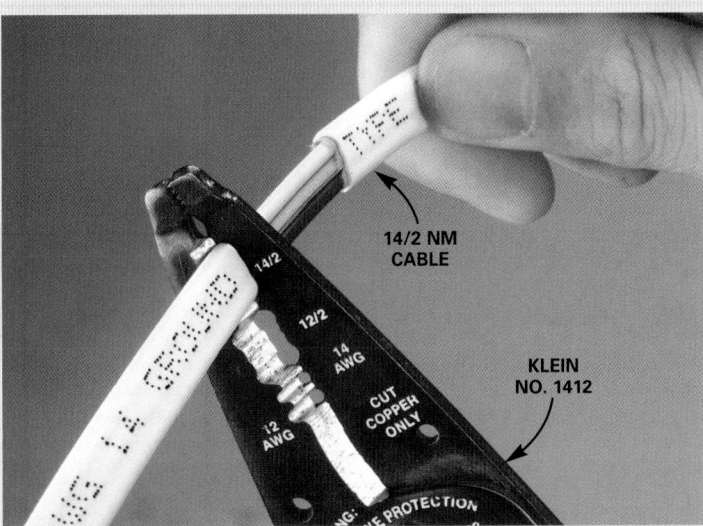

14/2 NM
CABLE

KLEIN
NO. 1412

1 ALIGN the plastic-sheathed cable with the notch that matches the wire gauge you're using—either 14/2 or 12/2—and squeeze down to cut the sheathing. Slide off the sheathing to expose the wires underneath.

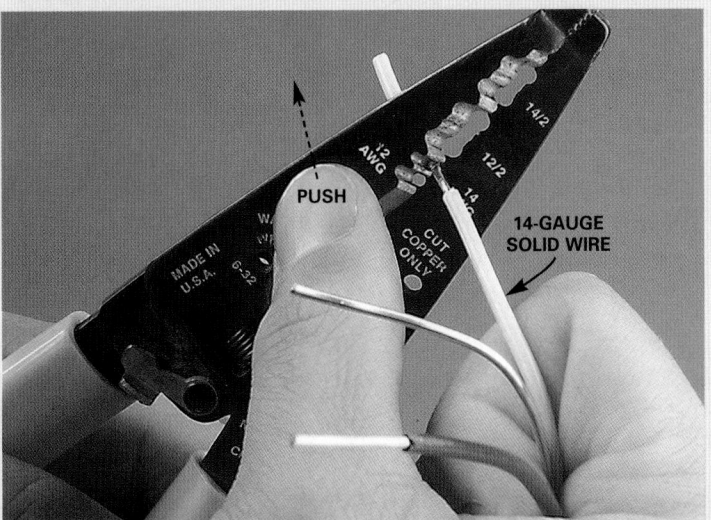

PUSH

14-GAUGE
SOLID WIRE

2 STRIP individual conductors by lining them up in the correct notch and squeezing the stripper to cut through the plastic. Keep the stripper perpendicular to the wire. Tilting the stripper can cause nicked wires. Push against the stripper with your thumb to slide the insulation from the wire.

Using Tools: Stripping Wire

Sheathed communication wires

With high-speed Internet lines and household computer networking becoming more common, you may soon find yourself installing new communication cables that can handle the greater bandwidths. Here's a $4 tool that makes short work of removing the outer sheath from these small cables without nicking the conductors inside. The cable size notches aren't labeled, so you'll have to experiment to find the one that works.

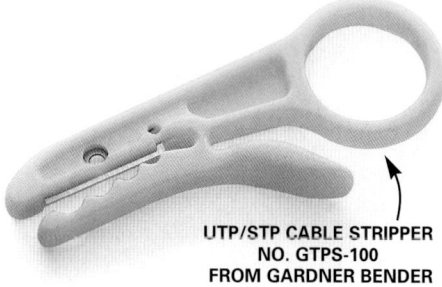

UTP/STP CABLE STRIPPER NO. GTPS-100 FROM GARDNER BENDER

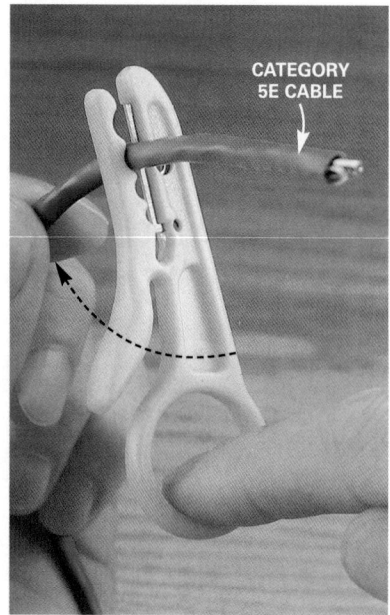

CATEGORY 5E CABLE

1 OPEN the jaws on the stripper slightly and slip the cable into the largest groove. Rotate the cutter clockwise. If it doesn't score the outer sheathing, move it to the next smaller slot and try again.

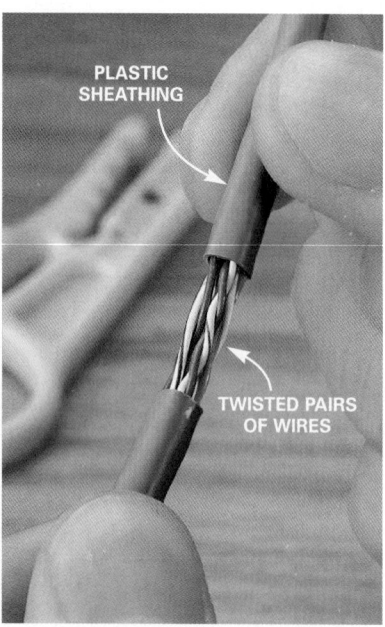

PLASTIC SHEATHING

TWISTED PAIRS OF WIRES

2 BEND the cable to break the sheathing. Then slide the scored sheathing from the wires. Inspect the twisted pairs of wires to make sure the insulation isn't sliced.

Thin wires

Tiny communication wires are tough to strip without nicking and weakening them. The key is to match the stripper to the wire you're using. For example, you may be surprised to discover that there's a special stripper for stranded wire (Photo 1) that's just slightly larger than the same size solid wire. There are also strippers for those tiny little wires you find on doorbells and telephone lines. Read the packaging before you buy to find the stripper that's right for your job.

FOR STRANDED WIRE

1 THIS stripper removes the insulation from 16- to 26-gauge stranded wires. Similar tools strip larger-gauge stranded wires and solid wires.

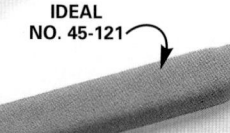

IDEAL NO. 45-121

Coaxial cable

Adding F-type connectors to coaxial cable requires a two- or three-step strip on the end of the cable, depending on the connector. With care, you can make the strip with a utility knife, and a regular wire stripper. But the dedicated tool ($19) we show here makes the job quick and accurate. Read the packaging to match the stripper to the type of coaxial cable you're using. The strippers you find in home centers work on common household coaxial cables.

Read the lettering on the sheathing to determine whether your coaxial cable is RG-58, RG-59 or RG-6, and adjust the slide on top of the cutter to match your cable type. Make a practice cut and adjust the blades if necessary (Photo 1).

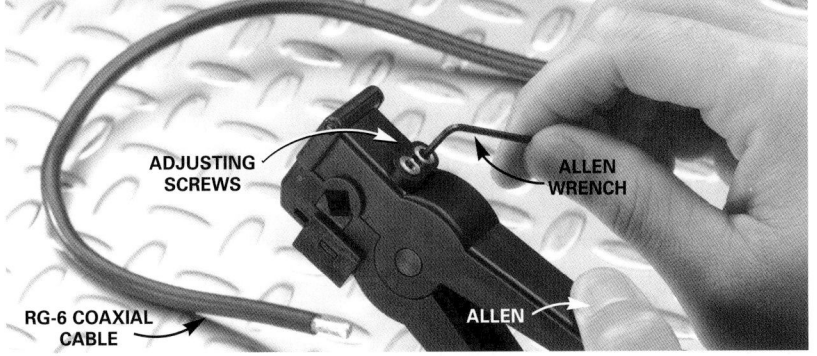

ADJUSTING SCREWS — **ALLEN WRENCH** — **ALLEN** — **RG-6 COAXIAL CABLE**

1 TEST cutter depth on a cable scrap. Adjust the two cutting blades one at a time to fine-tune the depth of the cut. Turn the adjusting screws clockwise with the Allen wrench (included with the tool) to make a deeper cut.

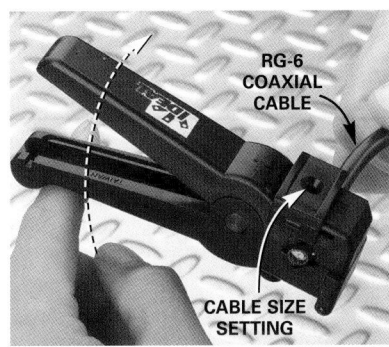

RG-6 COAXIAL CABLE — **CABLE SIZE SETTING**

2 SET the stripper to match your coaxial cable size. Open the jaws and position the cable as shown. Check the icon on the tool's handle to make sure the cut end of the cable is pointing the right direction. Rotate the cutter about five or six times clockwise.

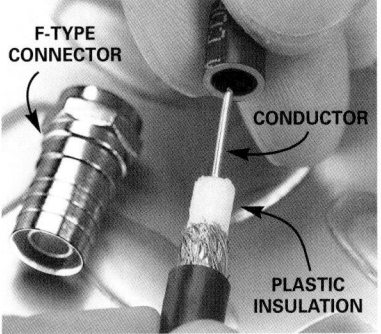

F-TYPE CONNECTOR — **CONDUCTOR** — **PLASTIC INSULATION**

3 REMOVE the cutter and slide off the sections of cut sheathing. Scrape the metal foil from the plastic insulation with your fingernail.

Underground cable

A special type of plastic-sheathed cable called UF (underground feeder) requires a slightly different technique. Since the sheathing surrounds each conductor, you can't just score it and slide it off. Photos 1 – 3 show how to strip UF cable.

This technique requires practice to master. Develop your skill before trying it on a real project. The key to success is controlling the depth of the cut by keeping the angle of the blade low, almost parallel with the cable. When you get it right, you'll be able to feel the blade riding along the top of the insulation of the wire underneath. Remember, if you gouge the insulation or nick the wires inside, cut off the cable at that point and try again. 🏠

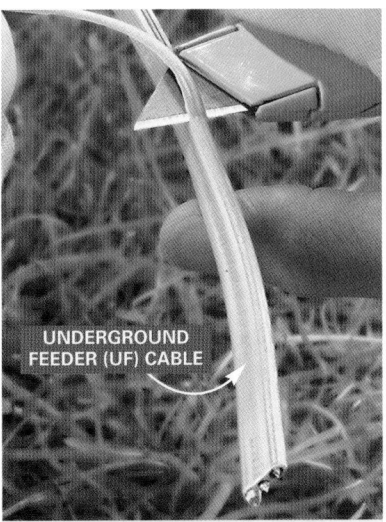

UNDERGROUND FEEDER (UF) CABLE

CAUTION: Use the sharp knife blade very, very carefully

1 PEEL the plastic sheathing from the wires underneath with a sharp utility knife. Slide your thumb along the underside of the wire while you pull the knife along the top to remove a thin slice of plastic. This technique takes practice. If you cut through the insulation on the wire underneath, cut off that segment of cable and try again.

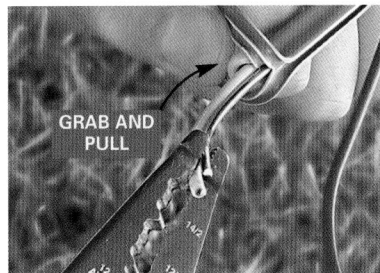

GRAB AND PULL

2 EXPOSE a few inches of wire at the end of the cable. Grab the ends of the wires with the stripper in one hand and the plastic sheath in the other, and peel the sheathing back to where you started the cut.

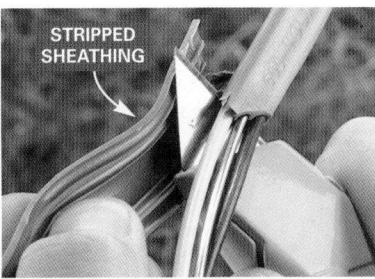

STRIPPED SHEATHING

3 SLIDE your knife between the loose sheathing and wires and cut toward the unstripped cable to remove the excess plastic sheathing.

GET
WIRED!

Install two types of cable now—and all your telephone, cable TV, computer and Internet needs will be set for the 21st century

by **Travis Larson**

You may not think you'll ever need an updated communication system, but with the increasing digitizing of our society, you will. The need is now. Within a few years, digital TVs will be the only show in town, and the high-speed links to the Internet will be more necessary and affordable. More and more, electronic components will need to "converse." And your old phone and cable wires just won't be up to the task.

It's easy to feel intimidated by all the electronic jargon. However, for now, all you need to know is that your telephone, TV, Internet and other communication needs can all be handled by running only two types of cable—all headquartered in a central distribution system you can install yourself. It's as easy as fishing in a new phone line, except that you'll need four cables (two phone and two coaxial) to each jack to do the job right.

We'll show you how to run the wires, install the proper jacks and hook up the central distribution box. The new system doesn't mean you have to scrap your old cables and jacks. Existing phone lines and jacks can coexist with your new system.

We recommend that you initially install new cables and jacks to rooms only where they're needed, and upgrade the system with new jacks and lines as your electronic needs change. The beauty of the installation system shown in this article is that it will be easy to reconfigure, enhance or expand it in the future. Eventually you'll be able to connect any compatible devices simply by "jumping" cable or phone lines in the distribution box (much like old-time telephone operators used to do in the first half of this century).

It's easiest to install the system when you're remodeling, adding on or building a new home. The walls are open and it's simple to route the cables to every room. But in most cases, you can also retrofit your existing home (although it'll take a little more effort fishing cable and sometimes cutting and patching walls). We'll show you some strategies that'll help.

Planning the installation

The key to an upgradable system is to place the main distribution panel in a location where it'll be easiest to fish additional wires and jacks to the rest of the house. In the example home (**Fig. A, below**), we show the laundry room as the logical place for the distribution box. From there, wires can be easily fished to the basement and to the attic and then on to selected outlet locations anywhere in the house. But the best location for the distribution panel may be different in your home—a furnace room, garage or even a closet. You'll also need to create an access into the stud space above and below the panel. For easiest access, position the panel in an open stud space so you can fish new lines into the panel. We show you how to

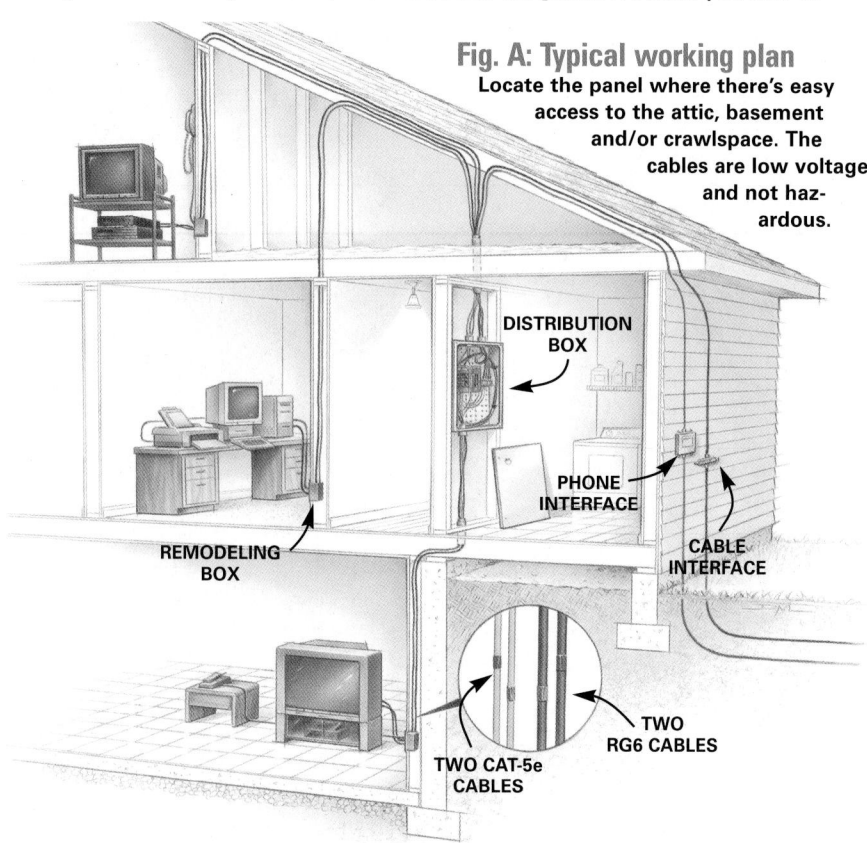

Fig. A: Typical working plan
Locate the panel where there's easy access to the attic, basement and/or crawlspace. The cables are low voltage and not hazardous.

DISTRIBUTION BOX

PHONE INTERFACE

CABLE INTERFACE

REMODELING BOX

TWO RG6 CABLES

TWO CAT-5e CABLES

do this with a panel that unscrews from the wall (Photo 18).

Next, plan your cable routing paths. Attics, basements, crawlspaces, garages and even closets offer the easiest unimpeded routes. Then you can usually drill holes through top or bottom plates and fish the cables in without opening up finished walls. But middle floors that are sandwiched between finished floors can be more challenging. Routing to those rooms by surface-mounting cables through closets is one good strategy, but sometimes cutting and

Capabilities of a new communication system

- One DVD, VCR, and cable or satellite TV receiver will be able to transmit to any television in the house.
- Computers can be networked to share files or computer peripherals like printers and scanners.
- Remote closed-circuit TV cameras can be hooked up to televisions anywhere in the house, and security-system hookups are a breeze.
- You'll have enough telephone-line capacity to run the Pentagon.
- Your home will be rigged for either cable- or telephone-based high-speed Internet service.
- The necessary lines will be in place to handle the inevitable switch from analog to digital TV.
- Whole-house audio systems can be routed over the same cables.
- Depending on the system, integrated home controls can be coupled with "smart appliances."

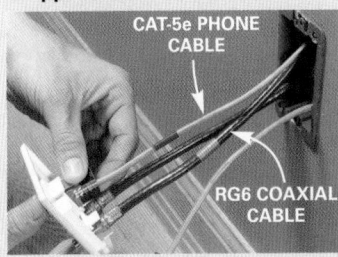

CAT-5e PHONE CABLE

RG6 COAXIAL CABLE

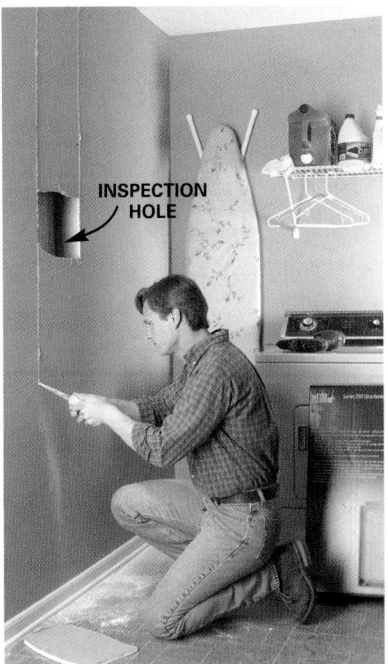

INSPECTION HOLE

1 USE a drywall saw to cut out the drywall between two wall studs. Stop the cuts at the top plates at the ceiling and 2 in. above the baseboards at the floor. (Cut a small inspection hole first to locate wires within the wall to prevent damaging them.)

DISTRIBUTION BOX

2"

2 SCREW the distribution box to the sides of the studs at a comfortable working height. Make sure the box projects past the drywall 1/2 in. to allow for the thickness of the access panels (Photo 18).

TOP PLATES

RIGHT-ANGLE DRILL

2-1/2" HOLE SAW

3 DRILL a 2-1/2 in. hole through the top and bottom plates to access the attic and basement for cable runs.

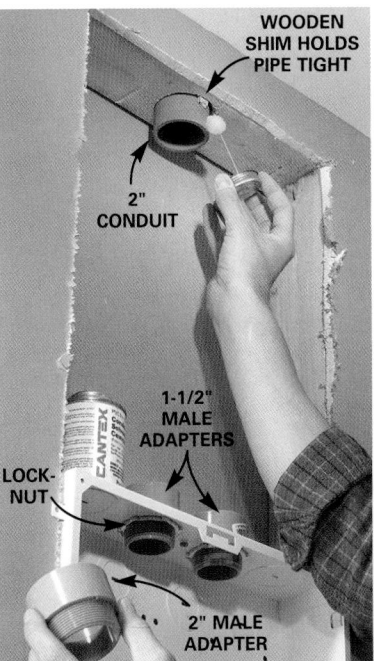

WOODEN SHIM HOLDS PIPE TIGHT

2" CONDUIT

1-1/2" MALE ADAPTERS

LOCK-NUT

2" MALE ADAPTER

4 INSTALL 1-1/2 in. male adapters with locknuts. Cut two 12-in. lengths of 2-in. conduit and cement 2-in. male adapters to one end. Drop one from the attic and poke one up from the basement (Photo 6).

WIRING & ELECTRICAL

patching holes in finished walls or even ceilings to run the wires is inescapable.

Here we show you the most useful jack configuration: two cable jacks and two phone jacks, all in the same cover plate. (A single cover plate will handle four different lines.) And a cable jack will handle video- or cable-based Internet. The extra two phone and coaxial cables will handle "interhouse" networking. You probably won't need all these lines right away, but pull the wires in anyway. However, you don't have to hook them all up. Just attach the jacks and snap them into the cover plate and coil the extra lines neatly inside the distribution box.

All four of the lines from each outlet go back to the distribution box. That calls for a lot of wires, but wiring and jacks are relatively cheap. If you know that you'll only need one cable or one phone jack, just run single lines and use a different cover plate.

Label the wires before and after fishing

When you fish wire from the jacks, label one cable of each pair with an "in" and the other with an "out." It's easy to get confused once all of the lines have been run. Use colored tape around both ends (**Photos 7 and 14**) of the cables and identify the outlet by writing its room location on the tape at the end you feed into the wall before you fish it. To keep everything straight, do the same on the outlet end after it's cut to length. We used orange tape to designate "in" and blue tape for "out." Retape and mark the ends as you cut the cables to final lengths within the distribution box for hookups (**Photo 16**).

Step B: Run the cables

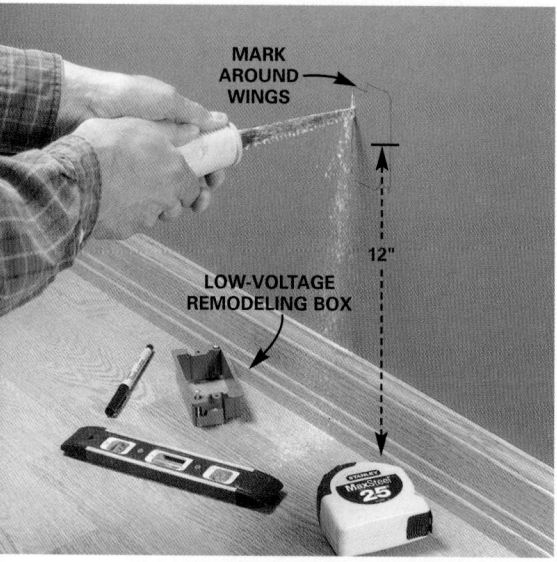

5 HOLD a low-voltage remodeling box against the wall between two studs so the center of the box is 12 in. above the floor (or match the heights of other outlets in the room) and draw around the box and holding wings. Then cut out the opening with a drywall saw.

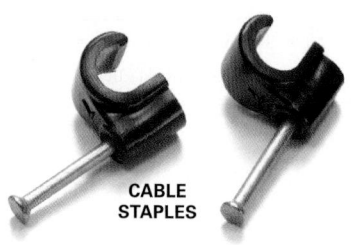

CABLE STAPLES

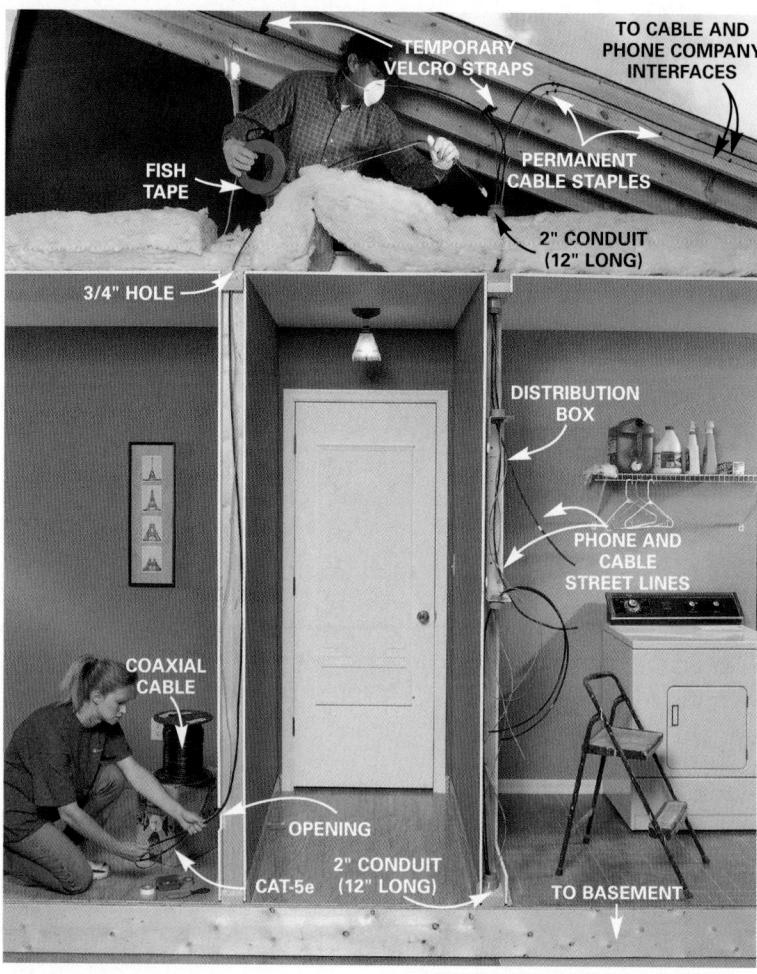

6 FISH the cables from the openings into the distribution box in pairs of coaxial and CAT-5e. Mark the ends of the cables with colored electrical tape for the outlet location. Run the fish tape down into the outlet stud cavity through a 3/4-in. hole drilled through the plates from the attic, then tape both of the marked cable ends to the fish tape. Pull them up into the attic and then push them down to the distribution box. Leave about 3 ft. of extra cable at the distribution box. Cut off the outlet end of the cables about 12 in. past the openings and mark the ends with more colored tape.

A cover panel keeps the wiring runs accessible

We opened up the stud space within a few inches of the ceiling and floor to mount the distribution box and to fish the cables (**Photo 2**). But that stud space has to remain accessible for running new cables later as your system grows. A handsome cover panel made from painted MDF (medium density fiberboard) screwed through the drywall into the studs makes access just a matter of unscrewing it from the wall.

CAT-5e—handle with care

CAT-5e cable is made to exacting standards with specially designed twists between each individual pair of wires. For best performance, follow these wiring guidelines:

- Make sweeping, gradual bends of no less than a 2-in. radius, not sharp bends.
- Gently pull phone cables when fishing, with no more than about 20 lbs. of force (about the tension you'd use for good, tight bootlaces). Don't jerk or yank on the wires or pull them around sharp corners.

Which Should I Buy?

You'll find all the materials and tools you need for your wiring project at most home centers in the telephone accessories department. If parts aren't available in your area, see the Buyer's Guide on p. 94. They'll be able to help you find suppliers in your area. The total cost for this arrangement was $600 for three outlets, including the specialty tools. But the big-ticket items are the distribution box and its components. After this initial investment, expanding the system is cheap.

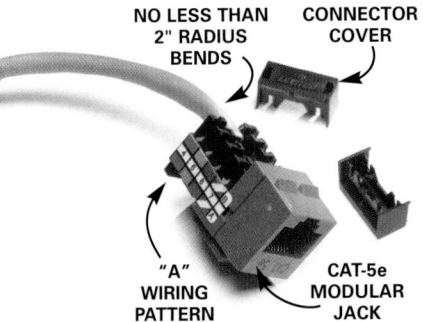

NO LESS THAN 2" RADIUS BENDS — **CONNECTOR COVER** — **"A" WIRING PATTERN** — **CAT-5e MODULAR JACK**

1. Cables

Buy your cable in bulk—it's much cheaper that way. CAT-5e phone cable is sold in 1,000-ft. spools for about $60. It's made to extremely high standards and contains four twisted pairs of wires, so it'll carry up to four different telephone lines per cable. RG-6 coaxial cable is sold in 500-ft. spools for about $60.

2. Distribution system

The heart of the system is the distribution box (**Photo 2**). If you think you'll only need six or fewer outlets throughout the house, buy a small box for about $50. But if you want to leave room for expansion with lots of outlets and space inside the box for networking, signal amplifiers or other hardware, get a larger one ($75).

Go to any electronics store or home center and you'll find plenty of hardware designed to speed up, expand or improve your basic system. The space needed for this hardware is one of the main reasons we recommend going with the larger distribution box.

The telecommunication module (**Photo 14**) is the nerve center for phone jacks and jack-to-jack link-ups. Also included in the module is a coaxial splitter. The splitter distributes the cable connection from the street and "splits" the signal to send it to any components you hook up to it. You can add more phone banks or splitters as needed. A starter module costs about $75 and will take care of your immediate needs. You can snap in banks of jacks or even more modules as required.

3. Jack materials

Modular telephone jacks cost about $8 each. At the outlets, you'll attach these telephone-plug receptacles that snap into the backs of the cover plates. Don't worry—they'll accept old and modern phone lines.

Crimp-on F-connectors cost $20 for a package of 10. End all coaxial lines with crimp-on male F-connectors, which then screw on to splitters within the distribution box or onto snap-on female F-couplings at the cover plates. F-connectors screw into these, which in turn snap into the back of four-port cover plates.

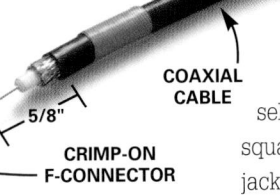

COAXIAL CABLE — **5/8"** — **CRIMP-ON F-CONNECTOR** — **F-JACK**

The four-port cover plates sell for about $2 each. The four square holes receive either modular jacks or F-jacks in any configuration.

In addition to buying the hardware, you'll have to spend about $100 on these must-have specialty tools for working with communication wiring and fittings:

- Coaxial stripper (**Photo 10**)
- F-connector crimping tool (**Photo 11**)
- Electrician's scissors (**Photo 8**)
- Plus, you'll need a right-angle drill ($17 per day rental; **Photo 3**) and a 2-1/2 in. hole saw (**Photo 3**) to drill the wire-run holes.

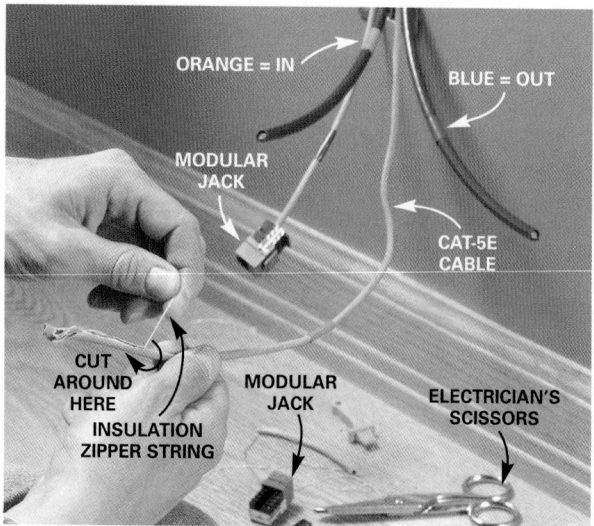

ORANGE = IN

BLUE = OUT

MODULAR JACK

CAT-5E CABLE

CUT AROUND HERE

INSULATION ZIPPER STRING

MODULAR JACK

ELECTRICIAN'S SCISSORS

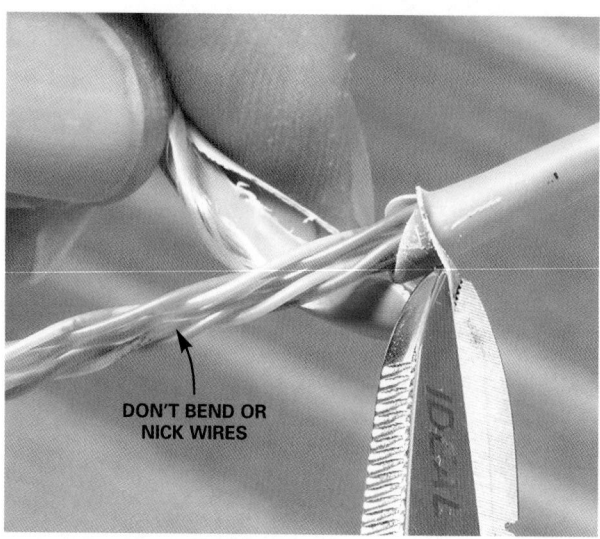

DON'T BEND OR NICK WIRES

7 INSTALL the remodeling box, then cut into the end of the CAT-5e cable about an inch with the electrician's scissors and peel back the insulation. Pluck out the internal string and use it like a zipper to peel open about 4 in. of cable.

8 SNIP around the base of the insulation with the scissors to remove it. If you cut it with a knife, you might nick the wires.

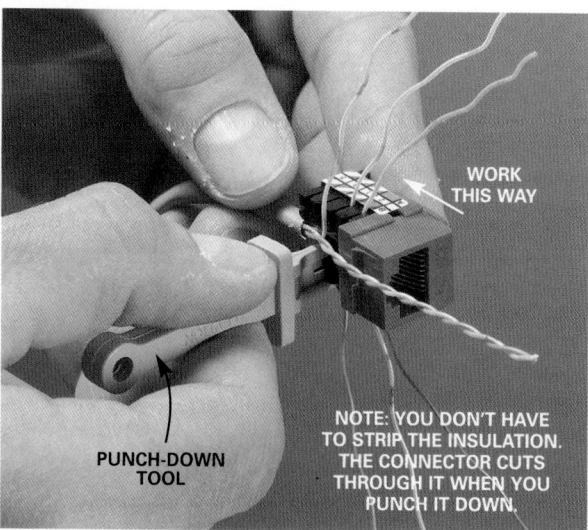

WORK THIS WAY

PUNCH-DOWN TOOL

NOTE: YOU DON'T HAVE TO STRIP THE INSULATION. THE CONNECTOR CUTS THROUGH IT WHEN YOU PUNCH IT DOWN.

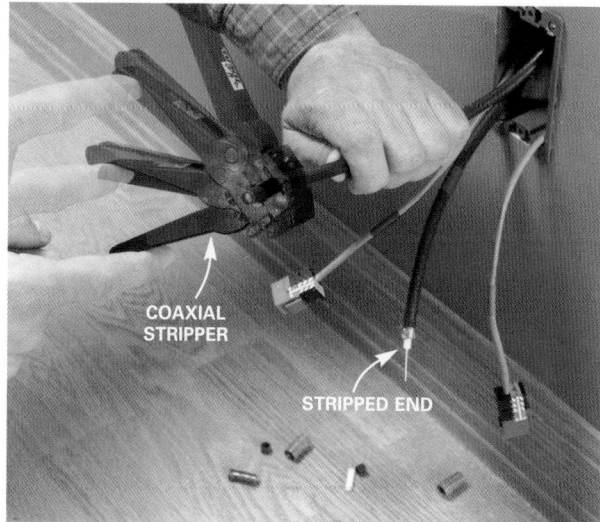

COAXIAL STRIPPER

STRIPPED END

9 GENTLY untwist the colored pairs and bend them into the matching terminals. Work from the front of the jack toward the back, using the punch-down tool that comes with the jacks. Push them in until you feel the little snap that tells you the connector has bitten into the wire. Using the scissors, cut off the excess wires flush with the side of the jack.

10 CLAMP the stripper tool around the coaxial cable with about 5/8 in. of the cable projecting past the tool. Spin it around the cable several times until the sound of cutting metal stops, then remove the tool. You may need to adjust the cutting depths of the little knife blades inside until it strips the cable. Expose the three layers of the cable by stripping with your fingernails to reveal the inner signal wire, white insulation and metal shielding.

- When you're installing jacks or punching down wires on the terminal board, untwist pairs carefully and punch down within 1/2 in. of the beginning of the untwist.

- Never crush CAT-5e with staples or other fasteners like bent-over nails. Instead, bundle it or strap it to framing with loose loops of Velcro and then use special cable straps after all the cables are run.

- Cross any existing electrical cables at 90-degree angles to avoid electrical interference. Never run them side by side unless there's at least a 2-in. separation.

It's easy to get confused by the "A" and "B" markings on modular jacks. The color-coded sticker on the side of the jack shows you where to punch down each wire. Generally, residential phone systems and telecommunication modules are designed

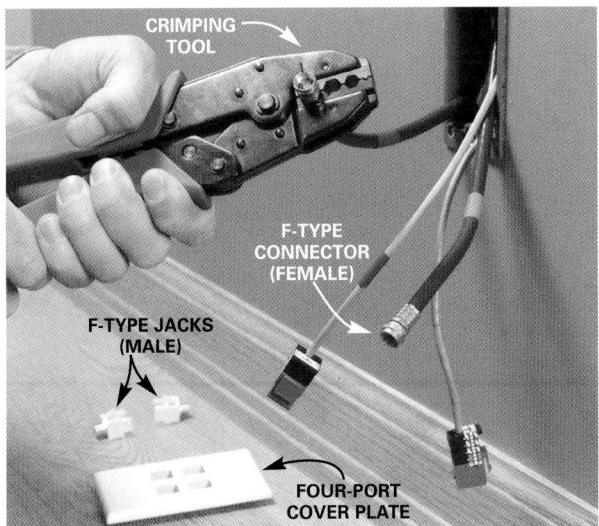

F-TYPE CONNECTOR (FEMALE)

CRIMPING TOOL

F-TYPE JACKS (MALE)

FOUR-PORT COVER PLATE

11 PUSH on the F-connector until the white insulation is tight against the back of the connector, and then crimp it on with a crimping tool. Snip off the copper wire so it projects 1/8 in. past the end of the F-connector.

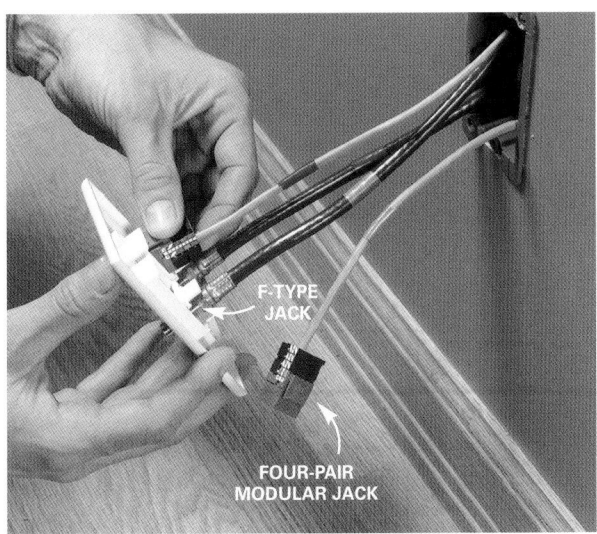

F-TYPE JACK

FOUR-PAIR MODULAR JACK

12 SCREW the F-connectors to the back of the F-jacks and tighten them with a wrench, then snap them into place in the cover plate. Snap in the modular jacks as well, then screw the cover plate to the remodeling box.

for the "A" layout while commercial systems are designed for the "B" system.

The punchdown markings on the module in the distribution box also can be confusing because the slots are marked with a color but no stripe designation. You'll have to study the instructions that come with the module to make sure.

Usually the mostly white wire with small colored stripes goes in the uppermost or farthest left slots followed by the mostly colored wire with the thinner white stripe (Photo 16). If you get either the module wires or the jack wires mixed up, your phones probably won't work, so be sure to consult the directions before hooking up either one. To further alleviate confusion after the system's installed, plan on using colored jacks, too (Photo 7).

Step D: Wire the distribution panel

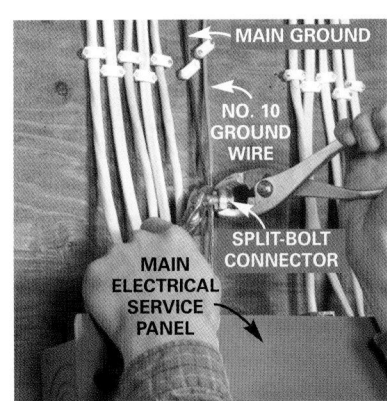

MAIN GROUND

NO. 10 GROUND WIRE

SPLIT-BOLT CONNECTOR

MAIN ELECTRICAL SERVICE PANEL

13 CONNECT a No. 10 ground wire with a grounding screw to the bottom of the box (Photo 14) and to the main ground line of the home service panel with a split-bolt connector.

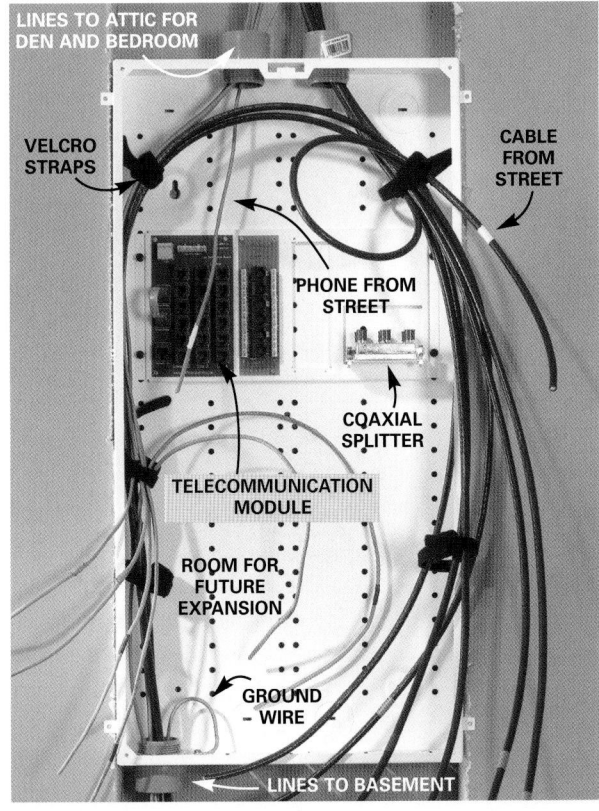

LINES TO ATTIC FOR DEN AND BEDROOM

VELCRO STRAPS

CABLE FROM STREET

PHONE FROM STREET

COAXIAL SPLITTER

TELECOMMUNICATION MODULE

ROOM FOR FUTURE EXPANSION

GROUND WIRE

LINES TO BASEMENT

14 SNAP in the telecommunication module and cable splitter and organize the phone and coaxial cables within the box for easy hookups using loose-fitting Velcro straps. Leave an extra loop in the main coaxial cable line from the street for a future signal booster. Route coaxial cables in from the top of the box for easier splitter hookups.

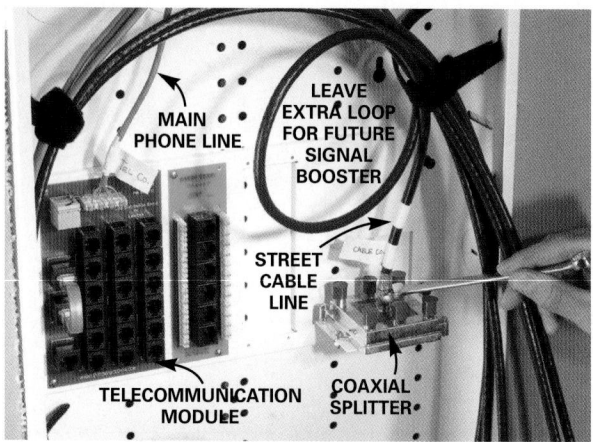

15 PUNCH down the main phone line (from the inter-face box) into the telecommunication module. Crimp an F-connector to the main coaxial cable (from the cable company's hookup box) and tighten it onto the center splitter port.

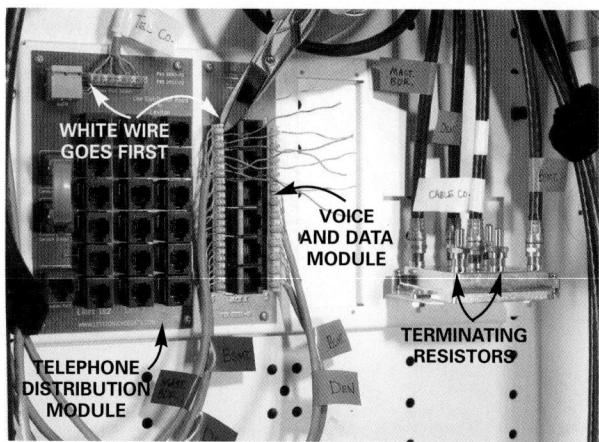

16 CRIMP F-connectors onto the "in" coaxial cables and screw them to the splitter terminals. Cap any unused terminals with terminating resistors. Strip the CAT-5e cables (Photos 7 and 8) and punch them into the terminals on the voice and data module, then clip off the excess wires with the electrician's scissors.

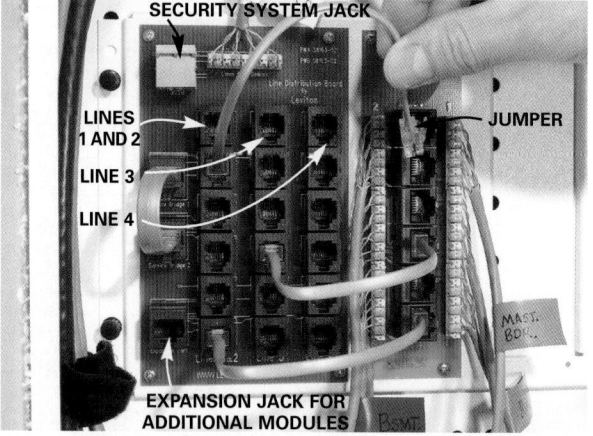

17 SNAP in jumper cables (included with module) to route phone lines to the jacks, according to the manufacturer's instructions.

18 CUT, ROUT AND PAINT 18-in. wide MDF cover panels and screw them through the drywall into the studs with 2-in. drywall screws and finish washers.

Remember to ground the system

It's important to ground the distribution box (Photos 13 and 14) before snapping in the telecommunication module. Even small static charges you introduce to the system from your body can damage delicate electronic components. We show connecting a 10-gauge wire from the ground screw in the box to the main ground wire of the electrical service panel. Hook the new ground wire anywhere on that main ground wire. You can also attach the ground to your main water supply pipe within 5 ft. of its entrance point, if the pipe is metal.

Let the phone and cable companies do the main interface hookups

The phone and cable TV interfaces (the boxes where the lines from the street hook up to your home lines) can be positioned either inside or outside the house. It's up to you to get the lines from the distribution box to the interfaces. Run them to the interface locations and leave a couple of extra feet of cable. Call the phone and cable TV companies to take care of the actual hookups. ⌂

4 Plumbing

IN THIS CHAPTER

Ask Handyman .96
   *Fiberglass shower over a concrete
   floor?, plumbing an island sink and more...*

Replace a Dishwasher 100

You Can Fix It .104
   *Repair a drippy shower, replace a
   leaking tub faucet, clean a sluggish toilet*

Handy Hints 109
   *Easier toilet mounting, power drain
   unclogger and faucet nut remover*

How to Clear Clogged Drains 110

Great Goofs 114

Ask Handyman™

HOW DO I INSTALL A FIBERGLASS SHOWER BAY OVER A CONCRETE FLOOR?

I'm ready to frame up the walls for my lower-level bathroom. There's a 2-in. pipe sticking up through the concrete floor. How do I position my fiberglass shower bay and connect it to the drain?

Sounds like your bathroom plumbing is already roughed in, although a call to the plumber or contractor who did the work will confirm it. The 2-in. pipe is typically the shower or tub drain. Line it up exactly with the drain hole in the bottom of your shower bay. This position determines the location of the stud walls around the shower. The supplier may be able to provide a dimensioned drawing of the shower bay, so you don't actually have to put it in first.

If the existing 2-in. drainpipe isn't where you want it, you'll have to break up the concrete and replumb the drain.

Make sure the drainpipe extends at least an inch above the concrete. If the pipe is too short, you'll have to break up the concrete and extend it. Also, you'll need at least a 1-1/2 in. space between the pipe and the concrete to accommodate the drain assembly (see photo above left). If there isn't, carefully chisel out the concrete around the pipe.

How to mount a leakproof drain assembly

After you frame the shower walls to fit the shower bay, lay the bay on its back and install the drain. Use a special leakproof drain assembly called the No-Caulk Shower Drain. It's available at home centers and plumbing supply houses. Although these drain baskets are available in plastic ($10), I'd opt for the brass one ($18). Follow these steps to attach the shower to the drain:

- Roll out a coil (about the diameter of a pencil) of plumber's putty (available at hardware stores) and wrap it under the drain basket flange.
- Hold the drain basket in position in the shower bay drain hole, slide on the washers, and then thread on and hand-tighten the exterior

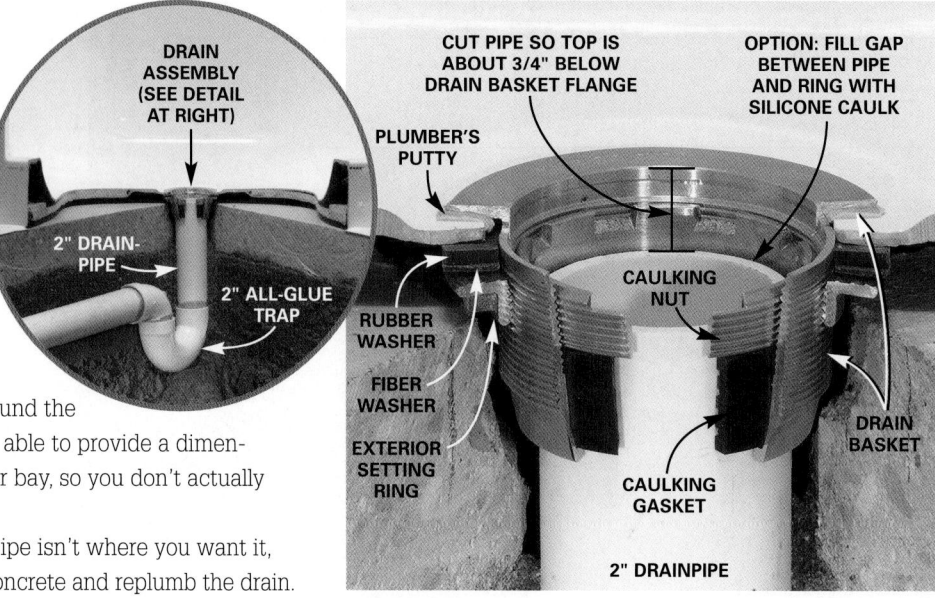

setting ring. Tighten the ring with a large slip-joint pliers until it's firmly in place. You shouldn't be able to move the shower basket by hand.

- Lower the shower bay and basket assembly over the drainpipe. Mark the pipe about 3/4 in. below the drain basket flange.
- Lift the shower bay out of the way and cut the drainpipe to length. Make sure to cut the pipe square, not angled.
- Set the shower bay and basket assembly back over the pipe. Slide the caulking gasket over the pipe and push it all the way down so it sits against the lip at the bottom of the drain basket. You may have to tap this gasket into place with a hammer and a thin piece of wood.
- Thread on the caulking nut and firmly tighten to compress the caulking gasket and seal the pipe. Use the slotted bar tool that comes with the drain assembly. Stick the flat blade of a screwdriver into the bar's slot and firmly hand-tighten.
- Snap on the perforated drain cover (not shown).

> **Tip**
>
> If you're considering a single-piece shower bay, make sure you can get it into the new bathroom space. You may have to bring the unit into the space before framing the doorway or walls. If access is a problem, check out multiple-piece units that will fit through doorways more easily.

GAS TUBE TO PILOT LIGHT

GAS TUBE TO MAIN BURNER

THERMO-COUPLE LEAD

WHOLE BURNER ASSEMBLY

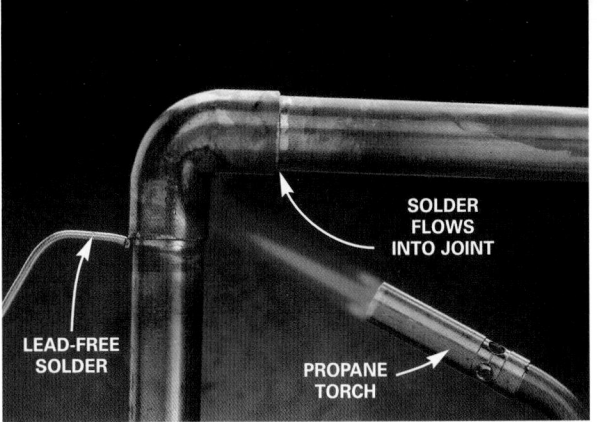

SOLDER FLOWS INTO JOINT

LEAD-FREE SOLDER

PROPANE TORCH

PLUMBING

NEW WATER HEATER THERMOCOUPLE

The pilot light on my gas water heater won't stay lit. Any ideas?

The No. 1 cause of this problem is a worn-out thermocouple. It's easy to replace and a new one costs $5 to $10. Rather than trying to unfasten the thermocouple inside the water heater's burning chamber, it's easier to remove the whole burner and thermocouple assembly. Then detach the thermocouple from the burner and take it with you to the home center or hardware store to ensure you buy the right replacement.

First shut off the gas valve on the water heater and the gas valve on the gas line near the heater. Then unfasten the three nuts that hold the thermocouple and the two gas tubes to the valve. The burner typically sits loosely—or under clips—in the burning chamber and just slides out. This is a good time to vacuum out the burner compartment, check for water leaks and remove debris in the burner ports.

Attach the thermocouple and reinstall the burner assembly. Light the pilot following the instructions on the water heater. Check for gas leaks by applying soapy water to joints and looking for bubbles while the main burner is firing.

STOPPING A PLUMBING LEAK

I have a small leak at an elbow joint in a copper water line. How do I go about fixing this?

Are you feeling lucky? Try this first fix and find out. This will be a quick and easy fix or it will try your patience.

Shut off the water at the main valve in your home and open up nearby faucets to completely drain the pipe with the leaky elbow. Dry the outside of the elbow and sand (120-grit paper or cloth) around the leaking joint to remove all surface corrosion. Apply soldering flux around the whole joint and apply heat with a torch until the old solder melts. Add new solder until a shiny ring of solder shows all around the joint. Let the pipe cool for five minutes, then turn the water back on and cross your fingers that you stopped the leak.

If the leak continues . . .

Turn off the water again, open faucets to drain the line and cut out the entire elbow. Then solder in new fittings.

A last ditch effort . . .

Sometimes you can't solder in the new fittings because there's a continuous slow trickle of water. If you don't want to wait for the water to completely drain, try this trick. Replace the elbow with a tee with a threaded fitting soldered on one end. This open end allows any moisture to escape as steam so you can heat the joint enough to melt the solder. When the pipe has cooled, screw in a threaded plug. Be sure to use Teflon tape or pipe compound on the threads.

For more information, see "Soldering Copper Pipe: Start to Finish," April '00, p. 83. To order a copy, see p. 288.

WATER HAMMER FIX FOR TOILET

I've installed water hammer arresters in the basement water supply lines. They alleviated much of the water hammering in the house with the exception of the upstairs toilet. Every time the toilet tank refills after a flush, the whole house reverberates. It's nearly impossible to install arresters near the toilets without ripping open the walls. Do you have any suggestions?

Here's a rather simple solution. Partially close the valve that feeds the toilet. The toilet will take longer to refill, but the hammering should be reduced because the volume of water going through the pipe is less. Then when the internal toilet tank valve shuts off the flow, the shock to the pipe will be less.

Ask Handyman™

WHY FROST-PROOF FAUCETS FAIL

This spring I hooked up the garden hose to my frost-proof sill cock, turned on the water and found water pouring into my finished basement. Apparently my frost-proof faucet had frozen and split. What can I do to prevent this from happening again?

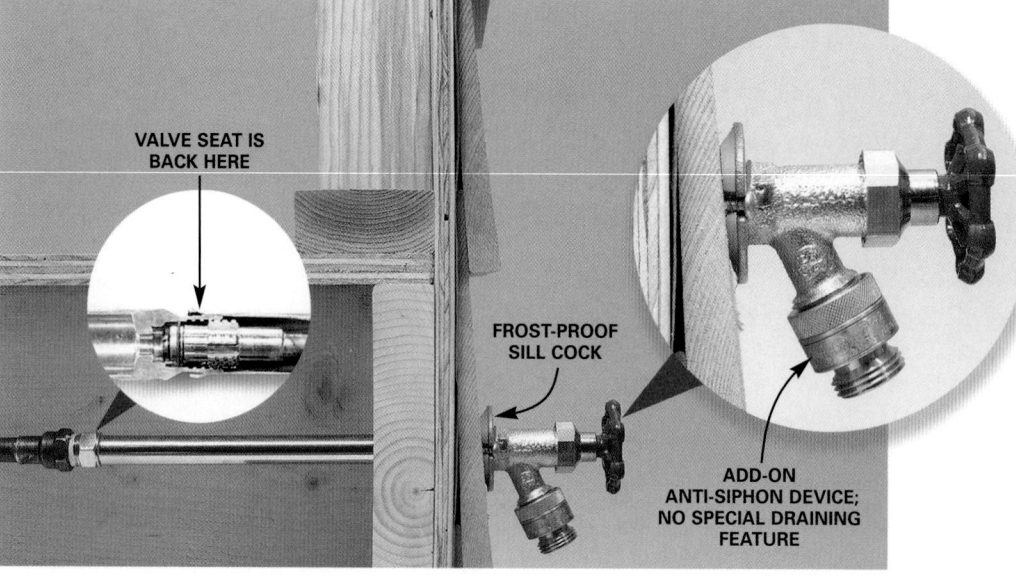

VALVE SEAT IS BACK HERE

FROST-PROOF SILL COCK

ADD-ON ANTI-SIPHON DEVICE; NO SPECIAL DRAINING FEATURE

A frost-proof faucet isn't freeze-proof if water remains in it. While the valve seat is located in the warmth of the house, where the water won't freeze, water trapped between the spout and the valve can freeze and split the pipe. The most common cause is a garden hose left screwed on when temperatures dive below freezing. Remember to disconnect your hose before winter hits.

A second cause is water trapped by an add-on anti-siphon device on the sill cock (photo above). Building codes require anti-siphon devices on outdoor faucets. Some types of anti-siphon devices won't let the water in the sill cock drain out. If the trapped water freezes, it can split the pipe.

The best way to avoid this is to install a self-draining, frost-proof sill cock that has a built-in anti-siphon device (One good one is Woodford model No. 25CP3, available on-line at www.plumbingmart.com for about $40.) Or install an add-on anti-siphon device that has a built-in draining feature. These allow the pipe to drain when the valve is turned off. Both are available at plumbing suppliers. Check with your local plumbing inspector to make sure the product you use meets code.

EASY-FLUSH WATER HEATER VALVE

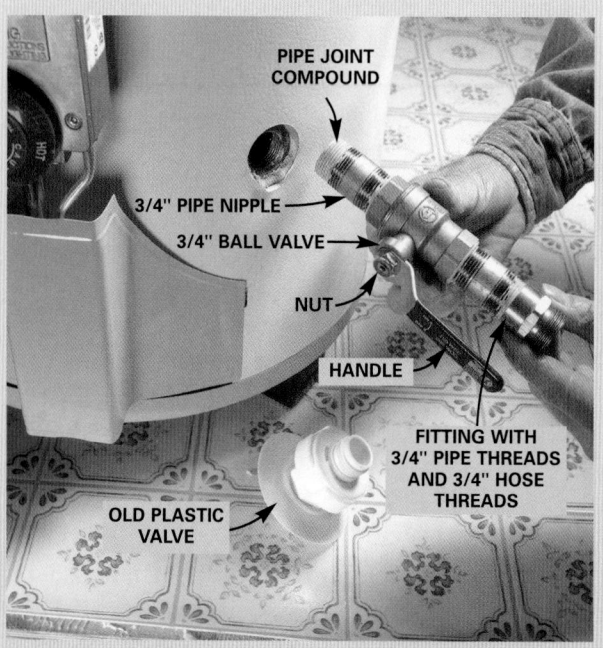

PIPE JOINT COMPOUND

3/4" PIPE NIPPLE

3/4" BALL VALVE

NUT

HANDLE

FITTING WITH 3/4" PIPE THREADS AND 3/4" HOSE THREADS

OLD PLASTIC VALVE

I have hard water and have been told that I should periodically drain my water heater to flush out the minerals. Is this true?

It's a good idea. Manufacturers recommend it to prevent mineral buildup that reduces heater performance and efficiency. In fact, research shows that for every 1/2 in. of sediment on the bottom of a gas-fired water heater, 70 percent more fuel is required to heat the water.

How often it should be drained depends on the mineral load in your water, the amount of hot water used and whether a water softener is part of your system. To judge this, drain the water heater, then wait six months and do it again. If the water seems clear after six months, then extend the time between draining. If it's heavy with sediment, drain your water heater more often.

PLUMBING AN ISLAND SINK

We want to add a sink to our kitchen island, but we've been told the plumbing is tricky. How should we handle it?

You're right. Plumbing an island sink is challenging. It can't be vented the same way as a regular kitchen sink.

Plumbing vents (a network of pipes that carry air and gas outdoors through a pipe exiting your roof) are essential to supply enough air to keep equal pressure in the plumbing system. They keep water and waste moving through the pipes at the right speed. A flow that's too slow leaves behind debris that clogs pipes. If it's too fast, suction siphons water from the P-trap (see photo), allowing harmful sewer gas to enter your home.

A regular kitchen sink, adjacent to a wall, has a vent hidden in the wall that connects to a vent. So it won't plug up, the vent must rise 6 in. above the overflow level of the sink before the pipe goes horizontal. Obviously, a vent pipe in a kitchen island can't do that.

As an alternative, most plumbers recommend a special type of vent (photo right) that loops as high as it can go inside the cabinet before heading under the floor and over to the main vent in the wall. Always get approval from your local plumbing inspector before installing this type of vent. A second cleanout may be required in the vertical wall vent pipe.

A second option—one that requires no outside venting, makes installation much easier, and is either loved or hated by plumbers—is called an air admittance valve. These are not the spring-operated cheater vents used in trailers; they're gravity-operated valves that open when water flow creates negative pressure, allowing air to enter to equalize pressure. But before you opt for this choice, you need to understand the pros and cons, as well as contact your local plumbing inspector to determine if an AAV is allowed (many local plumbing codes in the United States currently accept AAVs).

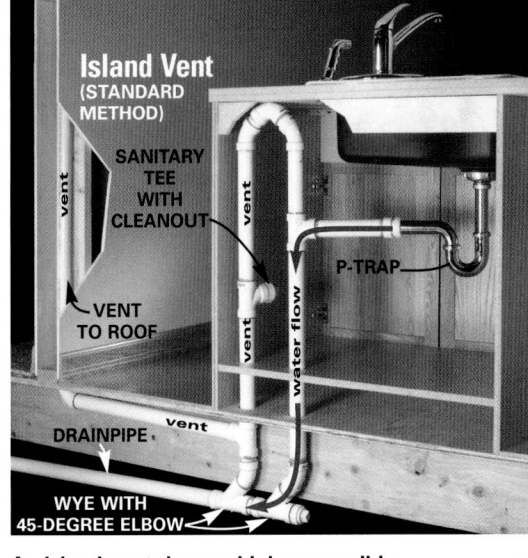

An island vent rises as high as possible under an island before running to a regular vertical vent. It keeps air in the drain system and prevents siphoning of the P-trap.

If installed correctly, they can work in most single-family homes, as long as there's one primary main vent that penetrates the roof to outside air. Drawbacks? Sometimes AAVs can't keep up with the venting needs of high-volume (18 to 22 gpm) discharge washers and dishwashers. And AAVs have a tougher time relieving pressure in the drainage and vent system of buildings five stories and higher.

For more information on AAVs, contact the following manufacturers:
- Ayrlett: (877) 338-7455, www.ayrlett.com
- Magic Vent: (800) 231-3345, www.rectorseal.com
- Oatey: (800) 321-9532, www.oatey.com
- Studor: (800) 447-4721, www.studor.com

To drain, first turn off the power. If your water heater is gas powered, twist the dial on the thermostat from the "on" position to "off." If it's electric, flip the circuit breaker off at the service panel that controls the water heater or flip off the main breaker. Next, shut off the cold water supply by twisting the water valve (located atop the heater) clockwise until it stops. Then attach a garden hose to the drain valve at the base of the heater and run the other end of the hose into a light-colored bucket in order to view the sediment.

Open the drain valve and turn the cold water supply back on to flush out the sediment. Be careful; the water is hot! The first water exiting the heater carries the most sediment. When water runs clear, shut off the drain valve, detach the hose and turn the power back on.

If you have sediment, replace the plastic drain valve with a ball-style valve. It's much less likely to clog with sediment and is easier to close than the factory-equipped valves. This type of valve also allows you to run a stiff wire into the tank bottom to loosen hardened sediment.

To replace, it's simply a matter of draining the tank (use steps listed at left), unscrewing the factory-installed plastic valve and threading in the new ball valve. And always use pipe joint compound or Teflon tape for a proper seal.

Water heater safety

Installing a ball valve eases the draining and flushing of a water heater, but it might pose a hazard to children who could easily open it.

The best method to prevent this is to loosen the nut on the handle and remove it. Then you can hang the handle nearby. Another option is to buy a metal cap with hose threads to fit over the hose end, attaching it with a rubber hose washer placed inside the cap for a proper seal.

REPLACE A
DISHWASHER

Our pros tell you how to avoid the most common mistakes

by **Jeff Timm**

Swapping out that old, noisy dishwasher for a new, quiet one is a lot easier than you might think. With a few basic tools and an hour or two, you'll have that new one in and can pocket the $100 installation fee. There's only one better deal: If installation is part of the purchase price, let the dealer do it!

In this article, we'll show you how to pull out your old dishwasher, slide in the new one, and make the new water, drain and electrical connections.

In most cases, you won't need any special tools or skills to do a first-class job. Most dishwashers are 24 in. wide, so you won't have to alter cabinets to get the new one to fit. (If you change sizes, you'll have to alter your cabinets. This requires more advanced carpentry skills that we won't show here.)

You may find that extra layers of flooring have raised the floor height in front of the old dishwasher. This can make it difficult to get the old dishwasher out and the new one in. In some cases, you have to either loosen the countertop or remove flooring. Consider consulting a professional installer if you don't feel confident about the best strategy.

Before you start

Get a blanket, an old rug or cardboard to protect your floor while you work. Gather two adjustable wrenches, a screwdriver, a tape measure, a pair of pliers and a level. You'll also need a shallow pan, bucket, sponge and rag to collect water that'll drain from the lines when you disconnect them.

Turn off the power to the dishwasher at the main panel or unplug it under the sink. Also turn off the water to the dishwasher at the nearest shutoff valve, usually the hot water shutoff under the sink. Or shut it off at the water heater.

Consider removing the cabinet doors from your sink base to make disconnecting the drain lines easier.

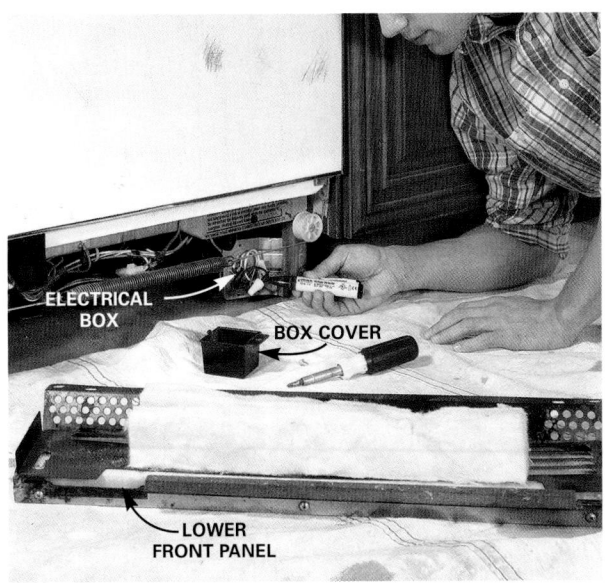

ELECTRICAL BOX

BOX COVER

LOWER FRONT PANEL

1 TURN OFF the power, remove the front panel and use a voltage tester to make sure the power is off. Disconnect the wires and pull the cable from the box.

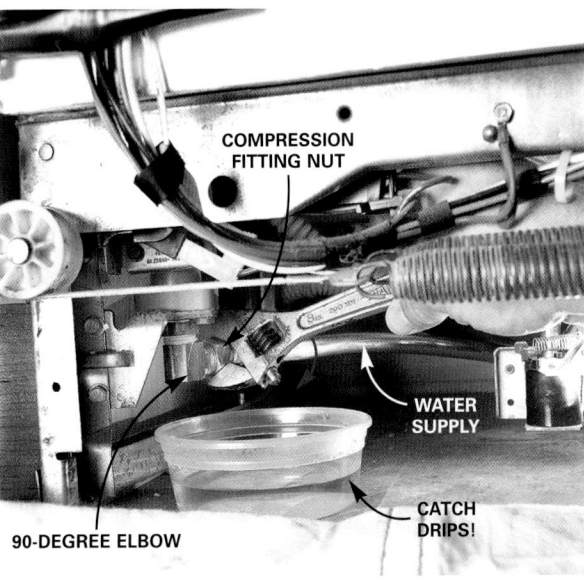

COMPRESSION FITTING NUT

WATER SUPPLY

CATCH DRIPS!

90-DEGREE ELBOW

2 REMOVE the compression fitting nut from the water supply line (water turned off). Note which way the 90-degree elbow points, then unscrew it.

COUNTERTOP SCREWS

INLET ARM

DISHWASHER DRAIN TUBE

3 SLIDE the dishwasher drain tube and off the inlet arm on the sink drain. Drain it into a bucket. Remove the screws securing the dishwasher to the countertop.

DRAIN TUBE

LEVELING FOOT

CARDBOARD

4 LOWER the dishwasher and slip cardboard under the feet. Then gently lift and slide the dishwasher out. Work the drain tube out through the side of the cabinet.

Disconnect the electrical cable and water line

The water and electrical connections are underneath the dishwasher, behind a lower front panel that you have to unscrew (**Photo 1**). Always test with a voltage detector ($2 to $12 at a home center or hardware store) to make sure the power is off. When you remove the electrical line from the box, leave the cable clamp on and reuse it on the new dishwasher (**Photo 12**). Sometimes dishwashers are plug-and-cord connected rather than "hard wired" as shown in our photos. If so, disconnect the cord and reuse it on the new dishwasher. If it's in bad condition, buy a new one

($12) from an appliance dealer.

Usually, the water supply line is flexible copper or braided stainless steel. In either case, remove the nut securing it to the 90-degree fitting on the dishwasher (**Photo 2**). As long as the nut and ring are in good condition (no nicks or gouges; **Photo 11**), leave them on the line for later reuse. You can bend the copper line slightly, but take care not to kink the line. If you do, you'll have to replace it. Flexible stainless steel lines are a good replacement. They cost $12 at a hardware store or home center. Make sure you buy them long enough and with fittings that match the old.

Remove the 90-degree fitting for use on the new dishwasher. It's important to orient it exactly the same direction on the new machine so that the water line feeds directly into it. Otherwise you might kink the line.

Sponge out any standing water inside the dishwasher before removing the drain line under the sink. It's the flexible hose that's clamped to an inlet arm on the sink drain or a garbage disposer (**Photo 3**). As you slide the old dishwasher out, you'll have to simultaneously work the drain hose back through the hole in the sink cabinet. Keep a rag handy to wipe up the water that'll run out of the line.

Lowering the dishwasher gives you more clearance to slide the dishwasher out. Chances are the leveling feet will be difficult to turn, but a shot of penetrating oil on the threads may make it easier. If you need more clearance, cut the feet off with a hacksaw blade and turn the screw out. Then be sure to slip cardboard or a rug under them to avoid gouging your floor when you pull out the dishwasher.

Prep the new dishwasher

Uncrate the new dishwasher according to the instructions on the box. Once it's uncrated, you'll find the manuals and installation instructions inside the dishwasher. Review them before proceeding; they may differ slightly from the details we show.

Tip the dishwasher on its back and attach the 90-degree fitting (**Photo 5**). Don't reuse your old drain hose; the dishwasher will come with a new one. To prevent dishwasher odors from entering the sink drain, be sure to loop the flexible drain line all the way up to the bottom of the countertop (**Photo 6**). Some plumbing codes require a special air gap fitting ($7) in the drain line. Call your local plumbing inspector to find out the rules.

The manual will tell you how to adjust the leveling feet and/or wheels to fit the height of the opening. It's easiest to set these before sliding in the dishwasher. Make minor adjustments after the dishwasher is in. But if your kitchen

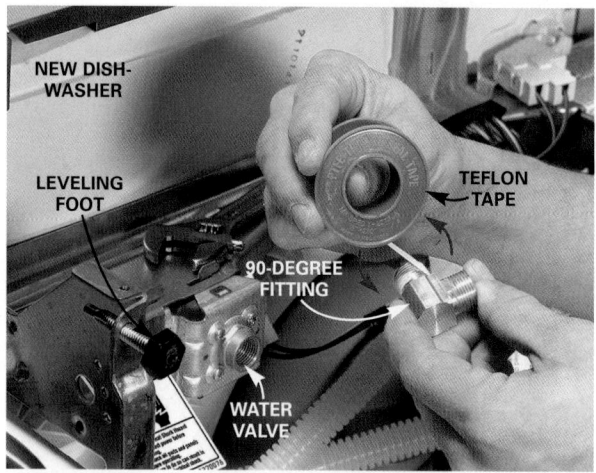

5 WRAP the 90-degree fitting twice with Teflon tape and screw it into the new water valve. Tighten it, aiming the elbow as on the old machine.

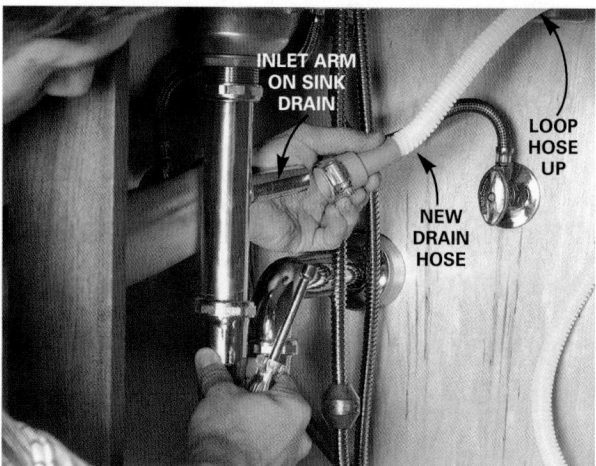

6 THREAD the new drain line into the sink base cabinet. Loop it higher than the inlet arm on the sink drain or garbage disposer. Slip it on and tighten the clamp.

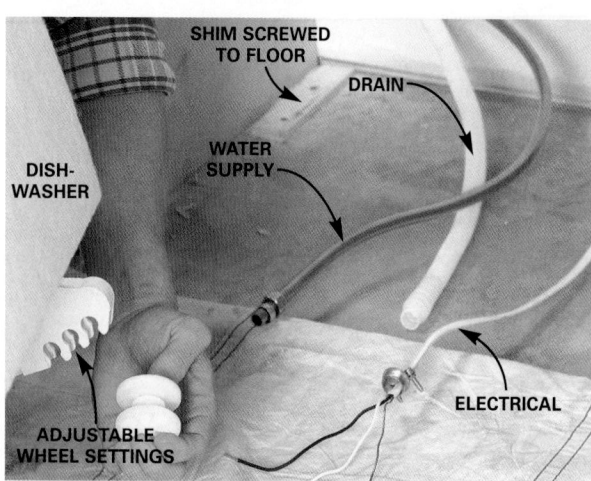

7 LAY the water supply, drain and electrical lines flat on the floor. Measure the height of the opening, then adjust the wheels and feet according to the manual.

8 GRASP the sides of the dishwasher, lift slightly and roll the dishwasher into the opening. Protect the kitchen floor with a tarp or cardboard.

floor is built up (higher than the area where the dishwasher sits), you'll have to adjust the feet after you slide it into the opening. If your dishwasher is equipped with rear wheels without adjusters in the back, you may have to set shims (Photo 7) to raise the back to the height of the finished floor. Tack them to the floor so they don't shake loose when the dishwasher runs.

Slide the dishwasher in and reconnect it

Slide in the new dishwasher (**Photo 8**), grasping it by the sides to avoid denting the front panel. Set the dishwasher in position according to **Photos 9 and 10**. But don't secure it to the countertop yet. Wait until you make all connections and adjustments.

Connecting the copper water line so it doesn't leak can be tricky. The secret is to align it so it slides straight into the threaded part of the elbow (**Photo 11**). If it's cocked to one side, the compression nut won't thread on right and

it'll leak. If necessary, turn the elbow on the dishwasher slightly with a wrench to align it, or gently bend copper lines about 8 to 12 in. from the end.

With the supply line, the electrical cable and drain connected, turn the power and water back on and check for leaks. Recheck the positioning, then screw the dishwasher to the countertop (some screw to the cabinet sides). If your countertop is a synthetic material or stone, and the old holes don't line up, follow the directions listed in the manual. ⌂

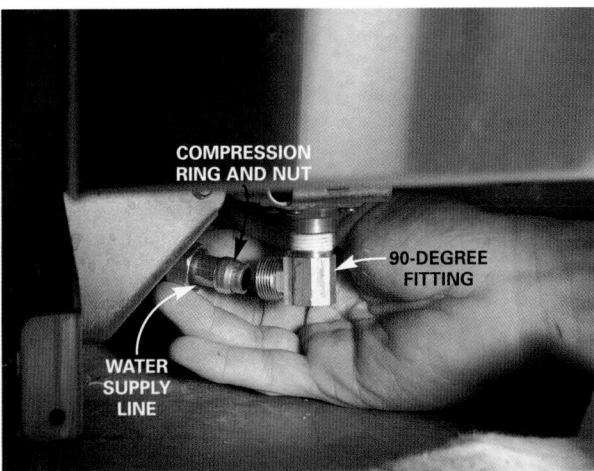

9 SLIDE the dishwasher back until it's flush to the cabinets. Positioning may vary slightly according to dishwasher styles and the style of your cabinets.

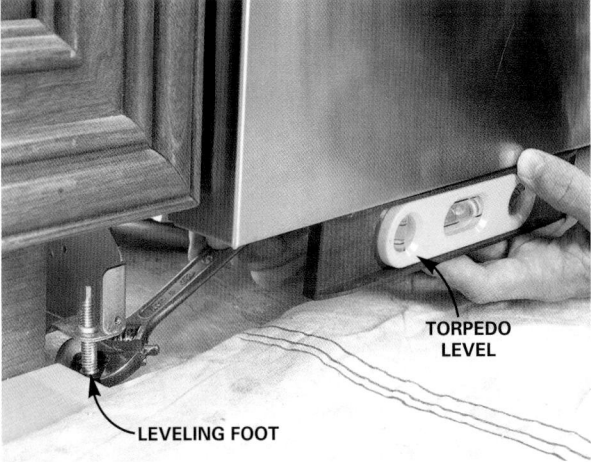

10 ADJUST the leveling feet with a wrench until the dishwasher is level (side to side) and plumb (up and down).

11 ALIGN the water supply line so it slides straight into the 90-degree fitting. Thread on the compression nut (no Teflon tape needed) and tighten with a wrench.

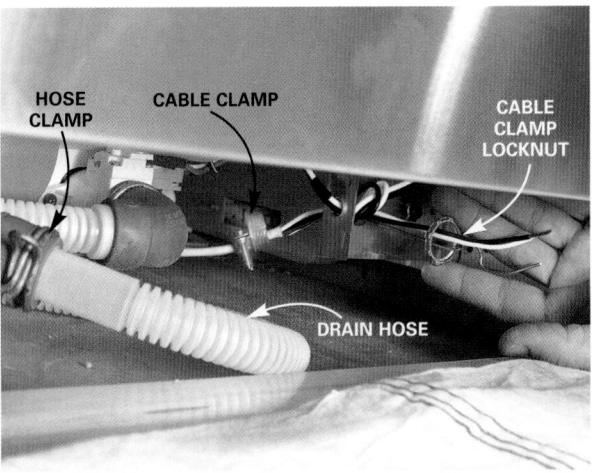

12 CLAMP the drain hose to the dishwasher. Then clamp the electrical wires and connect them. Finally, screw the dishwasher to the countertop bottom.

You Can Fix It™

REPAIR A DRIPPY SHOWER

When your single-handle shower faucet drips and drips, refusing to completely turn off, don't assume you have to replace the whole faucet. Most faucets can be repaired in an hour for less than $50.

In this article, we'll focus on fixing a cartridge-style faucet. Cartridge valves have a single handle and operate when the cartridge slides in and out. Don't confuse them with single-handle ball-style faucets, which have a dome-shaped casing under the handle.

We won't deal with two-handle faucets here, which may be either a stem-type valve or ceramic disc valve. For information about repairing stem valves, see "You Can Fix It," March '03, p. 19. To order a copy, see p. 288.

Turn off the water at the fixture shutoff valves or at your home's main valve. Turn on a faucet to make sure it's off. Remove the handle as shown in **Photos 1 and 2**. If the handle sticks, try heating it with a hair dryer set on "hot." If you still can't get

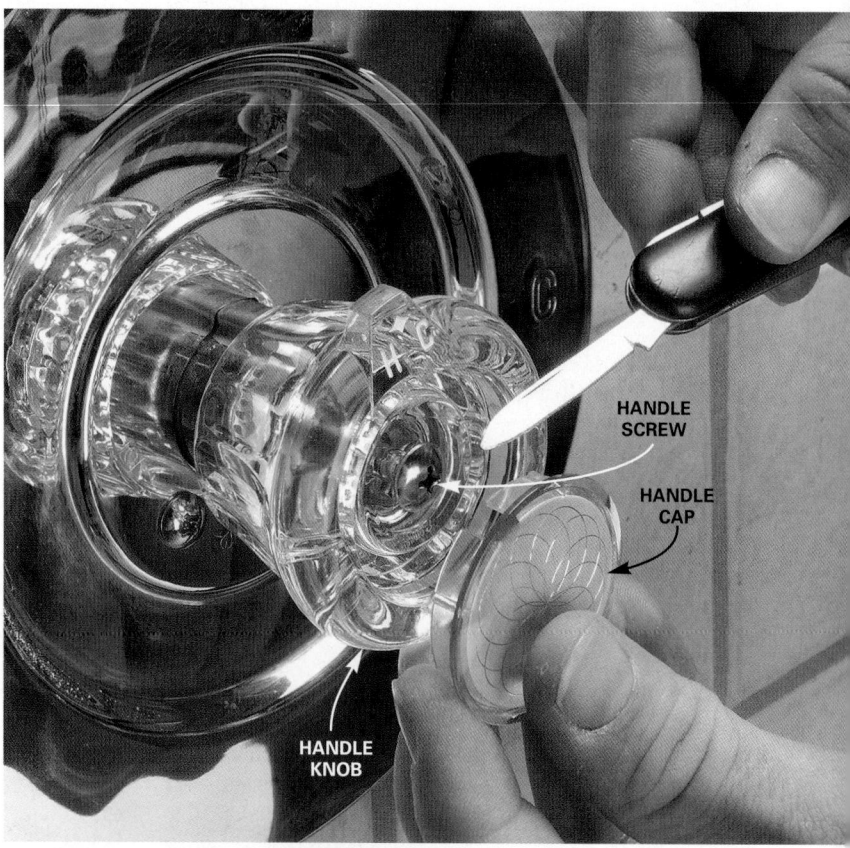

HANDLE
SCREW

HANDLE
CAP

HANDLE
KNOB

OLD CARTRIDGE

NEW CARTRIDGE

HANDLE
SCREW

1 TURN OFF the water supply to the shower. Then pry off the handle cap with a small pocketknife to expose the internal handle screw.

2 LOOSEN and remove the handle screw. Pull off the handle and set it aside.

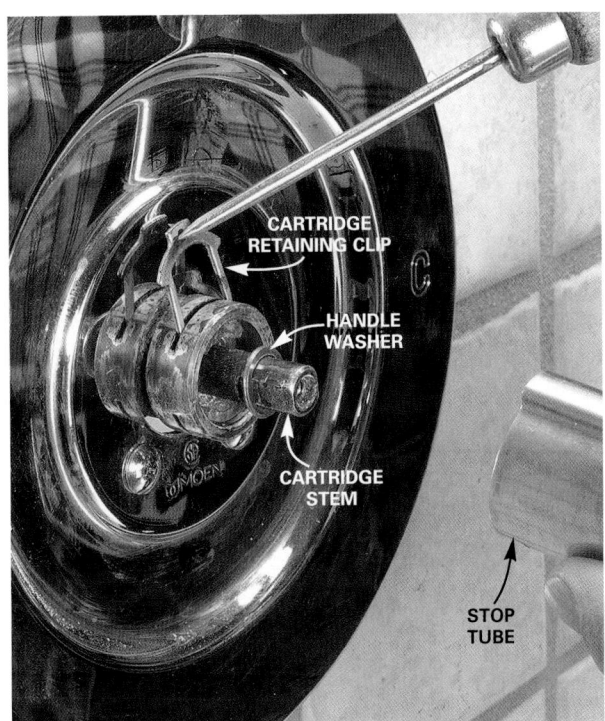

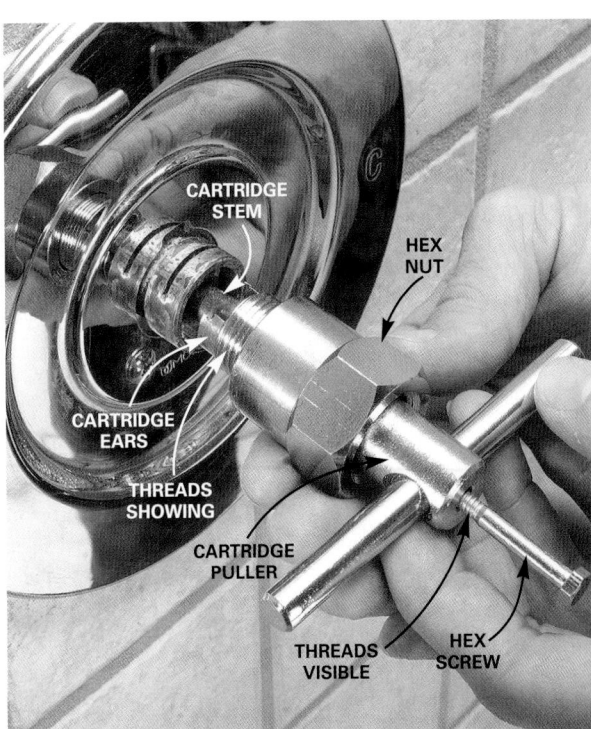

3 PULL OFF the stop tube. Pry up the cartridge retaining clip with a small screwdriver or awl. Remove the handle washer and then twist the cartridge stem loose and pull it out with a pliers.

4 IF IT'S STUCK, use a special cartridge puller. Unscrew the hex screw and hex nut until threads are visible. Slide the puller over the cartridge stem, aligning the tool ears with the cartridge notches, and twist to loosen.

it off, use a special handle puller ($10 to $20 from a plumbing parts distributor or home center). (See "You Can Fix It," March '03, p. 20. To order a copy, see p. 288.)

Virtually every faucet manufacturer has a different method of securing the cartridge to the faucet body. Look for a clip or spring and remove it (**Photo 3**). Cartridges are often difficult to pull out. Some manufacturers include a removal cap with new cartridges. Align the cap with the old cartridge ears and try to twist the cartridge loose. Then pull it out with a pliers.

If you can't budge the old cartridge, you'll need a cartridge puller ($20 to $30 from a plumbing parts distributor). Make sure the one you buy works on your brand of faucet. Look on the handle or trim for the faucet brand or manufacturer. A knowledgeable person at a plumbing parts store may be able to identify the brand and model from a photo. Review **Photos 4 and 5** for instructions on using a cartridge puller. Make sure you twist the cartridge loose before pulling it out (**Photo 4**). Take the old cartridge with you to a plumbing parts store or a home center to find an exact replacement ($15 to $25).

Lubricate the cartridge sides, O-rings, retaining clip, cartridge stem and handle screw threads with plumber's grease. Slide the new cartridge into the faucet body. Some cartridges can only be installed one way (to avoid reversing the hot and cold), so follow the enclosed instructions. Reassemble the remaining faucet components.

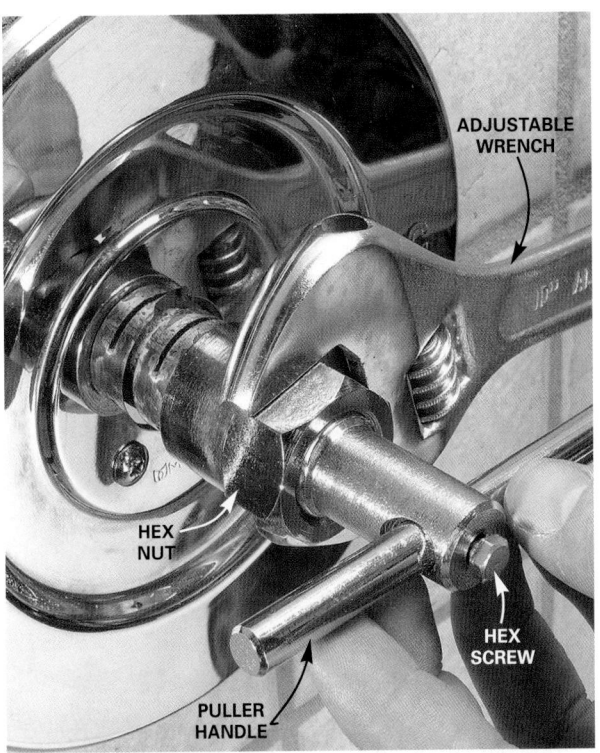

5 TURN the hex screw by hand until it bottoms out. Snug up the hex nut by hand and tug on the cartridge puller handle. If the cartridge won't pull out, hold the puller handle steady and tighten the hex nut two full turns. Pull the cartridge out of the faucet body. Buy an identical replacement cartridge, align it properly and reassemble the parts.

You Can Fix It™

REPLACE A LEAKING TUB FAUCET

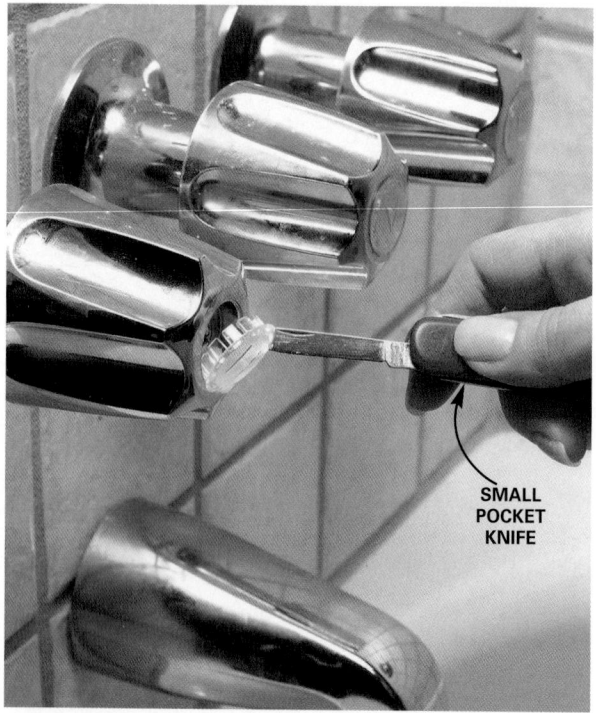

The drip, drip, drip of a leaking tub faucet is a constant reminder to fix it. Go ahead—you'll love the savings on your water bill!

The entire job, with special tools, may set you back $80 to $90, but that's a lot cheaper than hiring a plumber, and usually cheaper and easier than tearing out the old faucet and installing a new one.

Worn rubber washers, seals or gaskets in the valve assembly cause most leaks. In this article, we'll show you how to fix a stem-type valve, which is common in older, two-handle faucets (separate hot and cold). We won't cover single-handle faucets here.

You can fix most problems with the replacement parts available at hardware stores and home centers. A plumbing parts distributor will carry a much larger selection and may be able to special-order hard-to-find items (look under "Plumbing Parts and Supplies" in your local Yellow Pages).

There are thousands of different faucet replacement parts available, so bring your old parts to the store for a proper match. If your valve is highly corroded or the finish is wearing off, replace the entire faucet.

Removing the faucet handle is the toughest part of the

SMALL POCKET KNIFE

1 SHUT OFF the water supply to the faucet and open the valves to drain excess water from the system. Pry off the handle insert with the thin blade of a pocketknife.

HANDLE SCREW

2 REMOVE the handle screw. Then wiggle the handle and pull it off. If the handle doesn't come off, heat it with a hair dryer to free it. Be careful; if you pull too hard, it'll break.

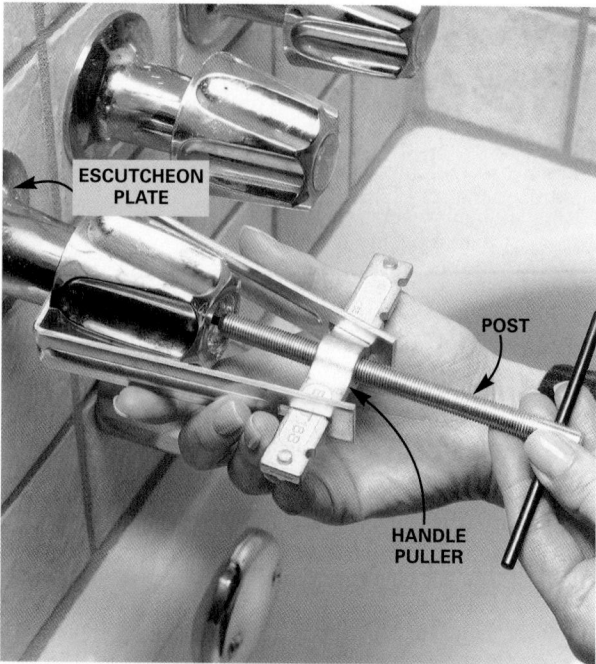

ESCUTCHEON PLATE

POST

HANDLE PULLER

3 TURN the handle screw about halfway back into the stem. Position the handle puller's post against the screwhead and press the arms together behind the handle. Turn the post clockwise until the handle pops loose. Remove the handle screw and handle. Then pull off or unscrew the escutcheon plate.

To replace the stem parts:

1. **Unscrew the packing nut. Twist the stem clockwise and back it out of the bonnet. Pry out the old packing washer with a small flat-blade screwdriver or pick. Grease the stem threads and reinstall the stem in the bonnet. Grease the new packing washer and slide it in place, and then grease the packing nut threads and firmly tighten the packing nut. Use special plumber's grease.**
2. **Remove the old seat washer screw and the old seat washer. Grease the new seat washer and the threads of the new screw and then reinstall them.**
3. **Pull off the old bonnet washer, grease the new one and slide it in place.**
4. **Apply pipe joint compound to the bonnet threads and reinstall it in the faucet body (Photo 4).**
5. **Grease the handle splines and replace the escutcheon and handle.**

Fig. A: Stem Assembly and Replacement Parts

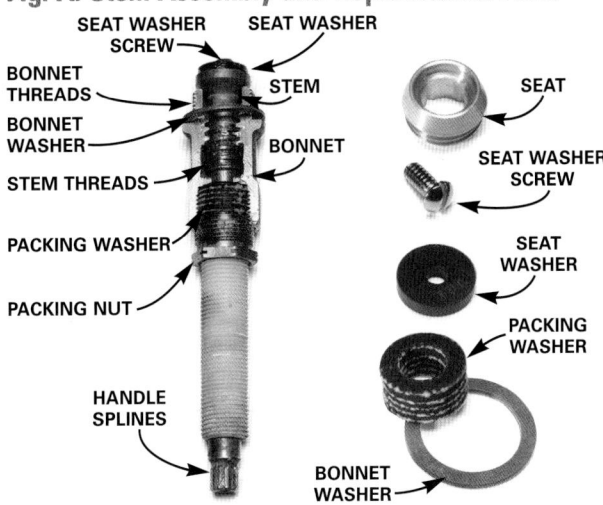

job. Over time, corrosion can virtually weld the handle to the stem. Remove the handle by following the instructions in **Photos 1 and 2**. If the handle won't come off, don't force it—it might break. Instead, remove it with a special handle puller ($10 to $20; **Photo 3**).

Once the handle's off, unscrew the escutcheon and stem assembly (**Photo 4 and Fig. A**). The stem assembly controls the amount and temperature of the water dispensed through the tub spout or shower head. Remove it with a special bath socket wrench, which looks like a spark plug wrench on steroids (**Photo 4**).

Leaks usually occur for two reasons. Over time, the seat washer stiffens and won't seal tightly. And water pressure gradually erodes the brass rim of the seat (Photo 5). Replace the seat using a special seat wrench ($10 to $20) as shown in **Photo 5**.

Fig. A shows the stem replacement parts and how to prepare the stem for reinstallation. Lubricate the parts with special plumber's grease. If you're working on a two-handled faucet, we recommend replacing the washers and seats in both the hot and cold valves.

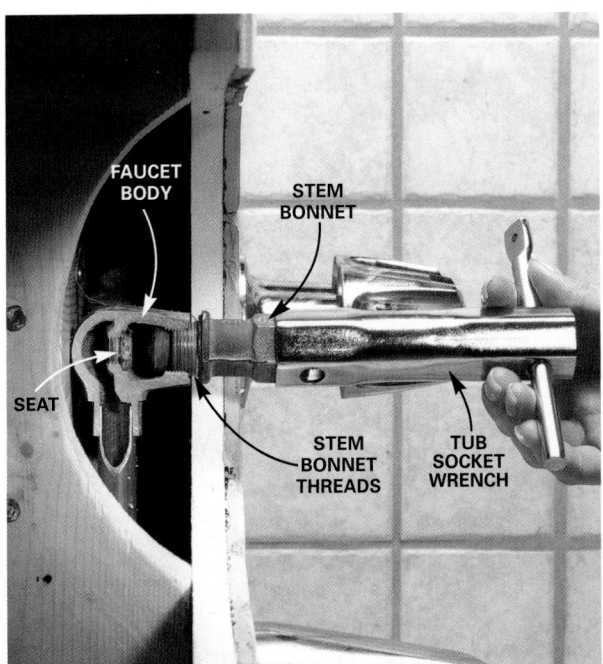

4 SLIDE the bath socket onto the stem bonnet and turn it counterclockwise to break the stem loose. If it sticks, soak it with penetrating lubricant. Unscrew and remove the stem.

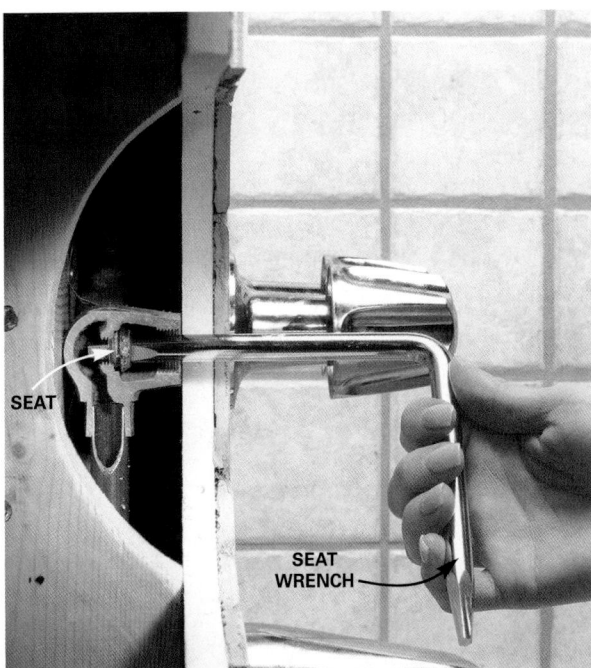

5 PRESS the seat wrench firmly into the center of the seat. Turn counterclockwise to snap the seat loose and remove it. If it sticks, soak it with penetrating lubricant. Coat the threads of the new seat with pipe dope and screw it into the fixture body with the seat wrench.

You Can Fix It™

CLEAN A SLUGGISH TOILET

If your toilet flushes slowly, the rinse holes under the rim may be clogged with mineral deposits. With a mirror and a coat hanger, you can clean out those clogged holes without ever getting your hands dirty. The photo says it all—look into the mirror to see if the holes are clogged and poke them clean with a coat hanger.

USE a hand mirror to see the holes under the rim of the toilet. Bend a coat hanger flat and probe the tip into the holes to poke out any mineral deposits.

REPLACE A SINK SPRAYER AND HOSE

Over time, sink sprayers often break or become clogged with mineral deposits. Or the sprayer hose can harden and crack or wear through from rubbing against something under the sink. The best solution in these cases is replacement.

You can pick up just the sprayer head ($5) or a head and hose kit ($10) at a home center or hardware store.

Photo 1 shows how to remove the entire sprayer head and hose assembly. You may be able to get a small open-end wrench up to the sprayer hose nipple, but space is very tight. If there isn't enough room to turn the wrench, you'll have to purchase a basin wrench ($15 to $25 at home centers and hardware stores). If your sprayer hose is in good condition, simply unscrew the head and replace it (Photo 2).

1 USE an open-end or basin wrench to unscrew the sprayer hose from the hose nipple. Pull the old sprayer and hose out of the sink grommet. Slide the new hose through the grommet on top of the sink and reconnect it to the faucet.

2 HOLD the base of the sprayer in your hand and twist off the sprayer head. Screw on the new head. Be careful to install the two washers in the correct order.

Handy Hints® from our readers

PLASTIC STRAW

TOILET FLANGE BOLT

EASIER TOILET MOUNTING

PLASTIC STRAW

Toilets are heavy and awkward to get over the flange bolts, especially by yourself. Make the job easier by putting straws over the bolts to lengthen them and guide them into the bolt holes.

POWER DRAIN UNCLOGGER

The plunger won't unclog your drain? And you don't want to use harsh chemicals? Try running a garden hose to the drain from an outside faucet. Hold the hose end in the drain and wrap a towel around it, packing it around the drain to make a tight seal and to prevent splashing. Then have someone turn on the faucet while you hold the hose in place.

FAUCET NUT REMOVER

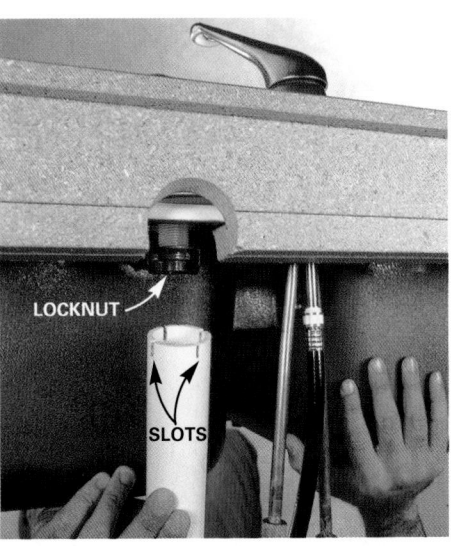

LOCKNUT

SLOTS

Having trouble loosening the plastic faucet locknut under the sink? Using a hacksaw, cut 1/4-in. deep slots corresponding to the locknut flanges in a scrap piece of 1-1/4 in. PVC drainpipe. Then just use the drainpipe as a wrench.

Great Goofs™

A quick shower

A few years ago, my father was remodeling the downstairs bathroom. To make the connection to the waste pipe, he had to cut it open at about eye level. He then announced that no one should use the bathroom upstairs until he finished connecting the waste pipes. After a bit, he heard the unmistakable sound of a toilet flushing. Before he could finish yelling my sister's name, a flood of water and solid waste hit his face. My sister's plea of forgiveness went unheard as he wiped himself off with a rag. He couldn't wash up right away because he had the water lines disconnected too. Like a dedicated do-it-yourselfer, he finished the job, then went straight to the shower!

PLUMBING

HOW TO CLEAR
CLOGGED DRAINS

With two simple tools—a plunger and a snake—you can clear 95 percent of your stopped-up drain problems

by **Paul Gorton**

A clogged kitchen sink can wreck a perfectly good evening in front of the tube. Instead of settling in to watch the big game, you'll find yourself staring at a sink full of dirty, backed-up water and wondering whether to call in a plumber ($80 to $120!). However, with two inexpensive tools and a little practice, you can fix this mess in less than an hour.

In this article, we'll show you how to use a plunger and snake to clear up all but the most stubborn drain clogs. Plungers cost $4 to $10 at any hardware store or home center (**photo below**). Those with larger rubber bells deliver more thrust, but most will work for kitchen drains.

Be sure it has a stout handle so you can apply plenty of force. A snake (sometimes called a hand auger) costs $5 to $20, depending on the size, length and turning mechanism. For all-around use, we recommend a 3/8-in. model that's about 20 ft. long, like the one in **Photo 6** ($15 at hardware stores and home centers). It's easy to turn down into the drain. But shorter, 1/4-in. types will work for most clogs too. In addition, keep several other items handy—a bucket or a plastic bin that fits under your drain, rubber gloves and a good flashlight.

You can avoid most clogs by not abusing your kitchen drain line. Don't overload your disposer with meat; foods high in starch, like pasta, potatoes and rice; or foods high in fiber, like celery and corn husks. Also, run plenty of cold water down the drain and let the disposer catch up after every cup of food you push into it. Never dump bacon grease or coffee grounds into the drain. If allowed to settle and cool, they solidify in the drain.

If you follow the steps of this article and still can't clear the blockage, don't hesitate to call in a plumber. You may have a clog far down the drain line beyond your reach, or stuck objects in the pipes.

Clear blockage with a plunger

One of the most common causes of a clogged drain is a clogged garbage disposer. If the side of the sink that has the disposer doesn't drain, plunge it first to remove the clog or force it down the drain.

And if you flip the switch to turn on your garbage disposer and all you hear is a low humming sound, your disposer is probably jammed. You can usually free it by turning the

CAUTION: Don't plunge or snake a drain if you've poured drain cleaners into the sink. The chemicals can cause serious burns if they splash on your skin. Use drain cleaners only if the sink is draining slowly and not completely clogged.

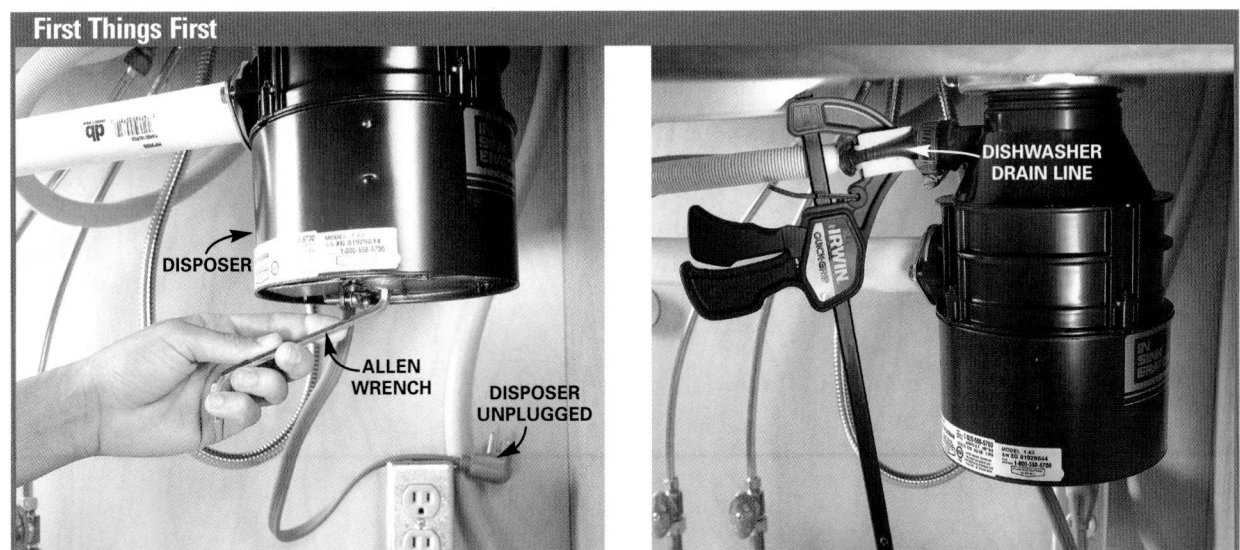

If you have a garbage disposer, turn it on. If it hums but doesn't spin, switch it off and unplug the unit. Then rotate the disposer blades manually by inserting an Allen wrench into the hole on the bottom of many disposers. If you have a dishwasher, tighten a clamp over the flexible part of the drain line before plunging the drain. This prevents dirty water from flowing back into the dishwasher cabinet.

blades manually (see "First Things First," above). (If the disposer doesn't make any sound when you turn it on, an internal breaker on the motor probably has tripped. Give the disposer a minute to cool off. Then press the reset button located on the bottom of the unit, and turn it on again.)

If the problem isn't in the disposer, plunge the drain. If you have a dishwasher, first clamp the drain hose (**photo**, above right). Then fill the sink with 3 to 4 in. of water to ensure that the plunger seals around the drain. Hold a wet

rag tightly over the other drain opening in double sinks or use the basket strainer to seal it (**Photo 1**). Then plunge away. Roll the head of the plunger into the water so you force water, not air, into the drain. Pump vigorously. On your last upstroke, pop the plunger off the mouth of the drain for extra pressure (**Photo 2**). If the water doesn't swirl straight down the drain, continue plunging for several minutes. Plunging can be quick and easy or it could be a wet mess. Keep towels handy to soak up spills.

1 HOLD a wet cloth tightly over one sink drain to seal it and set the plunger over the other drain. Plunge up and down vigorously for about 20 seconds.

2 POP the plunger off the drain on your last pull stroke in a final attempt to break the clog free.

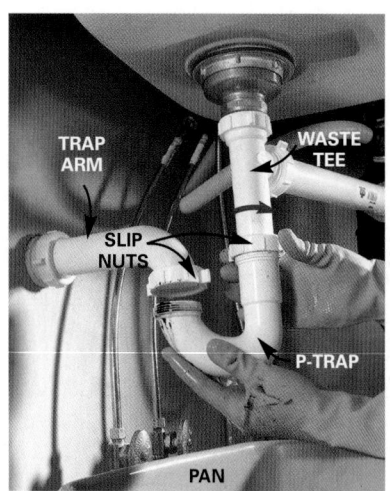

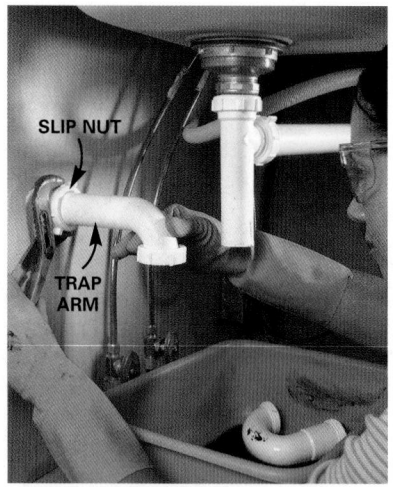

3 LOOSEN the slip nut on the trap arm assembly and the continuous waste tee and wiggle the trap free. Check the waste tee and remove and clean it if it's clogged.

4 CLEAN OUT any debris from the P-trap. Inspect both it and the trap arm for cracks or weak walls. If it's worn, replace it to avoid problems in the future.

5 LOOSEN the slip nut and slide the trap arm from the drain line stub-out. You will likely need a pliers to remove the nut.

Clean the P-trap

Clogs that occur in the P-trap and trap arm of the drain (**Photo 3**) most often occur when grease or coffee grounds stick. If intensive plunging doesn't remove it, disassemble and clean out the P-trap (10 to 15 minutes; Photos 3 – 5).

Begin by sponging the water from the sink to reduce the flow under the sink when you pull off the trap (**Photo 3**). Keep your pan or bucket underneath; dirty water will flow out. We show plastic drain lines, but many older kitchen sinks have metal traps and pipes. Metal slip nuts are usually more difficult to loosen than plastic, but either will probably require the use of slip-joint pliers to break

them free. Loosen them gently to avoid cracking or bending the trap assembly.

Unscrew the slip nut between the P-trap and the trap arm first, then the nut at the bottom of the waste tee. If the trap is clogged, clean it (**Photo 4**), reinstall it and test the line with warm water. Don't overtighten the slip nuts. Hand tight plus a quarter turn with a pliers should be enough.

If the P-trap isn't clogged, move on and remove the trap arm and clean it (**Photo 5**). Run a screwdriver around the inside of the pipe stub-out and pull out any debris that may have collected in the opening. If you still haven't found the clog, reach for the snake!

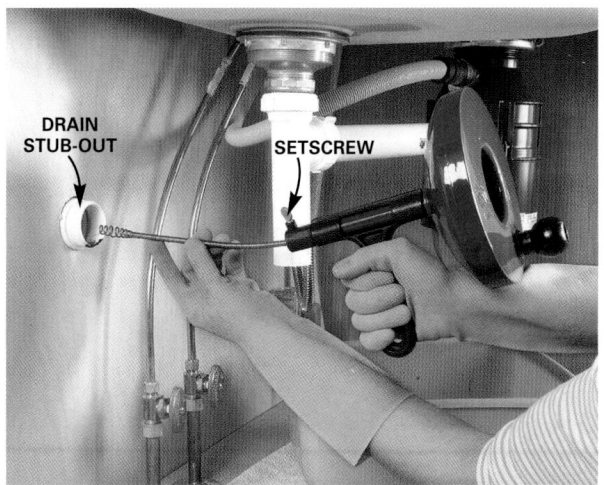

6 THREAD the tip of the snake into the drain stub-out. Tighten the setscrew and turn the crank clockwise to feed it into the drainpipe.

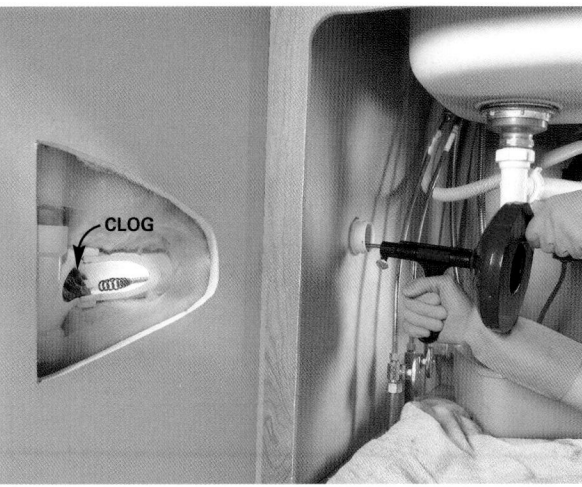

7 CONTINUE to turn the snake when you encounter resistance. The snake tip is designed to corkscrew through clogs and around corners.

Snake the line

Begin by loosening the setscrew at the tip of the snake and pulling out 6 to 10 in. of cable. Then tighten the setscrew and spin the snake down into the drain line (**Photos 6 and 7**). Initially you may feel an obstruction, but it's likely that the tip of the snake is just turning a corner. Loosen the setscrew, pull out another 6 to 10 in. of cable and continue to feed the snake into the line. If you feel the cable hit an obstruction, continue cranking and pushing the cable through the clog until you feel the tip bite through. This should be obvious because the tension in the cable will drop. When you are through the clog, turn the crank counterclockwise and pull out the cable. Clean the cable as you pull; it'll probably be covered with incredibly dirty gunk (**Photo 8**). You may get a large plug of material at the end of the snake, so keep that bucket handy. Repeat the process until you no longer feel blockage, then reassemble the trap and run plenty of warm water to flush the line. ⌂

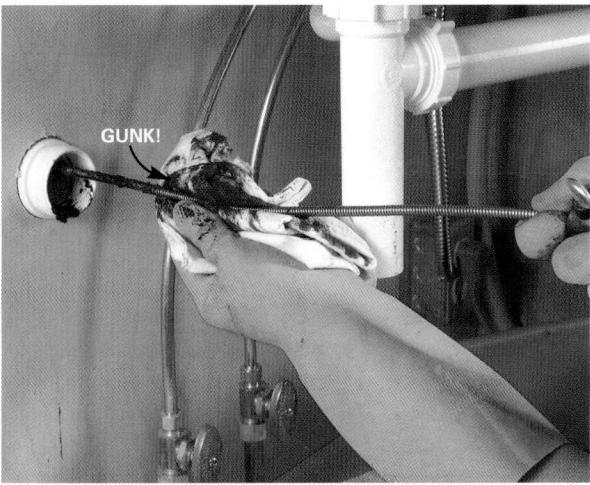

8 PULL the snake back out, cleaning the cable with a rag as you retrieve it. Reinstall the P-trap and run water to test the drain.

Tip
After the drain is open, pour 1/2 cup of baking soda and 1/2 cup of white vinegar into the drain. Cover both openings and let it sit for a few minutes. Then run another gallon or so of warm water behind it to flush out the mixture. The combination of baking soda and vinegar can break down any leftover fat deposits and will leave your drain smelling fresh.

Great Goofs™

Good idea, down the drain

Recently I used expanding spray foam to seal some cracks around the house. Trying to save money, I figured I could clean the nozzle and reuse it later. I rinsed it out in the sink with a small amount of thinner and water. After an hour, I tried to use the sink, but the drain was completely clogged. The foam had expanded in the drain. I called the plumber and he pulled out a big fat lump of hardened foam from the pipes below the sink. To add insult to injury, the next time I wanted to use the spray foam, the nozzle was clogged anyway.

A gush of plumbing
Great Goofs™
...wrenching true tales from our readers

Rough-in ruse

Not long ago, I decided to put a bathroom in the basement. My dad and I thought it would be easy to find the rough-in connections for all the fixtures, since most of the houses around here have them. We looked all over, but couldn't find them, so we rented a jackhammer to tie in to the main waste pipe below the concrete floor. Once the rough-in was completed and tested and the floor patched, it was time to frame the walls. The water softener was in the way, so we moved it. We couldn't believe our eyes. There were the rough-ins for the waste pipes! That water softener cost us a couple of weeks of work, a few hundred dollars and my sanity.

Soaking surprise

We hired a contractor to lay a new ceramic floor in the basement laundry room, so I decided to temporarily remove the water heater from that room to make the job easier. I shut off the cold water supply to the water heater, drained it and then cut the pipes just above the heater. The tile guy laid the tiles and was going to return the next day to grout.

The surprise came a few hours after he left when we ran the water in the upstairs bath. The cold water worked its way through the faucet into the hot water pipes and back to the open pipe above the water heater. The newly laid floor was completely flooded. I tried to mop up the water, but as I walked on the tile, the mortar oozed up between the tiles and ruined the tile job. Needless to say, the tile guy also got quite a surprise the next day! He had to completely redo the job. And not for free!

Wise geyser

We moved into an older home that needed lots of TLC. At the top of my list was fixing the leaky hot water faucet in the kitchen. I asked around for advice and a coworker told me I just needed to replace a washer. This sounded so easy that I got right to work. I grabbed my adjustable pliers and started to remove the faucet head. Just then my wife (a second-generation do-it-yourselfer) asked if I'd shut off the water. I confidently told her, "If it leaks, I'll shut off the water." Seconds later, the faucet handle flew toward the ceiling. I instinctively tried to cover the faucet with my hand only to get scalded. We finally got the water shut off and then mopped up the lake in the kitchen. And yes, I humbly fixed the faucet with a bandaged hand!

Good idea, down the drain

Recently I used expanding spray foam to seal some cracks around the house. Trying to save money, I figured I could clean the nozzle and reuse it later. I rinsed it out in the sink with a small amount of thinner and water. After an hour, I tried to use the sink, but the drain was completely clogged. The foam had expanded in the drain. I called the plumber and he pulled out a big fat lump of hardened foam from the pipes below the sink. To add insult to injury, the next time I wanted to use the spray foam, the nozzle was clogged anyway.

5 Interior Repairs & Appliances

IN THIS CHAPTER

Ask Handyman 116
Cutting wood doors, wet basements, drawer stops, doorbells, door stretching

Repair Washing Machine Leaks 120

You Can Fix It 125
Vacuum belt, bifold door, squealing hinge, doorknob and window crank

Handy Hints 128
Ultimate hanging tool, caulk smoother, easy-grip light switch and more...

Using Tools: Insulate 130

Ask Handyman™

WHAT'S THE BEST WAY TO CUT OFF WOOD DOOR BOTTOMS?

I recently installed carpeting and now the doors rub. What's the best way to trim off the door bottoms without splintering them?

Trimming a wood door with a circular saw without splintering the wood or damaging the finish is a challenge. Here's the method that works best for us.

First mark the clearance needed on the door. Then pull out the hinge pins and lay the door on padded sawhorses.

Mark the cutting line on the top face and edges of the door and apply a 6-in. wide strip of masking tape along the line to protect the door's finish from the circular saw's base plate.

Next, score the cutting lines 1/16 in. deep with a utility knife. I like to clamp a metal straightedge to the door on top of the masking tape along the cutting line. This helps to guide the knife, and then if the knife slips, it only scars

the waste side of the cut. You don't need to score the underside of the door.

Make sure your saw blade is sharp and has a minimum of 18 teeth. Hold the circular saw against the edge of the door as if you're ready to cut. With the blade teeth held just to the waste side of the scored line, mark the masking tape along the opposite edge of the base plate.

Position a straight saw guide at this mark, parallel to the cutting line, and clamp it at both ends. A 3/4-in. thick guide is thin enough to provide clearance under the saw's motor.

Hold the saw against the cutting guide and check the position of the blade's teeth. They should be just outside of the scored cutting line. Make the cut slowly. The scored line will stop the splintering. The bottom side of the door won't splinter because the saw teeth cut up into the wood.

Lightly sand all the edges along the new door bottom to soften them, then rehang the door.

MASKING TAPE

STRAIGHT EDGE

SCORED LINE

SAW CUT

DRAWER STOP

To keep a drawer from being pulled out, create a drawer stop with a 3-in. strip of 1/8-in. metal bar stock. Drill a 3/16-in. hole 1 in. from one end. Screw the metal strip to the back of the drawer about 1 in. from the top so it'll swing freely. Tip the strip and slide the drawer in. The heavier end of the strip hangs down and keeps the drawer from falling out.

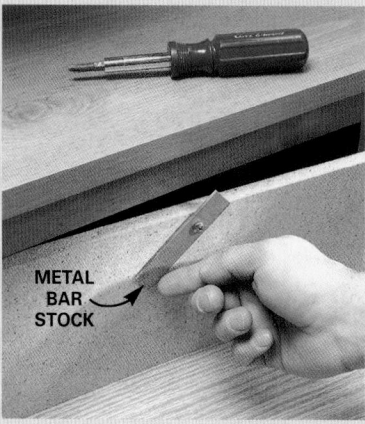

METAL BAR STOCK

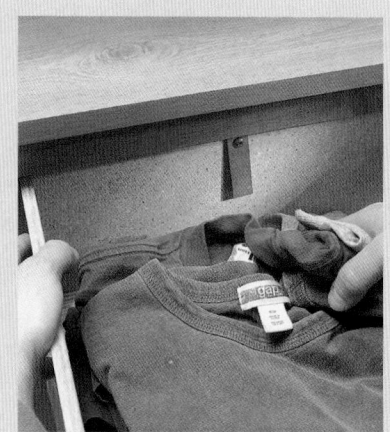

HOW TO DRY UP A WET BASEMENT

In the spring and after heavy rains, water leaks into my basement along the base of the foundation walls. How can I stop this?

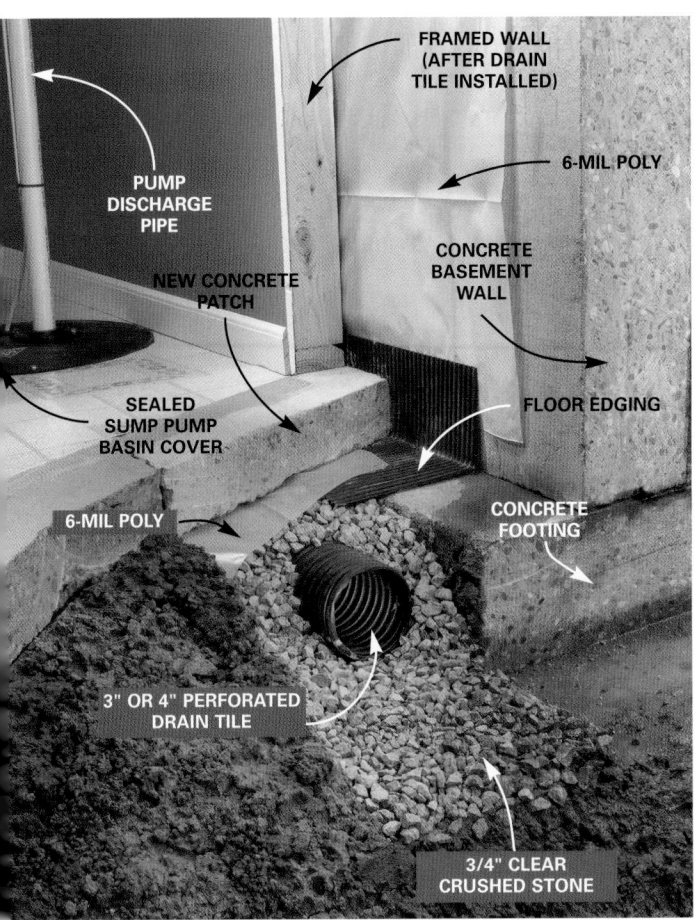

PUMP DISCHARGE PIPE

NEW CONCRETE PATCH

SEALED SUMP PUMP BASIN COVER

6-MIL POLY

3" OR 4" PERFORATED DRAIN TILE

FRAMED WALL (AFTER DRAIN TILE INSTALLED)

6-MIL POLY

CONCRETE BASEMENT WALL

FLOOR EDGING

CONCRETE FOOTING

3/4" CLEAR CRUSHED STONE

To install this system, follow these steps:

1. Break out and remove an 18-in. strip of concrete around the walls to expose the footing and underlying dirt. Rent an electric jackhammer ($65 per day) for this task.
2. Dig a 12-in. wide by 8-in. deep trench alongside the footing.
3. Find a location for the sump basin (an unfinished room is best). You'll need an electrical outlet for the sump pump and a way to run the discharge pipe outside. Break out additional floor, dig a hole and set the basin in place so the top is flush with the concrete floor.
4. Lay about 2 in. of gravel in the bottom of the trench (use crushed stone or river rock). Run the perforated drain tile in the trench and push its end through the knockout of the sump basin. Try to make a complete loop of the basement with the drain tile and run both ends into the basin. Fill the trench and around the basin with more gravel, leaving room for 3 to 4 in. of concrete.
5. Hang 6-mil polyethylene sheeting from the top of the foundation wall. Leave the bottom edge hanging just above the footing.
6. Lay the floor edging on the footing. Make sure the polyethylene runs behind it.
7. Lay a strip of polyethylene on top of the gravel and pour concrete to patch in the floor.
8. Install the sump pump in the basin and run the discharge pipe outside. Make sure the pipe runs at least 6 ft. away from the foundation so you aren't just dumping the water back against the foundation wall.

First, make sure that rainwater runs away from the house foundation. To pinpoint problem areas, go outside while it's raining and observe how the water flows off the roof and onto the ground around the house. Pay particular attention to areas below roof valleys where lots of water runs off.

Add soil to slope the ground away from the foundation. The grade should slope a minimum of 1 in. per foot for the first 4 to 6 ft. If necessary, direct roof water away with gutters and downspouts.

If these measures fail, you may have to install an interior drain tile and sump basin (**see photo**). The corrugated floor edging catches water running down the inside of the foundation wall and seeping under it and then directs it to the drain tile. The drain tile carries the water to the sump basin, where an electric pump automatically discharges it.

The materials are relatively inexpensive, but the labor is huge. You'll need to jackhammer out a strip of concrete around the perimeter, haul out concrete rubble and dirt, carry in gravel, and then patch the concrete floor. This is dusty, sweaty labor. Pros charge several thousand dollars for this job.

If you have a concrete block foundation, you'll have to drain the block cores by drilling 1-in. holes through the face of the block. Rent a rotary hammer with a 1-in. masonry bit; it's worth the $50-a-day fee.

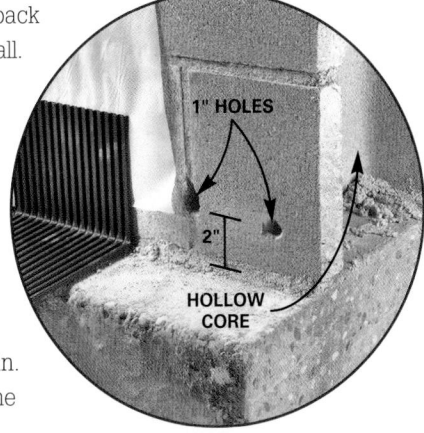

1" HOLES

2"

HOLLOW CORE

Buyer's Guide

- Floor edging: MTI, (800) 879-3348. Go to www.masonrytechnology.com to find a local supplier.
- Sealed basin: 18 x 22 in. with two drain tile holes, No. 5220 ($27), and lid No. 5225 ($26). Shelter Supply, (877) 207-7043. www.sheltersupply.com.

Ask Handyman™

CLEANING SOFFIT VENTS

I've noticed that my soffit vents look dirty. Do I need to clean them, and if so, what is the best method?

Yes, you should clean soffit (eave) and other types of attic air intake vents at least every couple of years, if not annually. The best way to clean them is with blasts of compressed air to blow away dust, dirt and any loose insulation that may have fallen into the soffit area (**see photo at right**).

Attic ventilation is critical to the health of your house. It begins with soffit vents that inhale outside air—necessary to create an airflow that moves warm attic air out the roof vents. Once the air enters the soffit, it usually proceeds through an air chute or some other opening along the underside of the roof into the attic where it helps push warm attic air out the roof vents (**photo below**). The plastic air chutes ($1 each from home centers and building suppliers) in each rafter space keep the air path clear between the rafters and the roof sheathing.

The benefits of ensuring good attic airflow are fourfold:

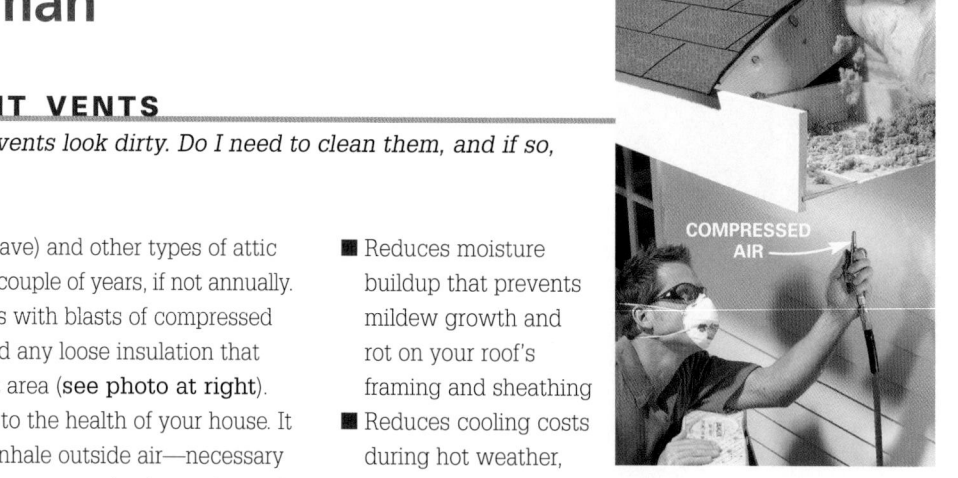

COMPRESSED AIR

- Reduces moisture buildup that prevents mildew growth and rot on your roof's framing and sheathing
- Reduces cooling costs during hot weather, which can be dramatic if your attic is underinsulated
- Extends shingle life by keeping the roof cooler in hot weather
- Reduces ice dams and the potential damage they cause during snow season.

To learn more about other common causes of poor attic ventilation and how to fix them, see "Improve Attic Ventilation," Nov. '00, p. 54, and "Defeat Ice Dams," Sept. '00, p. 35. To order copies, see p. 288.

AIRFLOW

ROOF VENT

AIR FLOW

AIR CHUTE

AIRFLOW

FIBERGLASS INSULATION PLUG

AIRFLOW

BLOWN-IN INSULATION

FLOW

AIR

SOFFIT VENT

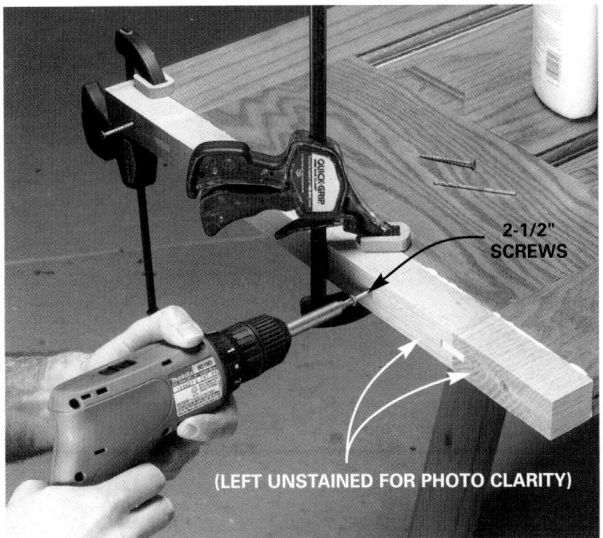

2-1/2" SCREWS

(LEFT UNSTAINED FOR PHOTO CLARITY)

HOW DO I 'STRETCH' A DOOR?

We bought a house and removed the long shag carpet. The solid oak panel interior doors are now too short. How can I "stretch" them to close up the gap?

It's easy enough to glue and screw a piece of wood to the door bottom, but it'll look bad unless you paint your door. For a nice-looking job, choose wood of the same species with a grain and color that closely match the door. A first-rate job requires a table saw, some woodworking skill and patience, but the results will be worth the effort.

Because the floor may not be level, swing the door to find the highest spot in the floor. Make a light pencil mark on the door 2 in. up from the floor at the high spot. The filler piece will be 1-1/2 in. tall and you'll want at least 1/2-in. clearance under the door.

Remove the door by pulling out the hinge pins and lay it on a pair of padded horses. Carefully cut off the door at the pencil mark to get a clean, square edge.

For the most seamless appearance, construct the filler from three separate pieces, matching the width, thickness and grain direction of the door's two stiles and rail (see photo). Glue the three pieces together using biscuits, dowels or splines.

Accuracy is essential. Make sure the finished filler piece is exactly the same thickness and width as the door. Then finish-sand it to 120 grit and stain and varnish it to match the door. The closer you can match the stain, the more seamless the fix will look.

Drill four clearance holes all the way through the filler piece. Apply wood glue to the door, align the filler and clamp it in place. Then drill pilot holes in the door through the clearance holes. Drive the screws tight, countersinking their heads, and wipe off excess glue with a damp rag.

SECOND DOORBELL CHIME

Can I add a remote ringer to the doorbell in my basement shop?

Yes, it's a simple job. The most difficult part is tracking down the cables. Although it's easy to connect a new "doorbell cable" (common is 18- or 20-gauge CL2 type or the equivalent) at the existing doorbell chime (**photo at right**), it may be difficult to run concealed wires to your basement shop. It may be easier to make the connection at the low-

ADDED PIGTAILS AND WIRE CONNECTORS

NEW CABLE TO NEW CHIME

EXISTING DOORBELL CHIME

voltage transformer that powers the doorbell, especially if it's near the shop. Often the transformer is mounted on the electrical service panel (**bottom photo**).

If you're connecting it at the chime, note the three screw terminals labeled "front," "back" and "transformer." Connect a wire to each and then simply make sure the three wires connect to the same terminals on the new chime. There's no uniform color-coding for doorbell wires.

Add a second chime cable at the transformer, exactly like the cable to the existing chime. Your existing transformer may not be powerful enough to handle both chimes. So if you get a weak sound, replace the transformer with a 15-20VA (volt amp) unit.

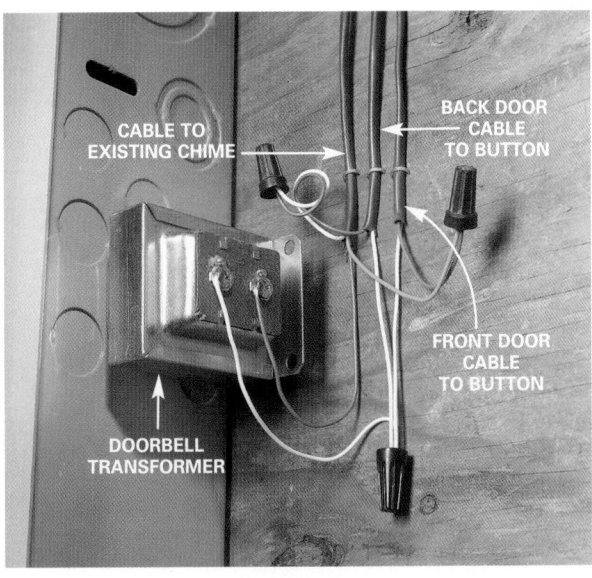

CABLE TO EXISTING CHIME

BACK DOOR CABLE TO BUTTON

FRONT DOOR CABLE TO BUTTON

DOORBELL TRANSFORMER

REPAIR
WASHING MACHINE LEAKS

Fix the most common leaks yourself and avoid that $75 service call

by **Jeffrey Larson**

When the washing machine starts leaking water all over the floor, you face a tough choice. Either call a service technician to fix the problem or purchase a new machine. Both decisions are expensive. Most service technicians charge $50 to $100 just to walk in the door and diagnose the problem, and labor expenses can quickly accumulate. After receiving the final bill, you may even wish you'd replaced the machine!

This article will help you avoid the service call by showing you how to diagnose and fix the most common washing machine leaks. We cover hose, pump and tub leaks, but there may be additional problem areas specific to your brand of machine.

There are two types of washing machines: belt drive and direct drive. If you open up the cabinet and don't find any belts,

> **Tip**
> Make sure the water on the floor isn't the result of a plugged floor drain. It happens!

then you've got a direct-drive machine. Repairs are similar for both machines, but generally easier on the direct-drive unit. The following photos are from a belt-drive washing machine. If you have a direct drive, refer to your owner's manual or diagrams (see "Buying Parts," p. 124) for brand-specific details.

Fig. A: Common leak locations
(BELT-DRIVE WASHING MACHINE SHOWN)

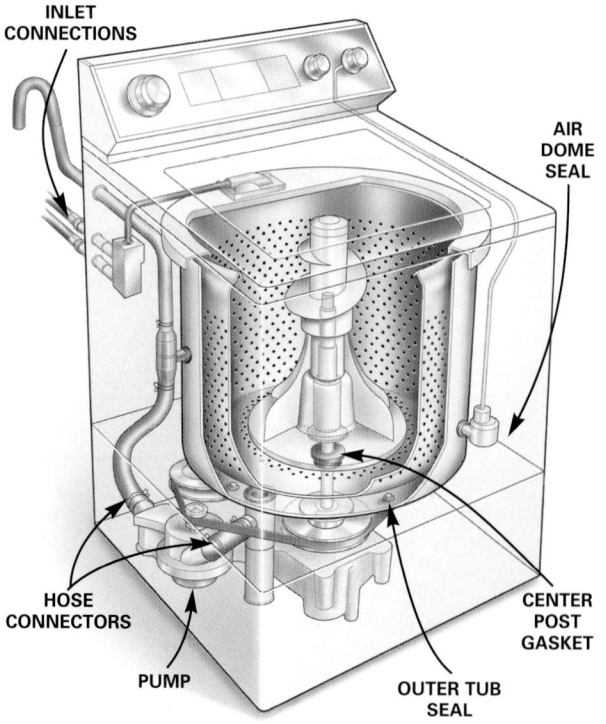

INLET CONNECTIONS

AIR DOME SEAL

HOSE CONNECTORS

PUMP

OUTER TUB SEAL

CENTER POST GASKET

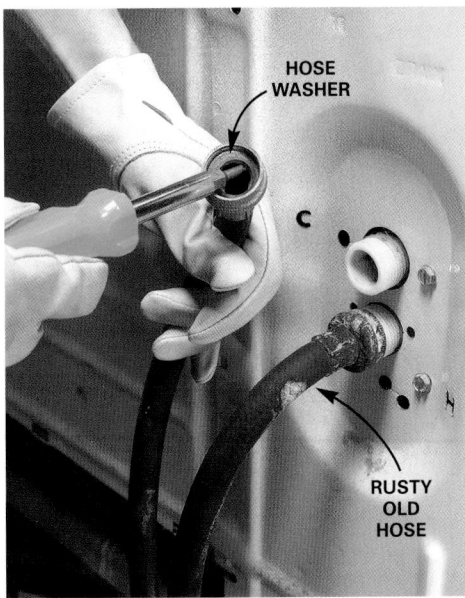

TURN OFF the water main or shutoff valve and unscrew the supply hoses from the back of the machine with an adjustable pliers. Pry out the old hose washers with a flat-blade screwdriver. Install new gaskets in both hoses and reconnect the supply lines.

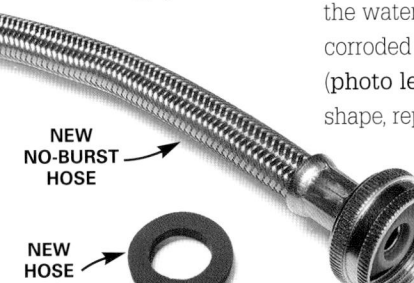

HOSE WASHER

RUSTY OLD HOSE

NEW NO-BURST HOSE

NEW HOSE WASHER

FIRST, replace leaky supply hoses

The first step is to locate the source of the leak. Empty the washing machine, move it away from the wall and start the fill cycle. Look for drips around the water supply hose connection at the back of the machine while it fills with water. Shut off the water and replace any old, heavily corroded or rusted hoses with new ones (photo left). If the hoses are in good shape, replace the internal washers only.

Special no-burst hoses ($10), regular hoses ($6) and new hose washers ($2 per 10-pack) are available at home centers and hardware stores.

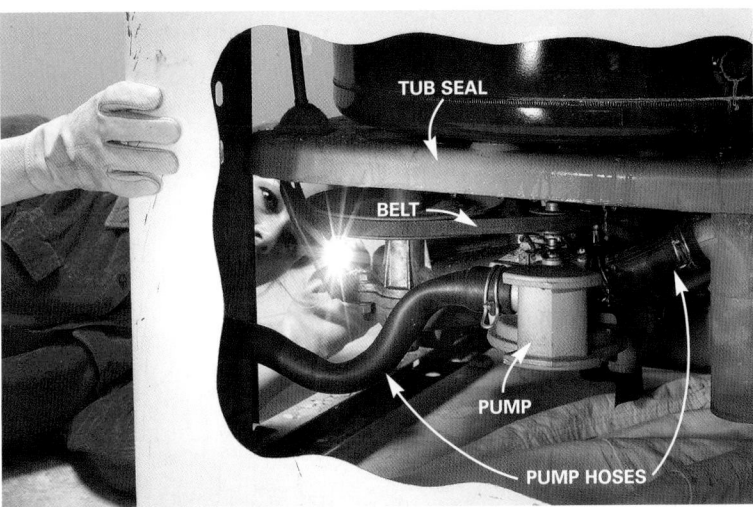

TUB SEAL

BELT

PUMP

PUMP HOSES

1 UNSCREW the access panel from the back of the machine or open the cabinet. Look for leaks while the machine fills with water. If you don't see any, advance the machine to the agitate cycle and check again.

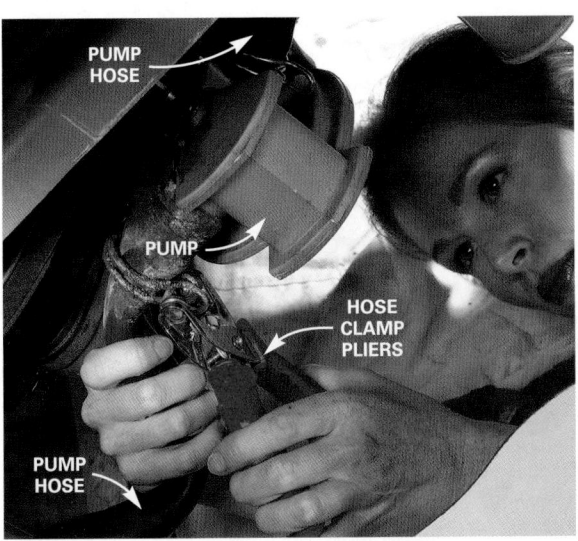

PUMP HOSE

PUMP

HOSE CLAMP PLIERS

PUMP HOSE

2 SQUEEZE the hose clamp together, slide it down the hose and pull off the hose. Keep a bucket or pan handy so you can catch any residual water left in the hoses. Replace the hose with an identical part and new worm-drive clamps (right).

SECOND, replace leaky internal hoses

If the supply hoses aren't leaking, open the cabinet and inspect the internal components. Belt-drive machines typically have a rear access panel that unscrews. Access direct-drive machines by removing the two screws on the outside of the control panel and flipping up the lid. Then pry up the cabinet clips and pull off the entire cabinet. With the cabinet open, restart the fill cycle to check for internal leaks (Photo 1). Look for additional clues like rust and calcium deposits. Most often you'll find the leaks in the spots we show in Fig. A, p. 120.

Hoses tend to leak around a worn-out spring clamp. First try to remove the spring clamp with an adjustable pliers. If you can't get it, you'll need a special $15 hose clamp pliers (Photo 2) available from your local parts supplier. Replace the old spring clamp with a new worm-drive clamp (photo below). If the hose itself is cracked and leaking, remove it and take it to the appliance parts supplier for a replacement.

WORM-DRIVE CLAMP

CAUTION: Unplug the machine before performing any repairs.

THIRD, replace a leaky pump

The pump usually leaks around the pulley seal (see **Photo 3**). If you spot water leaking from this spot, the pump is shot and will have to be replaced. A new pump costs $35 to $45.

To replace the pump, work from underneath the machine. Unplug the machine and tip it up against the wall. Block up the front with a car jack or 2x4s so it can't tip over while you reach underneath. Replace the pump as shown in **Photos 1 – 4**. If the belt is darkened from burning or is worn down to the threads, replace it, too.

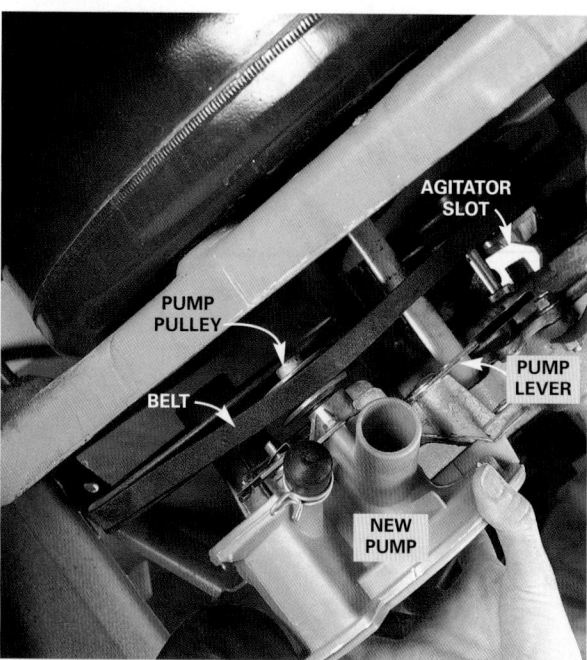

1 LOOSEN the two motor mounting bolts to relieve tension on the belt. One will be at the rear of the cabinet and the other is nearby.

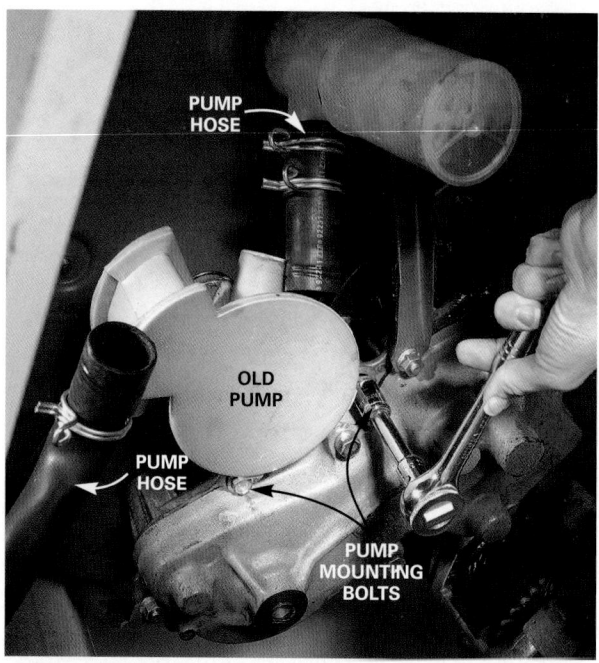

2 DISCONNECT the pump hoses. Then unscrew the pump mounting bolts, tip the pump pulley away from the belt and wiggle the pump loose. Direct-drive pumps will simply unscrew or unclip.

3 INSTALL the new pump by sliding the pump lever into the agitator slot and aligning the belt with the pump pulley. Line up the bolt holes and firmly tighten the mounting bolts. Reconnect all hoses and clamps.

4 PULL against the motor to tension the belt and then tighten the rear motor mounting bolt. The belt should deflect about 1/2 in. when you push against it. Then tighten the mounting bolt located on the opposite side of the motor.

FOURTH, replace worn-out tub fittings

The most challenging repair is fixing a leaking tub fitting, whether it's the air dome seal ($5), the center post gasket ($8) or the tub seals ($15 to $20). (See **Fig. A** and photos for locations.) Before proceeding, make sure that telltale drips are coming from around the tub. The details of this repair vary by brand and model. The details we show are for most Whirlpool and Kenmore belt drives. Study a schematic drawing or consult a parts specialist if your machine is different from what we show.

You'll need a special $15 spanner wrench (**Photo 4**) to remove the tub and replace the tub fittings on this type of machine. It's available at your local appliance parts supplier. Follow **Photos 1 – 5** to access the tub fittings. You can open the top of many machines by releasing the spring catches (**Photo 1**). However, on others you have to unscrew several screws and lift off the entire cabinet. Look in your owner's manual or at a parts diagram. (See the manufacturer's Web site or one of the sites listed in "Buying Parts" on p. 124.) You'll have to unscrew the water inlet and the tub snubber (**Photo 1**) before unclipping the

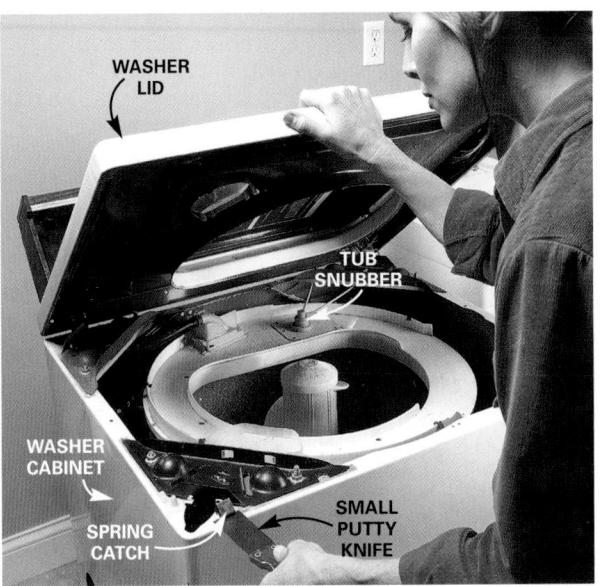

1 SLIDE a small putty knife between the washer lid and the cabinet. Push the putty knife against the spring catch while lifting up on the lid. Release both catches and fold the lid back.

2 POP OFF the tub ring clips, lift the tub ring out of the cabinet and set it aside.

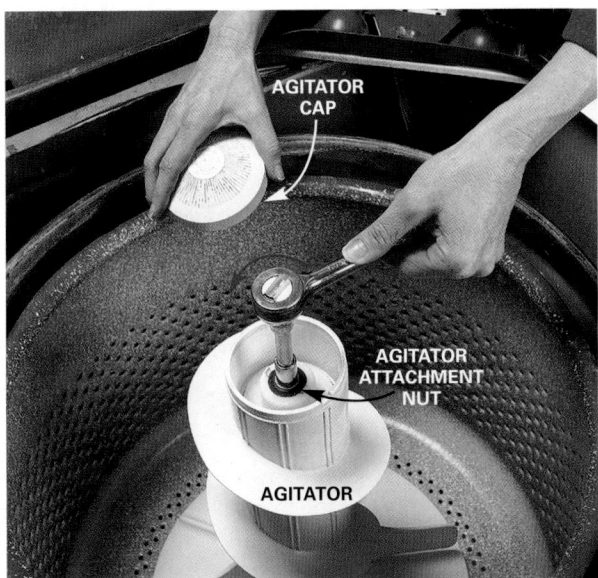

3 TWIST or pry the cap off the agitator. Then unscrew the attachment nut and pull the agitator up and off the drive shaft.

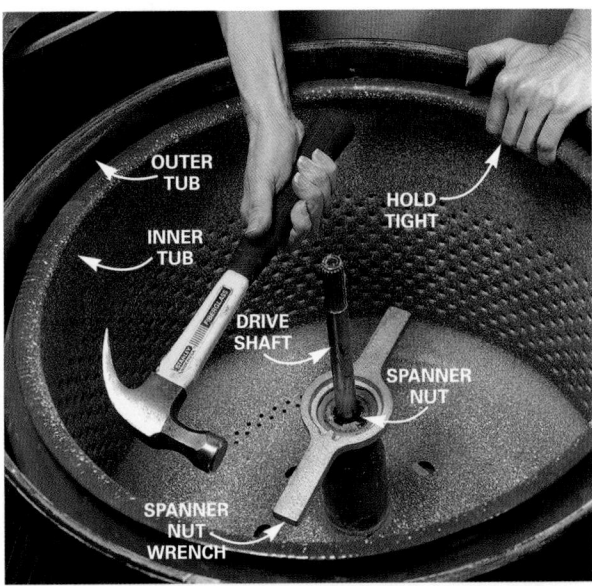

4 HOLD the inner tub tight to the outer tub. Rap the special spanner wrench to break the spanner nut free. Remove the spanner nut.

ring (**Photo 2**). Fastening systems for these vary by brand, as do attachment methods for the agitator (**Photo 3**) and inner tub (**Photo 4**).

There are four tub seals that secure the outer tub to the cabinet, each consisting of a bolt with a rubber and metal washer. Rust often develops around one of the tub seals, causing a tub leak. A new tub seal kit will come with four new bolts and oversized rubber and metal washers that will seal small leaks (**Photo 6**). But if the tub is completely rusted through around the bolt, it's time to buy a new washing machine. Replace all four tub seals as shown in **Photo 6**.

If the leaking occurs only when the machine is agitating, a bad center post gasket ("doughnut") is the culprit. Remove the outer tub to replace the center post gasket (**Photos 8 and 9**). While you're at it, replace the air dome seal as well (**Photo 8**). Reassemble the washing machine and run a test cycle. 🏠

Buying parts

Washing machine parts are available at appliance parts distributors. (Look in the Yellow Pages under "Appliance Parts.") Try to find a parts supplier with a well-informed staff, ideally ex–repair technicians, who can provide diagrams and help diagnose any problems specific to your brand of machine. A great Internet source is www.searspartsdirect.com. Enter your model number to access exploded-view diagrams and a thorough parts list for easy on-line ordering.

You'll need the brand and model number for proper part identification. Model numbers are usually stamped on a small metal plate (photo below) located under the tub lid or on the side or back of the machine. Copy down all the plate information and take it along to the parts distributor.

MODEL NUMBER 82374110

5 LIFT the inner tub up and off the drive shaft. You might have to wiggle it back and forth to help work it loose.

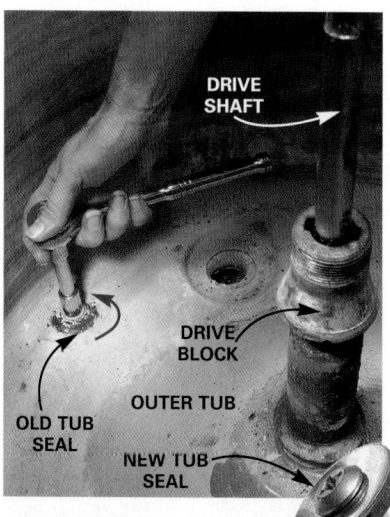

6 UNSCREW the old leaky tub seals from the outer tub. Later, install the new tub seals, making sure the metal washer is on top of the rubber washer.

7 TAP up on the drive block with a hammer to break it loose from the drive shaft. Pull off the drive block and set it aside. Lift the outer tub from the cabinet, twisting it back and forth to work it loose.

8 TWIST the air dome a quarter turn and pull it free from the outer tub. Pry off the old air dome seal and replace it with a new one.

9 SQUEEZE the center post gasket together and pull it from the bottom of the outer tub. Install a new center post gasket and reassemble the machine.

You Can Fix It™

FIX YOUR BIFOLD DOOR

Free yourself of the hassles of a broken bifold door faster than a fish fleeing a net. Often, heavily used bifold doors wobble and don't work because the top pivot has broken loose. We stumbled upon a neat repair gizmo called "The Bracket" (800-343-3275) that reinforces the pivot. It costs about $3 at hardware stores. To install it, grab the closed bifold door with both hands and lift up while you pull the bottom pivot free of the floor bracket. (To make reinstallation easier, first mark where the bottom pin sits in the floor bracket.) Set the door on a workbench or on sawhorses and remove the pivot (**Photo 1**). After you secure "The Bracket" (**Photo 2**), rehang the door by aligning the top pivot with its bracket, lifting the door and setting the bottom pivot back into the floor bracket.

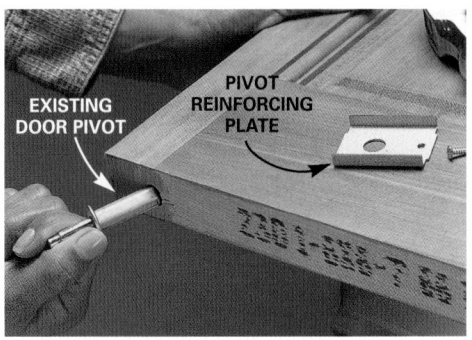

EXISTING DOOR PIVOT

PIVOT REINFORCING PLATE

1 REMOVE the bifold door and pull the top pivot from the top edge.

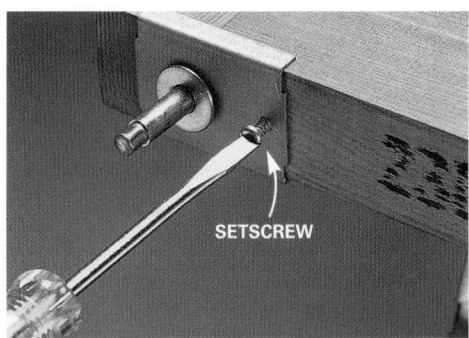

SETSCREW

2 CENTER the reinforcing plate over the pivot hole with the setscrew hole pointing toward the center of the door. Lightly tap the plate in place with a hammer. Secure it with the enclosed setscrew, and reinsert the pivot.

REPLACE A VACUUM BELT

When your vacuum starts to lose cleaning power, requiring multiple passes to get an area clean, or the self-propulsion loses its zip, chances are you need to change the vacuum agitator belt. After only a few months of use, most vacuum belts stretch out enough to slip, causing the agitator to spin more slowly.

Replacing the belt is quick and inexpensive. New belts are available for about $5 from a vacuum parts supplier (check the Yellow Pages for a store in your area). Belts come in numerous brands and sizes, so bring the old one to the store for a guaranteed match.

Fifteen minutes, two screwdrivers and a new belt are all you'll typically need to complete the job. **Photo 1** shows how to access the old belt. The cover on your vacuum may be held on by other arrangements of clips and screws.

After removing the cover, install the new belt as shown in **Photos 2 and 3**. Once the new belt's on and the agitator's back in place, turn the agitator by hand to make sure the belt spins smoothly, without rubbing or binding. Reassemble the bottom cover and test-run the machine.

1 UNPLUG the vacuum and turn it over, exposing the underside. Back out the casing screws that secure the bottom cover. Release the attachment clips with a flat-blade screwdriver and lift off the cover.

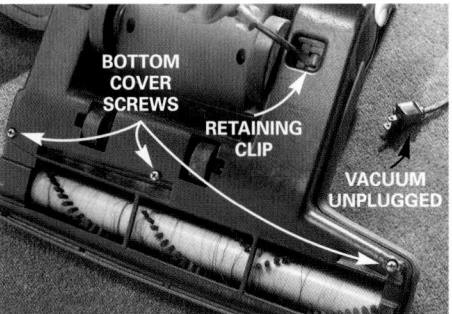

BOTTOM COVER SCREWS

RETAINING CLIP

VACUUM UNPLUGGED

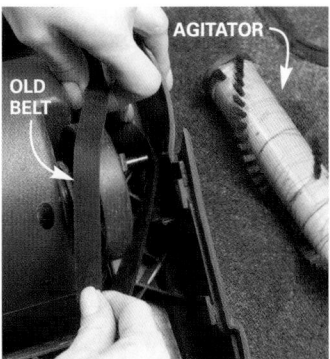

OLD BELT

AGITATOR

2 PRY out the agitator with a flat-blade screwdriver. Slide the old belt off the agitator pulley and motor drive shaft and slide the new belt on the motor drive shaft.

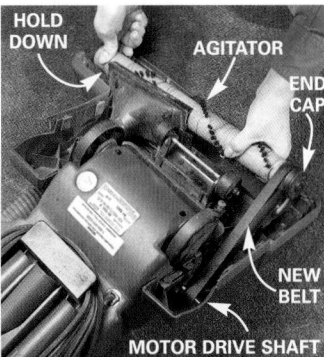

HOLD DOWN

AGITATOR

END CAP

NEW BELT

MOTOR DRIVE SHAFT

3 SLIDE the new belt onto the agitator. Replace the agitator, making sure the end caps are properly seated. Spin it with your hand to make sure it doesn't bind, and then replace the cover.

INTERIOR REPAIRS & APPLIANCES

You Can Fix It™

REPLACE A CASEMENT WINDOW CRANK OPERATOR

If your window crank handle just spins when it's turned, or it can't pull in the sash far enough to engage the lock, chances are the gears are stripped and it's time for a new crank mechanism. Replacing the crank mechanism is simple. But finding a new crank may take some time. Two excellent sources to call are Blaine Window Hardware, 17319 Blaine Drive, Hagerstown, MD 21740 (800-678-1919), and Replacement Hardware Mfg. Inc., 500 W. 84th St., Hialeah, FL 33014 (800-780-5051). You can mail them your old crank and you'll get back a match (Photo 1). The cranks can be expensive, from $25 to more than $100, but they may be a bargain if the overall condition of the window is still good.

Start by inspecting the old crank operator and handle for wear. If the teeth are missing inside the crank handle, simply replace it ($10 to $20 at home centers and full-service hardware stores). But if the operator has broken or worn parts (Photo 1), replace the entire operator mechanism.

Your operator may vary slightly from the one we show. However, the replacement process is similar. The first step is to disconnect the crank arm from the guide track. Take out the screen and crank the window open until the plastic guide bushing aligns with the guide track notch (Photo 2).

Next, look for trim mounting screws inside the screen track. Unscrew them to remove the casement cover and access the crank innards (Photo 4). If there aren't any trim screws, the casement cover is probably nailed or stapled in place. Slide a stiff putty knife between the window jamb and casement cover. Carefully pry up the casing so you don't damage the wood parts.

Close the window and lock it until the new crank arrives. Compare the new operator with the old, making sure they match. Install the new crank as shown in Photo 5.

1 INSPECT the old crank for wear. Worn and missing splines on the crank stud, stripped or broken gears, and worn-out crank arms mean you have to replace the entire crank operator.

SILENCE A SQUEALING HINGE!

If you've got a door hinge that squeals worse than a pig in a slaughterhouse, we've got the fix for you! A little petroleum jelly will rid the hinge of that annoying wail. The petroleum jelly works its way into the hinge and adheres well, so it won't run off and make a mess like oil or other lubricants.

Photos 1 and 2 show how to punch out a hinge pin and grease it up. After all the hinges have been lubricated, open and close the door a few times to work the petroleum jelly into the hinge joints.

1 LOOSEN each hinge pin by tapping an 8d nail up from underneath. Once the pin is loose, pull it out (lift up on the door handle to relieve pressure if the pin binds). Keep the door closed and work on only one hinge at a time.

2 LIGHTLY coat the hinge pin with petroleum jelly and dab a little in the top of the pin slot. Reinsert the pin and wipe off any excess.

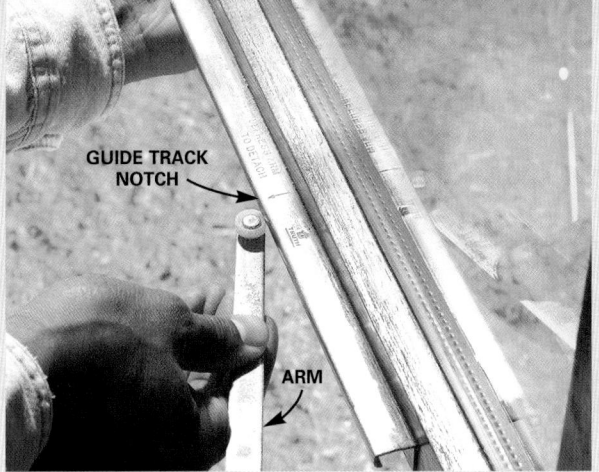

GUIDE TRACK NOTCH

ARM

TRIM SCREW

CASEMENT COVER

CRANK MOUNTING SCREWS

2 OPEN the window until the crank arm guide bushing aligns with the notch in the guide track (use a locking pliers for a crank handle and push out on the window to help it open). Press down on the arm to free the bushing from the track, and then push out the window until the bushing clears the track.

3 BACK out the trim screws and lift the casement cover off the window jamb. Remove all crank mounting screws and lift off the crank. Replace rusted or bent trim screws.

4 COMPARE the new operator with the old to make sure they match.

5 LINE up the new crank with the old holes. The old screw holes are often stripped. If so, stick a toothpick or two in them as filler and drive the screws. Then reattach the crank arm and casement cover.

TIGHTEN A LOOSE BIFOLD DOORKNOB

Tired of opening a bifold door and having the knob come off in your hand? Once loose, knobs always fall off again unless you fix them right. What's worse, overtightening the knob screws on hollow-core doors causes the screwhead to pull through the door's veneer.

Try these fixes. Add a finish washer behind the screwhead (**Photo 1**). Inexpensive, about 10¢ each, they're available at hardware stores and home centers in zinc or brass finishes.

Keep the doorknob in place with a glue like Loctite's Screw Tightener (about $4.50; **Photo 2**). The beauty of this type of glue is that it doesn't form a permanent bond. If you want to change knobs or refinish the door, you can still remove the knob (with some effort) using locking pliers and a screwdriver. Be sure you protect the knob's finish by padding it with a rag before gripping it with the pliers.

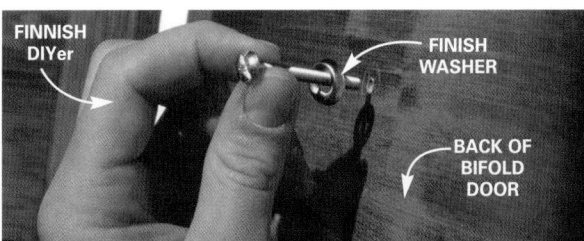

FINNISH DIYer

FINISH WASHER

BACK OF BIFOLD DOOR

1 PLACE a finish washer behind the screwhead to prevent it from digging into the door and to add a more finished look.

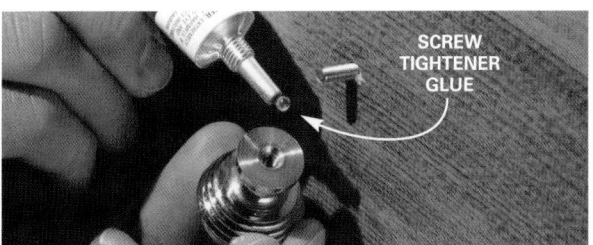

SCREW TIGHTENER GLUE

2 SQUEEZE three or four drops of glue into the doorknob and turn the knob on the screw. Wipe any glue from the knob face to prevent it from sticking to the door. Allow the glue to dry for an hour. (If you don't have glue, you can substitute fingernail polish.)

Handy Hints® from our readers

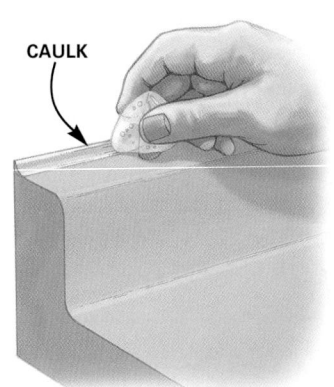

CAULK

ICE CUBE CAULK SMOOTHER

If you have difficulty smoothing a bead of latex caulk evenly, try this technique. Squeeze out the bead of caulk. Then shape the edge of an ice cube to the desired bead shape by melting it with your hand. Run the ice cube along the joint to form a perfect bead.

ULTIMATE HANGING TOOL

Mount pictures and other art at the same height and level with this slick trick! Glue a flexible sewing tape measure to the edge of a 4-ft. level. Measure down from the ceiling for uniform mounting heights. Level across the wall to locate and mark additional studs (usually spaced 16 or 24 in. apart).

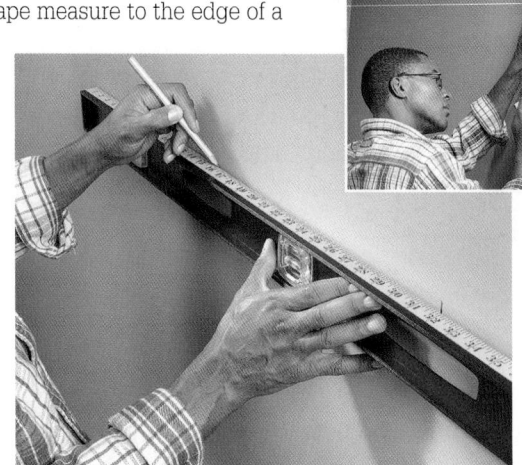

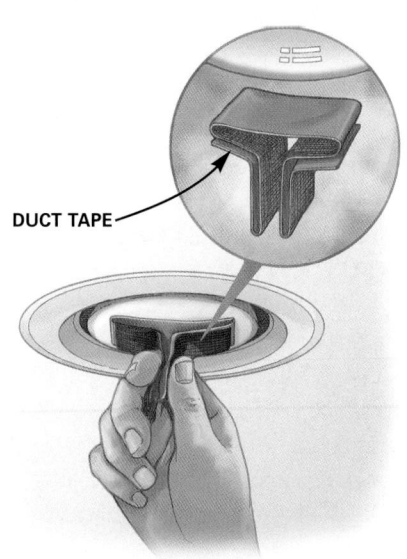

DUCT TAPE

EASY-GRIP LIGHT SWITCH

As we get older, our fingers aren't quite as nimble as they once were and even twisting a small lamp knob can be a chore. Put a drop of silicone in the bottom of a clean toothpaste cap and push it over a standard knob to make it more

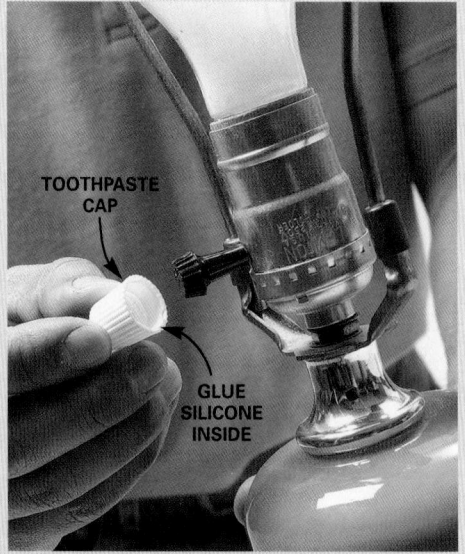

TOOTHPASTE CAP

GLUE SILICONE INSIDE

grabbable. The lampshade conceals the larger knob, but if you don't like the look, you can darken the cap with a permanent marker to match the old knob.

LIGHT BULB HANDLE

Removing a tight, burned-out light bulb from a recessed fixture can be next to impossible because there just isn't enough room for your fingers. Make a light bulb "handle" from a 15-in. strip of duct tape. Center the tape on the bulb; fold the two ends back to the middle, then fold each end over again on itself to form the handle.

CYLINDER
HOLE

1/8"
DRILL
BIT

2" NAIL

LATCH MARKER

Align a strike plate accurately on the very first try! Mark the cylinder and latch hole centers with the manufacturer's template, and drill out the cylinder hole. Then drill a 1/8-in. latch hole from the outside door edge into the center of the cylinder hole. Close the door against the doorstop. Press a 2-in. nail through the 1/8-in. hole and into the jamb to mark the exact center (height) of the strike plate.

SILICONE SIGHT

Create a caulk sight by marking the backside of the cut tip. The line makes it easy to maintain a constant angle for a straighter and smoother caulk line.

INTERIOR REPAIRS & APPLIANCES

NEW BOTTOM FOR HOLLOW-CORE DOORS

The next time you have to shorten a hollow-core door, try replacing the bottom rail with expanding foam instead of wood. Cut the door to the right length, clamp stiff boards to both sides of the bottom, and fill the bottom with expanding foam insulation. After the foam dries, trim off the excess with a utility knife and rehang the door.

EXPANDING
FOAM

CLAMP
DOOR BOTTOM
BETWEEN BOARDS
TO PREVENT
BULGING

Using Tools: Insulate

INSTALLING FIBERGLASS BATTS

You've only got one chance to do it right! Here's how:

Filling stud spaces with fiberglass batts is the cheapest, easiest way for you to insulate new walls. It's also the best way to upgrade wall insulation during remodeling. Installing the batts doesn't require any special skills, but it's slow, tedious, itchy work. It's often done poorly, and even small gaps can reduce efficiency as much as 25 percent. In this article, we'll show you how to cut and fit fiberglass batts and how to work around electrical outlets and cables to get the best job with the least hassle.

Fill all voids

The key to a high-quality insulating job is tight-fitting batts that completely fill the stud cavity with no voids or gaps. You can do top-quality work with only a few basic tools. You'll need a utility knife with a good supply of sharp blades, a tape measure and a straightedge, and a 3- or 4-in. putty knife for stuffing insulation around doors and windows. Fiberglass can irritate your throat and skin, so wear protective gear. Buy a two-strap mask rated for fiberglass insulation (3M No. 8210 is one example) and wear a hat, gloves, a long-sleeve shirt and goggles to keep fibers out of your eyes.

PUSH batts all the way to the back of each stud space and then pull out the front edges until they're flush with the face of the studs.

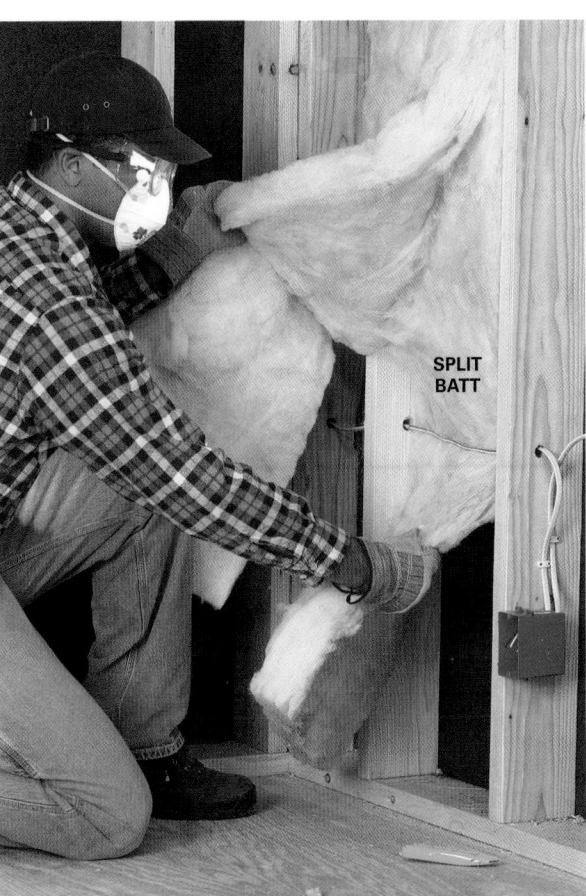

SPLIT batts to fit around electrical cables. Tear the batt in half, starting from the bottom. Slide one half behind the cable and lay the other half over the top.

Fit batts tightly around electrical cables and boxes

Running a full batt in front of electrical cables leaves an uninsulated space behind. Avoid this by splitting the batt as shown. Then when you come to an electrical box, trim the insulation to fit snugly around it. Run your knife blade against the outside of the box to guide the cut. But don't cut too deep or you risk nicking the wires. If you have plumbing pipes on an outside wall, insulate behind them, but leave the side facing the interior uncovered to allow heat from the house to keep the pipes warm.

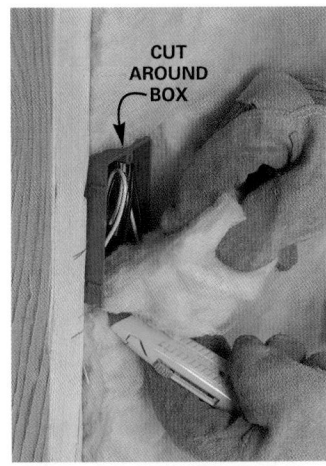

SPLIT AND CUT batts to fit behind and around electrical boxes. Slide half the batt behind the box. Then cut the front half to fit tightly around the box.

Using Tools: Insulate

Fit first, then cut to length

We're using unfaced batts that are sized to friction-fit into standard stud spaces (either 16-in. or 24-in. on-center studs). They're also available precut to lengths that fit standard 8-ft. and 9-ft. walls. Buying precut batts eliminates some work, but you'll still have to cut some batts to length. You could measure the space and cut the batt to fit, but a quicker method that's just as accurate is shown below. Leave an extra 1/2 in. of length for a snug fit.

We're using unfaced batts because they're easier to cut and install. In most climates, you'll have to staple 4-mil plastic sheeting over the batts to form a vapor barrier. Check with your local building inspector for the recommended practice in your area.

CUT batts to length by setting the top of the batt into the space and cutting against the bottom plate with a sharp utility knife. Leave an extra 1/2 in. of length for a tighter fit.

Trim batts in place

Accurate cutting is essential (actually, slightly oversized batts are best). A batt cut too small leaves gaps and one cut too large bunches up and leaves voids.

The photos show two methods of cutting batts to width. If you're having trouble getting an accurate cut with the "eyeballing" tech-

LEAVE the batt folded in half and hold one edge against the edge of the stud. Slice down the length while holding the top of the batt. Cut against the stud face.

Fill gaps around windows and doors

The shim space around windows and doors is a prime spot for air leakage. Stop these leaks by reaching to the back of this space with the straw-type nozzle included with a can of expanding foam insulation and applying a bead around the perimeter. Let it cure at least an hour before stuffing the remaining space with a thin strip of fiberglass. Don't pack the fiberglass too tight or it will bow the jambs and cause trouble with the operation of the window. ⌂

nique, measure the width of the stud space and use the straight-edge method instead. Add about 1/2 in. to the width to ensure a tight fit. It's better to compress the batts a little than to leave gaps. Don't worry if the batts bulge out a bit. The drywall will compress them tightly.

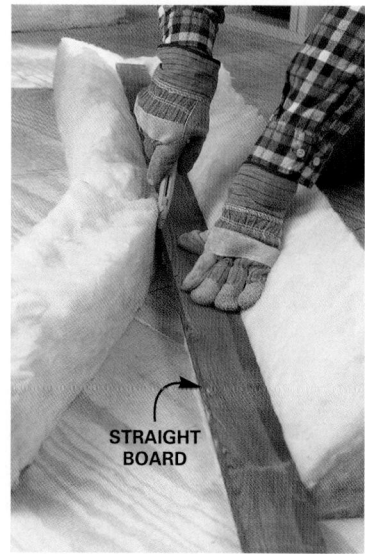

ALTERNATE METHOD: Press a straightedge down on the batt at the desired width and use it as a guide for the utility knife.

STUFF skinny strips of batting into spaces around windows and doors with a 3-in. wide putty knife. The insulation should fit snugly, but don't pack it.

6 Woodworking Projects & Built-Ins

IN THIS CHAPTER

Three-Hour Cedar Bench 134

Using Tools: Pocket Screws 139

Workshop Tips .142
  No-dent finish nailing, sanding
  bumper, photo sculptures and more...

Mission Oak Built-In Bookcase 145

Window Cornices 155

Fast Furniture Fixes 160
  Patch gouges, touch up scratches,
  clean gummy surfaces

3-HOUR CEDAR BENCH

Build it for 70 bucks in one afternoon!

by **Travis Larson**

The beauty of this cedar bench isn't just that it's easy to assemble and inexpensive—it's that it's so doggone comfortable. You can comfortably sit on your custom-fit bench for hours, even without cushions. In this story, we'll show you how to build the bench and how to adjust it for maximum comfort.

Sloping the back and the seat is the secret to pain-free perching on unpadded flat boards. But not all bodies are the same, and it's a rare piece of furniture that everyone agrees is seatworthy. This bench has a bolted pivot point where the back and seat meet that lets you alter the backrest and seat slopes to fit your build during one of the final assembly steps (**Photo 10**). The materials will cost about $70, and cutting and assembly will only take about three hours. Follow the step-by-step photo series for details on the simple construction.

SHOPPING LIST

DESCRIPTION	QUANTITY	DESCRIPTION	QUANTITY
1x3 x 8' cedar	2	3" deck screws	1 lb.
2x10 x 8' cedar	1	6d galv. casing nails	1/4 lb.
2x4 x 8' cedar	5	3/8" x 5" bolts with nuts and washers	2

Fig. A: Bench Parts

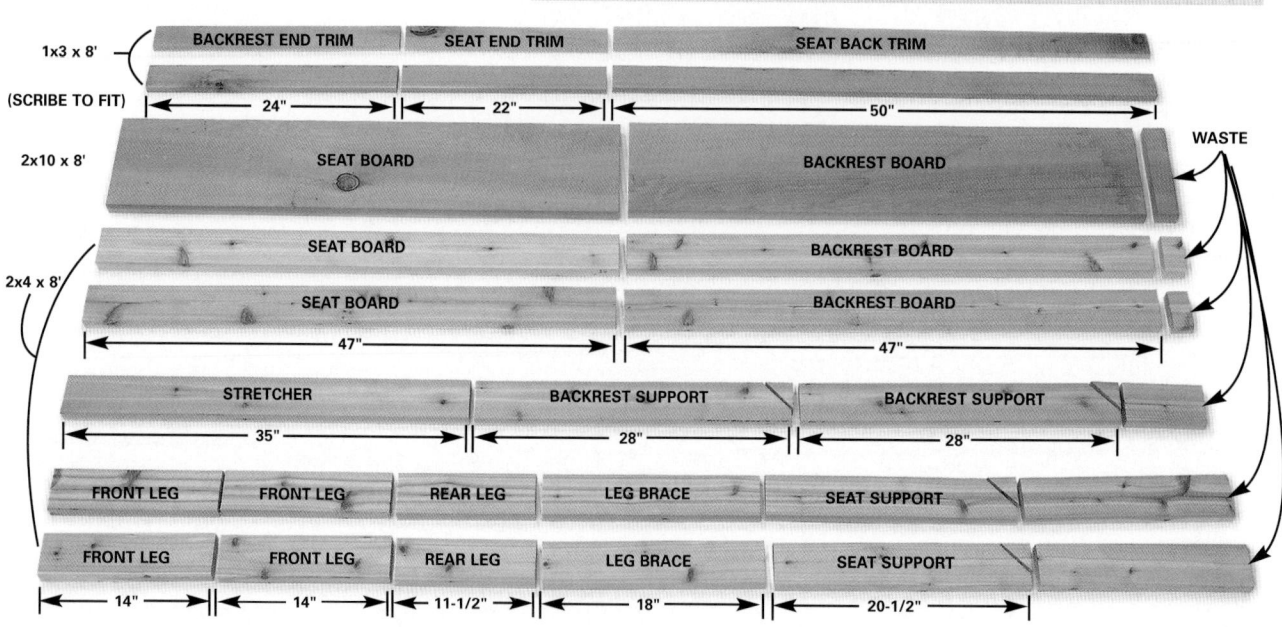

134

Build it from eight 8-ft. long boards and a handful of fasteners

A circular saw and a screw gun are the only power tools you really need for construction, although a power miter saw will speed things up and give you cleaner cuts. Begin by cutting the boards to length. **Fig. A** shows you how to cut up the eight boards efficiently, leaving little waste. When you're picking out the wood at the lumberyard, choose boards that above all are flat, not twisted. That's especially important for the seat and back parts. Don't worry so much about the leg assembly 2x4s because you

cut them into such short pieces that warps and twists aren't much of a concern.

After cutting the pieces to length, screw together the leg assemblies (**Photos** 2 – 6). It's important to use a square to keep the leg braces square to the legs (**Photo 2**). That way both leg assemblies will be identical and the bench won't wobble if it's put on a hard, flat surface. We spaced the leg brace 1/2 in. back from the front of the legs to create a more attractive shadow line. Then it's just a matter of connecting the leg assemblies with the stretcher (**Photo 7**), screwing down the seat and backrest boards,

1 **CUT OUT** the bench parts following the measurements in Fig. A. Use a square to guide the circular saw for accurate, square cuts. Cut 45-degree angles on the ends of the seat and back supports 1 in. down from the ends as shown (also see Photos 4 and 5).

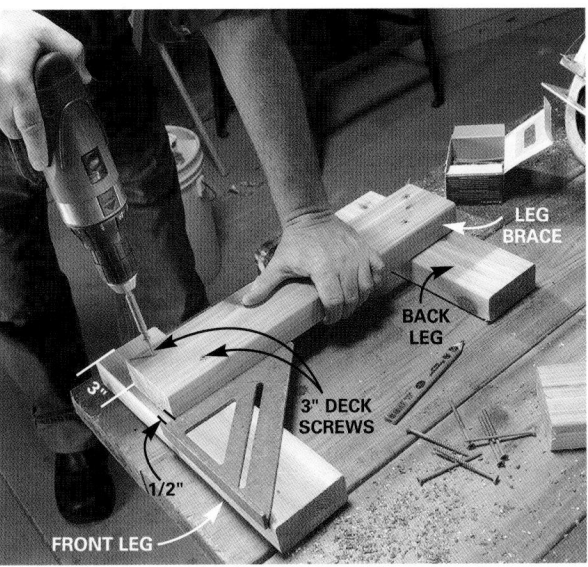

2 **FASTEN** the leg brace to the legs 3 in. above the bottom ends. Angle the 3-in. screws slightly to prevent the screw tips from protruding. Hold the brace 1/2 in. back from the front edge of the front leg. Use a square to make sure the brace and legs are at exact right angles.

3 **ALIGN** the second part of the front leg with the first one using a square and screw it to the leg brace as shown.

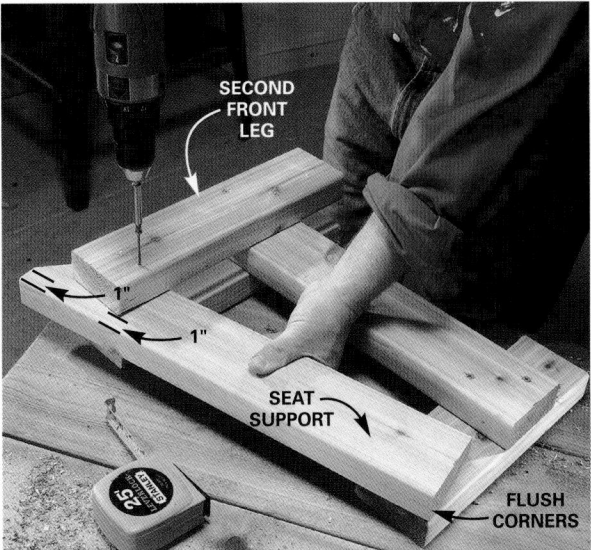

4 **SLIP** the seat support between the two front legs, positioning it as shown. Drive a single 3-in. screw through the front leg into the seat support.

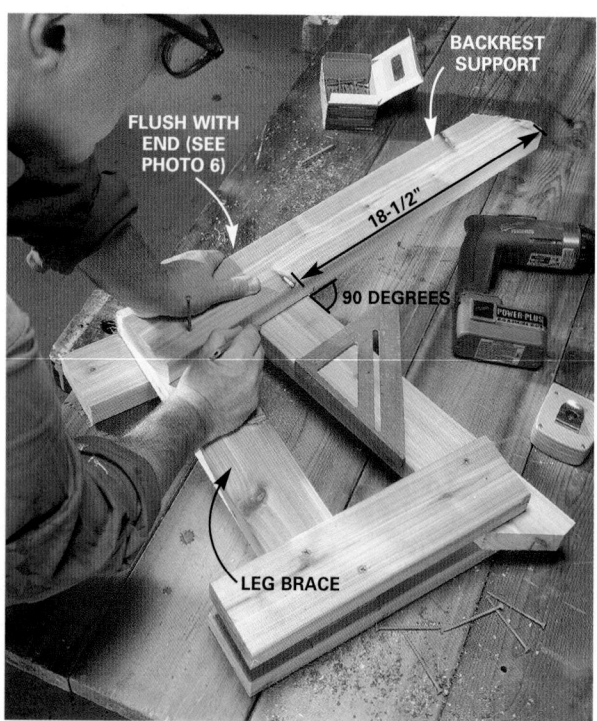

FLUSH WITH
END (SEE
PHOTO 6)

BACKREST
SUPPORT

18-1/2"

90 DEGREES

LEG BRACE

5 POSITION the backrest support on the leg assembly as shown, making sure it's at a right angle with the seat support, and mark the position on the seat support. Then drive a 3-in. screw through the middle of the backrest support into the leg brace.

3/8" x 5"
PIVOT BOLT

FLUSH AT
CORNER

6 CLAMP the backrest support, seat support and rear leg as shown using the line as a guide. Drill a 3/8-in. hole through the center of the assembly. Drive a 3/8-in. x 5-in. bolt fitted with a washer through the hole and slightly tighten the nut against a washer on the other side.

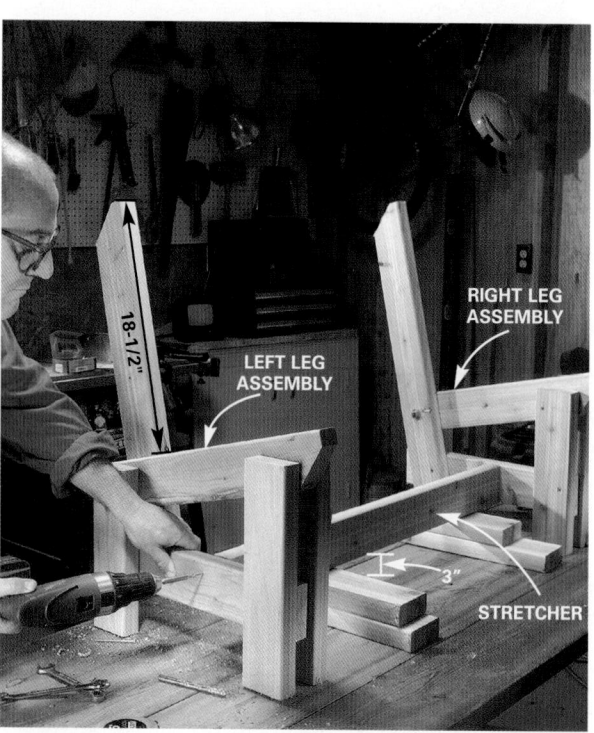

18-1/2"

LEFT LEG
ASSEMBLY

RIGHT LEG
ASSEMBLY

3"

STRETCHER

7 ASSEMBLE the other leg assembly to mirror the first as shown. (The back support and rear leg switch sides.) Prop the stretcher 3 in. above the workbench, center it between the front and rear bench legs and screw the leg braces into the ends with two 3-in. deck screws.

FIRST
BOARD

PENCIL
SPACER

FLUSH
EDGES

8 CENTER the first 2x4 seat board over the leg assemblies and flush with the front ends of the seat supports. Screw it to the seat supports with two 3-in. deck screws spaced about 1 in. away from the edges. Line up the 2x10 with the first 2x4, space it about 5/16 in. away (the thickness of a carpenter's pencil) and screw it to the seat supports with two 3-in. deck screws. Repeat with the rear 2x4.

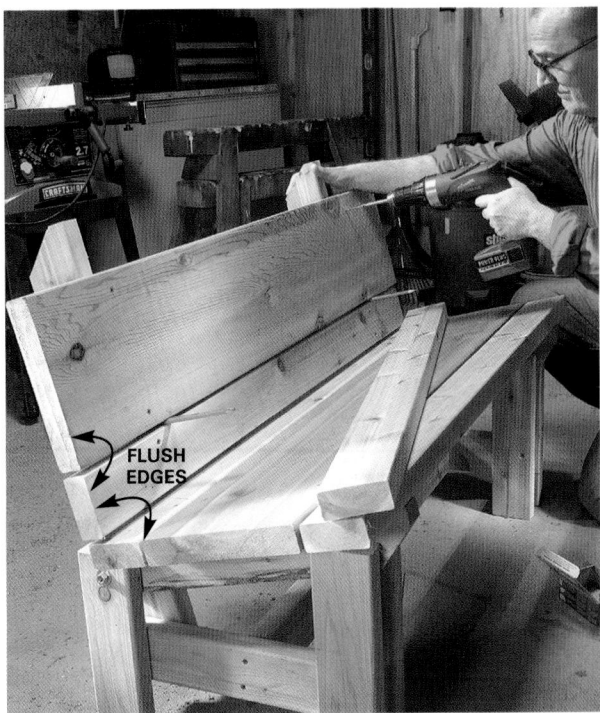

9 REST the bottom backrest 2x4 on carpenter's pencils, holding the end flush with the seat boards and screw it to the seat back braces. Then space and screw on the center 2x10 and the top 2x4 backrest boards.

FLUSH EDGES

and adjusting the slopes to fit your body.

The easiest way to adjust the slope is to hold the four locking points in place with clamps and then back out the temporary screws (Photo 10). To customize the slopes, you just loosen the clamps, make the adjustments, retighten and test the fit. When you're satisfied, run a couple of permanent screws into each joint. If you don't have clamps, don't worry—you'll just have to back out the screws, adjust the slopes, reset the screws and test the bench. Clamps just speed up the process.

Round over the edges

We show an option of rounding over the sharp edge of the 1x3 trim, which is best done with a router and a 1/2-in. round-over bit (Photo 12). Rounding over the edges can protect shins and the backs of thighs and leave teetering toddlers with goose eggs on their melons instead of gashes. So the step is highly recommended. If you don't have a router, round over the edge either by hand-sanding or with an orbital or belt sander. In any event, keep the casing nails 1 in. away from the edge to prevent hitting the nailheads with the router bit or sandpaper (Photo 12).

A bench with a past

About 15 years ago, I decided to throw together some simple outdoor benches so my growing family could relax outside and enjoy the yard. But they had to be better looking and more comfortable than the flat benches they were replacing. I wanted them to feel more like a chair, be light enough to move around easily and stand up to the elements. After much experimentation, I came up with a version of this design and used it to make three benches. At times they'll be arranged around the fire ring, or for larger social gatherings, placed on the patio or deck. Most often, however, all three encircle the herb garden, our favorite outdoor hangout.

After all those years without any shelter or finish, the benches are showing their age. The crisp, new look has long passed, now replaced with puppy teeth marks, a few cracks, a deep gray hue and even some rot at the bottom of the feet. But they're still as sturdy and comfortable as the day they were made. This new version has a few improved features. I wanted to make it easier to build (no fancy angles and fewer parts), even more comfortable (adjustable to fit), and even more durable (the feet bottoms are sealed).

— T.L.

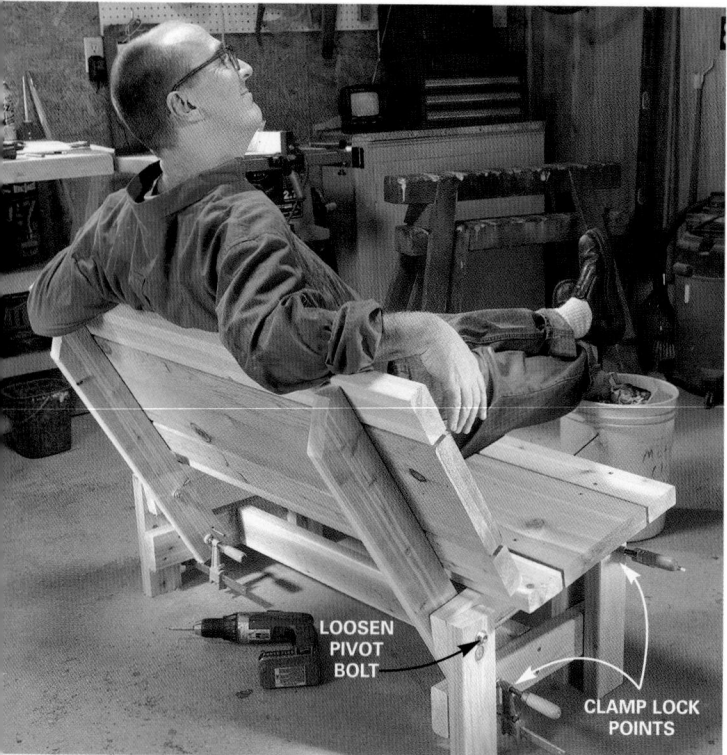

Building a longer bench

We demonstrate how to build a 4-ft. long bench, plenty of space for two. But you can use the same design and techniques for building 6- or 8-ft. long benches too. You'll just have to buy longer boards for the seat, back, stretcher and the trim boards. While you're at it, you can use the same design for matching end or coffee tables. Just match the double front leg design for the rear legs, and build flat-topped leg assemblies with an overall depth of 16-3/4 in.

Seal the legs to make it last

If you want to stain your bench, use a latex exterior stain on the parts after cutting them to length. After assembly, you won't be able to get good penetration at the cracks and crevices. Avoid clear exterior sealers, which will irritate bare skin. But the bench will last outside for more than 20 years without any stain or special care even if you decide to let it weather to a natural gray. However, the legs won't last that long because the end grain at the bottom will wick up moisture from the ground, making the legs rot long before the bench does. To make sure the legs last as long as the bench, seal the ends with epoxy, urethane or exterior woodworker's glue when you're through with the assembly 🏠

LOOSEN PIVOT BOLT

CLAMP LOCK POINTS

10 SIT on the bench and decide if you'd like to tilt the seat or the backrest or both to make the bench more comfortable. To make seat or back adjustments, loosen the bolts and clamp the bottoms of the seat back supports and the fronts of the seat supports. Then back out the four screws at those points. Loosen the clamps, make adjustments, then retighten and retest for comfort. When you're satisfied with the fit, drive in the four original screws plus another at each point. Retighten the pivot bolts.

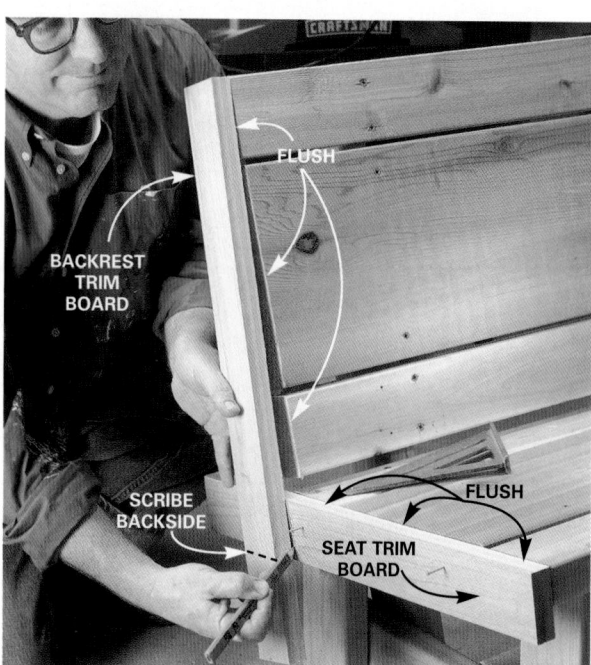

FLUSH

BACKREST TRIM BOARD

SCRIBE BACKSIDE

FLUSH

SEAT TRIM BOARD

11 TACK the seat trim boards to the seat with the ends flush with the front and top. Scribe and cut the trim boards to fit. Nail the boards to the seat and backrest boards with 6d galvanized casing nails, keeping the nails 1 in. back from the seat edges.

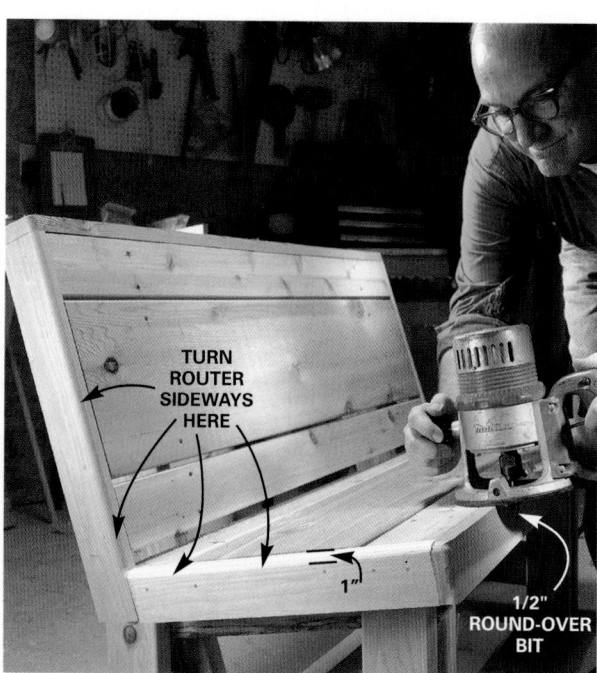

TURN ROUTER SIDEWAYS HERE

1"

1/2" ROUND-OVER BIT

12 EASE the edges of the trim boards with a router and a 1/2-in. round-over bit. Hold the router sideways to get at the seat/back corner.

Using Tools:
Pocket Screws

TIGHT JOINTS WITH POCKET SCREWS

This ingenious fastening system simplifies all types of wood joints. No fancy joints to cut, no clamps to install, no dowels or biscuits. Just drill and screw for a strong, tight joint.

Don't be put off by projects that call for tight joints or simple cabinet building. The pocket screw system is so easy to use that even a novice woodworker can make strong, tight joints. It works like this: You clamp the pocket hole jig onto your workpiece and drill angled holes with the special stepped drill bit. Then you simply align the two pieces to be joined and drive a pocket screw at an angle into the pocket to connect your pieces. The result is a tight joint that's as strong as a doweled or mortise-and-tenon joint but takes a fraction of the time to assemble.

In this article, we'll show you how to set up the jig and assemble joints using pocket screws. We'll show you techniques for assembling a face frame and a table leg and apron and for attaching shelf nosing.

Buy a top-quality jig

Less-expensive jigs that lack built-in clamps or alignment guides aren't worth messing with. The Kreg Rocket jig is a great midpriced tool. The $60 kit includes everything you'll need to get started: a pocket hole jig, a special stepped drill bit and stop collar, a 6-in. driver bit, a locking pliers–type clamp and a handful of pocket screws. Buy Kreg jigs at woodworking stores or on-line, or shop for a high-quality pocket hole jig with similar features (see the Buyer's Guide, p. 141).

ADJUSTABLE STOP COLLAR

STEPPED DRILL BIT

Setup is straightforward

Pocket screw jigs are ready to go right from the package. All you have to do is slide the stop collar over the bit, adjust the bit depth and tighten the collar (**Photo 1**). The jig is initially set up for joining 3/4-in. material with 1-1/4 in. screws. Add the plastic spacer included with the Kreg Rocket and use 2-1/2 in. long pocket screws to join 1-1/2 in. thick material like 2x4s. To join 1/2-in. thick material, reverse the stop on the front of the jig (refer to the instructions included with the jig) and use 1-in. long screws.

Using Tools: Pocket Screws

The stepped bit drills two holes at once

Photo 3 shows how to mount the jig and drill holes. Put the bit in the guide before you start the drill. Let the bit come to full speed before you push it into the wood. Withdraw the bit once or twice to eject shavings. It keeps the bit cooler and makes hole drilling easier.

Buy special screws

Pocket hole screws cost a little more, but they have three features that make them uniquely suited for pocket hole joinery: First, the self-drilling tips will easily penetrate even the hardest wood. Second, the heads are extra strong and have a square recess for slip-proof driving. For hardwood lumber, use fine-thread screws; for softer woods like pine, choose coarse-thread screws. And third, the washer head helps prevent overdriving the screws when you're joining particleboard or plywood.

There are a variety of screws available for specific applications. To check out the various types, order an assortment for about $25 from the Kreg Co. (see the Buyer's Guide, p. 141).

Hold the faces flush, then screw them together

Other than making sure your cuts are perfectly square, the only trick to getting flush, tight-fitting joints is keeping the faces lined up as you drive the screws. I've had great success using the locking pliers–type clamp included with the Kreg Rocket (Photo 4). Put the large round metal pad against the visible side of the joint and clamp the pieces together. The clamp holds the pieces while the screws pull the joint tight. Other pocket hole jig users I've talked to prefer to clamp both pieces down to a flat surface. Try it both ways and decide for yourself.

WASHER HEAD · SELF-DRILLING POINT · SQUARE RECESS

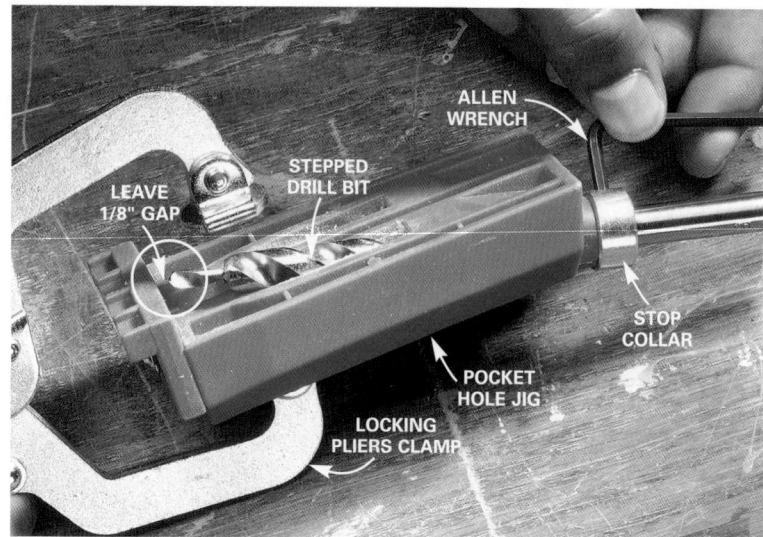

LEAVE 1/8" GAP · STEPPED DRILL BIT · ALLEN WRENCH · STOP COLLAR · POCKET HOLE JIG · LOCKING PLIERS CLAMP

1 TIGHTEN the stop collar onto the shank of the stepped drill bit. Leave a 1/8-in. space between the tip of the bit and the built-in stop on the end of the jig.

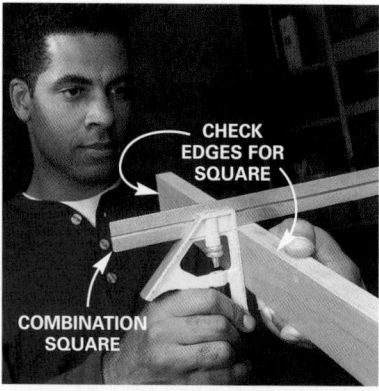

CHECK EDGES FOR SQUARE · COMBINATION SQUARE

2 CHECK to make sure the edges of the boards are square to the face. Also check the end cuts to make sure your miter box is properly adjusted to make perfectly square cuts.

3 SLIDE the stop against the end of the board, center it and clamp the jig in place. Bore two pocket holes for the screws. When you're building a cabinet face frame like this, drill the pockets parallel to the grain of the wood as shown.

POCKET HOLE JIG · SET SCREW · STOP · POCKET HOLE · FACE FRAME PART

Even though it's not necessary for a strong joint, it's good insurance to spread a thin layer of wood glue over both surfaces before screwing them together.

Pocket screws have some limitations

Most people are amazed at how easy it is to assemble strong, tight-fitting joints with pocket screws. But because the pocket holes are apparent even when they're filled, pocket screws aren't the best choice for assembling cabinet doors or other projects where both sides of the joint show. Despite this limitation, you'll find plenty of uses for a pocket hole jig around your home shop. 🏠

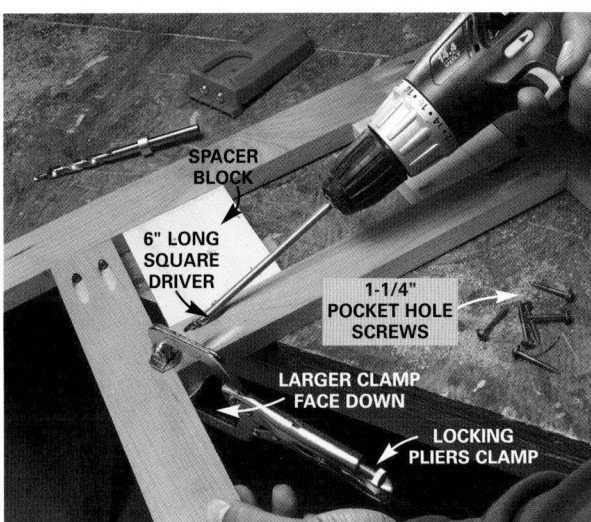

4 POSITION face frames precisely (use a spacer block here to ensure frame members are accurately aligned) and clamp the joint to hold the faces flush. Drive the pocket screws into the holes with the 6-in. long square driver bit until the joint is snug. Adjust the clutch on your drill to avoid overdriving the screw.

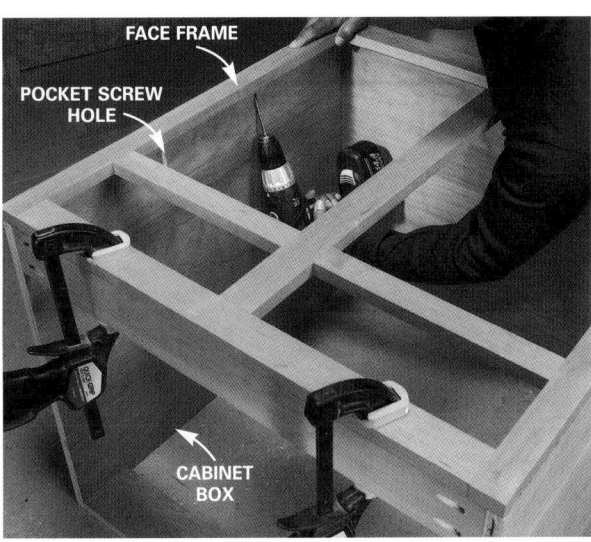

5 ASSEMBLE cabinet boxes with pocket screws by using the jig and drilling pocket holes every 8 to 12 in. along the edge of the plywood. Then glue, align and clamp the parts and screw them together. For a neater appearance, buy custom-shaped wood plugs to fill the pocket holes.

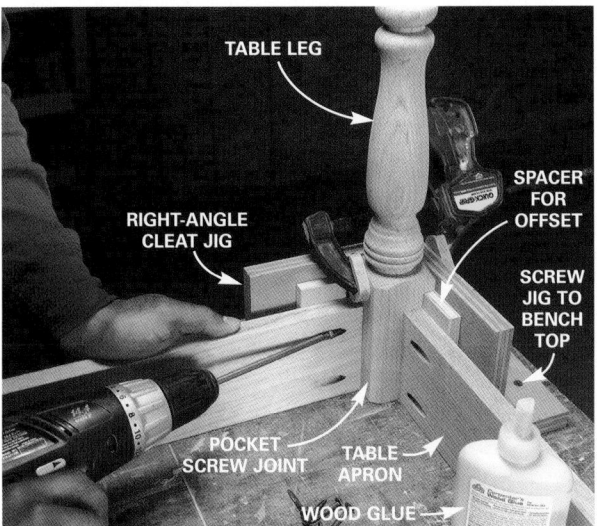

6 TO HOLD table legs in place while you attach the apron with pocket screws, build a simple right-angle jig as shown. Place spacers behind the apron boards as shown to create the desired offset.

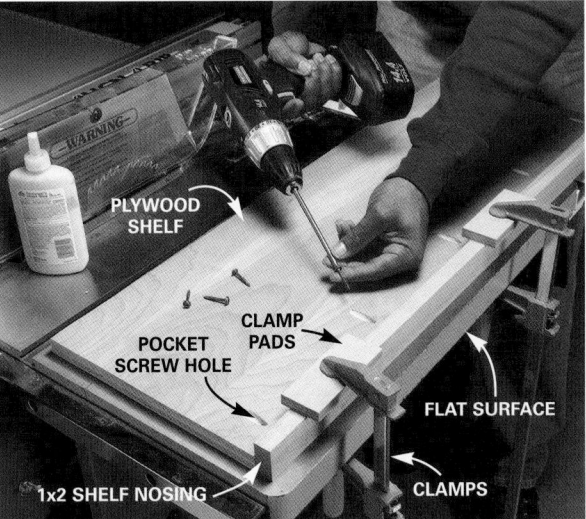

7 DRILL pockets along the edge of the plywood shelf. Clamp shelf nosing to a perfectly flat surface like the table saw top shown here. Spread a thin layer of glue along the edge of the plywood and screw the plywood to the shelf nosing. The pocket screws will draw the plywood down, resulting in a flush joint when you flip the shelf over.

Workshop Tips™

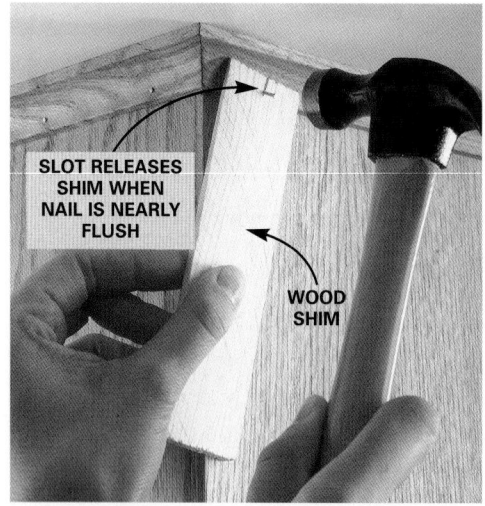

SLOT RELEASES SHIM WHEN NAIL IS NEARLY FLUSH

WOOD SHIM

NO-DENT FINISH NAILING

If you sometimes hit the wood and not the nail when applying trim or molding, try this tip. With a thin-bladed saw, saw a narrow kerf 1/4 in. into the end of a wood shim ($2 per pack at a home center). Press a finish nail into the slot, hold the shim against the molding, then drive in the nail. The soft wood shim lets you deliver a final firm blow to leave the nailhead nearly flush with the surface. Next, set the nail just below the surface with a nail set and apply wood filler.

IT'S IN THE BAG

It never fails. Every time I have an important meeting or social function, I find my hands stained from my latest woodworking project. Sound familiar? Now you can use this tip and take your hands out of your pockets on your next night out. Just slip a bread bag over your hand before you use that old sock as a stain applicator. The bag will keep the stain from penetrating the sock and getting into the pores of your skin.

SANDING BUMPER

Power sanders can really wreak havoc on inside edges of cabinets when the sander's base rubs on the adjoining edge. Avoid these unsightly scratches by taping a piece of poster board or a file folder to the side you're sanding

THIN CARDBOARD

against. When you're finished with one side, just move it to the next.

PERFECT ANGLE GLUE-UPS

Octagonal, hexagonal and even square pedestal bases for tables can be aligned perfectly for gluing with heavy-duty plastic sealing tape. Cut your bevels on the workpiece edge and lay them with the inside face

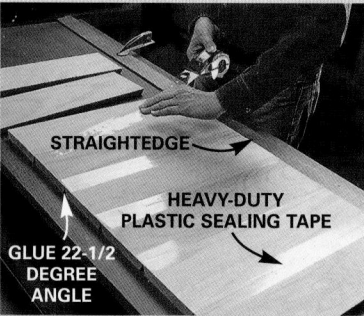

STRAIGHTEDGE

HEAVY-DUTY PLASTIC SEALING TAPE

GLUE 22-1/2 DEGREE ANGLE

BELT CLAMPS

down and one end butted to a straightedge. Align the bevels so they touch along their entire length and tape them securely. Next, carefully flip them over and apply glue to the joints. Then stand them up, fold them together, tape the final joint and pull the shape together with belt clamps. Tip: To get the angles for your shape, divide 360 by the number of sides you want, then divide this number by 2 to get the bevel angle for each side.

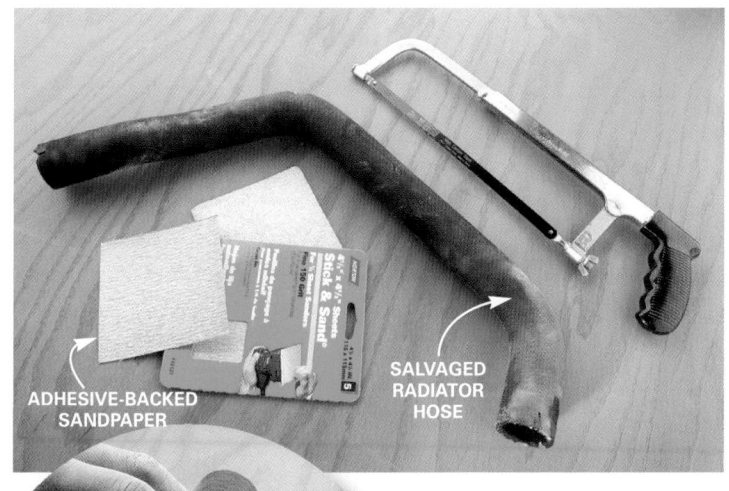

ADHESIVE-BACKED SANDPAPER

SALVAGED RADIATOR HOSE

RADIATOR HOSE CONTOUR SANDER

The "hose sander" is another great tool for sanding the curvy contours of your woodworking projects. Saw off a straight piece of discarded radiator hose with a hacksaw, clean it inside and out, and wrap a piece of adhesive-backed sandpaper around it. It works great when you bear down for coarser sanding and is just right for lighter-touch finish sanding too.

NAIL DRILL BIT

Drilling pilot holes in your latest project but can't find your itty-bitty drill bit? A nail will do the job. Cut off the nailhead with a wire cutter, then tighten the nail in the drill chuck and go to work. The chiseled tip on the end of the nail drills clean holes fast, especially in softer woods and plywood.

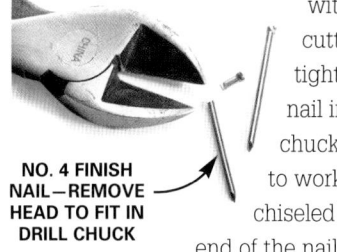

NO. 4 FINISH NAIL—REMOVE HEAD TO FIT IN DRILL CHUCK

GLUE-CLAMPING JIG FOR FRAME-AND-PANEL DOORS

Bravo—you're finally building those frame-and-panel doors to rejuvenate your kitchen. Here's a tip to ensure they turn out flat and square. Cut a piece of 3/4-in. Melamine ($8 for a 2 x 4-ft. sheet at a home center) several inches larger than the doors you're gluing. Screw a 3/4-in. x 2-in. fence board along one side, then dry-assemble the door parts and press them against the fence. Opposite the fence, screw two blocks at the door corners, angling them so there's room for a 10-degree wedge to slide in.

Now apply glue and clamp the door in the jig, tapping in the wedges to close all four joints. The flat surface of the Melamine ensures that the doors will be flat when the glue dries, and the all-wood clamping surfaces won't dent the door edges the way metal clamps often do.

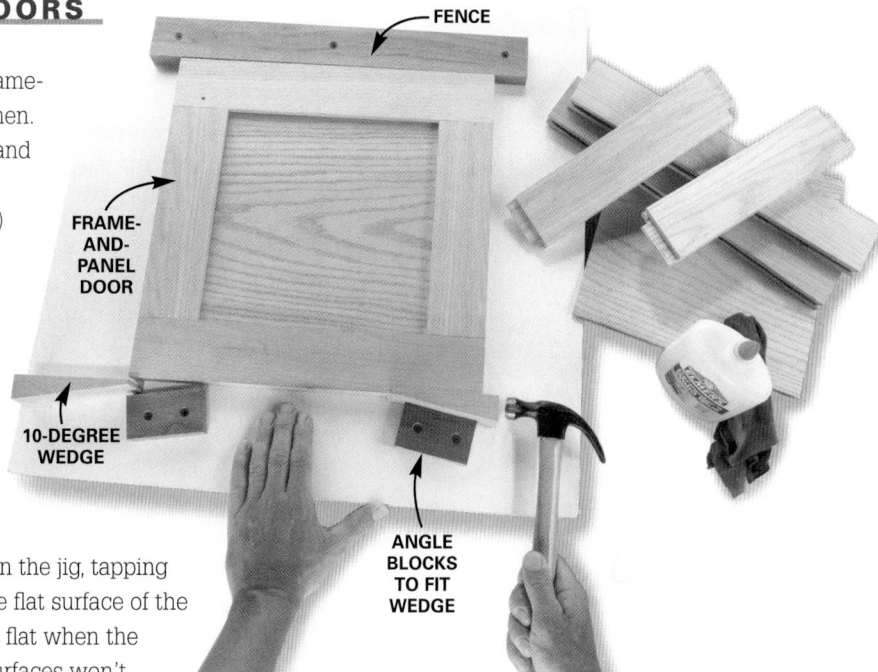

FENCE

FRAME-AND-PANEL DOOR

10-DEGREE WEDGE

ANGLE BLOCKS TO FIT WEDGE

Workshop Tips™

SPINNING PAINT STAND

Remember the last time you painted a project and halfway through realized you couldn't get at the backside? Just cut a 10-in. or larger diameter circle from a scrap of plywood or MDF and drive nails on a 1-in. grid pattern through the bottom as shown. Next, buy a lazy Susan base at a hardware store or home center. Screw the base to the disc and you're ready to paint any side with ease.

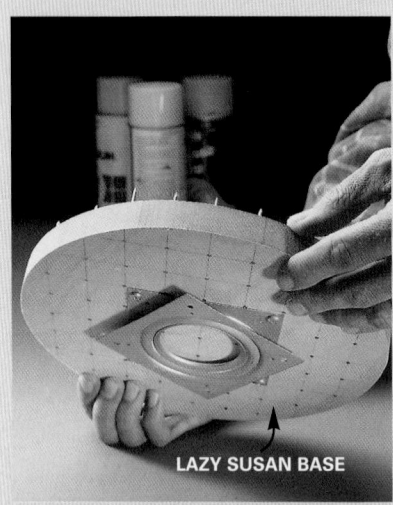

LAZY SUSAN BASE

PHOTO SCULPTURES

Surprise your friends and family with easy-to-make photo sculptures. Your favorite folks will "pop" from your photos when you use this easy technique.

CYANOACRYLATE GLUE

Here's how: Apply photo mount adhesive to pieces of 1/4-in. hardwood plywood, firmly press on the photos to be sculpted, then cut out the figures with a scroll saw. Make some wood bases from scrap wood and glue on the sculptured photos with Special-T cyanoacrylate glue (product No. 08X31; $10.99; Woodcraft, 800-225-1153). This glue will tightly bond the sculpture's bottom edge to the base, so you won't need to fiddle with notches or screws.

Hints for great-looking sculptures:

- Use a sharp No. 2 or No. 4 "skip tooth" blade ($7 for a package of 12 from Woodworker's Supply, 800-645-9292).
- Change blades when the sawn "paper edge" appears slightly ragged.
- Select a medium or high speed and feed the work at a slow rate, pressing the wood firmly on the table as you saw.
- When choosing photos to sculpt, look for clearly outlined subjects so it's easy to follow the cutting line. Hair or clothing that blends into the background is difficult to cut.

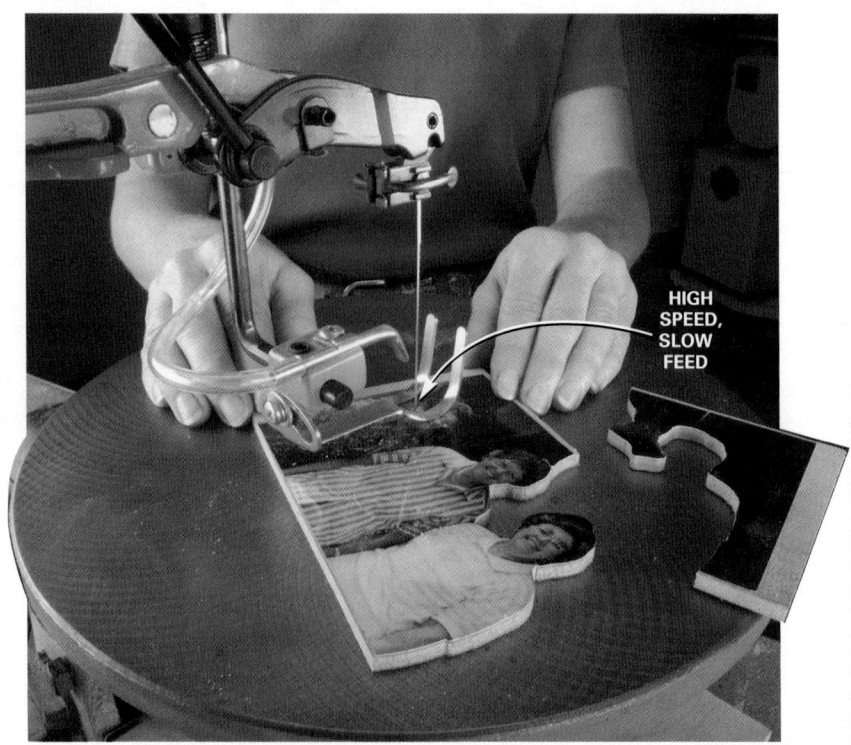

HIGH SPEED, SLOW FEED

MISSION-OAK
BUILT-IN BOOKCASE

This handsome bookcase may look difficult, but we've engineered it to go together easily without special woodworking skills

by **David Radtke**

This solid oak built-in bookcase has plenty of room for displaying your favorite books and collectibles plus lots of hidden cabinet space below. And it's easy to build. Just cut the 2x4 framework from standard lumber and screw it together. Then cut oak plywood and solid oak trim and nail them to the framework. You make the paneled cabinet doors with an ordinary table saw and join the face frames with an easy-to-use pocket hole jig.

Another plus is that you can pick up wherever you leave off at any time. You can prebuild most of it in your garage or shop and assemble the pieces as you go. Allow about five weekends for this project.

- ■ **Loads of adjustable shelf space**
- ■ **Vertical-grain solid oak construction**
- ■ **Easy-to-alter dimensions to fit your room**
- ■ **Tapered columns— simplified**

Customize it to fit your room

The bookcase measurements we give are based on our room, which has an 8-ft. ceiling and measures just a skosh over 12 ft. wide. If your room is a bit wider, just move each middle column away from the side walls by one-third of the difference. The columns near the wall stay where we've located them. For example, if your room is 12 ft. 9 in. wide, just move each center column one-third the difference of 9 in., or 3 in., farther from each wall than the measurement we give in **Photo 4**. If your room is taller, you'll need to stretch out the section of the bookcase above the cabinet doors; your columns will taper more gradually, but not enough to notice.

SHOPPING LIST

DESCRIPTION	QUANTITY	DESCRIPTION	QUANTITY
1x10 x 12' No. 2 pine arches (A)	2	1x6 x 16' oak base (V4)	1
1x4 x 12' No. 2 pine (B, K2, N2)	3	1x8 x 2' oak (X2)	1
1x6 x 8' No. 2 pine (Z2, U1, U2, V2)	3	1/2" x 5-1/2" x 12' cedar siding	1
2x4 x 12' pine (C)	2	No-mortise hinges	6 pr.
2x6 x 8' pine (V1)	1	Shelf clips	48
2x4 x 8' pine (G, D, H)	12	Wood glue	16 ozs.
1/4" x 4' x 8' oak plywood (F, T)	1	1" nails for nail gun	1 pkg.
3/4" x 4' x 8' oak plywood (J, L, K1, K3, Z1)	4	1-1/2" nails for nail gun	1 pkg.
1x4 x 8' oak (M, W, V3, X1)	5	2" nails for nail gun	1 pkg.
1x10 x 12' oak (N1)	1	10d casing nails	2 doz.
1x4 x 8' oak (P1, P2, P3, Q2)	8	Knobs and magnet catches for doors	6
1x6 x 12' oak (E, P4, Y1, Y2, Y3, R1, R2, S1, S2)	5	Stain	2 qts.
1x6 x 8' oak (Q1)	8	Varnish	3 qts.

CUTTING LIST

KEY	QTY.	SIZE & DESCRIPTION	KEY	QTY.	SIZE & DESCRIPTION
A	2	3/4" x 9-1/4" x 144" pine arch (cut to fit)	Q1	4	3/4" x 10" x 87" oak column blanks
B	11	3/4" x 3-1/2" x 10-3/8" cross ties	Q2	8	3/4" x 1-1/4" x 87" oak column sides
C	2	1-1/2" x 3-1/2" x 144" 2x4 base (cut to fit)	Q3	4	5/16" x 3/4" x 8" oak daggers
D	9	1-1/2" x 3-1/2" x 8-7/8" 2x4 cross ties	R1	12	3/4" x 2 1/2" x 11" oak door rails
E	2	3/4" x 5" x 11-7/8" oak fillers	R2	6	3/4" x 2-1/2" x 30" oak face frame rails
F	3	1/4" x 11-7/8" x 96" oak plywood rips (cut to fit)	S1	12	3/4" x 2-1/2" x 15" oak door stiles
G	10	1-1/2" x 3-1/2" x 96" vertical supports (cut to fit)	S2	6	3/4" x 4-3/4" x 20" oak face frame stiles
H	8	1-1/2" x 3-1/2" x 8-7/8" 2x4 filler blocks	T	6	1/4" x 10-7/8" x 10-7/8" oak plywood door panels
J	6	3/4" x 11-7/8" x 20" oak plywood cabinet sides	U1	6	3/4" x 3/4" x 39-1/2" pine face frame cleats
K1	3	3/4" x 11-7/8" x 41-1/2" oak plywood cabinet tops (cut to fit)	U2	8	3/4" x 1-1/4" x 60" pine upper column backers
K2	3	3/4" x 2-1/2" x 40" pine cleats (cut to fit)	V1	4	1-1/2" x 4" x 8-1/2" pine column base fillers
K3	12	3/4" x 10-3/4" x 40" oak plywood shelf blanks (cut to fit)	V2	4	3/4" x 4" x 8-1/2" pine column base fillers
L	6	3/4" x 11-7/8" x 70" oak plywood bookcase sides (cut to fit)	V3	4	3/4" x 3-1/2" x 11" oak column plinths
M	2	3/4" x 3-1/4" x 84" oak filler boards (cut to fit)	V4	16 ft.	3/4" x 4" oak baseboards
N1	1	3/4" x 9-1/4" x 144" oak arch (cut to fit)	W	10 ft.	3/4" x 1-1/4" oak capital molding
N2	1	3/4" x 1-1/4" x 144" pine filler (cut to fit)	X1	6	2-1/4" x 2" x 3-1/2" oak cornice blocks
P1	6 ft.	3/4" x 1-3/4" oak capital face molding (cut to fit)	X2	1	2-1/4" x 6" x 6" oak keystone
P2	12 ft.	3/4" x 1-1/2" cabinet top front molding (cut to fit)	Y1	12 ft.	3/4" x 2-3/4" oak cornice molding (cut to fit)
P3	12	3/4" x 1-1/4" x 40" oak shelf nosing molding (cut to fit)	Y2	12 ft.	3/4" x 2" oak cornice molding (cut to fit)
			Y3	12 ft.	3/4" x 5/8" oak cornice molding (cut to fit)
P4	12	3/4" x 1" x 40" oak shelf back reinforcing slat (cut to fit)	Z1	3	3/4" x 2" x 39" oak plywood cabinet top extensions (cut to fit)
			Z2	3	3/4" x 3/4" x 39" pine top extension cleats (cut to fit)

Undersize the upper apron and base assemblies

Measure the room width at the top, middle and base of your room. Take the narrowest measurement and subtract 3/8 in. from that. This will give you just the right amount of maneuvering room to get the apron assembly (Photo 3) off the floor and up to the ceiling without having to use a sledgehammer. Do the same for the 2x4 base assembly (Photo 4).

Fig. A:
Bookcase Details

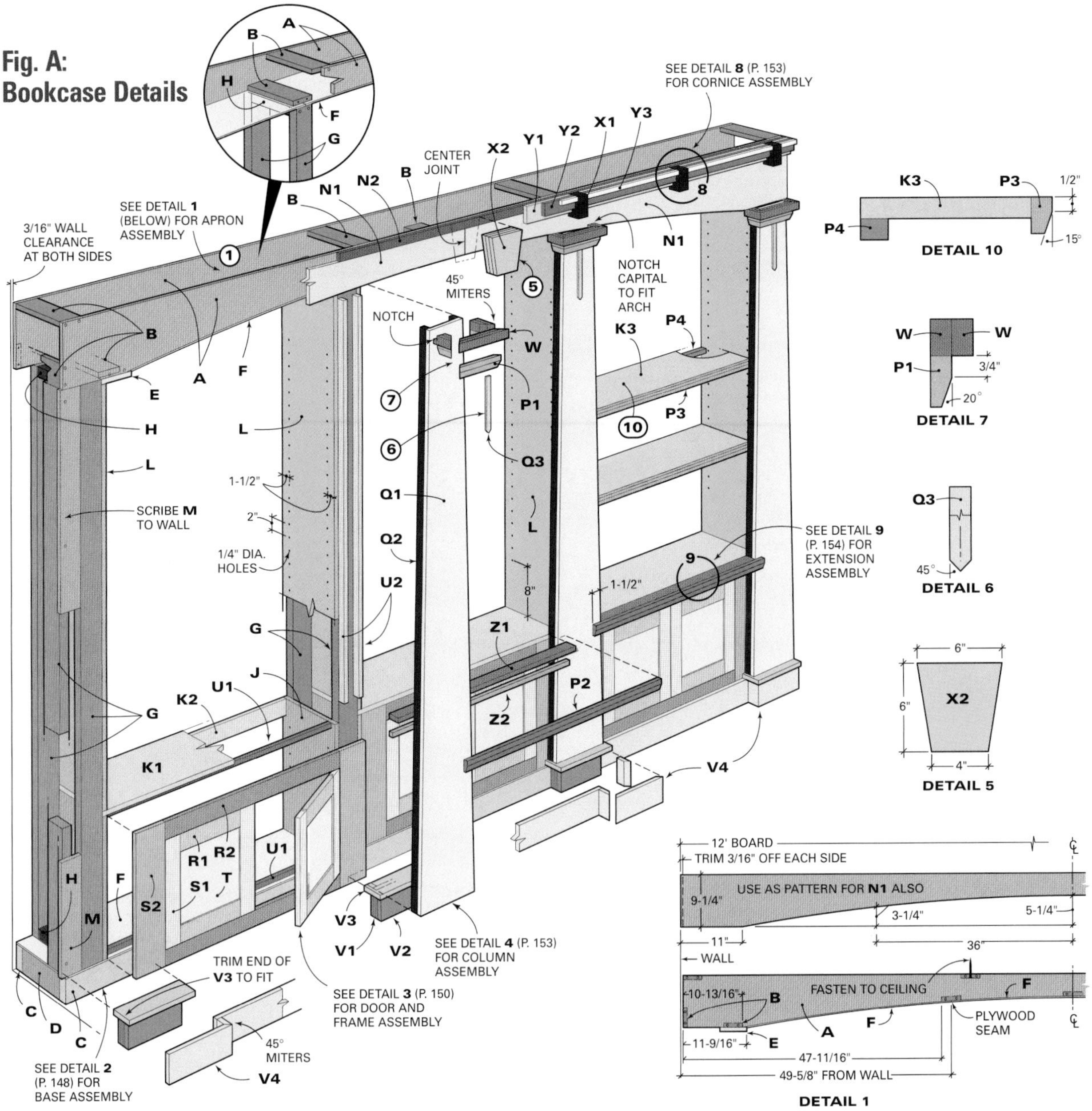

SEE DETAIL **1**
(BELOW) FOR APRON
ASSEMBLY

3/16" WALL
CLEARANCE
AT BOTH SIDES

SEE DETAIL **8** (P. 153)
FOR CORNICE ASSEMBLY

CENTER
JOINT

45°
MITERS

NOTCH

NOTCH
CAPITAL
TO FIT
ARCH

SCRIBE **M**
TO WALL

1-1/2"

2"

1/4" DIA.
HOLES

8"

1-1/2"

SEE DETAIL **9**
(P. 154) FOR
EXTENSION
ASSEMBLY

DETAIL 10

DETAIL 7

W
W
P1
3/4"
20°

DETAIL 6
Q3
45°

DETAIL 5
6"
X2
6"
4"

TRIM END OF
V3 TO FIT

45°
MITERS

SEE DETAIL **4** (P. 153)
FOR COLUMN
ASSEMBLY

SEE DETAIL **3** (P. 150)
FOR DOOR AND
FRAME ASSEMBLY

SEE DETAIL **2**
(P. 148) FOR
BASE ASSEMBLY

DETAIL 1

12' BOARD
TRIM 3/16" OFF EACH SIDE

USE AS PATTERN FOR **N1** ALSO

9-1/4"
3-1/4"
5-1/4"

11"
36"

WALL

10-13/16"
B
FASTEN TO CEILING
F

A
F
PLYWOOD
SEAM

11-9/16"
E
47-11/16"
49-5/8" FROM WALL

Our bookcase cost about $1,500, including the hardware and finish. That's not a lot of money compared with the price of a quality store-bought bookcase. If you shop around at local lumber suppliers, you may be able to save money. We used special rift-sawn oak, which we ordered from a local supplier. Its long, straight grain keeps the project from looking too busy and helps disguise glue joints like those in the center of the columns. The effect is a wide, evenly grained board. You can, however, sort through pieces at a home center and find nice-looking pieces that will match well. Whatever wood you choose, figure on spending about 40 hours or more to build and finish this project.

You'll need a table saw and a circular saw for this project, and we suggest using a pocket hole jig (see Buyer's Guide, p. 154) for the face frames (**Photo 10**) and

the cabinet top extensions (**Photo 21**). If you've never used a pocket hole jig, you'll find it easy to use with the instructions provided. It's a slick way to firmly hold wood joints without gluing and clamping. A doweling jig, however, is a good substitute for this part of the project.

If you don't have an air-powered finish nailer, here's a good excuse to buy one! You can buy inexpensive finish nailers at home centers or rent them when you do the major assembly work. I'd recommend an 18-gauge brad nailer ($100) for the smaller

Tip

Sand plywood sides, columns and door assemblies before you install them. You'll do a better job if you avoid working in difficult, strained positions.

pieces of trim and a 15-gauge finish nailer ($150) for nailing the columns and baseboards in place. You'll also need a screw gun, a belt sander and a finish sander along with your basic carpentry and layout tools.

Study **Fig. A** on p. 147 carefully for construction details, then read the text for added information and tips on building the doors, columns and cornice details. Follow the how-to photos as a step-by-step guide to the building process.

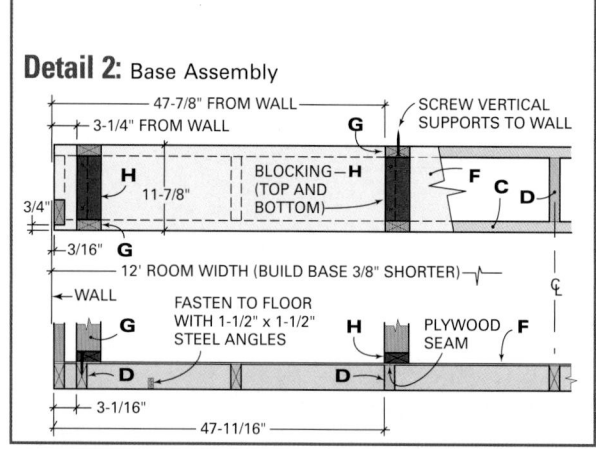

Detail 2: Base Assembly

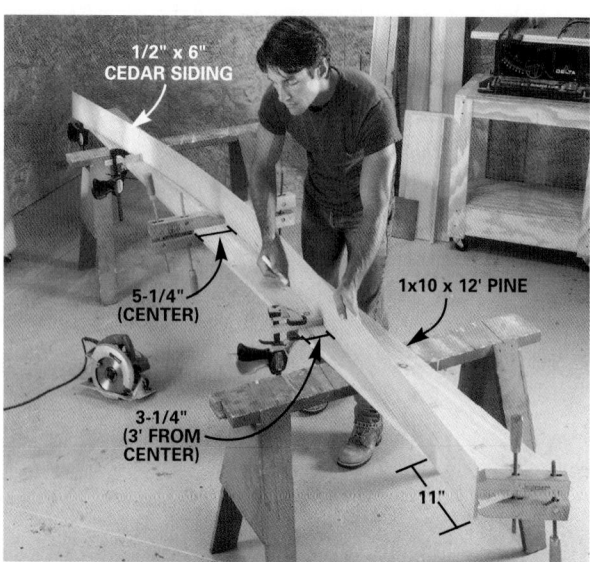

1 BEND a piece of clear cedar siding to form an arch. Trace the curves as shown onto the two 1x10 x 12-ft. upper arch pieces of the frame. Cut these pieces 3/8 in. shorter than the width of your room so you'll be able to maneuver it into position.

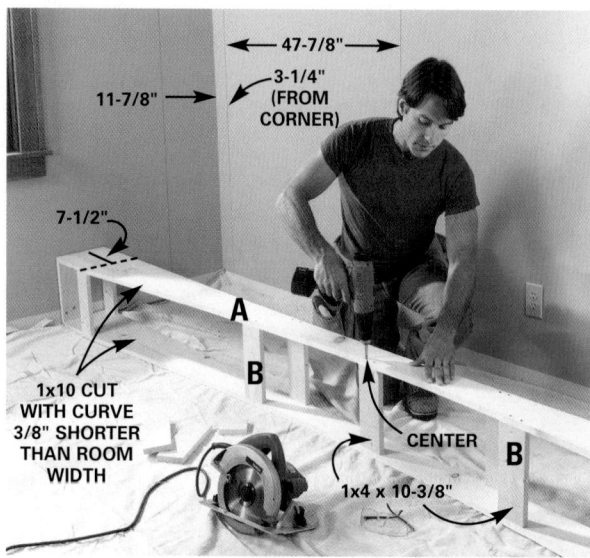

2 CARRY the two arched aprons into your room and screw 1x4s between them as shown with 1-5/8 in. wood screws. Drill pilot and countersink holes to avoid splitting the wood. Be sure to complete the layout lines on the wall (Photo 4 and Detail 2, above).

3 LIFT the apron assembly to the ceiling and build a temporary stand for each end to keep it tight to the ceiling as you screw it to the framing. If framing is difficult to find in key areas, use wall anchors (top photo, p. 149) to fasten it to the ceiling and side walls.

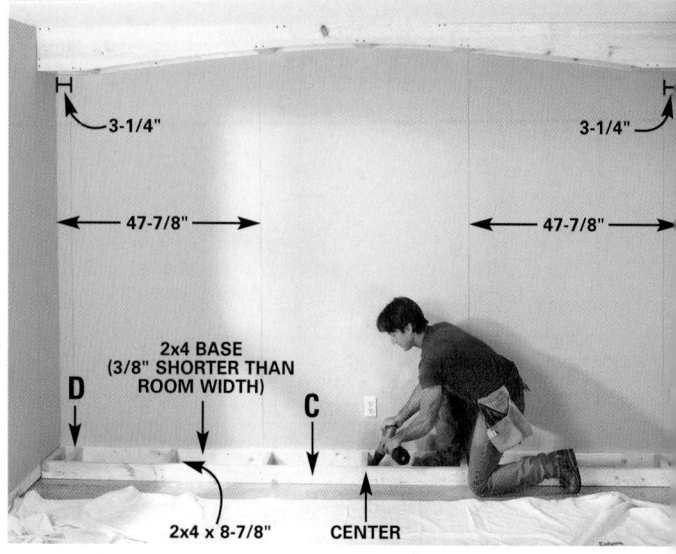

4 BUILD the 2x4 base as shown in Detail 2, above, and screw it to the floor with 1-1/2 in. x 1-1/2 in. steel angles. Space the 2x4 blocks so the vertical uprights marked on the walls will stand directly over them later.

Measure carefully as you lay out the room

The design of this project is forgiving for rooms that are a bit out of whack. If one of your side walls is out of plumb slightly, the taper of the columns will disguise it. If your floor slopes slightly from left to right, it's best to split the difference and make it flow with the room rather than trying to level the whole project. Just be sure to

Anchoring 2x4s to drywall

You'll most likely need to drill holes and screw the vertical supports to the drywall with screws and wall anchors. Place the 2x4 and drill 3/16-in. holes to mark the drywall. Remove the 2x4, then screw anchors into the drywall at these locations. If there's framing behind the 2x4, screw the support directly to it with 3-in. wood screws.

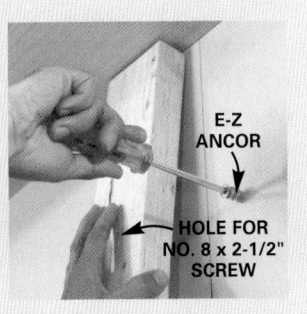

E-Z ANCOR

HOLE FOR NO. 8 x 2-1/2" SCREW

49-5/8" FROM WALL

I

F

11-3/4"

1/4" PLYWOOD RIPPED TO 11-7/8"

E

5 CUT two 3/4-in. x 5-in. blocks 11-7/8 in. long (E) and screw them to the underside of the aprons 11-3/4 in. from each side wall. These blocks will catch the edge of the 1/4-in. plywood top and hold it in place. Rip the 1/4-in. oak plywood to 11-7/8 in. and hold it tight to the apron while you mark the length. Install it so the splice will be hidden under the column as shown. Do the same to cover the base assembly as well. Use 1-in. finish nails in your nail gun to secure the plywood to each assembly.

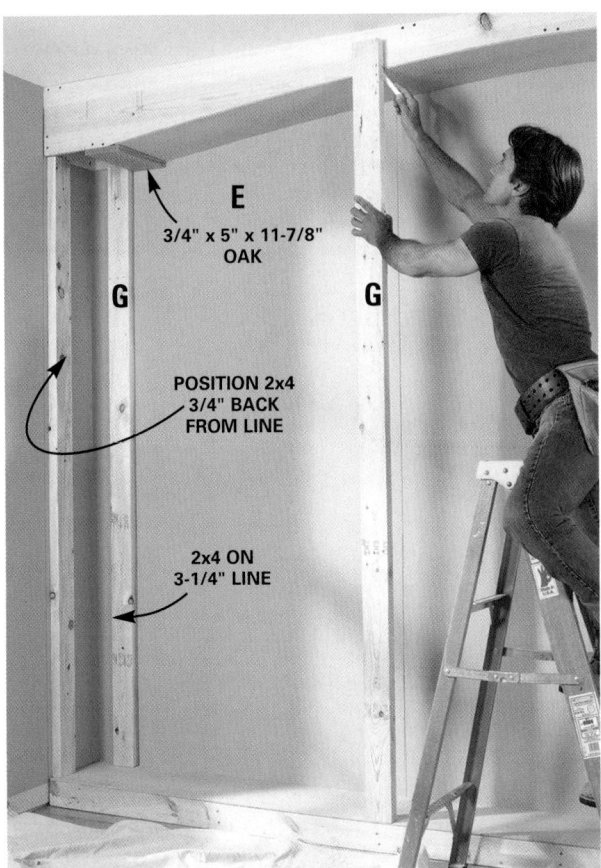

E
3/4" x 5" x 11-7/8" OAK

G

G

POSITION 2x4 3/4" BACK FROM LINE

2x4 ON 3-1/4" LINE

6 FASTEN the 2x4s to the wall as shown. Use E-Z Ancors (photo at top right) if wall framing isn't available behind the 2x4s. Scribe the 2x4 supports to fit under the curve. Note that the 2x4 supports on each side wall are set back 3/4 in. behind the 11-7/8 in. mark.

L

M

1/4" HOLES SPACED 2" APART

KEEP HOLES 1-1/2" FROM EDGE

L

L

K1

K1

J

3/4" PLYWOOD TOP

3/4" PLYWOOD SIDES

8"

7 RIP 3/4-in. oak plywood to 11-7/8 in. and then drill 1/4-in. holes for standard shelf clips. Use a strip of 1/4-in. Peg-Board as a template for the shelf clip holes. Drill the holes, positioning the template to the bottom of each piece to ensure the shelves will be level when installed.

install the 2x4 verticals plumb.

The odd measurement of 11-7/8 in. for the depth allows you to cut four sides (**Photo 7**) from a single sheet of 4 x 8-ft. oak plywood. We found that even oversized books fit comfortably on the bookcase, especially on the cabinet tops just above the doors. Here the depth increases to nearly 14-3/4 in. Follow **Photos 2 – 6** to get your layout lines in the right spots.

Buy good framing lumber

It's essential to use straight 2x4s and 3/4-in. boards to get the skeletal part of the bookcase correct. Bows and twists will make your job more difficult. Buy a couple of extra

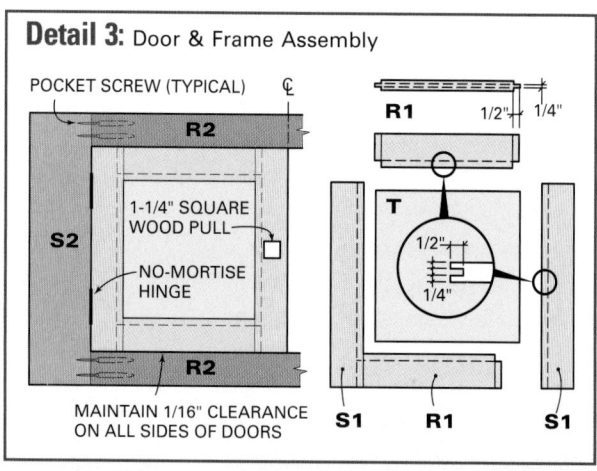

Detail 3: Door & Frame Assembly

8 NAIL a 3/4-in. x 1-1/4 in. filler to the top of the apron assembly, then nail the arched 1x10 oak pieces (cut in half to fit) to the apron assembly. Scribe the pieces to the side walls if necessary. The center joint will be covered by the keystone trim later.

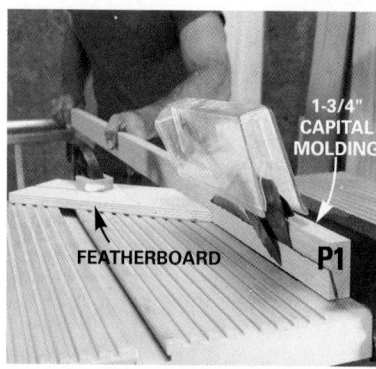

9 SET your saw to 20 degrees and taper the upper capital molding and the top shelf face molding (Fig. A). Make the front shelf molding in the same manner, only cut it from 1-1/2 in. strips.

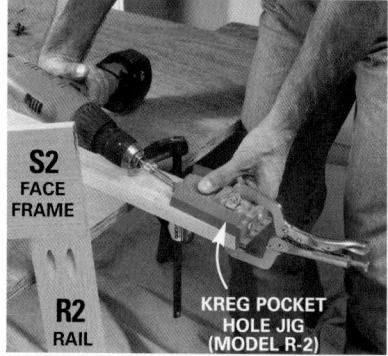

10 BUILD the face frames as shown in Detail 3 using the pocket hole jig (see Buyer's Guide, p. 154). The jig drills holes at sharp angles to connect the stiles and rails tightly without glue. If you have a doweling jig, this will work as well.

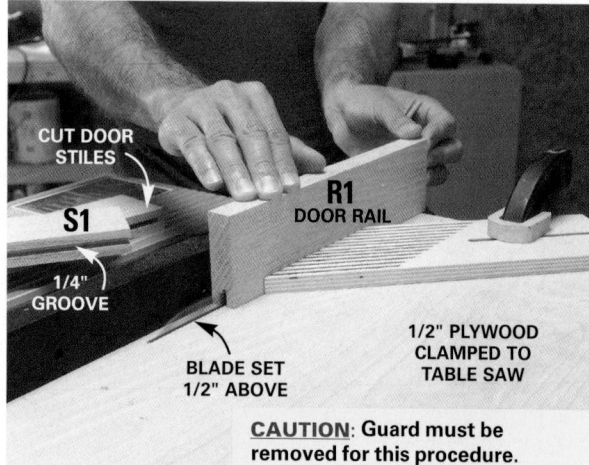

CAUTION: Guard must be removed for this procedure.

11 GROOVE the inside edges of stiles and rails for each door using a table saw. Cut the 1/2-in. deep grooves in the center of the edge. Run the piece through on one side, then flip it end-for-end and run it through on the other side to ensure the groove is centered. Because we had a wide throat plate space next to our saw blade, we measured to our fence first, lowered the blade, then installed a 1/2-in. piece of plywood on the saw table and raised the blade. This gave us a safe, stable, flat surface to cut the grooves.

CAUTION: Guard must be removed for this procedure.

12 CUT tenons on each end of the door rails using your table saw fence as a guide. The tongues should be 1/2 in. long and must fit snugly into the grooves of the stiles. Cut a test piece first to get the right setting.

pieces and store all your lumber in the house for about a week to acclimate it. Central heating has a way of taking a reasonably straight piece of lumber and quickly turning it into a banana. If you buy lumber at a home center where the stuff is reasonably dry and stored inside, you can usually assume it'll hold its shape.

Use a strip of 1/4-in. Peg-Board as a drilling guide

Getting precise holes into the 3/4-in. plywood sides for your shelf supports is a must for a project like this. To make a foolproof template, rip a 3-in. wide strip from a sheet of Peg-Board (use the rest of it to organize your shop space). Label the top and bottom, then use small brads to temporarily tack it to each panel. The holes on the Peg-Board are spaced every 2 in. Tape over the holes you won't be using. Then drill 1/4-in. holes 1/2 in. deep into the panels (J and L). Buy a stop collar and a new brad point bit to get clean, unsplintered holes. We left 8 in. free of holes on the bottom of each side panel, since it would be useless to position a shelf any lower. Reuse this same strip for each piece. Don't be sloppy here or you could widen the holes of your template and pay the price with uneven shelves.

Make the doors with your table saw

You won't need a router or a shaper or even a dado blade for your table saw to make these simple doors. A standard carbide blade set at the correct height and some careful fence adjustments will give you great results. The key to success here is to use sacrificial scraps to get your settings just right. It usually takes a bit of tweaking to get your setups just right.

Start by cutting the grooves. Set the fence just a hair over 1/4 in. from the blade, then lower the blade below the table. For safety, place a 1/2-in. piece of plywood over the blade area and against the fence and clamp it to the saw table (**Photo 11**). Start your saw and raise the blade until it comes through about 3/4 in. Shut off the saw and lower the blade until it's 1/2 in. above the plywood surface. Now, start the saw and run the scrap piece through the blade on edge as shown in **Photo 11**. When you've made

Tip	When you glue up your door pieces, apply glue both to the sides of the tenon and in the groove where the tenon will fit. Don't use too much glue or you'll have extra scraping and sanding to do when it oozes. A good glue job will force only tiny beads from the joint as you clamp it.

13 ASSEMBLE the doors as shown. First, glue the tenons of the top rail into the grooves of the stiles, then slip the plywood panel in place. No need to glue the plywood; just let it float in the grooves. The plywood should be 1/8 in. narrower and shorter than the distance from groove to groove to ensure a foolproof assembly. Clamp the doors, making sure they lie flat. Clamps can pull the frames and warp them if you're not careful.

14 INSTALL no-mortise hinges (see Buyer's Guide) on the stiles and the door edges before installing the face frames in the bookcase. Make sure to leave 1/16-in. clearance between the doors and the face frame. If necessary, use a belt sander to fit the doors precisely in the face frame openings. Attach the knobs to the doors, hang them on the hinges and nail the assembly to 3/4-in. x 3/4-in. pine strips set back and glued into the cabinets.

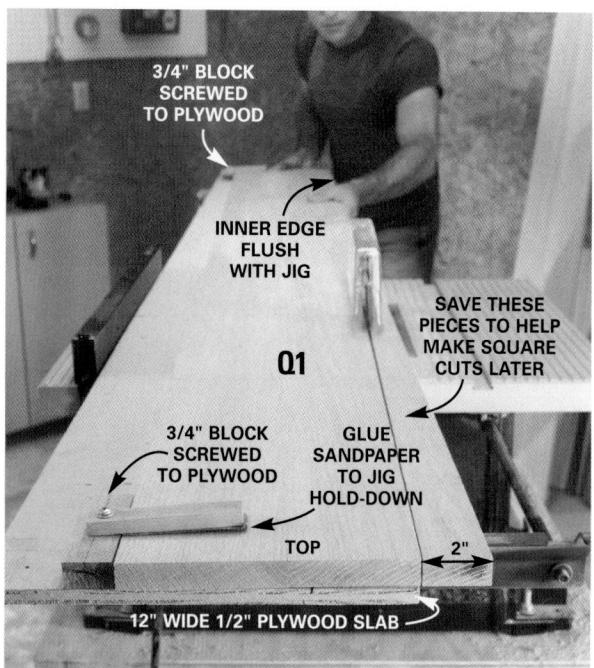

15 GLUE and clamp two pieces of 1x6 x 87-in. oak together and then rip them to 10 in. wide, keeping the glue joint at the center. Square both ends. Cut tapers on each side of each of the blanks using the homemade taper jig shown. Set the fence 12 in. from the blade, then rip a piece of plywood and cut it to 87 in. long. Cut a 2-in. taper on one side of each blank as shown, aligning the backside of the blank with the inner edge of the plywood and letting the side to be tapered hang over 2 in. as shown. Clamp the board with the jig levers over the board and run it through the saw.

16 REPOSITION the block in your jig and cut the opposite side of each blank. Always have the top of the blank at the tapered end of the jig and the wide base end even with the inner edge of the jig. Move the workpiece through, making sure the plywood is tight to the fence and have an outfeed stand to support the jig as it leaves the saw. Next, glue and finish-nail 3/4-in. x 1-1/4 in. strips (Q2) to the sides of each column as shown in Detail 4 to give the columns a heavier and deeper look. Once the glue is dry, sand them with 100-grit sandpaper followed by 150-grit sandpaper.

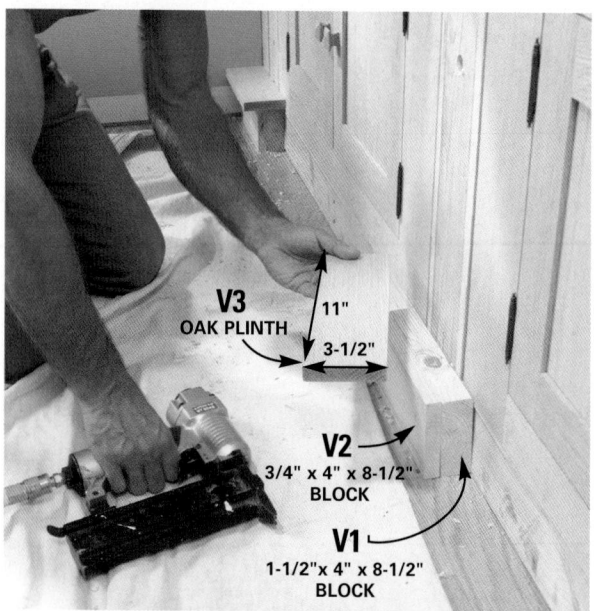

17 RIP 2x6 and 1x6 pine to 4-in. widths and nail them to the base assembly at the center of each 2x4 vertical support. These pieces will support the base cap. Next, wrap these supports with 3/4-in. x 4-in. oak base pieces and continue installing these base pieces between the column bases.

18 SET the columns onto the base caps and mark each side of the column where it meets the upper arch. Be sure the column is centered on the 2x4 support behind. Build up the upper face of the 2x4 supports with 1-1/4 in. deep strips to ensure the column lies 1-1/4 in. in front of the oak arch. Nail the columns to these strips and to the face of the 2x4 and face frame below with 10d finish nails.

Detail 4:
Column Assembly

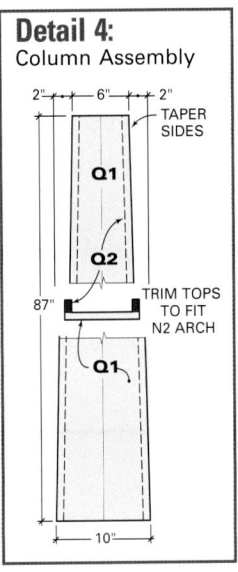

2" — 6" — 2"
TAPER SIDES
Q1
Q2
87"
TRIM TOPS TO FIT N2 ARCH
Q1
10"

the cut, flip the piece end-for-end and run the other side of the board through the blade, keeping it tight against the fence. Now test the groove by slipping in a piece of 1/4-in. plywood. It should slide into the groove without your pushing it firmly. If the fit is too loose, move the fence slightly away from the blade. If the fit is too tight, move the fence closer to the blade. Now cut all the inside edges of the rails and stiles.

Make your tenons by setting the fence exactly 1/2 in. from the blade (don't use the 1/2-in. plywood on top of your saw for

Tip

You'll find that your square is of little use when you need to cut the tops of your two side column assemblies to length. To mark a square cut, tape the discarded strip from your taper cut (**Photo 15**) to the side of your column. Then use your square to mark a straight line and your circular saw to make the cut.

19 FIT the capital moldings around the tops of the columns. Use a double layer at the top to build out the surface and notch these layers around the lower edge of the curve. Place the 3/4-in. x 1-3/4 in. tapered molding directly below and nail it in place with the brad nailer.

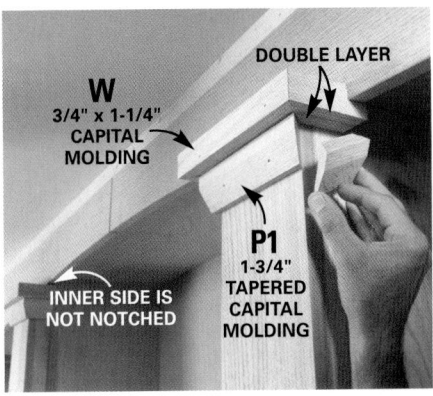

W
3/4" x 1-1/4"
CAPITAL MOLDING

DOUBLE LAYER

P1
1-3/4"
TAPERED CAPITAL MOLDING

INNER SIDE IS NOT NOTCHED

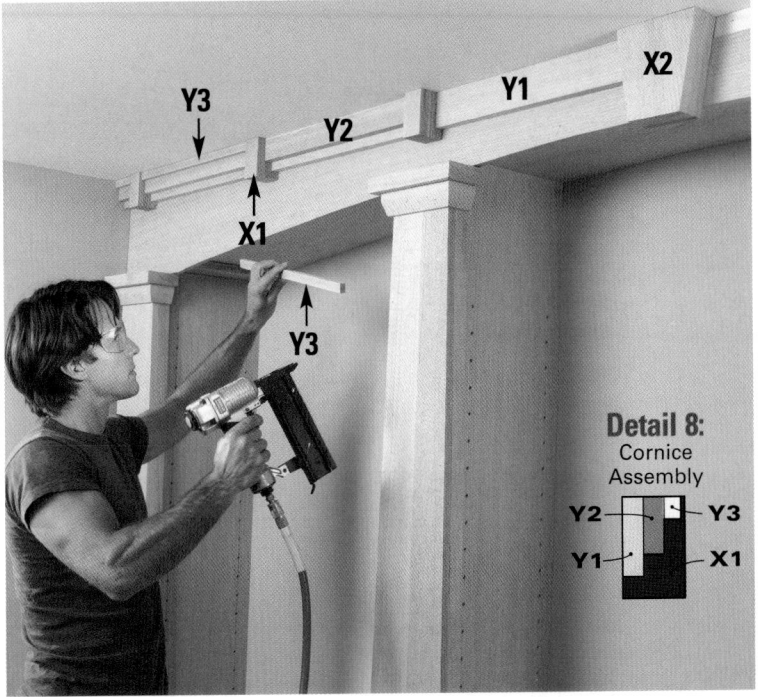

Y3 Y2 Y1 X2
X1
Y3

Detail 8:
Cornice Assembly

Y2 Y3
Y1 X1

20 CUT cornice blocks from 3/4-in. oak, then stack them in layers and glue them to achieve the 2-1/4 in. thickness. Make the tapered keystone center block in the same manner. Predrill, glue and hand-nail the cornice blocks to the curved apron with 10d finish nails. Next cut the cornice strips on the table saw and nail them in layers between the blocks with your finish nailer.

Great Goofs™

Lopsided bookcases

We found plans for a simple bookcase and decided to build it right away. We liked the bookcase so much that we decided to build two more. We cut all the pieces in an assembly-line fashion and finished the second bookcase quickly. While assembling the third bookcase, we noticed there were two left sides instead of a right and a left. After thinking it through, we decided to build one more bookcase and cut two right sides to fix our mistake. We assembled these bookcases just like the others. When they were in position, we noticed that two of the bookcases were leaning slightly. We checked our measurements and looked over the plans. Then we discovered that the two new right sides were 3/8 in. shorter than the left sides. In our assembly-line haste, we'd goofed on the measurements. To conceal our mistake, we shimmed the shelves slightly to create the illusion of level.

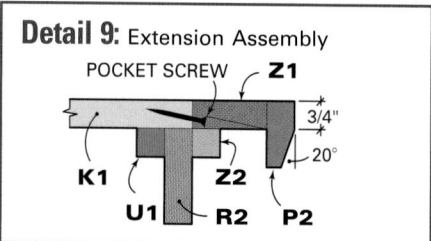

Detail 9: Extension Assembly
POCKET SCREW **Z1**
3/4"
20°
K1 **Z2**
U1 **R2** **P2**

21 FASTEN the front top extensions with your pocket hole jig. Nail a 3/4-in. x 3/4-in. strip to the top of the face frame and glue the extension to this for added support.

MINDS HIS
Ps AND Qs

← Q1
← Q2
Z1
Z2

22 GLUE and nail the top shelf edge molding to the top shelf, extending it 1-1/2 in. onto each column. To finish the building process, make the shelves as shown in Detail 10, p. 147, to fit between the vertical bookcase sides. (You'll also need to make three narrower shelves if you want extra storage inside the cabinets. Measure and cut them to fit.) Sand your bookcase with 100-grit sandpaper followed by 150-grit. Stain (see Buyer's Guide) then finish it with two coats of satin urethane or your choice of varnish.

P2

V4

this). Raise the blade 1/4 in. Make sure your miter gauge for your saw is set at 90 degrees. Push your scrap piece through the saw, keeping it firmly against the miter gauge and the fence. After one pass, move it away from the fence about 1/8 in. and send it through again. Continue until you've completed that side of the tenon. Then flip it over and do the other side. If there are some saw marks, scrape them off with a flat file. Test-fit your tenon in the groove you've just made. If it fits too tightly, raise the blade just slightly and recut the piece. If the fit is loose, lower the blade slightly and try another test piece. When you've got it right, cut the ends on all of the door rails as shown in Photo 12.

Make your cornice blocks from built-up strips

You could special-order thick slabs of wood for the cornice detail at the top of the bookcase (Photo 20), but that's impractical when you've got plenty of small scrap left over. Cut three strips to size from 3/4-in. oak for the cornice blocks and the keystone. Glue and clamp them. When the glue is dry, belt-sand them smooth on each side and then finish-sand them. Use your jigsaw or a miter saw to cut the keystone angles.

Buyer's Guide

- Get a pair of no-mortise hinges (part No. 90437; $2.99) from Rockler Hardware (800-279-4441; www.rockler.com). Package of 16 shelf clips (part No. 33894; $3.69).
- Buy the Kreg pocket hole jig kit (part No. Kreg R-2; $59.95) and an extra pack of 1-1/4 in. pocket screws ($5.50) from 7 Corners Hardware (800-328-0457). www.7corners.com
- Ace oil stain in Early American. Buy it at your local Ace Hardware.

WINDOW CORNICES

Custom-build your own window cornices for one-fourth the price of store-bought

by **Travis Larson**

Window cornices are a simple, inexpensive way to dramatically enhance any room. They'll hide ugly drapery rods and add a touch of custom-made detailing that makes an ordinary window or patio door look like something special. The top of the cornice can even serve as a display shelf for art or collectibles.

Cornices are surprisingly easy to build, even the elegant ones you see in home magazines. Using off-the-shelf trim from the home center and a compound miter saw, anyone with simple carpentry skills can create a beautiful window or door cornice in just a few hours.

If this sounds interesting, read on and we'll show you how to select the materials, assemble the parts and attach the cornice to the wall. We'll also share design tips to help you match a cornice style to your home's décor.

Build it yourself and save big bucks

Search the Internet for cornice suppliers and you'll see that you can save huge money by building your own. One site offers custom cornices for $3 to $7.50 per inch! Depending on the style, that's between $216 and $540 for a cornice for a 6-ft. patio door, plus shipping. Build your own and you can expect to spend about one-fourth of that. The materials for the style we show in the how-to photos add up to about $5.60 per foot, or about $45 per window, plus paint. Usually the materials are cheap, although selecting upscale trim like an elaborate crown molding will drive up the cost. For help selecting styles and materials, see "Designing Your Cornice," p. 159.

Selecting the wood

If you plan to paint your cornices, poplar and aspen are good choices for the box materials. They're stable and relatively cheap, and the grain won't show through paint. Pine and basswood moldings are usually the least expensive choices for paintable trim.

If you want a stained or natural wood cornice, look for oak, mahogany, cherry, maple and others at home centers. The biggest problem is finding hardwood moldings other than oak. You may have to special-order them or find a specialty millwork supplier by looking under "Millwork" in the Yellow Pages.

Using a compound or sliding compound miter saw

The best tool for cutting miters on wide boards (1x6s) is either a 10-in. compound miter saw or a sliding compound saw. Standard compound saws work like typical miter saws, but the motor and blade tip sideways, making them capable of cutting bevels. A sliding compound miter saw cuts compound angles too, but the motor and blade slide on tracks so it can handle wider stock.

Be sure to use a sharp finish-cutting blade in either one. Prices for standard compound miter saws start as low as $100, or you can rent one for about $35 per day.

You can predrill and hand-nail

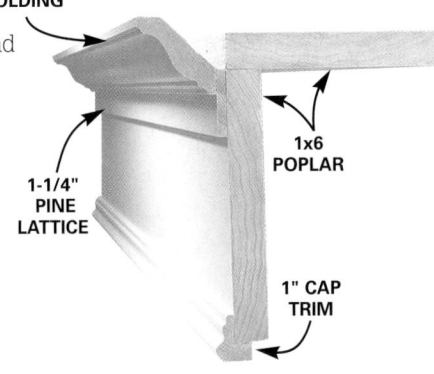

2-1/4" CROWN MOLDING

1-1/4" PINE LATTICE

1x6 POPLAR

1" CAP TRIM

most of the project, but an air-powered brad nailer with 1 and 1-1/2 in. brads makes the job much easier. Some of the cheaper ones sell for less than $100, or you can rent one for about $25 per day. (Rent one of the special airless ones and you'll save the price of renting a compressor.) But for the money, compound miter saws and brad nailers are far too useful and far too fun not to own yourself.

Build the basic box, then add the trim

Every cornice begins the same way, with cutting and assembling the three-sided, lidded box (**Photos 2 – 4**).

Then you add the trim of your choice (**Photos 5 – 9**) and finish the cornice (**Photo 11**). The cornice is then ready for mounting on the wall by screwing it to a 1x2 that's screwed to the wall above the opening (**Photos 12 – 14**).

Begin by measuring the curtain and curtain rod for length, depth and width (**Photo 1**). Measure with the curtains open so you take into account their thickness when bunched. Add an inch or so to the depth and the width of the curtain rod to make sure the cornice will cover everything.

Miter the ends and front box pieces first. It's easiest to

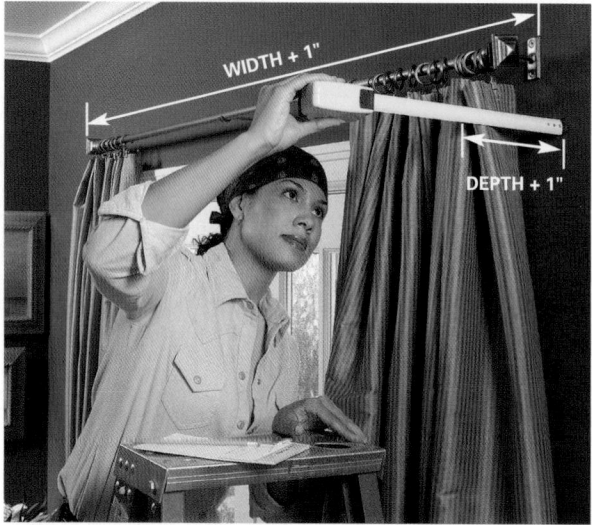

1 MEASURE the outside width and depth of curtains, curtain rods or shades that you want to cover and their distances from the wall. Add 1 in. to determine the inside box dimensions.

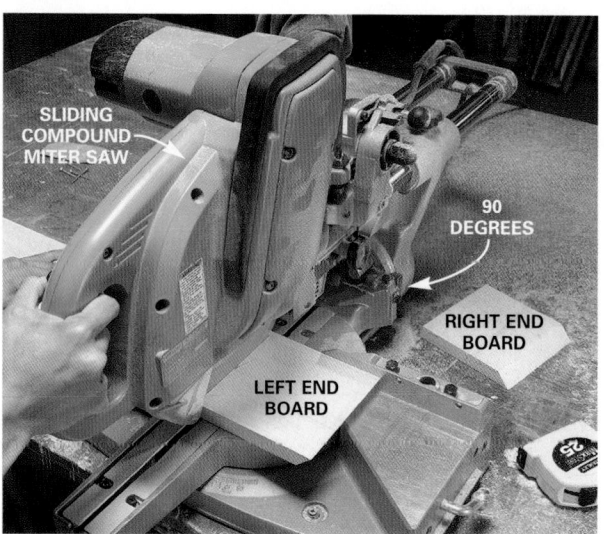

2 CUT the end boards and then the front board, cutting 45-degree bevels on one end of the end boards and both ends of the front board. If you want to match wood grain at corners on clear-finished cornices, cut the end boards from opposite ends.

3 SMEAR a little woodworking glue on the miters and tack the joint together with six 1-in. brads, three from each side.

4 CUT the top board to length to fit flush with the front and sides of the box (depending on the design). Glue and nail the top to the box frame with 1-1/2 in. brads spaced every 6 in.

square up the board, then tilt the miter saw to cut a 45-degree bevel for the first end piece and then square it up to cut the second end (**Photo 2**). The mitered corners are glued and nailed together with 1-in. brads. Measure the assembly to determine the exact length for the top.

When mitering the trim for the box, always start by first cutting and mounting an end trim piece, then the long front trim and finally the other

Tip Build up short fences to support crown moldings while cutting by screwing 1x4 boards to the saw fence through the predrilled holes in the fence (shown below).

end. That way, you'll be able to check fits and get crisp miters at each corner. Fit each miter, then scribe the length of each piece rather than measuring (**Photo 5**). It's faster and much more accurate. It's best to cut pieces just a tad long so you can shave them down until they fit perfectly. If you're new to woodworking, it's nice to have a helper by your side to hold the miters together while you're scribing lengths or fastening parts.

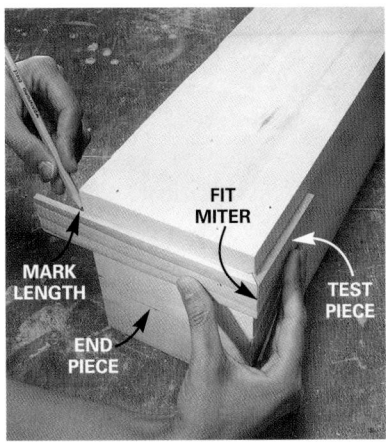

5 USING a short test piece, fit the end piece and mark and cut it to fit. Cut the miter on the long front piece of trim, fit it to the first piece, mark its length, then cut and fasten it. Repeat the steps for the other end.

6 CUT the two crown molding end pieces 1 in. longer than needed with opposite 45-degree angles on one end of each piece (you're cutting a right and a left corner).

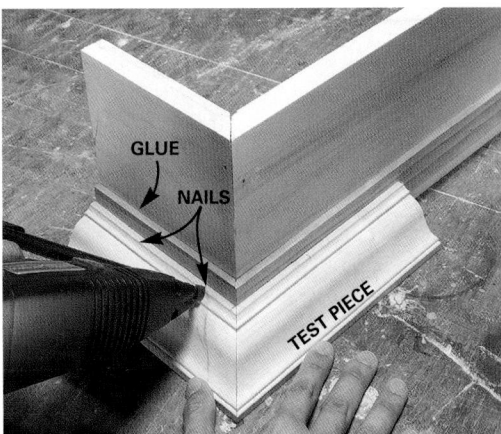

7 FLIP the box upside down and prop the crown molding end piece against the box. Use the other end as a test piece to line up the miters. Mark and cut the piece to length. Smear a little glue along the bottom and tack it to the cornice with a couple of 1-in. brads.

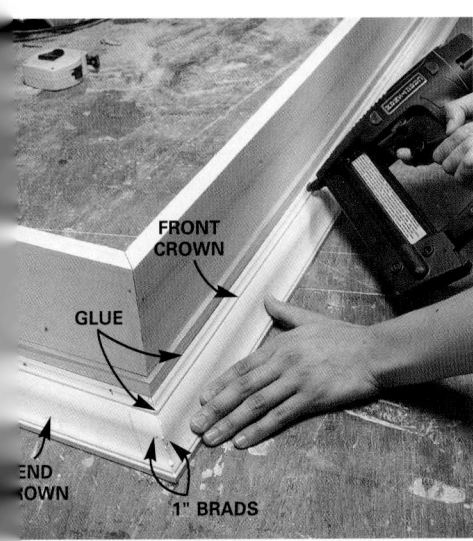

8 TEST-FIT, mark and cut the front piece of crown molding to length. Glue and nail the miters together, then nail the molding to the cornice box. Cut and install the last end piece of crown molding.

9 CUT, fit, glue and nail the bottom piece of trim to the box using the same techniques you used with the crown molding.

10 FILL nail holes and any miter gaps in joints with wood filler. Sand excess wood filler and file miters as necessary to remove any wood fibers or smooth out inconsistencies in profiles.

Cutting crown molding is a little tricky

The trick to cutting perfect crown molding miters is to rest the molding upside down and against the bed and fence while cutting the 45-degree angles (Photo 6). If you cut wide crown molding, you may have to extend the fence height by screwing a length of 1x4 to the miter saw fence through the holes in the back. Remember that the long point of the miter is always the top edge. That'll help you remember which way to angle the saw before cutting. To further eliminate the costly mistake of miscutting an angle, draw a light line while you're fitting the piece to indicate the proper angle (Photo 6).

Finishing

Fill nail holes and prime before painting. If your cornices have elaborate details like dentil blocking, you'll get better results with several light coats of spray paint instead of brushing. Finish highly detailed natural and stained wood with spray lacquer, shellac or polyurethane.

Prepaint the 1x2 cornice ledger to match the wall before you put it up if you think it'll show after the window covering is in place (Photo 13).

11 PRIME the wood and lightly sand it with 150-grit sandpaper before applying your choice of paint.

12 CENTER the cornice over the opening at the height that best covers the curtain rod and curtain. Then reach underneath and mark the bottom. Take down the cornice and extend the mark with a 4-ft. level.

13 CUT a 1x2 to fit between the curtain rod brackets. Screw it through the drywall into the framing with 2-1/2 in. screws spaced about every foot.

14 PREDRILL 1/8-in. pilot holes spaced about every foot in the top of the cornice 3/4 in. from the back edge. Angle the holes slightly toward the wall. Hold the cornice tight to the wall and run 2-in. screws into the 1x2.

DESIGNING YOUR CORNICE

Design elements within your home should dictate the wood type, molding style and finish that you select. Depending on the design, the top either overlaps the sides, sometimes with a routed edge, or is nailed to the top or inside of the box and doesn't show from below. The tops are best made from 1x4s, 1x6s or 1x8s. There's no need to cut the tops to width if you choose the right combination of top style and board size. The example we show is a 1x6 nailed on top of the box, which gives an overall inside depth of 4-3/4 in. For the same look but with a shallower box, you could also nail a 1x4 inside the box flush with the top for a depth of 3-1/2 in. Choose whichever method it takes to clear your curtains.

Building mock-ups

Not sure what style to choose? Here's a tip. Buy short lengths of different types of trim along with some cheap 1x4s and 1x6s. Cut everything to 1-ft. lengths and mock up several different combinations. Just squirt a little wood glue on the pieces and clamp them together for about 10 minutes. Hold the mock-ups over the opening to get a feel for the final look.

We actually made about 30 cornice samples before deciding on the final design for the how-to photos and the designs on this page. Of course, the hard part is choosing one. 🏠

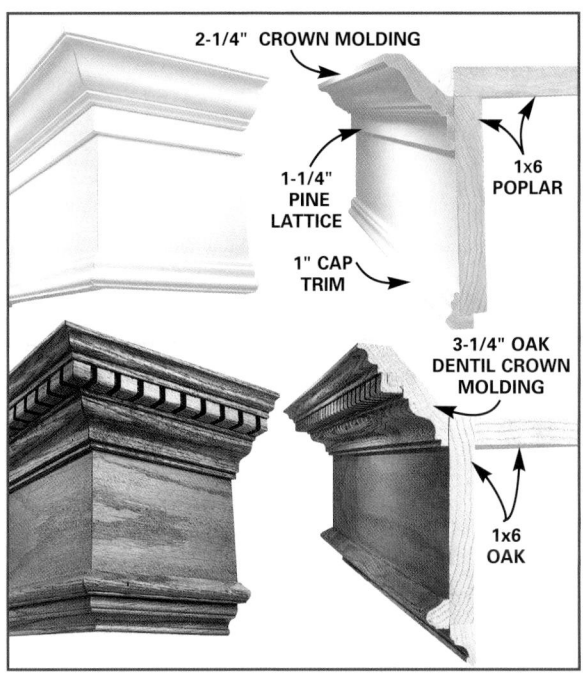

A. Simple 1x6 box technique
Tops that don't show from below can either lap over (upper photo) or butt against (lower photo) the top of the front board of the box. Further box depth adjustments can be made by using a narrower or wider top board or ripping it to a smaller width.

Labels: 2-1/4" CROWN MOLDING; 1-1/4" PINE LATTICE; 1" CAP TRIM; 1x6 POPLAR; 3-1/4" OAK DENTIL CROWN MOLDING; 1x6 OAK

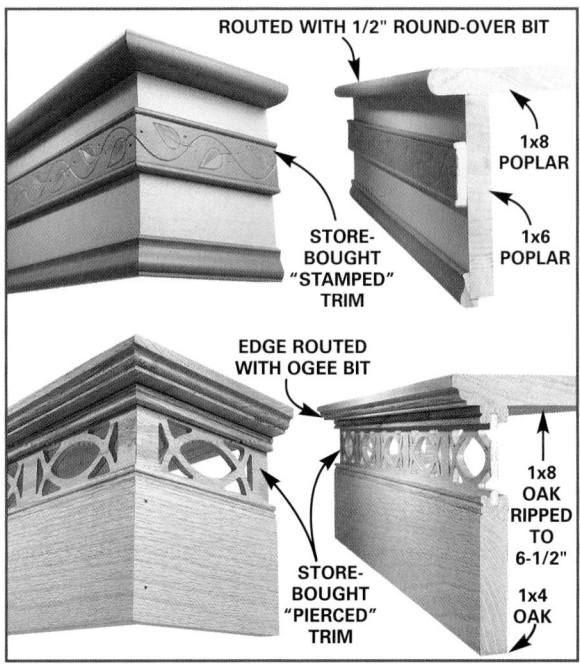

B: Overlapping top with routed edge
Overlapping tops simplify construction and are good to use when the top of the cornice will be seen from above. Use a router to carve a profile on the outer lip of the top before you assemble the cornice. "Stamped" moldings (upper photo) and "pierced" moldings (lower photo) offer another unique look and are widely available at home centers.

Labels: ROUTED WITH 1/2" ROUND-OVER BIT; 1x8 POPLAR; 1x6 POPLAR; STORE-BOUGHT "STAMPED" TRIM; EDGE ROUTED WITH OGEE BIT; 1x8 OAK RIPPED TO 6-1/2"; STORE-BOUGHT "PIERCED" TRIM; 1x4 OAK

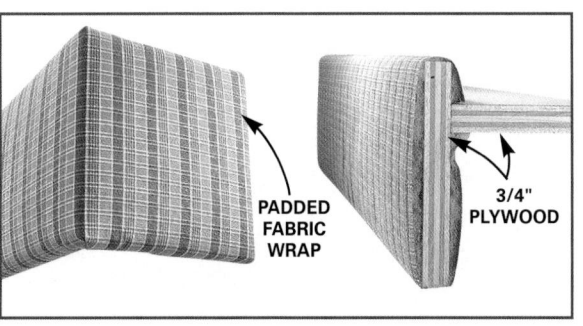

C: Fabric wrapped
Fabric-covered cornices can be built from 3/4-in. plywood, since the wood is hidden. If you'd like to wrap a cornice in wallpaper, build it from poplar or a smoother plywood.

Labels: PADDED FABRIC WRAP; 3/4" PLYWOOD

FAST **FURNITURE FIXES**

Make those nicks and scratches go away with just a few minutes' work

by **Art Rooze**

Furniture looking a little shabby with all those little scratches and dings? You know, the vacuum cleaner bumps here and there, and the Hot Wheels hit-and-runs? Not to worry. We'll show you simple touch-up techniques that will make these minor eyesores disappear quickly and painlessly.

We're not talking about refinishing or even repairing here, which are different games altogether. This is about hiding flaws so only you will know they're there.

The procedures and materials shown in this article won't damage the original finish on your furniture if it was made in the last 50 years.

However, if the piece of furniture you're touching up is very old, or an antique, it may have a shellac finish. With shellac, you shouldn't attempt the scratch-removal process shown on p. 162. And if the piece is an antique, think twice about doing any touch-up, which could actually devalue it.

You can test for a shellac finish with a few drops of alcohol in an out-of-sight spot. Alcohol will dissolve shellac.

Think safety: Even though all the fluids and sprays we show here are everyday hardware-store products, most are both flammable and toxic. Read and follow the directions on the label. Don't use them in a room where there's a pilot light, or near open flames or in an unventilated space. If you'll be doing anything more than a few quick passes with the sprays shown here, work outdoors and wear a respirator mask with organic cartridges. And if you're pregnant, stay away from these materials altogether.

CLEAN DIRTY, GREASY, GUMMY SURFACES

The results of a simple surface cleaning with mineral spirits may amaze you. Polish buildup and the dirt embedded in it muddy the finish but will wipe away. Don't use stronger solvents; they might dissolve the finish itself.

1 **SOAK a coarse, absorbent, clean cloth with mineral spirits and wipe the finish. Keep applying and wiping until the cloth no longer picks up dirt. Then do a final wipe with a fresh, clean rag.**

2 **CLEAN crevices, grooves and carved areas with cotton swabs dipped in mineral spirits.**

PATCH GOUGES

Fill in gouges with colored putty sticks, sold at most hardware stores and home centers. This putty works well for small holes and nicks but is somewhat trickier to use as a fill for larger damage like we show here. Unlike hardening putties, it remains soft and somewhat flexible, so you have to shape it carefully. And it won't hold up under heavy wear.

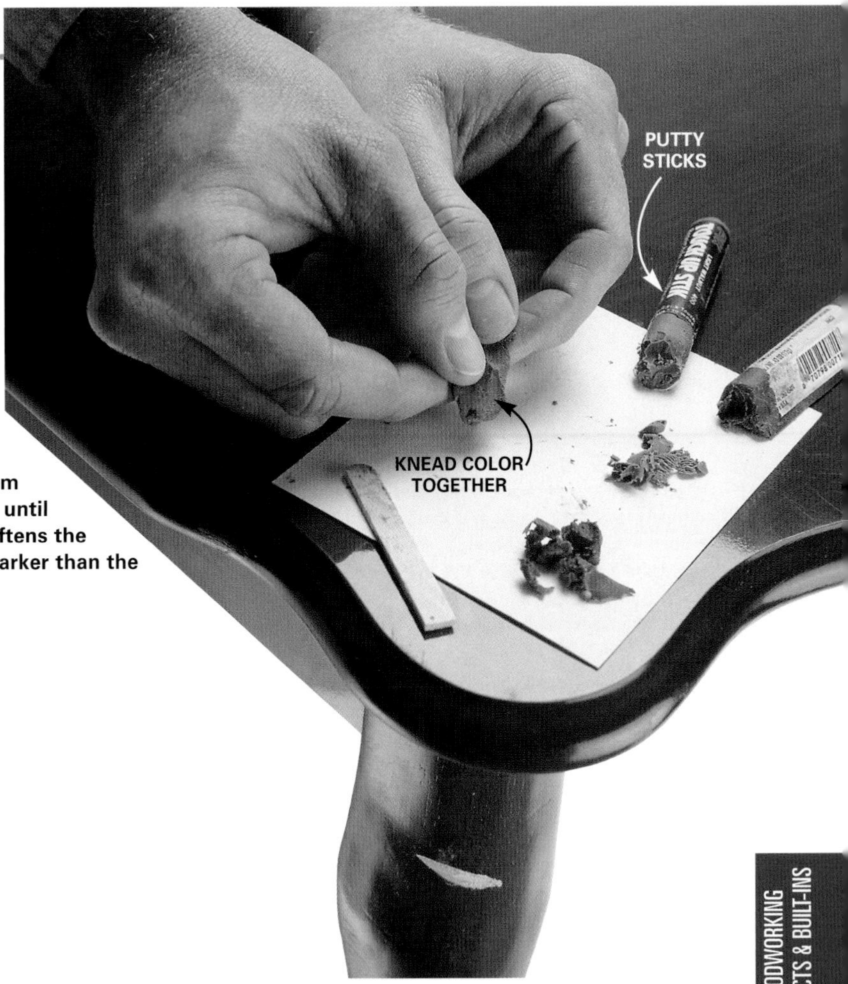

PUTTY STICKS

KNEAD COLOR TOGETHER

1 BUY several sticks of putty similar to the color of the stain you want to match. Scrape flakes from each, then mix and knead them with your fingertips until the color is right. The heat from your fingers also softens the putty for easy application. Make the patch slightly darker than the furniture; lighter will be more obvious.

2 PRESS putty tightly into the gouge with a small flat stick, then flatten it and scrape away the excess with the stick's long edge. Round the end of the stick with sandpaper.

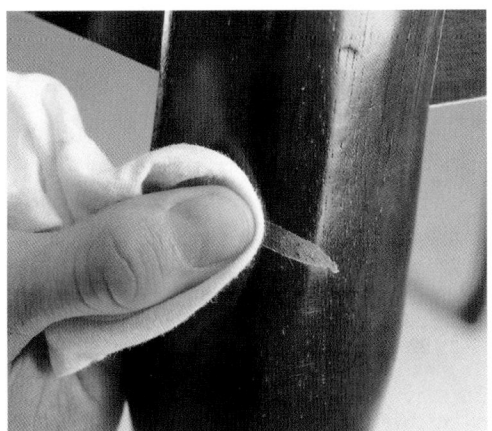

3 WIPE AWAY any putty adhering to the wood around the gouge, and smooth the surface of the putty with a clean cloth. A thin, light-colored line will usually appear around the perimeter of the patch. Use a matching marker to color this line, as shown on p. 162.

4 SPRAY the patch with a few quick passes of shellac, then after it dries, a few quick passes of spray lacquer—either high gloss or satin, depending on the finish. Never apply lacquer or polyurethane/varnish directly over a putty patch; it will leave a permanently soft mess. Shellac will harden; however, the patch will remain somewhat pliable under the finish, so don't attempt this on a heavy-wear surface.

WIPE AWAY SCRATCHES AND RECOAT THE SURFACE

You can buff out fine scratches using very fine (0000) steel wool saturated with clear Danish oil. (You can also use ultra-fine automotive rubbing compound.) The process shown here only works for scratches in the finish itself, not scratches that are all the way into the stain or the wood.

1 POUR a generous amount of clear or neutral Danish oil onto a very fine steel wool pad. Rub the surface with the oil-saturated pad using your flat hand. Rub with the grain, never against it or at an angle to it. Continue rubbing until you remove enough of the clear surface finish to eliminate the scratches, but be careful not to remove any of the stain below the clear finish. Rub not only the scratched area but also the area around it in gradually decreasing amounts. Be careful not to rub edges or corners excessively; they wear through quickly.

2 WIPE AWAY all the Danish oil with rags or paper towels, then thoroughly clean the entire surface with mineral spirits several times to make sure all the oil is removed. If any oil remains, the lacquer (Photo 3) won't adhere. Allow the surface to dry overnight before applying lacquer.

3 SPRAY the entire surface with clear lacquer. Move the spray can in one continuous, straight stroke, allowing the spray to extend beyond the edges in all directions. Wipe the nozzle with a rag after each stroke to prevent drips. Move with the grain, and make sure the angle of the spray remains the same all the way across. Keep the spray aimed away from other surfaces that you don't want coated, or mask them with newspaper.

CAUTION: Rags and steel wool saturated with Danish oil can spontaneously combust if left bunched up. Dry them outdoors, spread out loosely. When the oil has dried, you can safely throw the rags and steel wool in the trash.

TOUCH UP SCRATCHES

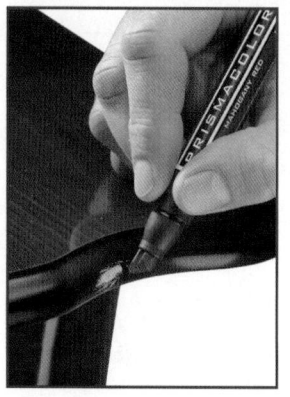

1 HIDE scratches with permanent-ink felt-tip markers. You can either use the furniture touch-up markers available at hardware stores and home centers, or, to get an exact match, buy markers at an art supply store that carries an array of colors (check the Yellow Pages). For thorough coverage, you may need to dab the ink onto the scratch, let it dry, then even out the color by stroking lightly across it with the tip. Keep in mind that colors tend to darken when they soak into wood fibers.

2 TOUCH UP thin scratches with a fine-tip permanent marker. When filling in scratches, steady your hand against the furniture for accuracy; as much as possible, flow the ink only onto the scratch.

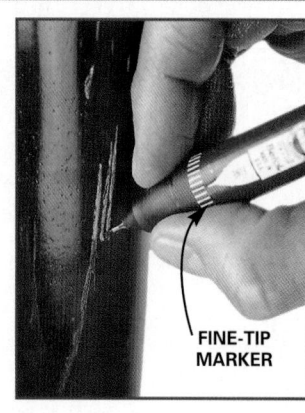

FINE-TIP MARKER

7 Workshop Tools, Tips & Storage

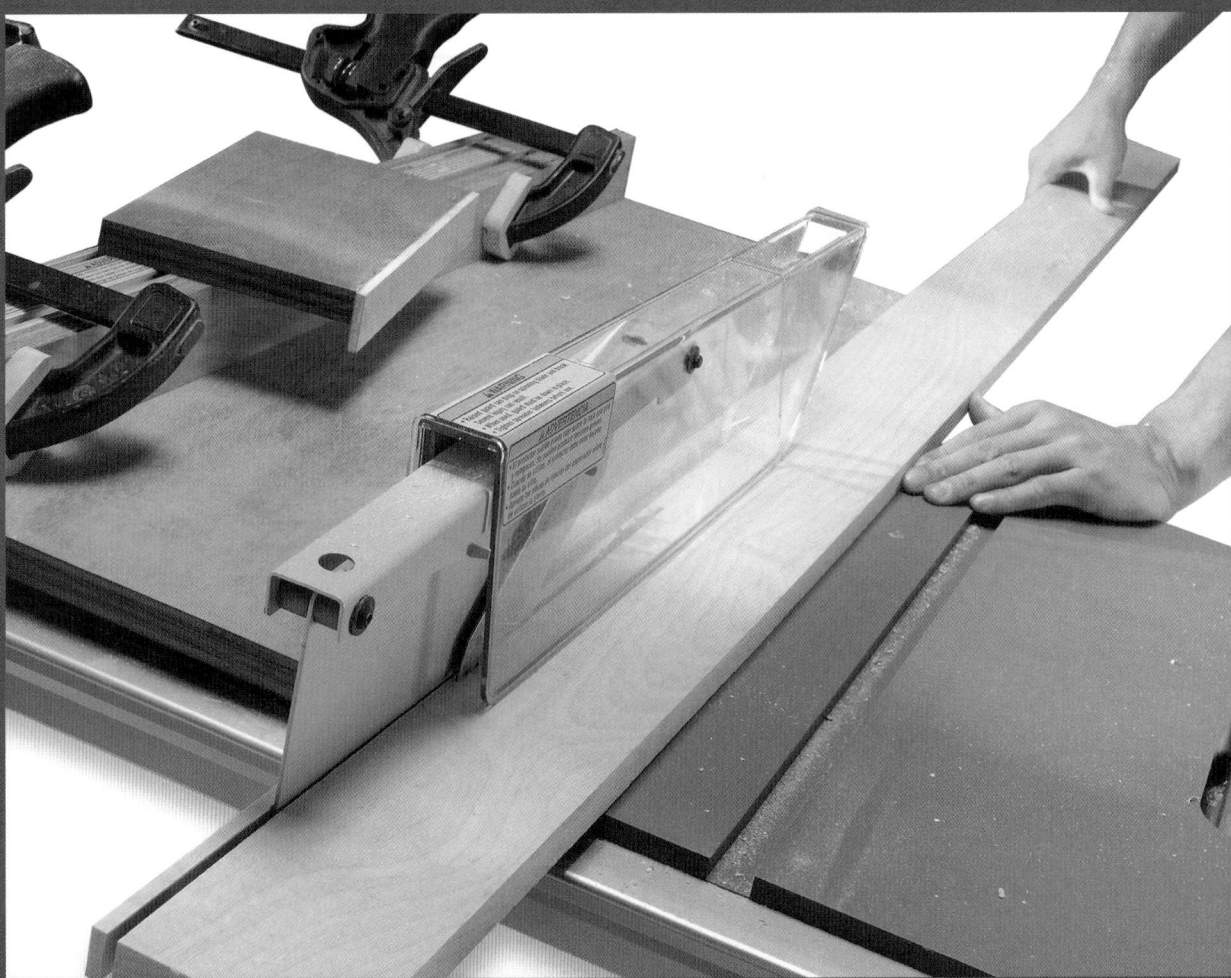

IN THIS CHAPTER

Small Shop Tips 164
   Adjustable sawhorses, storage rack,
   space-efficient workbench

Using Tools: Table Saw 166

10-Minute Workshop
   Storage Projects 170

Using Tools: Angle Grinder 174

Ask Handyman .177
   Sizing pilot holes and air compressors

Workshop Tips .178
   Torch caddy, table saw extension
   table and more...

Small Shop Tips

ADJUSTABLE-HEIGHT SAWHORSES

Every shop needs horsepower. These adjustable horses are easy to build from construction-grade 1x4s and 2x4s. Add the adjustable-height jig and these horses will hold projects at the perfect working height. Use a pair of them as a stand for portable or bench-top power tools, or make a temporary workbench by throwing a piece of plywood on top.

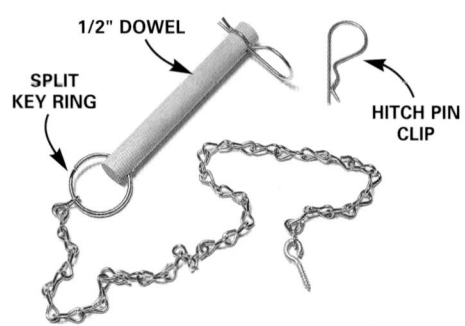

1/2" DOWEL

SPLIT KEY RING

HITCH PIN CLIP

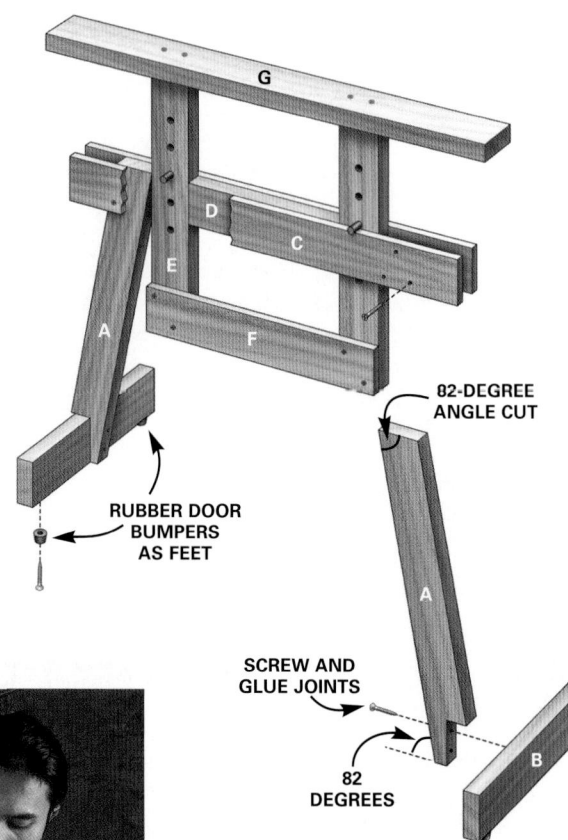

G

D

C

E

A

F

RUBBER DOOR BUMPERS AS FEET

82-DEGREE ANGLE CUT

A

SCREW AND GLUE JOINTS

82 DEGREES

B

CUTTING LIST		
KEY	**PCS.**	**SIZE & DESCRIPTION**
A	2	1-1/2" x 3-1/2" x 25" legs
B	2	1-1/2" x 3-1/2" x 18" footers
C	2	3/4" x 3-1/2" x 36" top rails
D	1	1-1/2" x 3-1/2" x 13" spacer block
E	2	1-1/2" x 3-1/2" x 21" adjustable slides; drill 1/2" dowel holes 2" apart
F	1	3/4" x 3-1/2" x 20" slide support
G	1	1-1/2" x 3-1/2" x 40" work rail

FLIP-THROUGH STORAGE RACK

Unless you live in an art gallery, wall space is always at a premium. Build this booklike storage rack, and expand your wall space exponentially. Grabbing a tool is as easy as flipping through a magazine.

Mount two parallel 2x4s on the wall spaced 24 in. apart. Cut the leaves from 3/4-in. plywood and hang them from the 2x4s with 3-in. door hinges. Fur out the hinges with 3/4-in. plywood blocks so the pages can pivot without binding. Mount the leaves at least 4 in. apart to allow room for them to fold back. Let your imagination run wild creating holders for your various tools.

For you Peg-Board fans, sandwich a 1x3 frame between two pieces of Peg-Board. Now your collection of hooks and holders will work with this tool storage system.

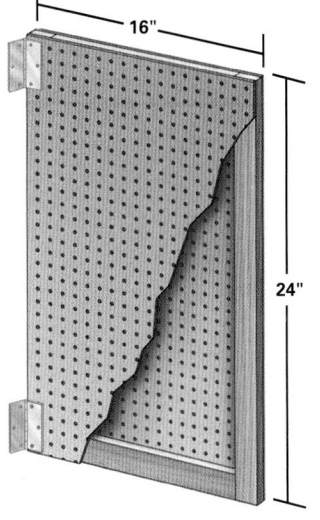

PEG-BOARD LEAF

16"

24"

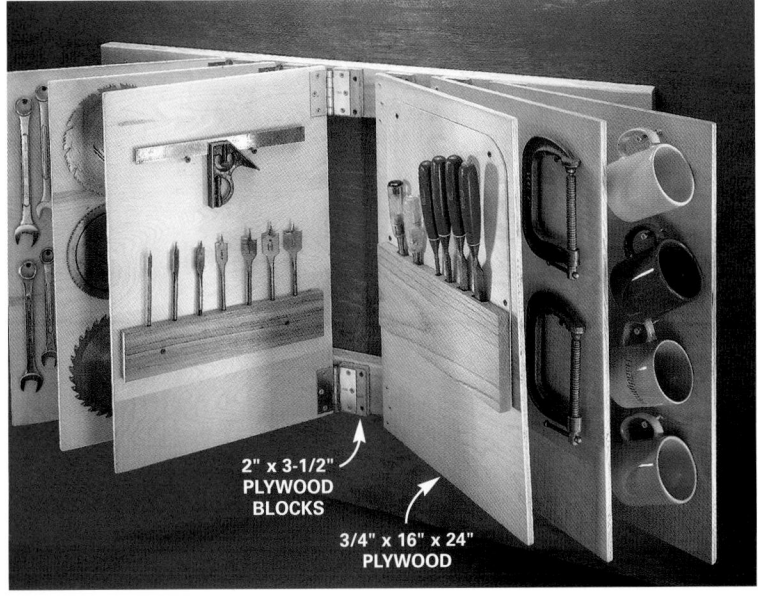

2" x 3-1/2"
PLYWOOD
BLOCKS

3/4" x 16" x 24"
PLYWOOD

WORKBENCH WITH BUILT-IN STORAGE

At the heart of every small shop is a multipurpose workbench. Build this workbench with tons of storage space underneath. While ours is configured for lumber storage, you can put cabinet doors on the front and store tools and materials. For our 8-ft. long bench, we built four 2x4 frames; that left about 27 in. between them. This spacing provides plenty of support for the double 3/4-in. plywood top and long lengths of lumber underneath. 🏠

12"

53"

20"

36"

3"
SCREWS

32"

BASIC FRAME

Using Tools: Table Saw

RIPPING SAFELY WITH A TABLE SAW

Cutting boards lengthwise, called ripping, is the task a table saw does best. But ripping on a table saw is so simple that it's easy to become complacent and forget that a table saw is one of the most dangerous tools in the shop. Fortunately there are techniques and safety equipment that can eliminate most table saw injuries. In this article, we'll show you the safe way to make a variety of rip cuts including long rips, skinny rips and even rips to straighten a crooked board.

- Blade guard savvy
- Favorite push sticks
- Rip thin strips safely
- Straighten crooked boards

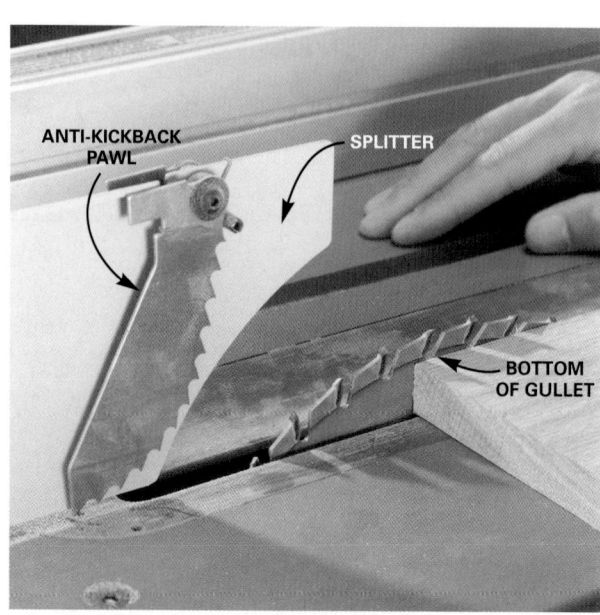

1 ADJUST the blade height so the bottom of the saw blade gullet is even with the top of the wood you're ripping.

Install the blade guard that came with your saw

A blade guard assembly that includes a splitter and an anti-kickback pawl is standard equipment with every table saw. If you've set yours aside, now's the time to dust it off, dig out your instruction manual and reinstall it. Keeping this safety equipment on your saw and in good working condition is crucial for safe cutting. The plastic guard keeps your fingers away from the blade and deflects flying debris. The splitter keeps the board from pinching the blade and kicking back at you. Kickback danger is further reduced by the anti-kickback pawl, which has little teeth that grab the board and prevent it from hurtling toward you if the blade pinches or binds during the cut.

Safe ripping starts with adjusting the blade height. In general, the less blade exposed, the safer your sawing operation. Photo 1 shows the safest height for good cutting perfomance.

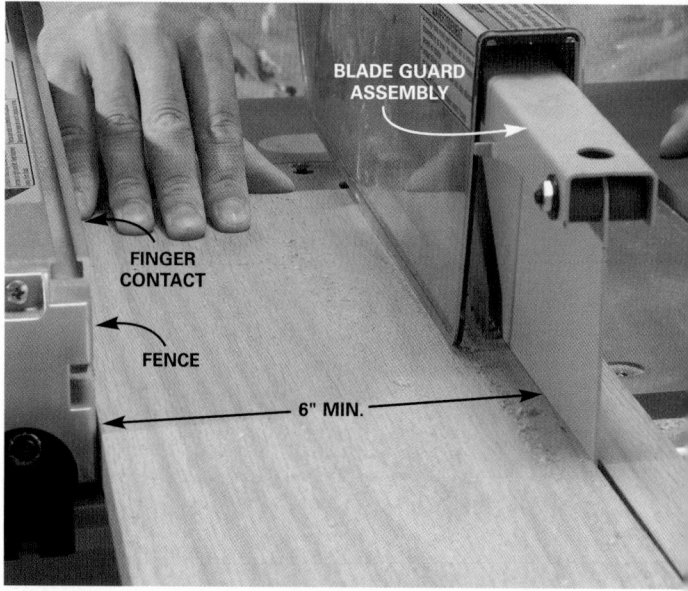

2 HOOK your thumb behind the board and keep your little finger in contact with the fence to rip boards 6 in. and wider. Concentrate on keeping the edge of the board in full contact with the fence while you push it through the blade at a slow, steady rate. Push the board completely past the blade and kickback pawl. Then switch off the saw, being careful to stay out of the path of the blade in case the ripped board or cutoff piece catches in the blade and kicks back.

Save your fingers with a push stick

Even with a blade guard in place, you don't want your hand anywhere near the spinning blade. A moment's lapse in concentration or one little slip is all it takes to lose a finger. Push sticks allow you to keep your hands a safe distance from the blade while ripping skinny pieces. Woodworkers we talked to prefer the push shoe design (**Photo 4**) over the push stick (**photo below**). The handle on the shoe shape gives you a better grip for more control over the wood and reduces the chances of your hand slipping off. Make a push shoe using the pattern we've provided, or buy one for about $20 from Sears or a store specializing in woodworking supplies (**photo below**). Always make push sticks out of plywood, not lumber that could split and fall apart while you're pushing. Push sticks and shoes

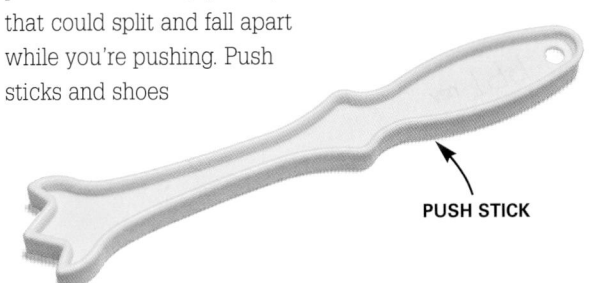

PUSH STICK

are the only safe way to guide a thin board past the spinning saw blade. Make a habit of keeping a push stick or shoe within easy reach whenever you use the saw.

While there are no hard and fast rules about how narrow a strip you can rip before needing a push stick, it's a good idea to establish a safe distance and stick to it. We recommend using a push stick for any rip narrower than 6 in. (**Photo 4**).

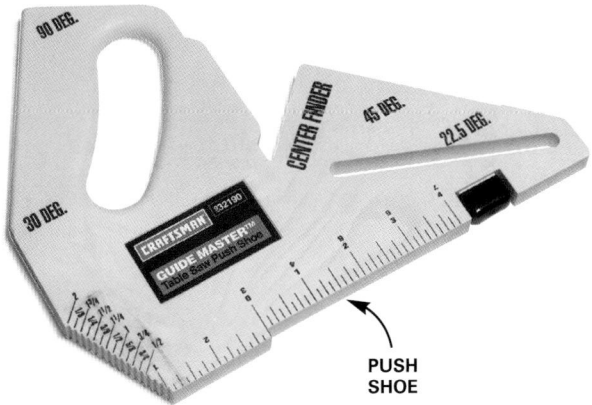

PUSH SHOE

Support long rips with an outfeed table

Ripping long boards is tricky because the board falls off the backside of the table, tempting you to reach over the spinning blade to catch it. To do it safely, you must support the end of the board as it comes off the back of the saw. You can buy manufactured stands that incorporate rollers and other devices to support this "outfeed" lumber. But a better solution is to build a small table that's the same height as your table saw (**Photo 3**). Or if room permits, build a permanent outfeed platform. Just make sure to support the lumber behind the saw so you're not tempted to reach over the blade to catch it.

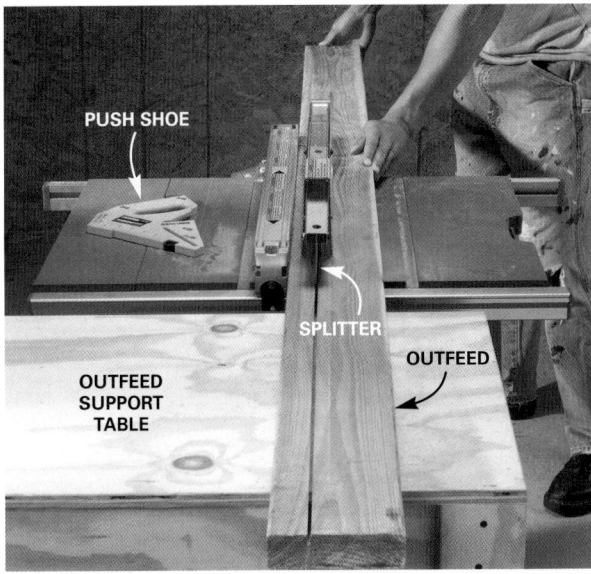

PUSH SHOE

SPLITTER

OUTFEED

OUTFEED SUPPORT TABLE

3 RIP boards narrower than 6 in. using the same technique as for wider boards. When your right hand reaches the edge of the saw table, pick up the push shoe and hook it over the back edge of the board. Stand to the side of and not directly behind the blade as you're ripping. Use a table or other outfeed support to hold the board as it leaves the saw.

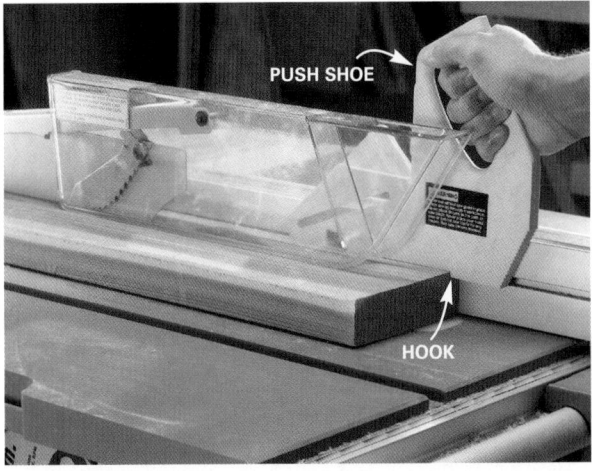

PUSH SHOE

HOOK

4 COMPLETE a narrow rip by pushing the board past the blade and anti-kickback pawl with a push shoe or push stick. Switch off the saw before retrieving the ripped board.

Using Tools: Table Saw

You can rip thin strips safely too

A table saw is the best tool for cutting thin strips of wood for plywood edging, jamb extensions or lattice. The problem is that the blade guard assembly interferes with the fence and doesn't provide enough space for a push stick. **Photos 5 and 6** show how to rip thin strips with the blade guard in place using a couple of easily constructed table saw accessories.

Build the fence extension by screwing a 3/4-in. x 2-1/2 in.

strip of plywood to the long side of a 10-in. x 24-in. rectangle of 3/4-in. plywood. Simplify fence adjustments by ripping the finished assembly to exactly 10 in. wide. Then simply add 10 in. to your desired ripping dimension when you set the distance from the blade to the fence. Glue and clamp a 1-3/8 in. wide strip of 1/4-in. plywood or hardboard to a 6-in. x 8-in. rectangle of 3/4-in. plywood for the push block. Don't use metal fasteners to attach the thin strip.

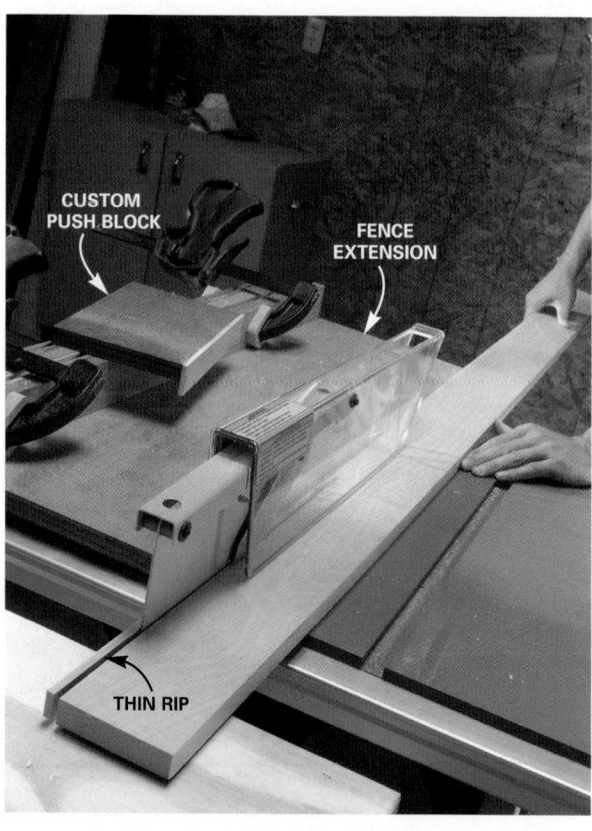

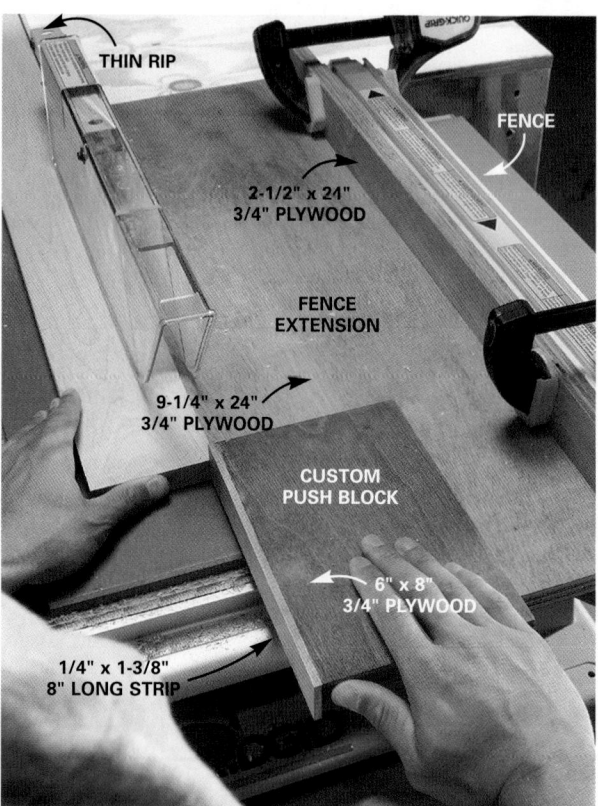

5 CLAMP the L-shaped plywood extension to your fence. Adjust the fence to the desired ripping width. Rip the thin strip by guiding the board along the plywood fence extension.

6 COMPLETE the rip by using the L-shaped push block to push the thin strip past the blade and anti-kickback pawl.

Follow these commonsense safety rules

- ■ To avoid being hit by a board if it kicks back, stand to the side of the blade when you're cutting, not directly behind it. Also keep onlookers away from this danger zone. If possible, orient the saw so that doors, windows and walkways aren't in the blade's path in case a kickback occurs.
- ■ Unplug the saw whenever you perform a blade change or adjustment that puts your fingers close to the blade. Also unplug the saw when you're not using it.
- ■ Wear safety glasses and hearing protection. Wear a dust mask if you're sawing in a confined space.
- ■ Unplug the saw before resetting a tripped circuit breaker or replacing a fuse.

Here's a trick for straightening crooked boards

Have you ever wanted to rip a straight edge on a crooked board, or rip an odd-shaped piece of wood like a stair baluster in half? The trick is to attach your workpiece to a straight strip of plywood. Then run the straight plywood edge against the fence to create a perfectly straight edge on your crooked board or odd-shaped piece.

This technique works only for boards with an edge that isn't straight. Don't try to rip boards that are twisted or cupped. They'll likely bind in the blade and could kick back. ⌂

7 RIP a 6-in. wide strip from the straight factory edge of a sheet of plywood. Use screws or finish nails to temporarily attach the crooked board to the plywood strip. Keep the fasteners away from the edge where they might come in contact with the saw blade.

8 SET the fence to remove the least amount of material and trim the attached board. Using the standard ripping procedure shown in Photo 2, guide the edge of the plywood against the fence as you run the board and plywood through the saw blade. Unscrew the board from the plywood and rip it again with the newly created straight edge against the fence.

HOMEMADE PUSH SHOE

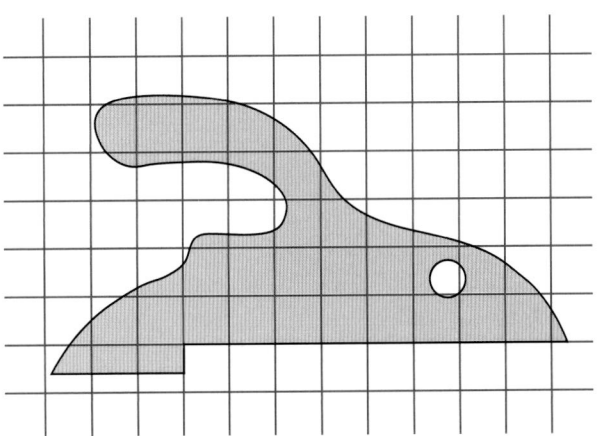

Plan is at 25%. Enlarge 400% on copy machine

10-MINUTE WORKSHOP
STORAGE PROJECTS

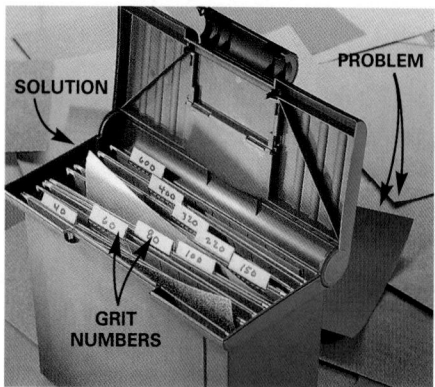

SOLUTION

PROBLEM

GRIT NUMBERS

FILE BY GRIT

Organize sandpaper by grit in a handy plastic file box ($9) available at office supply stores. Just list the grits on the tabs and you can instantly find the right one. The box is also a good place to store those partially used pieces that often find their way into the trash can prematurely.

A SWEET LITTLE BOTTLE O' TWINE

Can't find your twine to bundle that pile of recyclables? Try this slick solution. Cut the bottom 4 in. off a 1/2-gallon plastic milk or orange juice jug and load the container with a fresh spool of twine that unwinds from the middle. Then thread the twine through the jug opening and tape the jug back together. Cut an "X" in the cap with a utility knife to keep the twine from falling back into the jug!

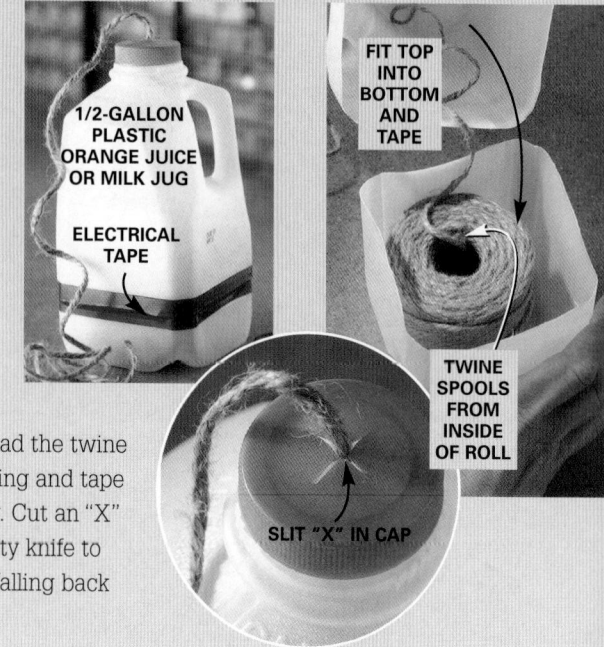

1/2-GALLON PLASTIC ORANGE JUICE OR MILK JUG

ELECTRICAL TAPE

FIT TOP INTO BOTTOM AND TAPE

TWINE SPOOLS FROM INSIDE OF ROLL

SLIT "X" IN CAP

HANG YOUR HANDYMAN

Here's an orderly tip: Hang issues of *The Family Handyman* and *American Woodworker* on Peg-Board hooks for easy reference during project production. Drill a 1/4-in. hole in the upper right corner of the magazines, clamping them between a couple of strips of scrap wood to drill a clean hole. Now when you hang the magazines, they overlap one another and you can read each issue's date without moving adjacent magazines out of the way.

PEG-BOARD HOOK

ISSUE DATES ARE VISIBLE

CLAMP FIRMLY FOR CRISPLY DRILLED HOLE

Handyman
Water Garden

FASTENER BINS FOR FREE

Save those 100-oz. laundry detergent bottles and use them to hold jumbo supplies of screws and nails. Cut the top off the bottle to create a wide mouth bin with a built-in handle. Label the bins, load them up, and you're ready to snag a handful when needed or carry a bin or two right to the job site.

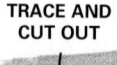

TRACE AND CUT OUT

100-OZ. LAUNDRY DETERGENT CONTAINERS

GRAB AND CARRY

ADD LABELS

TENNIS BALL BIT KEEPER

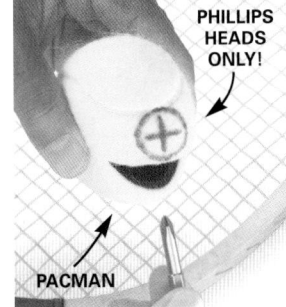

SOCKET SYMBOL

PHILLIPS HEADS ONLY!

PACMAN

Old tennis balls still serve well! Cut 2-in. slits in the balls with a utility knife, then squeeze them to open and load them with driver bits, small sockets or assorted small hardware like screws and brads. Use a permanent marker to identify the contents. Stored in a drawer, tool chest or nail apron, these bright balls will organize a lot of small parts.

CHISEL POCKETS

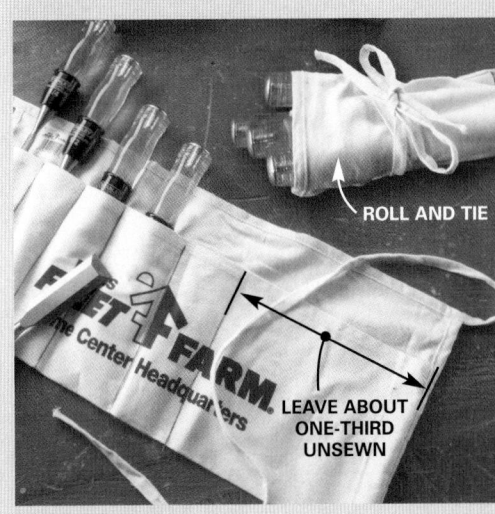

ROLL AND TIE

LEAVE ABOUT ONE-THIRD UNSEWN

Here's a nifty way to store chisels, files, carving knives and spade bits. Sew 1- to 1-1/2 in. wide parallel pockets in a carpenter's apron ($2 at a home center). Leave a third of the apron's width free of pockets so you can roll up the tools in a neat bundle. The apron strings tie the whole thing together, and your cutting tools stay sharp, dry and organized between jobs.

ODDS-AND-ENDS STORAGE

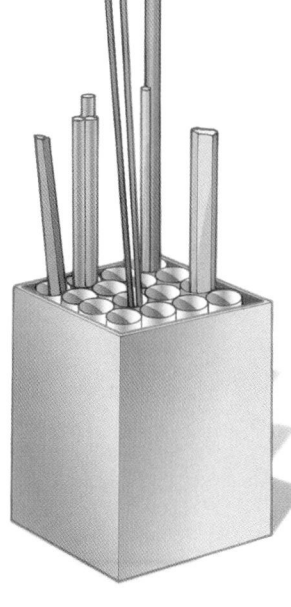

Fill a sturdy cardboard box with sawed-off shipping tubes or scraps of larger PVC pipe. Then use it to store and organize all those short pieces of molding, pipe and dowels.

SUPER-DUTY STEEL STUD SHELF BRACKETS

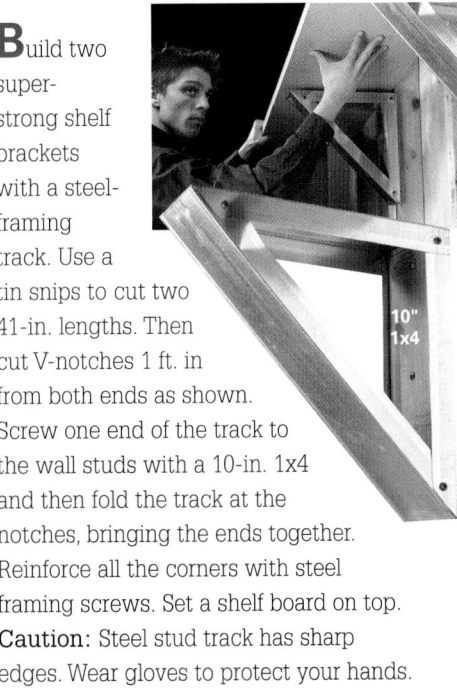

10" 1x4

Build two super-strong shelf brackets with a steel-framing track. Use a tin snips to cut two 41-in. lengths. Then cut V-notches 1 ft. in from both ends as shown. Screw one end of the track to the wall studs with a 10-in. 1x4 and then fold the track at the notches, bringing the ends together. Reinforce all the corners with steel framing screws. Set a shelf board on top. **Caution:** Steel stud track has sharp edges. Wear gloves to protect your hands.

WORKSHOP TOOLS, TIPS & STORAGE

CORD KEEPER

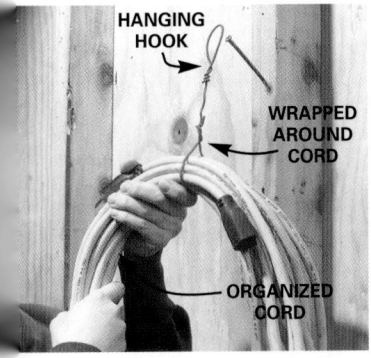

INDIVIDUAL WIRE STRAND

ELECTRICAL CABLE

HANGING HOOK

WRAPPED AROUND CORD

ORGANIZED CORD

Individual strands of electrical cable make great cord and hose wraps. Cut 12- or 14-gauge electrical cable into 12-in. to 18-in. sections. Grip a single strand with a needle-nose pliers, hold the casing and pull out the individual strand. It's easy to wrap and unwrap the wire around cords or hoses. Twist a loop on the opposite end of the wire for hanging.

TIDIER TOOL TRAYS

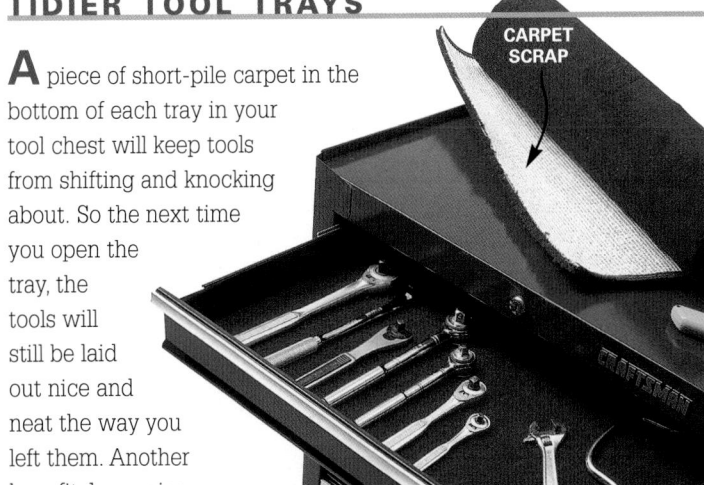

CARPET SCRAP

A piece of short-pile carpet in the bottom of each tray in your tool chest will keep tools from shifting and knocking about. So the next time you open the tray, the tools will still be laid out nice and neat the way you left them. Another benefit: less noise.

COFFEE CARRYALL

DRYWALL ANCHOR VARIETY PACK

FOUR-CUP COFFEE CARRIER

Here's a witty use for takeout coffee four-pack cartons. The ones we used are made of stiff cardboard and offer 3-1/2 in. wide square bins for jumbo plastic drinking cups. (Whoppers malt balls cartons cut in half are also great bin liners.)

I loaded my carryall with a 10-year supply of four styles of drywall fasteners—I always need them but can't find them in my heap of surplus hardware. Heck, now that I think of it, I gotta head out for another four-pack of coffee. I'll be wired, but I'll know where my wire spools are for years to come!

MAGNETIC MINI STORAGE

Want to build this handy storage roost for all the little screws, earplugs, nuts and washers in your shop? Pick up a pack of Glad 4-oz. cups, a magnetic strip, several 7/16-in. washers and a tube of E6000 glue ($4 at craft and hobby stores). Apply glue to the cup's concave bottom, press in a washer flush with the bottom rim and let the glue set for 24 hours. That's it. Mount the magnet, load the cups, snap on the lids and all your itty-bitties are easy to spot, nab and put away. Magnetic strips are available from Rockler (800-279-4441, www.rockler.com) and Magnaproducts (800-338-0527).

The magnetic strip provides more than enough magnet power to hold a cup crammed with screws.

SEE-THROUGH SIDES

WIDE MOUTH FOR EASY GRABBING

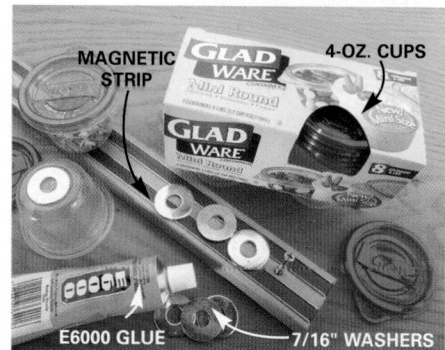

MAGNETIC STRIP

4-OZ. CUPS

E6000 GLUE

7/16" WASHERS

PVC SOCKET SHELVES

Here's a great way to use leftover pieces of PVC pipe. Cut them into various shorter lengths and glue them to a 4-in. wide board with construction adhesive. Attach the boards to a shop wall with corner irons ($3 for a four-pack at a home center) bent downward 15 degrees or so. Then fill the pipe pieces with screws, nails, glue, spray paint and, sure, a hot cup of coffee.

With the shelves angling a little downward, it's easier to see and grab the contents. Two-inch pieces of 3-in. dia. pipe are great for screws and nails, and 5-in. long pieces of 1-1/2 in. dia. pipe are neat holsters for pencils, files, paint brushes and Popsicle sticks.

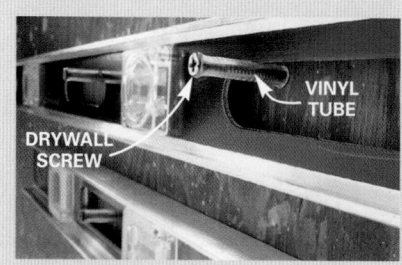

DRYWALL SCREW

VINYL TUBE

CUSHIONED TOOL PEGS

Screws make great pegs for holding tools on the wall, and here's a way you can make them even more useful. Buy a length of 3/16-in. tubing, cut pieces about 1 in. in length, and slip them over your 2-in. drywall or deck screw shafts. Drive each screw until the vinyl tube contacts the wood surface and the tapered head of the screw. Now you've got cushioned surfaces for hanging all your fine hand tools.

5" LONG x 1-1/2" DIA. PVC PIPE

3" LONG x 3" DIA. PVC PIPE

3" x 3" ANGLE BRACKET

2" LONG x 3" DIA. PVC PIPE

20" MACHO PIPES

BOLTS

WASHERS   **NUTS**

MUFFIN PAN PARTS TRAY

When I work on small projects or take something apart, I use muffin pans to keep everything organized. Stack several pans together for extra workspace or storage.

RUST-FREE NAIL STORAGE

For rust-free storage of expensive air nailer fasteners, use steel ammunition boxes from an army surplus store. They have a watertight seal to help prevent corrosion and they're cheap (about $5).

NAIL GUN AMMO CASE

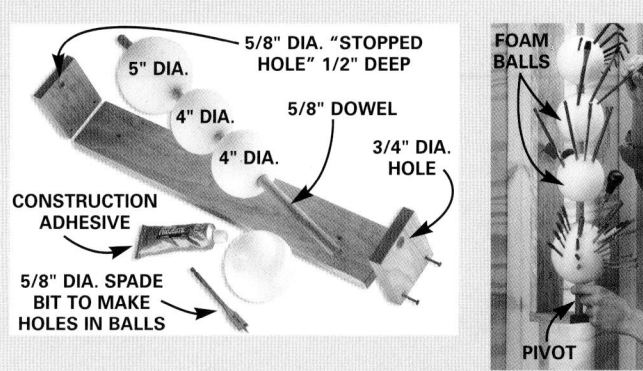

5/8" DIA. "STOPPED HOLE" 1/2" DEEP

5" DIA.

4" DIA.

5/8" DOWEL

4" DIA.

3/4" DIA. HOLE

CONSTRUCTION ADHESIVE

5/8" DIA. SPADE BIT TO MAKE HOLES IN BALLS

FOAM BALLS

PIVOT

FOAM BALL TOOL STORAGE

Here's a pointer on storing pointed tools for instant availability. Drill 5/8-in. holes through a few 4- or 5-in. foam craft balls ($3 each at a craft store), and skewer and glue them along a 5/8-in. dia. dowel with construction adhesive. Screw together a 3/4-in. wood bracket, drilling a stopped 5/8-in. dia. hole 1/2 in. deep in the bottom end and a 3/4-in. hole through the upper end. Screw the bracket at a convenient height, slide in the foam balls and load them with drill, router and spade bits; paint brushes; screwdrivers; Allen wrenches; awls; X-Acto knives; pencils and, well, you get the point.

NUTS AND WASHERS STORED ON PEG-BOARD

Old-fashioned shower curtain rings ($2 for a 12-pack at a home center) can organize and conveniently display nuts and washers on your Peg-Board. Load up the rings, add a tape label, and hang them near the wrenches. You can also toss them in a nail apron for on-the-go repairs.

SHOWER CURTAIN RINGS

1/4   3/8   1/2

PVC PIPE CLAMP RACK

FOR 3/4" IRON PIPE CLAMPS, USE 1" PVC

FOR 1/2" IRON PIPE CLAMPS, USE 3/4" PVC

Are your pipe clamps missing in action right when you need them? Never again, thanks to this slick snap-in, snap-out storage rack, made from PVC pipe. For 1/2-in. dia. iron pipe, use 3/4-in. PVC, and for 3/4-in. dia. pipe use 1-in. PVC.

To make the rack, cut 2-in. lengths of PVC, and with a hacksaw or band saw, slice them lengthwise about 3/16 in. past the diameter's center line. This creates the gripping action to firmly hold the heavy iron pipe. Drill and countersink two holes in each PVC piece, then space and screw them along a pair of 2-in. wide boards. Attach the upper board to your shop wall and snap a pipe clamp in either end to position the lower board for screwing to the wall. That's it. You've shaped AWOL pipe clamps into an orderly arsenal.

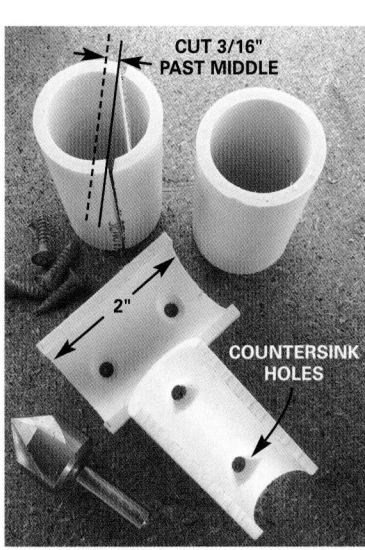

CUT 3/16" PAST MIDDLE

2"

COUNTERSINK HOLES

Using Tools: Angle Grinder

Not just for *grinding metal, this versatile tool cuts tile, routs out mortar, and sands* ***and polishes***

I used to think an angle grinder was only good for grinding metal. Then I saw a tile setter using an angle grinder with a diamond wheel to make intricate cuts for a tile backsplash and realized the tool's potential. Now that I own an angle grinder, I've found all kinds of uses for it. Cutting tile, mortar, stucco and pavers is easy with a diamond wheel. Wire brush attachments make quick work of rust and loose paint removal.

Special abrasive wheels can cut or grind steel. We'll show you how to use your angle grinder with special wheels to accomplish a number of common but difficult cutting, grinding and polishing tasks.

You'll find angle grinders anywhere power tools are sold. Larger grinders are available, but the popular 4-in. and 4-1/2 in. grinders are the right size for most tasks. You can buy an angle grinder for as little as $40, but for frequent use or for demanding jobs like cutting stucco or cement, I'd recommend spending $70 to $110 for a grinder with a more powerful motor (look for a motor that draws 5 to 9 amps).

The ability to handle different wheels and accessories is what makes angle grinders so versatile. Your angle grinder includes a spindle washer and spindle nut that you'll install in different configurations to accommodate thicker or thinner wheels or remove altogether when you screw wire wheels and cups onto the threaded spindle. Consult your manual for instructions on mounting wheels and accessories.

You'll find abrasive wheels for angle grinders in any hardware store or home center for $2 to $3. Although the wheels all look similar, they're designed for different tasks. Read the labels.

Metal cleaning

Wire wheels remove rust and flaking paint quickly. Wire wheel and brush attachments cost $15 to $25 and are designed for different types of stripping, cleaning and deburring tasks. Wire cup brushes work best for stripping paint or rust from broad, flat areas, while wire wheels fit into crevices and corners more easily (**photos, below**). Wheel and brush attachments come in a wide variety of styles. Read the packaging to find one that works for your application. Also make sure to match the threads to the spindle threads on your grinder. Most angle grinders have 5/8-in. spindle threads, but there are a few oddballs.

WIRE CUP BRUSH

WIRE WHEEL

WIRE CUP BRUSH

THREAD ONTO SPINDLE

CEMENT-COATED SHOVEL

BRUSH AWAY FROM EDGE

CLEAN rust and caked-on cement and dirt from garden tools with a wire cup. Secure the work with clamps or a vise. Make sure the brush is spinning away from, not into, the edge. Otherwise, the brush can catch on the edge and cause the grinder to kick back at you.

BRUSH AWAY FROM EDGE

CREVICE

WIRE WHEEL

REMOVE paint with a wire wheel. Again, be careful to work away from, not into, sharp edges. Wire wheels fit into crevices and tight areas.

Cut bars, rods and bolts

If you're patient, you can cut most metal with a hacksaw. But for quick, rough cuts, it's hard to beat a grinder. I've used an angle grinder to cut rebar (**left photo**), angle iron, rusted bolts (**right photo**) and welded wire fencing. Use a cutoff wheel ($2.50) for these and other metal-cutting tasks.

METAL CUTOFF WHEEL

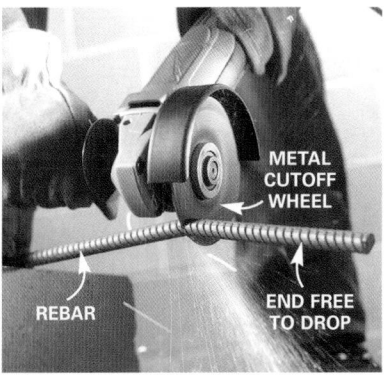

METAL CUTOFF WHEEL

REBAR

END FREE TO DROP

MOUNT a metal cutoff wheel in your angle grinder. Prop up the long side of the rebar and hold it securely. Drop the cutoff wheel through the metal, allowing the weight of the tool to do most of the work. Allow the short end to drop freely to avoid binding the blade.

BOLT

GRIND bolts flush to concrete. You can brush against the concrete, but don't try to cut into it with this wheel.

Cut tile, stone and concrete

Notching and cutting ceramic or stone tile to fit around outlets and other obstructions is difficult if not impossible with standard tile cutters. But an angle grinder fitted with a $25 dry-cut diamond wheel makes short work of these difficult cuts (**photos, below**).

DRY-CUT DIAMOND WHEEL

DIAMOND WHEEL

MARKED FOR OUTLET CUTOUT

SCORE TILE FACE

1 MARK the outline of the cut accurately on both the front and the back of the tile. Clamp the tile to your workbench and score the outline about 1/8 in. deep on the front with the diamond blade.

BACK OF TILE

EXTEND CUTS PAST CORNERS

2 FLIP the tile over and cut through the tile from the back. Extend the cuts slightly past the lines at the corners to make crisp, square corners.

Using Tools: **Angle Grinder**

Restore cutting edges

Outfitted with a grinding wheel ($3), an angle grinder is a great tool for restoring edges on rough-and-tumble tools like hoes, shovels and ice scrapers or for the initial grinding of axes, hatchets and lawn mower blades. If you need a sharper edge than the grinder leaves, follow up with a mill bastard file. The photo at right shows how to sharpen a lawn mower blade. Use the same technique to restore

GRINDING WHEEL the edge on other tools. Orient the grinder so that the wheel spins from the body of the blade toward the edge (refer to the arrow on the body of the grinder to determine which direction the wheel spins). Finally, with the grinder off, rest the grinding wheel against the blade and adjust the angle of the grinder to match the blade's bevel. This is the position you'll want to maintain as you grind the edge. Lift the grinder from the edge, switch it on and let it come to speed before moving it into the blade.

Stroke the grinder across the work in the direction of the handle rather than grinding back and forth. Then lift it off and repeat, concentrating on holding the grinder at a consistent angle throughout the stroke.

It's easy to overheat a metal blade with a grinder. Overheated metal turns a bluish black or straw color and won't stay sharp for long. To avoid overheating, apply only light pressure and keep the grinder moving. Also keep a bucket of water and sponge or rag handy and drench the metal frequently to keep it cool.

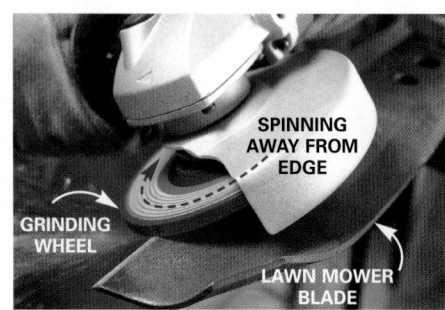

CLAMP the blade in a vise or to your workbench with hand clamps. Orient the grinder and adjust the blade guard to deflect sparks from your face and body. Align the grinding wheel with the angle on the blade. Start the grinder and move the grinding wheel steadily across the blade while applying light pressure.

Cutting out old mortar

Grinding beats a chisel and hammer for removing old mortar (**photo, right**). It would be worth buying a grinder just

DIAMOND TUCKPOINTING WHEEL to remove mortar if you had a lot of tuckpointing to do. Thicker diamond tuckpointing wheels ($50) remove old mortar quickly without disturbing or damaging the bricks. It's dusty, though, so wear a dust mask and make sure to shut your windows and warn the neighbors.

We've only touched on the jobs you can do with an angle grinder. Browse your local hardware store or home center to get a better idea of the attachments available. They can save you a ton of time. ⌂

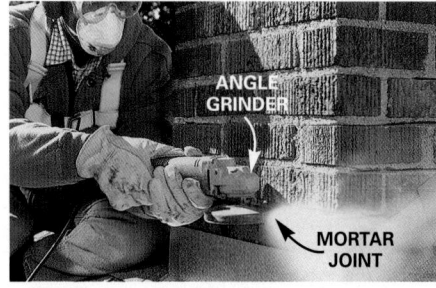

GRIND out old, loose mortar with an angle grinder and diamond tuckpointing wheel. Make two or three 1/2-in. deep passes to completely clear the joint. Stay about 1/8 in. from the brick to avoid damaging it.

Grinder safety

Unlike drill motors that run at about 700 to 1,200 rpm, grinders spin at a breakneck speed of 10,000 to 11,000 rpm. They're fast enough to be scary! Follow these precautions for safe grinder use:

- **Wear a face shield ($20) and gloves.**
- **Unplug the grinder when you're changing wheels.**
- **Attach the handle and maintain a firm grip with both hands.**
- **Use the guard if possible.**
- **Run new wheels for one minute in a protected area before using them to make sure the wheel isn't defective.**

- **Orient the work so debris is directed downward.**
- **Keep bystanders away. Everyone in the vicinity should wear safety glasses.**
- **Orient the work so the wheel spins away from, not into, sharp edges. Wheels, especially wire wheels, can catch on an edge and throw the workpiece or cause the grinder to kick back.**
- **Keep sparks away from flammable materials.**
- **Clamp or secure the workpiece in some fashion.**
- **Store angle grinders out of children's reach.**

Ask Handyman™

WHAT SIZE PILOT HOLES?

You're always talking about drilling pilot, clearance and countersink holes when working with wood screws. What size holes do I drill?

The purpose of the pilot hole is either to reduce the chance of splitting a board or to make a screw easier to drive. In both cases, the hole makes room for the body of the screw shaft, yet leaves enough material for the threads to bite. The drill bit should match the diameter of the screw body (not the threads). In practice, hold the screw up to the light and match a drill bit to the shank diameter.

A clearance hole allows the whole body of the screw to pass through. When it's important to draw one piece of wood tight to another, first drill a clearance hole.

The countersink allows the screwhead to sit either flush or below the surface. Special drill bits will cut clearance, pilot and countersink holes in one operation. While that's convenient, you have to buy a bit for each screw size.

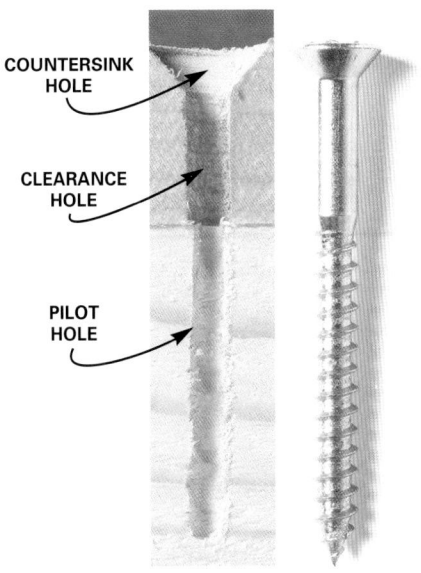

COUNTERSINK HOLE

CLEARANCE HOLE

PILOT HOLE

SIZING AN AIR COMPRESSOR

I need to buy an air compressor for my home woodworking shop. Could you give me some hints on the minimum airflow, power and tank capacity?

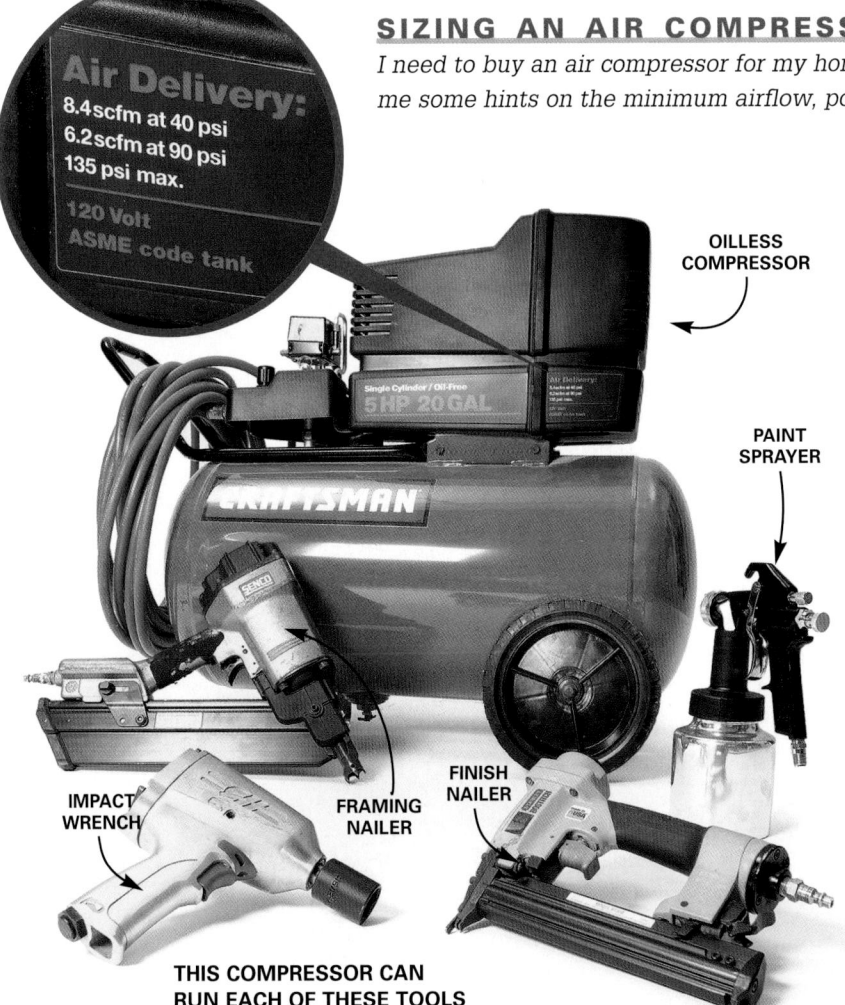

Air Delivery:
8.4 scfm at 40 psi
6.2 scfm at 90 psi
135 psi max.

120 Volt
ASME code tank

OILLESS COMPRESSOR

PAINT SPRAYER

FINISH NAILER

IMPACT WRENCH

FRAMING NAILER

THIS COMPRESSOR CAN RUN EACH OF THESE TOOLS

While it's tempting to go out and buy some big plowhorse of a compressor, the fact is that most shops can get by with a 1- to 2-hp unit. That's because most of us only use them to run trim nail guns and blow dust off projects. Smaller compressors are cheaper and don't require 240-volt circuits.

But if you plan to use paint sprayers or rotary tools like an orbital sander, then size the compressor to the tool that requires the highest volume of air. You'll find the specifications printed somewhere on the tool or in the accompanying literature (yes, the booklet you tucked away somewhere when you first unpacked the tool). Determine the tool's working pressure (pounds per square inch, or psi) and air usage requirements (square cubic feet per minute, or scfm). Choose a compressor that'll provide at least 1.2 times these specifications.

Finally, consider investing in an oil-lubricated one. It'll last longer and be much quieter than the oilless compressors.

Workshop Tips™

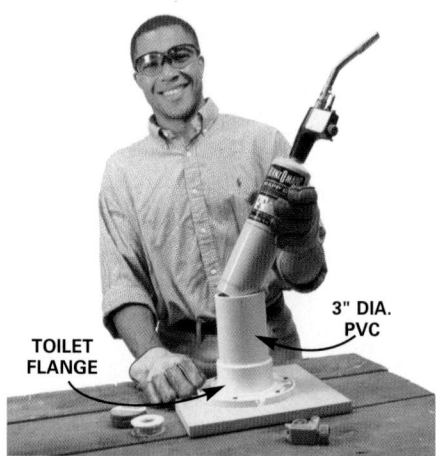

TOILET FLANGE

3" DIA. PVC

TORCH CADDY

Here's a caddy that holds hot torches steady and works as a third hand when you're welding. Mount a toilet flange to a 1-ft. square plywood base with 1-in. wood screws. Cut an 8-in. piece of 3-in. dia. pipe and glue it into the flange.

5/16" JAM NUT FILED TO FIT PENCIL

NUTTY, STAY-AT-HOME PENCIL

Does your pencil roll off the table while you're drafting your latest masterpiece? Twist a 5/16-in. "jam nut" (five for $1 at a hardware store) on the end and the pencil will stay put. For a perfect fit, file the nut's threads lightly with a rattail file. Jam nuts are narrower than standard-size nuts, so the little added weight won't bug you while you're sketching or writing. Add jam nuts to pens, X-Acto knives and other small cylindrical tools to keep them planted as well.

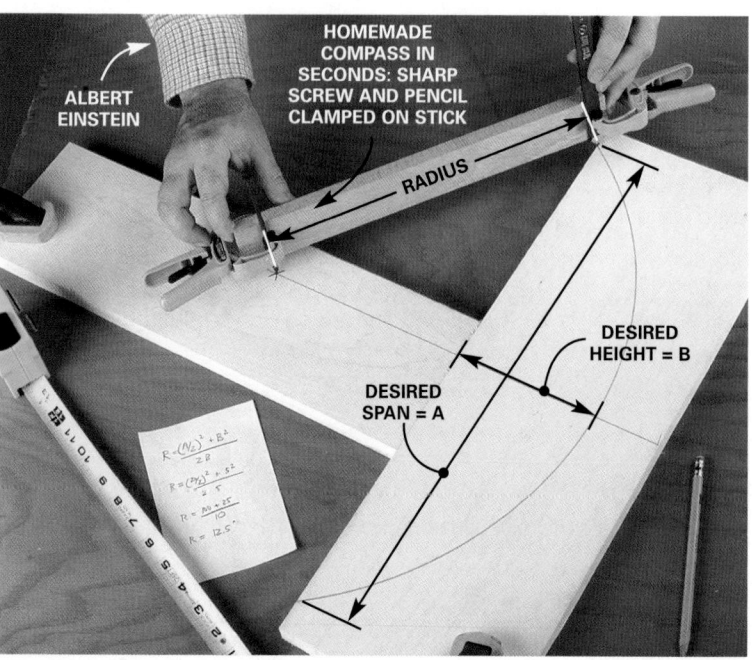

ALBERT EINSTEIN

HOMEMADE COMPASS IN SECONDS: SHARP SCREW AND PENCIL CLAMPED ON STICK

RADIUS

DESIRED HEIGHT = B

DESIRED SPAN = A

THE EXACT ARC YOU NEED

Guarantee: Use this formula to draw and saw an arc on a project workpiece and you'll never use guesswork or freehand tracing again. Measure the width of your desired arc's span (A) and the height (or depth) of the arc (B) and determine the arc's radius with this formula:

$$R= \frac{\left(\frac{A}{2} \right)^2 + B2}{2B}$$

Now (after realizing anew the pleasures of algebra!) set the radius on a compass and trace the arc. For larger arcs, mark the radius on a strip of wood and clamp on a pencil and a screw to make a jumbo compass for tracing the arc.

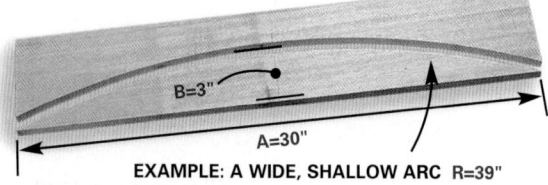

B=3"

A=30"

EXAMPLE: A WIDE, SHALLOW ARC R=39"

EASY-OPEN POLYURETHANE

Sometimes it's hard to pry off the lid of a half-used can of polyurethane because the lid is stuck in place by the hardened poly.

Next time, before tapping the lid in place, lay a piece of plastic wrap over the can. Later, when you go to open it, the lid won't stick, and the wrap seals the can better so a plastic skin won't form on the poly.

TABLE SAW EXTENSION TABLE

Make this knockdown table to support larger workpieces on your table saw. You'll need:

- 1-3/4-in. plywood tabletop sized to fit your saw
- four 1x2 border boards to reinforce the plywood top
- two 1-1/4 in. dia. iron pipe legs threaded on one end
- two 1-1/4 in. pipe flanges
- two 5-in. square x 3/4-in. blocks to attach the flanges to the table
- three 5/16-in. x 3-in. hanger bolts and wing nuts
- one 3/4-in. x 3-in. hanger bolt support board
- wood screws

Build the plywood tabletop (border included) to equal the table saw's front-to-back dimension. Make it wide enough to create at least 48 in. of overall support on the left side of the blade. Screw on the 5-in. square blocks and pipe flanges, then measure for the leg sizes while holding the table level with the saw. Have a home center thread and cut the pipes to length. Predrill the holes into the edge and support board to match the holes in the left edge of the saw table. Turn the hanger bolts into the support board with a locking pliers, then mount it to your saw by tightening the wing nuts. Adjust the legs to level the table with the table saw and go to work!

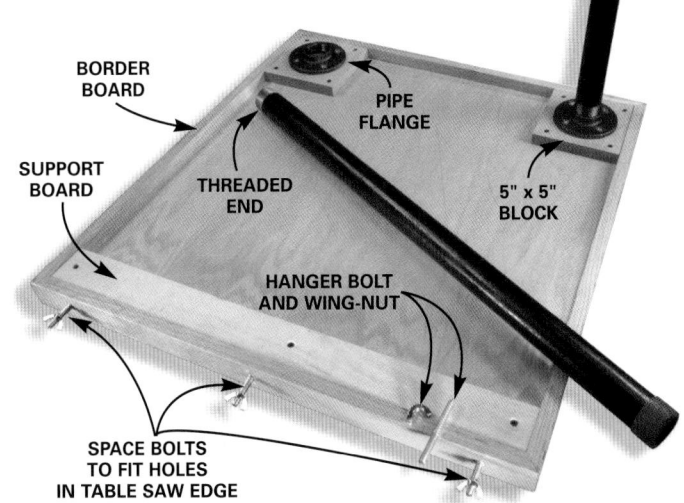

BORDER BOARD

PIPE FLANGE

SUPPORT BOARD

THREADED END

5" x 5" BLOCK

HANGER BOLT AND WING-NUT

SPACE BOLTS TO FIT HOLES IN TABLE SAW EDGE

48"

BOLT TO SAW HERE

CHEAP SPREADERS

Old laminate samples and scraps never die in my shop. I use them as glue spreaders, clamp guards and even as a note pad. I have two sources. I picked up a whole ring of discontinued samples from my local home center, and I save scraps that my local cabinet shop throws out and cut them down to size. Either way I've always got some around.

SIMPLE SANDPAPER

Use a fingernail emery board to sand tough-to-reach places. They come in varying lengths and sizes, many with a coarse and a fine side.

MERRY-GO-SHARPENING

Here's a fast, safe and easy way to rough-sharpen smaller shop tools like paint and glue scrapers. Buy a sanding disc kit ($6 at a home center) for an electric drill. The kit includes a rubber disc and several sanding discs in various grits.

Carefully clamp the drill in a vise without bending or distorting the drill's housing, then run the disc at low speed. Hold the blade so the disc rotates away from, not into, the blade so it won't cut into the disc. Move the blade from side to side, working near the outer edge of the disc for greatest control.

Use coarser grits to restore nicked edges and finer grits for touch-up sharpening.

Workshop Tips™

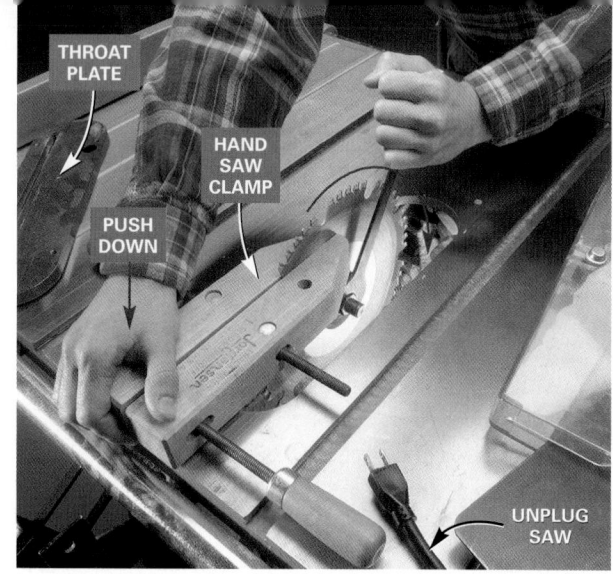

THROAT PLATE

HAND SAW CLAMP

PUSH DOWN

UNPLUG SAW

SPRING CLAMP STOP BLOCK

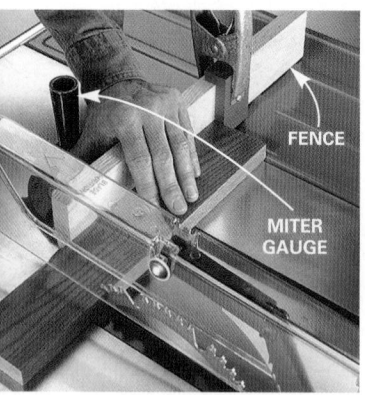

FENCE

MITER GAUGE

Here's a stop block that'll work great on every fence in your shop. Make an L-shaped block (the red piece in the photo) to ride upside down on the fence on your miter gauge. To make the L-block, cut a short 1-1/2 in. wide strip of 1/2-in. thick board, then cut a 1/2-in. piece off the end and glue it at a right angle to the end of the longer one. Screw the L-block to a strong spring clamp by drilling a screw hole in the tip of one clamp jaw, then screw the block inside the clamp with a fairly loose fit. When you snap the block in place on the fence, it'll snug up tight to both edges. Put adhesive-backed sandpaper on the fence side of the L-block to make it grip extra tight.

PAINLESS BLADE REMOVAL

Ever wondered how to remove a table saw blade without scratching your hand and fingers when you loosen the arbor nut? Here's the elegant and safe solution. Unplug the saw, lift out the throat plate and clamp the cranked-up blade in a handscrew. Now you can hold the handscrew—not the blade!—while untightening the arbor nut. The wood jaw surfaces can't ding up the blade. This method works just as well for tightening the blade on the saw.

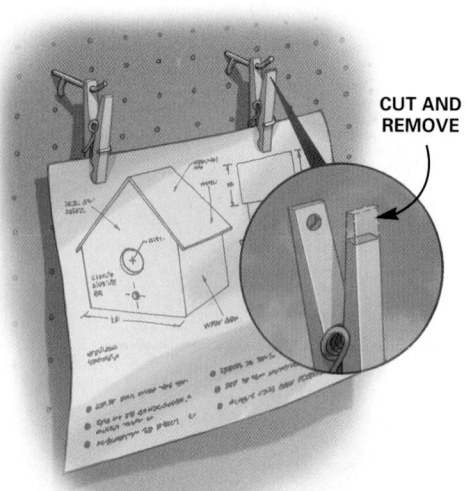

SCRAP WOOD TO SUPPORT WORK

HANGER STRAP

MITER GAUGE SLOT

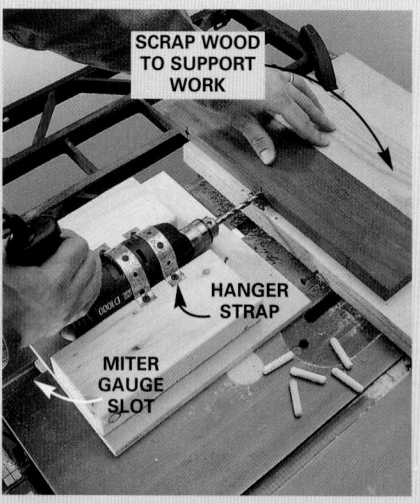

WOOD STRIP

WORKBENCH PLANS HANGER

If you have Peg-Board over your workbench and you need to hang plans or drawings where you can see them, use two clothespins with a hole drilled in one end of each. Then hang each clothespin from a Peg-Board hook and they're ready to hold those plans.

CUT AND REMOVE

HORIZONTAL DRILLING STATION

Use this simple wood jig to turn your table saw top into a horizontal drilling station for drilling repetitive holes. Cut a strip of hardwood the same width as your miter gauge slot and screw it to the bottom of a piece of 3/4-in. plywood. Cradle your drill between pieces of 2x4 fastened to the plywood. Strap your drill (a flat-top drill works best) to the 2x4 with plumber's hanger strap. You may need to use tapered shims to get your drill bit parallel to the saw table. Now you can slide this jig along the top with the strip below riding smoothly in the miter slot. When you drill your wood, be sure to clamp it to the top.

REPLACE A RANDOM ORBITAL PAD

Over time, hook-and-loop backing pads wear down and lose their grip. And if you use the sander too aggressively, the sanding pad will heat up and melt the plastic hooks slightly. This significantly reduces the grip between the sander pad and sanding disc. The first sign is when the sanding disc shifts off center, slipping out from under the pad. Eventually the sanding disc grabs onto your project and the sander continues on without it, mutilating the little plastic hooks and ruining the pad.

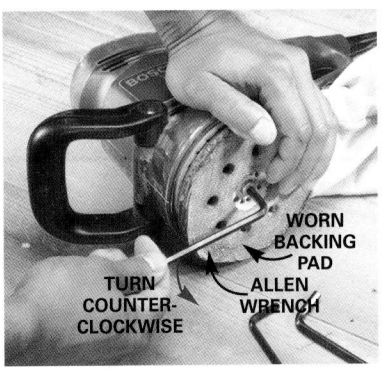

TURN COUNTER-CLOCKWISE — **WORN BACKING PAD** — **ALLEN WRENCH**

1 TURN the sander on its right side (for standard threaded bolts; flip it over for reverse threaded). Hold the base tight to the sander and firmly against the workbench. Turn the Allen wrench counterclockwise to break the bolt free. Remove the bolt and pull off the old backing pad.

To replace the backing pad, check the Yellow Pages under "Tools" for an authorized dealer for your tool brand. Bring the sander's model number to the dealer for the proper replacement backing pad (about $20). Also, ask the dealer if the mounting bolt has standard or reverse threads.

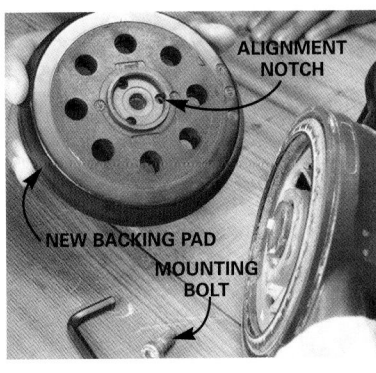

ALIGNMENT NOTCH — **NEW BACKING PAD** — **MOUNTING BOLT**

2 ALIGN the notches in the new backing pad with the tabs on the sander coupling. Apply thread-locking compound (Locktite) to the bolt and firmly tighten it down.

Remove the old backing pad as shown in **Photo 1**. Clean out any dust buildup inside the tool with compressed air or a small paint brush before installing the new pad (**Photo 2**).

You can also replace an adhesive pad with a hook-and-loop pad this way. Hook-and-loop systems have several advantages over adhesive-backed systems. Hook-and-loop systems allow frequent changing without damaging the sanding disc. Adhesive pads tend to collect dust and debris and lose their stickiness once removed, so you might consider switching over.

MAGNETIC FENCE FOR DRILL PRESS OR BAND SAW

Pick up a Shop-Mag ($7 at a home center or order from Magnaproducts, 800-338-0527) and use it as a fence for repeated accuracy on your drill press or band saw. This magnet can raise a 150-lb. outboard motor from a lake bottom, so it won't move when you use it to line up boards for drilling or sawing. Yet it comes loose with a sideways bump of your palm against the eye screw. Tap it along the base with a hammer for fine adjustments.

PUSH SIDEWAYS TO FREE MAGNET FROM TABLE — **MAGNETIC FENCE**

THE BOTTLE IS FULL

Is your glue bottle half full or half empty? For me, it's the latter. Every time I need to squeeze a little glue, I've got to wait for it to find its way down to the tip. Now no matter how much glue is in the bottle, it seems like it's full because I store the bottle upside down in this handy stand. To make it, take a 3 x 3-in. block of wood and drill a 1-1/4 in. hole in the middle a little deeper than the wide part of the cap. Next, drill a 5/8-in. hole for the neck as shown.

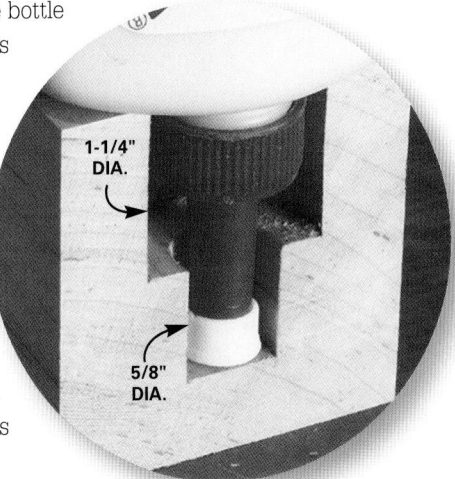

1-1/4" DIA. — **5/8" DIA.**

Workshop Tips™

NO GLUE ON YOUR HANDSCREWS!

Handscrews are the pros' choice for clamping face-glued boards and laminates. The only drawback is that the handscrew jaws can load up with glue, and if you're not careful, they could become a permanent part of the project! Besides, dried glue on the jaws will dent your projects. Here's the solution.

1. Wrap duct tape or clear packaging tape around the handscrew jaws to keep glue from penetrating and adhering to the clamps.
2. Remove the clamps once the glue is set but still pliable. Use a moist rag to clean the glue off the taped handscrews, or strip off the tape and apply new tape before your next messy job.

THE PROBLEM: A MESS OF HARDENED GLUE

THE SOLUTION: COVER JAWS WITH DUCT TAPE

TURNING BLANK FOR ROLLING PIN

SPILL-PROOF BOTTLE BASE

As a handyman pushing 90, I find my eyes and hands aren't as coordinated as they were a few years ago. When I'm using small craft-paint or similar bottles, one will occasionally tip over, making quite a mess. To avert this problem, drill a hole (slightly larger than the bottle) in a scrap 2x4 using a spade bit or other flat-bottom bit. Stick the bottle in the hole to keep it securely upright.

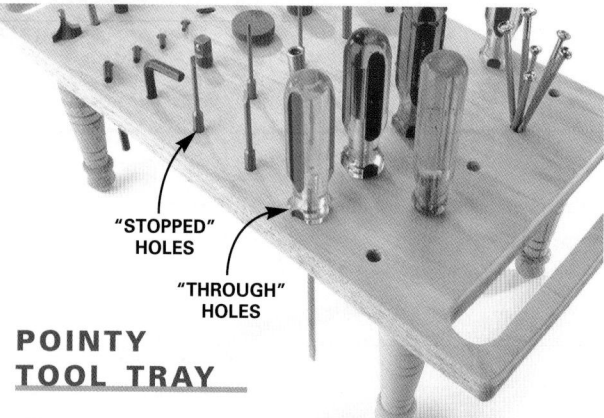

"STOPPED" HOLES

"THROUGH" HOLES

POINTY TOOL TRAY

A resourceful reader showed us a cool way to keep screwdrivers and all other pointy tools at hand. Drill a grid of holes in a 10 x 20-in. piece of plywood, leaving room on the ends for handle slots. To create the ends of the slots, drill 1-1/4 in. holes with a spade bit. Then connect the holes with parallel lines and saw out the slots with a saber or keyhole saw. Make or buy some short legs, screw them on and serve up your tools!

WORK LIGHT

SHOP VACUUM

POWER STRIP

WORK LIGHT CORD

SHOP VACUUM CORD

MITER SAW CORD

FLIP THE SWITCH

When I use my miter saw, I like to use a light to zero in on fussy cuts and a shop vacuum as a dust collector. To cut down on plugging and unplugging and flipping switches, I came up with this solution: I bought a power strip at the hardware store with key-holes in the back for mounting to the side of a cabinet. It's got a switch that turns the outlets on and off. I plugged in my light and vacuum so when I flip the switch on the strip, they both come on. Then I start my saw and I'm ready to go. Don't try to plug in too many things—most strips are rated at just 15 amps.

8 Exterior Maintenance & Repairs

IN THIS CHAPTER

You Can Fix It 184
  *Caulk cracked concrete, mend a
  leaky hose, asphalt repair and more...*

Vinyl Siding 192

Ask Handyman 198
  *Durable fix for a sinking driveway
  and sturdy stair posts.*

Making Paint Last 200

Handy Hints 205
  *Cleaner paint brushes, gutter
  straightener and more...*

Using Tools: Ladders 208

Great Goofs 209

You Can Fix It™

CAULK CRACKED CONCRETE

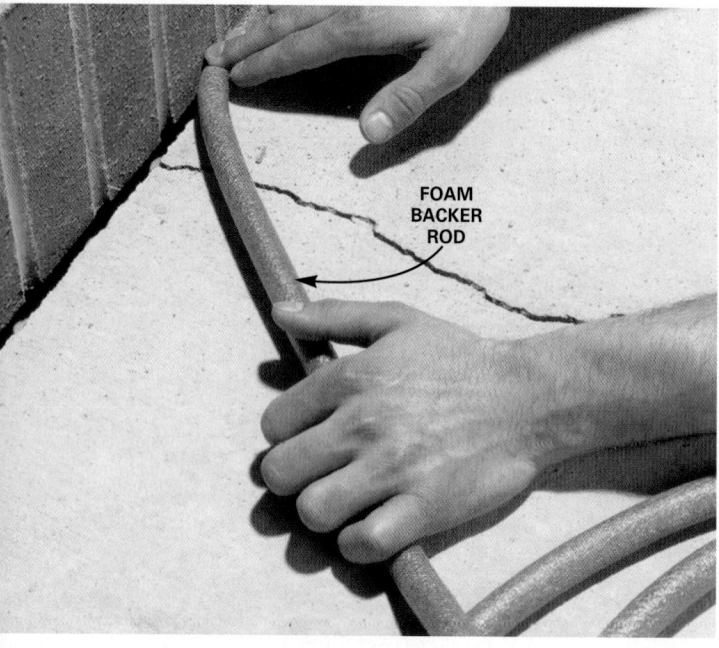

1 PUSH foam backer rod into the gap with your fingers. Set the rod 1/4 in. lower than the surface of the concrete.

Cracks and gaps in concrete are more than just an eyesore. Water can get into the joints, freeze and then expand, making the cracks even larger. Gaps against a house can direct water against the foundation, leading to more problems. Once a year, go around your home and fill these gaps and joints with urethane caulk to prevent problems. The caulk is available at contractor supply stores, well-stocked home centers and hardware stores for about $5 per tube. For gaps and joints more than 1/4 in. wide, install foam backer rod to support the caulk. You want the rod to fit tight in the joint, so buy it one size larger than the gap. It costs about 10¢ per foot.

A word of advice: Keep the urethane caulk off your bare hands and clothes; it's the stickiest stuff you'll ever touch. Wear disposable gloves when you're tooling the joints. If you get some on your skin, quickly wipe it off with a mineral spirits–dampened cloth.

2 FILL the crack with urethane caulk. Snip the opening of the tube at a 30-degree angle, making the opening the same size as your gap. Use a smooth, even motion, filling the crack flush with the surface, beveling it if it's against the house. Smooth the caulk in wide joints with the back of an old spoon. Wipe the spoon clean as needed with a rag and mineral spirits.

3 CAULK cracks 1/4 in. wide or less without using backer rod. Draw the gun down the crack, smoothing the caulk with the tip as you go.

REPLACE A DAMAGED SHINGLE

Asphalt shingles withstand years of abuse from wind, rain, sleet and snow, but they can tear like cardboard when struck by a falling tree limb or branch. Replacing the shingle will only take about 10 minutes— just be careful not to damage any other shingles.

If you don't have a few extra shingles stored in the garage or attic, take a scrap of the shingle to a home center or roofing supplier to find a match. You'll have to buy a full bundle ($10 to $25).

It's best to work on the roof when the temperature is between 50 and 70 degrees F. Walking around on a hotter roof can damage the shingles.

The first step is to remove what's left of the damaged shingle. Each shingle has an adhesive tar sealant strip down the center that grips the shingle above it. The tabs from the damaged shingle and the tabs directly above it will all have to be freed from the sealant strip (**Photo 1**). Break this seal to get at the nails and get the damaged shingle out.

The next step is to pull out the nails and remove the damaged shingle. There will be eight or nine nails holding the shingle in place (four in the damaged shingle and four or five from the shingles directly above it). Remove the nails as shown in **Photo 2**.

Pull out the old shingle and slide a new one in its place. If the old nails are in good condition, reuse them, but if they're rusty or bent, replace them with new galvanized roofing nails of the same length. Align the new shingle with the rest of the row and nail it off (**Photos 3 and 4**).

SHINGLE TABS

PUTTY KNIFE

SEALANT STRIP

1 PUSH a stiff putty knife under the shingle tabs to break through the sealant strip. Rock the putty knife back and forth to help it slice through.

2 SLIDE a flat pry bar under the head of the nails (tap it with a hammer if necessary). Slip a scrap block of wood under the pry bar to help leverage the nail loose. Remove nails in the shingle itself and the nails in the row directly above it. Slide out the old shingle.

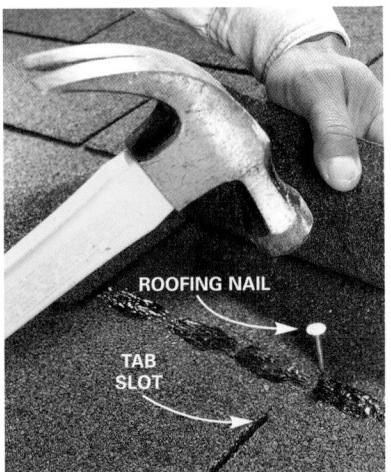

ROOFING NAIL

TAB SLOT

3 SLIP the new shingle into place. Gently lift the tab of the shingle above, position the nails just above the sealant strip and nail the new shingle above the tab slots and at the ends. Move up one row and nail and repeat the process until you've replaced all the nails.

4 SEAL the loose shingle tabs to the roof with roof cement and a caulking gun.

EXTERIOR MAINTENANCE & REPAIRS

You Can Fix It™

SCREEN REPAIR

Balls hit them, kids push on them and pets try to run through them. Whether your screens are aluminum or fiberglass, they'll get punctured or torn. But don't go ballistic and take it out on your cat. Repairing a damaged screen is easy and takes only a few minutes.

If the screen's aluminum frame is in good shape, you'll need only the following: a roll of new screen material, a package of spline (the thin rubber strip that holds the screen material on the frame) and a screen rolling tool. You'll find all these items at home centers and hardware stores.

The steps we show here apply only to aluminum frame screens. If your screens are wood frame, see "Repairing Wood Frame Screens," June '95, p. 25. To order a copy, see p. 288.

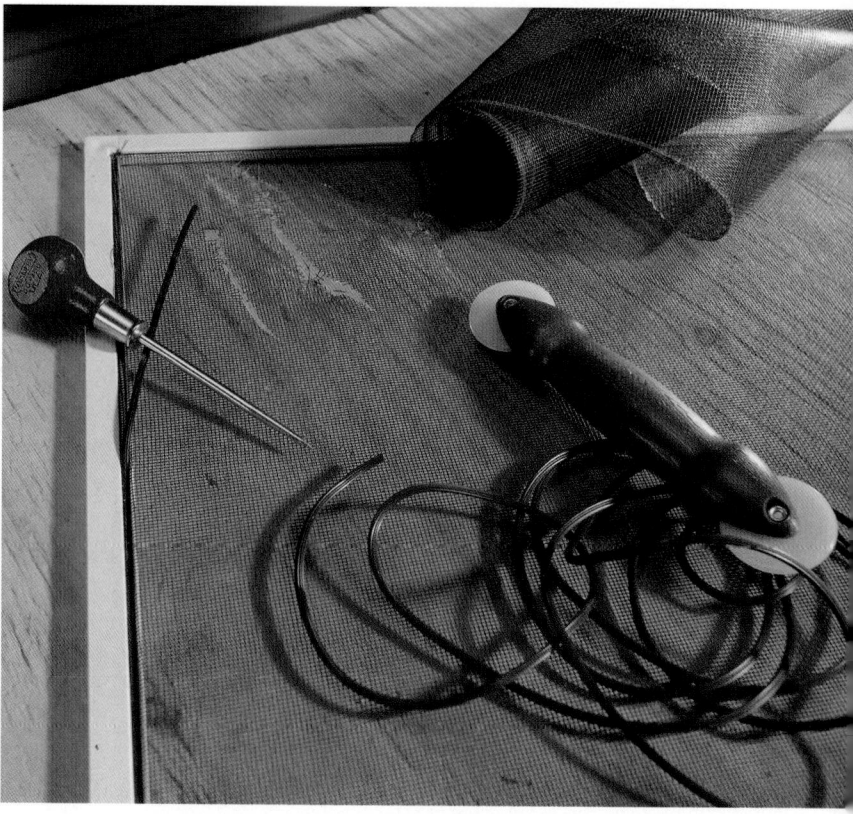

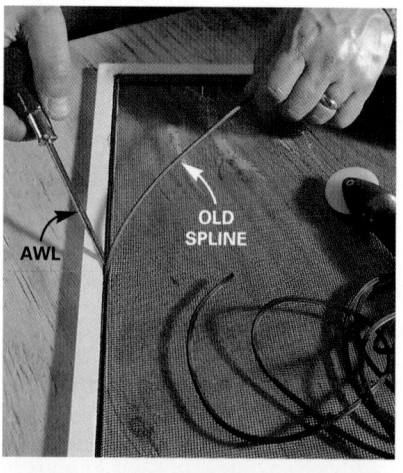

1 PRY out the old spline with an awl or a narrow-tipped screwdriver. Throw it away—spline gets hard and brittle as it ages and shouldn't be reused.

2 PLACE wooden blocks along the inside of the two longest sides of the frame and secure them to the work surface. The blocks keep the frame from bowing inward when you install the new screen material.

Selecting screen material

The most popular replacement screen material is fiberglass, the type we're installing. Its flexibility makes it the easiest to use—if you make a mistake, you can take it out of the frame and try again. Aluminum screen is sturdier, but you only get one chance. The grooves you've made with the screen rolling tool are there to stay.

A third type of screen material that's popular is sun-shading fabric. It blocks more sun, which means less load on your air-conditioning system and less fading of your carpet, draperies and furniture. It's also stronger than fiberglass and aluminum screening, so it's great for pet owners.

All three materials come in gray or black to match your other window screens. You can also get shiny aluminum as well as sun-shading fabrics in bronze and brown tones. Know the size of your window when you go to the home center. It will sell premeasured rolls to fit nearly any opening size. If your screen frame is taller than 36 in., it should have a center support to keep it from bowing in once the material is in place. Newer screens usually come with this support.

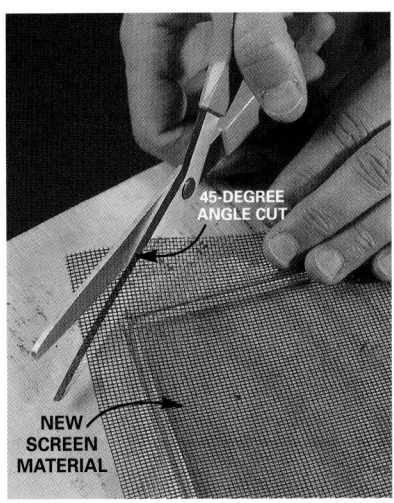

3 LAY the new screen material over the frame. It should overlap the frame by about 3/4 to 1 in. Cut each corner at a 45-degree angle just slightly beyond the spline groove. The cuts keep the screen from bunching in the corners.

NEW SCREEN MATERIAL

45-DEGREE ANGLE CUT

4 BEGIN installing the new spline at a corner. Use the screen rolling tool to push the spline and screen material into the groove. Continue around the frame. If wrinkles or bulges appear, remove the spline and reroll. Small wrinkles should tighten up as you get back to the starting corner.

SCREEN ROLLING TOOL

CONCAVE ROLLER

NEW SPLINE

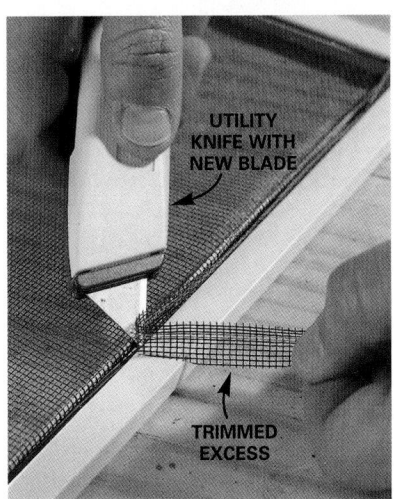

5 TRIM excess screen material using a utility knife with a new sharp blade. A dull blade will pull the material, not cut it. Cut with the blade on top of the spline and pointed toward the outside of the frame.

UTILITY KNIFE WITH NEW BLADE

TRIMMED EXCESS

Tip

If your long screens don't have a support, you can make one out of aluminum frame stock. It's located near the screening supplies in most stores. The aluminum stock can be cut with a tin snips and trimmed to fit.

ROTARY TOOL

TUNGSTEN CARBIDE CUTTER

SHAVE OFF the inside of the strike plate with a rotary tool and a metal-cutting carbide bit. Remove a small amount and test the latch by closing the door. Continue removing metal until the door latch catches.

FIX A DOOR THAT DOESN'T LATCH

As a house settles, doorknob latches and strike plates sometimes become misaligned, so doors won't latch shut. Usually you have to push the door in, and either pull up or press down on the doorknob in order to get the latch to catch in the strike plate.

If the movement has been slight, there's a very simple fix for the problem. Instead of moving the strike plate, simply slightly enlarge the latch opening in the strike plate as shown above. A rotary tool does this quickly and easily. Use a carbide-cutting bit specifically designed for metal cutting.

Judge the part of the strike plate that needs grinding by testing when the latch catches. If you have to push down on the doorknob, then the top of the strike plate hole needs grinding. If the door has to be pushed in, then grind the outside edge of the strike plate hole.

CAUTION: Grinding metal can throw sparks and fragments into the air, so wear safety glasses with side shields, or full goggles when grinding. Otherwise, use a small round file.

You don't want the latch slopping around inside a huge opening, so don't grind away half the strike plate. Remove small amounts of metal and then test the door. Repeat until the door latch effortlessly catches the strike plate.

EXTERIOR MAINTENANCE & REPAIRS

You Can Fix It™

METAL GUTTER REPAIR

GUTTER HANGER

CAUTION: Stay well away from electrical power lines.

GUTTER HANGER

METAL GUTTER

1 HOOK the gutter hanger under the front edge of the gutter and over the back edge. Then drive the hex head screw through the wood trim behind the gutter. The hangers will be stronger if you screw them into a rafter. Look for nailheads, which indicate rafter locations. Add new gutter hangers about every 3 ft. along the entire length of the gutters if the old ones have let go.

ROOF VALLEY

1/8" DRILL BIT

SPLASH GUARD

2 DRILL 1/8-in. holes through both the splash guard and the gutter.

If your metal gutters have developed a middle-age sag, it's time for a little tummy tuck. You'll find some version of a gutter support bracket that'll work on your gutters to lift the low spots. It'll help drain water better and help keep debris from accumulating. The style shown, made by Amerimax Home Products (800-776-8629, www.amerimax.com), is very easy to install and costs about $1 each. Another style of gutter hanger slides under the shingles and is nailed to the roof under the shingles. But test-bend your shingles first. Older shingles can be brittle and could break off when you lift them for the installation.

Rx for overflowing valley gutters

If rainwater cascading down your roof valley causes a waterfall that washes out the petunias every time it storms, install a splash guard. It takes about 20 minutes to complete. You can find these precut splash guards (about $3) in both brown and white aluminum at a home center, but you could easily make your own out of aluminum or sheet metal and spray-paint them to match your gutters. If you don't own a Pop riveter, attach the guards with 1/2-in. sheet metal screws instead.

POP RIVET GUN

3 PRESS the head of a 1/8-in. rivet into each hole. Place the Pop rivet tool over the shaft of the rivet and squeeze the handle once or twice to compress the rivet and break off the stem.

MEND A LEAKY HOSE

If you've got a cracked or punctured garden hose that sprays water all over, this fix is for you. If you cut out the leaky section and splice the hose back together, you won't have to throw it out. Garden hose splices are easy to install and are available at hardware stores, home centers and garden supply centers for about $3.

Cut off the leaky hose section (**Photo 1**). Several inches of hose around the leak will probably be stressed as well. Cut back to solid hose, removing all damaged or weakened sections. Measure the inside diameter of the garden hose to determine the splice size needed. The hose will be 1/2 in., 5/8 in. or 3/4 in. Buy the same size splice.

Install the splice between the two severed hose ends (**Photos 2 and 3**). Use liquid hand or dishwashing soap to lubricate the splice barbs and hose interiors so they go together smoothly.

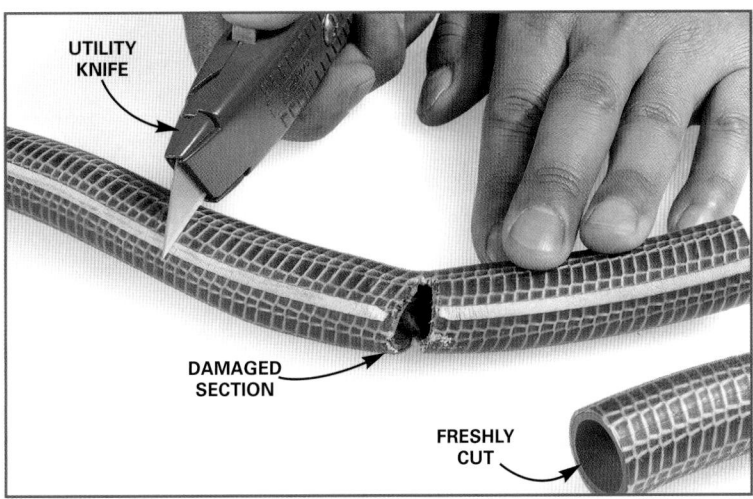

1 CUT the hose a few inches on each side of the damage to remove any weakened or stressed material. Use a sharp utility knife and keep the cut square.

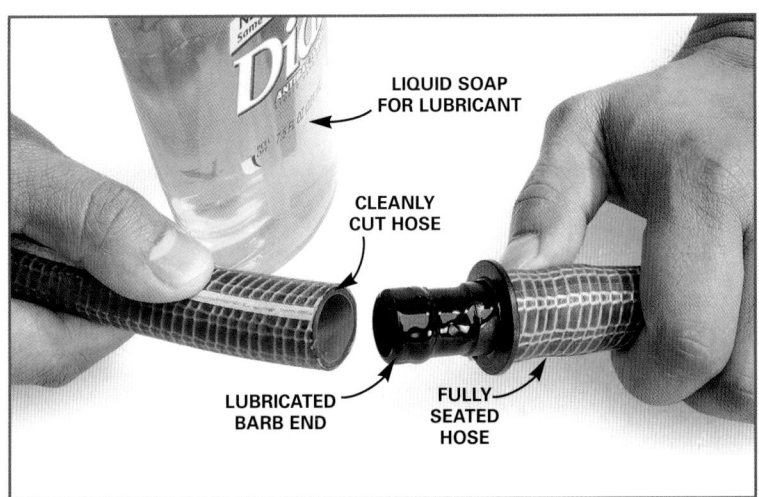

2 DISMANTLE the hose splice. Lubricate the splice barbs and hose interiors with liquid soap. Stand the splice upright on a workbench and push one cut end over the barb until the hose is fully seated. Twist the other cut end onto the other barb by hand until it's also fully seated.

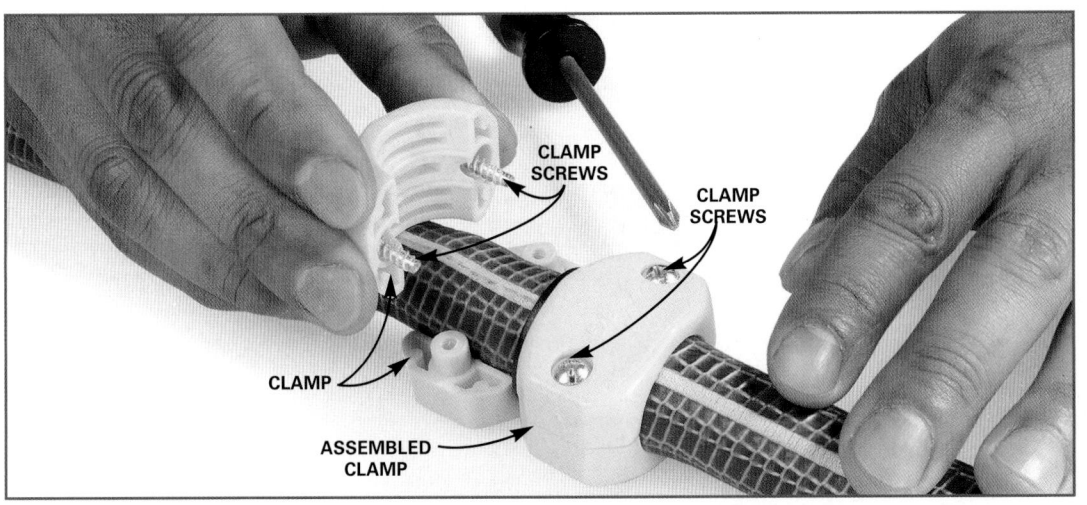

3 SANDWICH the clamps around the barbs and tighten the screws snugly. Don't torque the screws too hard or the plastic threads might strip.

You Can Fix It™

ASPHALT REPAIR

Are tufts of grass sprouting from your asphalt driveway? Well, if you don't do something about the pot holes and cracks in the pavement, they're not going to go away. In fact, they'll only get worse, especially if you live in a cold climate where ice and freeze/thaw cycles reign. Fix the little problems now and you'll add years to the life of your driveway.

Materials and equipment

Everything you need is available at home centers. You'll need liquid crack filler, a bag of cold-mix asphalt patch for filling holes and liquid driveway sealer to seal the entire driveway. You'll also need a degreaser if your driveway has any oil stains. Degreasers are usually stocked near the crack filler.

For tools, round up the following: a cold chisel for chipping away loose asphalt from around the edge of the holes, a garden trowel for putting the asphalt patch in the holes, and a 4x4 landscaping timber or post for tamping the asphalt patch into the hole. You'll also need a disposable brush/squeegee tool to apply the sealer. The total cost for materials and equipment will be $25 to $35.

Oh, and wear old clothes and old shoes, because none of these products will wash out.

The annual checkup

Do a quick inspection of your driveway and you're sure to find cracks. Hairline cracks will fill in when you apply the sealer. Cracks that are 1/8 to 1 in. wide should be filled with crack filler before sealing to prevent moisture from working its way into the asphalt. Moisture can break up the asphalt and weaken the base, which in turn leads to low spots in the surface and more water damage. Cracks that are wider than 1 in. should be repaired the same way you repair a hole (Photos 1 – 3).

COLD CHISEL

SQUARED CORNERS AND EDGES

1 CLEAN OUT all loose asphalt and any debris. Scrape around the edge of the hole until you have a solid edge. Don't be surprised if you make the hole a lot bigger.

If your driveway has a lot of wide cracks or broken-up areas, it's beyond this type of fix. Tree roots under the asphalt, an asphalt bed that's too thin (less than 4 in. thick) and eroding edges are major problems. Contact an asphalt contractor for advice and complete replacement.

Before making repairs

Sweep or hose off all dirt and debris. Next apply a degreaser to all oil stains. If you don't get rid of the stains, they'll bleed through the sealer. Scrub the areas thoroughly with a stiff-bristle brush and then rinse with the hose. Once everything dries, you can make the necessary repairs and apply the sealer.

Watch the weather

When you make your asphalt repairs is as important as how you make them. Select a day when the temperature is at least 50 degrees F. The higher the temperature, the easier the sealer is to apply and the faster it dries. And if there's rain in the 24-hour forecast, you're off the hook, at least for today.

2 FILL holes with asphalt patch. If the hole is more than 1-1/2 in. deep, fill it in layers. Add about 1 in. of asphalt patch, tamp it and then add more.

3 TAMP the asphalt into the hole with a 4x4 post. If the tamped area is lower than the driveway surface, add more asphalt patch until it's about 1/2 in. above the driveway surface and tamp again. Do this until the filled area is flush with the surface.

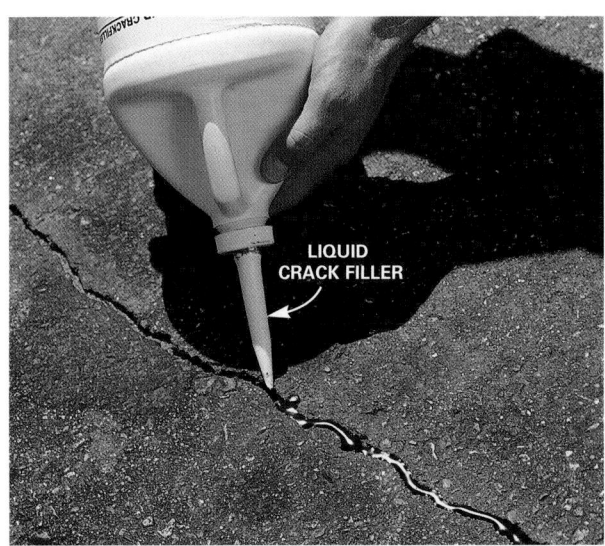

4 POUR in crack filler until it's flush or slightly below the driveway surface. If the filler settles, add more. Follow the manufacturer's instructions for drying time before applying the sealer. Remove any vegetation growing in the cracks before filling them.

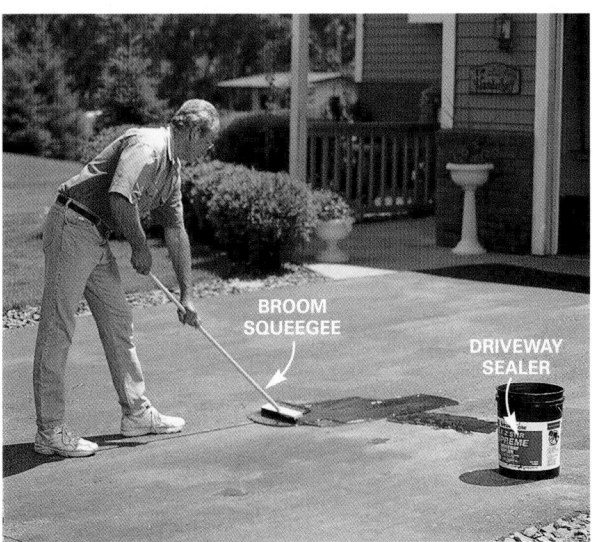

5 APPLY driveway sealer every two to three years. First scrub away oil stains with a degreaser and rust stains with a detergent and water solution. Then, rinse the area with water. Stay off the asphalt for 24 to 48 hours after applying sealer.

VINYL
SIDING

Don't be intimidated. Our staff pro shows you the steps for removing and installing it.

by **Carl Hines**

Don't let the fact that you have vinyl siding deter you from that repair or remodeling project. If you want to shift a window, replace a door or even put on an addition, you can remove, alter and reinstall vinyl siding much more easily than any other type of siding.

In this article, we're going to demonstrate how to rework the siding around a new set of windows. We'll show you how to remove it, install new parts and then cut it, fit it and nail it back up. Most important, we'll show you how to make the installation watertight.

While we'll cover the basics, we won't cover every detail you might run into with your own project. Most manufacturers offer complete instructions; ask for them wherever vinyl siding is sold.

The parts

Working with vinyl doesn't require special skills, but you do have to understand the system. The only special tool you'll need for reworking areas is an unlocking tool, often called a zip tool ($5; **photo below**). (You'll need a snap-lock punch if you intend to cover new areas.)

You'll probably need new trim pieces. We bought two types—J-channel to go around the new, larger windows (**Photo 9**), and undersill trim (see "When to Use Undersill Trim," p. 197). You may also need additional siding.

Unique installation

Vinyl siding is designed to hang loosely on the sheathing so that it can expand and contract with temperature changes. To prevent the relatively thin panels from buckling, observe these fitting and nailing rules.

1. Leave a 1/4-in. gap at all ends. The siding slides behind trim pieces that hide the gap and the cut end.

2. Lock the panel into the one below it, then gently snug it up before nailing. Marking the position of each piece before you remove it

ZIP TOOL

192

1 **SLIDE** the zip tool under the butt edge of the siding, hook the locking edge and pull down. Then slide the tool horizontally along the lock to release it. Lift the unlocked siding to expose the nailing hem of the siding piece below. Draw a line on the wall along the top of each siding course before you pull the nails.

NAILING HEM
LOCKING EDGE
DIFFERENT COLOR FOR CLARITY

2 **DRIVE** a flat bar between the nailheads and siding and carefully pull the nails. Then slide the piece down to unlock and remove it. Number each piece and set it aside. Remove siding until you expose enough wall to replace the window.

(Photo 2) will help you reposition the siding without stretching it.

3. Center the nails in the nailing slots and drive them, leaving 1/16 in. to 1/8 in. of the shank exposed (**Photo 14**). The vinyl must be free to expand and contract.

Remove the siding

The beauty of vinyl is that you can remove a piece anywhere on the wall. Locate the piece you want to remove and unlock the one above it with the zip tool (**Photo 1 inset**).

It might be tricky hooking the zip tool onto the locking edge if your siding is tight. Try starting at an end or look for a loose spot. Sometimes you can unzip it just with your fingers. If you're having difficulty with a particular lock, try moving up a course. New vinyl siding is quite flexible, especially in warm weather, but older siding becomes more brittle with age, so work carefully.

It should be easy to slide a flat bar behind the nailheads since they're not driven tight (**Photo 2**). Don't slide the flat

bar behind the siding itself. You'll risk breaking it.

You may have to bow each length of vinyl to release its ends from the trim moldings, and you may have to slide short pieces up or down past the window to release them from the J-channel.

Building paper and window flashing

Building paper is an important part of the wall's waterproofing. It's a barrier to any water that may work its way behind the siding, so be sure upper pieces lap over lower ones. Tape any tears or holes with housewrap tape (available at home centers).

Flashing is critical for a watertight window or door. Aluminum works best with vinyl. Buy a 10-in. wide roll of aluminum ($10 at home centers), and cut it

Tip

If you're working over foam sheathing, place a piece of plywood between the foam and flat bar to avoid crushing the foam.

into 5-in. wide strips for the top and sides of the window.

The width of the bottom flashing will vary. It must go under the window nailing fin and lap over the nailing hem of the vinyl siding (**Photo 3**). This will direct water to the front of the siding.

When you're done flashing the window, stand back and imagine water running down the wall. Start above the window and visually check that all building papers and flashing lap over the piece below it so water can't run behind.

Install J-channel around the window

You have to wrap the window with vinyl J-channel to divert water and to cover the ends of the siding (**Photo 9**). You'll probably have to buy new strips for this. Start with the bottom piece and work up to the top (**Photos 6 – 10**).

3 **LEVEL and tack the new window in place, then cut a piece of aluminum flashing to width so it extends from the new window to overlap the nailing hem of the siding below. Slide the top edge under the window fin, then nail off the fin with roofing nails.**

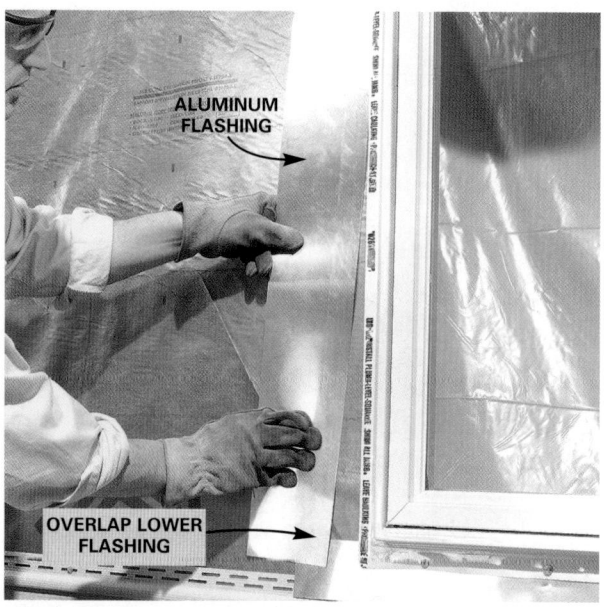

4 **SLIDE 5-in. wide side flashing under the window's nailing fin. Make sure it laps over the bottom flashing at least 2 in. and extends 2 in. above the window's top. Nail off the window.**

5 **SLIT the building paper about 2 in. above the window and slide 5-in. wide flashing behind it. Lap it over the side flashing and window nailing fin. Drive roofing nails at each corner to secure it.**

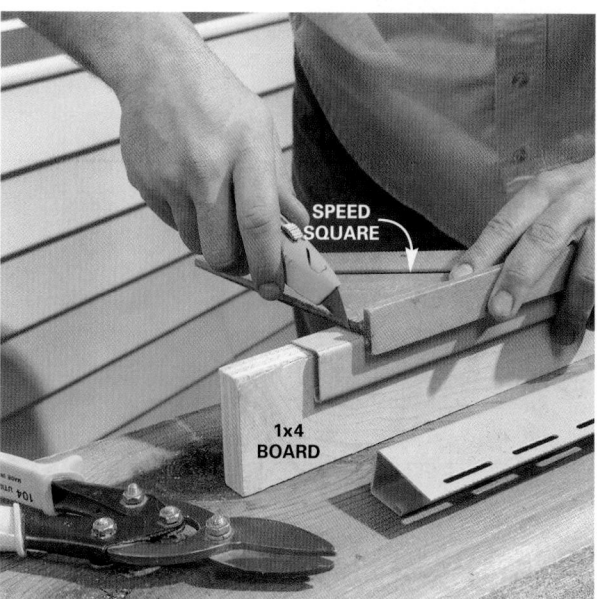

6 **CUT a section of new J-channel 2 in. longer than the width of the window. Mark out a notch 1 in. in from each end and deeply score the inner cutting line with a utility knife.**

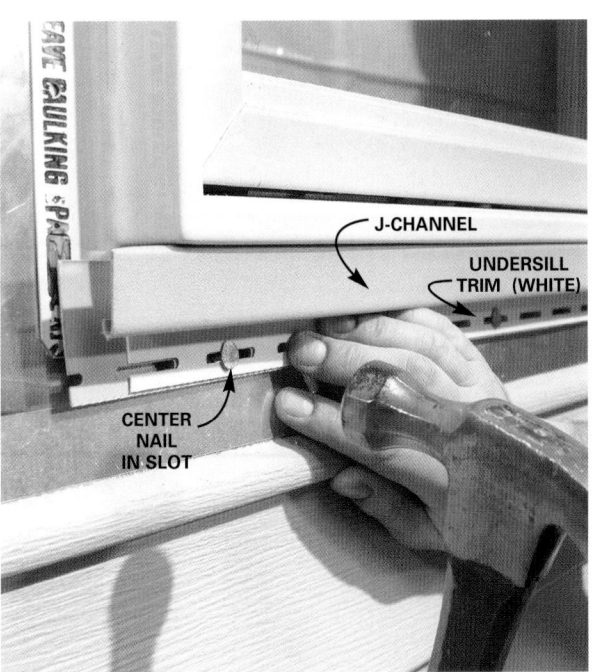

7 MAKE the last two cuts with snips. Bend the tab back and forth to snap it off (see Photo 8).

8 POSITION the J-channel under the window. Cut and position an undersill trim if necessary (see "When to Use Undersill Trim," p. 197). Drive roofing nails every 8 to 10 in. through the middle of the slots. Don't drive them tight. The trim pieces should slide back and forth slightly.

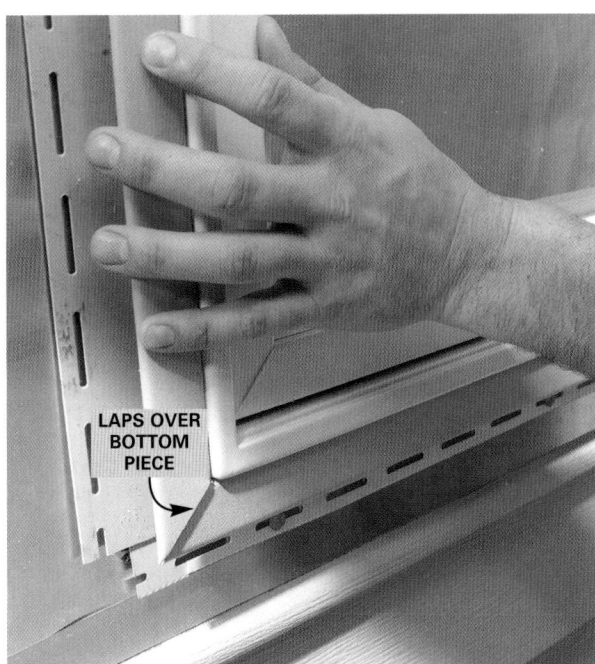

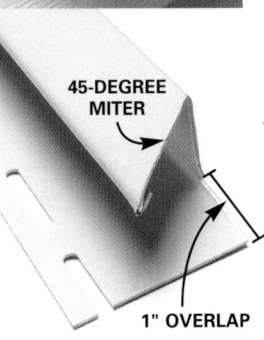

9 CUT the side J-channel 2 in. longer than the height of the window. Make the miter cut on the bottom with shears. Cut a 1-in. notch on the top end as you did on the bottom J-channel. Lap the side over the bottom as shown. Drive roofing nails every 8 to 10 in. to secure it.

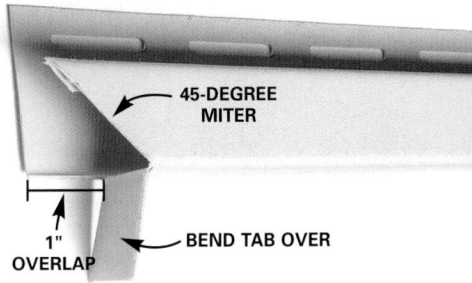

10 CUT the top J-channel 2 in. longer than the window width. Cut and bend the profile shown (see detail) on both ends. Lap it over the sides as shown and nail it into place.

EXTERIOR MAINTENANCE & REPAIRS

Make sure the pieces overlap to keep out water.

Mitered corners give a clean and finished appearance. Be extra careful to fit the top channel correctly over the side pieces (**Photo 10**) because a lot of water can run over these joints.

Install the siding

Maneuvering long pieces of vinyl into place can be tricky. Push one end of longer pieces into the trim, then bow the siding slightly and guide the other end into the trim. Then slide it up and snap the butt into the locking edge of the piece below. Feed the shorter pieces alongside the window into the channel at the top of the window, and slide them down into position.

Installing the piece above the window (**Photo 15**) was especially tricky because it was also the last piece (it would have been easier to remove one more course above). We had to cut the piece and put a joint directly above the window. Then we cut a long length of extra siding to complete the row. Be sure to overlap butt joints 1 in. This method wouldn't work if you had to splice in new vinyl, because the colors wouldn't match. 🏠

11 POSITION the siding to be notched below the window. Mark it on each side of the window, allowing an extra 1/4-in. gap on each side for expansion. Measure from the locking tab of the siding below to the undersill trim to determine the depth of the notch.

12 CUT through the nailing hem with shears, then score deeply along the rip line with a utility knife. Bend back the piece to snap off the notch.

13 POSITION the notched piece under the window, sliding it into the undersill trim and pushing the butt edge against the locking tab in the lower siding course to snap it in place. Make sure the top edge is on the layout line, then drive roofing nails at each stud.

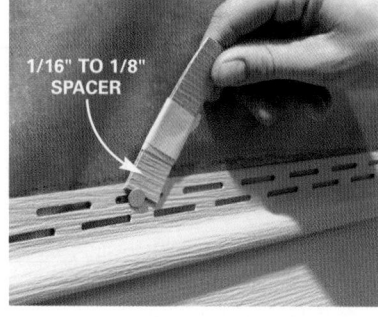

14 DRIVE nails so that the exposed shank equals the thickness of two layers of siding (1/16 in. to 1/8 in.). Don't drive nails all the way in.

TOP LOOSE PIECE

BUTT JOINT OVER WINDOW

15 MEASURE and notch the top piece over the window. If necessary, put a butt joint above the window to make it easier to install these final pieces. Lock the piece to the one below it, then nail it into place.

ZIP TOOL

16 FINALLY, pull the last loose piece down and over the lock with the zip tool. Using your hand, push or pound the piece to lock it back into place. Work the piece into the lock down its length.

WHEN TO USE UNDERSILL TRIM

Because the siding is beveled, the cut edge under a window may end up about 1/2 in. out from the wall. If it falls 1/4 in. or less away, add the undersill trim to lock it in place (shown). If it falls more than 1/4 in. away, skip the undersill trim and simply rely on the J-channel.

UNDERSILL TRIM (WHITE)

J-CHANNEL (BLUE)

MATCHING YOUR SIDING

Remove a piece of siding and identify it. Take it to a siding retailer or distributor. They'll identify the brand and style and should be able to direct you to the right source.

Unfortunately, vinyl siding fades with age, so an exact color match may be impossible. Be sure to save and reuse all the siding you remove. The trim pieces aren't as critical. If you have to add new siding, position it in an obscure spot, like the base of a wall or behind the garage. In fact, you may want to re-side an entire wall with new vinyl.

Ask Handyman™

DURABLE FIX FOR A SINKING DRIVEWAY

My asphalt driveway has sunk a couple of inches in front of my garage door. Now there's a big gap that water runs into. What should I use to fill the gap?

Filling the gap will help keep out water and reduce potential damage to your garage foundation. But it's only a band-aid, not a long-term fix. The best solution is to remove the settled asphalt, compact the underlying soil and patch the driveway. Although the soil correction is a do-it-yourself project, asphalt work is not. The bagged asphalt at the home center isn't intended for this type of patch; it won't hold up. On the other hand, an asphalt contractor will charge up to $600 to make the repair.

Another approach is to make an apron from paving brick. It's attractive, you can do it yourself, and you can easily reset the pavers if the soil settles again. Follow these steps:

1. **Snap a chalk line** parallel to the garage door. Make sure it's out far enough to include all the settled asphalt. Lay out a row of your paving bricks, starting against the garage floor slab to position the chalk line at a full brick.
2. **Rent a gas cutoff saw** with an asphalt-cutting blade ($60 per day) and cut through the asphalt (it's usually 2 to 3 in. thick) along the chalk line. Be sure to wear hearing and eye protection.
3. **Remove the asphalt** and dig a 12-in. deep trench. Angle the wall of the trench slightly under the remaining asphalt. Rent a plate compactor ($50 per day) and run it along the trench at least four times to compact

the soil. Line the sides and bottom of the trench with landscape fabric. It's available from landscape suppliers.

4. **Spread a 2-in. layer of Class V** or other compactible gravel, dampen it and run the compactor over it four times. Continue to spread and compact the gravel in 2-in. layers until it's 3 in. below the existing driveway.

SWEEP SAND INTO JOINTS

PAVER BRICK

1" LAYER OF COARSE SAND

9" COMPACTED CLASS V GRAVEL

COMPACTED SOIL

LANDSCAPE FABRIC

(For detailed instructions, see "Build a Patio with Brick and Stone," April '00, p. 34. To order a copy, see p. 288.)

5. **Install paver edging** along grass edges and spread a 1-in. layer of coarse sand. Don't compact it.
6. **Set your pavers,** compact them with the plate compactor and fill the joints with sand. Be sure to use joint-stabilizing sealer to keep the sand from washing out.

STURDY STAIR POSTS

How do I anchor rail posts at the bottom of my deck stairs? I don't want to set them in concrete, so what's the best alternative?

The bottom post is the toughest post to make solid. My favorite technique is to bolt it to the stair stringers (the frame). But it'll only be solid if the stringers are solid. That's the challenging part.

First, build a level landing pad for the stair stringers. You don't need to pour a footing. Just dig out and compact a minimum 4-in. thick gravel base, then pour a concrete slab or lay paving stones.

Lay out and cut the stringers. (See "Building Deck Stairs," March '02, pp. 64–71. To order a copy, see p. 288.) Make the bottom tread cut 1-1/2 in. shorter than the others. You'll fill out this space with a 2-by "subriser" (**see photo**).

Fasten the top of the stringers to the deck. Rip a piece of treated 2-by lumber to match the height of the bottom riser, then screw this "subriser" to the bottom ends of all three stringers. The finished riser (cedar in our case) will cover it.

Cut each post to length, allowing them to run alongside the stringer to the ground. Then cut a 1-1/2 in. deep notch into the post so it sits over the stringer, flush with the outside face.

Tack the post into the framing, making sure it's tight to the stringer and subriser. Then cut and nail treated 2-by blocks between the stringers and tight to the backside of the posts. Next drill two 1/2-in. holes through the stringer and the post. Hold them 1-1/2 in. from the top and bottom. Drill another 1/2-in. hole through the subriser, the post and the block behind it.

You'll need either an extra-long drill bit or an extension bit. Install 1/2-in. galvanized carriage bolts with washers and nuts. Tighten them firmly.

Finally, install the risers and treads as shown in the photo. The post won't be as rock-solid as one set in concrete. You'll still feel some give when you lean on it. But it's strong—it won't move unless the stairs move.

Note: Confirm the handrail detail on this post design with your local building inspector to make sure it's acceptable in your region.

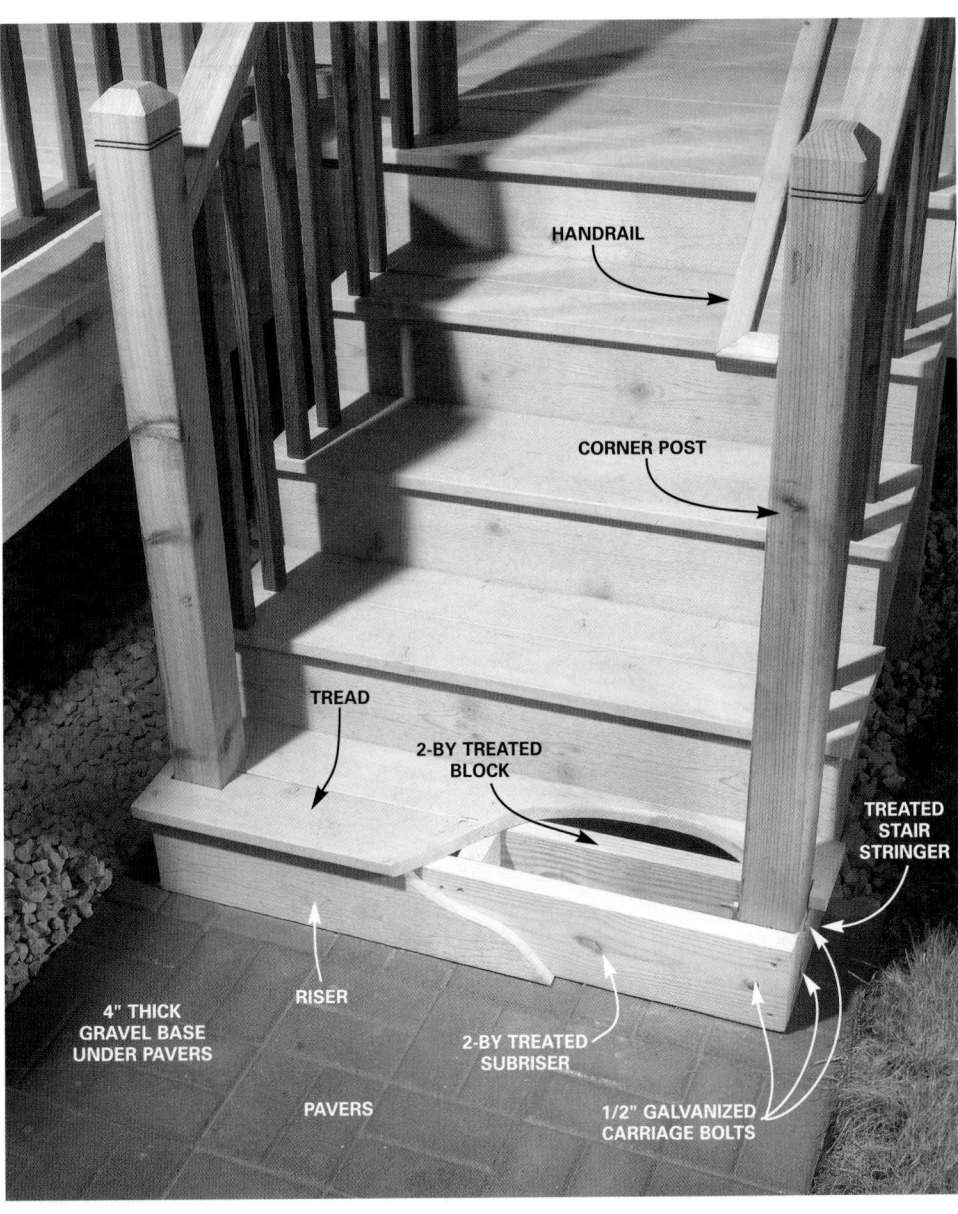

HANDRAIL

CORNER POST

TREAD

2-BY TREATED BLOCK

TREATED STAIR STRINGER

4" THICK GRAVEL BASE UNDER PAVERS

RISER

2-BY TREATED SUBRISER

PAVERS

1/2" GALVANIZED CARRIAGE BOLTS

EXTERIOR MAINTENANCE & REPAIRS

MAKING PAINT LAST

Prep tips and techniques for wood siding and trim

by David Radtke

Tired of your paint job peeling when it's only two years old? Paying close attention to the prep work can add years to the life of your finish coat of paint. In this article, we'll give you tips and techniques on cleaning, scraping, filling and priming so your paint will stay put. We'll also help you identify and solve some specific problems that may have caused your paint to fail prematurely.

Applying the paint is easy. But creating a sound, dry surface for the new coat of paint is tough and time consuming. However, it's the key to any successful paint job.

PRESSURE WASHERS CLEAN DEEP & FAST

Paint just won't stick to dirty or dusty surfaces (see Fig. A, p. 202). You'll need to clean it even if there's very little scraping to do, and the fastest way is with a pressure washer. You can rent a pressure washer (Photo 1) from a rental store for about $60 a day and get a lot of loose paint and grime off your old painted surfaces fast.

These washers kick out a hard stream of water, so try it out on an inconspicuous spot on the house to get the hang of handling the wand. Be careful not to hit windows (they can break), and don't work the spray upward under the laps of siding. Remember, this is for cleaning, not blasting off all the old paint. Of course, some of the old loose paint will fall off, but too much pressure will gouge the wood.

Don't try to pressure-wash while standing on a ladder. The recoil can knock you off balance. And finally, keep in mind that you won't be able to do any scraping and sanding for a couple of days until the surface dries thoroughly.

If the prospect of using a pressure washer is just too intimidating, you can get a stiff brush on a pole and a bucket with mild detergent and scrub the surfaces. Follow the scrub immediately with a rinse from your garden hose.

1 **PRESSURE WASHING** removes loose paint and built-up grime and improves paint adhesion. Use the high pressure carefully, especially around windows. High-pressure water can break the glass. Avoid directing water up under the laps, and keep the nozzle at least 16 in. away from the wood.

2 **SOME LOOSE PAINT** will flake off while you wash the surface. But don't try to strip the paint—you'll gouge the wood.

KEEP YOUR **SCRAPER SHARP**

GRAIN DIRECTION

1 FOLLOW the grain of the wood with long strokes. If nails are sticking up, pound them in. If the nail won't stay put, pull it and drive a new galvanized nail 1/2 in. away.

Old, flaking paint must be scraped from your wood surface or your new paint will eventually let go. Make sure the surfaces are dry. Then scrape in the direction of the grain to avoid tearing the wood fibers and creating an unstable surface for your primer. Obviously, a sharp scraper is the best. You can buy hardened steel scrapers (**Photo 1**), or for about twice the price, you can buy carbide scrapers (**Photo 2**). Good-quality scrapers all have replaceable blades. You can easily sharpen a steel scraper blade using a fine metal file. The carbide blades last up to 10 times longer but must be sharpened with special tools. Buy replacement blades to have on hand.

WINDOW FRAME

SIDING

2 PULL DOWN firmly with a sharp scraper to remove loose paint. Remember, you don't need to remove all the paint, just the stuff that flakes away with the scraper. Keep your scrapers sharp with a fine file. Tip: Don't scrape wet wood. You'll tear away the fibers and dig deep gouges into the wood.

3 GET INTO tight areas with a small 1-in. scraper. Heavy buildup of paint in corners will eventually crack and let moisture in. Scrape and cut excess paint out of the corners with a sharp putty knife.

4 WHILE YOU'RE SCRAPING, dig out any loose caulk around doors, windows and trim. Old, dried-out caulk loses its elasticity and will usually crack later. If your caulk is sound and adhering well, leave it in place.

EXTERIOR MAINTENANCE & REPAIRS

DIAGNOSE COMMON **PAINT PROBLEMS**

Take a good look at your house before you start painting. You may have to correct some of the wrongs that the previous painter overlooked in desiring to get the job done fast. You may have peeling paint as shown in **Figs. A – C**.

contractor to help you solve the problem. Then scrape and sand to remove the loose paint.

Poorly prepared surface

You may notice the finished coat of paint peeling away from another coat underneath (**Fig. A**). This is the result of painting over a poorly prepped surface. Usually the surface wasn't cleaned before painting or the primer coat was left too long before the finish coat of paint was applied. You can remedy this situation by firmly scraping away the paint to get at the surface below. Scrape until you get down to a solid surface that may be part bare wood or a sound, previously painted surface. Sand and clean the surface thoroughly, let it dry, and prime all bare wood and spot-prime any small bare spots.

Excess moisture

Sometimes you find paint and primer falling away from the bare wood surface (**Fig. B**). This is most likely caused by water getting behind the wood or even moisture from the home's interior. You can't repaint here unless you stop the source of the moisture migrating through the walls, especially from bathrooms and kitchens. Adding ventilation such as an exhaust fan in the room can frequently help the problem. Many older homes have no vapor barrier, but sometimes applying a vapor barrier paint on the inside will do the trick. If you're stymied, consult a building

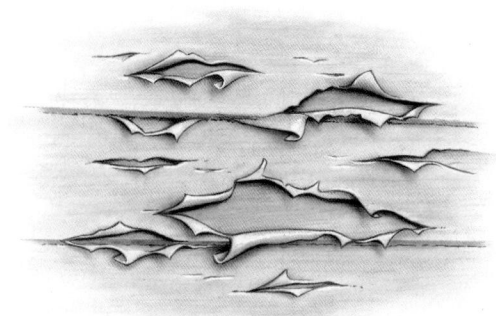

Fig. A:
Painting over a poorly prepared surface

Fig. B:
Excess moisture getting behind the siding

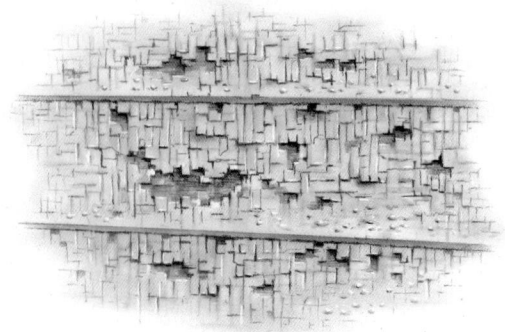

Fig. C:
Alligatoring from too many layers of oil-based paint

Alligatoring

Another common problem is cross-grain cracking, sometimes referred to as "alligatoring." The source of this problem is usually paint buildup from several layers of oil-based paints. Unfortunately, there's no magic bullet for this fix. You'll have to scrape off all the old paint down to bare wood and then sand the surface. Take precautions and gather this paint onto dropcloths or plastic for disposal because it may contain lead. Don't keep applying layers of paint to areas that don't need it such as porch ceilings and eaves where the surfaces are protected. Often a good cleaning is all they need.

Other problems

You may find dark mildew spots on the finished coat of paint along shady areas of the house. Buy a special cleaner at paint supply stores to scrub the surface. You can usually stop mildew by increasing exterior airflow in that area, trimming plants close to the house, and channeling water away with gutters and downspouts. If the area is tough to air out, you can get mildewcide additives for your finish coat of paint. Another problem is chalking, where old paint surfaces get powdery. This is natural for old paints, but you'll have to power wash or scrub the surface and do some light sanding to remove the chalking before applying paint.

FILL LARGE GOUGES BEFORE PRIMING

Fill large holes and gouges with a two-part resin filler such as Minwax High Performance Wood Filler. You have to mix these setting types of fillers, but they stick better to wood than other fillers. Remove any paint around the area before filling. You can fill nail holes with them too.

For small, shallow blemishes, use an exterior spackling compound. Cracks can be filled with exterior caulk after priming.

TWO-PART WOOD FILLER

OVERFILL each repair and then shape it, once it has set, with a file, sharp chisel and sandpaper. Blemishes deeper than 1/2 in. will need additional applications. Once the patch is dry, shaped and sanded, prime it to protect it from moisture.

SAND THE **RIDGES**

PAINT RIDGE

Power sanders cut fast. Use a 60-grit paper for heavy ridges followed by 100-grit for a smooth look. Also sand shiny, old paint surfaces to give the topcoat better bite.

FEATHER the edge of your scraped areas with a power sander to get rid of sharp edges. These ridges can break the finished paint surface later and allow moisture to get behind the paint. After sanding (use 80 to 100 grit), use a dry brush to whisk away any surface dust, especially on horizontal surfaces like windowsills.

Tip — Sand all old, bare wood. Paint won't stick to wood once it has weathered.

USE A **STAIN-BLOCKING PRIMER**

You can choose either an oil or a latex primer and get great results. Oil primers, however, are generally more effective on new wood, metal and previously chalked surfaces. If you're priming over bare woods that have a high tannin content, such as cedar and redwood, ask your paint supplier for a special stain-blocking exterior primer. Stain-blocking primers will prevent a "bleed-through" of tannin through the primer and the topcoat and stop old, rusty nailheads from bleeding through as well (**Photo 1**).

Tip

Your paint supplier can add pigment to your primer to get it close to the topcoat color. This is especially helpful when your topcoat is a darker color. You may be able to cover the primed area and old paint surface with one coat of paint.

1 SPOT-PRIME nailheads and knots with a special stain-blocking primer to prevent unsightly bleed-through from rust or wood resin. A pigmented shellac (BIN, for example) is a good product for this use.

EXPOSED NAILS

2 WORK the primer into cracks and especially where trim pieces meet siding. Even out the primer with long brush strokes and check for drips. Remember to work the primer under the siding laps and into tight spaces and hard-to-see spots. Surfaces that still have old paint that's adhering well don't need a primer.

CAULKING WILL HELP MAKE PAINT LAST

With all the caulks available today, it can be hard to know what kind of caulk to buy to seal gaps. Most professionals agree that acrylic caulk and siliconized acrylic caulk are the best for caulking around windows and doors and against corner boards. These caulks are paintable, long lasting and easy to clean up.

Caulk after priming; caulk sticks best to a primed surface. Squeeze enough caulk into the gaps to get a smooth bead that fills the void. Excess caulk will look sloppy and will increase the possibility of working loose over time. ⌂

Tip

Always try to avoid priming or painting in direct sun. The extra heat can dry the primer and paint too quickly and prevent adequate penetration. It can also cause oil paints to develop blisters that'll ruin the skin of the finish coat of paint.

CAULK all the seams and cracks once you've primed the surface to keep out moisture and hide unsightly dark lines. Wipe excess acrylic caulk and shape it with a moist rag as you apply it. Let the caulk set (usually a couple of hours) before painting over it.

Handy Hints® from our readers

HANG 'EM OUT TO DRY

Painting objects like louvered shutters can be a real problem. It's much easier to get all the areas painted by first making a hanging paint and drying rack. Take two stepladders and a long 2x4. Then hook a metal coat hanger through one of the louvers of the shutter and slip the hanger over the 2x4. Now you can paint all sides and edges without having to handle the shutter.

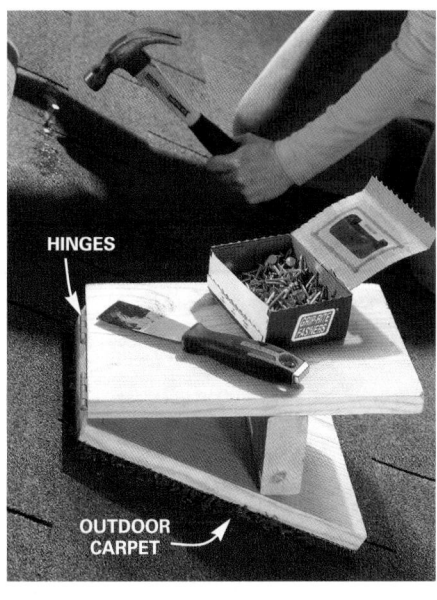

HINGES

OUTDOOR CARPET

CAULK RESCUE

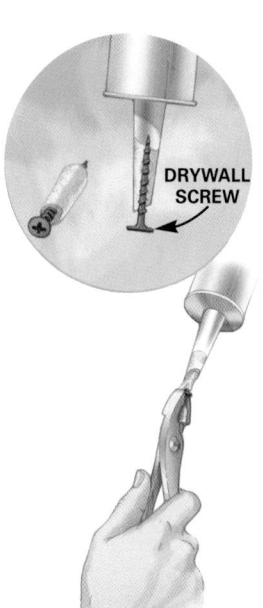

DRYWALL SCREW

If you leave the tip of your caulking tube uncovered and the caulk hardens behind the opening, here's the best way to get it flowing again. Cut the tip back so the hole is slightly larger. Then drive a screw into the plug of hardened caulk and use the screw to pull out the plug. A screw with coarse threads, such as a drywall or deck screw, works best.

ROOF BENCH

Here's a slick way to keep tools from sliding off the roof! Cut two 12-in. long boards (any width) and hinge them together. Glue a scrap of outdoor carpet to the bottom of one board. Set the boards on the edge of the roof with the hinges toward the peak (the carpeted board will grab onto the coarse shingle surface). Slide a 2x4 scrap between the two boards until the top board is level and fasten the 2x4 in place with drywall screws.

WALLET RULER

Never have a tape measure when you need one? Photocopy a 1-ft. section of your tape measure, cut it out and keep it in your wallet. Make sure the copier reproduces at 100 percent!

CLEANER PAINT BRUSHES

Get your paint brushes really clean by using an ordinary kitchen fork to comb out the paint. The strong tines of the fork penetrate all the way into the core of the brush, especially up near the base of the bristles where hardened paint accumulates.

EXTERIOR MAINTENANCE & REPAIRS

Handy Hints from our readers

GUTTER BUCKET

Snip the wire handle of a 5-gallon bucket in half and bend the free ends into small hooks. Hang the bucket on the edge of your gutter, then slide it along and fill it as you clean out the gutter.

HANG 'EM HIGH CAULK TUBES

We finally got the hang of preserving partially used caulk tubes. Seal the tube by twisting a screw eye or hook into the nozzle, then hang it on a nail or Peg-Board. Use 3/16-in. or 3/8-in. dia. screw eyes or hooks depending on the size nozzle opening you like. The screw threads create a nearly air-tight seal by burrowing into the plastic nozzle, but you can reinforce the seal by wrapping electrical tape around the nozzle.

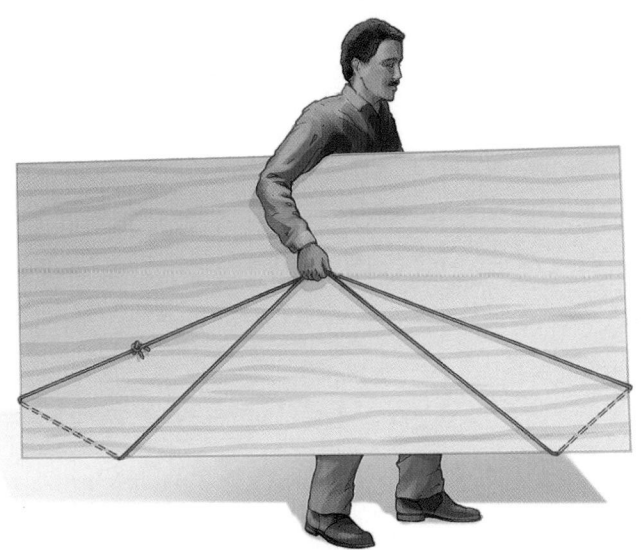

BIG-SHEET CARRIER

You don't have to struggle trying to lug around full sheets of plywood or drywall. Simply tie the ends of an 18-ft. length of rope together. Then loop the rope around the two bottom corners of the sheet and hoist from the middle.

TRASH-CAN SAWHORSES

When your other sawhorses aren't handy or they're already loaded up, a couple of 32-gal. trash containers will serve in a pinch. Remove the lids and you're ready to go.

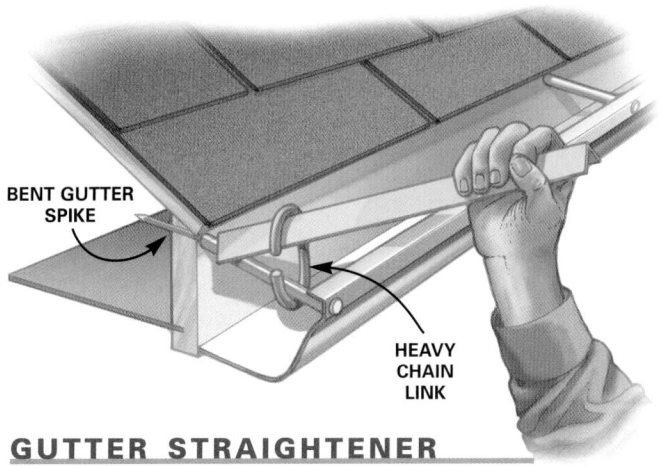

GUTTER STRAIGHTENER

BENT GUTTER SPIKE

HEAVY CHAIN LINK

Ice coming off your roof can bend the spikes that secure your gutters to the fascia board. One simple way to straighten them without removing them is to use a 2-ft. length of angle iron and a link of heavy metal chain. The angle iron and chain link provide sufficient leverage to straighten the spike and pull the gutter back into alignment.

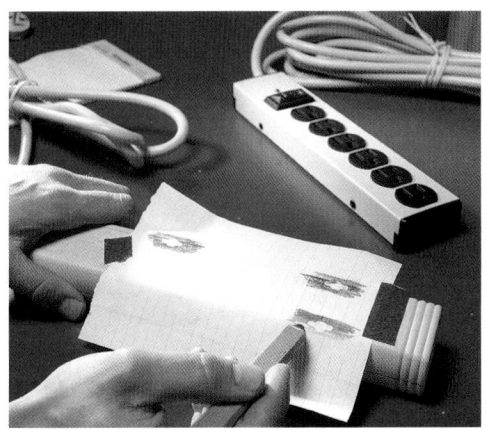

MOUNTING TEMPLATE

It's a real pain in the neck trying to line up all those keyhole slots when you're mounting an outlet power strip. One easy solution is to tape a piece of paper over the mounting slots. Rub a pencil over the slots to create a mounting template, and use it to accurately lay out the mounting holes.

DAMAGED SHINGLE

SHINGLE COOLER

I was replacing some damaged shingles on a hot August day and struggling to break through the sealant strip. Then I came up with a cool trick to ease the job. Rest an ice bag on the shingle for a couple of minutes before trying to break the sealant strip. The hot, sticky adhesive will cool down and pop up with ease.

LADDER APRON

Screw a cloth nail apron to the top back edge of your stepladder to hold nails, screws and small tools. To empty it, simply flip it upside down.

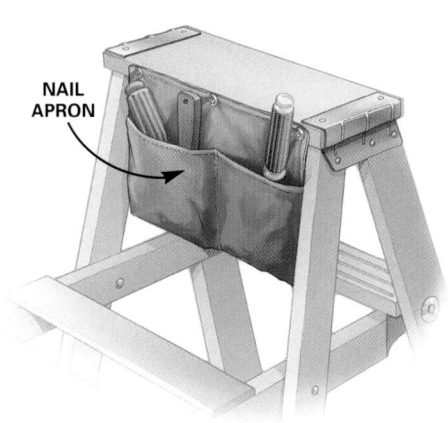

NAIL APRON

NO-TIP GARBAGE CANS

There really is a simple way to keep those garbage cans from getting blown or knocked over. For each garbage can, all you need are two 3/4-in. screw eyes and a 30-in. hook-end elastic cord from the hardware store.

Using Tools: Ladders

WORKING UP HIGH

Ever climbed halfway up an extension ladder and felt it sliding off to one side beneath your feet? You quickly realize you should have spent a few more minutes making sure the ladder feet were solidly set before starting your climb. Climbing a ladder can be safe, even under the less-than-perfect situations you find around your home. We'll show some easy ways to provide solid footing and a stable top to avoid heart-stopping experiences.

EXTEND ARMS

PALMS TOUCH RUNG

LADDER AT CORRECT ANGLE

TOUCH TOES TO LADDER BASE

SET your ladder at the correct angle. Put your toes against the ladder's feet. Stand straight up and extend your arms. The palms of your hands should just reach the ladder's rung.

Get the angle right

Setting the ladder at the correct angle is one of the most important steps to a safe ladder setup. Too steep and it could tip over backward. Too much angle and it could bend or the bottom could slide out. The photo shows how to get the angle just right. If an obstacle prevents you from setting the ladder at the correct angle, don't take chances—consider using methods like scaffolding instead.

DIG a trench under the high-side foot when your ladder is on uneven ground. Flip the shoes up when you're setting up the ladder on soft ground. The spurs will dig in and prevent the ladder from slipping.

Provide a level base

Even with the ladder at the correct angle, it can still tip sideways if the feet aren't level with each other and on solid ground.

It's unsafe to stack boards, bricks or other stuff under one of the feet to level the ladder. Instead, scrape out a shallow trench under the high-side foot (**photo above**). The claw of a hammer is perfect for this task, and it's almost always handy.

If digging is impractical because your site is steeply sloped, or you want to set the ladder on stairs or some other uneven, hard surface, don't opt for a makeshift solution.

Instead, buy adjustable leg-leveling extensions ($40 to $80) that bolt onto the bottom of your ladder. You'll use them often if you live on a sloped lot. To see what's available, check the ladder manufacturer's catalog or a store that sells your ladder brand.

JUMP on the lowest rung to set the ladder firmly and to test for stability. If the ladder tips to one side, move it aside and adjust the depth of the hole.

Secure the feet

In addition to establishing a level base, make sure the feet can't slip backward. On soft ground, flip up the ladder shoes so the spurs poke into the ground (**top left photo**). On decks, it's a simple matter to screw down a cleat (**photo below**). Before you set up the ladder on hard surfaces, clean the bottom of the ladder feet and sweep away sand and dirt that could cause the ladder to slip.

If it still seems like the ladder could slip, tie ropes to both ladder legs beneath the lowest rung and tie the other end of the ropes to a solidly anchored object at or near the base of the wall.

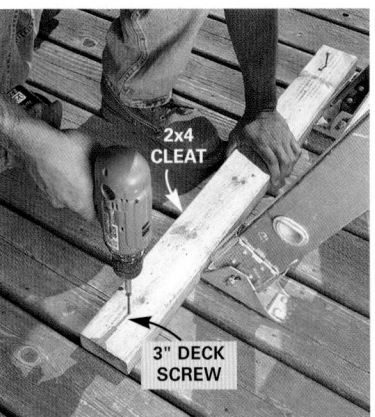

SCREW a 2x4 cleat to the deck behind the ladder's feet to prevent the ladder from slipping backward.

Using Tools: Ladders

Tie the top for extra security

If you plan to make several trips up and down while the ladder is in the same location, it pays to secure the top to keep it from sliding. This is especially important if you'll be stepping onto a roof (**photo below**). Ties will prevent the ladder from sliding sideways as you step to and from the roof. Using the setup we show has the added advantage of protecting the edge of the shingles. It will only take a few minutes to screw the two eye screws into a 2x4 and the 2x4 to the fascia board. You can keep the rig handy for future use. You'll be left with a few small screw holes in the fascia, but that's a small price to pay for this extra measure of security.

Here are a few more tips for steadying the top of the ladder. If you have a choice, set up the ladder where there's an adjoining wall, chimney or other structure to hold it in place. Also, if you regularly set the ladder against the same location on your metal gutters, add extra gutter straps to strengthen the gutter in the area where the ladder top rests. Then install eye screws out of sight above the gutter to provide anchors for securing your ladder with rope or wire.

Secure the top against a wall

Providing a stable base is only half the battle. You also have to make sure the top of the ladder can't slide when the rails rest against a wall. Make sure the ladder is vertical and the top is resting on an even surface. Angling the ladder to the left or right to reach a remote spot is asking for trouble.

There are a couple of add-on accessories that help stabilize the top of ladders. The first is a pair of rubber or soft plastic "mitts" ($9 to $12 at hardware stores and home centers) that slip over the top of the ladder's rails. They provide a better grip on the siding and protect it from ladder damage. Ladder stabilizers are another great add-on accessory (**photo below**). The large rubber pads grip almost any surface to keep the top from slipping sideways and help spread out the load to prevent damage to fragile siding materials like vinyl or aluminum. Stabilizers also span window openings and hold the ladder away from the building to allow work on gutters and overhangs. These range in price from $45 to $70 and are available almost everywhere ladders are sold. We highly recommend them for any kind of extensive work, such as washing and painting. 🏠

Tip Carrying tools in a tool belt allows you to use both hands when climbing.

3/8" x 2" EYE SCREW

2x4

ROPE TIE

SECURE the top of your ladder by tying it to a solid anchor. Make a reusable anchoring rig by screwing two 3/8-in. x 2-in. eye screws into a 32-in. length of 2x4. Then screw the 2x4 to the fascia with 3-in. deck screws.

LADDER STABILIZER

BOLT ON UNDER TOP RUNG

ADD a ladder stabilizer accessory to the top of your ladder to span windows and to provide extra stability. Follow the stabilizer installation instructions carefully.

9 Outdoor Structures & Landscaping

IN THIS CHAPTER

Garden Fountain 212

Ask Handyman 218
Grow a great lawn, staining a fence,
decking standards

Planning a Backyard Path 220

Weekend Projects 226
Trench edging & mulch borders,
paver path that grows, rustic plant cage,
chimney flue planters, paint-on moss

Buying Deck Lumber 230

Handy Hints .235
Stay-put vinyl edging, crevice
weeder and more...

Gallery of Ideas 238
Garden shed, garden pond & deck,
hammock hideaway, stone fire ring

You Can Fix It 240
Cure a patchy lawn, rock-steady
birdbath, dog-proof shrubs

GARDEN FOUNTAIN

Cast this fountain in a weekend with a few bags of concrete and some hardware odds and ends

by **Jeff Gorton**

This little fountain, modeled after an old millstone, is the perfect size to tuck into a spot near your patio or kitchen window. There you can enjoy the sound of water trickling over river stones and watch the birds and butterflies that come to bathe and drink.

We'll show you how to build this fountain using bagged concrete mix and common construction materials. You can build the sheet metal forms and pour the concrete in less than a day. The next day, you can finish up by removing the forms, burying the tub, and assembling the concrete fountain and the pump.

With the increased popularity of water gardens, many home centers now stock fountain pumps and plastic liner tubs. We purchased a pump with a flow rate of 130 gallons per hour and a maximum pumping height of 4.5 ft. Make sure the pump you buy has similar specifications. You can substitute any large plastic container for the 7-in. deep tub we used as long as it's at least 26 in. wide. Fifteen-inch deep plastic whiskey barrel liners work well. The increased depth calls for a little extra digging, but you won't have to refill the fountain as often. Increase the height of the concrete column to compensate for the extra depth. For Internet and mail-order pump sources, see the Buyer's Guide on p. 217. The total cost of the materials, including a $30 pump and $20 plastic liner, is about $100 (see the Materials List, p. 217).

In addition to basic tools, you'll need a plastic tub or wheelbarrow and a hoe for mixing concrete, and a steel trowel to finish the top of the wheel.

Solid forms are the first step to a successful concrete pour

When you build the forms for the concrete, take care to cut the plywood circle accurately and wrap the metal tightly around it (**Photo 1**). The double-faced tape holds the band of sheet metal to the plywood disc while you screw it in place. We lined the metal with foam sill sealer to create the ridges you see on the outside of the wheel. You can customize the wheel to your liking by substituting seashells, rope or other decorative items for the sill sealer. Attach

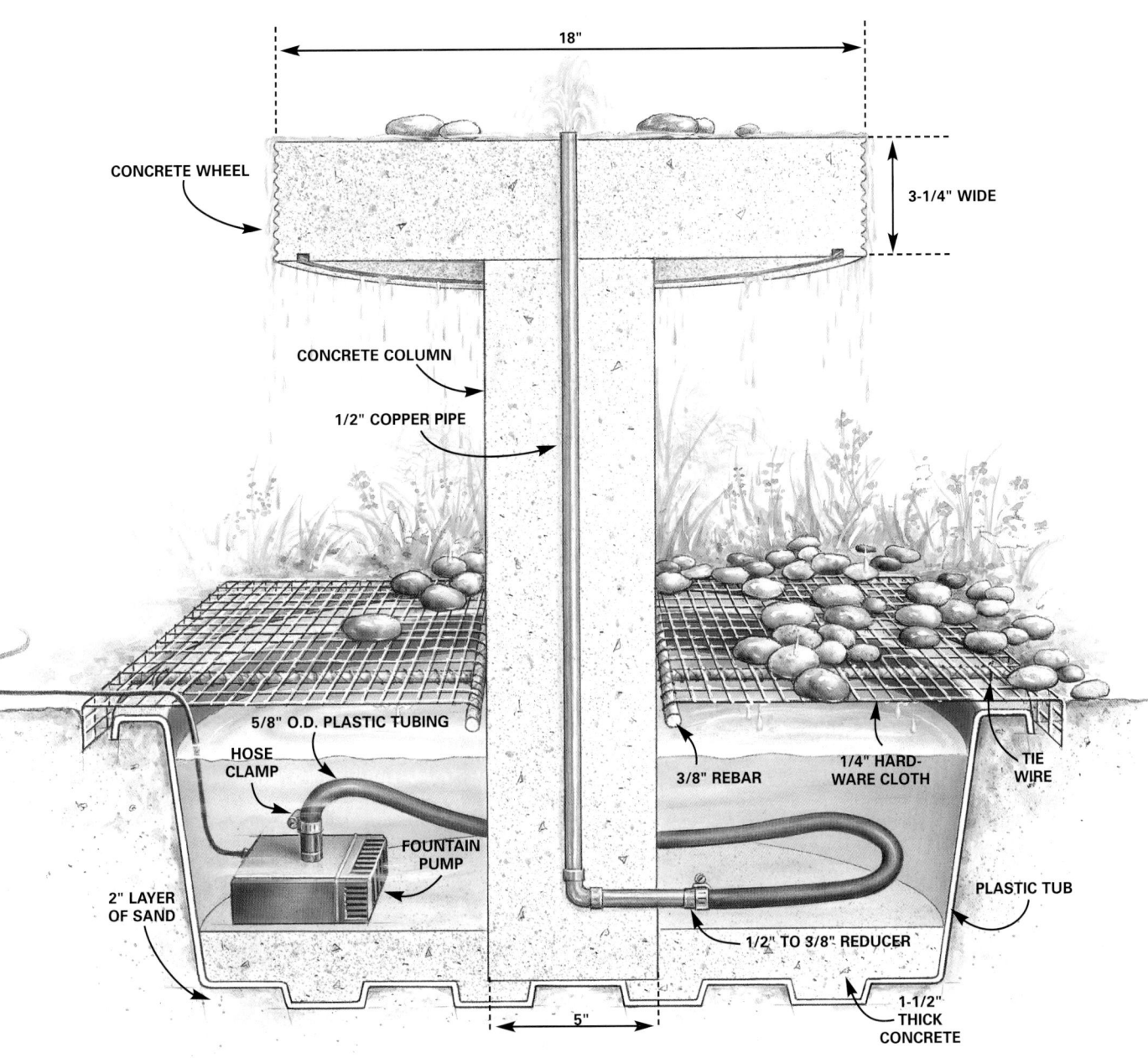

Fig. A: Fountain details

Labels in figure:
- 18"
- CONCRETE WHEEL
- 3-1/4" WIDE
- CONCRETE COLUMN
- 1/2" COPPER PIPE
- 5/8" O.D. PLASTIC TUBING
- HOSE CLAMP
- 3/8" REBAR
- 1/4" HARD-WARE CLOTH
- TIE WIRE
- FOUNTAIN PUMP
- 2" LAYER OF SAND
- PLASTIC TUB
- 1/2" TO 3/8" REDUCER
- 1-1/2" THICK CONCRETE
- 5"

them to the metal with hot-melt glue or double-faced tape.

We made the form for the column by snipping one locking edge and the end from an 8-in. round duct and rolling it into a 5-in. diameter cylinder (**Photo 4**). Allow the extra sheet metal to overlap. Complete the form by assembling and installing the copper pipe and taping the whole thing together with duct tape (**Photo 5**).

Don't forget to coat the inside of the forms, including the short copper pipe, with oil to prevent the concrete from sticking. We used a heavy layer of WD-40. The band of rope caulk in the bottom of the form creates a recess in the concrete that directs the water to drip from the edges, rather than run under the wheel.

Strong concrete mix has just the right amount of water

Too little water and the concrete mix will be stiff and unworkable. Too much water results in weak concrete prone to cracking and breaking. Start by dumping 1-1/2 bags of concrete mix into a wheelbarrow or plastic mixing tub. Then measure out the amount of water recommended on the bag and add it slowly while mixing the concrete with a hoe. Check for the proper consistency by making a trench with the hoe. The concrete should stand up on both sides of the trench. If it sags and fills the trench, it's too wet. Add more dry powder to make a stiffer mix. It should be about the consistency of potato salad.

It takes a little more effort to get this thick concrete mix to settle into the forms. The trick is to tap on the outside of the forms after they're filled with concrete (Photo 7). Tapping eliminates air pockets that would otherwise show up as holes in the concrete surface.

After filling and tapping the forms, you have to let the concrete harden for a while before smoothing the top surface (Photos 8 and 9). The length of time will vary between 45 minutes and three or four hours depending on the weather and other factors. The concrete is ready when the surface water is gone and you can barely indent the surface with your thumb.

1 DRAW an 18-in. diameter circle on 3/4-in. plywood. Saw it out with a jigsaw. Drill a 5/8-in. hole in the center. Cut a 60-in. length of 4-in. wide galvanized metal flashing. Run a strip of double-faced carpet tape along the top and bottom edge. Then wrap the flashing around the plywood circle.

2 DRIVE 1/2-in. sheet metal screws through the flashing at 8-in. intervals to secure it to the plywood. Line the flashing with a 60-in. length of foam sill sealer. To make a flush seam, cut through both thicknesses of foam with a utility knife where they overlap.

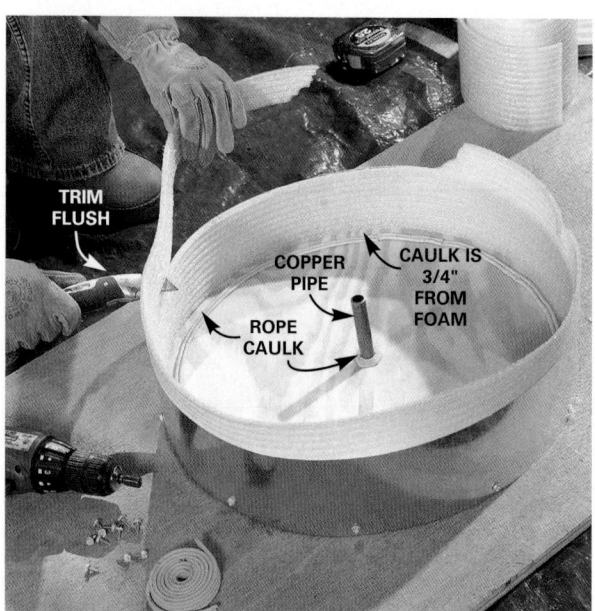

3 INSERT a 4-in. length of 1/2-in. copper pipe into the hole and hold it in place with a wrap of rope caulk. Press a double-wide bead of rope caulk in a circle around the bottom of the form about 3/4 in. away from the foam liner. Trim the foam flush with the top of the metal.

4 CUT a 20-in. length of 8-in. round metal duct with a tin snips. Then cut the locking edge from the length of the duct. Drill a 5/8-in. hole in about the center of the sheet, 3-1/2 in. from the bottom edge.

Labels on image: 5" COUPLER, 1/2" COPPER, TWO-PART EPOXY, TUBING CUTTER, 1/2" TO 3/8" REDUCER, 5" END CAP, DUCT TAPE

5 COIL the duct with the remaining locking edge to the outside and slip it inside the 5-in. end cap and 5-in. coupler to form a cylinder. Wrap the cylinder with three layers of duct tape to secure it (see next photo). Cut 20-in. and 4-in. lengths of 1/2-in. copper pipe and join them as shown with epoxy. Slip the assembled pipe into the cylinder. Reinstall the pipe and glue a 1/2- to 3/8-in. reducer to the short pipe that exits through the side of the form. Hold the pipe in place with duct tape.

Label on image: TAP ON PLYWOOD BOTTOM

7 SETTLE the concrete and remove trapped air by tapping the bottom of the form with a hammer. Add concrete if necessary to fill the form. Continue tapping and circling for about two minutes.

CAUTION: Wear long rubber gloves and safety glasses when you're working with concrete. Wet concrete can seriously burn bare skin.

Labels on image: WATER, MIXED CONCRETE, COLUMN FORM, FORM FOR TOP, SPRAY LUBRICANT, 12" LENGTH OF 3/8" REBAR

6 COAT the entire inside surface of both forms with a layer of oil (spray lubricant is easy to apply). Mix 1-1/2 bags of concrete mix to form a stiff, not runny, batch. Mix with a hoe for at least five minutes. Fill the tall cylinder while holding the pipe in the center. Tap the outside with a scrap of wood to settle the concrete and release trapped air. Fill the foam-lined top half-full. Lay 12-in. lengths of 3/8-in. reinforcing bar (rebar) in a tick-tack-toe pattern on top of the concrete. Continue adding concrete until it's flush to the top of the form.

Smoothing the top surface requires two steps: floating and troweling. Float the surface by rubbing the concrete in a circular motion with a block of wood (**Photo 8**) until a thin layer of soupy, rock-free cement covers the surface. Next, flatten and smooth the surface with a steel trowel (**Photo 9**).

Remove the forms after the concrete has set up for at least 12 hours. If you don't plan to assemble the fountain immediately, cover the column and wheel with plastic and store them in a shady spot until you're ready. Otherwise, keep the fountain running for at least a week to keep the concrete wet while it cures.

Photos 11 – 14 show how to assemble the fountain and connect the pump. Use a hacksaw to cut the rebar to length. Be very careful when you're working with the hardware cloth—the cut edges have razor-sharp points. Wear leather gloves and bend all cut edges down before you install the cover over the tub. Don't cover the hardware cloth with stones until you've filled the tub with water and tested the pump. To avoid the risk of electrical shock, make sure the circuit you plug the pump into is GFCI protected.

Fountains require a little maintenance

Keep the tub full of water. If it dries up while the pump is running, it will ruin the pump. Check the intake grate or screen on the pump occasionally and remove leaves and debris. If you live in a cold climate, drain the fountain in the fall. Then clean out the liner and store the pump inside for the winter. ⌂

8 LET the concrete harden until the water on the surface has soaked in or evaporated and your thumb pressed into the surface just barely leaves an indentation. Then rub a block of wood in a circular motion over the surface to bring a layer of soupy cement and sand to the surface.

10 REMOVE the sheet metal screws and unwrap the concrete wheel. Carefully place the wheel upside down on the bucket and remove the plywood. Protect the top surface by placing strips of foam between the bucket and concrete. Grab the copper pipe with a locking pliers or pipe wrench and twist and pull to remove it from the concrete. Remove the metal form from the tall cylinder.

9 SMOOTH the soupy layer of cement with a steel trowel. Let the concrete harden overnight.

11 LAY 30-in. lengths of rebar over the plastic tub to create a 5-in. square opening in the center for the concrete column. Drill two small holes through the tub at the end of each rebar and secure the rebar with twists of wire. Leave the end of one rebar loose until the column is in position. Dig a hole deep enough to accommodate the tub plus a 2-in. deep layer of sand.

216

PACK WITH BLOCK

1-1/2" DEEP CONCRETE

TWISTED WIRE

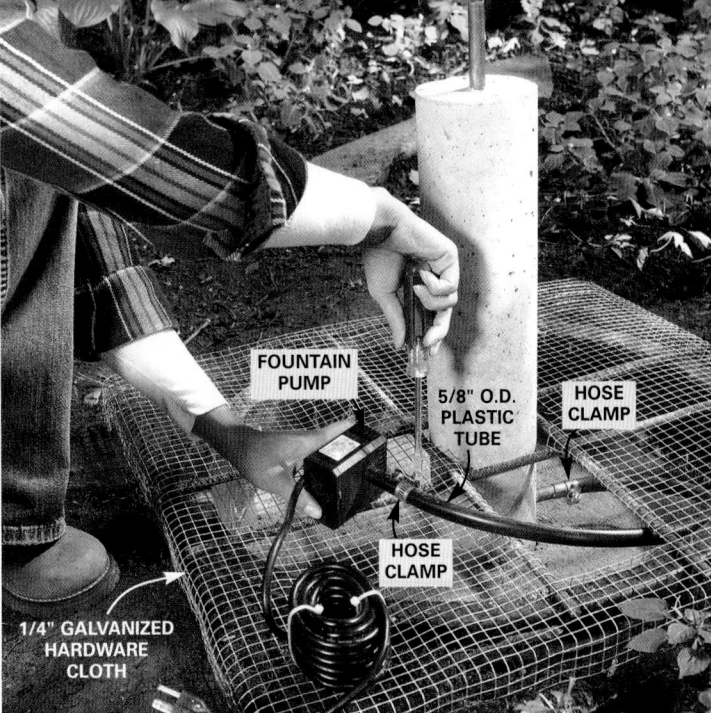

FOUNTAIN PUMP

5/8" O.D. PLASTIC TUBE

HOSE CLAMP

HOSE CLAMP

1/4" GALVANIZED HARDWARE CLOTH

12 LEVEL the sand base and set the tub in place. Pack dirt around it to the bottom of the rim. Set the column in place and use a level to make sure the sides are vertical and the flat area on top is level. Pour a 1-1/2 in. layer of concrete into the bottom of the liner to stabilize the column. Let the concrete set overnight.

13 CUT a square of 1/4-in. hardware cloth 4 in. larger than the diameter of the tub and bend down a 2-in. lip to form a mesh cover. Leave an extra inch of mesh when you cut the opening and bend it around the rebar to hide the sharp edges. Cut another small rectangle of hardware cloth to cover the opening. Connect the pump to the copper pipe with 5/8-in. plastic tube and hose clamps.

DRIP GROOVE

POLYURETHANE CONSTRUCTION ADHESIVE

14 PLACE a bead of polyurethane construction adhesive around the top of the column and lower the concrete wheel over the copper pipe. Check the top with a level and shim between the column and wheel if necessary to level the top surface. Use strips cut from plastic bottles for shims.

Materials List

- ◼ Square of 3/4-in. plywood, minimum size of 18 x 18 in.
- ◼ 5-ft. length of 4-in. wide sheet metal flashing
- ◼ Roll of double-faced carpet tape
- ◼ 5-ft. length of ribbed foam sill sealer (cut from roll)
- ◼ Twenty 1/2-in. sheet metal screws
- ◼ 5-in. round duct cap
- ◼ 5-in. round duct coupling
- ◼ 2-ft. length of 8-in. round metal duct
- ◼ Duct tape
- ◼ 2-ft. length of 1/2-in. copper pipe
- ◼ 1/2 in. copper elbow
- ◼ 1/2- to 3/8-in. copper reducer
- ◼ Two-part epoxy (five-minute type)
- ◼ Roll of rope caulk
- ◼ 16 ft. of 3/8-in. steel rebar
- ◼ 4 ft. of 14- or 16-gauge wire
- ◼ 3 ft. of 5/8-in. outside diameter (O.D.) plastic tubing
- ◼ Two hose clamps for above tubing
- ◼ Pump
- ◼ Two 60-lb. or 80-lb. bags of concrete mix
- ◼ 36 x 36-in. square of 1/4-in. galvanized hardware cloth
- ◼ 1-1/2 to 2-1/2 in. dia. river rock to cover hardware cloth
- ◼ Plastic tub

OUTDOOR STRUCTURES & LANDSCAPING

Ask Handyman™

HOW TO GROW A GREAT LAWN THIS SPRING

I've had lousy success trying to grow a decent lawn from grass seed. What's the trick?

Water, water, water. Turf specialists make it clear that watering is a key step to a successful lawn. The seeds need to stay moist not only for germination but also for seedling root development. The germinating seeds and the new seedlings are very vulnerable to even short dry periods.

Seed an area that you can realistically keep moist. It may require watering several times a day. An in-ground irrigation system is ideal, but hoses and sprinklers will work. Water long enough to wet the soil to a depth of 3 to 4 in.

Monitor the soil's moistness with the same attention you'd give to a sick child. Be aware of weather conditions; hot sun, high temperatures and wind will dry out the soil quickly. As the soil surface dries, its color will lighten—a sure sign to water again. You won't harm the seeds with too much water unless you're creating runoff and washing the seeds and soil away.

After the seeds have germinated (5 to 20 days), water less often but for longer periods. This deeper watering encourages the seedlings' roots to go deep. After the first mowing, you can begin to cut back on the daily watering.

Other key factors
Plant when temperatures are moderate

Avoid planting in the summer when you'll be fighting the hot sun and high temperatures. Also don't plant when the soil is too cold, which prevents germination. A good rule of thumb is to check nearby mature grass. If it's growing (not dormant), then the soil's temperature is OK for seeding. An ideal time to plant is at the end of summer when the soil is quite warm, but cooler days are ahead.

Choose the right seed for your yard and region

Talk to a turf specialist (from a garden center, university extension service or landscaping service) about the right seed for your climate and your specific soil and sun/ shade

Three key steps

Step 1. Loosen the ground to a depth of 4 to 6 in. A power tiller ($50 rental) makes this job easier. Rake the loosened soil to remove debris. Break up clumps and finish with a smooth surface.

Step 2. Apply starter fertilizer and then the grass seed. Sow the seeds in two directions with a drop spreader. Lightly rake the seeds into the soil with a leaf rake. You don't need to bury all the seed, just most of it.

Step 3. Water to keep the top few inches of soil moist until germination. After germination, apply more water but less often to promote deep roots.

conditions. This is one advantage to growing a lawn from seed. It allows you to fine-tune the type of grass for your yard. Sod, on the other hand, is best suited for those conditions found at the sod farm.

Feed the sprouts

Let's face it: Lawns eat like teenagers, so feeding is a fact of life. Just before seeding, apply a starter fertilizer. Read the product's directions to determine the amount to spread. After the grass has been cut a few times and is established, move to a maintenance feeding schedule consistent with the climate in your region.

STAINING A TREATED WOOD FENCE

Can I stain my green-treated wood fence?

Yes, you can. In fact, green-treated wood, like any other wood, needs protection. While treated wood is insect and rot resistant, it's still subject to splitting, cracking and warping caused by wetting and drying. We recommend that you use a semitransparent, water-repellent penetrating stain. It'll color the wood and help keep out moisture. There are lots of products on the market, so carefully read the label to make sure it provides water resistance. Also, some products require two coats to be effective, so follow the application directions. If you're applying the finish with a roller or sprayer, be sure to brush the stain into the wood as well.

New treated wood is often quite wet from the treatment process. You don't want to apply the stain to a damp surface, so let wet wood dry for a couple of weeks. Then test the wood by sprinkling water on it. If the droplets are quickly absorbed, it'll absorb the stain. If not, let it dry longer and test again.

DO COMPOSITES MEET DECKING STANDARDS?

My local building inspector told me to remove my new composite decking because it hadn't been approved. What's going on?

You just got caught in the growth pains of a new industry. Building codes require that materials being used, including decking, conform to certain minimum standards. This is to ensure they're strong, durable and safe.

Unfortunately, many brands of composite decking (plastic/wood blends) and other decking materials that substitute for wood are fairly new and haven't undergone the required testing for approval. Or the manufacturers simply haven't submitted them for approval before marketing them.

To avoid this problem, call your local building inspector and ask if the brand you intend to buy is on the approved list.

PLANNING A
BACKYARD PATH

Attractive, inexpensive and easy to build

by **Jeff Timm**

Tired of getting your shoes muddy every time you cross the yard or walk through the garden? A path is a simple solution that'll also add a handsome feature to your back yard. In this article, we'll describe a variety of path-building materials that you can install yourself. We'll help you decide which looks best for your yard and which best fits your budget, available time and skill level.

GRAVEL PATHS

Gravel is the easiest to handle and least expensive path material. It feels soft underfoot, but it's solid enough to handle a loaded wheelbarrow. And although it looks informal, it can complement a formal garden, especially if you add a stone border.

But gravel has several limitations. It's not ideal for a walkway right to the back door—pebbles will stick to your shoes and end up on the kitchen floor. It's not the best choice if you have to shovel snow off it in winter. You'll end up picking rocks out of your garden and yard. And it's tough on bare feet!

Design factors

- ■ **Best use:** Gravel paths are best for light to moderate foot traffic.
- ■ **Longevity/maintenance:** A gravel path will last indefinitely, but it needs upkeep. To keep it looking sharp, rake it and pull weeds monthly. Every few years, topdress it with a few buckets of new gravel.

1 GRAVEL paths are the easiest to build. Although these paths look informal, a limestone border like this one really dresses them up.

- **Drainage:** No special sloping needed. You can follow the grade of your yard, but avoid low spots.
- **Slopes:** Avoid steep inclines. A heavy rain will wash all your hard work away. For steps, use timbers or stone.
- **Borders:** Include a border in your plans. It's essential for containing the gravel.

Materials

Gravel is available in many sizes and colors. Ask for gravel that compacts well. It'll typically have stones ranging in size from 3/4 in. down to a powder. Smaller stones (3/8 in.) are the most comfortable underfoot. Larger (3/4 in.) stones stay put better during rainstorms.

CRUSHED LIMESTONE

CRUSHED WASHED GRAVEL

PEA ROCK

Tip Have your gravel dumped on your driveway. Shoveling gravel off a lawn or tarp wastes time.

Buy your gravel from a landscape supplier or directly from a quarry. (Look under "Sand and Gravel" in your Yellow Pages.)
- **Cost:** Figure 50¢ per sq. ft. (3 in. deep).

Borders

- **Metal edging:** Thin metal edging offers a crisp, clean, "borderless" look. To contain the gravel, set the edging 1 in. higher than the path. Anchor it with the metal stakes provided. Metal edging is available in green or brown painted steel or aluminum in 8-ft. and 16-ft. lengths. Cut

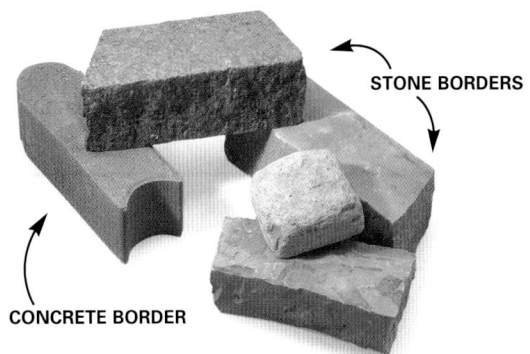

STONE BORDERS

CONCRETE BORDER

it with a circular saw equipped with a metal-cutting blade or a hacksaw. **Cost:** $2 to $3 per lin. ft.
- **Stone:** Almost any stone can be used to border a path. Landscape suppliers will have several types. If possible, fit the stones tightly for a smooth appearance. Install the stones on an inch or so of gravel, then set them with a whack from a rubber mallet. **Cost:** $1 to $4 per lin. ft.
- **Brick:** The brick border is a traditional style. Set the bricks upright at an angle or flat in the ground. Install them in a 2-in. sand bed, then surround them with the gravel and soil to lock them in place. **Cost:** $2 to $4 per lin. ft.

Key construction details

Laying a gravel path is mostly shovel and wheelbarrow work. You first flatten the pathway with a spade, skimming off sod if you're crossing a lawn. Then set the borders and pour in about 3 in. of gravel.

You're moving a lot of weight. A strong back is essential—enlist a neighborhood teenager to help out.

2 METAL edging is easy to install, makes nice curves and costs less than other materials.

3 TUMBLED stone and other stone borders require fitting, but they look the most natural.

4 BRICKS fit together easily and form highly traditional border patterns.

OUTDOOR STRUCTURES & LANDSCAPING

STONE PATHS

Stone is rich in color and texture. Each piece is unique. And it's timeless: A path installed yesterday may look as if it's been there for generations. It's the most expensive path material. This stuff is heavy, but surprisingly easy to install. In most cases, you simply set each piece on a layer of sand and level it. In high-use areas, fit each piece more tightly to lessen the chance of tripping.

Design factors

- **Best use**: Stone is highly decorative and good for light to moderately heavy traffic. Best for foot traffic. It's not so good for bikes, wheelbarrows and lawn mowers. The rough, uneven surface is difficult to shovel in winter.
- **Versatility**: Ideal for minimal disturbance of gardens and lawn. Great for around trees because you don't have to disturb the roots. Good material for an indecisive gardener— it's easy to shift the entire path for a new rosebush!
- **Longevity/maintenance**: The stones will last forever. You may have to lift and reset them if they dip or stick up too high.

1 STONE paths are highly decorative and easy to lay. You fit them like a long, freeform puzzle.

- **Drainage**: Let steppingstones follow the lay of the land. Water will run off into the joints. For tightly fitted stone, pitch the path about 1/4 in. per ft. to the side.
- **Slopes**: Build stone steps to match the path. Buy riser stones and large tread stones from the stone supplier.

Material selection

Limestone, granite, sandstone and slate are the most common types, all available in various colors, sizes and shapes. Set them apart as steppingstones or fit them tightly for a more solid pathway. Select material that's at least 1 in. thick to avoid cracking.

Here are the basic categories:

- **Steppers** are small (15 in. across or less), light and easy to handle, but laying them is slow because you have to fit and level each one. Steppers are prone to

GRANITE

FAKE STONE (CONCRETE)

LIMESTONE

LIMESTONE

LIMESTONE

SANDSTONE

BLUESTONE

SANDSTONE

DOLLY

150-LB. STONE

2 STEPPERS are smaller, irregular-shape stones. They look best when fit more tightly.

3 FLAGSTONES are larger, irregular-shape stones. They cost more than steppers but look more dramatic and are more stable underfoot.

4 CUT STONE is easy to fit and appears more formal than irregular-shape stones. Use a saw with a diamond blade to trim them.

wobbling and have to be reset more often than larger stones.

- **Flagstones** are large (24 to 48 in. across) irregular pieces. They're slightly more expensive than steppers, but they're versatile. You can always break a big piece to make smaller ones for tighter fits. Their size and weight helps keep them stable, and they're less likely to shift and need resetting.
- **Cut stone** is the most expensive but easiest to fit tightly. It looks especially good when set between borders. However, cut stone will probably require more cutting to achieve the more exact fits.

Order your stone from a landscape or masonry supplier. The supplier will tell you how much coverage (square feet) to expect per ton.

- **Cost:** $3 to $9 per sq. ft.

Key construction details

Setting stone is a lot like putting together a big, heavy jigsaw puzzle. You first skim and flatten the proposed pathway, then dump in and smooth out a couple of inches of sand as a setting bed. Patience is essential when it comes to fitting. Spread out the stones and pick and choose for a pleasing pattern.

The stones will weigh 60 to 200 lbs.! Use a dolly to move the big pieces into place.

Finish by filling all the joints tightly with sand, soil or mulch (packed in). Plant a ground cover in the joints for an attractive appearance and to help hold the soil in place.

PAVER PATHS

Pavers have been around since the Romans cut stones and placed them on a gravel bed to make incredibly durable roads. They can withstand heavy use. Modern versions are made from concrete, clay or stone. A paver path is a labor-intensive project that requires the rental of a heavy plate compactor (p. 225) for proper installation. But the result is a permanent, tight-fitting, relatively smooth path that rivals solid concrete for durability.

Design factors

■ **Best uses:** All-around excellent material for paths, walks and even driveways, since paver construction can withstand heavy weight. They're highly decorative. You can choose from a variety of colors and patterns, creating anything from a formal English garden walk to an ancient-looking cobblestone path.

1 PAVERS are designed to lie in a tight pattern. Colors and patterns vary widely.

■ **Versatility:** Ideal for straight or curved paths. However, since pavers require a compact gravel base, changing the path later is a huge job. Use with caution around mature trees, so as not to damage the roots.

■ **Longevity/maintenance:** This type of path will last a lifetime. To avoid weeds, sweep off dirt so it doesn't accumulate in the joints. Every few years, sweep more sand into the joints to keep the pavers secure.

■ **Drainage:** Set the path to drain at 1/4 in. per ft. to the side. Set the pavers slightly above the surrounding grade.

■ **Slopes:** Pavers can be laid on steep inclines (if you can walk up it, pavers can be laid on it), but don't use them for steps. Use stone, concrete or wood for the steps instead.

CONCRETE PAVERS

CLAY PAVERS

GRANITE PAVER

ANTIQUE CLAY PAVER

Materials

■ **Concrete pavers** are the most common and diverse, available in different colors and shapes. You can arrange each shape in a number of patterns. They have beveled edges for easier fitting and shoveling. Expect them to last 30 years or more. The color will fade slightly as they weather.

■ **Clay pavers** were commonly used for streets in the 1900s. Many versions are available today, from soft-textured molded styles to crisper "wire cut" types. Color retention and durability are excellent. Set them

PLATE COMPACTOR

2 CONCRETE pavers are cast in a wide variety of geometric shapes and colors. Most have rounded edges.

3 CLAY pavers offer the traditional brick look. Most have crisp, square edges.

4 STONE pavers are cut from natural stone and are a uniform size. They often have rough faces.

perfectly even; the edges on some types can chip. Be sure what you buy is a paver, not a house brick, which is softer and will deteriorate.

■ **Stone pavers** are the most expensive, at least twice the price of clay or concrete pavers. They're often tumbled to make them look old. They're incredibly hard and difficult to cut, but they're attractive and will last a lifetime.

You'll find the largest selection of all types of pavers at a landscape, brick or stone supplier. You can usually find concrete pavers at home centers as well.

■ **Cost:** Concrete and clay pavers: $2 to $4 per sq. ft. Stone pavers: $7 per sq. ft. and up. Add about $3.50 per sq. ft. for a 7-in. thick bed of base material plus edging.

Key construction details

Setting pavers is a lot of repetitious work and isn't a job for a novice. You first dig a pathway about 9 in. deep and fill and compact the base material (gravel that packs well) with a special plate compactor ($60 per day to rent). Then you lay the edging, spread and level a bed of sand and drop in the pavers. You usually have to cut some pavers to fit with a saw and diamond blade. To finish, you set the pavers with the plate compactor and then sweep sand into the joints. ⌂

WEEKEND PROJECTS

Beautify your yard with these done-in-a-snap projects

Do you feel your backyard needs a little pizzazz or sprucing up? Well, sometimes it's the smallest projects that make the biggest impact. Here are 5 uncomplicated, inexpensive projects.

TRENCH **EDGING** & MULCH **BORDERS**

Trench edging looks great in informal garden settings. Use trench edging as a border around spreading evergreens or groundcovers or in areas where vinyl or other permanent edging material would look too formal and unnatural. You can easily shift it if plants outgrow the bed. An open trench (**Photo 1**) holds back the adjacent grass better than a trench filled with mulch. But if you prefer a more finished look, fill it with mulch (**Photo 2**). You'll have to redig the trench once in a while to keep it neat and to hold back the lawn, but it doesn't take long and you can add the trimmings to your compost pile.

1 DIG a trench 4 to 6 in. deep and about 4 in. wide with a straight spade. Angle the sides outward at the top.

2 FILL the trench with wood chips or other organic mulch for a more finished look and to deter weeds.

Popular mulches

WOOD CHIPS

COCOA BEANS

CYPRESS BARK

A **PAVER PATH** THAT GROWS

A perfect paving solution for erosion-prone paths are these 15-3/4 in. x 23-5/8 in. grid-shaped concrete pavers, called Turfstone (Photo 1). The concrete grid holds soil and grass in place even on steep slopes while providing good traction for wheelbarrows and lawn mowers. Manufacturers recommend installing these pavers over a compacted gravel base for driveways or other heavy use areas, but if you're just laying a walking path like ours, you can lay them on any solid, well-drained soil.

Turfstone is a specialty item. You'll probably have to order it from a landscape supply center or a local concrete block supplier. Each block costs about $7 and covers 2.6 sq. ft. If you lay two blocks side by side with the long sides together as we did, your path will be about 32 in. wide.

We chose to plug the holes with squares of sod, but growing grass from seed is another option. Once the grass is established, you can mow it just like the rest of your lawn.

1 SKIM the sod and dirt to a depth of 3-1/2 in. below the surrounding lawn. Rake the soil smooth. Set the pavers end to end to create the path. Don't worry about gaps between pavers caused by curving the path. You won't notice them after the grass fills in.

2 FILL the recesses with good-quality, lump-free soil. Lightly tamp the soil in each square to make room for the sod.

3 CUT small squares of sod from the sod roll with a utility knife. Press the sod squares into the recesses in the Turfstone pavers. Tamp soil alongside the pavers to hold them in place. Water the sod when you're done planting.

OUTDOOR STRUCTURES & LANDSCAPING

RUSTIC PLANT CAGE

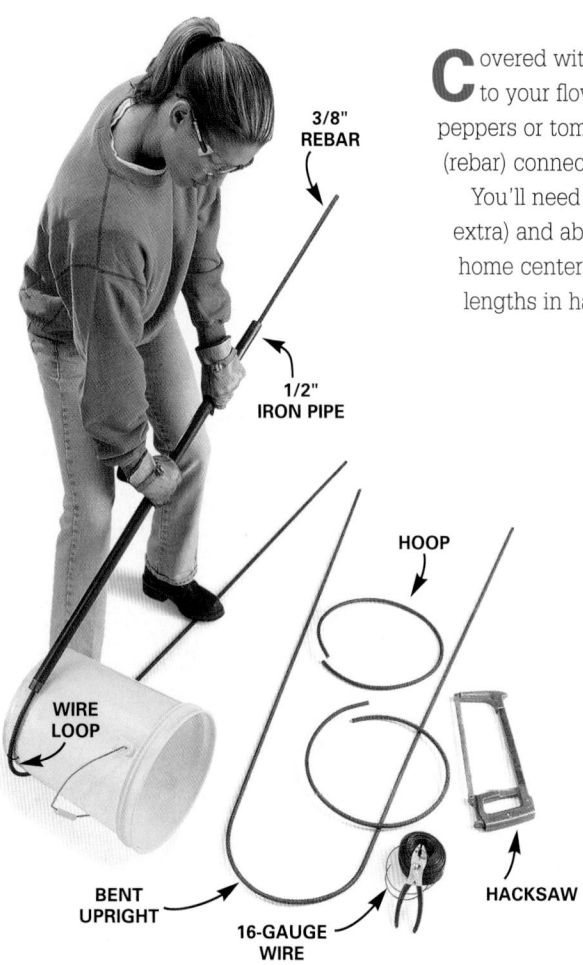

3/8" REBAR

1/2" IRON PIPE

HOOP

WIRE LOOP

BENT UPRIGHT

16-GAUGE WIRE

HACKSAW

Covered with vines, this rustic metal plant cage makes an attractive addition to your flower garden. In the vegetable patch, it's a great support for peppers or tomatoes. It's built from inexpensive concrete reinforcing steel (rebar) connected by twisted wire.

You'll need three 10-ft. lengths of 3/8-in. (No. 3) rebar (you'll have a little extra) and about 20 ft. of 16- or 18-gauge wire. You'll find 3/8-in. rebar at home centers ($6 for a 20-ft. length). Ask the supplier to cut standard 20-ft. lengths in half to make it easier to haul.

1 BEND 10-ft. lengths of 3/8-in. rebar around a 5-gallon bucket to form two arches as shown. Drill two holes in the side of the bucket and loop a wire through the holes and around the rebar to hold it in place while you do the bending. Slip a 3-ft. length of 1/2-in. pipe over the rebar for better leverage and control. Use the same technique for bending the hoops, but wrap the rebar completely around the bucket to form a circle. Then cut the straight section off with a hacksaw, leaving the hoop and a few inches of overlap. Wrap and twist-tie wire around the overlap to form the two hoops.

2 STACK the two hoops on the ground. Poke the ends of the two arches a few inches into the ground inside the hoops. Twist a 12-in. length of wire around the intersection of the two arches to secure them. Cut off the extra wire. Then slide the first loop up to about 16 in. from the top and wire it in place. Stand back and eyeball the hoop to make sure it's level and the uprights are evenly spaced before you tighten the tie wires. Repeat this process for the second hoop, leaving about 16 in. between hoops.

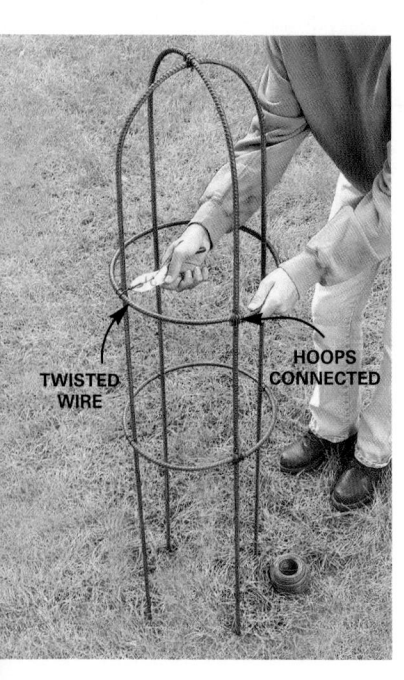

TWISTED WIRE

HOOPS CONNECTED

CHIMNEY FLUE **PLANTERS**

Want unique, tough terra cotta planters? Go to a brick supplier and buy 3-ft. lengths of clay chimney flue liner ($15 each). Cut them to different heights using a circular saw fitted with a masonry cutting blade ($2). Each blade will cut about two liners before wearing out.

The possibilities are endless: You can put the liners on a deck or patio to make a patio garden or accent your landscaping wherever you like—just pick your spots and bury the ends in the soil a little. Group the liners for an elegant herb garden or use them to border landscaped stairs.

Fill the liners with gravel for drainage, leaving at least 8 in. at the top for potting soil. Because the water can drain, the liners won't crack if they freeze. Or simply set plastic pots right on top of the gravel and you'll be able to bring in the plants for the winter.

PAINT-ON **MOSS**

MOSS MILKSHAKE

50/50 MOSS AND BUTTERMILK

CONCRETE POT

If you like the soft, weathered look of moss-covered pots but don't feel like leaving the process to the whims of nature, try this trick. Search cool, shady spots for moss and gather two or three cups. Put equal parts moss and buttermilk in your blender and mix it up to make a moss milkshake. Paint the moss solution onto any porous, unglazed masonry pot or planter. Place the pot in a shady spot and keep it moist by misting once or twice a day. Depending on the temperature and humidity, you'll start to see moss growing in a month or two. You don't have to wait to add a shade-loving plant to the pot. ⌂

OUTDOOR STRUCTURES & LANDSCAPING

BUYING
DECK LUMBER

Ten things you need to know about how to buy the good stuff, how to lose the bad stuff and where to use the ugly

by **Spike Carlsen**

You may have picked the perfect site, size and design for that new deck, but you still have one big thing left to select: the lumber. It doesn't matter whether you hand-pick your lumber and haul it home yourself or have it delivered sight unseen from the local lumberyard or home center: Choosing and using the right pieces in the right place can make your deck look better, last longer and go together faster.

1. Buy pressure-treated lumber with the right amount of treatment for the job

Pressure-treated lumber is the logical choice for the structural part of your deck—the posts, joists, beams and other members you normally don't see. Pressure-treated lumber can support more weight and span longer distances than cedar, redwood or other woods commonly used for building decks. It's also much less expensive.

Pressure-treated lumber is rated according to the pounds of preservative retained per cubic foot of wood; the higher the number, the better the protection against fungi and insect attack. Select boards with the preservative concentration suitable for their use.

| "ABOVE GRADE" .15 TO .25 LBS./CU. FT. | "GROUND CONTACT" .40 LBS./CU. FT. | "BELOW GRADE" .60 LBS./CU FT. |

The three common ratings:

1. **Above-grade use** (.25, sometimes .15). Typically used for decking, fence and railing material.

2. **Ground-contact use** (.40). Typically used for posts, beams, joists and, again, decking.

3. **Below-grade** (.60). Typically used for support posts that are partially buried below grade and for permanent wood foundations and planters.

Your boards will be tagged with the concentration and treating solution used. Use .40 material if you can't find .25. CCA (chromated copper arsenate) is being phased out because of health concerns. ACQ (Alkaline Copper Quat) and other preservatives are replacing it.

2. Avoid treated lumber that has a lot of heartwood

Since heartwood—wood from the center of the tree—is denser, it accepts pressure treatment less readily than sapwood—wood cut from the outer edges. This isn't as great an issue with dimensional lumber like 2x10s and deck boards; these boards are thin enough that the preservatives are usually driven throughout.

But with 4x4 and 6x6 posts, the preservatives may not penetrate the dense heartwood. However, it can be difficult to find posts not cut from heartwood.

3. When buying cedar or redwood decking, select boards cut from heartwood

Heartwood contains the natural preservative oils that give these woods their resistance to decay and insect attack. Heartwood in these species is the darker core of the tree. Sapwood—lighter in color and cut from the outer edges of the tree—lacks these natural oils. If you're purchasing redwood, you may find two grades. Look for lumber labeled "heartwood common," which has more heartwood than "construction common."

Install deck boards "good side up." Some swear deck boards should only be installed "bark side up," the theory being, if a board cups, boards laid "bark side up" will warp into a hump that water will run off rather than a dip where water can settle. But tests have shown there are many reasons boards cup and they don't always cup according to "bark side."

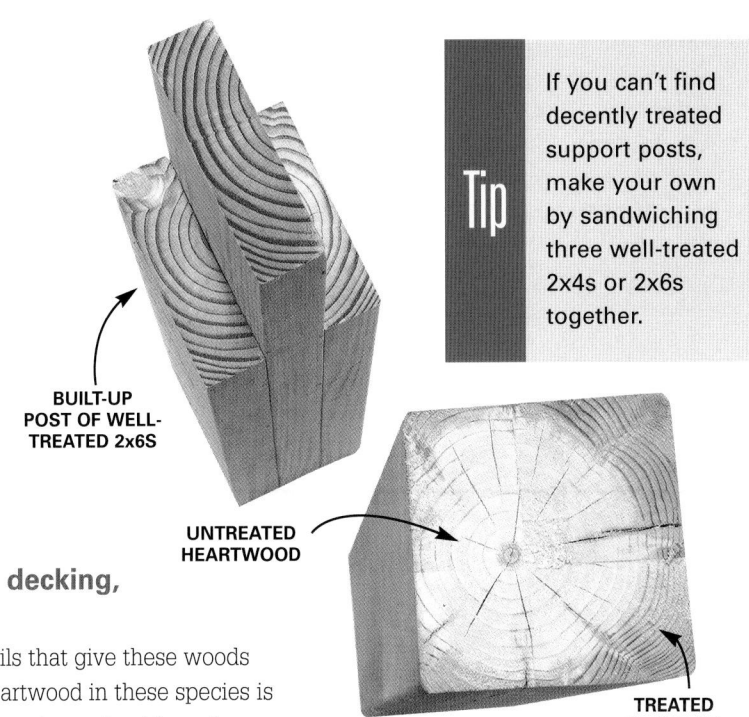

Tip If you can't find decently treated support posts, make your own by sandwiching three well-treated 2x4s or 2x6s together.

BUILT-UP POST OF WELL-TREATED 2x6S

UNTREATED HEARTWOOD

TREATED SAPWOOD

CEDAR BOARDS WITH TOO MUCH SAPWOOD

BOARD INSTALLED "BARK SIDE DOWN" WITH ACCEPTABLE AMOUNT OF SAPWOOD

BOARD INSTALLED "BARK SIDE UP" WITH NO SAPWOOD

4. Buy wood that's dry

If you're buying treated wood, buy boards that have had time to dry after they've been treated. Boards still saturated with the water used to carry the wood preservative into the wood cells can be literally twice as heavy as dry wood. The extra weight makes wet boards harder to work and to cut, and they shrink when they dry. This means joists can "rise up" out of their hangers, making them bouncier and less well supported. Fasteners can loosen and your deck can wind up with uneven and unsightly wide gaps between the boards. If you're unsure whether a board is too wet, compare its weight with that of an untreated board the same size; if it's twice as heavy and feels damp, it may need time to dry.

You can "sticker" the wood and let it dry for a few weeks (see photo). For deck boards, look for wood that's labeled KDAT (kiln dried after treatment).

STICKERS TO SPEED DRYING

WET DECKING

DRY DECKING

OUTDOOR STRUCTURES & LANDSCAPING

5. Use posts with some heft, especially if your deck is more than 2 ft. off the ground

Tall decks look spindly and awkward perched on 4x4 posts. Use 6x6 posts instead; they look and are more solid and substantial. They'll also last longer and support extra weight if you add a structure to your deck somewhere down the road. And avoid posts that already have a twist or bow; chances are the defect will only get worse.

3-1/2" x 3-1/2" POST

5-1/2" x 5-1/2" POST

12.25-SQ.-IN. CROSS SECTION

30.25-SQ.-IN. CROSS SECTION

6. Every type of deck board has its pros and cons

There are three main categories of deck boards, each with its own advantages and disadvantages.

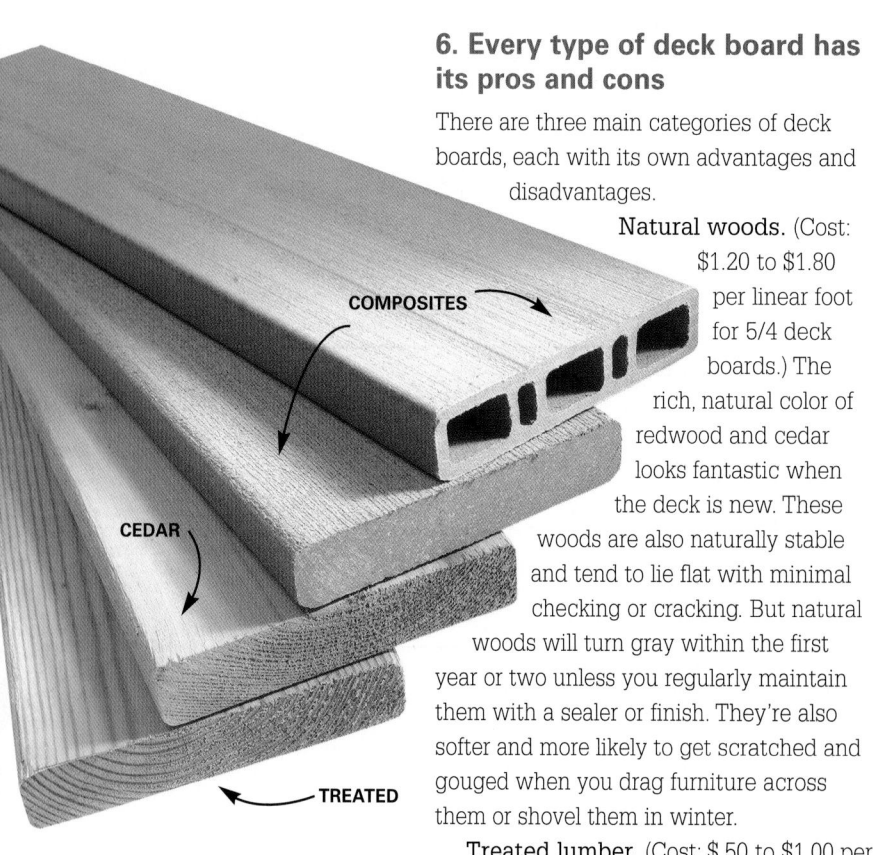

COMPOSITES

CEDAR

TREATED

Natural woods. (Cost: $1.20 to $1.80 per linear foot for 5/4 deck boards.) The rich, natural color of redwood and cedar looks fantastic when the deck is new. These woods are also naturally stable and tend to lie flat with minimal checking or cracking. But natural woods will turn gray within the first year or two unless you regularly maintain them with a sealer or finish. They're also softer and more likely to get scratched and gouged when you drag furniture across them or shovel them in winter.

Treated lumber. (Cost: $.50 to $1.00 per linear foot for 5/4 deck boards.) This material is strong, long lasting and the least expensive of your options. But often boards that aren't kiln dried after treatment will shrink appreciably after they're installed, creating wider spaces between the boards. And treated lumber has a greater tendency to crack once in place; apply a water repellent every year or two to stabilize it.

Composite deck boards. (Cost: About $1.25 to $2.00 per linear foot.) Composite boards are made from wood and plastic (often recycled materials) and resist rot and insect attack. Since there are no defects, there is very little waste, and many now come in a variety of colors. They have their drawbacks, however. Not all brands are code compliant in all communities. Some people object to their homogenous look and "plasticky" feel. And like any other outdoor material, they can become dirty and stained; expect to do an occasional pressure washing. And the colors do tend to fade eventually.

7. Consider all three dimensions when selecting your deck boards

Width: Six-inch wide boards are ideal in most cases. Four-inch wide material takes longer to install, creates more gaps and requires a lot more fasteners—but you can use it. Eight-inch wide boards, because of their greater width, have more of a tendency to crack and cup; avoid using them.

Thickness: Radius-edge, 5/4 material (which can measure anywhere from 1 to 1-1/4 in. thick) has become extremely common. In most cases, it

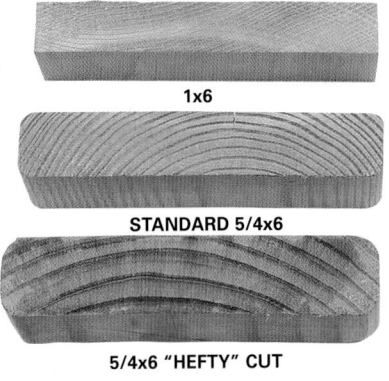

1x6

STANDARD 5/4x6

5/4x6 "HEFTY" CUT

requires a joist spacing of 16 in. for proper support. If your joists are spaced at 24 in. or you're running your deck boards at a diagonal, you may need to use 2-by (1-1/2 in. thick) boards. Avoid boards that are only 3/4 in. thick. They have a wimpy feel underfoot even with closer joist spacing.

Length: When possible, buy decking that can run the full length of your deck. All lumberyards and home centers carry 16-ft. deck boards, but many also stock or can order 20- and 24-ft. boards, though they may cost more. Full-length material allows you to avoid butting boards end to end, which can invite trouble; the ends of boards are more absorbent, slower to dry out and more susceptible to rotting, swelling and splintering. Fasteners driven close to the ends also tend to split the wood, making the ends even more vulnerable.

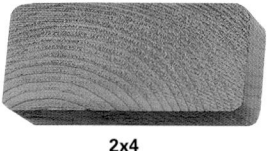

2x4

2x6

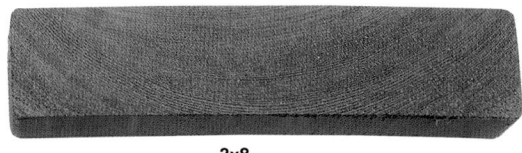

2x8

8. A little curve, twist or crown to your joists is OK (but "scalped edges" and uneven depths are a pain)

It's actually preferable to use joists with a slight crown, an upward bow of 1/4 to 1/2 in. (**Fig. A**, p. 234). Joists will settle and sag slightly as they support weight and movement. A perfectly flat joist will wind up with a dip. Check the crown by sighting along the edge of the board. Then check that crowned edge for scalped edges, called "wane" (**see below**). Wane on the bottom of a joist is OK, but

wane on the top means there's less wood for driving fasteners into—and you can't butt two deck boards on an uneven joist.

The depths of joists can vary by as much as 3/8 in.; the 12-ft. long 2x10s at your lumberyard may measure 9-1/8 in. in depth, while the 16-footers measure 9-1/2 in. Deck boards secured to uneven joists will flex more and the fasteners will creak and pop. Use joists that vary less than 1/8 in.

UNEVEN JOINT

WANE

JOISTS OF UNEQUAL DEPTH

OUTDOOR STRUCTURES & LANDSCAPING

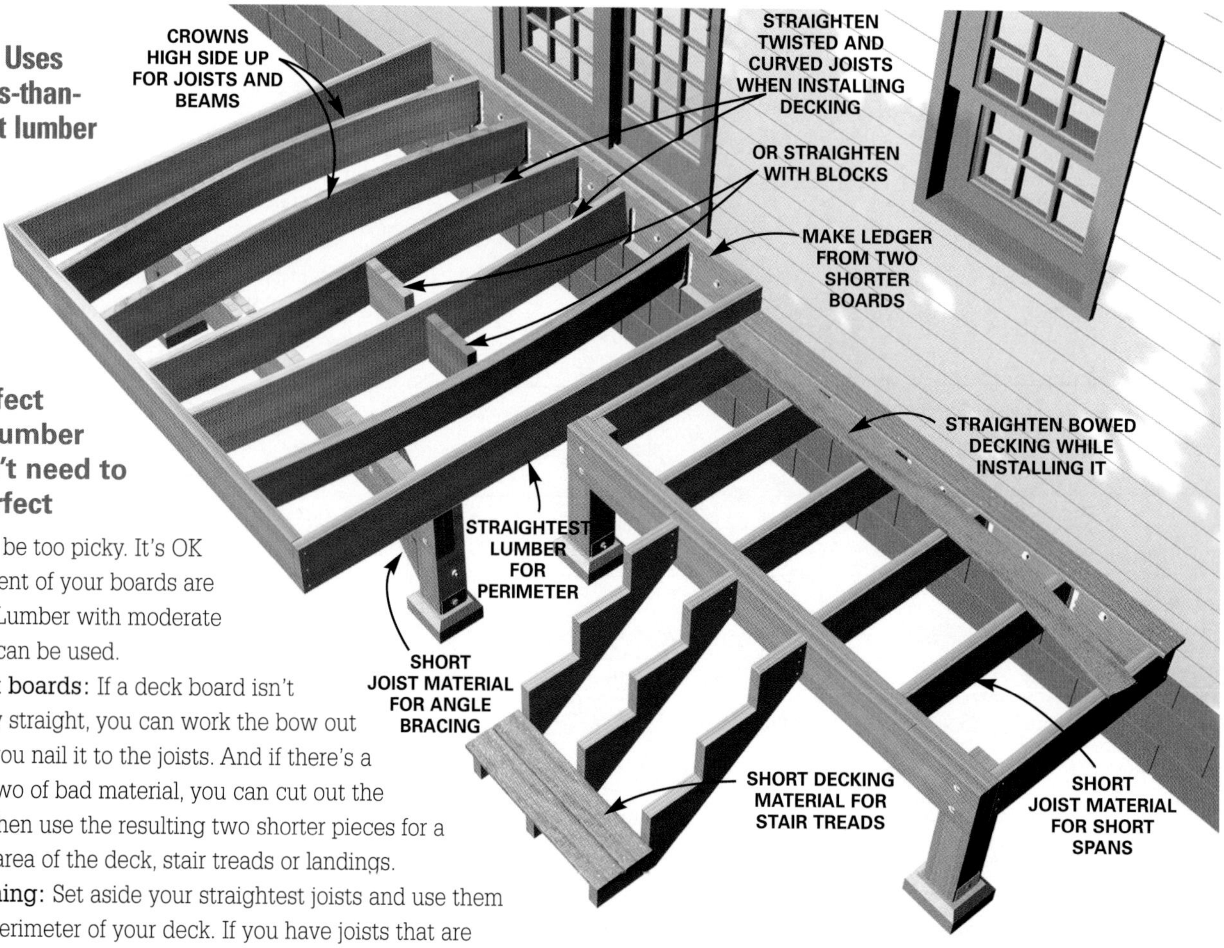

Fig. A: Uses for less-than-perfect lumber

CROWNS HIGH SIDE UP FOR JOISTS AND BEAMS

STRAIGHTEN TWISTED AND CURVED JOISTS WHEN INSTALLING DECKING

OR STRAIGHTEN WITH BLOCKS

MAKE LEDGER FROM TWO SHORTER BOARDS

STRAIGHTEN BOWED DECKING WHILE INSTALLING IT

STRAIGHTEST LUMBER FOR PERIMETER

SHORT JOIST MATERIAL FOR ANGLE BRACING

SHORT DECKING MATERIAL FOR STAIR TREADS

SHORT JOIST MATERIAL FOR SHORT SPANS

9. Perfect deck lumber doesn't need to be perfect

You can be too picky. It's OK if 5 percent of your boards are "dogs." Lumber with moderate defects can be used.

Deck boards: If a deck board isn't perfectly straight, you can work the bow out of it as you nail it to the joists. And if there's a foot or two of bad material, you can cut out the defect, then use the resulting two shorter pieces for a smaller area of the deck, stair treads or landings.

Framing: Set aside your straightest joists and use them for the perimeter of your deck. If you have joists that are curved or twisted, straighten them with blocking or as you install the decking (**Fig. A**). Extremely bowed or knot-filled boards can, again, be cut up and used as blocking or as joists for smaller landings and deck sections.

STRONG JACK

WEAK JACK

10. Buy straight, solid 12x12s for your stair jacks

Be fussy here. Look for material that's straight, with no splits or large knots. You'll cut deep triangles into each 2x12 to accommodate the treads; avoid splits along the top edge and knots along the lower edge, which can weaken the already thinned body of the jack. 🏠

Tip

As you haul your material from the driveway to the back yard, stack it into piles of "pretty" and "ugly," then use them accordingly.

Handy Hints® from our readers

SPACE-SAVING TOMATOES

If you're short on space and want to grow tomatoes in pots, you can train them to grow upward like a vine instead

GARDEN TWINE

BAMBOO STAKES

12" TO 24" POT

of sprawling all over. Make sure you don't buy the bush-type "determinate" tomato, which won't get tall enough to be trained as a vine. "Indeterminate" plants are later maturing, but they will continue to grow and branch until the growing tip (central leader) is cut off. If the label on the plant doesn't say which type of plant you're buying, ask the salesperson.

CENTRAL LEADER

SIDE SHOOT

Buy a roomy pot so roots can spread out and the soil won't dry out too quickly. (The 24-in. dia. plastic tubs that hold young trees at the nursery are ideal, although 12- to 24-in. pots will do.) You'll need five 6-ft. long by 3/4-in. dia. bamboo stakes. Cut one of them into 12-in. lengths. Tie these pieces with twine to the nodules on the vertical stakes, like rungs on a ladder. Push one end of each trellis 1 ft. deep into the pot, placing one trellis in front of the tomato plant and the other behind it.

To train the plant to grow upward like a vine, wind the stems through the trellis and secure with twine. Pinch out some of the side shoots to encourage growth of the central leader.

Tip — Tomatoes need lots of food and water, but even more when you grow them in pots.

SELF-LEVELING FEET

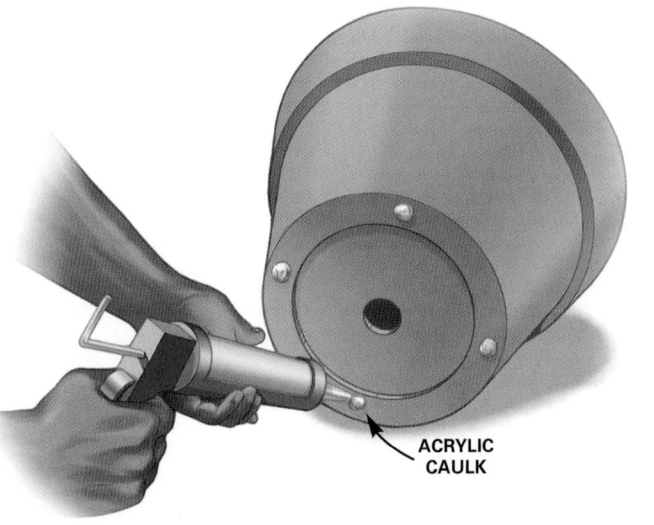

ACRYLIC CAULK

Here's how to make flower pots, vases, planters, boxes or almost any not-quite-flat-bottom object sit flat on the floor without scratching or slipping. Apply four blobs of acrylic caulk to the bottom, and let them dry until they're almost set. Then turn over the object and place it on a sheet of wax paper until the caulk cures. You'll get four stable feet.

Handy Hints® from our readers

STAY-PUT VINYL EDGING

Black vinyl edging is easy to install and economical. But after a few seasons it can start to look shabby, especially at the seams, where it tends to buckle and pull apart. Here's how to splice lengths of new edging to prevent them from separating or lifting.

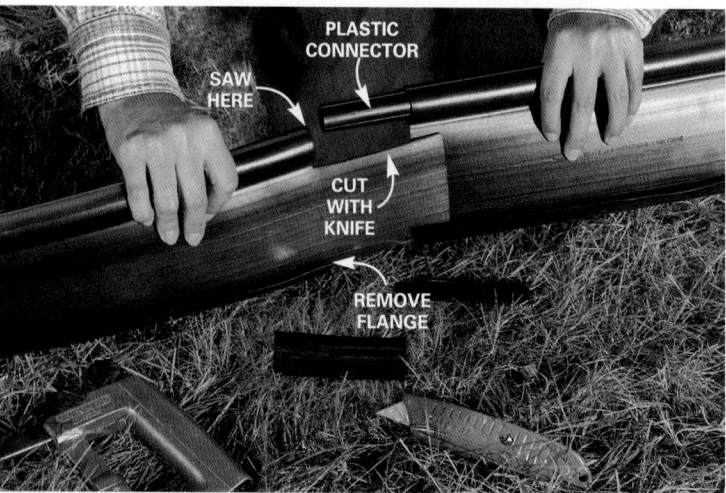

PLASTIC CONNECTOR

SAW HERE

CUT WITH KNIFE

REMOVE FLANGE

1 SAW through the tubular top and about 5 in. from the end of the edging with a hacksaw. Use a utility knife to complete the notch as shown. Cut off the bottom flange even with the top notch. Slip the plastic connector into the top tube and slide the two ends together.

COMPLETED SPLICE

METAL STAKE AT 45-DEGREE ANGLE

2 DIG a trench for the edging with the vertical face on the grass side. The top of the edging should be flush with the grass. Drive a steel edging stake at about a 45-degree angle through the overlapping section of edging into the ground. Bury the lower 2 in. of edging, but leave about 3 in. exposed on the garden side to make a pocket for mulch.

CREVICE WEEDER

Three-tine hand cultivators are easy to find at any garden supply store ($6 to $9), but I've never liked them for breaking up hard soil or getting into tight spots between plants. So I decided to convert mine by cutting off the two outside tines. Now the cultivator is easy to pull through hard soil and works great for weeding the cracks on the stone patio.

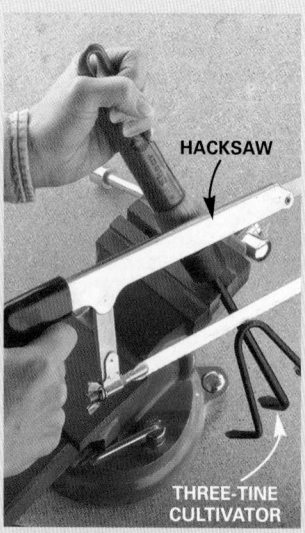

HACKSAW

THREE-TINE CULTIVATOR

Clamp the hand cultivator in a vise and saw through the weld with a hacksaw. File off any sharp edges with a mill bastard file.

Tip

Sidewalk cracks are a weeding nightmare. Make short work of those tenacious crack-hugging weeds by slicing off their tops with a string trimmer. You won't get the roots, but at least it will look good until the next time you trim.

THE PLUMPEST PUMPKIN

You might not be able to grow a pumpkin the size of Cinderella's coach—but with a bit of custom care, you can grow a monster. Pumpkins take three or four months to mature, so if Halloween is your target date, plant your seeds in May. Follow these steps:

1. Purchase seeds developed to grow big pumpkins; most nurseries and mail-order sources have them.
2. Dig a hole the size of a bushel basket and dump in compost or rotted manure. Then cover the area with a 4- to 6-in. layer of black dirt.
3. Plant three seeds about 1 in. deep. After the seeds sprout a few leaves, thin to the single healthiest plant.
4. When three pumpkins begin to develop, remove any additional female flowers—the ones with the pumpkin-shaped bulge immediately behind them.
5. When the three pumpkins are softball-size, thin to just one pumpkin.
6. Keep the plant weeded, well watered and fertilized with a high-phosphorus fertilizer.
7. Harvest your pumpkin before the first hard frost, leaving the stem attached. Place it in a warm room for a week, then store it in a cool place until you're ready to carve it.

LAUNDRY JUG WATERING CAN

Instead of throwing away empty laundry detergent containers, rinse them out thoroughly and then recycle them for watering plants. Drill 1/8-in. holes in the top of the cap, and a 1/2-in. hole just above the handle to relieve pressure so the water flows freely.

COLLAPSIBLE BARREL

The beauty of the Kangaroo Container is that when you don't need it, it collapses to a 3-in. thick disk that hangs on the wall. Unclasp the plastic toggles and it springs into service as a 30-gallon soft-sided barrel ready for dirty clothes, leaves, sporting goods or whatever. A 10-gallon size also is available. Sold at most home centers for about $15 to $20. Fiskars Brands Inc., (608) 259-1649. www.fiskars.com

Gallery of Ideas

GARDEN SHED

If you're an avid gardener—or have a lot of lawn and garden equipment in need of a home—check out this garden shed. It has an 8 ft. x 9-1/2 ft. storage area, plus a 5-1/2 ft. x 8 ft. potting shed. It even has a mini-patio and arbor! The concrete paver floor, natural cedar siding and steel roofing add up to a low-maintenance shed that will last for generations.

Project Facts:
Cost: $3,600
Skill level: Intermediate to advanced carpentry skills
Time: 4 weekends for two people

GARDEN POND & DECK

If you like the sound of running water and enjoy relaxing on a deck, you'll love this garden pond and deck project. Simple wood walls made from treated lumber frame the pond and form the base for the deck. A single-piece rubber liner keeps the water in place. Tropical hardwood decking called Ipe creates the attractive, extremely durable walking surface.

Project Facts:
Cost: $3,000
Skill level:
 Intermediate do-
 it-yourself skills
Time: 4 to 5 days

HAMMOCK HIDEAWAY

Here's a home improvement project you'll want to dive right into. One of the great features of this project is that it lets you choose the ideal location and bring your shade with you. An optional awning cover lets you nap out of the sun and out of the rain. The project is built around two 6x6 treated posts that you set in concrete. The rest of the project is made from ordinary cedar lumber and screws and hardware you can get at your local hardware store or home center.

Project Facts:
Cost: $600 + cost
  of hammock
Skill level: Basic
  carpentry skills
Time: 2 to 3 days

STONE FIRE RING

An outdoor fire is a natural gathering spot for family and friends, whether for a cookout or casual conversation on a cool evening. Those gatherings can be more comfortable and safe by building a simple fire ring with retaining wall stone. This project requires no special tools or skills. In fact, the primary tool for this project is a strong back.

Project Facts:
Cost: $200 for 24 granite retaining
  wall stones, $800 for 200 sq. ft. of
  flagstone surrounding the fire ring
Skill level: Beginner project
Time: 1 weekend

To order photocopies of complete plans for the projects shown here, call 715-246-4344 or write to:
Copies, The Family Handyman, P.O. Box 83695, Stillwater, MN 55083-0695.
Many public libraries also carry back issues of *The Family Handyman* magazine.

You Can Fix It™

CURE FOR A PATCHY LAWN

Prepare your lawn and enjoy lush grass every spring

If your lawn looks a little tired and bare after a summer of badminton games and dry spells, don't worry. Fall is a great time to rejuvenate it. The weather is good for seed germination and competition from weeds is at its lowest. Here's how to seed your lawn to thicken it. Start by loosening compacted soil to stimulate growth.

Many patchy lawns suffer from compacted soil, which deprives grass roots of needed oxygen. Removing plugs of soil with a core aerator ($40 per half day to rent) allows air and water to penetrate the ground and leaves space for surrounding soil to expand and loosen. Plan ahead and reserve the core aerator for at least half a day for an average-size lawn. It's best to use the aerator when the soil is moist. You'll need a truck or trailer to haul the core aerator home. The machine weighs 150 to 200 lbs., so it takes some muscle to move around. If you're not up to the task, consider hiring a lawn service for this part of the job (it may not cost much more than renting the aerator). Allow a day between aerating and seeding to let the soil plugs dry. Dry plugs will break up easier when you blend them in along with the dressing of topsoil.

Pick a grass seed mix that fits your climate as well as soil and shade conditions. There are many great sources of information. If you have Internet access, check www.seedsuperstore.com or a similar site. You can also call your local county extension office or ask at the nursery for advice. Make note of your soil type, whether it's heavy clay or well-drained loam, and how much sunlight the area gets. Pick seed that's meant to grow best in these conditions and in your climate.

Measure your lawn and calculate the amount of seed you'll need based on the coverage rates for your seed (listed on the package). For small areas, throw out the seed as if you were feeding birds. For larger areas, use a drop spreader or broadcast spreader. Divide the seed in half and apply it in two passes at right angles to each other. Set the spreader for half the recommended application rate, or to about 20 percent open if there are no settings, and spread the first half of the seed. Keep a close eye as you're applying it so you don't run out. It's better to err on the side of spreading it too thin at first. You can always go over the area again.

The final step in the renovation is to cover the seed

1 LOOSEN the soil with a rented core aerator. Make four or five passes over the lawn at angles to each other. Let the cores dry a day or so before seeding.

2 SPREAD the grass seed at about half the rate recommended for new seeding of bare soil. Seed small areas by hand. Use a drop spreader or broadcast spreader to seed large areas.

with a thin layer of soil. Buy bags of soil from the nursery for small areas. If you're reseeding an entire lawn, it'll be more economical to order topsoil delivered. Call a nursery or landscape supply company and say you want screened and pulverized black dirt for top dressing your lawn. You can also use dry, screened soil from your yard. One cubic yard of soil will cost about $30 plus delivery and cover about 1,300 sq. ft. at 1/4 in. deep. Spread the soil and rake it to create a thin, even layer over the seeds.

Lightly water the seeded area two or three times a day for 5 to 20 days until the seed sprouts. As the grass reaches 1 to 2 in. tall, water once a day, but leave the sprinkler on long enough to wet the roots, which are 1 to 2 in. deep. You can mow the grass when it's about 3 in. tall. See "Ask Handyman," April '03, p.10, for more information on growing grass from seed. To order a copy, see p. 288.

TIPPY BATHS AREN'T FOR THE BIRDS

Leveling a paver stone under your bird feeder is a slick way to keep your birdbath from tipping over and the water in the bowl level. Round or square paving stones like the one we're using are readily available at garden centers ($3 to $6).

Dig a hole about 2 in. deeper than the thickness of the paver. Spread and roughly level a 2-in. layer of sand in the hole. Set the paver on the sand and check it with a short carpenter's level. Lift one edge of the paver and add or remove sand to level it.

3 SPREAD a 1/4-in. layer of topsoil over the seeded area. Fling the soil from the shovel to distribute it evenly.

TOPSOIL

4 RAKE the surface with a fan or leaf rake to break up the soil plugs and spread the topsoil over the seeds. About 10 percent of the seeds will show. Water the new seeds with a sprinkler.

1/4" LAYER OF TOPSOIL

OUTDOOR STRUCTURES & LANDSCAPING

You Can Fix It™

TIN SNIPS

SHALLOW TRENCH

LANDSCAPE FABRIC STAKES

CYPRESS BARK MULCH

BURIED EDGE

1 CUT chicken wire with a tin snips to fit around bushes and other plants. Dig a 3-in. deep trench under the edges and bend the chicken wire down into the trench. Push stakes into the ground 12 in. apart in every direction.

2 FILL the trenches with soil and pack it down to anchor the edges of the chicken wire. Then cover the chicken wire with mulch or a thin layer of soil.

DOG-PROOF YOUR SHRUBS

Our dog loves to get out of the hot sun by relaxing in a nice, big, cool hole he's dug under the shrubs along the house. And, of course, one hole just isn't enough. I read somewhere that chicken wire laid over the ground would solve the problem, and sure enough, dogs hate getting their nails caught in the mesh. But if you want the wire to stay put, you have to take time to carefully bury all the edges and put in plenty of stakes.

Chicken wire, also called poultry netting, is available at home centers and hardware stores in widths from 24 in. to 4 or 5 ft. Measure your bed and, if possible, buy a piece wide enough to cover it without a seam. We bought metal landscape fabric stakes from a landscape supply center and used them to hold the chicken wire in place. Bent coat hangers or other stiff wire also would work.

DIGGING UP A COOL SPOT

10 Auto & Garage

IN THIS CHAPTER

Auto Fast Fixes 244
  *Paint chip repair, replacing fuses,
  DIY oil change*

Epoxy Floor 251

Handy Hints 256
  *Trailer dolly, elastic cord storage
  and more...*

Mower Tune-Up 258

Foldaway Workshop 264

You Can Fix It .271
  Car door opener

AUTO **FAST FIXES**

Keep your car looking good and running great with these easy fixes

PAINT CHIP REPAIR

Do it now before it mushrooms into a huge expense

Remember that gravel truck traveling at 70 mph that suddenly switched lanes in front of you and bounced a few marble-size rocks off your hood? Now you've got several tiny chips in your paint finish that could grow to quarter-size rust spots in a few years. Take care of the problem right away for less than $10, and you'll save yourself big money later on, not to mention the embarrassment of driving a premature clunker.

The fix we show here is for fresh chips that haven't started to rust yet. If you see a rust spot like the one on p. 245, or have a dent along with your chip, you'll need to do a more challenging fix than we show here. Keep in mind that this repair will be visible under close scrutiny, but if you buy the right touch-up color, it'll be unnoticeable from a few feet away.

Buy auto primer and the right paint

At an auto parts store, you'll find a display of auto touch-up paints. Look up your car's year, make and model in the booklet at the display. You'll find a list of factory colors that cars like yours were painted that year. If you have a white vehicle and there is only one white listed for it, just buy that one. If you don't know the color number for your car, you'll have to find it on your vehicle identification plate. This can be challenging. The plate may be located under the hood on the cowl, near the radiator shield or on the jamb of the driver's door. Some owner's manuals will tell you where to look, or a

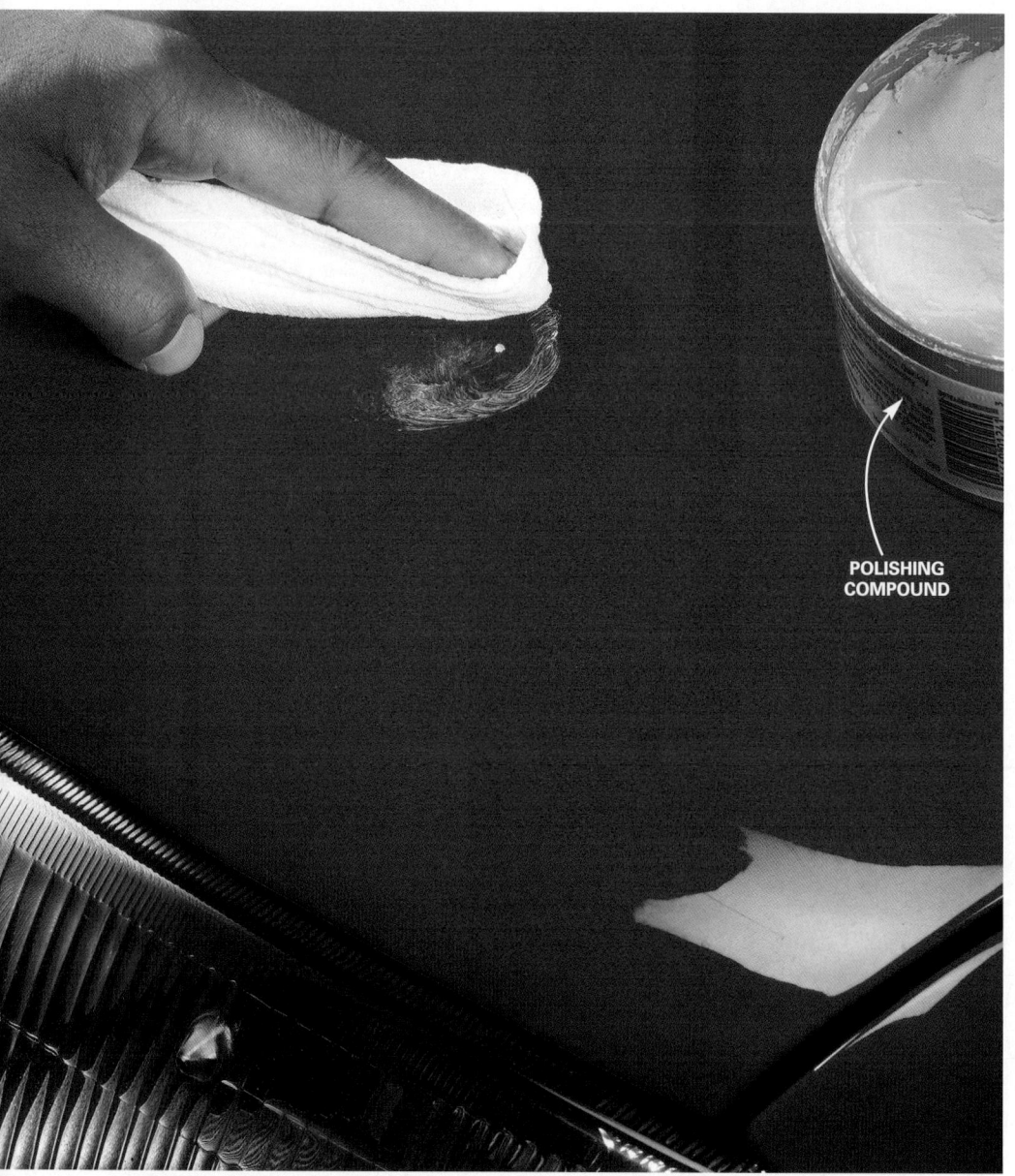

POLISHING COMPOUND

1 CLEAN the chip with soap and water and then dry it with a soft cotton cloth. Rub a dab of automotive polishing compound over the chip to gently soften any ragged edges. Just a dozen swirls or so will do the job. Too much rubbing could damage the clearcoat over the paint and make a cloudy mess.

quick call to your dealer will help. Once you find the number, buy a small bottle of touch-up paint. If you can't find the correct color at the display, check with the dealer. Dealers often carry colors for the cars they sell. Also, buy a small can of auto primer.

Now just follow our photo sequence to fix that chip, and remember, don't do this repair in the direct sun or if the temperature is below 50 degrees F.

2 CLEAN the finish with denatured alcohol. Don't flood it with alcohol. Just a few wipes with a soft cloth will do. The alcohol will remove any wax or remaining grime.

> **Tip** If you can only find spray paint with the right color number, you can use it by spraying a bit of paint into the cap and applying it with a fine artist's brush.

Fix it before it's too late

The top photo shows a typical rock chip that you can fix with this procedure. In fact, even if the chip is about one-fourth the size of a dime, you can still repair it.

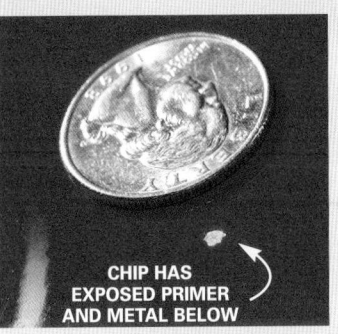

CHIP HAS EXPOSED PRIMER AND METAL BELOW

The bottom photo shows a chip that should have been repaired long ago. The metal inside the chip has rusted and started to lift the paint at the edges. This fix is less do-it-yourself–friendly and requires sanding, priming and painting.

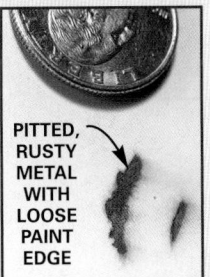

PITTED, RUSTY METAL WITH LOOSE PAINT EDGE

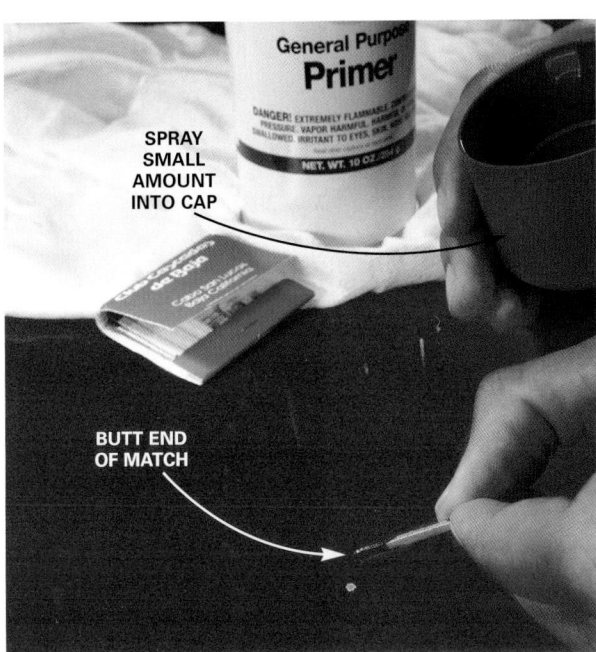

SPRAY SMALL AMOUNT INTO CAP

BUTT END OF MATCH

3 APPLY a spot of primer with the butt end of a paper match. Fill the area within the chip, just touching the edges of the surrounding paint. Let the primer dry for at least a half hour.

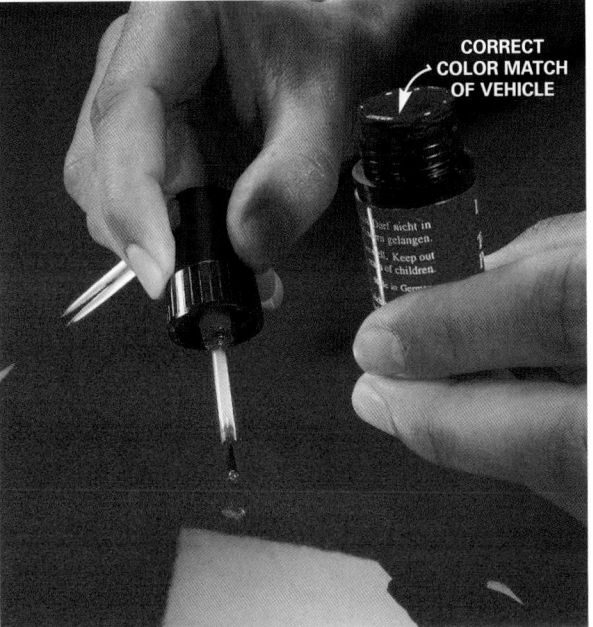

CORRECT COLOR MATCH OF VEHICLE

4 PUT a small amount of paint over the primer coat. Always test the color on a piece of paper to make sure it matches. The test will also give you a feel for how much paint to load onto the applicator brush. Apply a second coat about one hour later. Let the paint cure for several days and rub it out again gently with polishing compound to feather the edges of the repair.

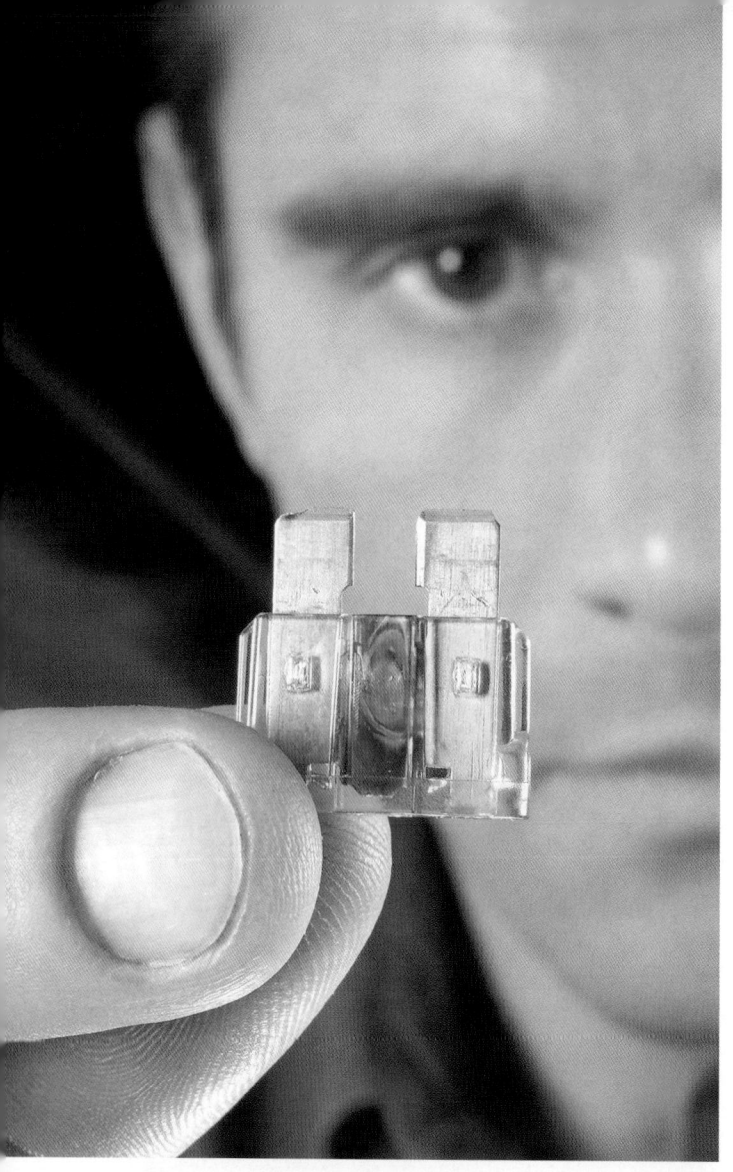

REPLACING
AUTO FUSES

Check your fuse box before you make an appointment at the repair shop

Your vehicle runs on electricity as much as it does on gas. And almost every electrical device in your vehicle, from your lights to your ABS brakes, is protected by a fuse, so it pays to know how to find and replace them. It takes about five minutes, costs about $1, and even better, it'll save you the hassle of a trip to the repair shop.

Vehicles today have 40 or more fuses grouped in two or more places. Usually located in or around the instrument panel near the dash, fuses can also be found under the hood and even under the rear seat.

Next time your radio, lights or other device stops working, chances are, a blown fuse is the culprit. Look under "Fuses" in your owner's manual for help finding your fuse panels. Most manuals have a diagram showing you where each fuse box is. Each fuse panel cover should have a diagram listing each device and the corresponding fuse.

Fuses are color coded by amp rating. For example, a standard blue fuse has a 15-amp rating, yellow is 20 amps and green is 30. Before you buy fuses, keep in mind that the fuse panel cover often contains spare fuses and even a fuse puller (**Photo 2, inset**). Just be sure to replace the spares so they'll be there the next time you need them. You can buy them at any auto parts store and at well-stocked service stations.

Note: If your new fuse blows soon after installing it, you could have problems in that circuit. Schedule an appointment with your service station or dealer for an expert diagnosis to repair the problem.

WARNING: Never replace a blown fuse with a higher-amp fuse. Always replace the fuse with one with the specified amp rating. You may install the next-smaller-rated fuse to get you by in a pinch until you can purchase a replacement.

1 CHECK your owner's manual for the location of your fuse box. It may be under the hood, under the dash, beneath the side kick panels or under the rear seat.

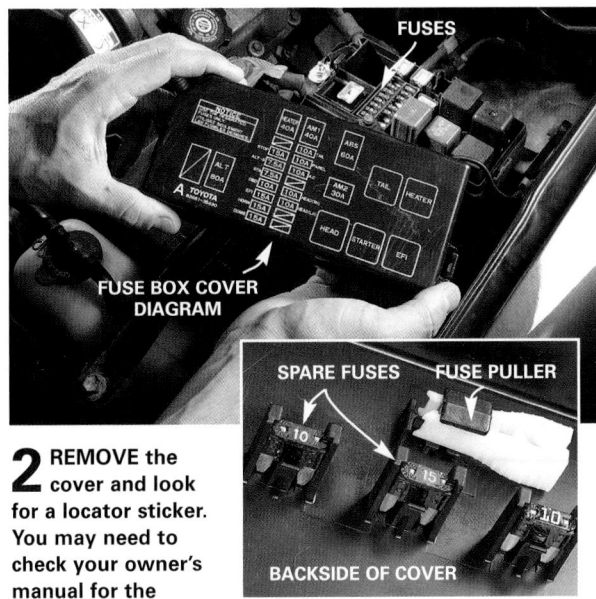

FUSES

FUSE BOX COVER
DIAGRAM

SPARE FUSES   FUSE PULLER

BACKSIDE OF COVER

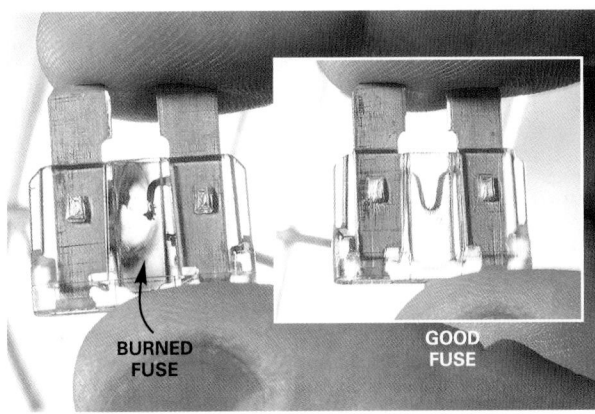

2 REMOVE the cover and look for a locator sticker. You may need to check your owner's manual for the location of the fuse you're looking for. Many fuse covers contain extra fuses and fuse pullers on the backside (inset photo). If you use one of them, replace it the next time you go to the auto parts store.

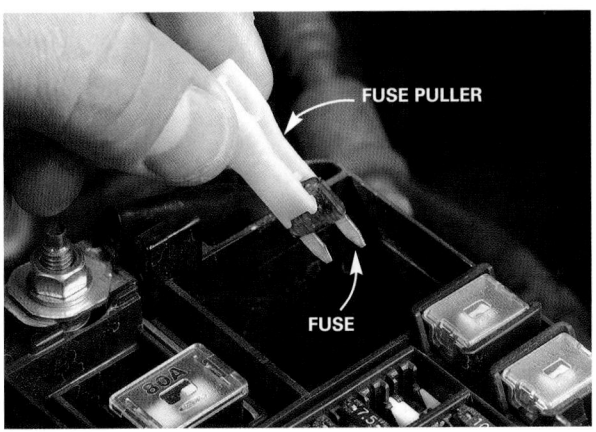

FUSE PULLER

FUSE

3 REMOVE the fuse that's labeled for the device that's not working, for example, the fan, radio, lighter or marker lights. Use a needle-nose pliers or a fuse puller (available at auto parts stores).

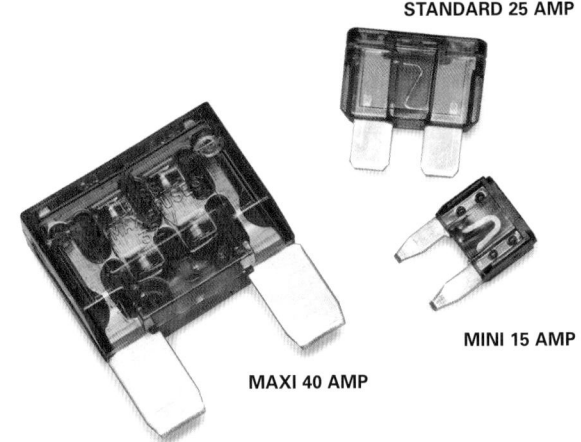

STANDARD 25 AMP

MINI 15 AMP

MAXI 40 AMP

BURNED
FUSE

GOOD
FUSE

4 HOLD the fuse up to the light to see if it's burned out. You'll see a fine wire connecting the two sides if the fuse is good. If a section of that wire has burned away, the fuse is bad.

5 MOST fuses used in vehicles today are one of three types: mini, standard or maxi. The mini and standard are fast-acting fuses that protect the majority of your vehicle's circuits, including those for lights and radios. The maxi fuses are slow-acting fuses that protect circuits with a large current draw such as those for anti-lock brakes, rear window defogger and traction control.

In-line Fuses

Some accessories that aren't factory installed may have a remote in-line fuse. These fuses can be located under the dash, under the hood or even in the trunk depending on the circuit they protect. They most likely protect an aftermarket accessory like fog lights or a CD changer. The best way to find an in-line fuse is to trace the wire from the accessory to the fuse panel. Along the way, you'll notice a fuse container that looks like one of these shown. Open the housing to pull out the fuse and examine it. Replace it with one of the same size and amperage and snap the housing back together.

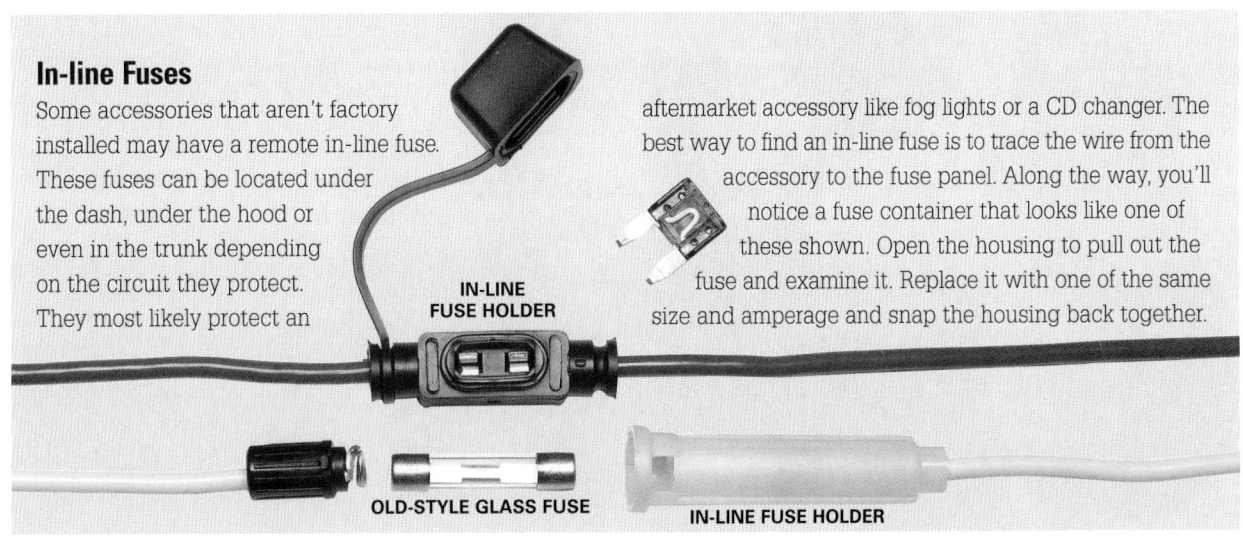

IN-LINE
FUSE HOLDER

OLD-STYLE GLASS FUSE

IN-LINE FUSE HOLDER

THE COMPLETE DO-IT-YOURSELF OIL CHANGE

Save money and do the job right

Changing your oil regularly is the single best thing you can do to prolong the life of your car's engine. And if you do this simple 20-minute job yourself, you can save money and know that it was done right.

However, it's not a task for everybody. Most of the job is easy, but you'll probably have to raise your car to get at the drain plug. You'll need a sturdy set of ramps for your car or a floor jack and safety stands designed for your car's weight. Some people have a phobia about getting under their car. If you're one of them, stop here and make an appointment at a lube shop.

Also, before you start, look under the car and make sure you'll be able to get at the filter to remove it. Some makes of cars have awkward setups that make it nearly impossible to get at and remove the filter with ordinary tools. If that's the case, call for an appointment and pay the $30 fee.

Check your owner's manual for the vehicle's oil capacity and drain plug location. For most jobs, you'll need 4 or 5 qts. of oil, an oil filter wrench, a box-end wrench the size of your filler plug, a funnel, rags and, of course, a new oil filter appropriate for your car or truck.

Tip: If your car's engine is cold, let the engine run for a few minutes to warm up the oil. This helps loosen the contaminants in the oil so they'll flow out into the drain pan. However, don't try to drain the oil if the engine is hot. Let it cool to avoid burning your hand.

OWNER'S MANUAL

2x12 RAMP STOP (EACH SIDE)

DRAIN PAN, FILTER AND NEW OIL

NON-SKID RUBBER MAT

1 DRIVE your car onto your ramps, or use an inexpensive floor jack along with a set of jack (safety) stands (not shown). Be sure to set your parking brake. Check the directions that come with the drive-on ramps or jack stands for details, then give the car a good shake from side to side to make sure it's solidly supported. If you use ramps, be sure they won't slide as you drive onto them. We used a rubber mat under the front of the stand and a 2x12 plank to keep the ramps from sliding forward. Have a helper guide you so you don't drive off the ramp.

CAUTION: Never work under any car using the factory-supplied jack—it's only for changing a flat tire!

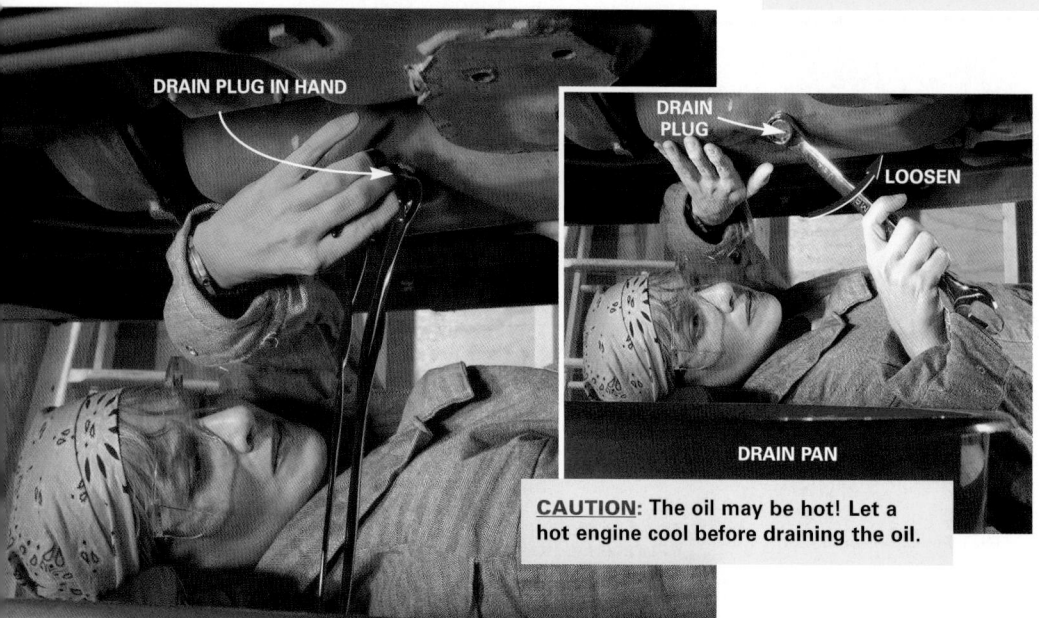

DRAIN PLUG IN HAND

DRAIN PLUG

LOOSEN

DRAIN PAN

CAUTION: The oil may be hot! Let a hot engine cool before draining the oil.

2 USING a box-end wrench, loosen the drain plug about a half turn. Avoid using an adjustable wrench because it's more likely to slip and eventually ruin the plug head. And remember this memory aid—lefty loosy, righty tighty. Slide the drain pan under the drain plug. Unscrew the plug. When the plug is ready to come out, quickly pull it out of the way. Hold on to the plug so it doesn't drop into the drain pan. Let the oil drain for at least five minutes, then reinstall the plug.

OIL FILTER

FILTER WRENCH

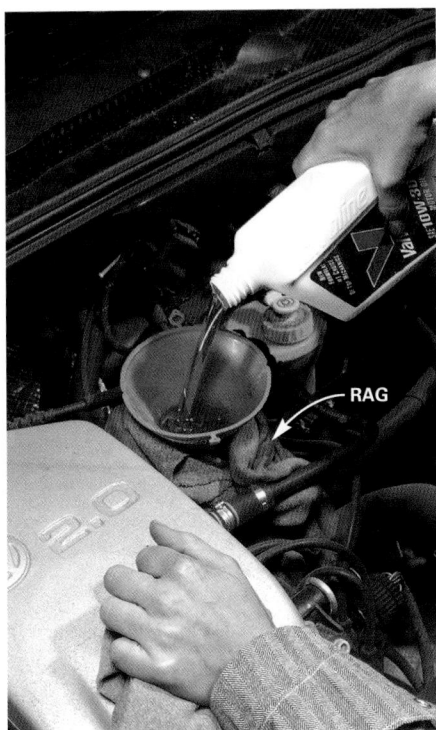

RAG

3 UNSCREW the oil filter, using an inexpensive oil filter wrench ($5 to $10). If you use the type pictured, make sure it's the right size and configuration. Some wrenches cinch around the filter and turn from the side. Others, like the one shown, fit the bottom of the filter and accept a 3/8-in. drive socket or a wrench. Room to move the tool is the key. Loosen the oil filter by turning counterclockwise. When the filter is loose, use a rag to unscrew it by hand. Be careful! The filter may be full of oil, so place the drain pan under it. Remove the filter and pour any oil into the drain pan. Wipe any old oil or dirt from the filter-mounting surface so the new filter will seal properly, and make sure the old oil filter ring gasket hasn't stuck to the engine.

5 LOCATE the engine oil fill hole and clean the area around the fill cap. Using a clean, dry funnel, add the new oil. Don't spill any on the engine. If you do, wipe it up immediately. Note: Refer to your owner's manual for the correct weight, API rating and amount of oil you'll need to add. Replace the oil fill cap, check the oil level on the dipstick (it may be slightly over the mark until you run the engine) and start the engine. Be sure the garage door is open so exhaust fumes can escape. Check the oil pressure gauge for the proper pressure reading or be certain the oil light on the instrument cluster is off. Look under the car for leaks. Lower the car and recheck the dipstick level to make sure the oil is up to the full mark.

RING GASKET

NEW OIL FILTER

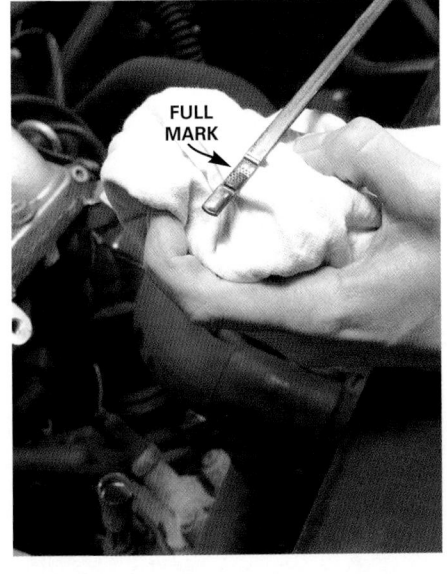

FULL MARK

4 SMEAR a few drops of clean oil on the new filter's ring gasket. Carefully spin the new filter on by hand. Be sure you don't pick up any dirt from the frame or other parts on the ring gasket as you position the new filter. Spin the filter on clockwise until the gasket seats against the engine. Then turn the filter—by hand—approximately a half turn to fully seat the ring gasket. If you can't get your hand around it firmly because space is tight, use your wrench. Don't overtighten the filter—you may tear the gasket.

OIL **CHANGE** TIPS

If you're one of those few diehard shade-tree mechanics who still change their own oil, here's a product you gotta get. You know the oil-changing drill. First you have to find the right-size wrench and then skin your knuckles loosening the plug. Then hot oil drains down your arm as you unscrew the plug, ruining that nice shirt you shouldn't be wearing. Then you face the filthy job of pouring the old oil into some sort of recycling container and cleaning out the oil basin.

That's all dirty history with the new Sure Drain System from Fram.

The next time you change your oil, drain it and replace the oil pan drain plug with the drain actuator valve and finger-tighten the brass dust cap. When you're ready to change the oil again, just remove the dust cap, screw on the drain tube and the oil will start flowing. There's a little valve that gets opened when you screw on the tube assembly. Put the end of the tube into an empty milk jug and have another jug ready to go for when the first one is full. They're ready to be capped and sent to recycling. You'll never have to deal with a dirty catch basin again. Just make sure you check the Fram catalog for your vehicle's part number to buy the correct thread size for your oil pan. Sold at auto parts stores for $12.99.

Fram, (203) 830-7800 or (800) 862-7737. www.fram.com

INSTANT OIL FUNNEL

SECOND CONTAINER
FIRST CONTAINER
NO MESS

Don't have a funnel handy? An empty plastic oil container will do the job. Cut the bottom out of the empty container with a sharp utility knife. This funnel can hold an oil container snugly, so you don't have to stand around waiting for the last drop to drain.

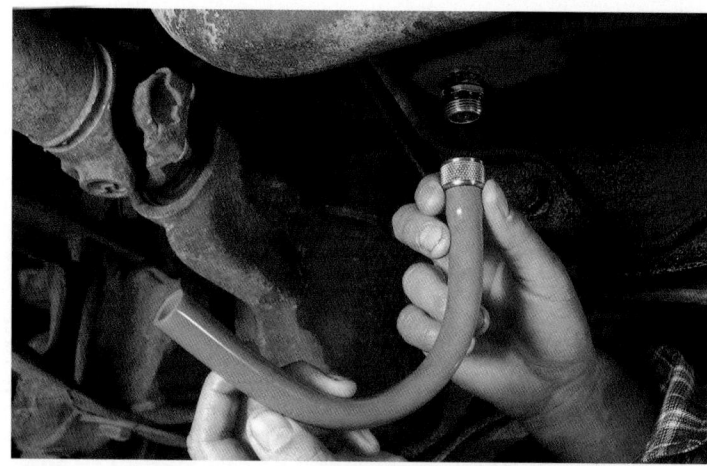

Tip

Dispose of the old oil by pouring it back into oil bottles (a rather messy job) or into an old container. Don't put the container out with the regular trash. Used motor oil is hazardous waste and must be disposed of properly. In many states, retail outlets that sell motor oil must accept used oil for recycling. If your store doesn't take back used oil, check with a repair shop, because many shops will dispose of used oil. Otherwise, contact your local waste removal company for instructions. Drain all the oil from your old filter and dispose of the filter in the trash.

OLD OIL
OLD CONTAINER

EPOXY
FLOOR

Achieve auto showroom brilliance in one long weekend for less than $500

by **Kurt Lawton**

Imagine pulling onto an auto showroom floor every evening after work. That's the feeling you'll get pulling into your own garage if you give the floor a durable epoxy finish. Epoxy is a tough, long-lasting coating that you paint onto the concrete. It resists grease, oil and many other substances that would ruin ordinary paint. It cleans easily and can be found in a variety of colors (if you look hard enough), so you can keep your garage floor sparkling clean and attractive for years.

However, the reality of this challenging project is, one, not all concrete floors will hold a coating, and two, preparing concrete can be labor intensive and tedious. That said, this story will help you assess your concrete's condition, show you how to clean and etch it, and demonstrate how to apply an epoxy surface that will handle car traffic, chemicals, oils, salt and scraping better than any other paint or stain.

As with any other paint job, success lies in the prep

Test your concrete

MOIST CONCRETE—
DO NOT APPLY EPOXY

Lift the corner of a plastic bag that's been taped to the garage floor for 24 hours. If it's dry underneath, you can proceed with an epoxy coating. *If you see moisture* under the plastic, don't coat the floor with epoxy; water pressure will break the bond.

CLEANER/
DEGREASER

DON'T SCRUB
OUTSIDE
STAINED AREA

1 DIP a stiff-bristle brush into a cleaner/degreaser and scrub oil stains aggressively. Wipe up with cotton rags or paper shop towels. Repeat the procedure until the greasy feel is gone and water droplets no longer bead up on the surface.

ENTIRE FLOOR
WET

2 WET the entire floor with a hose, then scrub back and forth using an electric floor scrubber with a brush attachment (or a coarse scrubbing pad if a brush attachment is unavailable). Pour cleaner/degreaser mixture onto the floor as you go to keep suds going.

work. Plan to spend the first day removing oil spots, cleaning/degreasing the floor, etching it with a mild acid, and scrubbing, vacuuming and rinsing (a lot!). Day two is for filling cracks and applying the first coat of epoxy, which is followed by a second coat on day three.

This job doesn't require many special tools. But to do the best job (and save your back), we recommend that you rent a walk-behind power floor scrubber (**Photo 2**) with a stiff brush attachment ($25 per day). Brushes work better than scrubbing pads on concrete, but buy two pads ($8 each) if a brush isn't available. Also, rent a wet vacuum ($18 per day) if you don't own or have access to one.

Analyze the floor and weather

Before you even consider epoxy paint for your floor, test to determine if dampness is coming up through the concrete from the ground (**top photo**). If moisture is evident, your floor isn't suitable for epoxy. Also, forgo the project if a concrete sealer was previously used (you'll know a sealer has been used if water beads up when applied to the surface). If you're dealing with a new slab, you must wait a minimum of 28 days, preferably two months, for the floor to cure and dry thoroughly before applying a garage floor coating. And if you're dealing with a previously painted floor, the best advice is to remove the paint, especially when you're applying a solvent-based epoxy that could soften any that remains.

If your concrete passed these tests, make sure the weekend weather passes too. The temperature of the concrete must be a minimum of 55 degrees F, with an air temperature between 60 and 90 degrees F for optimum epoxy curing/drying.

Sorting out epoxy

The final critical decision is what type of epoxy to use. Epoxy floor paints are tough resins that come in two separate parts that you mix together just before you apply them. You can divide them roughly into three types: 100 percent solids, solvent based and water based.

The 100 percent solid type is almost pure epoxy; it doesn't contain solvents that evaporate. These products are expensive and difficult to handle because they harden so rapidly. They're best left to the pros.

The solvent-based epoxies typically contain from 40 to 60 percent solids (epoxy). They penetrate and adhere well and are the choice of most pros. And they're often available in a wide range of colors, which is one reason we chose this type for our demonstration. But they do have some drawbacks. The solvents are powerful and potentially hazardous; you MUST use a respirator (a 3M 5000 series respirator with an organic vapor/acid gas filter, $14, or the equivalent in another brand). The respirator must fit tightly to your face so you don't breathe the fumes. In addition, you must ventilate the garage well and keep other people away from the odors.

Solvent-based epoxies also may be harder to find. Some paint specialty stores may carry them (Sherwin-Williams and ICI Dulux, among others), but otherwise you'll have to go to an industrial supply–type store. Check the Yellow Pages under "Paint, Wholesale & Manufacturers" or "Industrial Equipment & Supplies," or look on the Internet.

The water-based epoxies also have two parts that you mix just before application. And they also typically contain 40 to 60 percent solids. The benefit of this type of epoxy is that there are no hazardous solvent fumes. And, at least one brand, Rust-Oleum's EpoxyShield Garage Floor Coating, is widely available at home centers. (Colors are limited to gray or tan. See Buyer's Guide, p. 255, for details.)

Whether you're working with solvent- or water-based epoxy, we recommend that you apply two coats to get enough build for long-term wear and durability. "Build" refers to the thickness of the dried epoxy film. Typically, an epoxy with a higher solid content will give a higher build. And, in general, prices tend to reflect the amount of epoxy in the mix—the more epoxy, the higher the build and the higher the price.

For a two-car garage (450 sq. ft.), you'll need 2 to 3 gallons per coat (depending on the percent of solids in the epoxy you buy—read the container). The price of epoxy for two coats will range from $150 to $300. Check the cans for coverage to make sure you buy enough.

Day 1: Floor cleaning

To begin, use a flat-edged shovel or scraper to loosen hardened surface debris, then sweep it out with a stiff-bristle garage broom.

Next, mix up a 5-gallon batch of water and concrete cleaner/degreaser according to label directions (found at home centers and hardware stores for about $12).

Once spots are cleaned, power-scrub the entire floor (**Photo 2**). To clean a two-car garage floor, plan on scrubbing for 20 to 30 minutes (keep the floor wet at all times). Make sure you scrub with a stiff-bristle hand brush along the walls and in the corners where the machine cannot reach. Once you're satisfied with dirt removal, vacuum up the cleaner for proper disposal (**Photo 3**).

Don't just wash the product down the drive into the storm sewer. The environmental effects of cleaning products can vary widely. Check the product label or call the manufacturer for the proper waste disposal method. We looked up the Material Safety Data Sheet for the product we used (made by Behr) on the Web site www.msdssearch.com and learned we could pour the waste into the "sanitary sewer" (toilet). Also check the

3 PUSH a rubber squeegee along the floor and pool the soap mixture into smaller areas. Vacuum up the solution for proper disposal (see text, below, under "Day 1.")

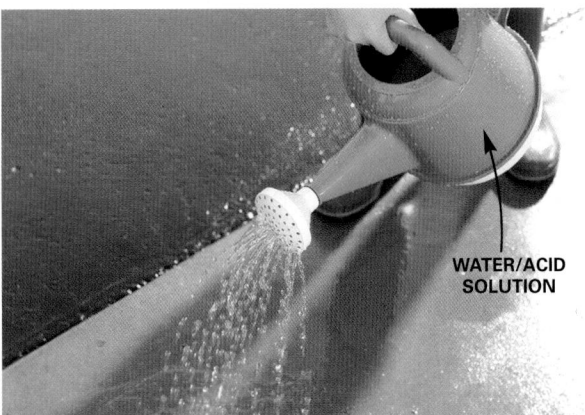

4 POUR 12 ozs. from a bottle of 32 percent muriatic acid (common formulation) into a gallon of water (1 part acid to 10 parts water) in a plastic sprinkler can, then sprinkle evenly over a 10 x 10-ft. area.

<u>CAUTION:</u> Always add acid to water, not water to acid and wear an organic vapor/acid respirator (*Photo 7*).

5 POWER-SCRUB the 10 x 10-ft. area for 5 to 10 minutes. Repeat sprinkling/scrubbing for each 100-sq.-ft. section, making sure the entire floor stays wet. When you're done, spray a large volume of water on the floor to flush the residue out. Power scrub again, then rinse two or three times. Let the floor dry overnight, until it appears white.

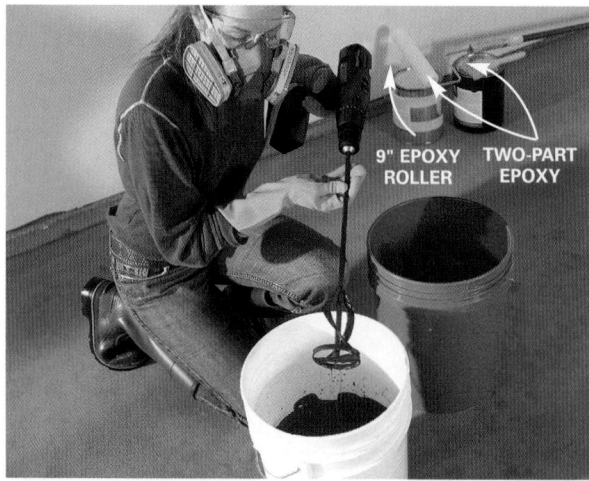

6 MIX the two epoxy components for five minutes using a drill and stirring bit. Then pour the entire contents into a second bucket and repeat the power mix to ensure complete blending of the entire mixture.

9" EPOXY ROLLER — *TWO-PART EPOXY*

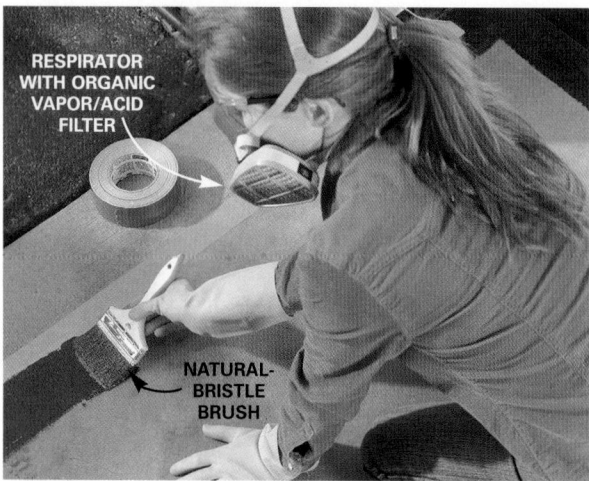

RESPIRATOR WITH ORGANIC VAPOR/ACID FILTER

NATURAL-BRISTLE BRUSH

7 TAPE the area directly underneath the garage door with duct or masking tape, then brush a 4-in. strip of epoxy along the walls and against the tape.

8 DIP a 9-in. wide, 3/16-in. short-nap epoxy roller into the bucket so only the bottom half of the roller is covered. (This helps keep epoxy out of the roller.)

label or call the manufacturer for instructions on safe disposal of all leftover product and containers. When in doubt, call your city or county environmental office.

Before etching concrete with the acid solution (**Photo 4**), hose down your entire driveway and several feet beyond the sides of the drive. This aids in the final rinse out of the garage so the material will flow more easily down the driveway.

Now sprinkle the 10:1 ratio of water to muriatic acid ($2 per gallon of 32 percent acid) mixture and power-scrub the floor (with a rinsed brush attachment or new pad; **Photos 4 and 5**).

Rinsing is key

When you're finished, take your hose and nozzle end and flood the floor with water, spraying the material out of the garage for a good 10 minutes (diluted muriatic acid can be rinsed with large volumes of water into a storm sewer, according to the manufacturer). Rinse off the power scrubber brush/pad, then scrub the wet floor one last time for 5 to 10 minutes. Finally, rinse out the entire floor and driveway two to three more times.

The concrete surface should now feel like fine-grit sandpaper. If not, you need to repeat the acid washing. Finally, to speed the drying process, squeegee out any remaining pooled water, and take a rag and dry any remaining spots, cracks or chipped areas. Leave the garage door open overnight to speed drying.

Day 2: First coat

First thing in the morning, after the floor has dried overnight, fill 1/4-in. cracks and larger, plus holes or spalled areas, with an epoxy crack filler, available at home centers for $24. Use a plastic putty knife to scrape the surface level and smooth. Let this dry for four hours (check label directions) before you begin painting your first coat of epoxy.

Mix the correct amount of epoxy (**Photo 6**) to cover the square footage of your garage floor according to label

> **Tip**
>
> Consider adding epoxy paint to the bottom 4 in. of drywall, wood or concrete wall along the floor to protect it when you hose the floor clean in the future.

directions. It's critical that you allow the mixed product to stand undisturbed for the specified time on the label before applying it. You also must apply the entire batch you mixed up before the specified time expires. We used a 40 percent solid, solvent-based epoxy from a local industrial supplier/manufacturer that had to sit for 30 minutes, and the batch had to be used up within 24 hours (and it was offered in almost 20 colors).

While waiting for the crack filler to cure, use a high-quality natural-bristle paint brush and cut in the floor edges (**Photo 7**). Also, tape the area directly underneath the garage door with masking or duct tape, allowing you to shut the door overnight. This is intended to keep out dust, dirt, pets and children until the floor is dry. And put a "Do Not Enter" sign along with tape across the doorway leading to the garage from the house.

Coating the floor

If you move at a steady pace (**Photo 9**), you should finish your two-car garage floor in less than one hour. (Remember not to paint yourself into a corner!) The solvent odors are powerful. Be sure to wear a respirator (**Photo 7**) and keep the garage door open at least an hour after coating.

Day 3: Second coat

Let the first coat dry overnight, for a minimum of 16 hours (or according to label directions, since epoxy products vary). Add a non-skid product ($3 per gallon) to the epoxy (**Photo 10**) for the second coat, especially if your vehicles

drag snow and moisture into the garage, or you'd feel safer on a less slippery floor. Repeat the "cutting in" and floor painting like the day before (**Photos 7 – 9**).

Wait another 16 hours (check label directions) after finishing before allowing foot traffic. You can start parking your cars on the floor after approximately three to seven days (depending on the epoxy label directions). A full cure for the floor takes approximately one month. ⌂

Oops!

Despite ardent cleaning and proper epoxy application, we experienced a few dime-size holes where a car tire removed some epoxy. Repainting fixed the problem, but this illustrates the importance of proper prep, enough time for the concrete to dry, and adequate curing time.

3'- 4'

3'- 4'

9 PAINT a big wet "W" pattern that's about 3 to 4 ft. square, then backroll to fill in the pattern—all in 60 seconds. Finish by going over it lightly to remove roller marks.

NON-SKID ADDITIVE →

10 LET the first coat dry according to label directions. For the second coat, repeat the steps in Photos 7 – 9. If you don't want a glossy floor (it's slippery when wet), add a non-skid floor coating additive into the epoxy and stir well to disperse the granules evenly.

Buyer's Guide

- ■ Dura-Seal 400 Epoxy: Durall Concrete Floor Coatings, (800) 466-8910. www.concrete-floor-coatings.com
- ■ Anti-slip floor coating additive and epoxy crack filler: Rust-Oleum, (800) 323-3584. www.rustoleum.com
- ■ Muriatic acid: Sunnyside, (800) 323-8611. www.sunnysidecorp.com
- ■ Cleaner/Degreaser: Behr, (800) 854-0133. www.behr.com
- ■ Respirator: ANI Safety & Supply, (847) 676-5800. www.anisafety.com

Handy Hints® from our readers

OIL RECOVERY SYSTEM

Being environmentally concerned, I try to completely drain oil containers when servicing vehicles and lawn equipment. My oil recovery system is made up of 1-in. PVC pipe and assorted 1-in. PVC fittings. Cut 1-in. PVC pipe into 3-in. and 6-in. lengths and glue everything together with PVC cement as shown. Build the oil recovery system as large as needed. Use pipe straps to mount it to the wall, placing it high enough off the floor so a gallon jug with a funnel can slide underneath to catch the last of the oil.

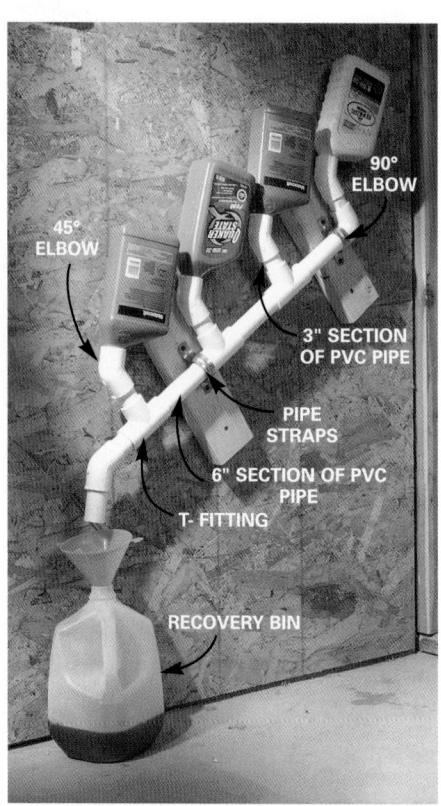

45° ELBOW
90° ELBOW
3" SECTION OF PVC PIPE
PIPE STRAPS
6" SECTION OF PVC PIPE
T- FITTING
RECOVERY BIN

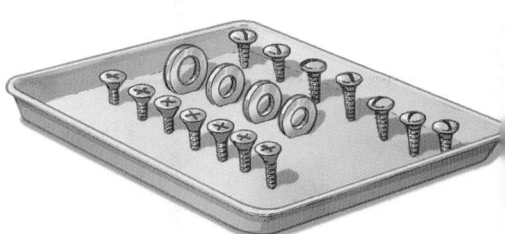

GAS CAN FUNNEL COVER

Prevent gas from splashing out of the funnel hole on the trip home from the station. Replace that missing funnel cover with the cap from a gallon milk or water jug. Snip off the outside rim of the gallon cap, leaving the center intact (tin snips held flat work the best). Put the cover over the inverted funnel and screw down the cap.

ROLL-DOWN WORKSHOP WALLS

If you have a workshop in the basement (or garage), you know how difficult it is to keep sawdust from spreading over everything. A simple solution for dusty work is a set of roll-down walls. Buy two 8 x 16-ft. plastic tarps, four 16-ft. lengths of 1x3, four Bungee cords and eight screw eyes. Staple the tarps to the 1x3s at the tops and bottoms, then screw the top 1x3 to the ceiling joists. Roll them down for dusty work and roll them up when you need more space. The Bungee cords hooked to the screw eyes hold the rolled-up walls in place.

1x3s
ELASTIC CORD

SMALL-PARTS ORGANIZER

Wash and save those foam meat trays to use when you're assembling a project that has lots of small screws, bolts, nails, etc. Just poke the parts into the tray bottom in the order you'll need them. It will help you determine beforehand whether you have all the parts you need, and will speed up the assembly considerably.

SHADOW

FIND THOSE LOST PARTS

Here's a slick way to locate small parts that fall to the floor. Turn off the lights and shine a flashlight beam across the floor. When the part is struck by the light, its large shadow makes it easy to find.

ELASTIC CORD STORAGE

Tie-down straps, both the rubber and the elastic-cord types, are great to use but a headache to store. They're always getting tangled. Try storing them on a length of PVC pipe. Cut the pipe slightly longer than the tie-down straps and hook the ends inside the pipe.

ORDERLY WRENCH CASE

If you find the contents of your socket wrench case in a mess every time you open it, try this. Cut a piece of 1/2-in. foam rubber to fit inside the lid, and glue it in place. When you fasten the catch, all the sockets will stay securely where they belong.

TRAILER DOLLY

As I've gotten older, it's become increasingly difficult for me to manually move my trailer around. So I drilled a hole in a dolly 1-1/2 in. from the edge, then stacked 10 washers onto a 1/2-in. carriage bolt, stuck it through the hole, and tightened it down with a washer and nut. Now I hook the bolt and washer assembly onto the trailer tongue and can easily pull the trailer around.

WRENCH FOR ROUNDED BOLT HEADS

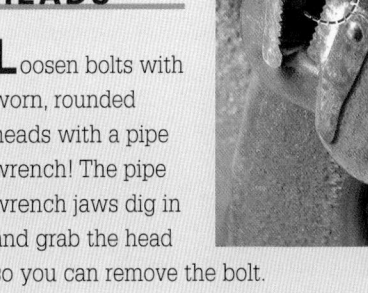

ROUNDED BOLT

Loosen bolts with worn, rounded heads with a pipe wrench! The pipe wrench jaws dig in and grab the head so you can remove the bolt.

MOWER TUNE-UP

Keep your mower running like new. Do these 5 simple fixes now.

by **Jeff Gorton**

Mowing is enough of a chore without having to deal with a rough-running, poor-cutting lawn mower. With just a few bucks' worth of parts and a couple of hours' work, you can get your lawn mower in prime shape to start the mowing season. We'll show you how to drain the old gas, replace the air filter, put in a new spark plug, change the oil and sharpen the blade—tasks that will keep your gas-powered mower starting easy, running smooth and cutting clean.

Add fresh gas at the start of the season

Fuel system problems top the list of lawn mower malfunctions. Many of these, like gunked-up carburetors, are often caused by gasoline that's been left in the mower too long. Although fall is the best time to take preventive measures (see "Storing Your Lawn Mower for the Winter," p. 262), you can at least get off to a good start in the spring by replacing the old gas in your tank with fresh gas. **Photo 1** shows one method.

Gasoline is highly flammable. Work outdoors or in a well-ventilated area away from sparks and flame. Wipe up

1 USING an old turkey baster, suck old gas from your tank. Squirt it into a container approved for gas storage and label it as old gas. Refill the tank with fresh fuel.

CAUTION: Always disconnect the spark plug wire from the spark plug (Photo 6) before reaching under your mower.

2 SEAL the gas tank by removing the gas cap and covering the opening with a plastic bag. Screw the cap back on over the plastic bag.

3 REMOVE the dipstick from the oil filler tube and tip the mower to drain the oil. Pour the used oil into a plastic milk jug or similar container and recycle it.

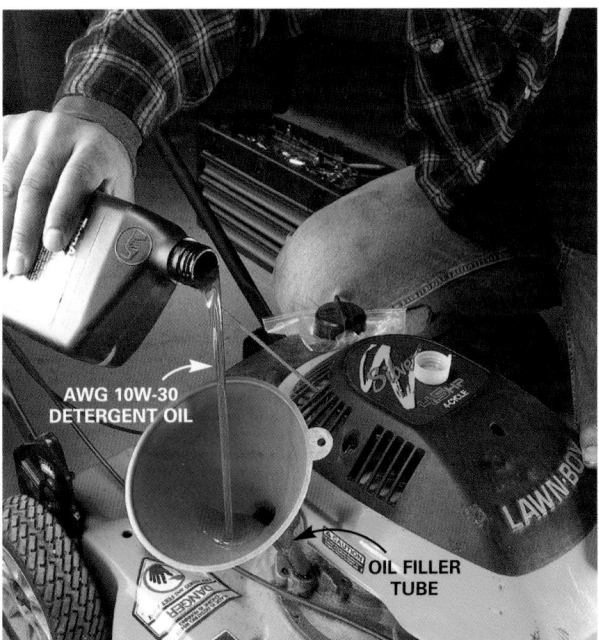

4 REFILL the engine with clean oil. Most engines require about 20 ozs. (5/8 quart). Insert the dipstick and check the oil level. Add oil if needed but don't overfill.

Alternate draining method

5 UNSCREW the plug located on the bottom of the engine and allow the oil to drain into a pan. Lower the mower down on its wheels to make sure all the oil drains. Replace the plug, set the mower on a level surface, and fill the engine with clean oil through the filler hole near the base of the engine.

spills immediately and store gas in approved sealed containers. To dispose of the old gas, call your local hazardous waste disposal site for instructions.

Most mowers have a mesh screen over the outlet at the bottom of the tank. If you can see the screen through the filler hole, use an old turkey baster to suck up dirt and debris that may be covering it.

Change your oil regularly

Changing the oil in your lawn mower takes about 15 minutes and costs less than $2. That's time and money well spent considering that changing oil at the recommended intervals will greatly extend the life of the engine. Most engine manufacturers recommend an oil change at least every 25 hours of operation or every three months.

AUTO & GARAGE

Older mowers have a fill plug close to the mower deck. Fill this type until oil reaches the threads of the refill hole. Two-cycle engines that use a gas/oil mix for fuel don't have an oil reservoir on the engine and don't require oil changes.

Before you drain the old oil, run the mower a few minutes to warm the oil and stir up sediment. Then disconnect the spark plug, drain the old oil and add new (**Photos 1 – 4**). Use SAE 30 W oil (check your owner's manual). There are two ways to drain old oil: through the filler neck (**Photo 3**) or out the drain plug in the bottom of the engine (**Photo 5**). It's quicker and easier to drain the oil through the filler neck if your mower has one. If you have an older mower without a filler neck, locate the drain plug on the bottom of the engine and remove it to drain the oil. Pour used oil through a funnel into a plastic milk jug or other container and label it for recycling.

Whenever you tip a lawn mower up on two wheels (**Photo 3**) to work on the underside, *only lift the side with the air cleaner.* This prevents oil from running into the carburetor and soaking the air filter. Also, if your lawn mower has a fuel valve, turn it off.

Remember to check the oil level occasionally between oil changes, setting the mower on a level surface. Top it off as needed. Newer mowers have dipsticks with markings that indicate when to add oil. Don't overfill. Check your manual for instructions to see whether the dipstick should be fully screwed in or just set in when you're checking the level. If you accidentally add too much oil, follow the procedure shown in **Photos 3 and 5** to drain some out.

Add pep with a new spark plug

Often a new spark plug will make a big improvement in the way your engine starts and runs. Spark plugs are so cheap (less than $3) and easy to install that it's good insurance just to replace your plug every spring.

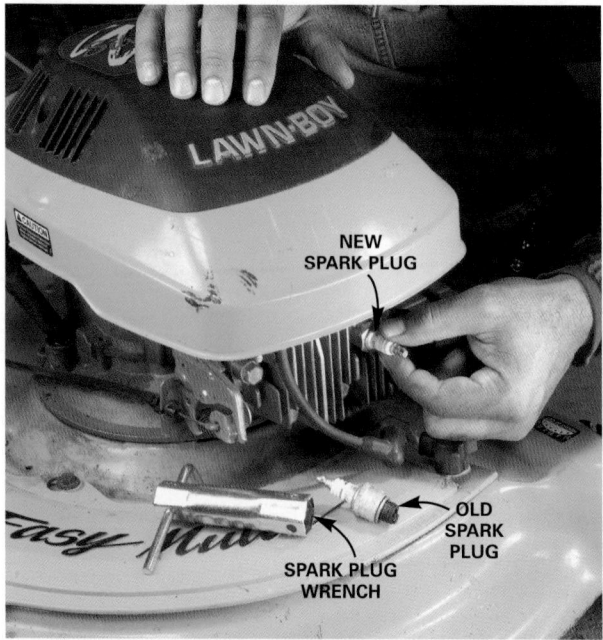

Check your owner's manual for the correct spark plug, or take the old plug with you to the store to match it up.

New spark plugs are factory set with a .030-in. gap between the electrodes at the tip of the plug. Inspect the plug when you buy it to make sure there's a gap about the thickness of a matchbook cover. If there's no gap, the plug may have been dropped and damaged. Choose another one.

If you don't own a socket wrench set with a 3/4-in. or 13/16-in. deep socket for changing the spark plug, pick up an inexpensive ($3 to $4) spark plug wrench (**photo above**).

6 REMOVE the spark plug wire by pulling it straight out. If it's stuck, try twisting it slightly as you pull. Wipe off dirt from the area. Use a 3/4-in. or 13/16-in. deep socket or spark plug wrench to unscrew the old spark plug. Turn the wrench counterclockwise.

7 INSTALL the new spark plug by turning it clockwise two or three complete revolutions by hand before switching over to the spark plug wrench to tighten it. Don't overtighten the spark plug. Manufacturers recommend tightening the plug about a half turn after it seats to compress the new washer. Complete the job by pressing the plug wire onto the plug.

Don't suffocate your mower—change the air filter

Air filters are cheap and easy to replace. Dirty air filters choke the engine, causing it to run poorly and lose power. If your lawn is dry and dusty, check the filter after every few mowings. Otherwise, check it a couple of times during the season. Replace it when it starts to get plugged with dirt and debris. One common test is to shine a flashlight through the filter. If you can't see the light through the filter, replace it with a new one.

Most newer mowers have pleated paper filters that are either flat or cylindrical (**Photo 9**), while many older mowers have foam filters (**Photo 10**). Both types of replacement filters are readily available for $3 to $6 at lawn mower retailers, hardware stores and home centers. Take your old filter along and have your mower manufacturer's name and model number handy.

In a pinch, you can wash foam filters in a solution of laundry detergent and water and allow them to air dry. But since replacements only cost about $3, it's best to just buy a new one. In either case, saturate the foam filter in motor oil and squeeze out the excess before installing it (**Photo 11**).

Keep your blade sharp for the best cut

A sharp blade will make your lawn mower cut like new. The cleanly cut grass will look better, and your mower won't bog down every time you hit a thick spot. If your

Pleated paper air filters

8 LOCATE the air filter near the carburetor. Unscrew, unsnap or twist off the cover to remove the old filter.

9 REMOVE the old air filter and replace it if it's dirty. Wipe grass and dirt from the filter cover and the mounting area with a clean cloth before installing the new filter. Be careful not to let dirt fall into the carburetor.

Foam air filters

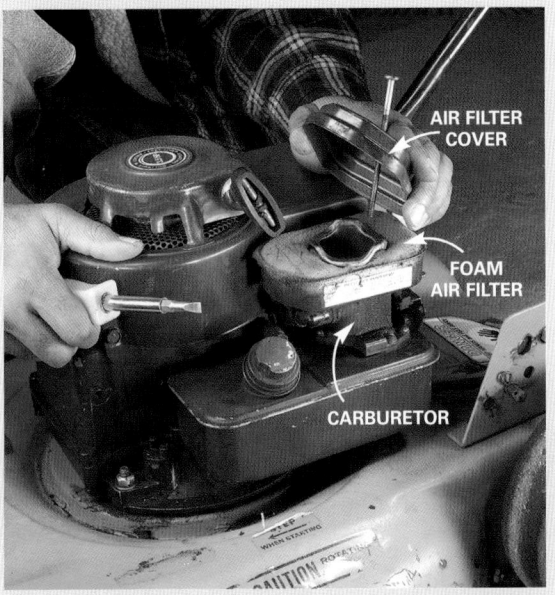

10 UNSCREW or unhook the cover and pull out the old filter. Wipe the filter cover parts with a clean rag to remove dirt and grime.

11 POUR about 1/4 cup of clean motor oil over the new foam filter. Wrap the filter in a clean cloth and squeeze it firmly to distribute the oil evenly and remove any excess. Install the filter, making sure the foam lip covers the top of the filter holder. Replace the cover and tighten the screw.

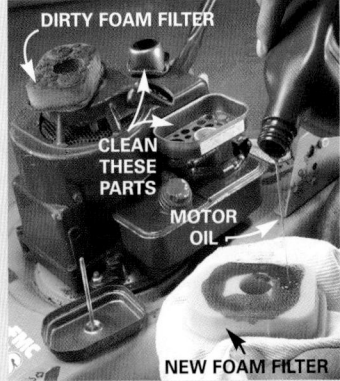

lawn is rough and you mow over rocks and dirt spots, your blade may need to be sharpened several times during the season. Otherwise, once or twice should be plenty. Keep on top of the sharpening task by tuning up the blade with a mill bastard file whenever it starts to dull (**Photo 14**). Once the edge of your blade becomes rounded or chipped, it's a lot faster to use a grinder to restore the edge (**Photo 13**). Most hardware stores and lawn mower mechanics will sharpen your blade for $3 to $5, but you have to remove it for them. Use a permanent marker to mark the bottom of the blade and other parts like washers and mulching accessories. Then number them so they'll be easy to reinstall in the right sequence and orientation.

Inspect the blade for cracks or worn-thin areas every time you sharpen it, paying special attention to the area at the base of the upswept section (**photo at right**). Replace the blade with a new one if the metal is worn thin or cracked ($10 to $15). You'll find the best selection of new blades at a lawn mower service center or your lawn mower retailer.

It's surprising how quickly you can put a new edge on a blade with a sharp file. Buy a 10-in. mill bastard file ($6) and keep it sharp by protecting it from moisture and contact with other tools when you're not using it.

Grinding is much quicker than filing, but you have to

follow a few safety precautions and avoid overheating and ruining the blade. Wear goggles or a full-face shield when grinding. Never wear loose clothes or jewelry that could get caught in the wheel. Keep your hands and face out of the path of the sparks, and make sure there are no flammable liquids or spilled gasoline nearby.

DON'T SHARPEN BLADES LIKE THIS — REPLACE THEM

WORN THROUGH

It's easy to overheat blades on a grinder by applying too much pressure or leaving the blade in one spot too long. Overheated metal loses its temper and won't stay sharp. You'll know if you've overheated the metal by the change in color from silver to dull, blackish blue. Proper grinding technique (**Photo 13**) and dipping the blade frequently in water will help keep it cool.

CAUTION: Always disconnect the spark plug when you check the blade or remove it for sharpening.

WOOD BLOCK

CLAMP

SOCKET WRENCH

TURN COUNTERCLOCKWISE

DULL BLADE

12 DISCONNECT the spark plug wire, turn off the fuel valve and seal the gas tank (Photo 2). Then clamp a block of wood to the lawn mower deck with the sharp edge of the blade against the block. Remove the blade by turning the large nut counterclockwise with a socket wrench.

STORING YOUR LAWN MOWER FOR THE WINTER

Gasoline left in your mower during storage can deteriorate and leave gum deposits that clog the fuel system. There are two storage methods: completely draining the system or leaving it filled with fresh, stabilized gasoline.

Most manufacturers of newer mowers recommend draining the gas completely. Do this by opening the drain valve or drain bolt on the carburetor bowl and draining the gas into a container. If your carburetor doesn't have a drain valve, check with the manufacturer or lawn mower repair center for instructions.

Older lawn mowers with a foam filter and carburetor that's screwed to the top of the gas tank should be filled with stabilized fuel for the winter. Purchase a container of fuel stabilizer, available at hardware stores, home centers, gas stations or lawn mower service centers, and mix as recommended with fresh gas. Fill the empty lawn mower tank with the stabilized gas and run the mower for about 10 minutes. Then top off the fuel tank with stabilized gas and shut the fuel valve. Check your owner's manual for storage instructions.

WATER TO COOL BLADE

BENCH GRINDER

13 SHARPEN blades with nicks or rounded cutting edges on a grinder. Hold the blade firmly and tilt it so the grinding wheel contacts it at the original angle (about a 30-degree bevel). Move the blade steadily across the grinding wheel while applying slight pressure. Dip it in water after each pass to cool it.

10" MILL BASTARD FILE

FILE CARD (BRUSH)

14 FILE previously ground or slightly dulled blades with a 10-in. mill bastard file to hone the edge. Align the file with the angle of the blade and push down across the blade. You should feel the teeth cutting the metal. Maintain the same angle throughout the stroke. Files cut only on the push stroke. Use a file card to clean built-up metal from the file's teeth.

Some maintenance is best left to the pros

The basic maintenance tasks we show above will go a long way toward keeping your mower in good running condition. But there are two more items that would normally be included in a professional tune-up. The first is disassembly and cleaning of the carburetor and linkage. This may be necessary if you've left untreated gas in the tank over the winter and the lawn mower won't start or runs poorly. This repair requires some mechanical experience.

Cleaning grass and debris from the engine's cooling fins (the cooling fins are the metal ridges that cover the engine) is another maintenance task that should be performed periodically. On mowers with exposed cooling fins, this is an easy do-it-yourself job. Use a stiff-bristle brush to clean gunk from between the fins. On many newer mowers, however, the plastic or metal covering on top of the engine has to be removed first, which may also require disconnecting the fuel tank. Use a flashlight to inspect the cooling fins under these covers. If they look clogged, you'll have to decide if you're up to the challenge or would feel more comfortable letting a pro handle the job. Most lawn mower mechanics charge $80 to $120 for a basic lawn mower tune-up that includes all the items in this story, plus cleaning and adjusting the carburetor.

BALANCING CONE

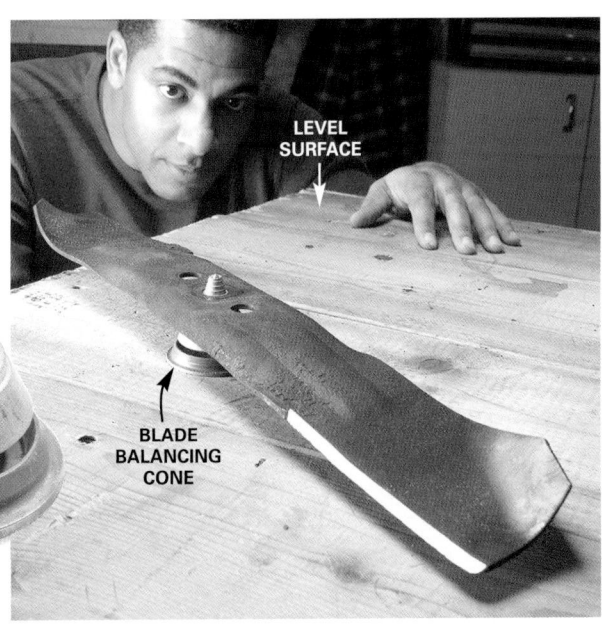

LEVEL SURFACE

BLADE BALANCING CONE

15 BALANCE the blade on a balancing cone ($4 at hardware stores) before reinstalling it. Working on a level surface, set the blade on the cone and eyeball each end. Mark the heavy end. Grind some metal from the blunt part of the heavy end. Recheck the balance and repeat until the blade balances. Reinstall the blade, washer or other parts in the reverse order you removed them.

FOLDAWAY
WORKSHOP

This space saver will keep your work area clutter free and your tools within reach

by **David Radtke**

Before I built this nifty foldaway workshop, I had tools and fasteners spread out on every horizontal surface I could find. It got so bad that I'd spend more time looking for fasteners and tools than using them. This workshop is designed to fix that problem and more. It has loads of storage for all your gear and yet keeps it easily accessible. Best of all, when you're finished for the day, you can put everything away, shut the doors and lock it up. You'll also appreciate its modest profile. With the doors shut, it protrudes a mere 14-1/2 in. from the wall, so no sweat, you'll still be able to pull your car into the garage—and even get out.

This workshop is also designed to be easy to build with simple woodworking tools. In fact, all you'll need besides your measuring and marking tools is a circular saw, a jigsaw and a drill. And it doesn't have any tricky wood joints to slow down the building process—just screws and nails. If you have basic carpentry skills, you'll find you can easily work your way through the how-to steps in a single weekend. You'll also like the price; the whole thing will only cost you about $350.

You'll be able to buy everything at a home center except the folding L-brackets. These heavy-duty brackets will support up to 750 lbs. and we found they live up to the claim. The brackets have four positions: straight up for tabletop work and flat down for storage, as well as two in-between locking positions that transform the worktop into a handy drawing board. Check the Buyer's Guide on p. 270 for a mail-order source.

Besides the fold-down worktop, you'll appreciate the adjustable shelves in each door recess that'll hold boxes of nails and screws, paint, glue bottles, spare parts—you name it. And the sturdy piano hinges are strong enough to hold nearly anything you can pack into the shelves. The tried-and-true Peg-Board is great for visually organizing your hand tools, and we've included space for an overhead fluorescent light and an outlet strip for power tools. There's plenty of room on the bottom shelf for bigger tools like your circular saw, belt sander and router. The foldaway workshop is also great for hobby, craft and even gardening supplies and tools. So whether you're building one or several, get your materials and follow our step-by-step photos and clear shop drawing.

Choose straight lumber

Go to a home center and choose your lumber carefully. The main frame of the project is built with sturdy, dry, construction-grade 2x10s and 2x4s. Buy them as straight as you can find. If they have a twist or bow, they'll throw off the frame and the doors will be difficult to fit. The plywood should be 3/4 in. and flat. You can get by with construction grade, but we used birch plywood because it's nice looking and perfectly flat. The door sides and shelves should be hardwood for

strength. Our home center had a nice selection of maple that matched the birch plywood. You can substitute poplar, oak or birch. Here again, make sure the lumber is straight. Boards that aren't perfectly straight can be cut up for the shorter shelves.

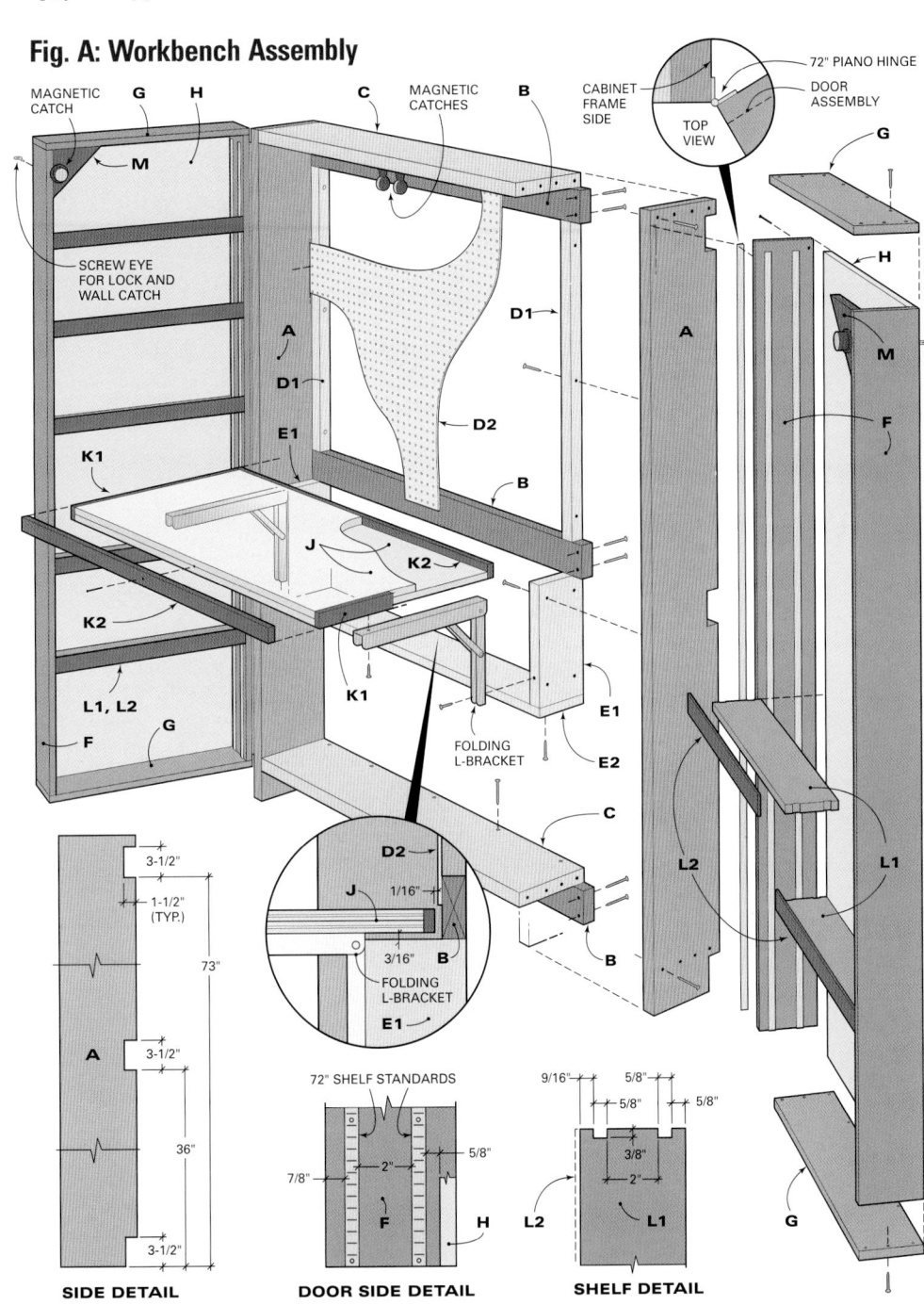

Fig. A: Workbench Assembly

SIDE DETAIL

DOOR SIDE DETAIL

SHELF DETAIL

Note: Assemble the project on an even, flat surface. You can end up with some unintentional twists in the main frame and the doors if you build them on an uneven surface. Choose a flat area in your garage or driveway for the assembly work.

Notches in the frame keep it square

Ripping your 2x10s to 9 in. wide gives you a nice, square edge on the face of the frame to mount your piano hinges to later. Once they're ripped, notch the backsides of the frame sides as shown in **Photo 1** to accept the horizontal stretchers. Set your saw to a 1-1/2 in. depth of cut and make multiple passes about 1/4 in. apart the width of the 2x4. Break out the notches with a chisel and file the bottom of the notches smooth.

Take care to get the frame square as you screw the stretchers (B) into the notches and screw the top and bottom panels (C) into place. The best way to ensure the frame is square is to measure the diagonals and adjust the frame until they're equal.

Find the right spot in your garage

There may be a few snags to look out for in your garage. If you're installing the foldaway workshop near the garage door, make sure it will clear the track. The height of the project is 78 in. Low-clearance overhead doors may have a track in the way. Also keep in mind that it opens to a full 8 ft. You'll find you still have 3-1/2 in. behind the doors when they're open so you can hang rakes and shovels behind it.

Your garage may have a row of concrete block near the floor that sticks out past the wall surface. If so, plan ahead

and cut the side pieces longer past the bottom stretcher to accommodate the block and then notch them to fit around it. Also feel free to make the project shorter or a bit taller to suit your needs and adjust the worktop to a height that suits you. Ours sits at a comfortable 36 in. off the floor.

The Peg-Board stiffens the frame

Once the basic frame is assembled, cut your Peg-Board and center it onto the top and middle stretchers. You'll know if your frame is out of square because the panel should fall into place (**Photo 3**). Fasten the Peg-Board every 6 in. to the stretchers and 2x2s with 1-1/4 in. wood screws.

L-brackets make a rock-solid top

Position the brackets carefully as you install them on the bracket supports to make sure they'll open and close once the project is complete. Keep them flush with the inside edge of the supports and make sure they extend 3/16 in. past the top (**Photo 4**). This little extension gives a bit of room for the folding L-brackets to release properly when it's time to fold them down.

Take the same care later (see **Photo 9**) when you attach the top to the folding L-brackets. Make sure the top is 1/16 in. from the Peg-Board and that the tops of the L-brackets are parallel to the sides of the worktop.

SHOPPING LIST

DESCRIPTION	QTY.
2x10 x 8' spruce, pine or fir	3
2x4 x 14' spruce, pine or fir	1
2x2 x 8' spruce, pine or fir	1
1x6 x 12' hardwood (door sides and shelves)	4
1x8 x 4' pine shelf (under-bracket blocks)	1
37" x 44-15/16" Peg-Board (1/4" thick)	1
3/4" x 4' x 8' birch plywood	2
1x2 x 12' hardwood worktop edging	1
6' piano hinges	2
6' shelf standards and brackets	8
1/4" x 1-3/4" x 10' pine or hardwood lattice (shelf edging)	2
6d nails	1 lb.
3" wood screws	2 lbs.
2-1/2" wood screws	1 lb.
1-5/8" wood screws	1 lb.
1-1/4" wood screws	1 lb.
1/4" x 4" lag screws and washers	6
Folding L-brackets (see Buyer's Guide)	1 pr.
Magnetic catches (see Buyer's Guide)	2
Wall anchors, bolt snaps, door handles	
Mini-tube fluorescent light	1

CUTTING LIST

KEY	PCS.	SIZE & DESCRIPTION
A	2	1-1/2" x 9" x 78" pine sides
B	3	1-1/2" x 3-1/2" x 48" pine stretchers
C	2	1-1/2" x 9" x 45" pine top and bottom
D1	2	1-1/2" x 1-1/2" x 33-1/2" pine backers for Peg-Board
D2	1	1/4" x 44-15/16" x 37" Peg-Board
E1	2	1-1/2" x 6-1/8" x 12-3/4" pine bracket supports
E2	1	3/4" x 6-1/8" x 45" fixed pine shelf
F	4	3/4" x 5-1/2" x 73" maple door sides
G	4	3/4" x 5-1/2" x 23-7/8" maple door tops and bottoms
H	2	3/4" x 22-3/8" x 73" birch plywood door panels
J	2	3/4" x 22-3/8" x 43-3/8" birch plywood worktop pieces
K1	2	3/4" x 1-1/2" x 22-3/8" maple
K2	2	3/4" x 1-1/2" x 44-7/8" maple
L1	10	3/4" x 4-7/16" x 22-3/8" maple shelves
L2	10	1/4" x 1-3/4" x 22-1/4" maple shelf stops
M	2	3/4" x 5-1/2" maple triangular braces

* Cut to fit

1 RIP 2x10 lumber to 9 in. wide to create a flat edge and ensure that all the frame pieces are uniform. Then mark and cut the 1-1/2 in. deep notches for the rear stretcher pieces (Fig. A).

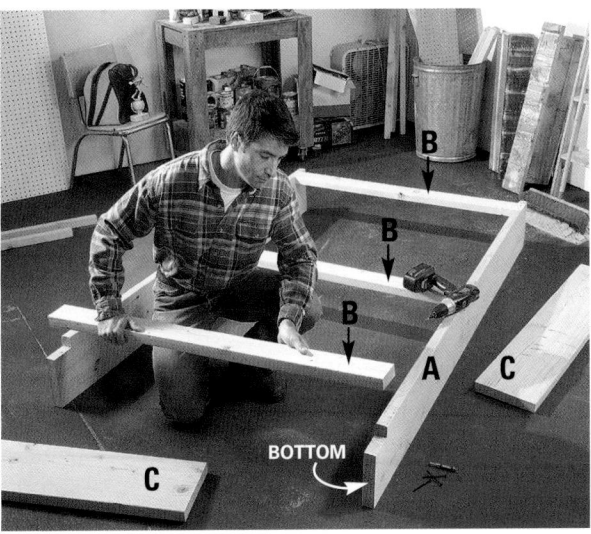

2 SET the rear stretchers (B) into the notches of the sides (A) and screw them into place. Next, screw the top and bottom pieces (C) to the sides and stretchers.

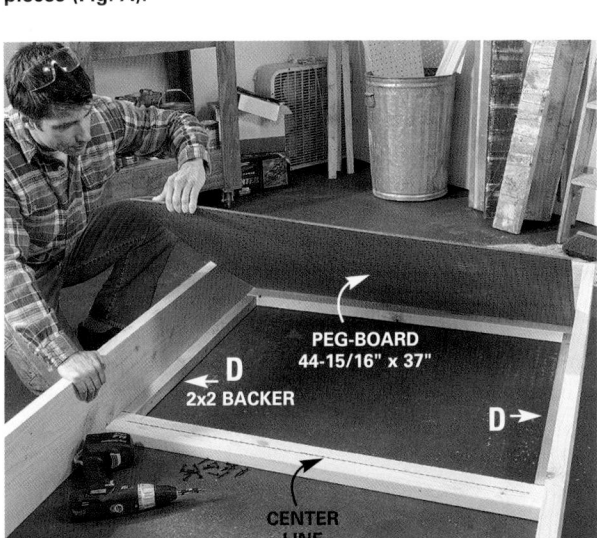

3 FLIP the assembly over onto its back. Measure and cut a pair of 2x2 backers to fit between the center and upper stretchers. Next, screw the Peg-Board to stretchers and the 2x2s.

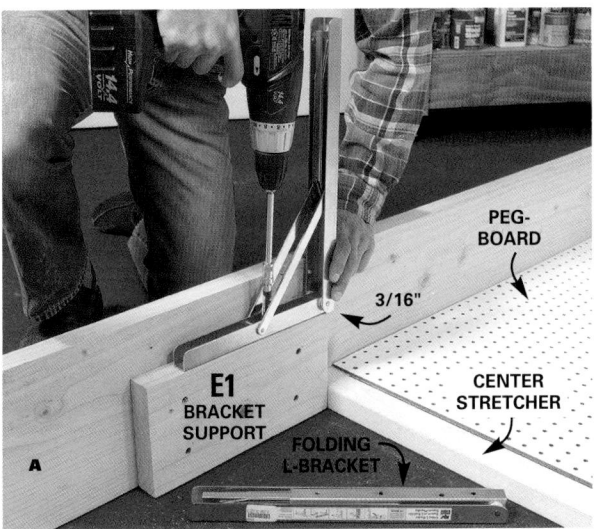

4 SCREW the folding L-bracket supports (E1) to the sides. Position the brackets 3/16 in. past the top of the support and flush with the support's inside edge. Screw the brackets into the support with No. 8 x 1-1/4 in. pan head screws.

Install the shelf standards precisely

The shelf standards support the shelves, and the notches in the shelves hold them in place so they don't fly out when you open the door. Set your combination square to the dimensions shown in **Fig. A** and slide it up along the edge of the door frame sides (F) as you nail the standards into place. Also make sure you flush the standard bottoms to the bottom of the door sides so all the shelves will be level.

Rip your shelves to width and again be precise with the layout of the notches in the ends of the shelf. These are a bugger to cut, but making multiple passes from each end

with a jigsaw works well. You can clean up the cuts with a file.

Cutting your plywood door panels

We used a table saw to first rip the panels for a nice, straight edge. If you don't have a table saw, use a circular saw and a long straightedge guide. Once the panels are cut for width, mark the length using a framing square as a guide. Cut each panel carefully with your circular saw equipped with a sharp 40-tooth blade.

Attach the door sides, making sure they're flush with the plywood door panel face. If a little glue oozes out, wipe

5 CUT the door frame sides (F) and top and bottom pieces (G) to length from 1x6 boards. Position the 6-ft. shelf standards flush with the bottom edge of each door side (F) and nail them every 6 in.

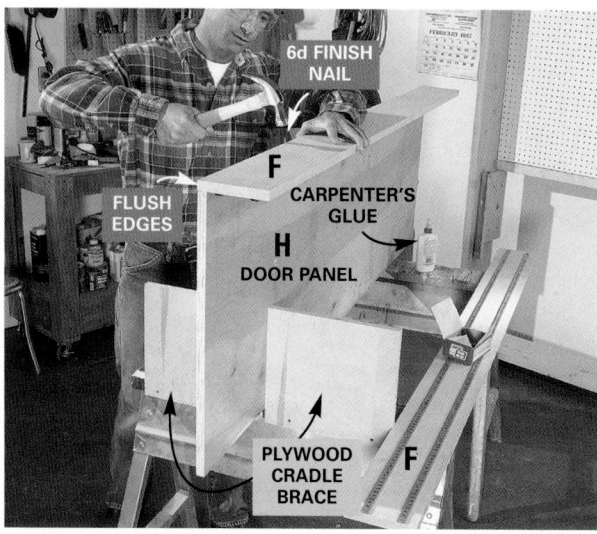

6 CUT the door panels (H) and place them into a cradle brace as shown. Spread glue on the edge of the plywood and predrill and nail the sides (F) to the plywood door panels every 6 in. Once the sides are fastened, predrill and glue and screw the door tops and bottoms (G) to the door panels.

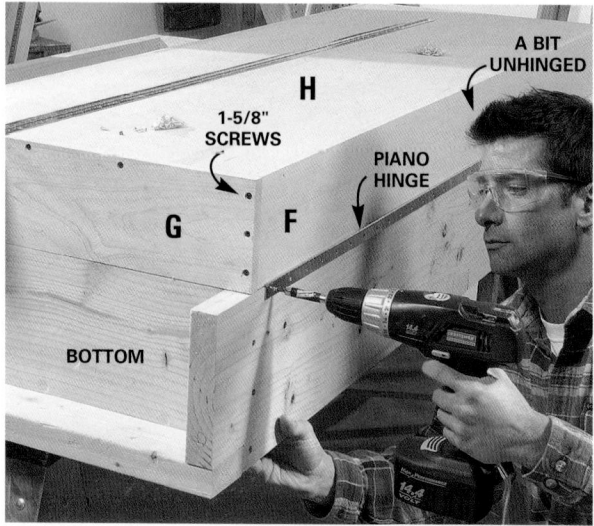

7 SET the door assemblies onto the frame assembly as shown. Fold the top flap of your piano hinge so it's trapped between the door edge and the side of the frame to position it evenly. Screw it to the frame, then open the hinge and screw it to the door.

8 CUT and glue two pieces of 3/4-in. plywood (J) to make the work surface. To complete the worktop, cut 1x2 boards to length and nail them to the sides with 6d finish nails.

it off with a wet rag right away to keep it from showing through your finish later.

Screw the top and bottom of the door frame (parts G) to the panel (H) instead of nailing them. The 1-5/8 in. screws, along with the glue, bond the door sides and plywood panel together for a rock-solid door. To complete the door frame, cut a pair of triangular pieces of maple (M) 5-1/2 in. on a side and glue and nail them to the top inside corners of the doors to hold the closing plates of the magnetic door catches.

Piano hinges give total door support

Piano hinges can be a pain to install, but you can simplify the process by tucking the top flap between the door and the frame (**Photo 7**) to hold it in place while you screw the lower exposed flap to the frame side. To predrill perfectly centered holes, use a No. 3 Vix bit in your drill. This nifty bit has a tapered front edge that fits into the hole on the hinge and exactly centers itself. As you push on the bit, the spring-loaded bit pilots itself dead center. Drive the screws as you go to keep the hinge from shifting.

Once the bottom flap of the hinge is secured, lift the

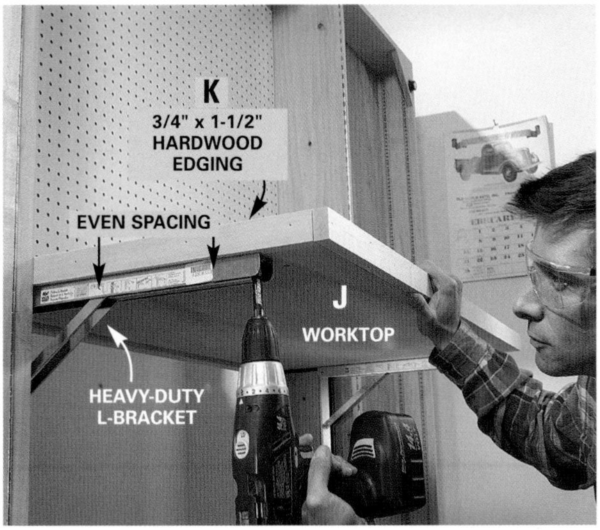
K
3/4" x 1-1/2" HARDWOOD EDGING
EVEN SPACING
J
WORKTOP
HEAVY-DUTY L-BRACKET

9 **CENTER the worktop (J) between the sides and leave a 1/16-in. gap from the face of the Peg-Board. Make sure the folding L-brackets are evenly spaced front-to-back along the edge of the worktop. Screw the L-bracket to the underside of the worktop with No. 8 x 1-1/4 in. pan head screws.**

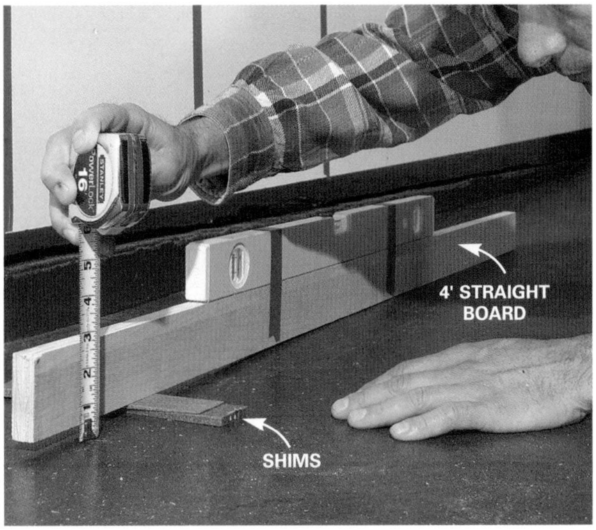
4' STRAIGHT BOARD
SHIMS

10 **CHECK your floor with a level placed on a 4-ft. board to see how much you may need to shim the cabinet sides. Our garage floor had a 1/2-in. slope in 4 ft. from front to back.**

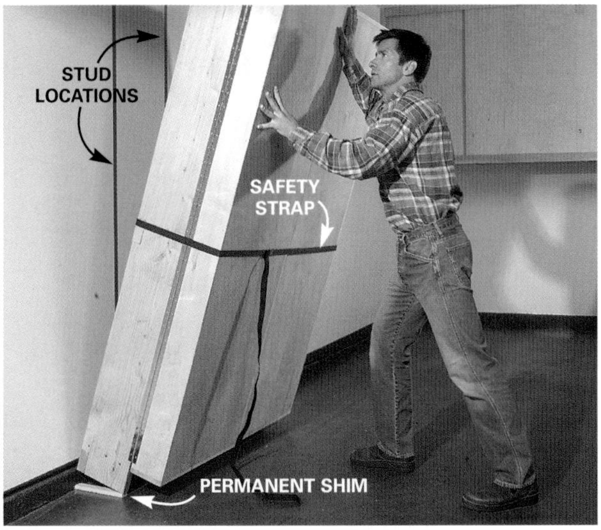
STUD LOCATIONS
SAFETY STRAP
PERMANENT SHIM

11 **MARK the stud locations. Cut and set the shim. Tip the cabinet up slowly with the doors closed. Slide it into position.**

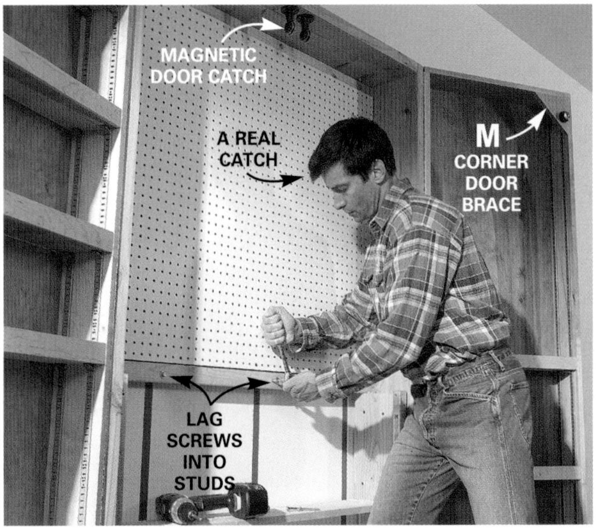
MAGNETIC DOOR CATCH
A REAL CATCH
M
CORNER DOOR BRACE
LAG SCREWS INTO STUDS

12 **DRILL 3/16-in. pilot holes through the stretchers into the studs. Insert 1/4-in. x 4-in. lag screws and washers and use a wrench to tighten the cabinet to the wall. Add the magnetic catches and the shelves.**

door, pivot the top flat out, position the door side even with the frame and secure the hinge to the door frame in exactly the same way.

Use a double layer of plywood for a solid worktop

Cut your worktop pieces (J) from 3/4-in. plywood and glue them (Photo 8) together with carpenter's glue spread liberally between. Screw the pieces together on the underside with 1-1/4 in. wood screws. Once the glue sets, cut 1x2 maple and nail it around the edges as shown in Fig. A.

Position the top carefully onto the folding L-brackets. Hold the top securely, align the brackets parallel to the edge and screw it into place. You'll need a bit extension for your power screwdriver to get inside the bracket mechanism. If you don't have one, you can mark it, predrill it and then use a long-blade screwdriver to drive the screws. At this point, test the mechanism to make sure it folds down. If the bracket binds, loosen the screws and shift the bracket until it works.

Lag-screw the frame to the studs

Every installation situation has its own set of problems, and ours was no exception. The floor was out of level, so we had to shim one side to get the project to sit level on the floor. The concrete foundation at the bottom of the wall stuck out 1/2 in., so we added 1/2-in. strips to the backside of the frame to move it out from the wall a bit. Use your ingenuity to get past any problems you might find. We also secured some bolt snaps to the wall (see **photo**, below) with wall anchors and screw eyes to keep the doors open when in use. The screw eyes on the front of the door also double as a place to slip in a padlock to keep out unwanted visitors.

Caution: The doors of this project can fly open when you're moving it into position. Use a strap hinge and brace the bottom of the doors until you get it secured to the wall.

Flip the top down, close the doors and secure the padlock until you're ready for your next project.

Finishing touches

The magnetic catches for the doors are actually interior door catches (see Buyer's Guide, below). Screw the ball section to the top of the frame and the steel plate onto the door. We found a mini-tube fluorescent light fixture at a home center and screwed it to the underside of the top. An outlet strip mounted to the side of the frame makes plugging in power tools a snap. We drilled a 1-1/2 in. hole in the frame side to slip the plug end through to the nearest outlet.

Although not completely necessary, two coats of furniture oil or polyurethane will help preserve the project, especially if your garage gets seasonally damp. Just remove the hardware and apply your finish. Be sure to wait a couple of days for the project to dry before using it.

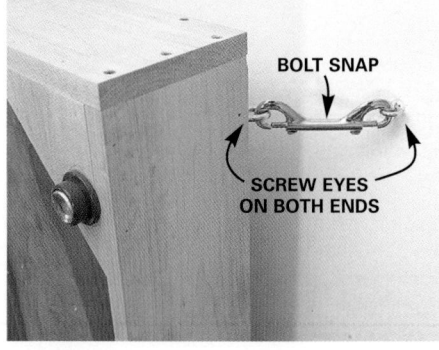

Keep the doors open with a wall anchor and double-ended bolt snap.

Buyer's Guide
- Folding L-brackets ($15.99 each) and Vix bits: Woodworker's Hardware, (800) 383-0130 or www.wwhardware.com
- Magnetic door catches (No. 47175, $8 each) shown on p. 269: (800) 642-2112. www.improvementscatalog.com

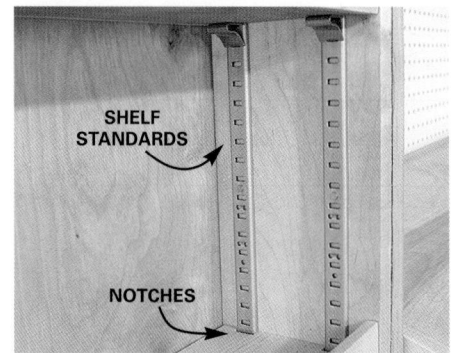

The notches in the shelves keep them secure as you open and close your doors.

You Can Fix It™

REVIVE A DEAD CAR DOOR OPENER

Remote car door openers are sweet when they work properly, but having to push the button a dozen times to open the door is irritating. If your door opener only works at close range, sporadically or not at all, a dying or dead battery may be the cause.

Replacement batteries cost a couple of bucks and are available at home centers, hardware stores and discount stores like Wal-Mart and Target. The identification number will be stamped on the battery back (**photo below**). Buy a new battery with a matching identification number.

The door opener will either snap or screw together. **Photos 1 and 2** show two opener styles. Before removing the battery, note its position— printed side up or down —and then install the new battery the same way (**Photo 2**).

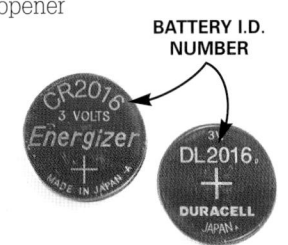

BATTERY I.D. NUMBER

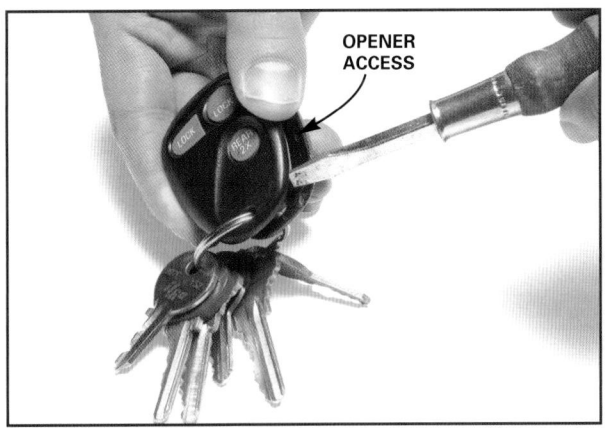

OPENER ACCESS

1 POKE a flat-blade screwdriver into the recess on the edge of the opener. Twist the screwdriver to pop the opener apart (on some you have to remove a small screw).

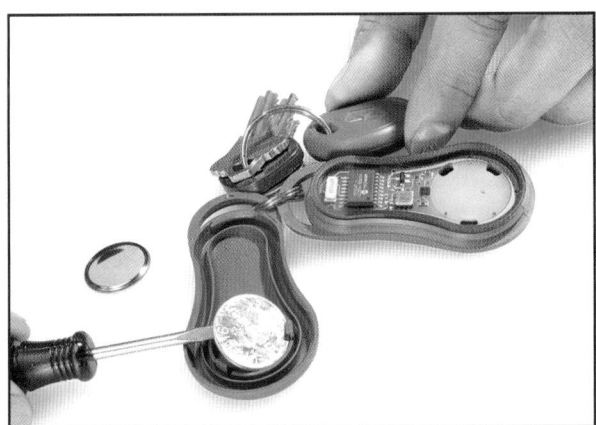

2 FLIP out the old battery with a small screwdriver or pocketknife (there may be two batteries stacked together). Install the new matching battery just like the old one and snap the opener back together.

New Product

GARAGE DOOR MONITOR

RECEIVER

SENSOR

You know the scenario. You're padding around in your slippers getting ready to hit the sack and wonder . . . did I close the doggone garage door? Save yourself those cold, reluctant reconnaissance trips by installing the Wireless Garage Sentry. It's simple. Just attach the battery-powered sensor to the backside of the garage door, place the wireless receiver within 300 ft. of the sensor, plug it in and you're set! Keep it next to your bed, in the kitchen or anywhere else that's convenient. It's a bit pricey at $69.95 plus shipping, but it may be worth the cost for garage-door peace of mind. Order from Smarthome.

Smarthome, (800) 367-9836. www.smarthome.com

Handy Hints®
Hall of Fame

Handy Hints has been the most popular department in The Family Handyman magazine since it was launched in 1951. It's the way our ingenious readers show their ingenious solutions to everyday problems. Here are the best of the best.

BEST HANDY HINT FOR **PAINTING:**

DOOR PAINTING HELPER

Paint both sides of a door with ease with this nifty trick. Purchase three 3/8-in. x 4-in. lag bolts at a hardware store. Screw one into the center of the top edge and the other two into the bottom edge 6 in. in from each end. Paint one side of the door, then lift the door by the two bolts and flip it over using the single bolt as a pivot. Now paint the edges and other side of the door. When the door is dry, remove the bolts, fill the holes with putty and touch up with paint.

3/8" x 4" LAG BOLT

BEST HANDY HINT FOR **WORKING FASTER:**

LIPSTICK TRANSFER FOR DRYWALL

Here's one from our library of classic hints: When you're hanging drywall, it's a hassle measuring and transferring the location of the cutout holes for electrical boxes. Make the task easier by coating the rim of the box or mud ring with lipstick. Then gently position and press the drywall in place. You'll have perfectly positioned and sized markings for the cutout.

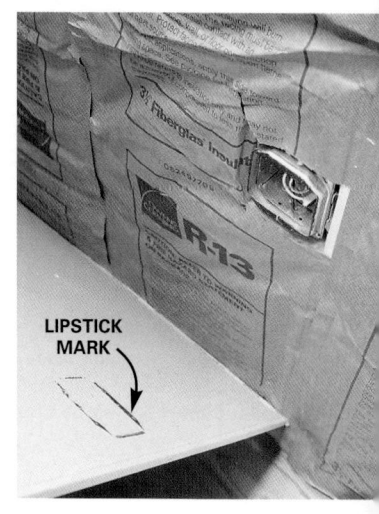

LIPSTICK MARK

BEST HANDY HINT FOR **TICKING OFF YOUR SPOUSE:**

PONYTAIL HOLDER FOR ELECTRICAL CORDS

I've got a confession to make. When my wife's not around, I sneak into her makeup bag and steal her ponytail holders. They're perfect for wrapping power tool cords and lightweight extension cords. Now I have to figure out how to explain the $100 Handy Hints check to my wife if you decide to use this tip!

[If there's no one to steal from in your house, get a dozen from any discount store for about $3.]

*Got your own Handy Hint?
See how $100 can be yours at
www.familyhandyman.com*

BEST HANDY HINT FOR
IMPRESSING YOUR DATE:

CORKSCREW IN A PINCH

It's difficult to remember everything for that important date. You've picked up your suit at the cleaners; coordinated the tablecloth, napkins and candle; and chilled the wine, but then you discover you've forgotten the corkscrew. But your date is resourceful and, as always, has her tools. She drives a coarse-threaded deck screw into the cork, grabs the screwhead with a pliers, carefully pulls out the cork and rescues the evening.

COARSE-THREADED DECK SCREW

HANDY DATE

PLIERS

BEST HANDY HINT FOR
USING DUCT TAPE:

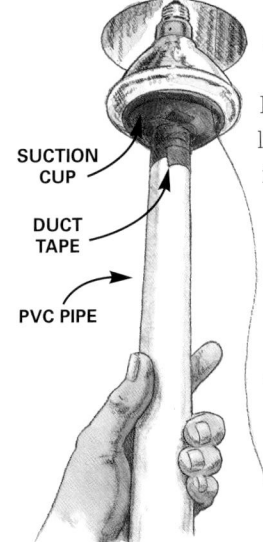

SUCTION CUP

DUCT TAPE

PVC PIPE

BULB CHANGER

I use this handy gizmo to get light bulbs out of high ceiling fixtures. It's a length of PVC pipe with a hardware store suction cup taped to the end. Just wet the rim of the suction cup, stick it to the bulb, and turn. The trick: a small hole near the rim with a string attached, to make it easier to get the darn suction cup back off.

BEST HANDY HINT FOR
ATTRACTING STRANGE STARES FROM YOUR NEIGHBORS:

LAWN TOOL CARRIER

An old golf bag with a cart makes a perfect holder for garden tools. The large wheels make it easy to haul the tools over long distances and rough terrain.

BEST HANDY HINT FOR SAVING MONEY:

REUSABLE PAINT THINNER

Whenever you clean your paint brushes after using oil-based paint, you can recycle the paint thinner. Clean the brushes and then let the paint solids settle to the bottom of the container. Then slowly pour the clear thinner back into the original container and reuse it. The solvent doesn't lose its cleaning ability.

BEST HANDY HINT FOR
SAVING FRUSTRATION:

STRAW HOLDER

Here's the perfect way to keep a spray-can straw from getting lost: Store it in a ballpoint pen tube taped to the side of the can.

PEN TUBE

BEST HANDY HINT FOR
RECYCLING SHOES:

LADDERS THAT LAND ON THEIR FEET

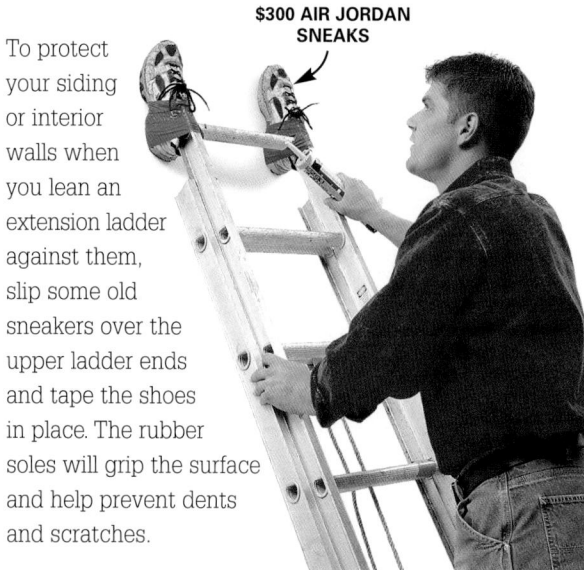

$300 AIR JORDAN SNEAKS

To protect your siding or interior walls when you lean an extension ladder against them, slip some old sneakers over the upper ladder ends and tape the shoes in place. The rubber soles will grip the surface and help prevent dents and scratches.

BEST HANDY HINT FOR
SAVING ENERGY:

FINALLY—A LIGHT THAT TURNS ITSELF OFF

My kids are always switching on the lights in the laundry room, storage room and pantry and never turning them off. Sometimes they burn all night, even for days, before I discover the light streaming under the closed doors. Here's my solution: I bought a wireless motion-sensing light adapter ($20 at home centers) and aimed the sensing unit straight down the wall inside the top of the door. The light automatically turns on when it senses that someone is after a can of SpaghettiOs or wants that special T-shirt out of the wash, and then turns off..

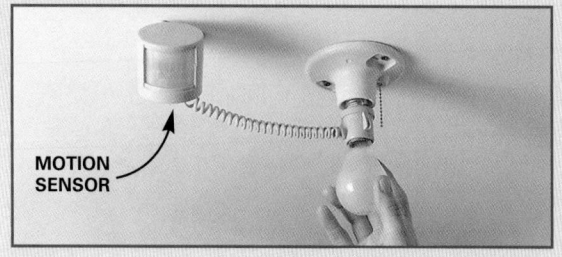

MOTION SENSOR

BEST HANDY HINT FOR
GETTING YOU OUT OF A JAM:

STRING SAW PIPE CUTTER

Amaze your friends and mystify your neighbors by cutting PVC pipe with a string. It's a great trick to know if you have to cut pipe that's buried in a wall or some other tight spot.

When we tried this amazing hint, we used a mason's line to cut through 2-in. PVC pipe in less than a minute.

BEST HANDY HINT FOR
WORKING SAFELY:

LISTEN TO THE MUSIC!

Instead of running upstairs, let the Rolling Stones help you find the right breaker.

Find circuit breakers by plugging a loud radio into the outlet you're working on. You'll know you have the right circuit breaker when the music dies. But don't assume the electricity is off in all the other outlets or lights in the room. Before doing any wiring, plug the radio into other outlets you plan to work on. Some duplex outlets can have different circuits running to adjacent outlets. To be safe, test both the top and bottom with the radio. For lights, turn the light switch on and off to be sure.

I CAN'T GET NO... SAT·IS·FAC·TION

YOU'RE THE MAN, MICK!

BEST **WACKY** HANDY HINT:

BACK MASSAGER

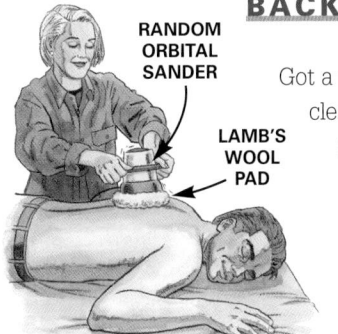

RANDOM ORBITAL SANDER

LAMB'S WOOL PAD

Got a tired back and aching muscles after a long day of banging nails? Put a lamb's wool pad on your random orbital sander and have your spouse give you a massage. You'll feel like a new person.

BEST HANDY HINT FOR **REALLY, REALLY LAZY PEOPLE:**

NEVER-LOSE-IT REMOTE CONTROL

Tired of losing the bedside remote? Attach half of a self-adhesive Velcro strip to the back of the remote and the other half to your headboard. You'll never have that remote slip between the mattress and the wall again.

VELCRO TAPE

BEST HANDY HINT FOR **STORAGE:**

CLOSET ROD BIKE HOLDER

The brackets made for holding a closet rod make a super rack for your bike. Screw the brackets to the wall studs, high or low, wherever you have space. Line them with a soft material like felt or leather to protect the bike's finish. You can even drop a shelf board on top to hold your helmet and water bottles. ⌂

BEST AND **MOST COMMONLY SUBMITTED** HANDY HINT OF ALL TIME:

FIX A LOOSE HINGE

Over time, many doors get heavy use, causing the hinge screws to strip out and the hinges to loosen. Here's a quick fix.

Completely remove the loose hinge from the door and frame. Remove only one hinge at a time so you don't have to take the door down. (If you have several hinges with stripped screws, however, you may want to remove the entire door.) Locate the stripped screw holes and repair with golf tees as shown in **Photos 1 and 2.** Once the hole is plugged, reattach the hinge and screws. Screwing through the golf tee will cause it to expand and tighten the hinge even more, restoring your doors to proper working condition.

GOLF TEE

TIGER WOODS

1 UNSCREW the loose hinge. Squirt wood glue on a golf tee and tap it into the stripped hole until tight. Let the glue dry for an hour.

2 CUT the golf tee flush with the door frame using a sharp utility knife, then screw the hinge back in place.

10 "UNDER-AN-HOUR" STORAGE PROJECTS

for every room in the house

SPICE STORAGE

Small spice containers use shelf space inefficiently and are difficult to find when surrounded by taller bottles and items. Use a small spring-tension curtain rod ($3) as a simple shelf. It's easy to install and strong enough to support the spices.

BETTER PAINT STORAGE

Here's a tip that makes pouring and storing paint a breeze. Save all your liquid laundry detergent jugs. Wash them out and you won't find a better way to store paint. No more rusty, unopenable lids, paint splatters from tapping the lids closed, dried-out paint or runs down the side of the can when filling paint trays. The spout works great for dispensing paint. Just fill the jugs using a funnel and you're good to go. I wonder why the paint manufacturers haven't thought of this!

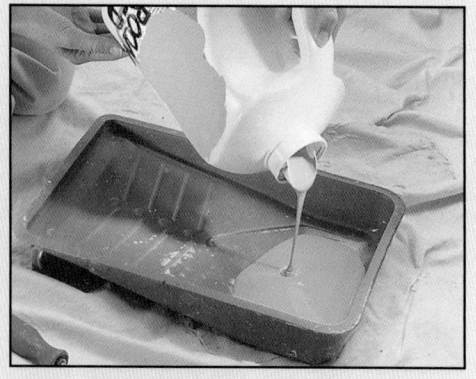

UTILITY SHELVES

This sturdy, free-standing shelf unit is made from any inexpensive 1-by lumber (3/4 in. thick) for the legs, and plywood or particleboard for the shelves. Glue and nail the four L-shaped legs together with 6d finishing nails. Clamp the shelves in place, getting them evenly spaced and level, then secure each shelf with eight 2-in. screws through the legs.

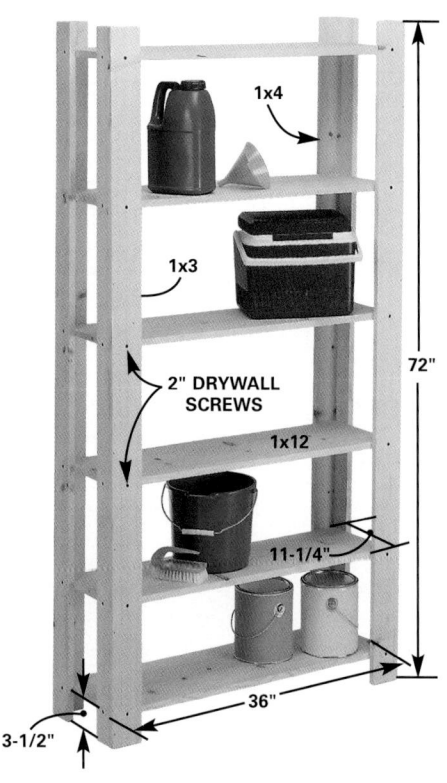

PLASTIC BAG HOLDER

An empty rectangular tissue box makes a convenient holder for small garbage bags, plastic grocery bags and small rags. Simply thumbtack it to the inside of a cabinet door.

EASY-TO-BUILD DISPLAY SHELVING

Assemble this simple shelf from 1x4s and tempered glass. Fasten the side boards to the 4-ft. back sections with carpenter's glue and 6d finish nails. Paint the brackets and screw them to wall studs. Buy round-cornered tempered glass shelves and slide them into place.

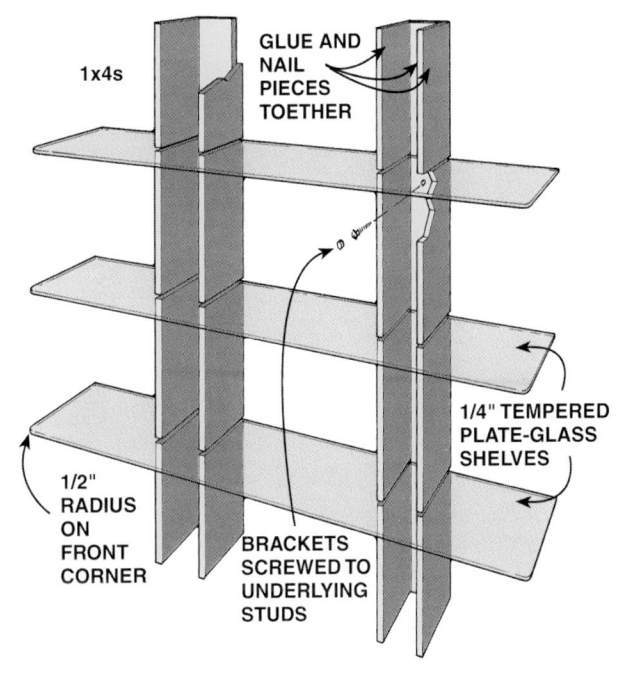

1x4s

GLUE AND NAIL PIECES TOETHER

1/4" TEMPERED PLATE-GLASS SHELVES

1/2" RADIUS ON FRONT CORNER

BRACKETS SCREWED TO UNDERLYING STUDS

PVC FOR TWO TYPES OF STORAGE

Here's how to tansform scrap pieces of PVC pipe into storage sites for dowels and fasteners.

Fastener trough (below)—Cut a 2-ft. length of 4-in. PVC pipe lengthwise with a scroll saw, creating a trough that's a little more than half the pipe's diameter. Glue or screw in 1/2-in. thick wood partitions to create compartments for often-used screw and nail sizes. To make it tip-proof, trace the pipe's curve on a couple of scrap 2x4 blocks, power-sand or saw out the curve, and screw the pipe on this scrap block base.

Dowel quiver (right)—Use a saber saw to cut lengthwise notches in a 30-in. long piece of 3- or 4-in. dia. pipe then glue on a PVC end cap. Drill pilot holes in the pipe opposite the notches and screw the quiver to a shop wall. Your notched-out quiver will hold any size dowel—from standard 36-in. lengths to stubby leftovers—for instant access.

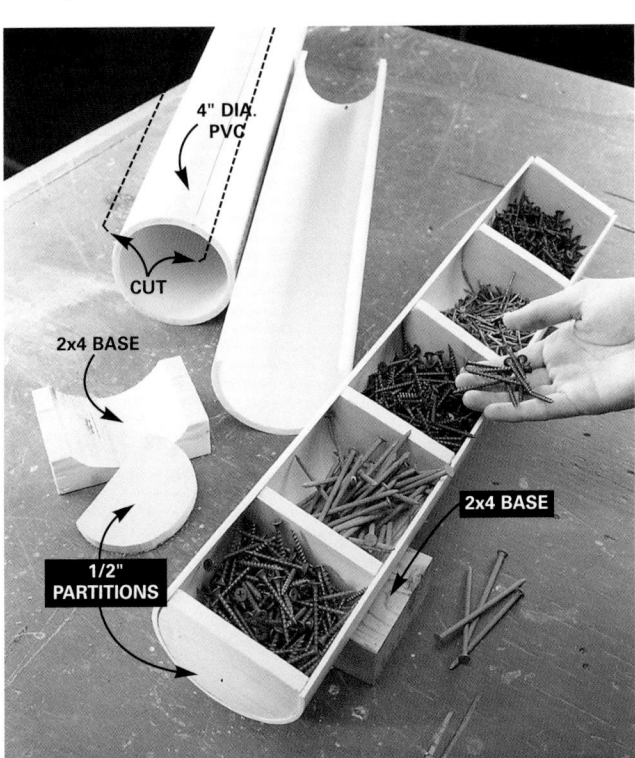

4" DIA. PVC

CUT

2x4 BASE

1/2" PARTITIONS

2x4 BASE

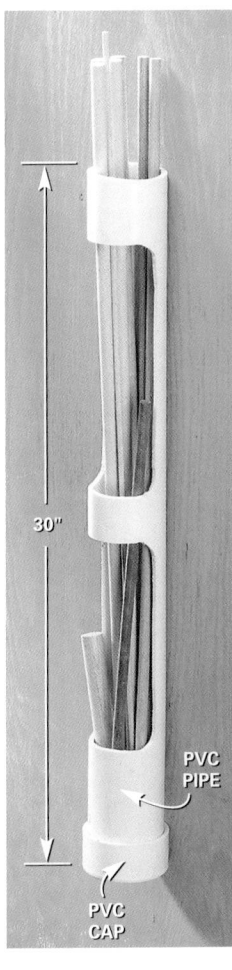

30"

PVC PIPE

PVC CAP

COMPACT SHOVEL RACK

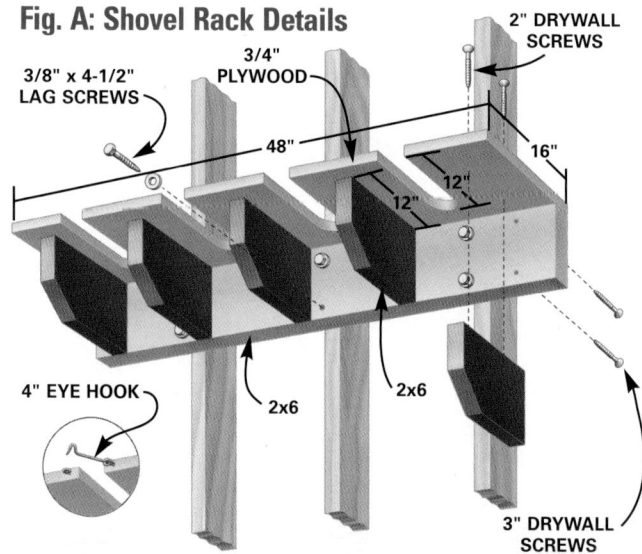

If you have more tools than a handful of 16-penny nails pounded into a 2x4 will accommodate, this shovel rack's for you. It looks simple and it is, yet this is a serious storage rack that will put its store-bought counterparts to shame. It will hold more than 14 items—ranging from shovels and rakes to sledgehammers and pickaxes—with room to spare. It's constructed from a 16-in. x 48-in. chunk of 3/4-in. plywood, supported with 2x6s and lag-screwed to the wall. Take an early morning break from your yard chores and put the rack together in a couple of hours for less than $20.

After cutting your pieces to size as indicated on the materials list, lay them out and cut the slots for the handles. We've made some suggestions about spacing, but feel free to customize the spacing to fit your tools. **Tip:** Make your slot wide enough to fit the "flare" where a handle meets a blade. The flare is usually wider than the handle itself.

Use a circular saw to make the straight cuts, then a jigsaw to finish out the inside curve (Photo 1). We used the bottom of a spray paint can to mark the curve on the inside of the slot.

Next tack a 2x6 ledger board to the plywood with a couple of 2-in. drywall screws, and then attach the supports (**Photo 2**), centering them between the slots. These short pieces of 2x6 reinforce the plywood and keep it from sagging. We knocked the ends off at a 45-degree angle so the sharp corner wouldn't catch someone's noggin.

Position the rack about 6 ft. off the floor and attach it to the wall studs with lag screws (**Photo 3**). Don't skimp on the lag screws. You need their holding power to support the weight of the rack and the tools.

Caution: If you have young kids or toddlers, attach an eye screw and hook to secure each slot so the tools won't accidentally fall out (**Fig. A**).

The rack is now ready for use. Load off-season items at the back and frequently used ones in the front. Unless you own a small farm, you should have some spare room to store new items as the need arises.

Fig. A: Shovel Rack Details

3/8" x 4-1/2" LAG SCREWS

3/4" PLYWOOD

2" DRYWALL SCREWS

48"

16"

12"

12"

4" EYE HOOK

2x6

2x6

3" DRYWALL SCREWS

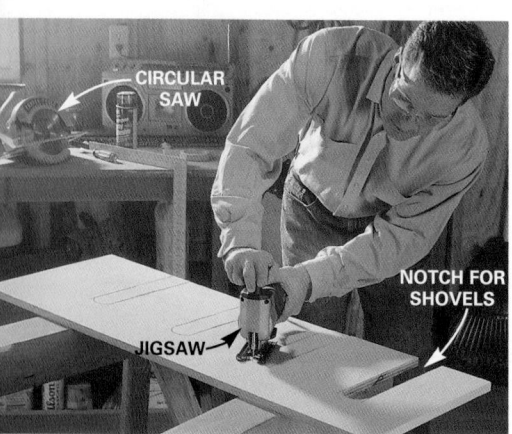

1 LAY OUT tool slots on the plywood top piece and make the straight cuts with a circular saw. Finish the inside curve with a jigsaw.

CIRCULAR SAW

JIGSAW

NOTCH FOR SHOVELS

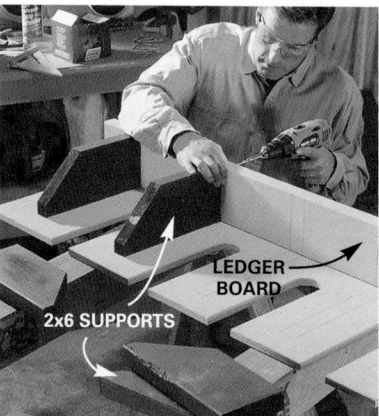

2 TACK 2x6 ledger board to plywood with 2-in. drywall screws. Fasten 2x6 supports to 2x6 ledger board with 3-in. drywall screws. Then flip rack over and anchor the plywood to 2x6s with 2-in. screws spaced every 8 in.

LEDGER BOARD

2x6 SUPPORTS

3 LEVEL the back against a wall and attach it to the studs with 3/8-in. x 4-1/2 in. lag screws and washers. Predrill holes with a 5/16-in. bit.

3" SCREW TEMPORARY SUPPORT

LAG SCREWS WITH WASHER

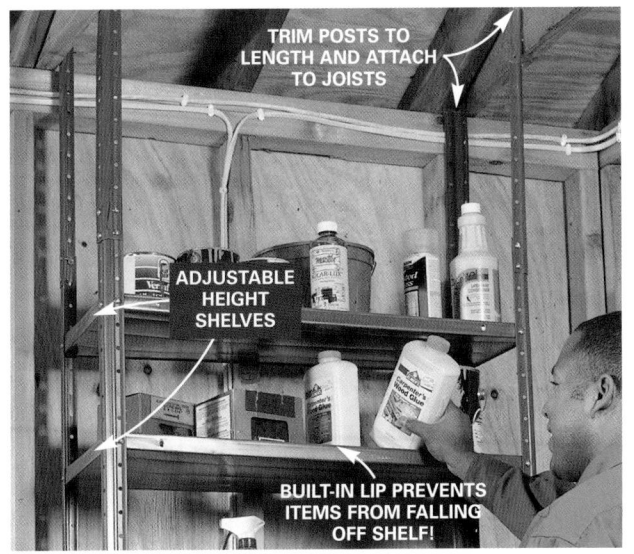

UPSIDE-DOWN SHELVES!

Here's some neat and fast storage for your shop's upper regions. Bolt together a set of inexpensive metal shelves (about $12 at a home center) and attach them upside down to the ceiling joists with lag bolts. The spacing between shelves is completely adjustable. Hang the shelves so they're easy to reach, or set them high so you won't bonk your head. Trim the shelf posts to just the right height with a tin snips.

(Photo labels: TRIM POSTS TO LENGTH AND ATTACH TO JOISTS; ADJUSTABLE HEIGHT SHELVES; BUILT-IN LIP PREVENTS ITEMS FROM FALLING OFF SHELF!)

SWING-DOWN COOKBOOK RACK

When counter space is at a minimum and counter mess at a maximum, this swing-down rack will keep your cookbook up and out of the fray. The special spring-loaded brackets allow you to swing your cookbook down when you need it, then out of the way when you're done.

Our cookbook platform tucks under a single cabinet. But you can make your platform larger to hold larger books, then mount it beneath two cabinets. With a little creativity, you can use this same hardware to create a swing-down knife rack or spice rack too.

Fold-down brackets (No. 00S30.02) are available for $19.60 plus shipping from Lee Valley Tools, P.O. Box 1780, Ogdensburg, NY 13669; (800) 871-8158. www.leevalley.com

1 CUT the 1/2-in. thick plywood base to size. Glue and nail the 3/4 x 3/4-in. lip to the front of the base, then "picture frame" the plywood with L-moldings. For an exact measurement, cut one end at 45 degrees on a miter saw, hold it in position and mark the other end. Put a "reminder mark" on the board so you remember which direction to cut the angle. Secure the pieces with carpenter's glue and 3d nails.

2 MOUNT the hinges to your base using wood screws. Hold the assembled unit in position under the cabinet, then mark the holes for the brackets (a two-person job). Drill the holes, then secure the brackets to the cabinet using short machine screws, washers and nuts.

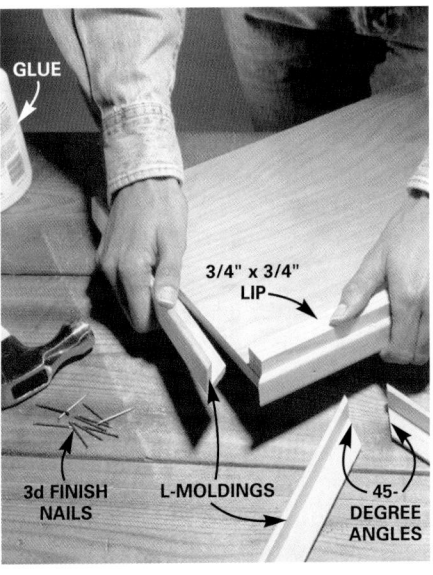

(Photo labels: GLUE; 3/4" x 3/4" LIP; 3d FINISH NAILS; L-MOLDINGS; 45-DEGREE ANGLES)

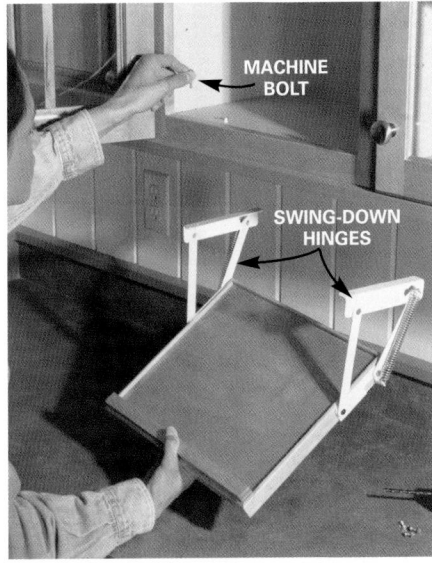

(Photo labels: MACHINE BOLT; SWING-DOWN HINGES)

(Illustration labels: MACHINE BOLT WITH WASHER AND LOCK NUT; OVERALL DIMENSIONS CAN VARY ACCORDING TO SPACE AVAILABLE; PLYWOOD; 3/4" x 3/4" LIP; 3d FINISH NAIL; SWING-DOWN HINGES; 1" x 1" L-MOLDINGS)

1 CUT AND FASTEN the 2x2 frame with 3-in. drywall screws. Then screw the Peg-Board to the frame using 1-in. drywall screws.

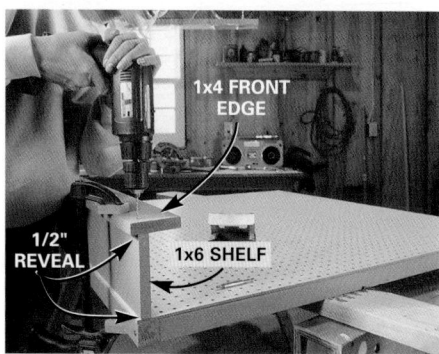

2 CLAMP the 1x4 front edge and 1x6 shelf board to the frame using two small bar clamps. Screw the front ledge to the shelf with 2-in. drywall screws spaced 12 in. apart.

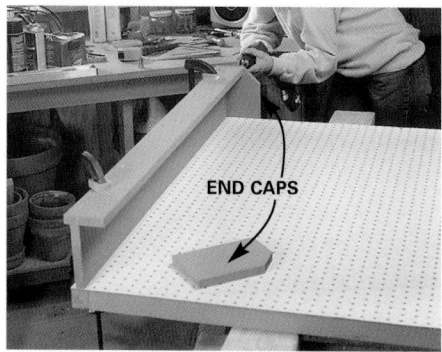

3 ATTACH end caps to each shelf with six 2-in. screws, two driven into each component.

4 FASTEN the Peg-Board to the wall with 3-in. drywall screws driven through the frame into the wall studs.

10 "UNDER-AN-HOUR"
STORAGE PROJECTS

PEG-BOARD AND BIN

Probably the most essential storage item in any garage is a Peg-Board system. It puts your most commonly used tools within quick and easy reach. Add a bin to the bottom of the Peg-Board to catch all those odds and ends that don't have a home, and you won't have any excuse for not keeping your workbench or gardening bench clear of clutter.

The construction only takes about two hours. Start by cutting all the parts to size with a circular saw. See **Fig. A** (below) for sizes.

Caution: Cut the short end caps from the long 1x6s. Don't try cutting short pieces from short boards.

Build a frame of 2x2s with one running across the center, connecting all joints with a 3-in. drywall screw. We then fastened 1/4-in. Peg-Board to the frame (**Photo 1**).

One-quarter inch has a little more heft than 1/8-in. and the larger hooks it requires stay put better. Some home centers and lumber yards stock the Peg-Board prefinished in white. If you can find it, it's worth it. It'll brighten up the garage and save you painting time.

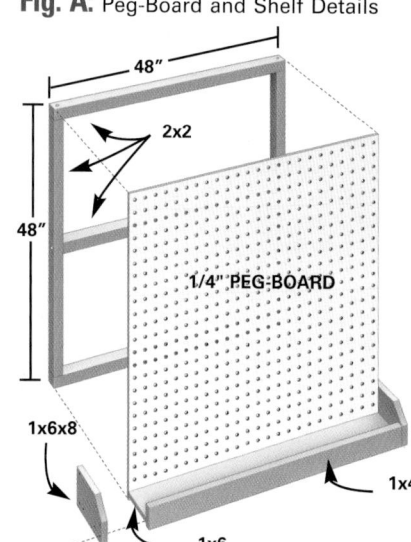

MATERIALS LIST	
DESCRIPTION	**QUANTITY**
4-ft. x 4-ft. piece of 1/4-in. Peg-Board	1
4-ft. 2x2s	5
4-ft. 1x4	1
6-ft. 1x6	1
1-in. drywall screws	24
2-in. drywall screws	24
3-in. deck screws	12

The trickiest part is attaching the front edge to the shelf. Using a couple of small bar clamps takes the frustration out of this step (**Photo 2**). Align the 1x4 front edge so it's 1/2 in. down from the shelf and clamp it to the Peg-Board and frame. Set back the shelf with that same 1/2-in. reveal. This 1/2-in. reveal strengthens the shelf. Predrill your screw holes with a 1/8-in. bit.

Next attach the end caps (**Photo 3**) to secure the shelf to the frame and to keep the front edge from tipping forward.

Finally, mount the Peg-Board low enough so you can easily reach your tools (**Photo 4**). If you're working alone, level and screw a 2x6 to the studs to temporarily support the Peg-Board while you attach it to the wall. Drive 3-in. screws through each member of the frame into every stud the Peg-Board covers.

Fig. A: Peg-Board and Shelf Details

48"
2x2
48"
1/4" PEG-BOARD
1x6x8
1x4
1x6

15 INGENIOUS WAYS TO TACKLE
TOUGH-TO-CLEAN STUFF

Simple ways to clean everything from sawblades to flower vases

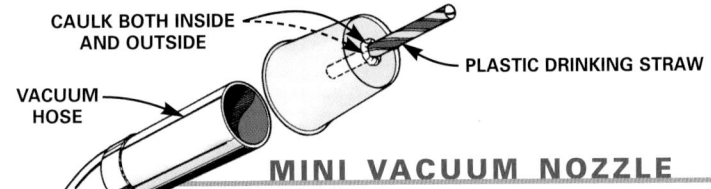

CAULK BOTH INSIDE AND OUTSIDE

VACUUM HOSE

PLASTIC DRINKING STRAW

MINI VACUUM NOZZLE

Ever try to vacuum dirt from that tiny space where the windshield meets the dashboard? From inside an electric motor? Or from all those little nooks and crannies around your house?

Concoct this gizmo for tight spots: Poke a long plastic straw through the bottom of a stiff paper cup and run a bit of caulk around the straw. Just plunk the cup on the end of your vacuum hose and the suction will hold it in place. Use a straw with a flexible neck for reaching around curves and corners.

CORNER CLEANER

My husband and I bought a very dirty house and found it frustrating to clean all the tight corners in the cabinet doors and windows. So I went to the store and bought a cheap electric toothbrush. Now it's quick and easy to clean all those hard-to-reach places.

VEGETABLE OIL SKIN CLEANER

Remove oil-based stains, paints and tar from your skin with vegetable oil. It works beautifully, with no irritation or smell—and it's environmentally friendly.

CREVICE TOOL FROM COPPER FITTINGS

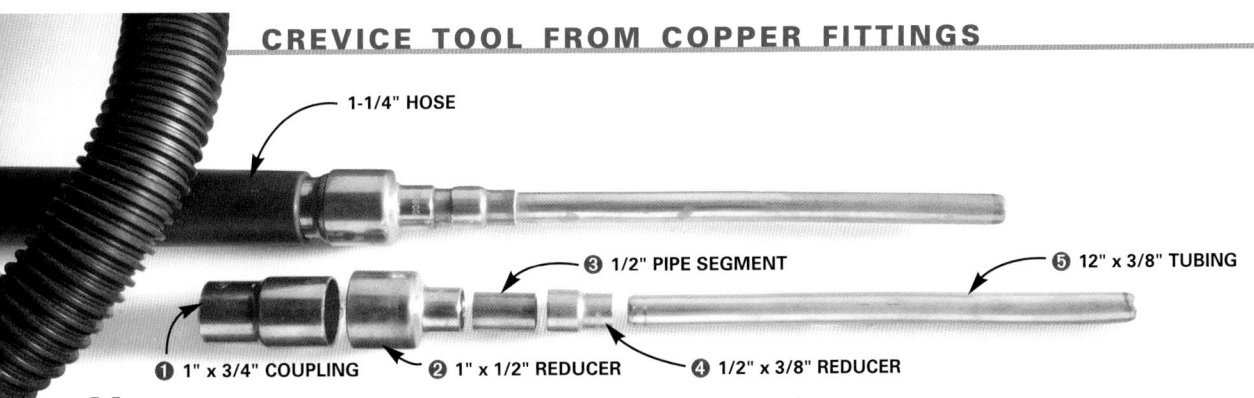

1-1/4" HOSE

❸ 1/2" PIPE SEGMENT

❺ 12" x 3/8" TUBING

❶ 1" x 3/4" COUPLING   ❷ 1" x 1/2" REDUCER   ❹ 1/2" x 3/8" REDUCER

You only need a few copper pipe fittings and short pieces of copper pipe to make this dual-purpose nozzle for your 1-1/4 in. shop vacuum. It'll blow dust like an air compressor nozzle or vacuum the tightest crevice. Just switch the vacuum hose from the exhaust port to the intake port on the vacuum. To make one, you need:

1. A 1-in. x 3/4-in. copper reducing coupling with stop
2. A 1-in. x 1/2-in. copper fitting reducer
3. A 1-in. piece of 1/2-in. inside-diameter copper pipe
4. A 1/2-in. x 3/8-in. copper fitting reducer
5. A 12-in. piece of 3/8-in. soft copper tubing

Glue the parts in the order shown with epoxy or cyanoacrylate glue. Now press-fit the 1-in. outside-diameter copper end into the 1-1/4 in. hose nozzle (the inside diameter is 1 in.) and put it to work. When using the vacuum as a blower, you can either grip the nozzle and hose so the nozzle won't blow out of the hose, or duct-tape the connection.

MAGNETIC STRIP

GLUE

DUSTPAN

OUTDOOR LIGHT CLEANING BRUSH

It's frustrating to clean the inside glass of outdoor lamps. Reaching my large hand into the glass left me with nicks, scratches and a sore wrist. My solution was to buy a 2-in. foam brush, spray glass cleaner onto it and scrub the lamp glass clean.

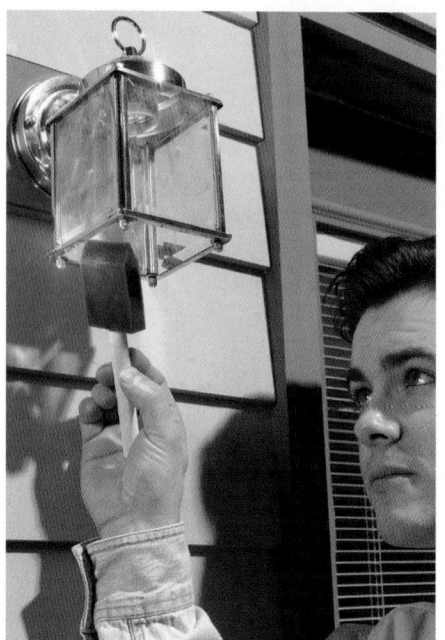

MAGNETIC SWEEP

Purchase a strip of flexible magnetic tape and glue it to the edge of your dustpan (some magnetic tapes are self-adhesive). When you're sweeping up your workshop, all those nuts, bolts and screws you've dropped will cling to the strip.

EASY BLIND CLEANER

Keep some cheap but thick cotton gloves around the house for cleaning your blinds. Just put the gloves on and run your fingers over the slats. When the gloves get dirty, throw them in the wash.

MUDDY BOOT SCRAPER

Tired of scraping mud off your boots, or worse yet, off your floors? Near your shed, fill a 12 x 12-in. hole with concrete, then embed an old spade about 6 in. deep. Now you have a permanent boot scraper complete with a handle you can grab to keep your balance.

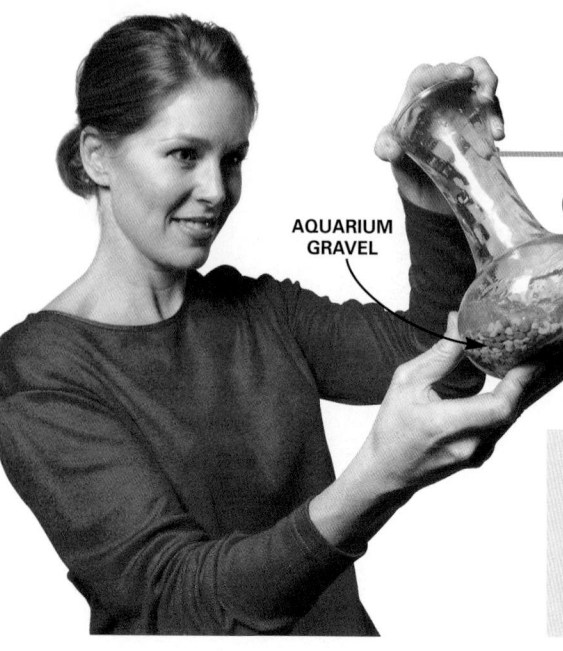

AQUARIUM GRAVEL

EASIER BOTTLE CLEANING

Clean those narrow-necked jars and vases with small gravel (aquarium gravel works the best). Fill one-third of the jar with water. Add a handful of gravel, and then stir and shake the jar. The gravel will scour the inside of the jar clean. Dump the gravel into a strainer, give it a quick rinse (so it doesn't stink!) and save it for next time.

SCUFF MARKS

Scuff marks on the kitchen wall? Try rubbing gently with a ball of fresh white bread.

REAL SHARP SCRAPER

Here's an easy-to-make, ultra-sharp scraper that's perfect for finish work. The blade corners project beyond the handle sides to easily reach gunked-up cracks and corners.

All you need is a utility knife blade and a 10-in. piece of 1-3/4 in. hardwood for a handle. First saw a 3/8-in. deep kerf in one end of the handle with a hacksaw or coping saw. Then saw or belt-sand 60-degree shoulders on both sides of the kerf so you can hold the scraper at a low angle. If the utility knife blade fits a little loose in the kerf, apply a layer or two of masking tape to create a snug fit. That's it; grip it firmly and go to work. When you're finished, slip out the blade with the pliers and store it until you need the scraper again.

MASKING TAPE
SHARP UTILITY BLADE
HACKSAW KERF
60-DEGREE BEVEL
3/4"

NOW-EASY-TO-REMOVE PAINT

REMOVING IVY FROM STUCCO

Before painting your stucco, painting experts say it's easiest to pull the vines down and let the clinging pieces dry. Then remove the bulk of them with either a hand-held wire brush or a wire wheel mounted to a drill or angle grinder. Don't worry about removing the disks that bonded the vine to the stucco because the paint will cover them just fine.

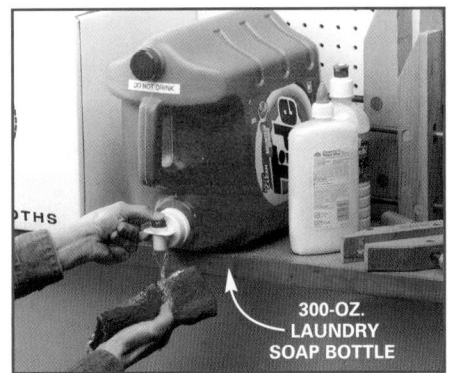

300-OZ. LAUNDRY SOAP BOTTLE

RUNNING WATER FOR YOUR SHOP

No utility sink nearby? Designate a 300-fl. oz. spigoted Tide laundry soap bottle as your shop's water supply. Thoroughly rinse out the bottle and fill it with fresh water, then set it in a convenient spot. The spigot can release a trickle or a torrent. Use it to moisten rags to clean up glue, freshen sharpening stones and clean your hands.

CHEWING GUM

Gum stuck to the chair seat? Hold an ice cube on the gum to harden it, then scrape it off with a butter knife.

SAW BLADE CLEANER

Clean resin and pitch from saw blades with spray oven cleaner. Suspend the saw blade from a dowel punched through a cardboard box. Spray both sides of the blade, close the box flaps for 10 to 20 minutes, then wash off the cleaner and gunk in warm water and dry the blade with a towel. Wear gloves for protection and work outside so you don't have to breathe the oven cleaner fumes. 🏠

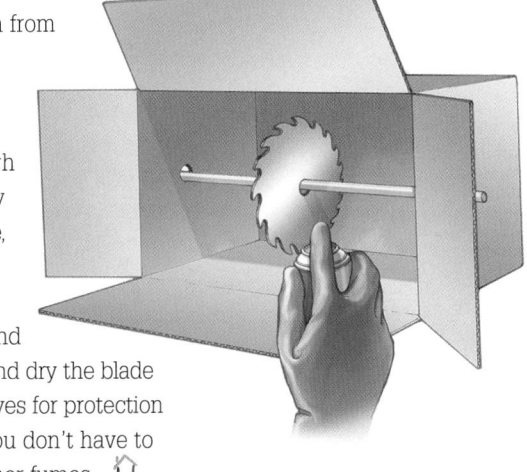
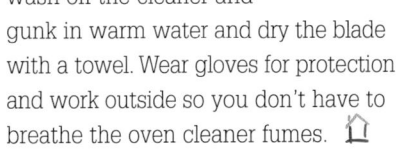

INDEX

For a complete 5-year index visit us at www.familyhandyman.com

A

Air compressors
sizing, 177
Angle grinders
uses of, 174–76
Arches
drywall, 24
Arcs
describing, 178
Asphalt
repairing, 190–91
Audio systems
wiring for, 88–94
Automobiles
fuses for, checking, 246–47
oil changes for, 248–50
paint repair for, 244–45

B

Band saws. *See* Outfeed tables; Push shoes.
Barrels
collapsible, 237
Baseboards
Craftsman-style, 29, 30
Basements
wet
correcting, 117
Bathtubs
stone-tile surround for, 60–63
whirlpool, 52
Benches
simple, 134–38
Bike holder
closet rod, 275
Birdbaths
leveling, 241
Bits
tile-cutting, 68, 70
Blinds
cleaning, 282
Bolts
rounded
removing, 257
sweeping up, 282
Bookcase
built-in, 145–154
lopsided, 153
Boot scrapers
shovels as, 282

Borders
dog protection for, 242
trenches for, 226
Bottles
cleaning, 282
spill-proof trays for, 182
Brackets
folding L-, 264, 266–67, 269
steel
making, 171
Brushes
cleaning, 205
electric toothbrush, for cleaning, 281
quality, 19–20
soaking, 11
Built-ins
bookcase, 145-154
Bungee cords
storage for, 257

C

Cabinets
doors for
new, 40
drawer fronts for
new, 41
face frames of
painting, 40
foldaway, 264–70
lighting under, 66–71
pantry
building, 54–57
wall
installing, 44, 50–51
racks for, 38, 39
raising, 38, 39, 41
Cable. *See* Wiring.
Carriers
from take-out boxes, 172
Casings
Craftsman-style, 29
Caulk
applying
sight line for, 129
hangers for, 206
paintable
applying, 19
for painting, 204
smoothing, 128
tip of
clearing, 205

Chair railing
installing, 12–15
Chewing gum
removing, 283
Chisels
storage for, 171
Circular saws
square crosscuts with, 135
Clamps
glue-proofing, 182
guards for, 179
PVC holders for, 173
Closet rods
installing, 44, 45
Communication
wiring for, 88–94
Computers
wiring for, 88–94
Concrete
cleaning, 253–54
cracked
repairing, 184
cutting
with angle grinder, 175
etching, 253–54
forms for
making, 214–15
mixing, 213
moisture checking, 33, 252
Coping
process of, 14, 15
Corkscrews
improvised, 273
Cornices
designing, 159
interior
building, 155–59
Countertops
scratched
repairing, 58
tile, 53
Coves
Craftsman-style, 29, 30–31

D

Decks
composite decking for, 219
lumber for, 230–34
around pools, 238
Dishwashers
replacing, 100–103

Doorbells
ringers for
adding, 119
updating, 82–83
Doors
bifold
fixing, 125
knob tightening for, 127
bolt snaps for, 270
clamping jig for gluing, 143
insulating around, 132
lengthening, 119
painting
both-sides aid for, 272
shortening, 116
and filling, 129
See also Screens; Trim.
Dowels
storage for, 276
Drains
clogged
clearing, 110-113
Drawers
basket, 41
lining, 171
spice, 43
stops for, 116
Drills
nail as drill bit, 143
sharpening with, 179
table saw drilling station for, 180
Driveways
sinking
repairing, 198
See also Asphalt.
Drywall
arches in, 24
corner bead
repairing, 16
cracks in
repairing, 17, 25
marking, 272
See also Joint compound.

E

Edgings
garden, vinyl
splicing, 236
for paths, 221
Electrical cord
keepers for, 171, 272

F

Faucets
  frost-proof
    failures with, 98
  leaking
    repairing, 106–7
    temporary fix for, 43
  nut remover for, 109
Feet
  levelers for
    applying, 235
Fences (machine)
  magnetic, 181
Fences (yard)
  staining, 219
Fillers
  applying, 18–19
  exterior, 203
  making, 11
Finishes
  cleaning, 160
  exterior, 138
Fire rings
  building, 239
Flooring
  finishes for, 25
  underlayment for
    installing, 34
  veneer
    installing, 32–35
  wood
    snap-together, 32–36
Floors
  concrete
    cleaning, 253–54
    etching, 253–54
  garage
    epoxy paint for,
      251–55
  leveling, 33
Fountains
  cast-concrete, 212–17
Furniture
  exterior
    finish for, 138

G

Garages
  door monitors for, 271
  door openers
    reviving, 271
  epoxy paint for, 251–55
  lighting for, 79
  workshops for
    foldaway, 264–70
Garbage cans
  hold-downs for, 207
Gardens
  tool carrier for, 273

Gas cans
  funnels for, 250, 256
Glass
  etching, 59
Glues
  angle gluing, 142
  bottle holders for, 181
  clamping jig, 143
  spreaders for, 179
Gouges. *See* Holes.
Grout
  dispenser for, 43
Gummy wood surfaces
  cleaning, 160
Gutters
  clean-out bucket for,
    206
  repairing, 188
  spikes of
    straightening, 207
  splash guards for, 188

H

Hammocks
  trellis stand for, 239
Hands
  oil cleaner for, 281
Hinges
  loose
    fixing, 275
  noisy
    greasing, 126
  piano
    installing, 268–69
Holes
  filling, 18–19, 203
  patching, 161
Hoses
  keepers for, 171
  repairing, 189

I

Insulation
  fiberglass
    installing, 130–32
Ironing board cabinet, 72
Ivy
  removing, 283

J

Joint compound
  mixing, 10
Joists
  lumber for, 233–34

K

Keyhole slots
  mounting template for,
    207
Kitchens
  facelifts for, 38–42

L

Ladders
  cushioning, 274
  placing, 208–9
  securing, 209–10
  stabilizers for, 210
  tool apron for, 207
Laundries
  organizing, 44–51
Lawns
  patchy
    reseeding, 240–41
  seeding, 218–19
Legs
  pocket-screw
    attachment for, 141
  weatherproofing, 138
Light fixtures
  bulb removal for, 128, 273
  in cabinets, 270
  chandelier
    installing, 74–78
  exterior
    cleaning, 282
  fluorescent
    cold-starting, 79
    colors of, 79
  motion-sensing, 274
  See also Switches.
Lighting
  under cabinets, 66–71
  for garages, 79
Liquids
  stirring, 11
Locksets
  strike plates for
    adjusting, 187
    setting, 129
Lumber
  for cabinets, 265
  choosing, 230–34
  composite, 232
  orientation for, 231
  pressure-treated, 232
  grades of, 230

M

Magazines
  hanging, 170
Magnetic strip
  for dustpan, 282

Massage
  with sander, 275
Metal
  cleaning
    with angle grinder,
      175
Miters
  in moldings
    corner, 13, 14
Moldings
  bed (*see* crown)
  coping, 14, 15
  crown, 12, 13, 14
    installing, 42, 156–57
  glass bead, 12, 15
  returns for, 14, 15
Mortar
  removing
    with angle grinder,
      176
Moss
  encouraging, 229
Mowers
  blades of
    balancing, 263
    sharpening, 261–63
  tuning up, 258–63

N

Nails
  as drill bit, 143
  holes from
    filling, 14, 31, 157, 158
  no-dent finish nailing,
    142
  storage containers for,
    170, 173
Nuts
  sweeping up, 282

O

Oil
  changing, 248–50, 259–60
  used
    collection system for,
      256
    disposing of, 250
Outfeed tables
  knock-down
    building, 179
  for ripping, 167

P

Paint
  auto
    repairing, 244–45
  basics of, 20–21
  can reminder, 10

caulk for, 204
cutting in, 21
drip catcher for, 10
epoxy floor, 251–55
exterior
  pressure washing
    for, 200
failing
  diagnosing, 202
latex
  qualities of, 20
masking for, 20–21
old
  removing, 18–19
peeling
  dealing with, 26
primers for, 204
scraping, 201
spinning stand for, 144
stirring, 11
storage for, 276
wiper for, 11
Paint thinner
  reusing, 273
Paneling
  attaching, 25
Pantries
  cabinets for, 54–57
Paths
  compacters for, 224, 225
  designing, 220–21
  edging for, 221
  grassed grid blocks for,
    227
  gravel, 220–21
  paver, 224–25
  stone, 222–23
Pencils
  jam nuts for, 178
Photo sculptures, 144
Picture frames
  hanging device for, 128
Pipe
  PVC
    as clamp holders, 173
    for storage, 171, 172,
      173, 276
    string cutter for, 274
  See also Plumbing.
Plans
  peg-board holder for,
    180
Planters
  from flue liners, 229
  leveling, 235
  moss for, 229
Plant supports
  from rebar, 228
  stakes for, 235
Plastic bag holder, 276

Plate rails
  Craftsman-style, 29, 31
Plumbing
  copper
    connecting, 101, 103
    fixing, 97
  for island sinks, 99
  unclogging
    with hose, 109
    with plunger or
      snake, 110-113
Plywood
  carrier for, 206
Pocket screws
  jigs for, 139
  screws for, 140
Pools
  constructing, 238
Posts
  choosing, 231, 232
Propane torches
  caddy for, 178
Pumpkins
  huge, 237
Push shoes
  for ripping, 167, 169

R

Racks
  drying, 205
  glass-plate, 38, 39
  for shovels, 278
  swing-down book, 279
  wall, book-style, 165
Roofs
  cleaning soffit vents, 118
  workbench for, 205
Routers
  rounding over with,
    137, 138
Rulers
  wallet-sized, 205

S

Sanders
  bumper for, 142
  contour, 143
  random-orbit
    pad replacement for,
      181
Sanding
  for painting, 203
Sandpaper
  boards of, 179
  filing, 170
Sawblades
  cleaning, 283

Sawhorses
  making, 164
  quick, 206
Saws, compound miter
  using, 155–57
Scrapers
  sharpening, 283
Scratches
  touching up, 162
Screens
  repairing, 186–87
Screws
  pilot holes for, 177
  storage containers for,
    170
  sweeping up, 282
  See also Pocket screws.
Sharpening
  with angle grinder, 176
  with sanding discs, 179
Sheds
  garden, 238
Shelves
  brackets for
    steel, 171
  display, 277
  foldaway, 264–70
  installing, 44, 45
  lightweight, 276
  liner for, 43
  spring-tension rod, 43
  swing-down, 279
  upside-down, 279
Shingles
  cooling
    for repair, 207
  replacing, 185
Shovels
  storage rack for, 278
Siding
  protecting from ladders,
    274
Showers
  fiberglass
    installing, 96
  leaking
    repairing, 104–5
    temporary fix for, 43
  slippery
    fixing, 59
Shrubs
  dog protection for, 242
Shutters
  drying rack for, 205
Sinks
  in islands
    plumbing, 99
  new, 52
  shelves under, 44, 47
  sprayers of
    replacing, 108
  unclogging, 110-113

Small parts
  finding, 257
  sweeping up, 282
Smart appliances
  wiring for, 88–94
Soap dispensers
  installing, 44, 46
Soffit vents, 118
Spark plugs
  changing, 260
Spray-can straw
  storing, 273
Spices
  shelves for, 276
  storage for, 43
Stain
  mixing, 10
  protecting hands from,
    142
Staircases
  exterior
    jacks for, 234
    posts for, 199
Steel
  cutting
    with angle grinder,
      175
Stenciling
  process of, 22–23
Stencils, 22–23
Stone
  cutting, 175
Stop blocks
  from spring clamps, 180
Storage
  foam-ball, 173
  for little stuff
    magnetic, 172
  in muffin tins, 173
  peg-board, 280
    bin for, 280
  PVC for, 171, 172, 173,
    277
  rust-free boxes for, 173
  tennis balls for, 171
  tool pegs for
    padding, 172
  wall
    for nuts, washers, 173
String
  holder for, 170
Stucco
  ivy removal for, 283
Studs
  straightening, 54
Surface preparation
  for painting, 18–19
Sweeping
  magnetic strip for, 282
Switches
  dual-outlet, 182
  easy-grip, 128

T

Tables
 wall-folding, 44, 48–49
Table saws
 blade removal for, 180
 ripping with, 166–69
 See also Outfeed tables;
  Push shoes.
Tabletops
 workbench
  plywood, 269
Tape
 masking
  for windows, 31
 painter's, 21
Telephones
 wiring for, 88–94
Television
 remote control holder
  for, 275
 wiring for, 88–94
Tilework, 175
 backerboard for, 61
 bits for, 68, 70
 countertop, 53
 cutting, 61, 62, 63
 grouting, 43
 painting, 58
 stone
  for tub, 60–63
Toilets
 hammering
  fixing, 97
 mounting, 109
 sluggish
  cleaning, 108
Tomatoes
 in containers, 235

Towel bars
 installing, 46, 58
Trailers
 dolly for, 257
Trays
 for bottles, 182
 lining, 171
 for small parts, 256
 for tools, 182
Trellises
 with hammocks, 239
Trim, 27–31
 Craftsman-style, 27–31
 painting, 18–21
 rosettes for, 15
 undercutting
  for flooring, 33
T-trap, 112

V

Vacuums
 belts of
  replacing, 125
 crevice tool for, 281
 nozzle for
  mini-, 281
Vanities
 new, 52
Vapor barriers
 need for, 26
Varnish
 cans of
  sealing, 178
 polyurethane
  over water-based, 25
Vinyl siding
 flashing under, 193–94
 installing, 192–93
 J-channel for, 194–97
 removing, 193

W

Walks. *See* Paths.
Walls
 moisture in, 26
 roll-down, temporary,
  256
 scuff marks on, 282
 stenciling, 22–23
Washing machines
 leaking
  repairing, 120–24
Water heaters
 draining, 98–99
 gas pilots on
  fixing, 97
Watering cans
 from soap containers,
  237
Weeding
 in cracks, 236
 crevice tool for, 236
Whirlpool tub, 52
Windows
 casement
  crank replacement
   for, 126–27
 cornices for, 155–59
 flashing, 193–94
 insulating around, 132
 masking, 31
 See also Screens; Trim.
Wiring
 aluminum, 67, 78, 103
 boxes for
  extending, 81, 83
  low-voltage, 90
  sizing, 69, 74–75
  tying in to, 80

CAT-5e
 handling, 91
circuits in
 checking, 274
flex cable for, 66–70
grounding, 81, 94
insulating around, 131
loads on
 figuring, 68–69
 polarity of, 76
 stripping, 84–87
 temperature rating of, 74
 for undercabinet lights,
  66–71
upgradable
 installing, 88–94
Wood surfaces
 cleaning, 160
 recoating, 162
 repairing, 161, 162
 scratches
  touching up, 162
Woodwork. *See* Trim.
Workbenches
 storage in, 165
Workshops
 foldaway, 264–70
 roll-down walls for, 256
 water jug for, 283
Wrenches
 case for, 257

ACKNOWLEDGMENTS

FOR THE FAMILY HANDYMAN

Editor in Chief	Ken Collier
Editor	Duane Johnson
Executive Editor	Spike Carlsen
Senior Editor	Dave Radtke
Associate Editors	Jeff Gorton
	Travis Larson
	Kurt Lawton
Senior Copy Editor	Donna Bierbach
Senior Art Director	Bob Ungar
Art Directors	Hope Fay
	Becky Pfluger
	Marcia Wright Roepke
Office Administrative Manager	Alice Garrett
Technical Manager	Shannon Hooge
Reader Service Specialist	Roxie Filipkowski
Office Administrative Assistant	Shelly Jacobsen
Administrative Assistant	Lori Callister
Production Manager	Judy Rodriguez
Production Artist	Lisa Pahl Knecht

CONTRIBUTING EDITORS

Jeff Larson	Jeff Timm
Mike J. Preble	Mac Wentz
Eric Smith	Bruce Wiebe

FREELANCE ART DIRECTORS

David Farr	Barb Pederson
Mark Jacobson	Gregg Weigand

PHOTOGRAPHERS

Mike Habermann, Mike Habermann Photography
Mike Krivit, Krivit Photography
Phil Leisenheimer, LA Studios
Craig McNitt and Shawn Nielsen, Studio Central
Ramon Moreno
Bill Zuehlke

ILLUSTRATORS

Steve Björkman	Don Mannes
Gabe De Matteis	Doug Oudekerk
Roy Doty	Frank Rohrbach
John Keely	Eugene Thompson
Bruce Kieffer	

OTHER CONSULTANTS

Charles Avoles, plumbing
Al Hildenbrand, electrical
Kathryn Hillbrand, interior design
Jon Jensen, carpentry
Bob Lacivita, automotive
Dave MacDonald, structural engineer
Mary Jane Pappas, kitchen and bath design
Ron Pearson, environmental issues
Tom Schultz, drywall
Dean Sorem, tile
Costas Stavrou, appliance repair
John Williamson, electrical
Ron Zeien, appliance repair
Les Zell, plumbing

For information about advertising in *The Family Handyman* magazine, call (212) 850-7226

To subscribe to *The Family Handyman* magazine:
- By phone: (800) 285-4961
- By Internet: www.familyhandyman.com
- By mail: The Family Handyman
  Subscriber Service Dept.
  P.O. Box 8174
  Red Oak, IA 51591-1174

We welcome your ideas and opinions. Write to:
The Editor, The Family Handyman,
2915 Commers Dr., Suite 700, Eagan, MN 55121
Fax: (651) 994-2250
E-mail: fheditor@readersdigest.com
Web site: www.familyhandyman.com

Photocopies of articles are available for $3.00 each. Call (715) 246-4344 from 8 a.m. to 5 p.m. Central, Monday through Friday or send an e-mail to FHMcustserve@cdsfulfillment.com. Visa, MasterCard and Discover accepted.